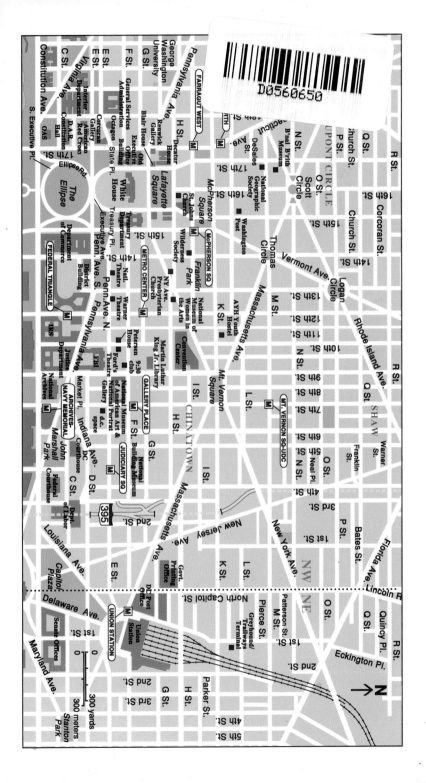

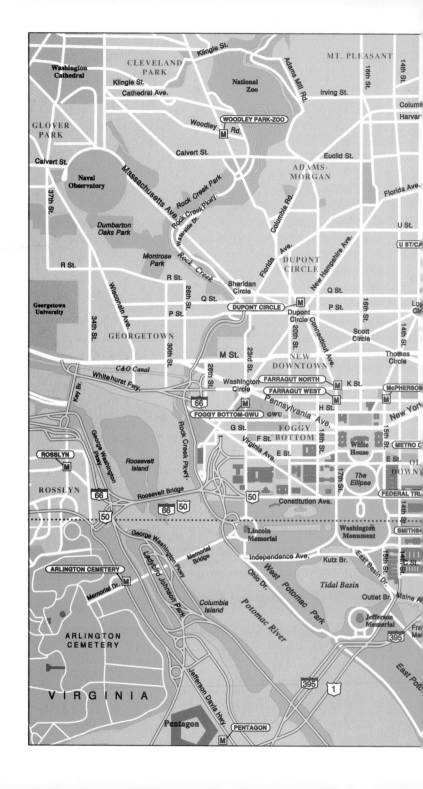

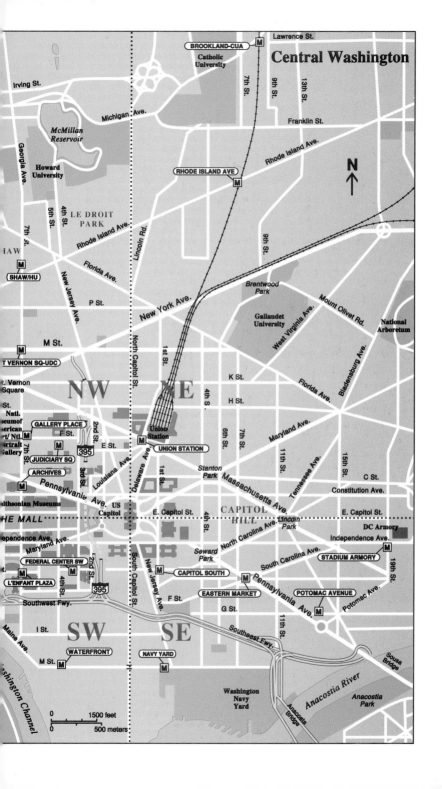

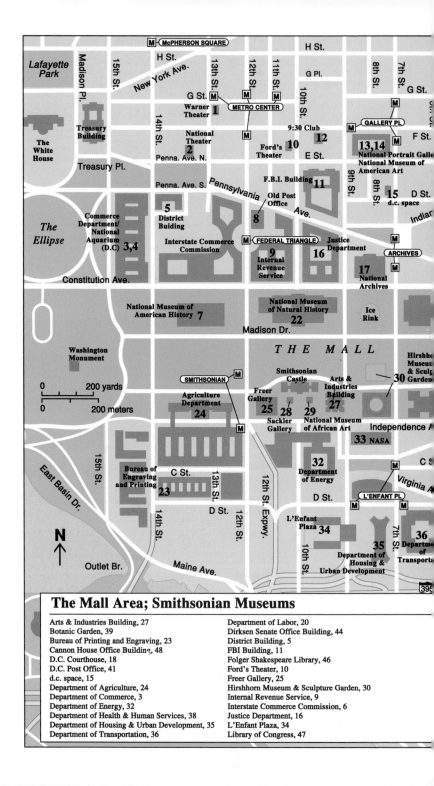

The Mall Area; Smithsonian Museums

Arts & Industries Building, 27
Botanic Garden, 39
Bureau of Printing and Engraving, 23
Cannon House Office Building, 48
D.C. Courthouse, 18
D.C. Post Office, 41
d.c. space, 15
Department of Agriculture, 24
Department of Commerce, 3
Department of Energy, 32
Department of Health & Human Services, 38
Department of Housing & Urban Development, 35
Department of Transportation, 36

Department of Labor, 20
Dirksen Senate Office Building, 44
District Building, 5
FBI Building, 11
Folger Shakespeare Library, 46
Ford's Theater, 10
Freer Gallery, 25
Hirshhorn Museum & Sculpture Garden, 30
Internal Revenue Service, 9
Interstate Commerce Commission, 6
Justice Department, 16
L'Enfant Plaza, 34
Library of Congress, 47

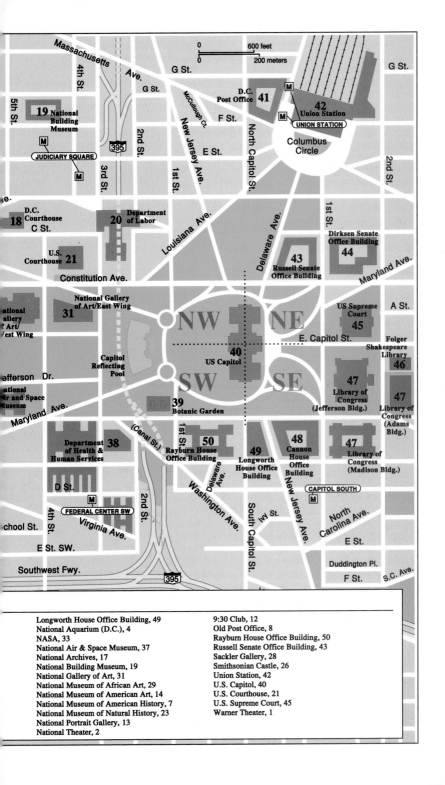

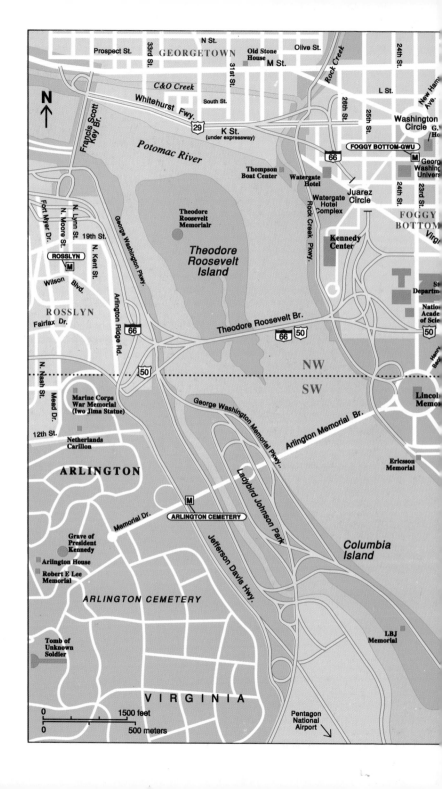

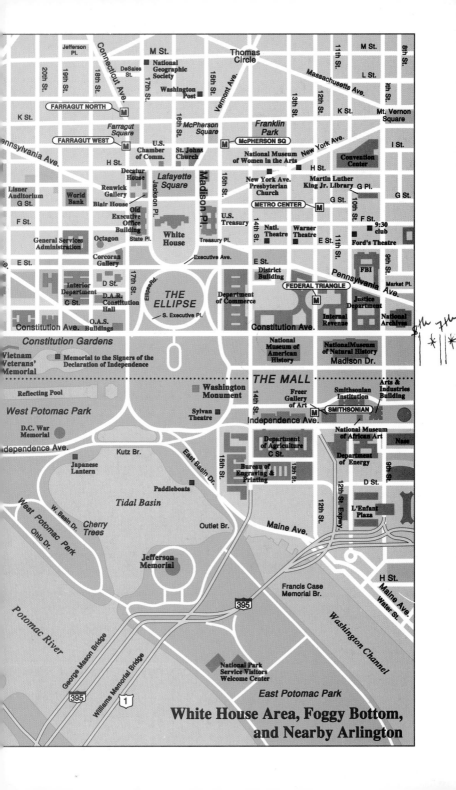

White House Area, Foggy Bottom, and Nearby Arlington

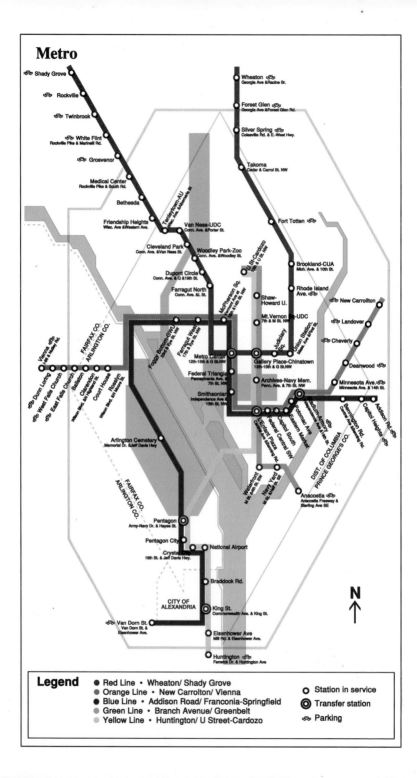

"Value-packed, accurate, and comprehensive..."
—*Los Angeles Times*

"Unbeatable..."—*The Washington Post*

LET'S GO:
WASHINGTON, D.C.

is the best book for anyone traveling on a budget. Here's why:

No other guidebook has as many budget listings.

We list over 20 places in or near Washington where you can spend the night for under $50. We tell you how to get there the cheapest way, whether by bus, plane, or thumb, and where to get an inexpensive and satisfying meal once you've arrived. There are hundreds of money-saving tips for everyone plus lots of information on student discounts.

LET'S GO researchers have to make it on their own.

Our Harvard-Radcliffe researchers travel on budgets as tight as your own—no expense accounts, no free hotel rooms.

LET'S GO is completely revised every year.

We don't just update the prices, we go back to the places. If a charming café has become an overpriced tourist trap, we'll replace the listing with a new and better one.

No other budget guidebook includes all this:

Coverage of both the city and daytrips out of the city; directions, addresses, phone numbers, and hours to get you in and around; in-depth information on culture, history, and inhabitants; tips on work, study, sights, nightlife, and special splurges; detailed city maps; and much, much more.

LET'S GO is for anyone who wants to see Washington, D.C on a budget.

Books by Let's Go, Inc.

Let's Go: Europe
Let's Go: Britain & Ireland
Let's Go: France
Let's Go: Germany, Austria & Switzerland
Let's Go: Greece & Turkey
Let's Go: Israel & Egypt
Let's Go: Italy
Let's Go: London
Let's Go: Paris
Let's Go: Rome
Let's Go: Spain & Portugal

Let's Go: USA
Let's Go: California & Hawaii
Let's Go: Mexico
Let's Go: New York City
Let's Go: The Pacific Northwest, Western Canada & Alaska
Let's Go: Washington, D.C.

LET'S GO:

The Budget Guide to

WASHINGTON, D.C.

1993

Michael C. Vazquez
Editor

Alexander E. Marashian
Assistant Editor

Written by
Let's Go, Inc.
a wholly owned subsidiary of
Harvard Student Agencies, Inc.

ST. MARTIN'S PRESS
NEW YORK

Helping Let's Go

If you have suggestions or corrections, or just want to share your discoveries, drop us a line. We read every piece of correspondence, whether a 10-page letter, a tacky Elvis postcard, or, as in one case, a collage. All suggestions are passed along to our researcher/writers. Please note that mail received after May 5, 1993 will probably be too late for the 1994 book, but will be retained for the following edition. Address mail to:

Let's Go: Washington, D.C.
Let's Go, Inc.
1 Story Street
Cambridge, MA 02138

In addition to the invaluable travel advice our readers share with us, many are kind enough to offer their services as researchers or editors. Unfortunately, the charter of Let's Go, Inc. and Harvard Student Agencies, Inc. enables us to employ only currently enrolled Harvard students.

Maps by David Lindroth, copyright © 1993, 1992 by St. Martin's Press, Inc.

Distributed outside the U.S. and Canada by Pan Books Ltd.

ISBN: 0-312-08252-5

First edition
10 9 8 7 6 5 4 3 2 1

Let's Go: Washington, D.C. is written by the Publishing Division of
Let's Go, Inc., 1 Story Street, Cambridge, Mass. 02138.

Let's Go® is a registered trademark of Let's Go, Inc.
Printed in the U.S.A. on recycled paper with biodegradable soy ink.

Acknowledgments

To Alex Marashian goes my most heartfelt and honest thanks and comradely greetings. I never imagined that two minds could meet at such an explosive loggerhead; the scattered remains of our combination are the meat and substance of this book.

Andrew Kent returned from the European midlands to help clean up our mess, proofing, calling, and chumbling with dead-on wit and straight-arrow eyes. In this he redoubled his performance on the *Slit* and once-again revealed to me one of the essential wellsprings of friendship: being around for the stupid shit.

Two more Alexes provided sometimes keen clippings from the thick undergrowth of the District. Ross and Star, a community from afar, kept me in touch with area goings-on and in the process kept hope alive that all of this, my moral firmament, will not extinguish in the long, post-graduate night.

Another community, our trusty office group, kept us in shape, making the days pass with ease and curtailling our excesses. Moondog, Elijah "Döh" Siegler, David, Kayla, Jane, Nell, and July kept us honest, or at least credible. July put up with our aggressive disorganization without freaking; she also accepted most of our glib linguistic trinkets, shared a grin and a cackle, and allowed us to swing lightly through our forested prose. We would have produced a sadder book without her.

Our researchers triumphed despite short funds and long itineraries.

Trusty stalwart Joe Mejía trounced his assignment, sent back steady, friendly prose and intimate portraits of his psychogeographical landscape. His humor and natural good looks left us constantly impressed; his company and proofing work at the final hour helped us recover our spirits. He also introduced us to that cute little drunken office girl—way to go, Joe. (Way to go to you, too, Abby!)

Caroline Kenney showed enormous dedication and aplomb in coping with our constantly changing needs and comments. If it wasn't right, she'd fix it; if it was right, she'd fix it anyway. Her keen eye spotted dozens of new restaurants, which she captured with a solid and expressive touch—that girl had language by the handle. She also pulled through up to the very end, driving miles to check on points far distant and fedexing us great gobs of prose. Hurrah, Caroline.

Steve "Freestyle" Burt and Carolyn McKee, the original Team WAS, were around to answer odd questions and defend themselves against our surly charges. Jill Kamin typed for us, Andrew and Nora plied us with food, rubbings, and voicemail, Bart did just what we told him to, even when it was lame, Jane made us happy, Mark "Candyman" Templeton kept us up and running, and David kept our cynicism from getting the better of us. Kayla made good on a longstanding promise of friendship, while Pete gave me a job and forgave me bad table manners.

Thanks, finally to a host of others: Marlies and Minna, longtime friends who directly or indirectly lent inrigue to my summer; Nell of the smiling curls and zebra skull, whose plotting grin and gypsy spirit were my most treasured find; Milena, whose grizzled sweetness kept me company at odd times; Ethan, who took me and Al through a North End carnival and into the urban blightscape; and Orah, whose warm company rounded out my summer in Cambridge.

Like most of the things I do, this book is offered to my parents, Lois and John. With love, thanks, and longing.

—MCV

My biggest thanks to Mike V., who found me floundering in a post-graduate netherworld, plucked me out, and steadied me before this screen. Wishbone headphones linked us to *Lost and Found* (88.1) and to a molten substratum of language where a mutual upchuckle is community agreement and a neighborly guffaw the signal for further excavations. I really wouldn't have done this for anyone else. Then there's

8

Mark Nevins, the lad who put me up, kept me roasty, and smackled my dab with a boundless generosity, a likemind taste in all but ramen, and a fulsome humanity. Nip out for a pop, Dr. Mahfooz? Could do.

Time and space constraints will constipate the brain; I love all of you who didn't slip through–here are those who did: Julianne my sister/ Kayla Alpert my other sister/ Nick Pirok/ Dave Cookieboy Thorpe, even for duties not discharged/ July, for a loose hand on our gimcrackery/ Muneer the hustler/ eggywhite Elijah/ Nell and Jane/ Geoff Rodkey/ Jeff Ferguson and the Gin Soon T'ai Club/ Steven McCauley for the pinpoint of light at the end of the summer/ Robert Kiely and Vicky Macy/ Katherine Ross/ Tina Merrill for Typing Tutor/ Gameboy and Gelcap/ the Gold Star 5 for the promise of another Cambridge summer (jizzes of thank go out to Troy and Tanya Selvaratnum for towing me two years back over a plate of enchiladas, and to Miguel "Kid" Sancho for ditching *Eye Clod*)/ Ethan Gold for reminding us that the summer is just begun/ Michelle Ponti for the sofa/ Josh Pashman and Dmitri Tymoczko, my fellow Young Curmudgeons/ Bohumil Hrabal/ Radio 1430, though it caused Rump Inglenook to pause: "a.m.?" the burly lineman pondered between goldfish, "fuck that shit"/ Ray / Andrew Kent, our whiffleball pitcher and crashdummy proofreader/ Gia-Cass/ Craig Mullen, who has his hand on the udder of language and milks it for all it's worth/ John Kelly and Rick Hawkins for the occasional pint/ Liz/ Randolf "Glitch" Chutney, class of '23/ Cafe o' India boyz/ thomas lauderdale/ the pit at Shaze where we hatched our nuts and swore we wouldn't speak of work/ Dr. D'am (if only he knew)/ yo last I want to thank my girlfriend, Cremora Melby (sorry about the whole Fiona McKenna thing, ok?). It's like my friend Joe Blunsten says: there *is* no justice for the working man in this country.

For my part, this book is dedicated to my parents, Edward and Janet, who are beyond thanks.

—AEM

CONTENTS

10   Contents

List of Maps

About Let's Go

A generation ago, Harvard Student Agencies, a three-year-old non-profit corporation dedicated to providing employment to students, was doing a booming business booking charter flights to Europe. One of the extras offered to passengers on these flights was a 20-page mimeographed pamphlet entitled *1960 European Guide,* a collection of tips on continental travel compiled by the HSA staff. The following year, students traveling to Europe researched the first full-fledged edition of *Let's Go: Europe,* a pocket-sized book with tips on budget accommodations, irreverent write-ups of sights, and a decidedly youthful slant.

Throughout the 60s, the series reflected the times: a section of the 1968 *Let's Go: Europe* was entitled "Street Singing in Europe on No Dollars a Day." During the 70s *Let's Go* evolved into a large-scale operation, adding regional European guides and expanding coverage into North Africa and Asia. In the 80s, we launched coverage of the United States, developed our research to include concerns of travelers of all ages, and finetuned the editorial process that continues to this day. The early 90s saw the introduction of *Let's Go* city guides.

1992 has been a big year for us. We are now Let's Go, Incorporated, a wholly owned subsidiary of Harvard Student Agencies. To celebrate this change, we moved from our dungeonesque Harvard Yard basement to an equally dungeonesque third-floor office in Harvard Square, and we purchased a high-tech computer system that allows us to typeset all of the guides in-house. Now in our 33rd year, *Let's Go* publishes 17 titles, covering more than 40 countries. This year *Let's Go* proudly introduces two new entries in the series: *Let's Go: Paris* and *Let's Go: Rome.*

But these changes haven't altered our tried and true approach to researching and writing travel guides. Each spring 90 Harvard University students are hired as researcher-writers and trained intensively during April and May for their summer tour of duty. Each researcher-writer then hits the road for seven weeks of travel on a shoestring budget, researching six days per week and overcoming countless obstacles in the quest for better bargains.

Back in Cambridge, Massachusetts, an editorial staff of 32, a management team of six, and countless typists and proofreaders—all students—spend more than six months pushing nearly 8000 pages of copy through a rigorous editing process. By the time classes start in September, the typeset guides are off to the printers, and they hit bookstores world-wide in late November. Then, by February, next year's guides are well underway.

A NOTE TO OUR READERS

The information for this book is gathered by Let's Go's researchers during the late spring and summer months. Each listing is derived from the assigned researcher's opinion based upon his or her visit at a particular time. The opinions are expressed in a candid and forthright manner. Other travelers might disagree. Those traveling at a different time may have different experiences since prices, dates, hours, and conditions are subject to change. You are urged to check beforehand to avoid inconvenience and surprises. Travel always involves a certain degree of risk, especially in low-cost areas. When traveling, especially on a budget, you should always take particular care to ensure your safety.

Let's Go: Washington, DC

Washington, DC's strange experiment—an infant nation building a capital from scratch—has matured into one of America's most interesting, and consequently most visited, cities. Its existence depends on the federal government, the national network that sucks in revenue, borrows money, and spits out laws and programs from around DC's hub and Congress' home, the United States Capitol. Monuments, departments, and the Smithsonian museums pull visitors in from all over the world for a brush with lunar landers or a look at the President. But north, south, west, and east of the federal enclave, Washington swirls with non-governmental neighborhoods and delights; there's more inside the Beltway than double-talk, and more along Pennsylvania Ave. than the White House. John F. Kennedy called the capital "a city of Northern charm and Southern efficiency," but that was just Presidential sour grapes: the high-speed information flow of downtown sends demands, promises, leaks, and laws scurrying at the touch of a button, while Old Town Alex andria's manicured cuteness competes for charm with anything in Old Virginny. The arts multiply in Dupont Circle, while youngsters and ethnic residents divide very "in" Adams-Morgan. The Kennedy Center bows and pirouettes with high culture almost every night. And indigenous music scenes pump out high-quality, honest tunes.

Let's Go's energetic, knowledgeable researchers have scoured the capital for comfortable budget lodging, good cheap eats, unknown sights (and better ways to see familiar ones), and a comprehensive roll call of nightlife. Where competitors deliver familiar platitudes or marvel at every manifestation of democracy, Let's Go strives for honesty, explaining and evaluating what we list. We travel the subway, buses, and streets, demystify the government for Americans and foreigners, explore hip and/or obscure neighborhoods, and make any guided tour superfluous. Let's Go researchers pay attention on behalf of travelers with kids or specific needs. Interns trying to improve their Washington summers will find Let's Go attentive to longer-term visitors, while international travelers can use this book to decide what and where to stay, eat, look, and listen in DC. This book also includes daytrips and farther-away destinations in Maryland, Virginia, West Virginia, and Delaware. Those looking for special attention paid to Washington's African-American, Latino, international, or gay communities won't be disappointed. Whether you drop in for a week or a year, to speed through the Smithsonian or soak up Adams-Morgan, we can save you money and show you the whole city like nobody else's business.

Life and Times

History

Founding and Early Years

> No nation had ever before the opportunity offered
> them of deliberately deciding on the spot where
> their Capital City should be fixed.
> —Pierre L'Enfant, letter to George Washington
> (1789)

Like many a young adult fresh out of college, Congress after the Revolutionary War realized independence meant little without a place to stay. While the weak Articles of Confederation governed the new United States, the Continental Congress convened in Philadelphia in 1783 and tried to decide where to park itself for good. Kingston, NY, Nottingham, NJ and Williamsburg, then the capital of Virginia, were all candidates for the capital honor. Before the Congress could make a decision, a mob of Continental

Washington, D.C. with Map Key

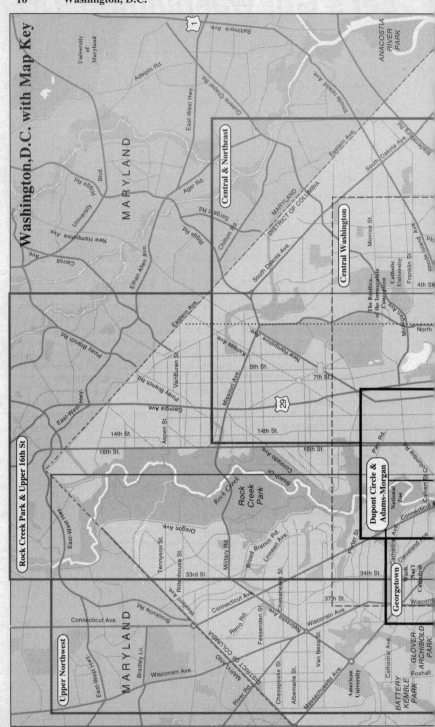

Central & Northeast

Central Washington

Rock Creek Park & Upper 16th St

Dupont Circle & Adams-Morgan

Georgetown

Upper Northwest

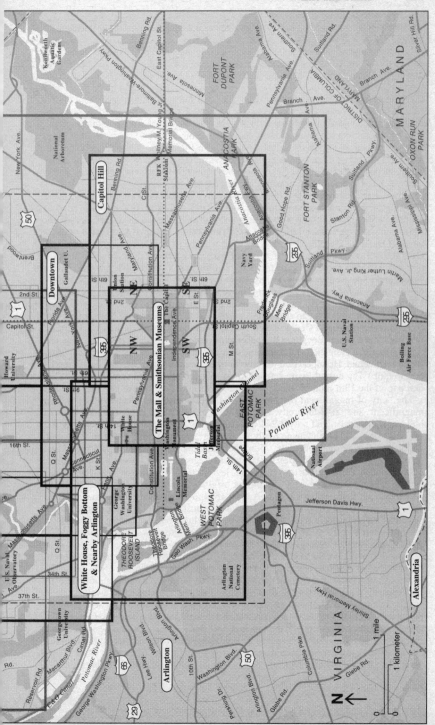

Army veterans converged on Philadelphia demanding back pay, and the scared legislators hightailed it to Princeton, NJ, Annapolis, MD, Trenton, NJ and finally to New York City, where George Washington's inauguration (socialists take note) took place on Wall St. By this point, Congress had two pressing questions: where to put the permanent capital, and whether the U.S. should fund the states' leftover war debt. Politicians from the mercantile northern states, led by the wily Alexander Hamilton, wanted the capital for themselves, but also yearned for debt relief. The prosperous, agrarian South didn't want to subsidize the North, but also sought the capital. Congress assumed the state obligations and decided on a southern capital, instructing George Washington to pick a spot "no more than ten miles square" along the Potomac River. GW picked the Potomac's intersection with the Anacostia River: closest to Mount Vernon, his home, but also ideal, in theory, for a port. Maryland and Virginia together agreed to donate a diamond-shaped parcel of 100 sq. mi. ("ten miles square"), French engineer Pierre L'Enfant was hired to design Washington City, and the real fun began.

L'Enfant was enchanted by stately Paris (who wouldn't be?) and wanted to make Washington the French capital's more rational cousin. The "L'Enfant Plan" laid out central Washington in a grid pattern with an overlay of diagonal avenues, named for states and radiating (mostly) from the Capitol and White House to an effusion of monumental squares. The plan covered only what was then called "Washington City," not Georgetown, Alexandria, or the miles of farmland around their edges. L'Enfant planned a central canal and port facilities, but his real love seemed to be the public spaces and wide avenues of his design. There lay the rub. The plan had already offended the area's landed gentry by seizing more land for roads than they expected, and L'Enfant's exacting "artistic temperament" hardly endeared him to political superiors. When L'Enfant tore down an aristocrat's porch (it stood in the way of New Jersey Ave. SE), not even his friend George could save him from the wrath of the rich. L'Enfant was fired; his deputies Benjamin Banneker and Andrew Ellicott replaced him. (The African-American Banneker, an excellent astronomer, may have been America's first Black intellectual. He supervised the city for three months before age and health forced him to quit.) The ousted Pierre refused to take Congress' offered sum, then spent the first part of the 19th century wandering around Washington trying to get paid.

The "city of magnificent distances" (DC's 19th-century nickname) was far from magnificent, and far from a city. In 1800 the capital village held scattered wooden buildings, dirt roads, and only 3,244 residents, with 123 free African-Americans and over 500 slaves. (The nickname really meant there was very little between the public buildings.) Early "improvements" didn't help matters: Tiber Creek was diverted and dammed to form the Washington Canal, whose stagnant water proved a boon to mosquitoes and bred the enduring, but false, legend that Washington was "built on a swamp." The paint was barely dry on the original Capitol before the War of 1812, which brought British troops here in August 1814 to burn the city down (in a civilized way, of course). The government buildings bit the dust, and Dolly Madison (the fourth President's wife) made a name for herself by carrying from the flaming White House one of Gilbert Stuart's many portraits of George Washington. Washingtonians have fled August ever since.

Though rain put out the blaze the Brits began, Congress was almost ready to throw in the towel; a postwar vote on a proposal to move the capital lost by only eight votes. The Capitol stayed, but so did the problems: as a port city between two plantation states, the District made a logical first stop for slave traders, whose shackled cargo awaited sale in crowded pens on the Mall and near the White House. Foreign diplomats were properly disgusted, deeming DC definitely "southern." Between the slave trade and the swamp air, elected officials understandably decided DC was no place for families: America's elected elite lived in all-male boarding houses, chewed tobacco and fought frequent duels in a famous valley near Bladensburg, MD. National politics became an affair of personalties: after one debate on the Senate floor, a South Carolina Representative clobbered aged anti-slavery Massachusetts Senator Charles Sumner with a cane. A Senator's marriage to Peggy Eaton, the beautiful daughter of a tavern-keeper, began a chain of social snubs and reactions that caused the resignation of Andrew Jackson's Vice President—John Calhoun, later a firebreathing secessionist.

Though subject to severe race prejudice, a town-within-the-town of free African-Americans was growing faster than the rest of the city. By 1850 Washington held 2,000 slaves, 8,000 free Blacks, and 30,000 Caucasians. White fear of uprisings had already created discriminatory laws and social unrest (like the Snow Riots of 1835), but the thriving community close to the "upper South" plantations continued to draw African-American migrants. Enterprising Black people established 15 schools in Georgetown and Washington City before the Civil War.

During the 1830s and 40s British travelers felt compelled to publish their Washington journals, which make delightful reading—a long record of unpaved streets, courteous officials, half-erected buildings, broad vistas, and horrifying slave traffic. Charles Dickens, who dropped by in 1842, called DC "the City of Magnificent Intentions":

> *Spacious avenues, that begin in nothing, and lead*
> *nowhere; streets, mile-long, that only want houses,*
> *roads and inhabitants; public buildings that need*
> *but a public...One might fancy the season over, and*
> *most of the houses gone out of town forever with*
> *their masters.*

The Civil War to World War I

"Such as it is, it is likely to remain," began Dickens' next paragraph. He hadn't counted on the War Between the States, whose outbreak in 1861 turned all military eyes on Washington and turned the capital from the Union's appendix to its jugular vein. The city's social elite brought picnic baskets to the First Battle of Bull Run, but an unexpected Confederate victory forced the Union military to harden up the capital. Soon forts encircled the city, soldiers slept in government offices, and bevies for the army overran the Mall. (Military Rd. NW still links some of these forts.) While Lincoln sent troops to keep Maryland loyal, DC society turned out to help the Union, and the President himself attended a skirmish in his trademark stovepipe hat. (When he stood for a better view of the battle, a Union officer shouted "Get down, you fool!") Though every other building seemed full of troops, Lincoln directed that work continue on the Capitol dome: "It is a sign," he reasoned, "that the Union shall go on." An 1862 *Harper's* magazine cover showed "Convalescent Troops Passing Through Washington," an everyday sight in the overcrowded wartime capital.

The Civil War and Reconstruction sent tens of thousands of former slaves north for a better life; for a time, they found a worse death instead in spontaneous shantytowns like Murder Bay, a few blocks from the White House. After Lincoln's assassination in 1865, the postwar Republican ascension spelled better times for Black people. The five years after 1868 were called the "Golden Age of Black Washington," with new, enforced civil rights laws, Black senators and congressmen, a Black public school system, an African-American at the helm of Georgetown U., and the founding of Dunbar High School and Howard University, for fifty years a two-step path into DC's Black elite. President Grant appointed abolitionist Frederick Douglass the District's Recorder of Deeds. With Sella Martin, Douglass edited the aptly named *New Era;* his 1877 "Lecture on the Nation's Capital" angered Congressmen and still makes good reading.

In May 1870 Congress gave Washington the right to choose a mayor. Holdover official Sayles J. Bowen kicked off a program of public works with a boneheaded move, paving Pennsylvania Ave. with wooden blocks that sank in the mud. Deputy Mayor Alexander "Boss" Shepherd took *de facto* charge in 1871; protected by his friendship with President Grant, Boss Shepherd resurfaced the streets, planted trees, and employed thousands of laborers in his super-efficient city improvement plan, just as L'Enfant would have wished. He tore down decrepit buildings, built sewers, parks, and new roads, and installed streetlights. Of course, all this cost money; the controversial, fast-acting Shepherd sent the city into record-breaking debt, and the federal bailout that followed reattached control of the city to Congress and robbed DC of self-government for over 100 years.

As DC temporarily prospered, federal Washington floundered. The political patron-
age system plus the corruption of the Grant years led a torrent of office-seekers to
Washington, interrupting executives and grinding down Congressmen with persistent
requests for favors and jobs. Charles J. Guiteau, universally described as a "disgruntled
office seeker," shot President James A. Garfield in 1881. Not long afterward, in 1885,
new President Grover Cleveland (by most accounts the first honest Chief since Lincoln) stayed up all night reading job applications patronage-seekers had hand-deliv-
ered; it was time for a change, and Cleveland made one by enforcing the 1882 Civil
Service Act, setting in place the not-entirely-partisan federal bureaucracy we know and
love today. Cleveland struggled through his early-1890s second term, as national de-
pression brought strikes to Chicago and Coxey's Army of 300 unemployed workers to
Washington in search of relief. It was DC's first big protest march, and Cleveland dith-
ered while federal police crushed the encampments.

Washington had more or less turned modern, with apartment houses, telephones, and
electric streetcars. But the capital was hardly a place of beauty. Vigorous President
Theodore Roosevelt, who charged in in 1901, appointed the McMillan Commission to
give the adolescent city a shave and a haircut. The Commission—architects Daniel
Burnham and Charles McKim, sculptor Augustus Saint-Gaudens, and landscape bigshot Frederick Law Olmsted—was the principal planner of DC's current public spaces
and monuments, and it shares responsibility for the "feel" of the city with L'Enfant.
The Commission decided to make the muddy Mall a permanent lawn, build a Lincoln
Memorial at one end of it, designate land elsewhere for parks, erect Memorial Bridge,
and build Union Station (among other things).

Meanwhile DC's African-Americans were losing economic power, even as their
numbers (and artistic achievements) increased. As employment segregation tightened,
most had to work in service industries (driving taxis, catering); the gains of Reconstruction were long gone. While T.R. himself listened to the Black community, Geor-
gia-born Woodrow Wilson supported a segregation so thorough that Black leader
"Lady Mollie" Mary Church Terrell couldn't get young poet Langston Hughes considered for a job at the Library of Congress—not even as a page. Newspapers fanned
white "Negrophobia" into the race riots of 1919. Cafeterias and even public parks became segregated facilities; at the 1922 dedication of the Lincoln Memorial, world-famous educator Booker T. Washington was made to sit in a "colored" section. Though
activists tried to increase hiring, "more federal jobs meant more messengers and janitors," in the words of historian David Lewis. Black Washington in these years was almost an autonomous city, with its own movie houses, theaters, shops, social clubs,
political leaders, and demographic patterns. The city-within-a-city was hardly unified,
though; middle-class Black people in LeDroit Park had little to do with the impover-
ished "alley dwellings" in SW and SE.

FDR and WWII

After the stock market crash of 1929, President Hoover responded to the Great De-
pression with platitudes instead of money. The "Bonus Army" of unemployed veterans
marched to the Mall to demand new benefits, but got dispersed by the National Guard
instead. The election of Franklin Delano Roosevelt in 1932 gave the country a New
Deal: to DC, it brought a herd of idealistic liberals anxious to make the "Alphabet
Soup" of new agencies and relief programs work. NRA, WPA, AAA, YCC, FHA, and
SEC were just a few of the novel acronyms FDR's "try-anything" philosophy spawned;
his liberal ideas enraged Washington's old-money "cave dwellers," who snubbed the
government from Sixteenth St. and Dupont Circle while newcomers with Ph.D.s
moved into Georgetown. The influx began to change the tenor of the city, from "sleepy
southern town" to an expanding young metropolis eternally envious of New York's sophistication.

As the professionals kept moving into Washington, Nazi Germany began invading its
neighbors, and DC had to prepare for war. In 1940 and '41, the President had to dis-
creetly persuade a country still scarred by World War I to help Great Britain try to save
Europe. Isolationist pickets surrounded the White House, Nazi puppet ambassadors
showed up along Massachusetts Ave., and Congress, as late as 1941, renewed the mili-

tary draft by only one vote. After the Japanese attacked Pearl Harbor on December 7, 1941 and the U.S. entered the war, Washington's bureaucracy ballooned. Soldiers on leave filled Washington's ballrooms, FDR's handpicked coordinators (like Leon Henderson and Donald Nelson) tried to straighten out the wartime economy, the War Department seized hotels for office space, and civilians of both sexes poured into DC as war-related clerical jobs opened up daily. A 1943 guidebook called the District "the Cinderella City."

Black Washington was changing, too, but more slowly. The city's segregation came to national attention when the Daughters of the American Revolution barred African-American opera star Marian Anderson from singing at Constitution Hall. Anderson sang instead, on Easter Sunday 1939, on the steps of the Lincoln Memorial, to an audience of 75,000. It had, unfortunately, only a symbolic effect on segregation in Washington. Black labor leader A. Phillip Randolph threatened to organize a march on Washington unless Roosevelt demanded fair federal hiring; he got what he asked for, but the decree did little good. The "alley dwelling" problem was worse than ever; a federal agency "cleared" the slums by kicking out the poor and creating (as a brochure actually announced) "Low-Income Housing for White Families." The tradition of the sit-in began in the 40s when Howard University students entered Thompson's Restaurant and refused to leave until they were served. (Mary Church Terrell led a more successful sit-in there years later.)

FDR's successor, Harry S Truman, dropped a bomb on Washington's racism when his appointed commission released its 1947 report. The Supreme Court's 1953 "Lost Laws" ruling (that civil rights laws from 1872 could still be enforced) essentially desegregated most of the city. Paradoxically, the integration of movie theaters, stores, and eating establishments destroyed many Black-owned businesses, and the African-American commercial districts north of Massachusetts Ave. began to deteriorate. In a similar vein, Dunbar High School—so good that Black families moved here from the Deep South just to send their children to Dunbar—became nothing special after 1954's *Brown v. Board* decision integrated America's schools.

Sen. Joseph McCarthy's witch hunts for Communists terrorized the bureaucracy in the early 1950s, but the government and its city kept getting bigger. (McCarthy finally disgraced himself in the famous, televised Army-McCarthy hearings of 1954.) A crew of Cold Warriors conducted affairs of state throughout the 50s and 60s; John F. Kennedy's narrow victory in 1960 enchanted the press and brought a new cultural savvy to the still-provincial capital. His Texan successor, Lyndon Johnson, once the Senate's shrewd Majority Leader, stampeded the Congress into civil rights action, then steered the nation deep into the Vietnam War. The District had meanwhile grown beyond its borders—the area's population doubled from 1950 to 1970, but much of the increase came in suburbs, where the 1950s bourgeoisie loved to live.

The Last Few Decades

During the turbulent, politicized 1960s, Washington was the nation's March Central, with one demonstration after the next. Martin Luther King, Jr. led two of the most important. The 1963 March on Washington, site of his "I Have a Dream" speech, gathered 250,000 people of all races on the Mall. The '63 marchers, Black and white, middle-class and poor, demanded an end to legal segregation (they got one), while those who came to DC in the 1968 Poor Peoples' Campaign demanded economic empowerment (still waiting). When news of King's assassination (on April 4, 1968) reached Washington, days of riots destroyed parts of DC. As in the Los Angeles Watts riots, desperate African-Americans burned down their own communities, especially the commercial corridors along 14th St., 7th St., H St. and U St. NW.

Goings-on around Washington held the nation rapt during the Watergate years of 1973-4, when the break-ins he authorized and the White House audiotapes he made brought disgrace and resignation for President Richard Nixon. The U.S. bicentennial in 1976 drew more tourists than ever to the capital. The Carter administration (1977-81) brought in Democratic outsiders from Georgia, while the Reagan administration (1981-89) imported conservative outsiders and smooth operators, many from his native California. The two Reagan inaugurals were the most expensive ever. During these years, conservative appointees clashed with more moderate federal workers, pro-business attitudes paralyzed regulators, and the Pentagon's $1000 toilet seats became the stuff of legend. While the "Teflon President's" popularity cowed Congress for several years, the Iran-contra scandals of 1986-88 demonstrated either astounding disregard for the law or incredible ignorance at the top. President Bush's administration bore witness to the passing of communism in Eastern Europe and the Soviet Union, and fought a high-profile but ultimately unsuccessful war in the Middle East. One of DC's last big parades, the Operation Desert Storm victory celebration, emulated the war itself: big, short, weirdly festive, and laden with hidden costs. The District tried to stop the parade's tanks from tearing up 16th St. NW, and helicopters landing on the Mall caused irreparable damage to the Hirshhorn's Sculpture Garden. Amidst the pompous circumstance, scandals, ranging from the very small (the House banking scandal) to the very large (the B.C.C.I. scandal) sent voter confidence plummeting. As the economy continued to deteriorate, H. Ross Perot ran an undeclared but briefly effective outsider campaign for President in 1992, energizing the political process and weakening the Republican hold on the Executive branch. Marches on Washington continued apace, with a largest-ever manifestation for abortion rights in 1992 and a national convention of "Riot Grrrl," pro-sex feminist rockers.

The rest of the city has seen good mixed intimately with bad in the last few decades. Downtown developers kept the economy moving from the late 70s to the late 80s, though often at the expense of residential areas. While city population dropped to 617,000 in 1988, the suburbs ballooned, producing pseudo-urban areas like Rockville, Maryland—that state's second largest city. Burgeoning Black middle and upper classes live in places like upper 16th St. NW, parts of NE, and the Maryland suburbs. DC in 1988 was 70% African-American, 25% white. The white population in the District itself tends to live west of Rock Creek Park; some white residents are moneyed, many are not. While the 70s produced flight to suburban outposts, the '80s lured many back to the townhouses of formerly rundown or blue-collar neighborhoods in the controversial process of gentrification. And hopeful immigrants keep arriving in city and suburbs, especially in Mount Pleasant, Adams-Morgan, Arlington, and Montgomery County. All these groups together fuel the metropolitan area with plenty of cultural and commercial vitality. But a large (and more publicized) segment of Washington sees fewer reasons for optimism: the mid-80s advent of "crack," a cheap, condensed, smokeable form of cocaine, incapacitated thousands of addicts ("pipeheads"). Teens without functional families or schools saw crack as their only career opportunity; dealers' turf wars, often fought with machine guns, made the body count higher than ever. As the long rise in crack use seems to be halting, despair and easy access to guns keep some areas dangerous and bleak.

A century of rule-by-Congressional-committee came largely to an end in 1973, when Congress passed the Home Rule Act, giving DC an elected Mayor, a City Council, and a non-voting delegate in Congress. The first Mayor, Walter Washington, represented the native, middle-class Black establishment; the second one, Marion Barry, grew up in rural North Carolina. Elected in 1976 by a multi-racial coalition, Barry was known as a 60s civil rights leader. Though he promised reforms, his first term was noted mostly for attracting business to the city; the downtown real estate boom was a Barry boast, as was a program that guaranteed summer employment for every enrolled youth. In the 80s, though, the shine wore off. Barry hadn't reformed the city, and some of his close associates wound up in jail on corruption charges. With the advent of crack and the decline of DC's infrastructure, city politics got uglier, with some talking of a white "plan" to retake the city. The Mayor was caught smoking crack (some say entrapped) by undercover federal agents in January 1990. Political outsider Sharon Pratt Dixon, who campaigned with a broom in her hand, was elected Mayor in November 1990. The articulate Dixon has tried to slash bureaucracy, cut down corruption, and restore the city's fiscal health; her rapid, sensible reaction to the Mount Pleasant riots convinced many voters that, given time, Dixon might ameliorate DC's urban crises.

U.S. Government and Politics

The structure of the U.S. government is mostly dictated by the **Constitution,** a famous document penned by smart 18th-century aristocrats (mostly by James Madison) and designed to prevent the twin horrors of executive tyranny and mob rule. The Constitution divides power between the U.S. government and those of the 50 states; there's a list of powers accrued to Congress and to the President, an "elastic clause" letting Congress do other things, and an Amendment (the Tenth) stating that all the leftover powers belong to the states. The federal government has three branches: **legislative, executive,** and **judicial,** each of which limits the power of the others (the "checks and balances" system). **Congress** drafts and votes on **bills; the President** (the Chief Executive) can sign them (making them **laws**) or veto them. A vetoed bill returns to Congress, which has to vote for it by a two-thirds majority the second time around to override the Prez and make the bill law. (If Congress is soon to adjourn, the President can ignore a bill and make it go away—a "pocket veto.") The **federal court system,** capped by the **Supreme Court,** interprets federal laws; the Supremes interpret the Constitution and throw out laws that violate it (even state laws). The real wheels of the government are oiled by more than just elected officials. Thousands of staffers grind away each day researching for Congressfolk, communicating with constituents, and running campaigns. And millions of civil-service bureaucrats spread funds and forms around the nation.

Congress has two levels: the 435-member **House of Representatives** and the 100-member **Senate.** House Members serve two-year terms and are popularly elected and represent numbered **districts** of about 575,000 people within a state, redrawn every 10 years after the Census. 1992 saw new seats created in growing states like California, and incumbents running against other incumbents in declining states like Michigan or Pennsylvania. (A flurry of recent lawsuits has suggested that minority ethnic groups are sometimes entitled to their own districts.) Senators serve six-year terms; each state, even Delaware, gets two. Until the 17th Amendment joined the Constitution in 1913, most Senators were chosen by state legislatures; now state voters elect them. As the original "representative" chamber, only the House may initiate bills that change taxes. Originally the elite chamber, the Senate, gives "advice and consent" to Presidential appointments like federal judges, Supreme Court justices, Cabinet secretaries, and ambassadors. In practice this means the Senate must **confirm** them before they can officially assume their jobs; lower-level nominees are often taken "hostage" by Senators who block their confirmations pending some favor from the executive branch. Recent Supreme Court nominees have faced publicity-heavy **confirmation fights,** with some Senators wondering aloud whether strong disagreement with a judge's beliefs justifies voting against him or her.

Though the whole House or Senate can meet to debate and vote on a bill, almost all their work gets done in **standing committees;** the House has 22, the Senate 16. These committees consider facts and write and edit bills; each one has separate staff members whose job is to be more informed than the Members on whatever issues the committee deals with. **Select** or **special** committees are convened to hold investigations (as for the Iran-contra scandal), administer Congressional affairs (like the House gym), or make members look good (e.g. the Select Committee on Aging). Especially powerful standing committees are the **House Ways and Means Committee** and the **Senate Rules Committee,** which decide when and how a bill will be debated when it gets "reported" from the committee to the House or Senate floor. Most Members have urgent desires to sit on committees related to their state or district (forestry for Oregon, transportation for Detroit). Most also yearn for powerful committees, especially House Appropriations or Senate Finance, which get to mark up and vote on all budgets. Other committees, especially Ethics, are near-powerless pariahs.

The **party leadership,** the top Democrats and Republicans in each chamber, decide who gets to sit on what committee; all the committees are led by chairpersons from the majority party (Democrats, as we went to press) and ranking minority members from the other side (Republicans). Both houses have **majority** and **minority leaders** and **whips** (deputy leaders). While the **Speaker of the House**, chosen from the majority party, presides *de jure* and *de facto* over that chamber, the official head of the Senate is the Vice President, who has little real power and only votes to break ties. Speaker of the House (now Tom Foley, D-Washington [the state]) and **Senate Majority Leader** (currently the pragmatic George Mitchell, D-Maine) are therefore roughly equivalent jobs. (The House Majority Leader is Richard Gephardt, D-Mo.; the Minority Leader is Bob Michel, R-Illinois. The Senate Minority Leader is the often caustic Bob Dole, R-Kansas.) These guys also coordinate and orchestrate each party's legislative agenda. The whole setup depends on the **two-party system,** and would sink into confusion if more parties showed up; on the other hand, America's split into D and R prevents splinter groups and minor parties from holding the influence they sometimes wield in parliamentary systems like Italy's or Israel's.

President George Bush, besides signing off on laws, is Commander-in-Chief of the armed forces and head of the Executive Branch. (That's why the oath of office made him promise to "take care that the laws will be faithfully executed.") Cultural backwater-boy Dan Quayle, his Vice President, does almost nothing, unless the President dies or gets too sick to do his job, in which case the Veep takes the office of the President. Presidents are elected for four-year terms; the 22nd Amendment, a reaction to Franklin Roosevelt's four terms, has banned presidents since from serving more than two. The President is the summit of the complex pyramid of federal bureaucracy, where those near the top are political appointees, those lower down career civil servants. Fourteen **departments** together do most of the government's work; their Secretaries together make up the **Cabinet.** The State Department, now run by James Baker, conducts foreign policy; the Treasury Department, run by Nicholas Brady, formulates economic policy and collects taxes and fees (through the IRS). The Defense Department, headed by former Wyoming Rep. Dick Cheney, presides over military matters. The Attorney General steers the Justice Department, which acts as the government's law firm, representing the executive branch in civil and criminal cases. Independent **regulatory agencies,** like the Environmental Protection Agency and the Food and Drug Administration, enforce their designated laws outside the purview of government departments. The White House also has its own, ever-expanding **executive staff,** which writes the President's speeches, draws up his schedules, and digs up information for him; the supposedly advisory National Security Council was a favorite tool for illegal covert action in the mid-80s.

The **Supreme Court's** nine justices are appointed for life by the President, but must be confirmed by the Senate. The current Chief Justice is the quite conservative William Rehnquist. The Supremes hear and vote on cases involving Constitutional issues; since they interpret the law rather than deciding facts, no jury is involved in their deliberations. The Court is the ultimate guarantor of civil liberties and civil rights, the protections from government intrusion contained or implied chiefly in the Bill of Rights (the first ten Constitutional amendments) and the Fourteenth Amendment. The First Amendment promises freedom of speech, press, assembly, and religion; the Fourth stops warrantless searches and seizures; the Fifth, Sixth, Seventh, and Eighth regulate trials and punishments; and the Fourteenth guarantees no deprivation of life, liberty, or property without due process of law—just one of its several wondrous provisions. The Supreme Court accepts cases for review from federal appellate courts or state supreme courts; it only takes about 5% of the ones it's asked to hear, though. Presidents understandably try to appoint justices who share their philosophies. Until recently they've often been surprised; Eisenhower said the worst mistake he made as President was appointing the groundbreakingly liberal Chief Justice Earl Warren. (Even the Reaganauts have had slight surprises, like the reluctance of David Souter and Anthony Kennedy to go all out for the conservative agenda.) The Court has become increasingly conservative as Reagan and Bush nominees replaced justices from the 60s and 70s who died or retired in ill health; today's Supreme Court is slowly rolling back the broad civil liberties created and guaranteed in recent decades, issuing muddy rulings on civil rights and racial issues, taking the government's side against criminal defendants, curtailing the right to privacy, making the death penalty easier to impose, and edging toward overturning the watershed 1973 *Roe v. Wade* abortion-rights decision.

Most elected officials want to get reelected. Swarms of **interest groups** are happy to aid them, for a price: "lobbies" for specific corporations, industries (like tobacco or steel), or constituencies (like small businesses, gun owners, or teachers) contribute to the campaigns of Congresspeople and other elected officials, generally as a reward or an incentive for certain votes or positions. These organizations, especially the non-corporate ones who can't compete in the contribution race, can pull their members together and swamp Congressional offices with calls, letters, and reasons to favor their cause. In the mid-70s, concern over the power of rich people and corporations led to a law limiting individual giving; the law, in turn, led to **Political Action Committees (PACs)**, organizations which collect and disperse contributions. Congressional incumbents (especially in the House) are more likely than not to get reelected, so PACs like to give to them, rather than to their challengers; this in turn widens incumbents' financial edge, making them even more likely to win again.

Arts and Culture

Architecture

L'Enfant aimed to make central Washington a unified work of art; you may have to look at a map to know it, though. The L'Enfant plan makes the Capitol DC's architectural focus; low government buildings with similar façades were supposed to flank the broad avenues, making most of Washington's vistas converge on the Congress and the dome above it. L'Enfant also expected—and got—plenty of trees all over the city (and that's not counting Rock Creek Park). The Mall was to be a central promenade, leading from the Capitol to some sort of Washington Monument, with trees on either side.

Early DC architects were self-consciously designing for a republic—in their eyes, the first important one since the Romans; their "Federal Style" unapologetically echoed Athens and Rome with columns, pediments, friezes, and marble, marble, marble. Many of these designs—William Thornton's original Capitol and James Hoban's White House, for example—were selected in anonymous competitions entered mostly by amateur builders. The mid-1800s saw the advent of the professional architect; the new breed was more interested in modern European than in ancient Greek models, and many of their works were homes or churches. The outstanding designer among these was Benjamin Latrobe, whose St. John's Church and Decatur House (near the White House) were models of the new sophistication.

Boss Shepherd (in charge 1871-74) sunk megabucks into new sewers, paved roads, and trees. He also paved the road to Victorian excess by authorizing A.B. Mullet's State, War, and Navy Building (now the Old Executive Office Building); the gingerbread windows delight tourists now, but the severe Neoclassicists of the early 1900s were understandably underwhelmed, and kept trying to get the building demolished. Where the OEO goes overboard on ornaments, the Smithsonian's Arts and Industries Building is a garish flood of contrasting colors—fun to look at, but hard to imagine wanting to build. The Library of Congress' Jefferson Building, the magnificent Pension building (now the National Building Museum), and the Old Post Office are more dignified examples of Victorian style.

The budget-inspired freeze on building which followed Boss Shepherd's fall from power thawed around the turn of the century, when Daniel Burnham brought the Beaux-Arts style to Washington. The McMillan Commission (see History above) revamped Washington's public spaces and commissioned Burnham's Union Station. The Commission also proposed the Lincoln Memorial, which heralded a return to Neoclassicism, though this time bigger and sparer. The neoclassic work of the 1930s exposed an unintentional irony: the buildings often seemed too massive or too ornate for their Greek models—the same error the Romans made. Both on Pennsylvania Ave. NW, the National Archives and the Federal Triangle complex are good examples of this mistake. John Russell Pope, the undisputed Emperor of 30s and 40s pseudo-Greco-Roman building, made his masterpiece the domed West Building of the National Gallery of Art on the Mall.

When the dust of World War II cleared, European avant-garde architects had settled in America, and brought with them the International Style office building, unaffectionately nicknamed the "glass box." As always, Washington was about a decade behind New York City in the adoption of this style. DC firms strived to blend international modernism's clean lines and brutal simplicity with the monumental marbleness of already-extant buildings; the Kennedy Center and the National Geographic building are two fairly successful examples. I.M. Pei's popular 1978 East Wing (of the National Gallery of Art) obeys the letter of modernist dictates (big planes, no ornaments, no paint, exposed structural elements) but certainly violates its spirit—the quite beautiful array of glass and white triangles was emphatically not designed for efficiency. In this it heralded the postmodern architecture that moved here in earnest from New York in the late 80s. Postmodern buildings rewrite old styles in modernism's plainer, planar vocabulary, with unusually-shaped windows (for example) set into two-color blocks of sheer granite; the Canadian embassy, which puts Greek elements where the Greeks would never think to put them, is certainly the best "postmodern" building now standing in DC. A few especially nice pomo offices stand among mediocre older buildings at 20th and M St. NW (at the northwest corner) and along K St.

A few considerations make all architecture in Washington unusual. The most obvious is the height limit: nothing in DC can be taller than the Capitol dome (roughly 13 stories). On the one hand, this means that truly big office buildings nearly always turn out sprawling and ugly; on the other hand, you can always see the sky downtown, and many feel it's worth the trade. Many 20th-century buildings have had to occupy awkward acute angles where avenues and circles or numbered or lettered streets intersect; there are as many answers to this as there are angles, though the East wing and the otherwise boring office building at Dupont Circle, Connecticut, and P St. NW provide two interesting solutions. Architects of new embassies have to decide how much the building should fit into Washington, and how much to reflect the style and culture of the relevant nation instead; the Canadian Embassy succeeds at the first, the British and Japanese at the second. Finally, there's the omnipresent classical vocabulary (you've noticed if you've read this far) of domes, columns, long steps, and such; every Washington architect has to adjust to the inevitable monumental atmosphere and the overriding plan of the capital city.

Visual Arts

The body politic's craze to commemorate has burdened DC with a profusion of public art. Eagles squint from cornices, workers labor heroically from the neo-Hellenic friezes above public buildings, and generals and statesmen gesture from horseback in almost every traffic circle. Most public statues date from between the 1870s, when public art remembered Civil War figures, and World War II, when the government found more urgent ways to spend its money. Though few of these statues are worthy of a Phidias, most of them still merit interest: some bear curious anecdotes (like General Scott in Scott Circle or Benito Juarez on Virginia Ave. NW), others have curious inscriptions (like the modern memorial on Roosevelt Island), and still others might actually teach you some history. Aesthetic delights may be had in Lafayette Park, at the Grant Memorial near the Capitol, from the statue of Robert Emmet near Dupont Circle, or the hard-to-get-to Adams Memorial in Rock Creek Cemetery.

The public memorial as its own art form, half sculpture and half architecture, may have reached its zenith in Washington. Though it's really an outgrowth of the same old outdoor statue idea, memorials give designers more room to innovate and viewers more space to contemplate. (Though he ordered trees removed to watch the Jefferson Memorial being built, FDR said he wanted his own monument to be no bigger than his desk.) DC's monuments reach their highest concentration west of the Mall, where the Washington Monument and the Lincoln and Jefferson Memorials lurk; designs range from copycat Greek to the spare self-reflection of the Vietnam Veterans Memorial, the simplest and most affecting piece of outdoor art in Washington. Since 1986, the government has laid down the law on future monuments: the honoree must have been dead for at least 25 years, three commissions must say yes to the project, and the construction must not use federal funds.

Collector Duncan Phillips' museum was showing off modern art while New York's MOMA was still just a building fund, but DC had no indigenous painters till a generation later, when Kenneth Noland's clean-lined abstractions, Gene Davis's parallel stripes, and the experimental canvases of critics' darling Morris Louis were said to form the Washington Color School. Look for Color Schoolers in the Hirshhorn and the Phillips, though there's no guarantee you'll see them even there.

Though it's not a hotbed of visual innovation, Washington is still world-class in terms of the art in its museums. Everybody goes to the National Gallery of Art, whose West Building holds masters everybody should know, from Giotto to Raphael to Vermeer. Twentieth-century and/or touring exhibitions happen in the Gallery's Pei-faced East Wing. The Hirshhorn's one cylinder is powered by two engines: contemporary art and 20th-century sculpture, one indoors, the other outside in the adjacent Sculpture Garden. Off the Mall, check out the Phillips Collection; the Corcoran Gallery for 19th-century American and 1980s art; the Renwick for American crafts; and the National Museum of American Art.

Music

Music in Washington began inauspiciously with John Philip Sousa, who led the Marine Corps Marching Band from the 1880s to the 1900s. The peppery Sousa taught the band to play, then initiated the bevy of military brass concerts and parades that toot, stomp, and honk near the Mall to this day. Later, things began to swing: the Howard Theater and other jazz venues nurtured a string of Washingtonian artists, most importantly the immortal Duke Ellington. Jazz songstresses from DC include Roberta Flack and Shirley Horne; the latter still performs in Washington clubs. Classical music-related performances took off with the building of the Kennedy Center, which gave the National Symphony Orchestra, the Washington Ballet, and many lesser musical groups a home as shiny and multi-chambered as a nautilus shell.

DC didn't go far in rock-and-roll until punk touched down in the early 80s; then, inspired by charismatic bands like Minor Threat, "straightedge" punks shaved their heads and drew Xs on their hands to parade their abstinence from drugs and alcohol. Where rock elsewhere affected combativeness with leather, studs, or long-winded guitar fuzz, DC punk's pre-teen art threat, clothed in T-shirts and jeans, packaged honest teen angst in three-minute songs. As the decade wore on they combined their no-nonsense attitude with real political activism: all-ages shows in rented halls to benefit the likes of the Washington Free Clinic and the American Civil Liberties Union are the best place to take in what's left of "harDCore," as the music is and was called. The winnowing of the punk moment has made space for a profusion of new trends and sounds: bratty feminist girl-rockers and unrepentant old-time punks have taken to heavy percussion (often performed at outdoor festivals at monuments or on the Supreme Court steps), while a new generation of bands is quietly reinventing the New Wave, running record labels out of their basements, and sparring with Olympia, Washington and Providence, Rhode Island for the title of capital of the International Pop Underground. The city recoiled when d.c. space, a punk-friendly fixture of the DC scene, closed down on New Year's Day, 1992. The 9:30 Club picks up some of the slack; after a show there, you can follow the performers to their 3am snacks at Dante's on 14th St. Record-hunters should seek out Dischord Records vinyl by Scream, Gray Matter, or Rites of Spring, or LPs by Government Issue; important bands still around include Wingtip Sloat, Unrest, and nationally-known (to their regret) Fugazi.

Though rap music is as strong here as in any urban center (Basehead lives in SE), the indigenous dance sound of DC is go-go. Repeated efforts to turn go-go music from a DC thing into a national (African-American) craze have failed; some say producers and promoters have failed to do it justice, while others maintain that the experience of live go-go just can't be copied on vinyl. The best go-go bands blend African percussion and instrumental virtuosity with the trimmings (and attitudes) of rap; some have over ten performers. One premier act, E.U. (once known as Experience Unlimited), went national with their dance hit "Da Butt." Other perennials include Rare Essence and Chuck Brown and the Soul Searchers. Hear live go-go outdoors at festivals like Malcom X

Day, Marvin Gaye Day, or Adams-Morgan Day, or call CJ, the TJ (telephone jockey), at 543-GOGO for chill recorded listings of the week's performances.

Theater

Washington has had professional theater for a while, and that's not counting Congress or the President. The "Washington Theatre" in 1821 and the National Theater in 1835 started a trend that flowered over a hundred years later, when Zelda Fichandler's Arena Stage gave birth to the American regional theater movement. Mounting new productions with its own repertory company, Arena succeeded hundreds of miles from Broadway, launching (among other shows) Lorraine Hansberry's *Raisin in the Sun*. While the multi-performing-art Kennedy Center allures, the cup of small-stage innovation has passed to the theater district of 14th St. NW, where several young companies experiment their hearts out.

Literature

> The White House of future poems, of dreams, of dramas, there in the soft and copious moon—
> —*Walt Whitman*, Specimen Days

More than a pit stop, but less than Parnassus, DC has briefly inspired and housed many of America's famous writers. Though British novelists like Dickens and Trollope have left vitriolic records of their visits to Washington, the first first-class scribbler to settle in the capital was poet Walt Whitman, whose years of volunteer work as a Union Army nurse are recorded in his memoir *Specimen Days*. Whitman's Lincoln elegies and his Civil War poems (collectively titled *Drum-Taps*) were surely influenced by his DC days, when cattle milled around the Washington Monument and Union encampments filled the avenues. (Contemporaries recall the poet as skilled and tender in his care of the wounded.) Frederick Douglass (see *History* above) lived in Anacostia when he finished his *Autobiography* in the 1870s and 80s; just beginning to be studied as literature, the book records the trials and experiences of the former slave, Abolitionist, orator, and diplomat. Historian and grumpy belletrist Henry Adams "took it for granted" (in his own words) he would someday live in the White House, just like his grandpa John Quincy Adams; he didn't get the White House, but he did get a well-appointed house nearby, where he and his wife gathered diplomats and historians like Henry Cabot Lodge and George Bancroft in a turn-of-the-century literary salon.

More poetry, and perhaps better writing, emanated from the African-American community in the early 20th century, when the famous Harlem Renaissance established a DC outpost around U St., through Shaw and in LeDroit Park. Ballad-poet Paul Dunbar's move to DC was emulated by Langston Hughes and Jean (*Cane*) Toomer. The MuSoLit club gave Black intelligentsia a gathering place. Later poems of Black Washington emanated from residents Sterling Brown and E. Ethelbert Miller and native daughter Elizabeth Alexander. (And that's not even counting rap.) Other poets made strange pilgrimages to see *Cantos* verse-maker Ezra Pound, confined in St. Elizabeth's for criminal insanity. Literary lions and doves converged on the city for the 1968 March on the Pentagon, led by novelist Norman Mailer and Robert Lowell, whose poem "July in Washington" may be the best ever written about the city. Since World War II, the Library of Congress has attracted important poets for the two-year job of Poetry Consultant; in the mid-80s the title changed to Poet Laureate (held now by Mona Vanduyn). The post has made the LoC the only place for consistently high-class literary events in Washington.

More demotic art forms have found Washington more congenial: popular interest in the machinations of government spawned its very own genre, the "Washington novel." The movies haven't passed DC by either: Jimmy Stewart (*Mr. Smith goes to Washington*) tried to make it honest, Klaatu (*The Day the Earth Stood Still*) landed a spaceship in it, and the journalists of *Broadcast News* seemed to ooze right through the city.

If, like the ancient Greeks and Romans, English-speaking peoples counted persuasive writing as literature, we'd have to admit that Washington had produced a whole genre of American writing: the memorable line (now known as the soundbite) has flourished here at least since Daniel Webster's toast "Liberty and Union, now and forever, one and inseparable." Today's equivalents sound more folksy than sonorous, but Presidents and their speechwriters still specialize in the ringing quip. FDR said "We have nothing to fear but fear itself" when he promised Americans a New Deal. Truman convinced Congress to send millions in postwar aid to Europe partly by invoking the name of its planner, General George Marshall. Martin Luther King, Jr. came to DC to tell the world he had a dream. The past two decades of political follies have brought a new irony to political talk; though more dough than ever goes to media gurus, the most memorable lines are the ones that ring false, from Nixon's laughable "I am not a crook" to Reagan's summary of Iran-contra: "Mistakes were made." One recent entry, President Bush's "This will not stand" (referring to the Iraqi invasion of Kuwait), had, at least, the virtue of honesty. ("He's a rabbit," H. Ross Perot's cryptic depiction of President Bush, shares that virtue.) No matter what you think the U.S. stands for, Washington has always been a favorite place to scribble a speech, stand up, and be heard.

International Washington

Though it certainly experienced a British Invasion, DC didn't start out very international. German-Americans worked in Foggy Bottom, Chinese-Americans hung on to Chinatown, and the African-American community, of course, maintained its Washington presence. 1800s embassies served a social function: a diplomat succeeded by impressing Americans and moving in Senators' circles. (Some embassies did other things, too, like espionage.) An unsupported legend maintains that European governments classed DC as a "hardship post," akin to tropical Asia, where diplomats could dress informally and received higher pay. Ambassadors, especially the British and French, were automatically social lions; since embassies are technically foreign territory, they lasted through Prohibition as legal speakeasies. (Underage Georgetown U. students rent them out for similar reasons.) Though ambassadorial business has become more complicated and more official, diplomatic Washington still adheres to old-school rules, gathering socialites and officeholders in decorated mansions and seating them by arcane rules only the State Department knows for sure. (The *Washington Post Style* section can tell you more than you possibly want to know about the embassy party scene.) The "dean" of the diplomatic corps is the one who's been in DC the longest; until recently, this was the Latvian ambassador, stranded here after World War II when Stalin grabbed his nation for the Soviet Union. (Presumably the elderly gentleman got home in time for Baltic independence.) For all this upper-class aloofness, international catastrophe can make any diplomat into just another budget traveler: when Iraq invaded Kuwait and the U.S. froze both nations' funds, the Kuwaiti embassy employees had to beg their bank for money to buy groceries. You can see, if not touch, diplomatic DC by looking for the foreign flags or national crests that hang outside almost all embassies; Embassy Row, around Massachusetts Ave. near and west of Dupont Circle, holds an especially high concentration.

Another kind of international Washington comprises the DC-area neighborhoods immigrants have imbued with their cultures. The large Hispanic community anchors itself in Adams-Morgan and Mount Pleasant, along with a substantial first-generation African and Afro-Caribbean culture. Southeast Asian immigrants have ringed DC, establishing communities in the suburbs and around Arlington's "Little Saigon." (See the write-ups of these neighborhoods for more on DC's ethnic communities.)

Statehood?

It is not easy to ever estimate the influence of the
people of the District of Columbia. Aside from

American women, they are now the only people in
the Republic denied the elective franchise.
    —*Frederick Douglass, "Lecture on the Nation's*
                            Capital" (1877)

Although District residents have been able to vote for Presidential electors since 1961 and have enjoyed limited home rule since 1973, many Washingtonians feel that they are being denied the rights due to them as American citizens. Although they must pay an income tax imposed by Congress, District residents have no representation in the Senate and only a non-voting delegate, Eleanor Holmes Norton (D), in the House. Congress is still able and frequently willing to meddle in Washington's local affairs, blocking, for example, changes in DC's sex laws and preventing the District from imposing a tax on commuters from Virginia and Maryland. That Congress is mostly white and the District population mostly African-American casts additional doubt on the justice of the arrangement.

Some Washingtonians feel that the only sure path to equality is for most of the current District to become the 51st state, leaving a small enclave of federal buildings as the Constitutionally-mandated Federal district. Sure, the new state would be kind of puny, but there are more residents of the District than of Alaska or Wyoming, and those Americans get full representation and self-determination. Thinking along these lines, members of the small Statehood Party have advocated statehood since 1969. Their efforts peaked in the early 1980s when DC voters called for a convention to write a constitution for the proposed state and later approved the resulting document. Since then, however, scandals in the DC government, a declining population, and dwindling interest among Washingtonians have lessened the chances that a 51st star will be added to the flag anytime soon.

Journalism and Publications

As a rule, the newspaper correspondents in Wash-
ington were unfriendly, and the lobby sceptical.
    —*Henry Adams,* The Education of Henry Adams
                                        (1902)

Where industrial cities might depend on oil or ore, Washington depends on information. Politicians prepare proposals, release reactions, and seek soundbites for newspapers and TV, then scour the next day's news to find out how they look. Ambitious bureaucrats and White House insiders conduct their infighting through press statements, unattributed quotations, "leaks," and surreptitious traffic with journalists ("Sources close to the President said today..."). And the government needs hard facts on everything from rutabagas to rent rates just to make its regulations and mete out funds. All this makes DC a veritable ant farm of journalists: in addition to the Washington-based papers and magazines, newspapers from all over America send their own correspondents here, a welter of trade publications pursue specialized data from their target agencies, and a neglected nest of foreign reporters sweat out their days in the State Dept.

Washington papers began as political organs for individual politicians. The Abolitionist movement produced independent papers with their own agenda, and "advocacy journalism" arose; the African-American community got its own newspaper, the *Washington Bee,* before the turn of the century. President Woodrow Wilson got hip to the power of the press in the 1910s and began to take reporters' questions at semi-regular conferences. Though wealthy publishers hated President Franklin Delano Roosevelt's New Deal, FDR wowed reporters with weekly conferences and regular access, though he also bypassed them and addressed America directly in his radio "fireside chats." JFK coddled reporters (and consequently improved his press), but journalism became more adversarial as race riots, youth movements, and the Vietnam War began to fracture America. Nixon spewed venom at the liberal press via Vice President Spiro Agnew and appointed inquisitional White House "plumbers" to stop the leaks. Perhaps driven by indignation, investigative reporting reached new heights. In 1970, Daniel Ellsberg and the *New York Times* published the famous "Pentagon Papers," which exposed government duplicity about Vietnam. A few years later, *Washington Post* reporters Bob Woodward and Carl Bernstein forced President Nixon out of office with their revelation of the Watergate scandal.

Today's Washington journalists often stay close to the government even as they try to dig up its dirt. Reporters must cultivate well-placed sources to hear the latest inside news; some say this makes the press inevitably partial. Conservatives say the Washington press is always out to get the President, while leftist critics like Noam Chomsky accuse it of accepting the Establishment's priorities. The National Press Club gathers elite journalists together, and the well-known annual Gridiron Dinner lets them "roast" elected officials. The investigative tradition continues, though the most established papers don't always take the lead; throughout the 80s good reporting on illegal covert operations took place on the margin, in the British *Financial Times*, New York's weekly *Village Voice*, and the *Miami Herald*. Televised press conferences let the President reward friendly journalists by calling on them for questions, though the Chief is sometimes tripped up by a sharp, unknown reporter. (Sometimes the Chief even manages to trip himself up unaided.) During and after the Reagan years, pundits worried that video charisma and sophisticated advertising would make political journalism irrelevant. And reporters complained of Pentagon "manipulation" during the bloody-on-one-side Persian Gulf war. Yet alongside the designer media firms, the made-for-TV statements, and non-events, the old-time religion of investigative journalism holds on to a mission and no small following.

In this town of news junkies, the *Washington Post* is the ubiquitous opiate, a newspaper of record with comprehensive, if not always incisive, political, national, and international coverage. Though the liberal *Post* hopes to repeat its Watergate glory days, in this decade of Republican politics its most obvious influence has been local. Disgraced Mayor Marion Barry rode to power on the white votes the *Post's* endorsement brought him in 1978; as if to make up for it, a *Post* endorsement spurred the 1991 election of relative underdog Sharon Pratt Dixon as the new mayor of DC. The *Metro* section covers local news, festivals and shootings; *Style* and Sunday *Show* take care of culture, arts, and fluff. Sunday's *Outlook* bursts with political opinion, while Friday's *Weekend* section helps readers (especially families) decide what to do with the next two days.

The Washington *City Paper* (Baltimore has one too) is a thick, free "alternative" weekly distributed (on Thursdays) to vending machines and cool stores all over town, with excellent local investigative reporting, feature stories, and better coverage of the arts in DC (especially theater and popular music) than the staid *Post* seems able to provide. (Use the *Post's* movie listings, but *City Paper's* movie reviews and club listings.) *CP* editor Jack Shafer's journalism columns persistently scold the *Washington Times*, a conservative daily left over from the early 80s "Reagan Revolution." The *Times'* quest for respectability has bogged down due to staff shakeups, hard-right columnists, and widespread awareness that Rev. Sun Myung Moon's Unification Church funds the paper. But once in a blue moon, the *Times* does find local stories the *Post* has missed.

Some national news-and-views magazines base themselves in Washington. The best-known is the highly-respected (and well-endowed) weekly *The New Republic*, which once carried the standard for American liberalism, and now devotes a fair share of its pages to mounting a legitimation campaign for Bill Clinton (expect to find a few *TNR* regulars in the Clinton cabinet). *TNR* prints news analysis and arts pieces from all over, including a roving "Diarist" column and a by-line by Michael Kinsley. The smaller, more focused *Washington Monthly* likes to boast that it broke famous stories, like Mayor Barry's corruption, National Security Council misdeeds, and design flaws in the space shuttle, years before better-known pages got hold of them. The scrappy *Monthly* is a favorite of aspiring policymakers; they keep tabs on the bureaucracy, but not always on the city as a whole.

Away from the bright lights of national news, Washington's communities run their own papers. The daily *Washington Afro-American* covers Black DC in a friendly, interested way, with attention to individual citizens' achievements. The well-written, free weekly *Washington Blade*, stacked in various stores (especially around Dupont Circle), is the strong gay and lesbian community's paper, with articles, listings, an events calendar, and a directory of gay professionals.

If it's Congress you're interested in, read *Roll Call*, which prints gossip, news and an events calendar for the House, the Senate, and their lucky staffers twice a week. Free *Intermission* serves Washington's smaller theaters. Monthly *Washingtonian* is almost the neighborhood paper of the affluent suburbs; plenty of articles on celebrities and real estate mix with interesting DC trivia, surprising, money-saving tidbits, and lots of lists ("top 10 delis," etc.). *Regardie's* magazine mixes business news with gossip and satire.

The Capitol Hill neighborhood cleans up twice weekly with *Hill Rag*, an area paper distributed all over downtown. The *In Towner* covers local issues (zoning, for example, and crime) for Dupont, Adams-Morgan, and points east (Scott and Logan Circles) and west (Cleveland Park). The *Georgetowner* does the same for guess where. The monthly *Old Town Crier* runs news and restaurant and gallery listings for Old Town Alexandria. Events listings of interest to the tourist community congregate in *Go* and *Where*, slick, free magazines distributed at downtown hotels, where even a budget traveler can pick one up.

Interns and Internships

> *Adams found even the government at his service,*
> *and everyone willing to answer his questions.*
> —Henry Adams, The Education of Henry Adams
> (1902)

From June to August each year, when sensible year-round Washington politicos start making plans to escape from their sweltering city, their ranks are fortified by an influx of collegiate go-getters from all over the country. To some, the pilgrimage to DC is the requisite first step toward the power and the glory. They are the summer interns, and for them, summertime Washington is The Future.

It's really not quite so glamorous. The projects most interns spend their summer pursuing are so far from the heartbeat of American politics that they might as well be working as a caddy. Interns are generally glorified receptionist/gofers who may, if they're lucky, get thrown a minor project to work on, at the behest of a low-level staffer. Still, proximity to power is a decent substitute for real power; even if interns have nothing to do with the day's debates and scandals, they at least hear and chat about them on a regular basis.

The central employer in the summer internship scheme is Congress; Senators might hire anywhere from five to fifteen interns, and the typical Representative's office has two or three. House interns usually hail from their boss's own district, whereas Senate internships are less bound by geography. Many interns work for a committee or subcommittee, meaning *de facto* that they work for the committee chair (invariably a Democrat). Other prime intern havens are think tanks, lobbying groups, and executive branch departments or agencies like the State Department or the Office of Management and Budget. If you're interested, start early; January is not too soon to be making inquiries. Connections help, obviously—this *is* politics.

The vast majority of these summer opportunities for college students are non-paying, and life in Washington is rarely cheap. Fortunately, there are ways to finagle some cash out of the deal. Some universities and foundations award grants to students to cover the summer expenses of working at an unpaid public sector job. Here and there a government branch might have some intern funds at their disposal; the House of Representatives, for instance, retains an endowment (the Lyndon Baines Johnson, or LBJ, fund) that gives each Member $2000 to split among any number of interns from his or her home district. In any case, interning in DC is rarely a profitable endeavor, and usually requires a bit of savings or a magical source of disposable funds. Interning for half the summer is a viable and common option that allows for some gainful employment; the wiliest get themselves out of Washington before the real dog days of August hit.

The intern social scene can be remarkably homogeneous; as a group, these upstart men and women are probably less diverse than the people that run our country (if that's possible). Most collegiate interns live in the dorms of George Washington U., American, or Georgetown (all of which are usually booked by April), or in a sublet townhouse in Georgetown, or (less probably) near Capitol Hill. Most of them also go to happy hours after work, hobnob in Georgetown or Hill bars at night, and play softball on weekends on the Mall for their college's DC summer intern squad. And *all* of them seem to take the oppressive #30/32/34/36 bus at 8:35am from the corner of Wisconsin and O St. NW. At all these locales—bus, bar, dorm—the unspoken main business of an ambitious Washington summer is going on: the schmoozing and smiling, the meeting and remembering, the shucking and jiving with peers that will someday pay off.

But for all the cynicism that a DC internship might inspire, it has the potential to be an unqualified winner. It is the most basic way of getting one's foot in the door of national politics and the best way to start learning how Washington really works. For every internship that's reserved for someone's kid as a political favor, there are four that aren't. And despite the heat, summertime Washington perpetually has a mysterious ability to convince young people that it is definitely the place to be.

Planning Your Trip

When to Go

> Even the Bostonian became simple, good-natured,
> almost genial, in the softness of a Washington
> spring… One could not stay there a month without
> loving the shabby town.
> —Henry Adams, The Education of Henry Adams
> *(1902)*

Keep three variables in mind as you decide when to take on DC. The first is **climate**: Washington tends toward wonderful springs, muggy to unbearably hot summers, cool falls, and chilly, erratic winters. The August humidity is legendarily repellent; a French foreign minister blamed the heat when he killed himself here in the 1890s. (The suicide note explained his aversion to iced drinks, one he shared with President Zachary Taylor, who died of a massive brain embolism upon drinking a mint julep one fateful day in 1850.) We moderns air-condition and endure; still, anyone planning to spend much time outdoors should avoid July and August. The second issue is **annual events:** DC brims with them, and a few (the Fourth of July, for instance) are worth changing your plans to attend. Read *Let's Go's Annual Events* section before you plan your stay. The third question is **where to stay:** most hotels offer summer discounts, and students who come in June, July and August have the added option of university summer housing. Between school vacations, weather, and cherry blossoms, spring is Washington's peak tourism season—if you're coming in April or May, reserve a place to stay way, way in advance. Fall visits provides a whiff of the spring climate, minus the spring crowd. Winter rides in on a raft of December-inspired events, then dumps its snow and departs in haste. And summer, for all its unpleasantness, carries its own hot pot of benefits: summer lodging options and discounts, outdoor concerts and festivals, and student internships. June can even be dry and pleasant; like good politicians, Washington's seasons will sometimes deliver more than the expected.

Getting More Information

Tourism Bureaus

Even if you're trying to travel incognito, contact the tourism bureaus in any city where you're planning to stay more than a few days, especially Washington. Ask them anything. They can provide invaluable last-minute advice about special deals on accommodations, tours, or newly opened establishments. Some will even make reservations for you. Don't be bashful either—they've probably heard it all before. Write or call the **Washington, DC Convention and Visitor's Association,** 1212 New York Ave. NW, Washington, DC 20005 (202-789-7000) or the affiliated **Visitor's Information Center,** 1455 Pennsylvania Ave. NW Washington, DC (202-939-5566). Foreign visitors should contact the **International Visitors Information Service,** 1623 Belmont St. NW, Washington, DC 20009 (202-939-5566). Volunteers speaking many different languages are on hand to answer questions.

The following offices may also be helpful: **Delaware Travel Office,** 99 King's Highway, Dover, DE 19903 (302-736-4271 or 800-441-8846); **Maryland Office of Tourism Development,** 217 E. Redwood St., 9th Floor, Baltimore, MD 21202 (301-333-6611, or 800-874-1313 or 654-9303); **Pennsylvania Visitor's Bureau,** 450 Forum Building, Harrisburg, PA 17120 (717-787-5453 or 800-847-4872); **Virginia Division of Tourism,** 1021 E. Cary St., Richmond, VA 23219 (804-266-0444), DC Branch, 1629 K St. NW 20006 (202-659-5523); and the **West Virginia Travel Office,** 2101 Washington St. East, Charleston, WV 25305-0317 (304-558-2200 or 800-225-5982).

Useful Organizations and Publications

When planning your itinerary, write to organizations and scrutinize the publications which specialize in Washington-area travel. The **U.S. Government Printing Office** offers a number of helpful bibliographies and publications, including the pamphlet *Travel and Tourism,* a very useful bibliography which covers travel within the U.S.; call or write ahead if you have time (write to: Superintendent of Documents, U.S. Government Printing Office, Washington, DC 20402, tel. 202-783-3238). Or stop by when you arrive in DC; the people at the office are congenial and happy to help. The **United States Travel and Tourism Administration,** Department of Commerce, #1863, 14th and Constitution Ave. NW, Washington, DC 20230 (202-377-4003 or 202-377-3811) also provides abundant free literature.

The **Council on International Educational Exchange (CIEE),** 205 E. 42nd St., New York, NY 10017 (212-661-1414) provides information on budget travel, volunteer opportunities, and work and study abroad. Administers ISIC, FIYTO, and ITIC cards. Write for *Student Travels* (free), CIEE's new biannual travel magazine for college students. **Council Travel,** one of CIEE's subsidiaries, provides low-cost travel arrangements and other useful publications. You can get good maps from the **Forsyth Travel Library,** 9154 W. 57th St., P.O. Box 2975, Shawnee Mission, KS 66201-1375 (913-384-3440 or 800-367-7984), a mail-order library that stocks a wide range of city, area, and country maps, or from the **American Automobile Association (AAA),** 100 AAA Dr. (Box 75), Heathrow, FL 32746-5063 (800-222-4357), which sells road maps and travel guides to the general public. (Additional services are available to AAA members; membership fees vary from region to region.) **ADC of Alexandria, Inc.** (800-232-6277) publishes great road and bike maps of the DC and surrounding vicinities ($9), and **Rand McNally** publishes a *Road Atlas* ($12) for the U.S., Canada, and Mexico, both available in local bookstores.

Documents

Carry at least two forms of identification, one of which should be a photo ID. Banks, in particular, will want to see more than one form of identification whenever you cash a traveler's check. Before you leave, photocopy both sides of your important documents, such as IDs and credit cards, and leave them with someone you can contact easily.

Senior citizens and students should bring proof of their age and status, respectively. (Don't expect the extensive student discounts on museum admission, entertainment, transportation, and accommodations available in Europe. Most DC museums are free anyway, though.) A current university ID card will usually suffice for U.S. students. Foreign students may want to purchase an **International Student Identification Card (ISIC),** (see *For International Visitors* below).

Those over 21 will often be required to show proof of age upon entering drinking establishments or purchasing alcohol. Often only a driver's license or passport will be accepted.

Money

No matter how tight your budget or how short your trip, you won't be able to carry all your cash with you. Even if you think you can—don't. Non-cash reserves are necessary. Personal checks will not be readily accepted out of state, no matter how many forms of identification you have.

If you're visiting Washington for more than a month, your best bet is to open a savings account in one of the local banks and get an **Automatic Teller Card (ATM)** which you can use 24 hr. all over DC (see the list of DC banks below). Your money will earn interest in the safety of the bank and be at your fingertips when you need it (albeit only about $250 per day). Shop around for banks without service and start-up charges. Most banks also belong to ATM networks, so you will be able to use the card in other cities if you travel on the weekends. Before you leave, you might also want to find out if your home bank is networked with any DC banks; **Cirrus** (800-424-7787) and **Plus** (800-843-7587) are both popular. Be careful not to rely too heavily on your home town card, though: heavy surcharges attach to such luxuries as using your Sporkie, Wyoming bank card in a Washington, DC bank.

If you're only passing through the city or if you're on the road a lot, **traveler's checks** will be most useful. Most tourist establishments accept them, and almost all banks will cash them. Get your checks in your hometown bank, usually with a 1-2% surcharge; the surcharge may be waived if you have a large enough balance or a certain type of account. Certain travel organizations, such as the **American Automobile Association (AAA),** offer commission-free traveler's checks to their members, but you must go to one of their offices to purchase them. While checks are available in denominations from $10 to $1000, try to purchase them in small denominations ($20 is best, never larger than $50)—otherwise, if you make a small-to-medium purchase you'll again find yourself carrying a large amount of cash. Remember that most exchangers will expect you to convert at least US$100 into traveler's checks.

Always keep the receipt from the purchase of your traveler's checks, a list of their serial numbers, and a record of which ones you've cashed. Keep these in a separate pocket or pouch from the checks themselves, since they contain the information you will need to replace the checks if they are stolen. It's also a good idea to leave the serial numbers with someone at home as a back-up in case of luggage loss.

American Express traveler's checks are perhaps the most widely recognized in the world, and the easiest to replace if lost or stolen—just contact the nearest AmEx Travel office or call the (800) number below. Other well-known banks also market traveler's checks. Major traveler's check or credit card companies offer a variety of free services when you buy their checks or apply for their cards, including emergency cash advances; travel information hotlines; medical, legal, and interpreter referrals; emergency message relays; guaranteed hospital entry payments; lost document and credit card cancellation assistance; travel insurance; and help with travel arrangements.

The following are reliable and well-known traveler's check companies:

American Express, 800-221-7282 in U.S. and Canada; from elsewhere, call collect at 800-964-6665, or contact the U.K. office at (0800) 52 12 12 and ask for the *Traveler's Companion*, which lists the addresses of all their travel offices. The *Check for Two* option allows for double signing with a travel partner.)

Bank of America, 800-227-3460; outside the U.S. call collect 415-624-5400. Connected with Visa/Barclay's under Interpayment. 1% commission for non-Bank of America customers. Checkholders may use the Travel Assistance hotline (800-368-7878 from U.S., 202-347-7113 collect from Canada), which provides free legal assistance, urgent message relay, lost document services, and, if you provide them with a credit card number, up to $1000 advance for prompt medical treatment.

Barclay's, 800-221-2426 in U.S. and Canada; in the U.K., (202) 67 12 12; from elsewhere call collect (212) 858-8500. Connected with Bank of America and Visa under Interpayment. Checks issued in US$ in Canada and U.S., CDN$ as well in Canada. 1% commission. Any branch will cash Barclay's checks free Mon.-Fri.; surcharge on Sat.

Citicorp, 800-645-6556; outside the U.S. call collect 813-623-4100. Commission 1%. Checks available in four currencies including both U.S. and CDN$. Commission of 1-2%. Checkholders enrolled automatically in Travel Assist Hotline (800-523-1199) for 45 days after purchase.

MasterCard International, 800-223-9920; outside the U.S. call collect 609-987-7300. Free from MasterCard, though bank commissions may run 1-2%.

Thomas Cook, 800-223-7373; outside the U.S. call collect 212-974-5696. Available at any bank displaying a MasterCard sign.

Visa, 800-227-6811 in U.S. and Canada; from abroad, call collect (212) 858-8500 (New York) or 71 937 80 91 (London). No commission if purchased at Barclay's.

Even the best-budgeted trip will present unexpected expenses and emergencies, and **credit cards** are the best way to make sure you're not sent home because of them. Many of the places *Let's Go* lists won't accept plastic, but virtually all transportation companies do. The cards are especially handy for renting cars, making reservations, and obtaining cash advances at most banks. Or use them for large purchases to avoid depleting your money at hand. While American Express may be more widely accepted abroad, Visa and MasterCard are at least as common in the U.S.

American Express cardholders pay a hefty annual fee ($55), but membership has its privileges: local AmEx offices will cash one personal check, domestic or foreign, per person per 7-day period. They can also cancel stolen credit cards, arrange for temporary identification, help change airline, hotel, and car rental reservations, send mailgrams and international cables, and hold your mail if you contact them well in advance. American Express operates machines at some major airports through which you can purchase traveler's checks with your card. For more information, call the American Express Card Division (800-528-4800) or AmEx Global Assist (800-333-2639), a 24-hr. helpline that provides legal and medical assistance.

Visa (800-227-6811) and **MasterCard** (800-223-9920) are accepted in more establishments than other credit cards, and they are also the most useful for getting an instant cash advance. Visa holders can generally obtain an advance up to the amount of the credit line remaining on the card, while MasterCard imposes a daily limit. Be sure to consult the bank that issues your card, however, since it may impose its own rules and restrictions. At a bank, you should be able to obtain cash from a teller, who will essentially "charge" you as if you had made a purchase. Not all ATMs will honor your credit card; those that do require you to enter your personal code number. You will have the option to set up a personal code when you receive a new card; if you do not have a code number for an old account, contact the credit card company to establish one. Expect a service charge for electronic cash advances.

Students or those with low income levels may run into problems trying to acquire a major credit card. Some of the larger, national banks have credit card offers geared especially toward students, even those who bank elsewhere. Otherwise, you may have to find someone older and more established (a parent or guardian, for example) to co-sign your application or request an extra card in your name.

Should you run out of money on the road and not have a credit card, you are at the mercy of the cash transfer and cabling systems, both reliable and costly choices. The most inexpensive option, and the one that makes the most sense within North America, is to have a **certified check** or **postal money order** mailed to you. It should arrive in about two days. All banks will cash certified checks, and post offices will redeem money orders upon presentation of two forms of identification (one with photo). Be sure the sender keeps the receipt for the money order, for they are refundable if lost.

Don't forget to write.

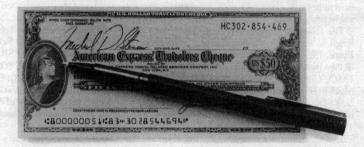

Now that you've said, "Let's go," it's time to say, "Let's get American Express® Travelers Cheques." Because when you want your travel money to go a long way, it's a good idea to protect it. So before you leave, be sure and write.

Cabling money is a more costly alternative. **Bank of America** (800-346-7693) will send money, drawn from a credit card, cash, or a cashier's check, to any affiliated bank. Have someone bring cash, a credit card, or a cashier's check to the sending bank—you need not have an account. You can pick up the money three to five working days later with ID, and it will be paid out to you in traveler's checks. If you do not have a Bank of America account, there is a $40 fee for domestic cabling, $45 for international. Other fees apply, depending on the bank at which you receive the money. **American Express' Moneygram** service (800-543-4080) will cable money domestically for $49 per $750-1000 and internationally for $70 per $750-1000. The first $200 may be received in cash, the rest in travelers' checks or as a money transfer check. Non-cardholders may use this service for no extra charge, but money can only be sent from England, Germany, and some locations in France; other European and Australian AmEx offices can only receive Moneygrams. **Barclay's** will wire money for their customers for the small fee of $15 for sums under $3000 within the U.S., for larger sums you may pay as much as $35-40. To take advantage of a classic, reliable, and expensive service, use **Western Union** (800-325-6000). You or someone else can phone in a credit card number, or else someone can bring cash to a Western Union office. As always, you need ID to pick up your money. Their charge is $40 for $500, $50 for $1000. There is an additional surcharge on money sent from Europe to the U.S, but it will usually be available within two days.

If time is of the essence, you can have money wired directly, bank to bank. A **cable transfer** is the fastest method of transport, requiring 24 or 48 hours to get to a major city or a bit longer to a more remote location. Cabling costs average $30 for amounts less than $1000, plus the commission charged by your home bank. Cheaper but slower is a **bank draft** or **international money order.** You pay a commission ($15-20) on the draft, plus the cost of sending it airmail (preferably registered). If nothing else works, your consulate will wire home for you and deduct a charge from the money you receive. But don't expect them to be happy about it.

Washington banks are usually open Mon.-Fri. 9am to 5pm and sometimes Saturdays 9am to noon or 1pm. All banks, government agencies, and post offices are closed on legal holidays (see *Official Holidays*).

The following banks have more than 15 branches in the District (the main branch is listed as well as the ATM networks to which the bank belongs): **American Security Bank,** 1501 Pennsylvania Ave. NW (624-4000); MOST, Plus. **CITIBANK, FSB,** 1775 Pennsylvania Ave. NW (857-6831; 24-hr. information 857-6700, outside DC 800 431-1350); Cirrus, MOST. **Crestar Bank,** 1445 New York Ave. NW (879-6378); Cirrus, MOST. **Riggs National Bank of Washington,** 1503 Pennsylvania Ave. NW (835-6000; from outside DC 800-368-5800); Cirrus, MOST. **First National Bank of Maryland and DC,** 555 13th St. NW (737-3060); MOST, Plus. **First American Bank,** 740 15th St. NW (637-7643); Cirrus.

Washington has numerous taxes to stymie your budget schemes. It's the government's town—what do you expect? Sales tax is 6%, food tax 9%, hotel tax 11% (plus a $1.50 occupancy surcharge per room per night), and the parking tax is 12%. Taxi drivers, waiters, and other service-industry folk expect a tip of 15%.

Safety

DC became the "Murder Capital of the U.S." according to *Newsweek,* with over twice New York City's murder rate, in 1942. Fifty years later, it's happened again. Widespread addiction to crack, a cheap derivative of cocaine, and the easy availability of high-powered weaponry has made Washington the nation's per capita murder capital. The murder epidemic is mostly an affair of drug dealers shooting one another, though innocents are sometimes hit by the crossfire. (Lately the murder rate has almost stopped rising, though the victims are younger than ever). Almost all of the killings take place in poor parts of the city, in NE, SE or east of 14th St. NW, in areas most visitors do not frequent. If you enter those areas try to do so in a car, and use extreme caution. For those not planning to enter the cocaine trade or move into a housing project,

Washington is among America's safer cities; count robberies instead of killings, and DC's not even in the top ten.

Which doesn't mean you shouldn't take precautions. Use common sense. Protect yourself first, then your money. Avoid public parks after dark. Walk on busy, well-lit streets whenever possible. When you're walking alone, walk fast, and look impatient to get where you're going—even if you don't know where you're going. Avoid proximity to dark alleys or doorways and stay in the light. Don't walk through parking lots at night. Whenever possible, *Let's Go* warns of unsafe neighborhoods, but only your eyes can tell you for sure if you've wandered into one; buildings in disrepair, vacant lots, public housing, and general desertedness are all bad signs. Some intersections have become open-air drug markets, where buyers (often in cars) pull up to street corners to make drug deals; if this seems to be happening where you are, skedaddle. Marginal areas like Logan Circle and Chinatown now host community patrols, civic-minded civilians in orange hats; these volunteers pound pavement to scare away drug dealers and reassure the neighbors that the streets belong to everyone. Count on the orange hats for reliable directions or other friendly assistance.

Homeless people are *not* a danger sign; they flock to areas like Georgetown where other pedestrians have money. (If you see *only* homeless people, that is a bad sign.) Both men and women may want to carry a small whistle to scare off attackers or attract attention. (Remember that you can call 911, for police or an ambulance, for free on a public phone.) The Metro system itself is almost crime-free, but some areas it stops in are not. When deciding where to stay, think about where you'll be going late at night, and how you'll get back—especially in Adams-Morgan, a wonderful neighborhood with lousy Metro connections. After the Metro shuts down, around midnight, DC's bizarre fare system makes taxis a good choice for getting back home.

Thieves prey on tourists for one good reason: they carry more money that the rest of the world. Your best bet is not to look like one, especially away from the Mall. (There are other reasons not to look conspicuously touristy; for one, Washingtonians will like you more.) The farther you go from the Smithsonian, the less you should stand out. Leave the three cameras at home, and don't hang the one you did bring around your neck. Don't gawk at buildings, don't unfold maps on the sidewalk, and use discretion in whom you ask for directions (when in doubt, try a storekeeper). You may even want to cover your cherished *Let's Go* in brown paper. Also, hide your wealth—leave your expensive jewelry and watch at home or at least buried under clothing. Never count your money in public and carry as little as possible. Also, be alert in public telephone booths. If you must say your calling card number, do so very quietly. And if somebody really insists on using the booth, give the phone up pronto—drug dealers often make transactions on public phones.

As for your property—don't carry your money in your back pocket; don't count it on the street or in front of strangers; and don't leave it dangling from a bag or pouch that can easily be grabbed off your shoulder. Keep your important documents—ID, passport, traveler's check numbers and receipts—separate from the bulk of your belongings, along with a small amount of emergency cash and a credit card. **Necklace pouches** that stay under your shirt are the best money carriers; they are not easily accessible, though, and large ones can be quite uncomfortable. **Money belts** can be worn around your waist and buried under one or all your layers of clothing—these are more convenient and nearly theft-proof.

Wherever you stow your belongings, either for the day or for the evening, try to keep your valuables on your person. In the dorm-style rooms of some hostels, consider this rule ironclad. Even a trip to the shower can cost you a wallet or camera. At night, sleep with your valuables under your pillow, and put the straps of your backpack or bag around the leg of your bed. Lockers at bus and train stations are safe. Label all your belongings (and maybe even yourself) with your name, address, and home phone. Try to memorize as many of your important numbers as possible in case they disappear: passport, ID, driver's license, health insurance policy, traveler's checks, credit cards. For more safe travel information, refer to *Travel Safely: Security and Safeguards at Home and Abroad*, from **Hippocrene Books, Inc.,** 171 Madison Ave., New York, NY 10016 (212-685-4371, orders 718-454-2360, FAX 718-454-1391). **Travel Assistance Inter-**

national, 1133 15th St. NW, Washington, DC (800-821-2828) provides a 24-hr. hotline for emergencies and referrals. Their year-long travel package ($120) includes medical and travel insurance, financial assistance, and help in replacing lost passports and visas. **Traveler's Aid International,** 918 16th St. NW #201, Washington, DC, 20006 (202-659-9468) provides help to individuals and families for theft, car failure, illness, and other "mobility-related" problems. They charge no fee but request donations.

One last note: remember to secure your home while you're away. Tell the police or a trusted friend when you'll be gone, but make your house or apartment look inhabited. Have someone pick up the mail and the papers; leave a light on a timer. Precautions taken before you leave will ensure a worry-free trip and a happy homecoming.

Health

Washington's sights are big enough to make racing through them doubly a blunder: not only will you exhaust yourself, but you'll have missed most of what you tried to see. Drink fluids in July and August, when heat exhaustion can become a real danger. Be especially good to your feet—some good walking shoes, clean socks, and a bit of talcum powder will go a long way. If you wear glasses or contact lenses, bring a prescription and/or an extra pair. Lens wearers can avoid dried-out contacts by drinking sufficient fluids and switching to glasses where the air is dry or smoky. Be sure all immunizations, such as tetanus shots, are up to date. All travelers should be concerned about Acquired Immune Deficiency Syndrome (AIDS), transmitted through the exchange of body fluids with an infected individual. Avoid unprotected sex and sharing intravenous needles. For more information you can call the AIDS Hotline at the **Centers for Disease Control** (800-342-2437).

Before you leave, check whether your insurance policy (if you have one) covers medical costs incurred while traveling (see *Insurance*). Always have proof of insurance and policy numbers with you. If you're a student, you may be covered by your family's policy. If you have insurance through your school, find out if the policy includes summer travel. If you choose to risk traveling without insurance, you still have avenues for health care that bypass hospitals and private practice. Call the local hotline or crisis center listed in *Let's Go* under *Practical Information*. Operators at these organizations have numbers for public health organizations and clinics that treat patients without demanding proof of solvency. University teaching hospitals usually run inexpensive clinics as well. If you require **emergency treatment,** call 911 or go to the emergency room of the nearest hospital. The following are the major hospitals in the District: **Capitol Hill Hospital,** 700 Constitution Ave. NE (269-8000); **Children's National Medical Center,** 111 Michigan Ave. NW (745-5000); **George Washington University Medical Center,** 901 23rd St. NW (994-1000); **Georgetown University Medical Center,** 3800 Reservoir Rd. NW (687-4600); **Howard University Hospital,** 2041 Georgia Ave. NW (865-6100); **Sibley Memorial Hospital,** 5255 Loughboro Rd. NW (537-4000); **George Washington University Medical Center,** 2150 Penn. Ave. NW (296-0816).

If you have a chronic medical condition that requires medication on a regular basis, consult your physician before you leave. Carry copies of your prescriptions and always distribute medication and/or syringes among all your carry-on and checked baggage in case any of your bags is lost. If you are traveling with a medical condition that cannot be easily recognized—such as diabetes, an allergy to antibiotics or other drugs, epilepsy, or a heart condition—you should obtain a **Medic Alert identification tag** (about $30) to alert both passersby and medical personnel of your condition in case of emergency. Such a tag is engraved with the wearer's primary medical condition, an identification number, and a 24-hr. hotline number that can provide critical medical information in an emergency. Contact Medic Alert Foundation International, Turlock, CA 95381-1009 (800-ID-Alert or 800-432-5378).

The **American Diabetes Association** (Attention: Patient Services, 1660 Duke St., Alexandria, VA 22314, (800-232-3472); DC office located at 1211 Conn. Ave., NW; 331-8303) also provides copies of the article "Travel and Diabetes" and diabetic ID cards. Contact your local ADA office for information. For more health-related advice, consult The Pocket Medical Encyclopedia and First-Aid Guide (Simon and Schuster, $5; write to Mail Order Dept., 200 Old Tappan Rd., Old Tappan, NJ 07675, or call 800-223-2348). In addition, the International Association for Medical Assistance to Travellers (IAMAT) provides members with free pamphlets and a directory of fixed-rate English-speaking physicians throughout the world. Membership is free, although donations are appreciated. Contact IAMAT at 415 Center St., Lewiston, NY 14092 (716-754-4883), or in Canada at 40 Regal St., Guelph, Ont. N1K 1B5 (519-836-0102). If you would like more information concerning health problems you may encounter in you travels, you can send away for the First-Aid and Safety Handbook ($14.95) from the American Red Cross. You can write to 99 Brookline Ave., Boston MA 02215, or to any local office in the U.S. to purchase this book. If you are interested in taking one of the many first-aid and CPR courses that the American Red Cross offers, contact one of their local offices. Courses are relatively inexpensive, and are usually very well taught.

If you are in the DC area and need an abortion, you may want to contact the **National Abortion Federation**, 1436 U St. NW, Washington, DC 20009 (667-5881). NAF is a professional association of providers of abortion. Call their toll-free hotline (800-772-9100, from DC 667-5881; open Mon.-Fri. 9:30-5:30) for information, counseling, and the names of qualified medical professionals in the area. NAF has developed informational publications available to individuals and health care clinics alike. The NAF will refer you only to clinics meeting certain safety and operational standards.

Alcohol and Drugs

In Washington, DC, the drinking age is 21 years of age and is, mostly, strictly enforced. Many places will want to see a photo ID when you order or buy alcohol. If you are 21 and you want to drink hard alcohol on Sundays, stock up Saturday night—only beer and wine can be sold on the seventh day. Possession and consumption of marijuana, cocaine, and most opiate derivatives is a federal offense subject to imprisonment.

Driving under the influence of alcohol or drugs is stupid. It is also punishable by law. Fines are stiff and a jail sentence is likely. By the way, officials at both the United States and Canadian borders also take drunk driving very seriously. No matter what kind of transportation you use for entry, if the customs guards discover a drunk driving conviction, you will be denied access.

Insurance

Before leaving home, check to see if your homeowner's insurance (or your family's coverage) will cover theft and accident while you're on the road; coverage usually includes loss of travel documents such as passports, plane tickets, and rail passes up to $500. For U.S. residents, **Medicare** covers travel in the U.S., Canada, and Mexico. **American Express** cardmembers automatically receive car-rental and flight insurance on purchases made with the card. If you need additional insurance, the **Council on International Educational Exchange (CIEE)** (212-661-1414) offers a **Trip-Safe Plan** that covers the entire U.S. for **ISIC** cardholders (see *For International Visitors,* below) and non-carriers alike. The Trip-Safe plan includes US$3000 of accident-related coverage and US$100 per day of in-patient health coverage for up to 60 days, US$1000 for 24-hr. all-risk death and dismemberment, as well as $25,000 for accidental death and dismemberment as an airline passenger. The plan also provides insurance for baggage loss, trip cancellation, and many other infelicities.

Most of the following insurance companies offer coverage for trip cancellation/interruption, baggage loss, accidents, and sickness, but ask individual firms for specifics. Some also provide on-the-spot hospital expenses, emergency cash advances, and guaranteed transferals, and most have 24-hr. hotlines. Senior citizens should be aware that many policies have an upper age limit of 70.

You can buy a policy directly from these firms or through a travel agent operating on their behalf:

Access America, Inc., P.O. Box 90310, Richmond, VA 23230-9310 (800-284-8300). A subsidiary of Blue Cross/Blue Shield. Covers trip cancellation/interruption, on-the-spot hospital admittance costs, emergency medical evacuation, and a 24-hr. hotline.

Carefree Travel Insurance, 120 Mineola Blvd., Mineola, NY 11501 (800-645-2424). Package includes coverage for baggage loss, accidents, medical treatment, and trip cancellation or interruption; the last can also be purchased separately. 24-hr. hotline.

Edmund A. Cocco Agency, 220 Broadway, #201, Lynnfield, MA 01940 (800-821-2488, in MA 617-595-0262). Coverage against accident, sickness, baggage loss, and trip cancellation or interruption. Emergency medical evacuation covered as well. Payment of medical expenses "on-the-spot" anywhere in the world. Protection against bankruptcy or default of airlines, cruise lines, or charter companies. Trip cancellation/interruption coverage $5.50 per $100 of coverage. Group rates available. 24-hr. hotline.

The Traveler's Insurance Co., 1 Tower Sq., Hartford, CT 06183-5040 (800-243-3174, in CT, HI, or AK 203-277-2318). Insurance against accident, baggage loss, sickness, trip cancellation or interruption, and company default. Covers emergency medical evacuation as well. Available through most travel agencies.

Travel Guard International, 1145 Clark St., Stevens Point, WI 54481 (715-345-0505 or 800-782-5151). Basic ($19), deluxe ($39), and comprehensive "Travel Guard Gold" (8% of total trip cost) packages cover baggage delay, car rental, accidental death, and trip cancellation or interruption. 24-hr. hotline for policy-holders.

No matter how you are covered, always have proof of insurance and policy numbers on hand during your trip. Keep police reports, doctor's statements, and receipts, as insurance claims can only be filed after you return home and must be accompanied by the relevant documents. Also, make sure that you file within the time limit.

Packing

Pack light. The number of stops on your itinerary should be inversely proportional to the amount of clothes you pack. In other words, if Washington is the one-and-only this time, you may pack a bit more than if you'll only be passing through on your way to Fresno. But don't go overboard. You'll have less to carry and fewer worries. A rule of thumb: set out everything you think you need, then pack only half of it.

The first order at hand when packing is what sort of luggage to carry. Backpacks are best suited to hiking and excessive traveling between cities. Duffel bags mush well into small spaces (like lockers at bus and trains stations, for example). No matter what bag you choose, be sure to bring a daypack for carrying valuables (traveler's checks, tickets, credit cards, ID), a change of clothes, and your trusty *Let's Go.*

As for what to put inside these bags—stick to the basics. The layering approach works well. Bring several t-shirts, a few pairs of shorts or long pants, a few sweatshirts and/or sweaters (depending on the weather), underwear, and socks, then add layers as the temperature drops. You may also need an outfit for going out in the evening—some restaurants, theaters, and events like to require an upmarket outfit. Sturdy and comfortable shoes are a necessity; bring two pairs. A winter coat, bathing suit, and towel should complete the wardrobe. Dark clothes will hide wear and tear more easily. And do yourself a favor, only take clothes that can be thrown in a washing machine or hand-washed. Travel and dry cleaning are incompatible.

Average Monthly Temperatures

> *There has lately been much suffering here from heat—I go around with an umbrella and a fan. I saw two cases of sun-stroke yesterday, one in Pennsylvania Avenue, and another in Seventh Street.*
> —Walt Whitman, *Specimen Days*

Washington weather can be sub-zero (rarely), pleasantly mild (most of the time) or unbearably hot and humid (July and August). Air quality also declines in the summer, so those with breathing problems should be careful; between the stop-and-go traffic and the low elevation, Georgetown sees the worst of the smog. The following are the mean monthly temperatures for the District:

January 35°F

February 38°

March 46°

April 57°

May 66°

June 75°

July 79°

August 78°

September 71°

October 59°

November 49°

December 39°

—*courtesy of the National Oceanic and Atmospheric Administration*

Keeping in Touch

Your friends and families will be able to keep in touch with you easily by phone or mail, provided they know where you'll be. It may be easiest for you to call them collect or with a credit card. To save everyone some money, you can try calling from a pay phone and having the person on the other end call you back. Some pay phones do not receive incoming calls, however; when this is the case, they are usually so marked where the phone number is printed. Beware of using phones in hotels; heavy surcharges are usually attached, even for local calls.

If you want to receive mail while on the road, it can be sent to you **c/o General Delivery.** Picking up mail sent to "General Delivery, Washington, DC" is more difficult than catching a bobcat with a titwillow: rather than going to a post office downtown, it goes to the main national sorting facility on Brentwood Rd. NE, miles from everywhere and not served by Metrorail. Worse still, you can't send General Delivery mail to another DC post office, even if you know the ZIP—it all ends up in Brentwood. Letters to you should be addressed with your name (last name capitalized and underlined, to ensure proper filing), the words "General Delivery," the city/town and state, and the General Delivery ZIP or postal code for the town (DC's main post office is 20066). Almost any morsel of DC-related postal information can be retrieved through the computer that answers the phone at the Postal Hotline (202-526-3920). The U.S. Postal Service has other ZIP code hotlines everywhere in America. The envelope should also say "Please hold until <...>," the blank filled in with a date a couple weeks after your correspondent expects you to pick up the letter. When you claim your mail, you'll have to present ID; if you don't claim a letter within two to four weeks, it will be returned to its sender.

American Express cardholders and checkholders can receive letters at those AmEx Travel Service offices that provide **"Client Letter Service."** For a complete list of offices and instructions on how to use the service, get the "Directory of Travel Service Offices" at any office or call 800-528-4800. The DC office is: 202-289-8800.

Official Holidays

Keep in mind the following dates when you plan your vacation. Government agencies, post offices, and banks are closed on certain holidays, and businesses may have special (shorter) hours. Many holidays are the occasions for parades and public celebrations.

U.S. National Holidays for 1993:

New Year's Day, Jan. 1

Martin Luther King, Jr.'s Birthday, Jan. 20 (observed)

Presidents Day, Feb. 17 (observed)

Easter, April 19

Memorial Day, May 25

Independence Day, July 4

Labor Day, Sept. 7

Columbus Day, Oct. 12

Veterans Day, Nov. 11 (observed)

Thanksgiving, Nov. 26

Christmas Day, Dec. 25

Specific Concerns

Student Travel

Students are often entitled to special discounts on admission prices, hotel rates, and airfares. Most places accept a current university ID or an **International Student Identity Card (ISIC)** as sufficient proof of student status. An ISIC for 1993 will cost you around $14 and you can obtain one from the student travel office of your university (if it has one) or else from one of the organizations listed below. When you apply for an ISIC, be sure to have up-to-date proof of full-time student status (usually a student ID, but sometimes official university documents), a vending-machine photograph (1 1/2 x 2-inch) with your name printed and signed in pencil on the back, and proof of your birthdate and nationality. The ISIC card is valid for up to 16 months, always expiring in December. Students must be at least 12 years old to be eligible. Non-students under 26 years of age should look into the **International Youth Card** from the **Federation of International Youth Travel Organizations (FIYTO),** which may help you take advantage of age-based discounts. Applicants must submit proof of birthdate, a photo, and a fee of $10. For further information, write to the FIYTO at Islands Brygge 81, DK-23X Copenhagen S, Denmark (tel. 31 54 60 80).

The following agencies specialize in travel for high school and university students. They sell ISIC cards and have tips on transportation discounts. For listings of similar organizations that serve foreign travelers, see *For International Visitors.*

Council on International Educational Exchange (CIEE) Travel Services. Advice on questions ranging from package tours and low-cost travel to work opportunities and long-distance hiking. Special academic and employment exchange programs. ISIC and International Youth cards. Write for *Student Travels* (free), CIEE's new biannual travel magazine for college students. **Council Travel,** a budget travel subdivision of CIEE, operates 30 offices throughout the U.S., including the following: **Boston,** 729 Boylston St. #201, MA 02116 (617-266-1926); **Chicago,** 1153 N. Dearborn St., IL 60601 (312-951-0585); **New York,** 205 E. 42nd St., NY, NY 10017 (800-223-7402 or 212-661-1450; one of three offices in the City—write or call the NY office for general information and for the address and phone of an office closer to you); **Los Angeles,** 1093 Broxton Ave. #220, CA. 90024 (213-208-3551); **San Francisco,** 919 Irving St. #102, CA 94122 (415-566-6222).

Let's Go Travel Services, Harvard Student Agencies, Inc., Thayer Hall-B, Harvard University, Cambridge, MA 02138 (617-495-9649). Sells railpasses, American Youth Hostel memberships (valid at all IYHF/HI youth hostels), International Student and Teacher ID cards, International Youth Cards for non-students, travel guides (including the *Let's Go* series), swell maps, discount airfares and a complete line of budget travel gear. All items are available by mail.

STA Travel, 17 E. 45th St., New York, NY 10017 (800-777-0112 or 212-986-9470) operates 10 offices in the U.S. and over 100 around the world. Offers discount airfares for travelers under 26 and full-time students under 32.

Travel CUTS (Canadian Universities Travel Service, Ltd.): 187 College St., Toronto, Ont. M5T 1P7 (416-979-2406). Canadian distributor of the ISIC, IYHF/HI, and International Youth Cards. Offers discount travel services and publishes a quarterly newsletter, *Canadian Student Traveler.* Write for address and phone of branches in Burnaby, Calgary, Edmonton, Halifax, Montreal, Ottawa, Quebec, Saskatoon, Sudbury, Victoria, Waterloo, Winnipeg, and London.

Senior Citizens

Discounts abound for the mature traveler. Don't lie about your age; take advantage of reduced rates on public transportation, museum, movie, theater and concert admissions, accommodations, and even dining. All you need is identification proving your age (a driver's license, a Medicare card, or a membership card from a recognized society of retired people).

Eight dollars will enroll you and your spouse in the **American Association of Retired Persons (AARP),** open to U.S. residents aged 50 and over. As members you can take advantage of **AARP's Purchase Privilege Program** with discounts at major hotel/motel chains, from car-rental and sight-seeing companies. For more information, write 601 E St. NW, Washington, DC 20049 (202-434-2277). For a fee, membership in the **September Days Club,** 2571 Buford Highway, Atlanta, GA 30324 (800-241-5050) entitles you to a 15-40% discount at Days Inns across the U.S. They also have a travel service for senior citizens.

Through the **National Council of Senior Citizens,** 1331 F St. NW, Washington, DC 20004 (202-347-8800), anyone of any age can get hotel and auto rental discounts, a senior citizen newspaper, use of a discount travel agency, and members over 65 years of age receive supplemental Medicare insurance. Fees are $12 per year or $150 for lifetime membership.

The **International Youth Hostel Federation/Hostelling International** sells membership cards ($15) at a discount to those over 54. Write the AYH National Headquarters, P.O. Box 37613, Washington, DC 20013-7613 (202-783-6161). The IYHF is currently in the process of adopting a new seal of approval. Members of the network will soon be using the trademark blue triangle and the name "Hostelling International" ("HI"). Look for these symbols to insure that you are staying at IYHF/AYH-affiliated hostels. (See Accommodations for information on hostels.) To explore the outdoors, U.S. citizens and permanent residents 62 and over can buy a **Golden Age Passport** ($20 at park entrances), that gives you free entry into all national parks and a 50% discount on recreational activities. Write or stop by the U.S. Department of the Interior, National Park Service, P.O. Box 37127, Washington, DC 20013-7127 or call 202-208-4747.

Helpful publications regarding travel for senior citizens abound. *Travel Tips for Older Americans,* a pamphlet put out by the U.S. Government, may be useful. For a copy, send $1 to the **Bureau of Consular Affairs,** Superintendent of Documents, U.S. Government Printing Office, Washington, DC 20402 (202-783-3238). The *International Directory of Access Guides* ($5) has listings specifically for the elderly; order from **Rehabilitation International USA,** 112 Broadway #704, New York, NY 10010. **Pilot Books** puts out two travel books for senior citizens: *Senior Citizen's Guide to Budget Travel in the United States and Canada* ($6 ppd.) and *The International Health Guide for Senior Citizen Travelers* ($5). Order from Pilot Books, 103 Cooper St., Babylon, NY 11702 (516-422-2225) and add $1 for postage. *Get Up & Go: A Guide for the Mature Traveler* ($10.95 plus $1.50 postage), by Gene and Adele Malott, is available from **Gateway Books,** 13 Bedford Cove, San Rafael, CA 94901 (415-454-5215). **Penguin USA,** 120 Woodbine St., Bergenfield, NJ 07621 (800-331-4624) distributes the *Discount Guide for Travelers over 55,* by Caroline and Walter Weintz (Dutton, $8 plus $1.50 postage).

Women Travelers

Women exploring any area on their own inevitably face additional safety concerns. Forgo cheap accommodations in city outskirts—the risks outweigh any savings—and stick to youth hostels, university accommodations, bed-and-breakfasts, and organizations offering rooms for women only. A woman should *never* hitchhike alone; it is dangerous even for two women together.

If you find yourself the object of catcalls or unwelcome propositions, your best answer is no answer. Always look as if you know where you're going (even when you don't), and maintain an assertive, confident posture wherever you go. If you feel uncomfortable asking strangers for information or directions, it may be easier to approach other women or couples. Always carry enough change for a bus, taxi, or phone call. And in emergencies, don't hesitate to yell for help.

Know the emergency numbers for the area you're visiting; *Let's Go* lists them in the *Practical Information* section of each area. More information and safety tips can be found in the *Handbook for Women Travelers,* available from Judy Piatkus (Publishers) Ltd., 5 Windmill St., London W1P 1HF, England (07 16 31 07 10). The folks who produced *Gaia's Guide* (no longer available) are now publishing *Women Going Places,* a new women's travel/resource guide, emphasizing women-owned and operated enterprises. The guide is aimed at lesbians, but useful to all women. Available from IN-LAND Book Company, P.O. Box 120261, East Haven, CT 06512 (203-467-4267).

Gay and Lesbian Travelers

American attitudes toward gays and lesbians are gradually improving, especially in the big cities, but complete acceptance has yet to be achieved. Washington itself has large openly gay and lesbian populations, but semi-rural communities in the region can be intolerant. In the District, pick up the weekly *Washington Blade,* DC's indispensable but dull gay newspaper, which covers restaurants, bars, services, meetings, and events. The *Gay and Lesbian Services Guide* lists businesses in the metro area that serve the gay community; you can pick it up at the bookstore **Lambda Rising,** 1625 Connecticut Ave. NW (462-6969). The **Gay and Lesbian Switchboard** number is 628-4667. The Gay and Lesbian hotline number is 833-3234. The **Gay Information and Assistance** office (667-5139) is located at 5020 Cathedral Ave. NW. The **Gay and Lesbian Alliance Against Defamation** (429-9500) is located at 1747 Conn. Ave. NW. The **Gay Men's V.D. clinic** (797-3532) is located at 1407 S St. NW. Wherever possible, *Let's Go* lists gay and lesbian information lines, community centers, bookshops, and special services. You may also want to check out the alternative *City Paper,* which includes an extensive listing of cultural events (films, theater, and museums) that may be of interest to gays and lesbians. [The *City Paper* also features the popular "Drunken Office Girl" comic strip—Ed.] In Baltimore, the *Baltimore Alternative* and the *Fun Map* cover bars, restaurants, and hotels for gays and lesbians. The number for the Gay and Lesbian Information Bureau in Arlington, VA is 703-578-4542.

For a continental directory of gay and lesbian establishments and services, consult the *Gay Yellow Pages* ($12). Order a copy from Renaissance House, P.O. Box 292, Village Station, New York, NY 10014-0292 (212-674-0120). You can also contact Renaissance House or write to 100 E. Biddle St., Baltimore, MD 21202 (301-727-5677) for a copy of the *Spartacus International Gay Guide* ($28), a worldwide touring guide; send a stamped, self-addressed envelope for a list of available publications. **Giovanni's Room,** 345 S. 12th St., Philadelphia, PA 19107 (215-923-2960), stocks many of the books mentioned in this section. Add $3.50 per book for shipping within the U.S.

The following publications provide additional listings and advice. *Bob Damron's Address Book, a Guide for Gay Men* ($12.95), *The Women's Traveler* ($10, plus $4.50 shipping), and *Inn Places: USA and Worldwide Gay Accommodations* ($14.95) are available from the **Bob Damron Company, Inc.,** P.O. Box 11270, San Francisco, CA 94101 (800-462-6654 or 415-777-0113).

Disabled Travelers

Most modern-day cities have been built by the physically-abled, for the physically-abled. Times are gradually changing, though, and with a little research and planning ahead, the disabled traveler can gain access to all but the most awkwardly built establishments. Call restaurants, hotels, parks, and other facilities to find out about ramps, the presence of easy trails, the width of doors, the dimensions of elevators, etc. Also inquire about restrictions on motorized wheelchairs. *Let's Go* indicates disabled access whenever possible.

Parts of Washington, especially the federally-owned parts, do their best to accommodate those with disabilities. Contact the National Capital Park service at 202-619-7222 or 202-619-7083 (TDD) for information about special services. The **Information, Protection, and Advocacy Center for Handicapped Individuals** (202-966-8081, TDD 202-966-2500) can help in any sort of emergency, large or small. Contact them for a copy of their book, *Access Washington: A Guide to Metropolitan Washington for the Physically Disabled* ($6), which lists the best-equipped accommodations, restaurants, and sights. Visually-impaired persons should write to Washington Ear, Inc., (301-681-6636), which sells large print and tactile atlases of the Washington area. **Columbia Lighthouse for the Blind,** 1421 P Street NW, Washington, DC 20005, (462-2900) distributes free tactile maps of the Metro system. The number for **Gay Deaf Assistance** is TDD 628-4669.

If you are planning to visit a national park or attraction run by the National Park Service, you should obtain a free **Golden Access Passport** ($20) available at all park entrances and from Federal offices whose functions relate to land, forests, or wildlife. The Golden Access Passport entitles disabled travelers and their families to enter the park for free and provides a 50% reduction on all campsite fees.

Arrange transportation well in advance to ensure a smooth trip. If you give sufficient notice, some major car rental agencies have hand-controlled vehicles at certain locations. Call **Avis** (800-331-1212, at least 24 hours notice), **Hertz** (800-654-3131, 2-3 days notice), or **National** (800-328-4567, at least 24 hours notice). Both **Amtrak** and the airlines must accommodate disabled passengers if notified in advance—simply tell the ticket agent when making reservations which services you'll need. Hearing-impaired travelers may contact Amtrak (800-872-7245, in PA 800-322-9537) using teletype printers. **Greyhound** buses will also provide free travel for a companion; if you are without a fellow-traveler, call Greyhound (800-752-4841) at least 48 hours before you plan to leave and they will make arrangements to assist you. Seeing-eye and hearing-ear dogs also ride Greyhound without charge. For information on transportation availability in DC (or any other U.S. city), contact the **American Public Transit Association,** 1201 N.Y. Ave. NW, Suite 400, Washington, DC 20005 (202-898-4000).

The **Travel Information Service** at the **Moss Rehabilitation Hospital,** 1200 W. Tabor Rd., Philadelphia, PA 19141 (215-329-5715), is an excellent source of information on tourist sights, accommodations, and transportation for the disabled; it charges only a nominal postage fee if you request the packet of information on travel accessibility. The **Society for the Advancement of Travel for the Handicapped,** 345 Fifth Ave., Ste. #610, New York, NY 10016 (212-447-7284); fax 212-620-2159), provides several useful booklets as well as advice and assistance on trip planning. Membership is $45 per year, $25 for senior citizens and students; non-members may obtain publications by sending a self-addressed stamped envelope and $2 to cover expenses. The **American Foundation for the Blind** recommends travel books and issues identification discount cards ($10) for the legally blind. For an ID application or for other information, contact the American Foundation for the Blind, 15 W. 16th St., New York, NY 10011 (800-232-5463 or 212-620-2159).

Other organizations specialize in arranging tours. **Evergreen Travel Service,** 4114 198th St., SW #13, Lynnwood, WA 98036 (800-435-2288), offers tour programs for travelers in wheelchairs, blind travelers, deaf travelers, and "slow walkers." **Directions Unlimited,** 720 N. Bedford Rd., Bedford Hills, NY 10507 (800-533-5343; in NY, 914-241-1700), also conducts tours for the physically disabled. To inquire about other organizations that plan tours for disabled travelers, write to the **Handicapped Travel Divi-**

sion, **National Tour Association,** P.O. Box 3071, Lexington, KY 40596 (606-253-1036). The **Federation of the Handicapped,** 211 W. 14th St., New York, NY 10011 (212-727-4268), leads tours for physically-disabled members, including daytrips, weekend outings, and longer excursions. **Flying Wheels Travel,** 143 W. Bridge St., P.O. Box 382, Owatonna, MN 55060 (800-535-6790, in MN 800-722-9351), provides general information and arranges domestic or international tours for groups and individuals. **Whole Persons Tours,** P.O. Box 1084, Bayonne, NJ 07002-1084 (201-858-3400), conducts tours and publishes the *Itinerary,* a bimonthly magazine for disabled travelers. (Subscriptions: $10 for 1 year, $18 for 2 years.

Read up in any of a number of books helpful to disabled travelers. One good resource is *Access to the World,* by Louise Weiss ($17). For a copy, contact **Facts on File, Inc.,** 460 Park Ave., New York, NY 10016 (800-322-8755). **Twin Peaks Press** publishes three books: *Directory for Travel Agencies for the Disabled* ($20), *Travel for the Disabled* ($20), and *Wheelchair Vagabond* ($10), which discusses camping and travel in cars, vans, and RVs. Order from Twin Peaks Press, P.O. Box 129, Vancouver, WA 98666 (800-637-2256 or 206-694-2462). Add $2 shipping per book for the first three ordered, $1 for each book after that. Twin Peaks also operates a worldwide traveling nurse network.

Traveling with Children

Family vacations can be recipes for disaster—unless you slow your pace and plan ahead a bit. Washington is overflowing with great opportunities for kids; some are obvious (the National Zoo), others are less so (the Folklife Festival). When deciding where to stay, remember the special needs of young children; if you pick a B&B, call and make sure they're child-friendly. If you rent a car, make sure the rental company provides a child safety seat. If you need to escape for a night, call **Sitters Unlimited,** 205 Yoakum Parkway, Alexandria, VA 22304 (703-250-5250 for individual service; 703-823-0888 for convention service). For counseling and referral service in DC, call the **baby hotline** at 202-547-2229.

Let's Go lists sights with particular interest to children. The most comprehensive lists of kid-friendly events, however, appear every Friday in the *Washington Post's Weekend* section. Smithsonian Kite Day in April and the Navy Band Lollipop Concert in August are always popular. The following books can help you avoid the constant complaints of boredom: *Going Places with Children in Washington, DC* ($9.95; taxes may apply), published by Green Acres School, 11701 Danville Drive, Rockville, MD 20852 (301-881-4100); and *Washington! Adventures for Kids ($6.95),* available from **Children's Innovations,** P.O. Box 1192, Washington, DC 20013. *My Travels in Washington, DC ($2.95),* a guidebook complete with crayons and color-in postcards, is available from **Havin' Fun Inc.,** P.O. Box 70468, Eugene, OR 97401-0124 (503-344-6207).

For more information, consult *Travel with Children* by Maureen Wheeler ($11 plus $1.50 shipping), available from Lonely Planet Publications, 155 Filbert St., Oakland, CA 94607 (800-229-0122), or Arlene Butler's *Traveling With Children and Enjoying It: A Complete Guide to Family Travel by Car, Plane, and Train ($11.95),* available from Globe Pequot Press, Box Q, Chester, CT 06412 (outside CT 800-243-0495, inside CT 800-962-0973). Written *for* children, the *Kidding Around* series ($10 each) includes a book on Washington, DC. Order copies from John Muir Publications, P.O. Box 613, Santa Fe, NM 87504 (800-888-7504); include $2.75 shipping for the first book requested and 50¢ for each additional.

Travelers with Special Diets

Vegetarians won't have any problem eating well and cheaply in Washington. (Vegetarian meals are almost always cheaper anyway—the ecosystem and your wallet are on the same side.) *Let's Go* lists a number of great, cheap vegetarian restaurants, but discriminating travelers will want more. You can order key books like the *International Vegetarian Travel Guide* and/or the *Vegetarian Times Guide to Natural Foods Restau-*

rants in the U.S. and Canada (each costs $15.95 plus $3 postage) from the **North American Vegetarian Society,** P.O. Box 72, Dolgeville, NY 13329 (518-568-7970).

Kosher travelers should contact DC synagogues for information about kosher restaurants and advice on how to eat kosher in non-kosher restaurants; your own synagogue or college Hillel should have access to lists of Jewish institutions across the continent. *The Jewish Travel Guide* ($11.50 with a $1.50 shipping charge) is available in the U.S. from **Sepher-Hermon Press,** 1265 46th St., Brooklyn, NY 11219 (718-972-9010). It lists Jewish institutions, synagogues, and kosher restaurants in over 80 countries.

Accommodations

In accommodation listings throughout this guide, "single" refers to one bed, which often sleeps two people; "double" means two beds. You should verify how many people the room accommodates, whether there is a fee for extra people, and whether cots are available.

Expect to pay at least $25-35 a night for a single in a cheap **hotel.** Most hotels and motels require a key deposit when you register. You will be told in advance if the bathroom is communal. Check-in usually takes place between 11am and 1pm, check-out probably before 11am. You may be able to store your gear for the day even after vacating your room and returning the key, but most proprietors will not take responsibility for the safety of your belongings.

Let's Go lists the best budget hotels or motels and ranks them in order of the best value, based on price, safety, and location. Ask the hotel owner if you can see a room before you pay for it. Motels tend to fill up by evening, so try not to wait until nightfall to look for a room.

Youth hostels offer unbeatable deals on indoor lodging, and are great places to meet budget travelers from all over the world. Hostels as a rule are dorm-style accommodations where the sexes sleep apart, often in large rooms with bunk beds. Expenses and frills are kept to a minimum. You must rent or bring your own sheets or sleep sacks

(two sheets sewn together); sleeping bags are often not allowed. Hostels often have kitchens and utensils for your use, and some have storage areas and laundry facilities.

American Youth Hostels (AYH) is the leading organization of U.S. hostels. (AYH is affiliated with IYHF/HI and treats IYHF/HI cards just like AYH's. Note that IYHF is currently in the process of adopting a new seal of approval for the hostels that belong to its network. Soon AYH and IYHF cards will be phased out and replaced by the new "Hostelling International" ("HI") cards. Look for the trademark blue triangle to identi-fy IYHF-affiliated hostels.) Most AYH/HI hostels have strict check-in and check-out times, a maximum stay of less than a week, and rules against pets and alcohol. All ages are welcome. Prices usually run $7-12 a night. AYH/HI membership is annual: $25 for adults, $15 for those over 54, $10 for those under 18, $35 for families. Nonmembers who wish to stay at an AYH/HI hostel usually pay $3 extra, which can be applied to-ward membership. For more information, contact AYH/HI, 425 Divisadero St. #310, San Francisco, CA 94117 (415-863-9939).

American Association of Independent Hostels (AAIH), includes more than 30 hostels nationwide, many of which were formerly AYH hostels. Because these hostels are all owner-operated, they often provide better service. For more information write to AAIH, 1412 Cerrillos Rd., Santa Fe, NM 87051 or call 505-988-1153 during business hours.

If you have a particular fondness for Hiltons and Marriotts beyond your means, con-sider joining **Discount Travel International,** Ives Bldg., #205, 114 Forrest Ave., Nar-berth, PA 19072 (215-668-7184). For an annual membership fee of $45, you and your household will have access to a clearing house of unsold hotel rooms (as well as airline tickets, cruises, and the like), which can save you as much as 50%.

Bed and Breakfasts (private homes which rent out one or more spare rooms to trav-elers) are a great alternative to impersonal hotel and motel rooms. B&Bs may provide an excellent way to explore with the help of a host who knows the region well, and some go out of their way to be accommodating—accepting travelers with pets or giving personalized tours. The best part of your stay will often be a home-cooked breakfast (and occasionally dinner). Many B&Bs do not provide phones, TVs, or showers with their rooms. Some homes give special discounts to families or senior citizens. Reserva-tions are almost always necessary, although in the off-season you can frequently find a room on short notice. Many bed and breakfasts close down during the winter, though.

As an alternative to standard B&Bs, contact the **U.S. Servas Committee,** 11 John St. #407, New York, NY 10038 (212-267-0252), an international cooperative system of hosts and travelers. This non-profit organization provides travelers with hosts for two nights; Servas is well-established in the DC area. Letters of reference and an interview are required. Participation in the program costs $45 per year per traveler, with a $15 de-posit on host lists, but travelers and hosts do not exchange money.

Many U.S. **colleges and universities** open their residence halls to other students and travelers during the summer when the school is not in session. This is especially true in the DC area and any person planning to be in Washington for the summer should defi-nitely look into housing at a city university; weekly rates come out to between $14-20 a day. All colleges tell you to write months in advance for summer rooms, but most still have a few beds come July. If you write as early as possible, not only will you assure yourself of a room, but the room you get will almost certainly be better. Colleges often make space available only to those with summer internships, or to those with summer jobs, or to students with ID (three very different restrictions). Be sure the room you take has air-conditioning—it's not worth the little you'd save to spend the summer bathing in sweat.

Camping and the Outdoors

For the hearty individual who prefers the vast outdoors to a dingy hotel room (and who is willing to do without certain comforts and conveniences), camping is an option worth considering. *Let's Go* lists several sites below (See *Accommodations*). Beware, however, that campsites in Maryland and Virginia are often far enough from DC to make the trip to the capital inconvenient.

FOR $15 YOU CAN STAY HERE OR GET YOUR SHOES SHINED AT THE HOTEL DOWN THE STREET.

The Washington International AYH-Hostel offers a clean, comfortable place to spend the night in the nation's capital. Plus the opportunity to meet and share experiences with travelers from all over the world. And while you may have to do without a few of life's little luxuries, at this price we don't think you'll miss them. For reservations or more information, call (202) 737-2333.

HOSTELLING INTERNATIONAL

The new seal of approval of the International Youth Hostel Federation.

HOSTELLING INTERNATIONAL®

Especially on the East Coast, National Parks offer the greatest expanses of wilderness. They charge a $3-5 entry fee for vehicles, and sometimes a nominal one for pedestrians and cyclists as well. The $25 **Golden Eagle Passport** covers the fee at all U.S. parks (most parks sell the Passports as well). Seniors and disabled travelers are entitled to free passes (see Specific Concerns above).

Woodall's Campground Directory ($16 U.S., $18 outside U.S.; 8 regional guides $5 back) covers campsites around the U.S. Also try Woodall's *Tent Camping Guide* ($11 in U.S., $13 abroad). If you can't find a copy locally, contact Woodall Publishing Co., 28167 N. Keith Dr., Lake Forest, IL 60045-5000 (800-323-9076 or 708-362-6700). For information about camping, accommodations, and regulations at National Parks, contact the **Forest Service/National Park Service, Outdoor Recreation Information Center,** 915 2nd Ave., Room 442, Seattle, WA 98174 (206-553-0170). The U.S. Government Printing Office publishes two useful pamphlets: *National Parks: Camping Guide* (S/N 024-005-01028-9; $3.50) and *National Parks: Lesser-Known Areas* (S/N 024-005-00911-6; $1.50). Disabled travelers should contact the Office of Public Inquiries, National Park Service, Washington, DC 20240 (202-343-4747) about accessible campsites. *How to Stay Alive in the Woods,* by Bradford Angier (Macmillan, $6), may come in handy as well.

When in Dire Straits

Every year, enterprising travelers sleep in locations ranging from cemeteries to sewage treatment plants in order to save on accommodations. While it is undeniably cheap, sacking out is generally uncomfortable, unsafe, and illegal. In Washington, DC, it's pretty stupid. Don't do it. If you arrive late in a city and don't know what else to do, ask for tips from employees at the bus or train station. If the situation looks hopeless, don't sleep outside or in your car; instead call **Traveler's Aid** (546-3120) for assistance (open 24 hr.).

For International Visitors

United States Tourist Offices, found in many countries, can provide you with arm-loads of free literature. If you can't find a U.S. Tourist Office in your area, write the U.S. Travel and Tourism Administration, Department of Commerce, 14th St. and Constitution Ave. NW, Washington, DC 20230 (202-377-4003 or 202-377-3811). USTTA has branches in Australia, Belgium, Canada, France, Germany, Japan, Mexico, and the United Kingdom; contact the Washington office for information about the branch in your country. For general tourist information, you may also want to direct inquiries to the state and city tourist offices listed throughout the book and under *Tourism Bureaus* above. In Canada, contact Travel CUTS, 44 George St., Toronto, Ont. M5T 1P7 (416-979-2406).

Student Travelers

The Council on International Educational Exchange (CIEE) has affiliates abroad that charter airline tickets, arrange homestays, sell international student ID cards, travel literature, travel insurance, and hostel cards. CIEE also helps students secure work visas and find employment through its work-exchange programs. In Australia, contact SSA/STA Swap Program, P.O. Box 399 (1st Floor), 220 Faraday St., Carlton South, Melbourne, Victoria 3053 (03 347 69 11). In the United Kingdom, contact London Student Travel, 52 Grosvenor Gardens, London WC1 (tel. (071) 730 34 02). In Canada write to Travel CUTS (Canadian University Travel Services Ltd.), 187 College St., Toronto, Ont. M5T 1P7 (416-979-2406). If you can't locate an affiliated office in your country, contact CIEE's main office: 205 E. 42nd St., New York, NY 10017 (212-661-1450; 800-223-7402 for charter flight tickets only) or the International Student Travel Confederation, Gothersgade 30, 1123 Copenhagen K, Denmark (45 33 99 93).

The Federation of International Youth Travel Organization (FIYTO) issues the International Youth Card (IYC) to anyone under 26, as well as a free catalog that lists special services and discounts for IYC cardholders. Write or call Council Travel.

STA Travel, based in the U.K., has over 100 offices worldwide to help you arrange discounted overseas flights. In the U.S. call 800-777-0112; if the number does not work, call local information for an office near you, or write to 74 and 86 Old Brompton Rd., London SW7 3LQ, England, or call (071) 937 99 71 for flights to North America.

If you wish to stay in a U.S. home during your vacation, many organizations can help you. The **Experiment in International Living** coordinates homestay programs for international visitors wishing to join a U.S. family for 3-4 weeks. Visitors over 14 live with host families. Homestays are arranged for all times of the year. For the appropriate address in your country, write to the U.S Headquarters, P.O. Box 676, Kipling Rd., Brattleboro, VT 05302-0676 (800-327-4678 or 802-257-7751). The **Institute of International Education (IIE)** publishes their "Homestay Information Sheet" listing many homestay programs for foreign visitors. Write to them at 809 United Nations Plaza, New York, NY 10017-3580 (212-883-8200). See Accommodations above for information on **Servas,** a similar inter-nation travel organization, which coordinates short (2-3 day) homestays.

Documents and Formalities

Foreign visitors who wish to travel to the United States should plan early so they can complete all the necessary paperwork in time.

Visas

Foreign visitors to the United States are required to have a **passport, visitor's visa,** and **proof of intent to leave.** That said, there are a number of exceptions. Visitors from the following nations do not need a visa to enter the U.S.: the U.K., Japan, Italy, Germany, France, the Netherlands, Sweden, and Switzerland. Without a visa, however, these travelers must fly into the country on one of a specified list of carriers, have with them a ticket to leave the U.S., and stay not more than 90 days. For more information, contact the nearest U.S. consulate.

Canadian citizens who enter the U.S. from Canada or Mexico do not need a visa or passport, nor do Mexican citizens with a form I-186. Mexican border crossing cards (non-immigrant visas) limit you to 72 hours or less in the U.S. within 25 mi. of the border. Always carry proof of citizenship (a driver's license or birth certificate).

Most visitors obtain a B-2 or "pleasure tourist" visa, valid for six months. If you lose your I-94 form (arrival/departure certificate attached to your visa upon arrival), replace it at the nearest **U.S. Immigration and Naturalization Service** office. (If you lose your passport in the U.S., you must replace it through your country's embassy.) Extensions for visas (maximum 6 months) require form I-539 as well as a $35 fee and are also granted by the INS. For a list of offices, write the Immigration and Naturalization Service, Central Office Information Operations Unit, 425 I St. NW #5044, Washington, DC 20536 (202-633-4316).

In most cases, no special vaccinations are required to enter the U.S. For exceptions contact a U.S. embassy or consulate.

Non-Tourist Visas for Work and Study

Working in the U.S. with only a B-2 visa is grounds for deportation. You must obtain a work visa. Apply at the U.S. consulate in your country with a letter from an American employer stating that you have been offered a job and listing its responsibilities, salary, and employment period. An American employer can also obtain an H visa (usually an H-2) for you.

To **study** in the U.S., foreigners must apply for a F-1 or J-1 visa, depending on whether they are exchange students or full-time students enrolled in degree-granting programs. F-1 and J-1 students may apply to the INS through their school for full-time **practical training,** employment at the school closely related to a student's field of study, beneficial to a student's professional development, and unavailable in the home country. Many foreign schools—and most U.S. colleges—have offices that give specific advice on study and employment in the U.S. Almost all institutions accept applications from international students directly. If English is not your native tongue, you will generally be required to take the **Test of English as a Foreign Language and Test of**

Spoken English (TOEFL/TSE), administered in many countries. Actual requirements are determined by each U.S. college or university. For more information, contact the TOEFL/TSE Application Office, P.O. Box 6155, Princeton, NJ 08541 (609-951-1100).

Before leaving the United States, foreigners holding some work or student visas must obtain a "Sailing Permit" from the **Internal Revenue Service** within 30 days prior to departure. (This is to ensure that you do not owe taxes to the U.S. government.) If you have any questions, write to the Director of International Operations, Internal Revenue Service, Washington, DC 20225.

International Driver's License

If you plan to drive during your visit, be sure to obtain an International Driver's License from your national automobile association before leaving (you can't get one here) and make sure you have proper insurance (required by law). To obtain a domestic driver's license, you must apply and be tested, a process that often takes weeks or months. Some foreign driver's licenses will be valid here for up to one year (check before you leave). And be careful: local authorities may not realize that your license is valid.

Members of national automobile associations affiliated with the **American Automobile Association** (800-222-4357) can receive services from the AAA while they're in the U.S. Automobile associations in 19 countries have full reciprocity agreements with the AAA. Check your country's association for details.

Customs

You may bring the following into the U.S. duty free: 200 cigarettes, $100 in gifts, and personal belongings such as clothes and jewelry. Travelers aged 21 and over may also bring up to one liter of alcohol, although state laws may further restrict the amount of alcohol you may carry.

You can bring any amount of currency, but if you carry over $10,000, you'll need to report it. In general, customs officers ask how much money you're carrying and your planned departure date in order to ensure that you'll be able to support yourself while here. In some cases they may ask about traveling companions and political affiliation. Travelers should carry any prescription drugs in clearly labeled containers and have a written prescription or doctor's statement ready to present to the customs officer. For more information, including the helpful pamphlet "Know Before You Go," contact the nearest U.S. embassy or write the U.S. Customs Service, 1301 Constitution Ave. NW, Washington DC 20229 (202-566-8195).

Currency and Exchange

The U.S. currency is a decimal system based on the dollar ($). Paper money ("bills") comes in six denominations, all the same physical size and color: $1, $5, $10, $20, $50, and $100. Each dollar is divided into 100 cents (¢). Coins, all worth one dollar or less, vary in size and color. The penny (1¢), made of copper, is smaller than the silver-colored nickel (5¢); both have smooth edges. The silver-colored dime (10¢) is the smallest coin. Both the dime and the silver-colored quarter (25¢), larger than the nickel, have ridged edges. Quarters are frequently used for laundry, soda, and stamp machines and for public transportation. Most banks will supply you a roll of 40 quarters for $10 (no extra charge). Half-dollar (50¢) and dollar ($1) coins are rarely used.

It is virtually impossible to buy anything in foreign currency, and in some regions you may even have trouble exchanging your currency for U.S. dollars. To avoid hassles, buy an established brand of traveler's checks. Some banks offer their own checks, which may not be easily cashed here. Buy checks in dollar amounts to simplify the task of cashing them. In addition, consider bringing along a credit card affiliated with a U.S. company, such as Interbank (affiliated with MasterCard), Barclay Card (affiliated with Visa), or American Express.

Sales tax is the American equivalent of the Value Added Tax. Amount and application differ by state. Expect to pay 5-10% in most places; DC is 6%. Restaurants, taxi drivers, and many other services (especially in more expensive hotels) will expect you to add a tip of 15 to 20% to the bill. Gratuity is rarely included. **Banking hours** are generally weekdays from 9am to 5pm, with some banks open on Saturdays from 9am to noon or 1pm. All banks, government agencies, and post offices are closed on legal holidays (see *Official Holidays* for a list). Be aware that most banks will not cash personal checks unless you are an account holder with them.

Communication

Mail

Individual offices of the U.S. Post Office are usually open Monday to Friday from 8am to 5pm and sometimes on Saturdays until about noon. All are closed on national holidays. **Postcards** mailed within the U.S. or to Canada or Mexico cost 19¢, **letters** up to one ounce 29¢. Postcards mailed overseas cost 40¢, letters 50¢ (1/2 oz.). **Aerograms** are available at the post office for 45¢. Mail from one coast to the other usually takes three days; to northern Europe, a week to 10 days; to southern Europe, North Africa, and the Middle East, two weeks; to South America or Asia, a week to 10 days. Of course, all of the above travel times for mail are dependent on the particular foreign country's mail service as well. Be sure to write "Air Mail" clearly on the front of the envelope for the speediest delivery. Large city post offices offer an **International Express Mail** service (delivery to a major city overseas in 48-72hr.).

The U.S. is divided into postal zones, each assigned a five-digit ZIP code. (Some businesses use an alternative 9-digit ZIP code for speedier delivery.) Writing this code on letters is essential for delivery.

The normal form of address is as follows:

Rump Inglenook (name)
Glencove Swingers Club (name of organization, optional)
356 Misty Lane, 5D (address, apartment number)
Nywas Falls, CA 93711 (city, state abbreviation, ZIP)
USA (country, if mailing internationally)

When ordering books and materials from the U.S., always include an **International Reply Coupon** with your request. IRCs should be available from your home post office. Be sure that your coupon has adequate postage to cover the cost of delivery.

Telephones

Phone numbers in the U.S. consist of a three-digit area code and a seven-digit number, written as 617-493-2007 or (617) 493-2007. In most parts of the U.S., only the last seven digits are used in **local calls. Non-local calls** within most area codes sometimes require that you dial (or press) "1" before the seven-digit number. **Long-distance calls** require that you dial "1," the area code, and then the number. For example, to leave a message for the President from outside of DC, dial 1-202-456-1111. Maryland, northern Virginia, and DC have three different area codes (**301, 703** and **202,** respectively). Calls to Arlington, Alexandria, and most of Fairfax, Montgomery and Prince Georges Counties count as local from DC (no charge from a private telephone), even though they're dialed as if long-distance.

Pay phones are plentiful on street corners and in public areas (restaurants, train stations, etc.). Insert your coins (10-25¢ for a 3-min. local call) in the slot before dialing. If there is no answer or if you get a busy signal (a series of beeps), your money will be returned when you hang up the receiver (what a deal). To make a long-distance direct call, insert your coins and dial the area code and number; an operator will tell you the cost of the first three minutes as the other person's phone rings. **Charge-a-Call** public phones are operated by American Telephone & Telegraph (AT&T), which is used for long-distance calls only and does not accept coins. Payment is made by telephone credit card or by reversing charges. Begin dialing all such calls with "0." The second type of phone is found in airports and is operated by independent long-distance companies. Generally these phones are operated by passing a credit card through a slot before dialing.

There are two ways to **reverse the charges** (i.e. bill the person receiving the call). In either case, you dial "0" (not "1"), then the area code and number. When you hear a beep, the operator will assist you. If you ask to make a **station-to-station collect call** and give your name, anyone who answers may accept or refuse the call. If you wish to speak only to a particular person, tell the operator you are placing a **person-to-person collect call,** and give both your name and the receiving person's name. In some areas, particularly rural ones, you may have to dial "0" only and then tell the operator the number you wish to call.

The cheapest times to make long-distance calls are between 11pm and 8am daily and from 11pm on Friday through 5pm on Sunday. Remember that collect calls cost more than direct calls, and person-to-person calls are far more expensive than station-to-station calls.

You can place **international calls** from any telephone. To make the call directly, dial the international access code (011), the country code, the city code, and the local number. In some areas dial "0" only and give the operator the number. To find out the cheapest time to call overseas, ask the operator (dial "0"). Remember to take time differences into account before dialing.

Most of the information you will need about telephone usage, including area codes and many foreign country codes, is in the front of the local **"white pages"** telephone directory. The **"yellow pages"** published at the end of the white pages or in a separate book, is used to look up the phone numbers of businesses and other services. To obtain local phone numbers or area codes of other cities, call **directory assistance** (411). Directory assistance is free from all public phone booths, but not from private phones. For long-distance directory assistance, dial 1-(area code)-555-1212.

Many large companies operate **toll-free numbers** to provide information to their customers at no charge. These consist of "1" plus "800" plus a seven-digit number. To obtain specific toll-free numbers, call 1-800-555-1212.

From all AT&T pay phones, you can reach an **operator** by dialing "0." The operator will help you make any call and can provide assistance in an emergency.

Cabling (Telegrams)

If a telephone call is impossible, cabling may be the only way to contact someone overseas quickly (usually by the next day). **Western Union** (800-325-6000) charges a base fee of $8, in addition to 51-66¢ per word, including name and address (the rate varying according to destination). If you're contacting England, Argentina, the Netherlands or the Philippines, you can send a **Telemessage** ($8.50 for the first 50 words or less, including name and address, $3.25 for each additional 50 words or less). Call to check rates to specific countries.

Measurements

The U.S. has retained the curious British system of **weights** and **measures.**

> **1 inch = 2.5 centimeters**
> **1 foot = 0.30 meter**
> **1 yard = 0.91 meter**
> **1 mile = 1.61 kilometers**
> **1 ounce = 25 grams**
> **1 pound = 0.45 kilogram**
> **1 quart (liquid) = 0.94 liter**

There are 12 inches (in.) in 1 foot (ft.), 3 ft. in 1 yard (yd.), and 5280 ft. in 1 mile (mi.). There are 16 ounces (oz.) in 1 pound (lb.), 8 oz. (liquid) in 1 cup, 2 cups in 1 pint, 2 pints in 1 quart, and 4 quarts in 1 gallon.

Electric outlets throughout North America provide current at 117 volts, 60 cycles (Hertz) A.C. Appliances designed for a foreign electrical system will not operate without a converter ($15-20) and a plug adapter, available at most department, hardware, and electrical equipment stores.

Temperature is measured by the Fahrenheit scale, rather than the Centigrade (Celsius) scale. The mathematically inclined can convert Fahrenheit to Centigrade by subtracting 32, then multiplying by 5/9. Others should just remember that 32°F is the freezing point of water, 212°F its boiling point, and 98.6°F normal human body temperature. Room temperature typically hovers around 70°F.

Time

U.S. residents tell time on the Latinate 12-hour (not a 24-hour) clock. Hours before noon are **ante meridiem** or am; after noon they are **post meridiem** or pm. Noon is 12pm and midnight is 12am. Although the North American continent is divided into six time zones, the entire East Coast is in the Eastern time zone (1 hr. before Central, 2 before Mountain, and 3 before Pacific). Shortly after midnight the first Sunday in April, continental U.S. clocks are switched one hour forward to **daylight savings time;** on the last Sunday in October, again shortly after midnight, clocks are moved back one hour to **standard time.** When times are given with time-zone abbreviations, take this into account (e.g. EDT—Eastern Daylight Time, MST—Mountain Standard Time).

Holidays

Some listings in *Let's Go* refer to holidays that may be unfamiliar to foreign travelers. **Martin Luther King Jr.'s Birthday** is celebrated on the third Monday in January, **President's Day** on the third Monday in February. **Memorial Day**, falling on the last Monday of May, honors all U.S. citizens who have died in wars and signals the unofficial start of summer. Patriotic Americans celebrate **Independence Da**y on July 4 with barbecues and fireworks. **Labor Day** is summer's finale on the first Monday of September, complete with back-to-school frenzies. **Christopher Columbus Day** comes on the second Monday in October, **Veterans' Day** on the second Monday in November. **Thanksgiving,** the fourth Thursday of November, celebrates the arrival of the Pilgrims in New England in 1620. Thanksgiving unofficially marks the beginning of the holiday season which peaks at **Christmas Day** (Dec. 25) and which runs through **New Year's Day** (Jan. 1). All public agencies and offices and many businesses close on these holidays, as well as on several others scattered throughout the calendar.

Getting to the U.S.

Transportation to and from Washington, DC, especially from outside the U.S., will probably be your major expense. The alternative to research and early planning is exorbitant rates; consult a travel agent whom you can trust. In addition, check the travel section of any major newspaper for bargain fares, and consult CIEE or your national student travel organization—they sometimes have special deals that regular travel agents can't offer.

From Canada and Mexico

Canadians and Americans are very welcome in each other's countries—border officials will accept a valid driver's license or passport as proof of citizenship (just don't carry any mace). Traversing the Mexican-American border can be more difficult. Mexican citizens may need a tourist visa for travel in the U.S.; contact the U.S. Embassy in Mexico City with questions.

Finding bargains on travel in the States may not be easy for residents of its neighboring countries. Residents of North America are rarely eligible for the discounts that U.S. airlines, bus, and train companies offer visitors from overseas (see *Getting Around* below). Canadian and Mexican carriers often fly to and from the U.S. and their respective country, as do U.S. airlines. Mexican residents who live more than 100 miles from the border may be eligible for "Visit USA" discount flight passes on some carriers; for information, see *Getting Around,* below. Otherwise, because flying in the U.S. is expensive, it may be cheaper to fly on a Mexican airline to one of the border towns, and then to travel by train or bus from there.

Most buses and trains from Mexico travel no farther than the U.S. border, but it is possible to arrange connections at San Diego, CA; Nogales, AZ; and El Paso, Eagle

Pass, Laredo, or Brownsville, TX. **Amtrak, Greyhound,** and their subsidiaries serve the towns along the U.S.-Mexico border.

From Europe

Travelers from Europe will experience the least competition for inexpensive seats during the off-season. This need not mean the dead of winter. Peak season rates are generally set on either May 15 or June 1 and run until about September 15. You can take advantage of cheap off-season flights within Europe to reach an advantageous port of departure for North America. (London is an important connecting point for budget flights to the U.S.)

Charter flights can save you a lot of money. You can book charters up to the last minute—some will not even sell tickets more than 30 days in advance. Many flights fill up well before their departure date, however. You must choose your departure and return dates when you book, and you will lose all or most of your money if you cancel your ticket. (Travel agents will cover your losses only in case of sudden illness, death of a close family member, or natural disaster.) Charter companies themselves reserve the right to change the dates of your flight or even cancel the flight a mere 48 hours in advance. Delays are not uncommon. To be safe, get your ticket as early as possible and arrive at the airport several hours before departure time. When making plans, try to investigate each charter company's reputation.

If you decide to fly with a scheduled airline, you'll be purchasing greater reliability, security, and flexibility. Major airlines do offer reduced-fare options. **APEX (Advanced Purchase Excursion Fare)** is one of the more sensible ways to go. It provides you with confirmed reservations, and you can make connections through different cities and travel on different airlines. Drawbacks include restrictions on the length of your stay (from 7-14 days minimum to 60-90 days maximum) and the requirement that you make reservations two weeks in advance (hence the name). APEX fares are generally not refundable, nor may you change your flight. You might also investigate unusual airlines that undercut the major carriers on regularly scheduled flights to an extremely limited number of cities. **Virgin Atlantic Airways** (800-862-8621) and **Icelandair** (800-223-5500) have particularly low fares. Competition for seats on these small carriers is usually fierce, so book early.

Student discounts will appear with a magical ease if you look around for them. Many major carriers will sell off un-purchased APEX seats at a further discount to persons under age 24, beginning 72 hours before the flight. These fares allow an open return date, but restrict your stay to a maximum of two weeks—the last part of which you will have to spend trying to secure your ticket back. Such deals are never really a predictable way to travel, and are especially risky in high season. They can, however, save you a considerable amount of money if your schedule is flexible enough for you to take advantage of them.

From Asia, Australia, and New Zealand

Whereas European travelers may choose from a variety of regular reduced fares, their counterparts in Asia and Australia must rely on APEX flights. From Japan, U.S. airlines such as **Northwest** and **United Airlines** offer cheaper flights than Japan Airlines. **Qantas, Air New Zealand, United, Continental,** and **UTA French Airlines** fly between Australia or New Zealand and the United States. Prices are roughly equivalent among the five (American carriers tend to be a bit less) although they vary seasonally, and the cities served by each carrier differ slightly. Super Saver fares from Australia have extremely tough restrictions. If you are uncertain about your plans, pay extra for a Super Saver that has only a 50% penalty for cancellation.

Getting Around the U.S.

By Air

Flight listings and airfares can leave you in a gnarly swamp of numbers, all but impossible to wade through. Again, your best bet is to ask a knowledgeable travel agent to help you; then check the weekend travel sections of major newspapers for bargain fares.

Super Saver fares can save you hundreds of dollars over the regular coach price. On the average, you save more than half on a 14-day advance-purchase fare, and a still-considerable amount on the 7-day advance-purchase fare. To obtain the cheapest fare, buy a round-trip ticket (not necessarily returning on the same route, if you want a stop-over) and stay over at least one Saturday. You will need to pay for the ticket within 24 hours of booking the flight, and you will not be able to change your flight reservation; the fare is also entirely non-refundable. By paying a bit extra, you can buy the ability to alter your plans, though there will still be some penalties for doing so. Also check with your travel agent for system-wide air passes and excursion fares.

There are a few principles to keep in mind when booking a flight. Traveling at night and during the wee hours of the morning is generally cheaper than during the day, and traveling on a weekday (between Monday and Thursday at noon) is cheaper than traveling on the weekend. Since airline travel peaks between June and August and around holidays, reserve a seat several months in advance for these times. Given the occasional appearance of sudden bargains and the availability of standby fares, advance purchase may not guarantee the lowest fare, but you will save some money and be assured a seat. The best deals usually appear between January and mid-May.

Many airlines offer special rates (usually 50% off regular fares) to children accompanied by an adult. These may still be higher than Super Savers, though. Very few airlines offer discounts for seniors. Chances of receiving discount fares increase on competitive routes.

Many major airlines offer special "**Visit USA**" passes and fares to foreign travelers. Purchase these tickets at home; one price pays for a certain number of "flight coupons," each good for one flight segment on a particular airline's domestic system within a certain time period. Often, the passes must be purchased when you buy a ticket to or from the States. Many different airlines offer these passes, but they come with innumerable restrictions and guidelines. Prices therefore vary a great deal. Consult a travel agent before you purchase any of these coupons to see whether you're really getting the best deal. Depending on the airline, the passes may be valid from 30 to 90 days. United Airlines offers special fares for travelers departing from many different regions of the world, including Asia, Europe, and Australia. When you purchase a pass, keep in mind the size of the airline. Eastern, United, American, and Northwest fly over the entire continent, while other airlines offer more limited or regional service.

Another discount option is to travel as a **courier.** In return for carrying packages with you, you receive dramatically reduced airfares. There are two catches, though. Only carry-on luggage is permitted (the company needs your luggage space), and flights mostly originate from New York City. Still, for the adventurous and the resourceful, courier services present opportunities for inexpensive travel. For more information, contact **Now Voyager,** 74 Varick St. #307, New York, NY 10013 (212-432-1616), or **Halbert Express,** 147-05 176th St., Jamaica, NY 11434 (718-656-8189).

Ticket consolidators sell unbooked commercial and charter airline tickets. The membership fee is $30-50, but fares can be extremely cheap. Inquire about cancellation fees and advance purchase requirements, and be prepared to be flexible about your dates of arrival and departure. For more information, contact **Air Hitch,** 2790 Broadway #100, New York, NY 10025 (212-864-2000). Or try **Unitravel Corporation**. Unitravel has departures from over 70 U.S. cities to more than 50 cities in Europe. The company holds all payments in a bank escrow until completion of the trip. Call 1-800-325-2222 and they will send a memo listing all of the flights departing from your city.

By Bus

If you are coming from rural America or have a seriously tight budget, buses may be your best bet. In the U.S., **Greyhound** (800-752-4841) operates the largest number of lines. Seniors receive a 5-10% discount off standard-fare tickets; children ages 5-11 travel for half-fare on standard-fare tickets; children ages 2-4 travel for 10% of the standard fare, and children under 2 travel free on laps. Restrictions do apply. If you plan to tour a great deal by bus within the U.S., you may save money with the **Ameripass.** Passes can be purchased for seven days ($299), 15 days ($319), or 30 days ($429), and each can be extended for $15 per day.

Always check bus schedules and routes personally, and don't rely on old printed schedules since listings change seasonally. Don't count on flagging down buses between stops—the driver might not stop. By all means avoid spending the night in a bus station. Though generally guarded, bus stations can be hangouts for deadbeats and down-and-outs. Try to arrange your arrivals for reasonable day or evening times. This will also make it easier for you to find transportation out of the station and another place to stay.

By Train

The train is one of the cheapest and most comfortable ways to travel in the U.S. Within the lower 48 states, **Amtrak** offers the "**All Aboard America**" fares for long-distance travel. Dividing the U.S. into three regions, Amtrak charges the same rate for both one-way and round-trip travel: $199 within one region, $279 between two regions, $339 between three (from Sept. 1-Dec. 17 and Jan. 4-May 27, rates are $179, $229, and $259). Amtrak discounts allow children ages 2-15 to travel for half-fare when accompanied by an adult. Senior citizens and disabled travelers may save up to 25% on regular one-way fares. Watch for special holiday packages as well. For information and reservations, call 800-872-7245 or look up Amtrak's local number in your area. Travelers with hearing impairments may use a **teletypewriter** (800-523-6590; 800-562-6960 in PA). Keep in mind that discounted air travel, particularly for longer distances, may be cheaper than train travel.

By Car

Interstate highways crisscross the country as part of a national network of highways originally designed primarily to aid the military in defending U.S. soil against foreign invasion. Even-numbered roads run east-west and odd-numbered ones run north-south. If the interstate has a three-digit number, it is a branch of another interstate (i.e. I-495 is a branch of I-95). An even digit in the hundreds place means the branch will eventually return to the main interstate; an odd digit means it won't. The national speed limit of 55 miles per hour has been raised to 65 mph in some rural areas, including parts of Virginia. The main routes through most towns are U.S. highways, often locally referred to by non-numerical names. State highways are usually less heavily traveled and may lead to down-home farming communities. Of course, U.S. and state highway numbers don't follow any particular numbering pattern.

If you plan to do a lot of driving, join an automobile club. Standing on the side of the road with a blown fan belt, you'll wish you had. Believe us. The best is the **American Automobile Association (AAA),** (800-222-4357; call them for the office nearest you). Annual dues vary with the size and location of the local AAA club—call the toll-free number or contact your local club for details. Membership includes free maps and guidebooks, trip-planning services, emergency road service anywhere in the country, discounts on car rentals, the International Driver's License, and commission-free traveler's checks from American Express. Your membership card doubles as a $5000 bail bond (if you find yourself in jail) or a $200 arrest bond certificate (which you can use in lieu of being arrested for any motor vehicle offense except drunk driving, driving without a valid license, or failure to appear in court on a prior motor-vehicle arrest).

Obeying the speed limit will save you gas and possibly your life. Oh, and buckle your seat belt—it's the law in the District of Columbia and in many states.

Renting

Although the cost of renting a car for days at a time can be prohibitively expensive, renting for local trips is often reasonable, especially if several people share the cost. In general, automobile rental agencies fall into two categories: national companies with thousands of affiliated offices across the country, and local companies that serve only one city or area.

Major rental companies usually allow cars to be picked up in one city and dropped off in another without any hitch. Their toll-free numbers enable customers to reserve a reliable car anywhere in the country. Drawbacks include steep prices and high minimum ages for rentals (21 with a major credit card or, frequently, 25). If you have a major credit card in your name, you can avoid having to leave a large cash deposit at a rental agency, and you may be able to rent where the minimum age would otherwise rule you out. Student discounts are occasionally available. Some major companies are **Alamo** (800-327-9633), **Avis** (800-331-1212), **Budget** (800-527-0700), **Dollar** (800-800-4000), **Hertz** (800-654-3131), **National** (800-328-4567), **Thrifty** (800-367-2271), and **Rent-A-Wreck** (800-421-7253).

While many local companies observe similar age requirements, they often have more flexible policies. Some require smaller cash deposits (on the order of $50-100). Others will simply accept proof of employment (check stubs, etc.). Local companies often charge less than major companies, although you'll generally have to return to your point of origin to return the car. *Let's Go* gives the addresses and phone numbers of local rental agencies.

When dealing with any car rental company, make certain the price includes insurance against theft and collision. This may be an additional charge, though American Express automatically insures any car rented with the card. Although basic rental charges run from $30-50 per day for a compact car, plus 30-40¢ per mile, most companies offer special money-saving deals. Standard shift cars are usually a few dollars cheaper then automatics. All companies have special weekend rates, and renting by the week can save you even more. Most packages include a certain amount of free mileage that varies with the length of time for which you're renting. If you'll be driving a long distance, ask for an unlimited-mileage deal. If you want to rent for longer than a week,

look into automobile leasing. Leasing is cheaper than renting, but make sure the car is covered by a service plan, or you could end up stuck with outrageous repair bills.

Auto Transport Companies

If you don't have a car and can't afford to rent one for a long trip, you might consider registering with an automobile transport company. These outfits hire drivers on behalf of car owners who need their automobile moved from one city to another. You can let the companies know where you want to drive, and if one of them is asked to have a car driven there, you'll get a call. You are provided with the first tank of gas; all other expenses are yours (gas, food, lodging, tolls). Before you leave you have to pay a deposit, which is refunded to you when you deliver the car. If the car breaks down or is damaged, the insurance of the car transport company covers it. You must be at least 21 years old and have a valid driver's license.

If offered a car, look it over first. Think twice about accepting a gas guzzler, since you're the one paying for gasoline. Driving for an auto transport company is most promising if your schedule is flexible: you may find a car within a week, or it may take several. One firm to try is the **Auto Driveaway Co.,** 310 South Michigan Ave., Chicago, IL 60604 (800-346-2277), which serves the U.S. and Canada. As the arrival deadline can be negotiated, you may be able to detour along the way. Auto Driveaway requires a $250 deposit.

By Bicycle

Travel by bicycle brings you even closer to the countryside—and the pavement. You move more slowly for more effort, but that doesn't mean you will be ill-rewarded. The leisurely pace gives you a chance to take in the view as well as the dust. Though you can carry much less than you could on a larger vehicle, assembling all the necessary equipment is, not surprisingly, the largest task you'll face as you prepare to tour by bike. Contact a local biking club if you don't know a great deal about bicycle equipment and repair. When you shop around, compare knowledgeable local retailers to mail-order firms. If the disparity in price is modest, buy locally. Otherwise, order by phone or mail and make sure you have someone in town with whom to consult. Make your first investment in an issue of *Bicycling* magazine, which advertises low sale prices. Wondrous **Bike Nashbar,** a mail-order catalog, will beat any nationally-advertised price by 5¢; write them at 4111 Simon Rd., Youngstown, OH 44512 (800-627-4227). Another exceptional mail-order firm which specializes in mountain bikes is **Bikecology,** P.O. Box 3900, Santa Monica, CA 90403 (800-326-2453).

Safe and secure bike use requires a quality helmet and a quality lock. A **Bell** or **Tourlite** helmet costs about $40—much cheaper than critical head surgery or a well-appointed funeral. **Kryptonite** locks begin at $20, with insurance against theft either for one or two years or up to a certain amount of money, depending on where you buy it. Make sure that you take care of the necessary paperwork when you buy both the bike and the lock, however, or you may have problems claiming your theft refund.

There are also a number of good books about bicycle touring and repair in general. *Touring the Washington, DC Area by Bicycle* ($10.95), by Peter Powers, available from Ten Speed Press, Box 7123, Berkeley, CA 94707, includes trails and topographic maps all around MD, DC, and VA. Two which discuss how to equip oneself and plan a bicycle trip are *Bike Touring* (Sierra Club, $11) and *Bicycle Touring* ($5) from **Rodale Press,** 33 E. Minor St., Emmaus, PA 18098 (215-967-5171). **10-Speed Press** publishes *The Bike Bag Book* ($4 plus $1 shipping), a bite-sized book of information with broad utility—just add creativity and stir. Write 10-Speed Press, Box 7123, Berkeley, CA 94707.

By Thumb

Hitchhiking is illegal in the District of Columbia, Maryland, and Virginia. In or near urban areas, it can also be dangerous; so many Americans think it's unsafe that anyone who will actually pick you up has a good chance of having at least one screw loose. By no means should anybody hitchhike in or near DC itself. *Let's Go* does not recommend hitchhiking. Some people, however, choose to hitchhike to, from, or around rural areas. It's easier to get a ride when alone, but it's considerably safer to hitchhike with someone. Women should *never* hitch alone. Before getting into a car, ask where the driver is going, and make sure the passenger door opens from the inside. Women especially should turn down the ride if the driver opens the door quickly and offers to drive anywhere. If there are several people inside, don't sit in the middle. Always place yourself so you can exit quickly, and don't let the driver place your belongings in the trunk. If you feel threatened or intimidated, ask to be let out no matter how unpromising the road looks. Don't ever worry about being embarrassed. Know in advance where to go if stranded and what to do in emergencies. Those who need a ride out of Washington not only shouldn't hitch, but don't have to: if you're staying in a youth hostel, for example, see if someone you like is planning to drive where you intend to go.

Practical Information

Emergency (Fire, Police or Ambulance): call 911; TDD: 727-9334.

Police non-emergency: 727-1010; answered in 24 hr.

Visitor Information: Visitor Information Center, 1455 Pennsylvania Ave. NW (789-7038), within the "Willard collection" of shops. A very helpful first stop. Ask for *Washington Visitors Map*, showing Metro stops near points of interest, and *Washington's Attractions*. Language bank service in over 20 tongues. Open Mon.-Sat. 9am-5pm. **Washington, DC Convention and Visitors Association (WCVA)**, 1212 New York Ave. NW (789-7000). Does not expect walk-ins. Write or call for copies of *Washington, DC: A Capital City* (for museum hours and exhibits to car rentals and accommodations) and the *Washington, DC, Dining/Shopping Guide*. Open Mon.-Fri. 9am-5pm. Daily Tourist Info: 737-8866.

International Visitors Information Service (IVIS): 1623 Belmont St. NW (939-5566). Language bank in over 50 languages (from 6am-11pm). Office open Mon.-Fri. 9am-5pm.

Traveler's Aid Society: Main office, 512 C St. NE (546-3120). Helpful in emergencies. Open Mon.-Fri. 9am-5pm. Desks at Union Station (371-1937, TDD 684-7886; open daily 9am-9pm), National Airport (684-3472, TDD 684 7884; open Mon.-Fri. 9am-9pm, Sat 9am-6pm), and Dulles International Airport (703-661-8636, TDD 471-9776; open Sun.-Fri. 10am-9pm, Sat. 10am-6pm). 24-hr. emergency aid, 546-3120.

Helplines: General DC Hotlines: 832-4357 (8DC-HELP); **AIDS Information Line**, 332-2437; **Dept. of Human Services Crisis Line** (24 hr.), 561-7000; **Rape Crisis Center**, 333-7273; **Disabled Persons Hotline** (emergency), TDD 727-3323; **National Organization for Victim's Assistance**, 1-800-879-6682; **Gay and Lesbian Hotline** (7am-11pm), 833-3234; **Ask-a-Nurse**, 703-760-8787; **Poison Control**, 625-3333; **Medical Referral, at George Washington University Hospital**, 994-4112; **Park Police** (emergencies in Rock Creek Park or on Federal park lands), 619-7310; **Disabled Persons Advice** (recording), 547-8081, TDD 547-6556; **Jewish Information**, 301-770-4848; **Montgomery County Hotline**, 301-527-4077; **Montgomery County Tourist Info**, 301-588-8687; **Prince Georges County Visitors Bureau**, 301-967-8687.

Embassies: Argentina, 1600 New Hampshire Ave. NW (939-6400); **Australia,** 1601 Massachusetts Ave. NW (797-3000); **Austria,** 2343 Massachusetts Ave. NW (483-4474); **Belgium,** 3330 Garfield St. NW (333-6900); **Brazil,** 3006 Massachusetts Ave. NW (745-2700); **Canada,** 501 Pennsylvania Ave. NW (682-1740); **Denmark,** 3200 Whitehaven St. NW (234-4300); **Egypt,** 2310 Decatur Place NW (232-5400); **Finland,** 3216 New Mexico Ave. NW (363-2430); **France,** 4101 Reservoir Rd. NW (944-6000); **Germany,** 4645 Reservoir Rd. NW (298-4000); **Greece,** 2221 Massachusetts Ave. NW (667-3168); **India,** 2107 Massachusetts Ave. NW (939-7000); **Ireland,** 2234 Massachusetts Ave. NW (462-3939); **Israel,** 3514 International Drive NW (364-5500); **Italy,** 1601 Fuller St. NW (328-5500); **Japan,** 2520 Massachusetts Ave. NW (939-6700); **Mexico,** 1911 Pennsylvania Ave. NW (728-1600); **Netherlands,** 4200 Linnaen Ave. NW (244-5300); **New Zealand,** 37 Observatory Circle NW (328-4800); **Norway,** 2720 34th St. NW (333-6000); **Philippines,** 1617 Massachusetts Ave. NW (483-1414); **Portugal,** 2125 Kalorama Rd. NW (328-8610); **Russia,** 1125 16th St. NW (628-7551); **South Africa,** 3051 Massachusetts Ave. NW (232-4400); **Spain,** 2700 15th St. NW (265-0190); **Sweden,** 600 New Hampshire Ave. NW (944-5600); **Switzerland,** 2900 Cathedral Ave. NW (745-7900); **United Kingdom,** 3100 Massachusetts Ave. NW (462-1340).

American Express: 1150 Connecticut Ave. NW (457-1300; TDD 775-6990). Travel service office provides traveler's checks, financial services, and other assistance. Call for other locations.

Car Rentals: Cheapest in Arlington, VA, across the Potomac from downtown and easily accessible by Metrobus. Cheaper rental outfits save their best vehicles for the most demanding rentals; if you say you're driving long distances, you may get a better automobile. **Easi Car Rentals,** 2480 S. Glebe Rd., Arlington (703-521-0188). Rates differ depending on season and make. Daily rates $21, plus 10¢ per mile. Weekly rates $141, with 200 free miles. Special weekend rates available. Must be 21 or older with major credit card or $300 cash deposit. Reservations advised. Open Mon.-Fri. 10am-6pm, Sat. 11am-4pm. **Bargain Buggies Rent-a-Car,** 6461 Gasall Rd., Alexandria (703-522-4141). $20 per day, or 10¢ per mile, $106 per week (local rental) with 200 free miles. Must be 18 or older with major credit card or cash deposit of $300. Those under 21 need full insurance coverage. Rates may alter depending on rental length and make of car. Open Mon.-Fri. 8am-7pm, Sat. 8am-5pm. **Quality Rent-a-Car,** 3166 Roanoke St., Fairfax (703-684-8880). $25 per day, $90 per weekend, $169 per week. Unlimited mileage. Major credit card deposit required. Open Mon.-Fri. 8am-5pm. **Enterprise Rent-a-Car,** 927 N. Kansas St., Arlington (703-243-5404 or 800-325-8007). $31 per day, $159 weekly (but expect rates to differ from branch to branch). Unlimited mileage. Major credit card deposit required. Open Mon.-Fri. 8am-6pm, Sat. 8am-noon.

Bicycle Rentals: Thompson Boat Center, 2900 Virginia Ave. NW (333-4861), between Rock Creek Pkwy. and Virginia Ave., near Watergate. 18-speed mountain bikes $6 per day or $22 per week, locks strongly recommended at 50¢ a day. Thompson also rents tandems and single-speeders. Open Mon.-Fri. 7am-6pm, Sat.-Sun. 8am-5pm. **Big Wheel Bikes,** 315 7th St. SE (543-1600). Regular bikes for as low as $3 per hour, $15 per business day; 3-hour minimum charge. For an extra $5, you can keep the bike overnight, giving you a full 24 hr. Major credit card or $30 cash per bike required for deposit. Open Mon.-Fri. 11am-7pm, Sat.-Sun. 10am-6pm. **Metropolis Bikes,** 709 8th St. SE (543-8900), across from the Marine barracks. All bikes $17 per business day, $70 per week. Ask about roller blade rentals. Open Mon.-Fri. 11am-7pm (Thurs. until 9pm), Sat. 10am-6pm, Sun noon-5pm. Credit card deposit required. Areas south and southeast of here can get pretty rough. **Better Bikes** (293-2080); call the phone number anytime (literally) and they will deliver a bike anywhere in the Washington area. Rates: 10-speeds $20 per day, mountain bikes $35 per day; Weekly rate $83. Helmet, map, backpack locks, and breakdown rescue service come free with every bike. $25 cash deposit and a driver's licence, credit card, or passport required for collateral. All transactions must be in cash. Open 24 hr. **City Bikes,** 2501 Champlain St. NW (265-1564), near the 18th St. and Columbia Rd. intersection under a big mural. Mostly mountain bikes and hybrids. Bike rentals $7 per hour, $20 per day, $90 per week. Tandems $14 per hour, $35 per day. Helmets $3 per day, locks $2 per day. Children's seats and trailers available. Major credit card deposit required, or cost of bike in cash. For international travellers, passport and plane ticket will suffice. Open Mon.-Wed. and Fri.-Sat. 10am-7pm, Thurs. 10am-9pm, Sun. noon-5pm. **Fletcher's Boat House,** 4940 Canal Rd., NW (244-0461). Located on the C & O towpath. Bicycles can only be used on canal towpath. $2.50 per hour (2-hr. min.), $9 per day. Some form of ID necessary as deposit. Open daily as weather permits.

Bike Repairs: The Bike Shop, 2003 P St. NW (659-8686). Open Mon.-Sat. 9am-6pm.

Public Library: Martin Luther King, Jr. Public Library, main branch, 901 G St. NW (727-1111 or TDD 727-2255). Open Mon.-Thurs. 9am-5pm, Fri.-Sat. 9am-5:30pm.

International newspapers: International newspapers and magazines are available at the following: **The News Room,** 1753 Connecticut Ave. NW (332-1489). Open Mon.-Fri. 7am-10pm, Sat. 7am-11pm, Sun. 7am-9pm. **News World,** 1001 Connecticut Ave. NW (872-0190). Open daily 7am-8:30pm, weekends 7am-7pm. **American International News,** 1825 I St. NW (223-2526). Open Mon.-Fri. 8am-6:30pm, Sat. 10am-4pm. **Key Bridge Newsstand,** 3326 M St. NW (338-2626) between 33rd and 34th St. NW. Open daily 8am-8pm. **Newsroom Farragut Square,** 1001 Connecticut Ave. NW (872-0190), at 17th and K St. Open Mon.-Fri. 7:30am-8:30pm, Sat.-Sun. 7am-7pm. **Editorial El Mundo,** 1796 Columbia Rd. NW (387-2831), in Adams-Morgan (Spanish-language papers only). **Open daily 10:30am-6pm.**

Saturday/Sunday currency exchange: **Deak & Co.,** 3222 M St. NW (338-3325), on the third level of Georgetown Park Mall. Open Sat. 10am-7pm, Sun. noon-6pm.

Telegrams: Western Union, 801 14th St. NW (624-0100). Metro: McPherson Square. Send and receive cables. See *Money.* Open 24 hr.

Post Office: Main office: indescribably inconvenient at 900 Brentwood Rd. NE (636-1532). ZIP code: 20066. Mail sent "General Delivery" always comes here—a good reason not to have anything sent General Delivery. Usually open Mon.-Fri. 8am-8pm, Sat. 10am-6pm. Call to be sure. **Capitol Hill:** North Capitol St. and Massachusetts Ave. NE (523-2628), across from Union Station. Open Mon.-Fri. 7am-midnight, Sat.-Sun. 7am-8pm. **Farragut Station,** in the new downtown: 1125 19th St. NW (523-2506). Open Mon.-Fri. 8am-6pm. **Temple Heights Station,** between Dupont and Adams-Morgan, 1921 Florida Ave. NW, near Connecticut Ave. (232-7613). Open Mon.-Fri. 8:30am-5pm. **Martin Luther King Jr. Station,** 14th St. between K and L St. NW (523-2000). Open Mon.-Fri. 8am-7pm and Sat. 10am-2pm. **Columbia Heights Station:** 1423 Irving St. NW (523-2399). Open Mon.-Fri. 8am-5:30pm. **Georgetown:** 1215 31st St. NW (523-2405). Open Mon.-Fri. 8am-5:30pm, Sat. 8:30am-2pm. Call 682-9595 to seek the post office nearest you. **Postal Hotline:** 526-3920.

Area Codes: DC 202; Maryland 301; northern Virginia 703. To reach any of the three from the other two, you must dial the area code, even though it's a local call. Unless otherwise noted all telephone numbers in this book have a 202 area code.

DC Population: 628,300 (4.6 million in the greater Washington metropolitan area).

See appropriate Sights sections for practical information for Arlington and Alexandria, VA.

Getting There

By Plane

Washington supports one bus station, one train station, and two airports. Flying is definitely a viable option, and with advance research and advice from a good travel agent, the fares just might not blow your budget. Start early and be flexible about the times and days you would like to travel. See *Getting Around the U.S.* for more information.

From New York's LaGuardia Airport, the **Delta Shuttle** and the **U.S. Shuttle** provide competing hourly flights to National Airport seven days a week. (From Boston, buy two tickets and take two one-hour shuttles—one to LaGuardia, one from it—and sit in the front of the first airplane so you can race through the terminal to the second.) While the shuttles were designed for businessfolk, with prices (over $130 each flight) to match, student and senior fares, available for anyone over 65 or under 24, stick to around $60 a flight. (If you qualify for these fares, expect to traverse this route frequently, and have the cash on hand, buy a 10-ticket JetPak for $440. You'll save over one-third of each flight's price.) Remember that discount fares from NYC don't apply during morning and evening rush hours, and that noise rules ban landings at National after 10pm, making 8:30pm shuttles from Boston a bad idea.

From within the U.S., it's best to fly into **National Airport** (703-685-8000). Doing so will save you money and headaches when you arrive, since National is on the Metro and close to Washington by car. Driving from downtown is easy (take I-395 south to the George Washington Pkwy. southbound. Follow signs for the airport); parking is not. In theory the ride from downtown to terminal should take about 20 minutes; in traffic, it can take much longer. Metrorail serves National Airport at a stop called National Airport (no duh), a few minutes' walk from the terminals themselves—just long enough to annoy if you're carrying heavy luggage. Cabs are probably the most convenient (albeit more expensive) way to get to and from the airport (about $10 from downtown).

While National is more convenient, **Dulles International Airport** (703-471-4242) is an *international* airport; no flights from abroad land at National. Some cheap domestic flights also touch down at Dulles. Driving from downtown Washington will take you about 40 minutes—more during rush hour. (Use the Dulles Access Rd. through Fairfax County, Va.; reach the road via the Capital Beltway or I-66 through Arlington.) Cabs to Dulles cost above $40. While there isn't a Metro station near Dulles, the **Dulles Express Bus** (703-685-1400) shuttles to and from the West Falls Church Metro every 20-30 minutes. (Mon.-Fri. 6am-10:30pm, Sat.-Sun. 8am-10:30pm; last bus from Metro, 11pm. One way trip $7.)

If you must, fly into **Baltimore-Washington International Airport (BWI),** about 10 miles south of Baltimore's city center. From Washington, take I-95 north to exit 47A. Then follow airport signs. From Baltimore, take 695 to exit 22A (the Baltimore-Washington Pkwy.) and then follow signs for the airport. Driving time is about 50 minutes from Washington and 30 minutes from Baltimore; but as always, allow for mega traffic. You can take Amtrak (40min.) or MARC from DC (see below).

The **Washington Flyer Express** (703-685-1400) also shuttles to and from National, Dulles, BWI, and their station at 1517 K St. NW. Buses leave Washington to National every 30 minutes from 6:05am-10:35pm on weekdays; hourly from 6:05am-1:05pm and every 30 minutes from 1:35pm-10:35pm on weekends. From National to downtown buses leave every 30 min. on weekdays; hourly from 6:25am-12:25pm and every 30min. from 1:25pm-9:25pm. on weekends. From downtown to Dulles (a 45-min. trip) buses leave every 30 minutes from 5:15am-9:45pm daily (Sat.-Sun., hourly departures from 6:15am-1:15pm). From Dulles to downtown buses leave every 30 minutes from 5:20am-10:20pm daily (Sat.-Sun., hourly departures from 5:20 am-12:20pm). From Washington to BWI daily every 90 minutes from 7am-8:30pm, from BWI to downtown DC from 7am-8:30pm. National one-way $7, round-trip $12; Dulles one-way $14, round-trip $22; BWI one-way $13, round-trip $23; under 7 free.

By Train

Amtrak's trains connect Washington to most other parts of the country through **Union Station,** 50 Massachusetts Ave. NE (484-7540). For most routes you can choose to take either a Metroliner or a regular train; Metroliners (800-523-8720) are speedier (though still much slower than European trains), more expensive, and usually not worth the money. Regular trains are efficient and quite pleasant. Call 800-USA-RAIL (872-7245) for Amtrak schedule information.

Amtrak may be the speediest route to **New York City,** although the Trump and Delta Shuttles give it a run for its money. Metroliners (three hours) leave approximately hourly from 5:50 am to 7pm from Union Station for Manhattan's Penn Station on weekdays; unreserved fares are $85 each way. Regular trains (three-and-a-half hours) leave about once an hour between 4:50am and 10:20pm; unreserved fares one-way $64, round-trip $89. Amtrak also stops in **Baltimore** (Metroliner (30min.) $21; regular (40 min.) one-way $12, round-trip $20) and **Philadelphia** (Metroliner (90min.) $51; regular (110min.) one-way $34, round-trip $51). Most New York trains continue on for another four hours to **Boston** (round-trip $128). Overnight trains depart daily at 4:05pm from Union Station on a 17-hr. exodus to **Chicago** (one-way $118, round-trip $212). Additional routes from Washington include: Richmond (one-way $21, round-trip $32-42 depending on demand); Williamsburg (one-way $28, round-trip $42-52); Virginia Beach (one-way $41, round-trip $62-82); and Atlanta (one-way $119, round-trip $156-210).

Maryland's commuter trains, **MARC** (1-800-325-7245), also depart from Union Station. These offer weekday commuter service to Baltimore, Kensington, Brunswick, Harpers Ferry, and Martinsburg, WV. Trains between Baltimore and Washington run in both directions during morning and late afternoon rush hours (5:30am-8am; 3:50-6:45pm). The trip takes about an hour and costs $5 one-way, $9 round-trip. Other trains run into DC mornings-only and out in the afternoon; fares range from $2.75-8 one-way. Call for schedule and fare information.

By Bus

Inter-city bus travel in America is slow, depressing, and often delayed. But it is cheap. The modern **Greyhound** station, 1005 1st St. NE (289-5155; 301-565-2662 for fare and schedules), at L St., rises over a rather decrepit neighborhood. Greyhound provides frequent daily service to: Philadelphia (every 2-3hr.; Mon.-Fri. $19 one way, $36 round trip; Sat.-Sun. $24 one way, $40 round trip), New York City (every 30min.-1hr.; Mon.-Fri. $32, $63 round trip; Sat.-Sun. $34 one way, $68 round trip), and Baltimore (every 30min.-1hr.; Mon.-Fri. $6.90, $13 roundtrip; Sat.-Sun. $8.50 one way, $16 round trip). Buses also go to Atlantic City, Pittsburgh, and Richmond.

By Car

DC is ringed by the Capital Beltway, **I-495** (except where it's part of I-95), bisected by **U.S. 1**, which incorporates several local thoroughfares, and intruded upon via Virginia by **I-395**. **I-95** shoots up from Florida, links Richmond, VA to Washington to Baltimore, then rockets up the East Coast past Boston. The high-speed **Baltimore-Washington Parkway,** predictably, also connects DC to Baltimore. **I-270** runs west through Montgomery County to link up with national east-west freeway **I-70** in western Maryland. **I-595** trickles off the Capital Beltway and scenically east and south to Annapolis. **I-66** heads west through Virginia. Most visitors who drive arrive from the north or south, on or parallel to I-95. To go downtown from the B-W Parkway, follow signs for New York Ave. From I-95, get onto the Capitol Beltway, then choose your exit. Wisconsin Ave. (to upper NW and Georgetown), Connecticut Ave. (exit 20, "Chevy Chase," to upper NW, Adams-Morgan, Dupont Circle and downtown) and New Hampshire Ave. (through Takoma to downtown) are three of the easiest and most useful. From the south, take I-95 (which becomes I-395) directly to the 14th St. Bridge or Memorial Bridge (both lead downtown). From the west, take I-66 East over the Roosevelt Bridge and follow signs for Constitution Ave. I-66 is simpler and faster than I-495. Vehicles on I-66 East (Mon.-Fri. 7-9am) and I-66 West (Mon.-Fri. 4-6pm) must carry at least three people (the "HOV-3" rule) or pay a hefty ticket. During the day, Maryland's major highways are sometimes congested; Virginia's usually are. Try to reach DC when it's not rush hour, especially if you're coming from Virginia.

Orientation

Street Plan

> *Make big plans, aim high in hope and work, remembering that a noble and logical diagram once recorded will never die, but long after we are gone will be a living thing, asserting itself with ever growing insistency.*
> *—Daniel Burnham (designer of Union Station),*
> *1899*

When Pierre L'Enfant laid out DC's streets, he had two things in mind: magnificent vistas and simple logic. Downtown Washington almost achieves both. The city is roughly diamond-shaped, with the four tips of the diamond pointed at the four compass directions. The irregular southwestern border is the Potomac River, flowing between DC and runaway Arlington, Virginia, which split off from the District in 1846. The other three borders are straight lines separating DC from Maryland. Washington street names and addresses split up into four quadrants, NW, NE, SE and SW, defined by their relation to the U.S. Capitol. NW is the largest; SW is tiny. The four quadrant names distinguish otherwise identical addresses: there are four intersections of a 7th St. and a G St., and consequently four addresses marked 700 G St.—SE, SW, NW and NE.

The basic street plan is a rectilinear grid. Streets that run from east to west are named in alphabetical order running north and south from the Capitol, from two A Streets two blocks apart (nearest the Capitol) out to two W Streets dozens of blocks apart. There is no A or B St. in NW and SW. Since the street plan was devised from the Roman alphabet, in which "I" and "J" were the same letter, there is also no J St. anywhere. After W, east-west streets take on two-syllable names, then three-syllable names, then (at the north end of NW) names of trees and flowers. These names run in alphabetical order, but sometimes repeat or skip a letter. The Mount Pleasant neighborhood, for example, contains the following streets, in order: Belmont, Clifton, Chapin, Euclid. (Don't blame L'Enfant for these discrepancies—his original plan stopped around Dupont Circle.) Streets running north-south get numbers (1st St., 2nd St., etc.) all the way out to 52nd St. NW and 63rd St. NE (both one block long). Numbered and lettered streets sometimes stop existing for a block, then keep going as if nothing had happened. (There is no Eye St. between 9th and 11th St. NW, for example.) Addresses on lettered streets indicate the numbered cross street (1100 D St. SE will be between 11th and 12th

St.). The same trick works with addresses on some avenues (Pennsylvania, but not Massachusetts or Wisconsin). The farther you get from the central city, the more these streets get interrupted or replaced by others not part of the alphanumeric system.

Downtown, the interruptions have a logic of their own. L'Enfant's plan included a sheaf of state avenues, radiating outward from the U.S. Capitol (Pennsylvania, New Jersey, Delaware, Maryland) or the White House (New York, Connecticut, Vermont) or otherwise crossing downtown (Massachusetts, New Hampshire, Virginia). Massachusetts Ave. runs NW-SE parallel to, but north of, Pennsylvania Ave. Rhode Island Ave. does the same for New York Ave., both running SW-NE. These diagonal avenues interrupt the grid streets; many are major thoroughfares. The U.S. added space while the city added streets; the Last Colony thus acquired avenues named for all 50 states. (Well, almost. California has a "Street" instead.) Besides the Capitol and the White House, downtown avenues meet at circles and squares: some important ones are Dupont Circle (Connecticut, Massachusetts, and New Hampshire Ave.); Washington Circle (New Hampshire and Pennsylvania); Scott Circle (Massachusetts, Rhode Island and 16th St.); and Mt. Vernon Square (Massachusetts and New York). Lafayette Square is the park north of the White House. (The Ellipse is south of it.)

A separate group of streets run in compass directions from the Capitol: North Capitol St., East Capitol St., and South Capitol St. separate the quadrants. The Mall, a huge green lawn with Smithsonian museums on either side, extends west of the Capitol in place of a "West Capitol St." An imaginary line down the middle of the Mall, extending west to the Potomac River, divides NW from SW. Independence Ave. runs east-west south of the Mall (where B St. SW should be); Constitution Ave. runs east-west north of the Mall (where B St. NW ought to be).

Some parts of the city's world have their own ideas of order. Crowded, eternally fashionable Georgetown runs west of 28th St. between K and (approximately) R St. NW. (Many visitors wrongly think it's far from downtown.) Though Georgetown's streets predate L'Enfant's plan, the older grid harmonized with his, and many of Georgetown's streets have numbers and letters; more than a few, however, retain older names (Thomas Jefferson St., Potomac St.). Wisconsin Ave. NW is Georgetown's north-south artery. Rock Creek Park interrupts the street plan with a near-unbroken transport to summery green. The few roads through it follow no pattern; Rock Creek Parkway is the north-south artery. Blighted Anacostia hides a more confused street plan than anywhere else in the city.

Some **major roads** are: **Pennsylvania Avenue,** which runs SE-NE from Anacostia to Capitol Hill to the Capitol, through downtown, past the White House and ends finally at 28th and M St. NW, in Georgetown; **Connecticut Ave.,** which runs north-northwest from the White House through Dupont Circle, past the Zoo and farther out through Chevy Chase, MD; **Wisconsin Ave.,** north from Georgetown past the Cathedral to Friendship Heights; **16th Street NW,** which zooms from the White House north through hotels, offices, townhouses, Adams-Morgan, and Mount Pleasant (in that order) then forms Rock Creek Park's eastern border until it continues into Maryland; **K Street NW,** a major artery downtown; **Constitution and Independence Avenues,** just north and south of the Mall; **Massachusetts Ave.,** from American University past the Cathedral, through Dupont and the old downtown to Capitol Hill; **New York Ave.,** whose principal arm runs from the White House through NE; **Rock Creek Parkway,** north-south through Rock Creek Park; and high-speed **North Capitol Street.**

Neighborhoods

DC isn't just for Congress anymore. Over 600,000 residents inhabit the federal city; rich and poor, African-American, white, and Latino are all well-represented. Since the 13-story height limit bans high-rise apartments, DC residents have conveniently arranged themselves into neighborhoods for your perusal, preferably on foot. Tourists who see the museums and the government, but don't escape the Mall and see the neighborhoods, haven't really seen Washington at all. **Capitol Hill** extends east from the Capitol; its townhouses and bars mix white- and blue-collar locals with legislation-minded pols. **The Mall** isn't a neighborhood but a long grassy stretch west of the Capitol along which spread the Smithsonian museums. West of the Mall proper, the grass grows around famous **monuments** like the Lincoln Memorial. The **SW** quadrant, south of the Mall, begins as federal offices, then passes under I-395 and becomes a low-income neighborhood (to the east) and the waterfront area (to the west). North of the Mall, the **old downtown** goes about its business, accompanied by **Foggy Bottom** (sometimes called the "West End") on the other side of the White House, and the **new downtown** around K St. west of 15th St. NW.

Georgetown draws crowds and sucks away bucks nightly from its center at Wisconsin and M St. NW. This townhouse neighborhood harbors plenty of students and a few millionaires. Business and pleasure, embassies and streetlife, straight and gay converge around **Dupont Circle;** east of 16th St. the Dupont Circle character changes to struggling **Logan Circle,** then to rundown **Shaw,** and then to Howard University and **LeDroit Park,** an early residence for Washington's African-American elite. A strong Hispanic community coexists with Black, white, and cool in **Adams-Morgan**, north of Dupont and east of Rock Creek Park; further north is the equally multi-racial but more troubled Mount Pleasant area.

West of the Park begins **"upper northwest,"** a big stretch of mostly white, more spread-out territory that includes several smaller, separately named neighborhoods, the National Zoo, and the Cathedral. The western edges of Washington hold American University and the affluent, landscaped Foxhall Road. Sixteenth Street zooms due north to Walter Reed Hospital, the peaceful Shepherd Park neighborhood and Silver Spring, MD. **Takoma Park** hangs out its batiks along the District's northeast edge. The NE quadrant itself, east of North Capitol St., includes the middle-class **Brookland** area, home of Catholic U., along with poorer neighborhoods and the expansive Arboretum. Across the Anacostia river, the rest of SE (including **Anacostia**), has been seriously damaged and further isolated by poverty, crack, and guns.

Getting Around

Metro

> The magnificent distances of old have been mastered by street railways in all directions. New lines of them have been built, old ones extended, and now splendid chariots have been added to the conveniences of the people in getting from one part of the city to the other.
> —Frederick Douglass, Lecture on the National Capital (1877)

Metrorail (637-7000), the Washington subway system, is a sight in its own right. (It's usually called simply the "Metro.") (Main office, 600 5th St. NW. Open daily 6am-around 11:30pm.) The Wheaton station has the world's longest escalator—230 feet from street to mezzanine level. (Before that, Dupont Circle had the longest non-Soviet one; the Metro broke its own record.) The sterile, monumental stations, with their high, curved ceilings and relentlessly brown-and-beige color scheme, zap first-time riders with their uniformity, efficiency, and artlessness; even the rows of parallel ceiling lozenges, meant to depress echoes, recede in both directions like a Bauhaus office building on its side. While the subway system has made tourists' lives infinitely easier since the first segment opened in 1976, designer Harry Weese's monotonous, futuristic plan has a lot to do with many visitors' mistaken impression of Washington as lifeless, efficient, and mostly governmental. Metro stations look alike—you'll feel at ease in all of them, or in none.

Trains themselves are clean, quiet, carpeted, and air-conditioned. Between the profusion of brown-capped Metro cops and the stations themselves, which give hoods no place to hide, the system so far has remained nearly crime-free. The Metro has just begun to serve inner-city Shaw; stations in troubled Anacostia opened in 1991. These stations offer overdue access to efficient public transportation for weary residents of areas ravaged by drug wars.

A computerized fare card must be bought from machines in the station before you enter the subway and passed through electronic readers at exit; if there's still money on it, you get it back. If you plan to connect with a bus after your ride, get a transfer pass from machines on the platform *before* boarding the train (transfers are not valid within four blocks of the station where they are issued). To use the subway several times, buy a $5 or $10 farecard. You will get a 5% bonus on farecards for $10 or more (max. value farecard is $30). The $6 family tourist pass lets a group of 4 ride Metrorail and Metrobus all day long any Saturday, Sunday, or holiday except July 4 (pass available at Metro Center stop and from some hotel concierges). Children age 4 and under ride free. Senior citizens and disabled persons are entitled to discount fares, but need a special Metro ID. Elevators help with wheelchairs and strollers. Trains run daily 6:30am-11:30pm. Peak hour fares range from $1 to $3.15, according to the distance traveled. At all other times, fares range from $1 to $2.

The extensive, complicated **Metrobus** (same address, phone, and hours as Metrorail) system reliably serves Georgetown, downtown, and the suburbs. Downtown, the bus stops every few blocks. Regular fare is $1 (flat dollar bills accepted), but again, rush hour fares vary. Seniors, disabled persons, and children ages 4 and under are entitled to discounts as on Metrorail. Schedules and route maps for buses operating near Metrorail stations are available in those stations. A comprehensive bus map is available from the main Metro office, assuming they haven't run out again. Call or write for availability and price. (ZIP code 20001). A **Flash Pass** allows unlimited bus (and sometimes Metro) rides over a two-week period. A DC-only pass costs just $20 ($21 for bus and Metro use), while the most expensive of the eight types, the Virginia Zone 3 pass, costs $34 (for bus and rail use). There is an unlimited one-day Metro pass for only $5—great for tourists. Passes are available at Metro Center, as well as at some banks and Giant food stores. Metro information (637-7000) can describe the alchemical mix of buses and trains needed to reach any destination.

Bus routes with a letter, then a number (D4, S2) make stops in DC and Maryland, or sometimes (like the "J" buses) only in Maryland. If the number precedes the letter (18L, 5D) the route runs in Virginia or in DC and Virginia. (Most Virginia routes somehow connect to the Pentagon Metro stop.) If they gave it a two-digit number and took away its name, the bus stops nowhere but in Washington itself. Thirtysomething buses (33, for example) run from downtown to some stretch of Wisconsin Ave. NW; 37 passes through Dupont Circle. 30, 32, 34 and 36 buses take Pennsylvania Ave. NW to Georgetown, then drive up Wisconsin. The immensely useful D2, D4, D6 and D8 lines zip from far NW to Glover Park, Q St. in Georgetown, Dupont Circle, the new downtown and Metro center before ending up in far NE at the Rhode Island Ave. Metro. The N5 and N8 buses run up Massachusetts Ave. NW from downtown past American University. L2 and L4 buses run from downtown up Connecticut Ave. NW. Alexandria (DASH) and Montgomery County (Ride-On) also have their own, smaller bus systems.

Taxis

Washington cab fares are lower, but weirder, than in other American cities: fares are based not on a meter but on a map which splits the city into five zones and 27 subzones. Despite its low fares, DC has more cabs per capita than anywhere else in America. Roundabout routes designed to push up fares by crossing as many zones as possible should be a thing of the past, since your fare is now based only on the zones you start and end the ride in. Zone prices are fixed, so your driver can—but probably won't—ask you for the fare at the beginning of your trip. A zone map and corresponding fare chart are posted in every legal cab. Be sure your destination is in the District before you hail that cab, though; cabs to, from, and within Maryland and Virginia are metered rather than zoned and exorbitant rather than affordable. (From downtown to National Airport: $10-15.)

Within zone 1, which surrounds the Capitol building and includes most of the downtown Mall area, your fare will be $3. Fares between other zones run $3 to $10.20, the maximum fare for any ride within DC. During rush hours (Mon.-Fri. 4-6:30pm), there is a $1 surcharge. Fares are doubled during official snow emergencies. Groups riding to the same destination are sometimes charged $1.25 for each extra person. Travel into Maryland or Virginia will cost you $2 for the first half-mile and 70¢ for each additional half-mile or part thereof, which quickly gets ridiculous. The Metro system obviates daytime taxi-riding; they're quite useful after dark, in subwayless Georgetown or Adams-Morgan, to get home from bars and clubs, or wherever you feel unsafe walking around.

Hail any cab downtown, but farther out, call **Yellow Cab** (544-1212). Be ready to give some directions or to send the first few cabs away. You can get a zone map and an informational brochure from the **District of Columbia Taxicab Commission,** 2041 Martin Luther King, Jr. Ave. SE, Washington, DC 20020 (767-8380). And remember, if you feel you're being ripped off, get the receipt, write down the cab number, and call either the DC commission or the Maryland and Virginia assistance number (331-1671).

Driving

> *Some diplomats are addicted to driving much faster*
> *than the law permits.*
> —*Evening Star (1890)*

Drivers from rapid cabbie-infested cities like New York City or Boston often think Washington drivers are wimps. They're right. DC drivers are fairly polite, which doesn't mean you can sleep all the way down North Capitol Street. Out-of-towners should map out their routes in advance and avoid driving whenever possible. Rush-hour commuter traffic can leave you in gridlock for hours. From 7-9:30am going downtown and 4-6:30pm leaving the city, especially to and from Virginia, your car will idle for so long you could probably get where you're going faster by walking. Lunchtime can also pose traffic problems, and Friday afternoons bring the worst nightmares. Most of the sights downtown are more easily accessible by Metro or by bus. In upper NW and NE, a car won't hurt: to some outlying attractions, you'd be lost without one. Around 8pm, when bureaucrats have all gone home, Washington driving becomes miraculously easy—know the street plan, and you'll get where you're going.

Downtown drivers fall into three groups: the first are white-collar workers with already-reserved parking, the second inhale deeply and shell out for garage space, and the third trade time for money and cruise the area for on-street parking. Cowards can expect to pay $12 for a day of parking or $4 per hour. Diehards should allot half an hour or more in search of daytime parking spaces around Georgetown, Dupont Circle, Bethesda, or Adams-Morgan; between K St. and the Mall, give up and take the Metro. Afternoon rush hour (Mon.-Fri. 4-6:30pm) turns most downtown spaces temporarily illegal. Read the signs where you've put your car, and take the time restrictions seriously: cops do, and they tow. Traffic tickets will hit you for $15 for an expired meter. Resist the urge to drive to the Smithsonian, or else park south of the museums along Independence Ave. SW or one of the numbered streets. (On weekends this may not be difficult.) Nighttime parking is tough only in Georgetown and Adams-Morgan—just the places you're most likely to drive to, since the Metro doesn't serve them.

With all those numbers and letters, Washington tries hard to make its streets comprehensible; though the city makes sense to pedestrians (see *Orientation*) its seeming order can turn to chaos behind a steering wheel. One-way streets and construction detours abound. If a one-way street isn't going your way, the next one up probably will be. Some streets, like Connecticut Ave., have "reversible lanes" whose directions depend on the time of day; a few turn one-way during rush hour. Watch for street signs indicating this. Certain intersections on the edge of Washington tend to plunge drivers into Virginia unawares. These are K St. NW west of 24th St., where the Whitehurst

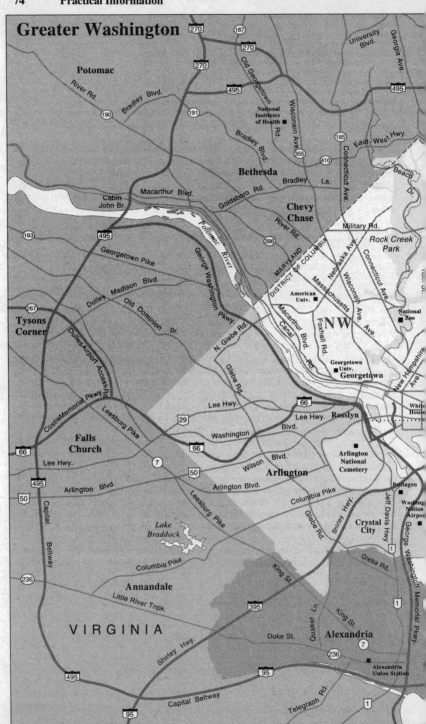

Greater Washington

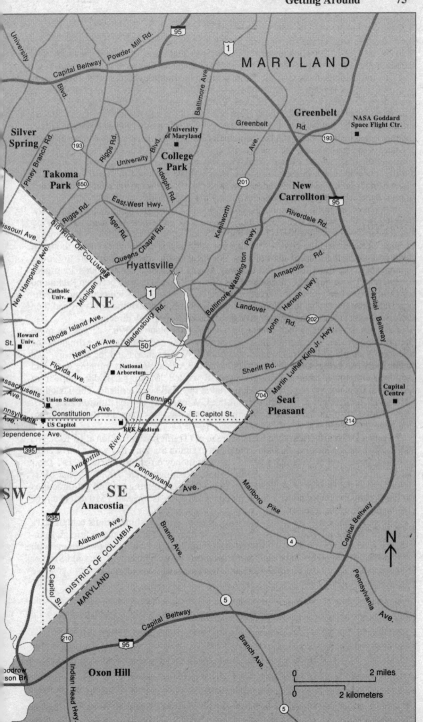

Freeway splits off above it; 8th St. SW south of D St., which sends drivers to Arlington or Anacostia—only; and the one-way spaghetti around the Lincoln Memorial, where drivers are like U.S. troops under fire—both may end up in Arlington Cemetery. DC roads are famously bad—for a good laugh, look at the pavement where a street crosses the line into Montgomery County. There's sure to be potholes on one of the sides.

Some parts of Washington have their very own logic, seemingly incomprehensible to outsiders. Congress is one. **Rock Creek Park** is another. Over the creek and through the woods is often the quickest way from one part of the city to another, since there are almost no traffic lights in the Park. But the park follows neither the grid nor the radial-avenue plan; instead, a few roads—principally Rock Creek Parkway—run north-south or across the park. Since the roads twist and confuse, check a map before you race through the park. Most of Rock Creek Parkway turns one-way during rush hour (south in the morning, north in the afternoon). Beach Drive is closed to motor vehicles Fri. 7pm-Sun. 7pm. In the few days after a snowstorm, try and route yourself through Rock Creek Park, where the Park Service promptly plows the roads.

Into, out of, or around the suburbs, you're bound to meet the behemoth known as the Capital Beltway, whose signs leave tourists panicked while their cars race past their exits at over 60 mph. A few hints: I-495 and I-95 both refer to the Beltway, which makes a huge circle around the city; I-95 continues north and south to other states, though it also completes the loop of the beltway. For local traffic, the two numbers are inter-changeable. The inner loop of the Beltway travels clockwise and the outer loop goes counterclockwise. Signs at entrance ramps often ask you to choose between Richmond or Baltimore when you want no part of either; read "south" for Richmond and "north" for Baltimore to resolve the dilemma. If you screw up, just take the next exit and then reverse course; local signs usually give good return-to-Beltway directions.

The 14th St. Bridge, which downed an Air Florida plane in 1983, serves the more helpful and prosaic function of linking downtown DC and the Mall to Arlington, the George Washington Parkway, and, through the GW, Alexandria and the Beltway. (It's technically two bridges, the George Mason and the Arland Williams, running north and south.) Arlington Memorial Bridge, universally called "Memorial Bridge," zips from Arlington Cemetery to the Lincoln Memorial at the Mall's western end. The Theodore Roosevelt Bridge, a.k.a. I-66, runs from the GW parkway to Constitution Ave. NW. Key Bridge, also on the George Washington Parkway, links austere Rosslyn, Va. to happening Georgetown.

To pay a DC traffic ticket, go to the Bureau of (Traffic) Adjudication at 65 K St. NE (727-5000; open Mon.-Fri. 8:30am-7pm; Metro: Union Station). Pay with cash or credit card (Mastercard or Visa). Or make a check or money order payable to the DC Treasurer and send it to the Bureau of Adjudication, Washington, DC 20002. If your car is towed, go to the Bureau of Adjudication to pay for your towing fee and get directions to the Brentwood Impoundment lot in far NE. Towing costs $75 and a $10 daily storage fee beginning 24 hr. after towing.

Any native has come up with a thousand reasons why Washingtonians cannot drive in snow. They're all true. Dangerous in any weather are the diplomats, foreign functionaries, and anyone with a weird, red-white-and-blue license plate that begins with "D" or "S." These jokers have *diplomatic immunity,* which means 13-year old Sven or Svetlana may be racing down Wisconsin Ave. in the ambassadorial family car. Give these vehicles a wide berth.

Accommodations

> On arriving in Washington I went to an hotel and re-
> mained there several days, but found the mode of
> living very disagreeable...I was glad to retreat to a
> private boarding-house, where there were several
> members of Congress, and everything was conduct-
> ed in an agreeable manner.
> —*John Finch, Esq.*, Travels in the United States and
> Canada *(1850)*

DC's accommodations crunch isn't new. B&Bs, hotels, and temporary lodgings have occasioned complaint at least since the Jackson administration (1829), when new officials and newcomers to Congress packed the boarding-houses, warning their families to avoid Washington's sordid streets and swampy climate. The streets have improved, but the climate hasn't—much: business travelers desert DC during the summer months, so business hotels discount deeply and swell with tourists during summer weekends. Students, Australians, and other downmarket *Let's Go* types fill up DC's amiable AYH/HI (Hostelling International) hostel. Other hostel-like accommodations gear themselves to longer stays; some favor international travelers over Americans, most give cheap weekly rates along with a chance to meet other visitors, and almost all want guests to call in advance. (Don't forget that IYHF-AYF hostels are in the process of adopting the new, blue triangle "Hostelling International" seal of approval. See the Accommodations section of the General Introduction above for more information.)

Interns and similar summer-long guests tend to stay in university dorms, where the rates are cheap and the students abound. Most college housing programs don't want, or even permit, non-student tourists; even college guys and gals who crave university summer housing should come up with a job or an official excuse to visit DC, then write or call several months in advance. Some colleges, at least in America, sponsor "summer in Washington" programs, which can put students in touch with DC alums who need housesitting or desire guests; if you're still in school, see if yours has one before you visit DC.

If you're lucky enough to hit the District without a car, and you don't want a hostel, the guest houses around Dupont Circle and Adams-Morgan should be your first try. These establishments are smaller, friendlier, and usually better-looking than any budget hotel. The automobile-encumbered may find it easier to stay in Arlington, VA or in Bethesda, MD, where the central-city real estate crunch doesn't preclude parking lots. Alexandria, VA, on average 20 minutes by car from DC, offers more motel-type options. If you need to keep a car downtown, call wherever you're thinking of staying and figure out where to park in advance.

Downtown hotels range from moderately to crazily expensive, but if you stay on a weekend in the off-season (read "sweltering summer"), you can live like a corporate executive for half the price, or less. Check the *New York Times* Sunday Travel section for the latest deals before you go, then bargain for a room as you would a used car. (Remember that DC adds an automatic 11% occupancy surcharge and another $1.50 per room per night to your bill.) If you're traveling in a group, keep in mind that hotels around here usually charge per room, not per guest. Even a $100 room becomes reasonable when you split it four ways. Most places will give your third or fifth occupant a cot for no extra charge.

Bulletin boards and newsletters can help you find rental housing; some are for everybody, others are special-interest. **Georgetown University's** housing office, 100 Harbin Hall (687-4560), publishes a weekly housing newsletter; stop by and pick one up at their on-campus office. (Other university housing offices just might provide similar help.) The **Food for Thought** restaurant in Dupont Circle (see *Food*) fills its bulletin board with all sorts of neighborhood requests, including those seeking apartments, tenants or roommates. A similar hodgepodge of needs accretes at **Takoma Traders,** in Takoma Park. Gay or lesbian travelers especially should check the resource centers at **Lammas** and **Lambda Rising** bookstores, also in Dupont Circle.

Help

Roommates Preferred, 904 Pennsylvania Ave. SE (547-4666). Metro: Capitol South or Eastern Market. Matches people who want roommates with those seeking rooms. The personable director will meet and talk with you, then suggest people with whom you might want to live. If you decide to use the service after the conversation, the fee is $50. They claim to have thousands of people on file. Open Mon.-Fri. 10am-7pm, Sat. 10am-noon. Call ahead for an appointment, or drop by.

1-800-VISIT-DC (a.k.a. 1-800-847-4832), 1730 Rhode Island Ave. Suite 302. An efficient telephone service that offers discounted rates in hotels around Washington. They claim to screen all hotels for security. Room rates vary with the season but can run from $55-120. Need credit card. Open Mon.-Fri. 8:30am-6:30pm, Sat. 9am-1pm.

Bed 'N' Breakfast Ltd. of Washington, DC, P.O. Box 12011, Washington, DC 20005 (328-3510). Reserves a wide range of accommodations, from budget to luxury, as well as apartments for families or guests requiring longer stays. Rates in private home B&Bs range from $40-100 for singles, $50-100 for doubles. Additional person charges are $15. Some historic properties. Interesting array of hosts and hostesses. Open Mon.-Fri. 10am-5pm, Sat. 10am-1pm.

The Bed and Breakfast League, Ltd., P.O. Box 9490, Washington, DC 20016 (363-7767). Reserves rooms in private homes, from Capitol Hill townhouses to Cleveland Park inn-style mansions. Check locations before you agree to anything: the cheapest B&Bs can parade far out in the suburbs. Room prices vary. Singles $35-55, $45-115 with private bath. Doubles $55-115 with private bath. Booking fee $10; non-refundable room deposit $25. Call for reservations during office hours (Mon.-Thurs. 9am-5pm, Fri. 9am-1pm).

University Dorms

Georgetown University Summer Housing is available only for summer educational (i.e. non-profit) pursuits; they gladly take interns and members of summer programs, but cannot house self-declared tourists. Air-conditioned singles ($19), non-air-conditioned doubles ($15), and air-conditioned doubles ($16), all with a strong college-dormitory mood. Woe to those stranded without air conditioning. Call or write G.U. Office of Housing and Conferences Services, Washington, DC 20057 (687-3999); the sooner you contact them, the better your room will be, although last-minute rentals are always a possibility. (Three-week min. stay. Bring your own linens. Requires mail application and 20% non-refundable deposit. Rooms available June to mid-Aug. Apartments with kitchens also available, but must be rented for the entire summer.) The housing office, 100 Harbin Hall, GU (687-4560), also lists off-campus sublets in a weekly newsletter. Drop by and pick one up when on campus (they won't mail them to non-Georgetown affiliates).

American University Summer Housing, write to 4400 Massachusetts Ave. NW, Washington, DC 20016-8039, Attn.: Housing Management (885-2598; Metro: Tenleytown Ave.), provides simple, air-conditioned dorm rooms for students and interns from late May to mid-August. Only double rooms available ($88 per week per person) with hall bathrooms and a required 2-week minimum stay. Come with a friend or they will invent one for you. Reserve early for check-in dates in early June; after that you can call 24hr. before you want to stay, and reservations will be accepted whenever the dorms aren't full. A university ID (from any university) and full payment for stay must be presented at check-in.

George Washington University Housing, write to: 2211 H St. NW, Washington, DC 20052 (994-6688). Metro: Foggy Bottom. For interns or students in academic programs only. Average dorm rooms, with hardwood floors and clean bathrooms. Suites are huge, spacious rooms and offer singles, unlike the triples or smaller combinations. In the freshman dorm, the five-person suite is a combination of a single and two doubles. Laundry in dorms; delis close by. All rooms have A/C. Singles with kitchen $19-25. Doubles with kitchen $38. Suites with microwave $22 per person.

Catholic University Housing: write to Office of Resident Life, 108 St. Bonaventure Hall, Catholic U., Washington, DC 20064 (319-5277). Metro: Brookland/CUA. Close to Metro, but far from almost everything else; try other college housing first. Housing available only to interns or students on academic programs (no tourists).The rooms in the new Centennial Village complex are spacious with huge bay windows and large closets, with A/C and private baths. Many disabled accessible. Stays of 13 days or less, singles with A/C $26. Stays of more than 14 days, singles with A/C $20. Stays of 30-79 nights discounted 5%; stays of 80 nights discounted 10%. Call ahead to request an application. Application must be in at least 24hr. before expected arrival; a 10% deposit is required in advance.

Howard University Housing is available for students working or studying in the DC are for the summer. Requests for applications should be directed to Reverend James Coleman at the Office of Special Programs (806-5661 or 806-5653). Not a great neighborhood. Affordable hostel-like rates in your choice of air-conditioned or non air-conditioned singles, doubles, and suites, in the university dorms. Air-conditioned single rooms $18; without A/C $14. Linen service $5 per week. Variable meal plans are available through university dining services. Available from the end of May through the first week of August. Advance payment required.

Hostels

Washington International Hostel (AYH/HI), 1009 11 St. NW (737-2333). Metro: Metro Center, take the 11th St. exit, then walk up 11th St. NW, away from the Mall, and turn right onto K St. Not only a cheapo place to stay, the AYH/HI hostel is one of the friendliest; international travelers from everywhere appreciate the college-age staff, bunk beds, bulletin boards, kitchen, and common rooms. Clean, air-conditioned rooms hold 4-12 beds, accessed by elevator. Lockers and laundry room available, as well as game room. No alcohol or drugs; smoking room in basement. Safe neighborhood, but not so safe northeast of here. Open 24hr. Bed $15; $3 membership charge on the first night for non-AYH/HI-members. Telephone reservations at least 48 hr. in advance, written reservations must be received 3 weeks in advance. MC/Visa accepted.

Washington International Student Center, 2452 18th St. NW (265-6555) on "restaurant row" in the heart of Adams-Morgan. This newly opened hostel accommodates out-of-state and international visitors in bunk beds in three very clean, though somewhat cramped, air-conditioned rooms. The friendly managers are helpful and eager to please newcomers to DC for only $13 a night (including free bed linen). Kitchen facilities on the premises, laundromat nearby on Columbia Road. Alcohol permitted, smoking on balcony, no curfew, no max. stay.

Women's Info Bank, a.k.a. **Bed and Bread,** 3918 W St. NW (338-1863). Peacefully west of Georgetown. Friendly but selective hostel accepts women (from all countries, including this one) and non-American men, at $15-20 (or less, according to need) for a shared single-sex room. Small but comfortable rooms with oriental rugs and comfortable beds; backyard bamboo trees conceal the Potomac River. House kitchen occasionally holds small buffets. Continental breakfast provided. Also a referral center for housing, in DC and elsewhere. Open house from 8pm-10pm, nightly. Those who want a place to stay should show up then. If the place is full, the owners promise to find rooms in the area for all who show up. No reservations necessary. To get here by public transportation, catch the D2 bus from Union station or from Georgetown, around Wisconsin and Q St.

Guest Houses and Hotels

Kalorama Guest House at Kalorama Park, 1854 Mintwood Place NW (667-6369), off Columbia Rd., in Adams-Morgan. Metro: Woodley Park/Zoo (a long walk). Well-run, impeccably decorated, immaculate guest rooms in three Victorian townhouses, in the upscale western slice of Adams-Morgan near Rock Creek Park. Enjoy evening sherry or lemonade among the oriental rugs, by the fire in winter or on the patio in summer. No wonder the guests call it home. All rooms have A/C and a clock radio. Refrigerator space, washing machines, and a guest phone for local calls. Free continental breakfast. Rooms with shared bath $40-70; $5 per additional person (all but two rooms come with private sink). Rooms with private baths $75-105. Call and reserve 1 to 2 weeks in advance; desk hours Mon.-Fri. 7:30am-9pm, Sat.-Sun. 7:30am-7pm.

Davis House, 1822 R St. NW (232-3196, 24 hr.). Metro: Dupont Circle. Charming and spacious wood-floored building perfect for short-term international visitors. Run by the American Friends Service Committee; accepts international visitors, staff of Quaker organizations, and "representatives of other organizations working on peace and justice concerns." Other visitors occasionally accepted on a same-day, space-available basis. Max. stay two weeks, reserve as early as possible (one night's deposit required). No smoking; no alcohol. Singles with half bath $25.

International Student House, 1825 R St. NW (232-4007). Metro: Dupont Circle. Welcomes longish-term international visitors grandly and warmly in an old townhouse with a mammoth dining hall, important-looking library, and neat entrance staircase. The house sponsors touring trips and athletic activities as well. In back, the modern, dormitory-like housing rents for $565-765 per person per month for doubles, triples and a quad; singles $765/month. Price includes daily breakfast and dinner. Minimum stay of 2 months during the summer, four months during the school year. Accepts a limited number of Americans (no passport or age restrictions). Write to them (ZIP 20009) for an application or more information. Reserve as far in advance as possible.

Thompson-Markward Hall, 235 2nd St. NE (546-3255), near the Capitol. For women (ages 18-34) only; male friends crowd the lavish lobby, which shares the first floor with lounges and a study room. Upstairs, dorm-like rooms line old but well-cleaned hallways. Small bedrooms (about 15 ft. by 10 ft.); bathrooms are large, well-kept, and public. Large, airy laundry room. Maid service provided but bring your own sheets. Two meals a day (old-fashioned cafeteria cuisine) in a pleasant dining hall. Piano. Popular with ivory-tickling Southerners and Hill interns. $130 a week; two-week min. stay.

Kalorama Guest House at Cathedral Park, 2700 Cathedral Ave. NW (328-0860). Metro: Woodley Park/Zoo. Two Victorian houses (one at 2116 Cathedral Ave. and the larger one at 2700 Cathedral Ave.) treat guests to frilly rooms of various sizes starting at $40 for a tiny single (double $45) with shared bath. High-class neighborhood. Enjoy continental breakfast and afternoon sherry in the living room. Laundry facilities. Reservations with full prepayment or credit card required; cancel for full refund up to two weeks ahead.

Allen Lee Hotel, 2224 F. St. NW (331-1224 or 800-462-0128), near George Washington University. Metro: Foggy Bottom/GWU. Large, rickety, blue hallways. Rooms vary widely in size, furnishings, and state of repair, so look at several before accepting one. Bedrooms and bathrooms normally old but clean. Collection of delivery menus behind the desk, for those who don't want to brave DC at night. Singles $32, with private bath $40. Doubles $40, with private bath $51. Twins $42, with private bath $55. Reservations required in summer.

2005 Columbia Guest House, 2005 Columbia Rd. NW (265-4006), southwest of central Adams-Morgan, a half-block from the Washington Hilton Hotel. An old Senator's house, with a creaky central staircase and seven rooms featuring a faded decor and sometimes lumpy beds. But the rooms are clean and quiet, and the rates are unmatchable. Two free swimming pools and tennis courts within walking distance. No alcohol allowed on premises. Call ahead. Singles $19-26. Doubles $28-39. Weekly rates available.

Adams Inn, 1744 Lanier Place NW (745-3600), behind the Columbia Rd. Safeway Supermarket, two blocks from the center of Adams-Morgan. Elaborate, elegant Victorian townhouses smothered in Persian rugs. Some rooms wood-paneled; all shared-bath rooms with private sink. Free breakfast. Outdoor patio, coin laundry facilities, pay phones, and eating facilities. Office hours Mon.-Sat. 8am-9pm, Sun. 1-9pm. Singles with shared bath $45, with private bath $60. Doubles with shared bath $55, with private bath $70. Weekly singles with shared bath $180, with private bath $220. Weekly doubles with shared bath $255, with private bath $295.

Carlyle Suites Hotel, 1731 New Hampshire Ave. NW (234-3200). Metro: Dupont Circle. Sparkles in renovated Art-Deco charm. Efficiency suites with small kitchenettes. Rates are negotiable, especially during slow summer months, but they usually hover in the $50-90 range.

Marifex Hotel, 1523 22nd St. NW (293-1885). Metro: Dupont Circle. Small, clean, linoleum-floored rooms, each with its own sink and shared bathrooms down the hall. Price includes various DC taxes (including the 11% occupancy tax). Singles $40.35. Doubles $51.45.

Swiss Inn, 1204 Massachusetts Ave. NW (371-1816 or 800-955-7947). Metro: Metro Center. Four blocks from Metro Center; close to downtown. Clean, quiet studio apartments with refrigerator, private bath, high ceilings, kitchenettes, and air-conditioning. Free local phone calls and free laundry(!). Once-a-summer cookout—featuring hot dogs, hamburgers, and bevies—all on the house. International crowd welcomed by French-speaking managers (one speaks Swiss-German also). Singles $58. Doubles $68. (Includes tax). Winter (Nov.-Feb.) discount 20%. Weekly rates available.

University Inn, 2134 G. St. (342-8020), across the street from George Washington U. buildings. Metro: Foggy Bottom/GWU. Narrow yellow building whose attractive hallways belie its small but air-conditioned and comfortable rooms. Clean communal bathrooms serve about three singles each. Mon.-Fri. singles $47, students $42; doubles $57, students $47. On weekends singles $39, doubles $49. Variable student (and faculty) discounts.

The Savoy Hotel, 2505 Wisconsin Ave. NW (337-9700), near Calvert St. north of Georgetown. Metro: Foggy Bottom, Tenleytown, or Friendship Heights—#30, 32, 34, or 36 bus from those stops or from Georgetown. Well-maintained, hotel-like rooms at motel-like prices, excellent for families strapped on a budget. Kitchenettes and jacuzzis in some rooms, and all have either a king or queen-size bed. Call in advance for their "star-spangled" deal: $60 for a double. (You must stay at least two nights.) Call as far ahead as you can—on big-event weekends like Georgetown U. graduation or major holidays, they're sold out months in advance. Singles range from $69-109 ($50 a day if you stay for a week or more) and doubles from $79-119, depending on how full the hotel is. Children under 18 stay free in same room as parents.

The Tabard Inn, 1739 N St. NW (785-1277), on the corner of 17th St. Metro: Dupont Circle. Romantic inn yields complimentary breakfast in a maze of darkened lounges, narrow stairwells and big heavy chairs. The wood-floored rooms are small but well-kept, with antique furnishings. Dining outdoors. Singles with shared bath $56-79.

The Connecticut Woodley Guest House, 2647 Woodley Rd. NW (667-0218). Metro: Woodley Park/Zoo. Modest furnishings in a motel-like atmosphere. Doubles with shared bath $48, about $10 more for rooms with a private bath. Small single rooms with shared bath for $39-43.

Windsor Park Hotel, 2116 Kalorama Rd. NW (483-7700). Metro: Woodley Park/Zoo. Cramped but clean rooms at reasonable rates. Stop here in the busy hotel season when other, larger hotels fill up. Singles $64. Doubles $74. All rooms have cable TV, phone, refrigerator and private bath.

Hotel Harrington, 11th and E St. NW (628-8140 or 800-424-8532). Metro: Metro Center. The businesslike center of the old downtown; three blocks from Smithsonian sights. International visitors abound. Ignore the dingy outside; the 275 rooms inside are large and clean, especially those on the recently-renovated upper floors. Five adults fit in an $80 "family room" with phone and TV. Ask about variable senior-citizen discounts. Singles $69, weekends $66, students $55. Doubles $79, weekends $67, students $62.

Best Western-Regency Congress Inn, 600 New York Ave. NE (546-9200). Metro: Union Station. Close to the Capitol and a half-block from Union Station. Standard motel rooms. Singles $52. Doubles $63.

Hotel Anthony, 1823 L St. NW (223-4320 or 800-424-2970). Metro: Farragut North. Space-age rooms are in their element among new downtown office buildings. Amply-furnished singles $79 in July and August, but it fills up quickly; make reservations in advance.

Holiday Inn, 1155 14th St. NW (737-1200 or 800-465-4329 for reservations), at Thomas Circle. Unhappy neighborhood. Unspectacular rooms $59 in the summertime. Call ahead for information.

Days Inn Downtown, 1201 K St. NW (842-1020 or 800-562-3350). Metro: Metro Center. Comfortable, standard-quality rooms recently renovated. Some rooms now sport kitchenettes. There's a bar/lounge as well as a rooftop pool. Parking garage nearby. Weekend rate $65 for a single or double. Regular rate singles $75. Doubles $85. (Ask about sporadic $50 rooms at 800-325-2525.)

Holiday Inn Central, 1501 Rhode Island Ave. NW (483-2000 or 800-465-4329). Metro: Farragut North. Free cable TV, a fitness center, and a rooftop swimming pool—should give you some idea of the ambience. Singles and doubles $69, at least in summer.

Envoy-Best Western, 501 New York Ave. NE (546-2855), 20 minutes from Union Station on the New York Ave. motel strip. Average motel rooms with TVs. Singles $50. Doubles $57. Military discounts.

Econolodge, 1600 New York Ave. NE (832-3200), on the motel strip two miles from Union Station; take bus D2, D4, D6, D8. Standard TV-equipped motel rooms. Be careful in this area at night. Singles $50. Doubles $53.

Embassy Inn, 1627 16th St. NW (234-7800). Metro: Dupont Circle. Same management as Windsor Inn rents small, somewhat faded rooms with a free nightly glass of sherry and continental breakfast. Singles $65. Summer weekends $55 (based on availability). Seniors 10% discount.

Windsor Park Hotel, 2116 Kalorama Rd. NW (483-7700). Metro: Woodley Park/Zoo. Very cramped but clean rooms at reasonable rates which rarely change. Stop here in the busy hotel season, when other hotels fill up. Singles $64. Doubles $74. Seniors 10% discount.

Holiday Inn, 2101 Wisconsin Ave. NW (338-4600). Pretty much what you would expect from a hotel chain. Neat rooms. Outdoor swimming pool and adjoining restaurant. Excellent packages throughout the year. From May-Sept. rooms go for $79 (including $6 breakfast coupon; if you want to eat out, ask for the $69 deal. Student rates are available, but vary during the year. Kids 19 or under traveling with parents sleep for free. 12 and under eat for free.

Weekend Rates and Specials

One Washington Circle Hotel, One Washington Circle NW (872-1680; 800-424-9671 for reservations). Variable summer weekend rates available for as low as $68 for a double. The dark blue hallways and plush carpets lead to well-appointed suites, each with a large refrigerator and lots of closet space. Interesting selection of carpets, wall paintings, and lobby furniture. First-class service; complimentary *Washington Post* delivered each morning except Sun.

Wyndham Bristol Hotel, 2430 Pennsylvania Ave. NW (955-6400; 800-822-4200 for reservations). This intensely decorated 240-room hotel runs a "summer promotion package"—three nights for the price of two, and those two nights at a bargain of $99 a night. Handicapped access, a kitchenette, and an extra phone in the bathroom. Airy, bright rooms and friendly service.

The Windsor Inn, 1842 16th St. NW (667-0300 or 800-423-9111) at S St. Metro: Dupont Circle. Clean guest house in an old 16th St. townhouse. 24-hr. reception desk. Continental breakfast and evening sherry served. All rooms feature private baths. Atmosphere quivers somewhere between traditional B&B and big hotel-style. Singles $69-99, doubles $79-110. Weekends all rooms $55, subject to availability. Prices negotiable during the off-season (late summer, winter).

Quality Inn Capitol Hill, 415 New Jersey Ave. NW (638-1616 or 800-228-5151), across from the Hyatt Regency. Metro: Union Station. Walk three blocks northwest on New Jersey Ave. from the Capitol building. Standard, well-maintained rooms, 24-hr. reception, and friendly front desk. Swimming pool on the top floor. Weekend rates vary seasonally, and can be hard to come by: singles and doubles from $59. Otherwise, singles $83-139, doubles $98-154. Call for reservations.

Pullman Highland Hotel, 1914 Connecticut Ave. NW (797-2000 or 800-424-2464). Metro: Dupont Circle. If you come at the right time of the year (weekends in July and August, for example), you can stay in a $160 room for $75 a night (one or two people). A terry cloth bed, two or three phones, an armoire with safe for valuables, a mini-bar, and a TV will greet you in your spacious room (which also includes a study). The hotel is wheelchair accessible but the bathrooms are not.

New Hampshire Suites Hotel, 1121 New Hampshire Ave. NW (457-0565 or 800-762-3777). Metro: Dupont Circle, Foggy Bottom. Fair-sized rooms with small refrigerators and even smaller microwaves. They offer weekend and summer or winter weekday packages (July-Aug. and Nov.-Feb.) of $79-$99 for up to two adults and two children, including a sideboard breakfast and health club passes. Call in advance for reservations.

St. James Hotel, 950 24th St. NW (457-0500). Chic European-style hotel just off of Penn. Ave. Cramped lobby belies almost 200 spacious rooms, complete with kitchens. Swimming pool in back with Roman mural—check it out. Coin laundry. Wheelchair accessible. Complimentary breakfast offered Mon.-Fri. 8-9am, weekends 8-10am. A first-rate hotel with special offers at various times during the year; call for details. Super weekend rate of $69 for those showing *Let's Go!*

Comfort Inn, 500 H. St. NW (289-5959). Metro: Chinatown. A standard upper mid-range hotel. Friendly service. Comfortable rooms. Prices vary by season and availability. Singles and doubles range $59-137. Summer special weekend rates for $99. Call to reserve or check on deals. 24 hr. check in.

Hotel Lombardy, 2019 I St. NW (828-2600 or 800-424-5486). An elegant, luxurious hotel with all the usual amenities. Rooms tastefully decorated with floral patterns; most come with kitchenette. Summer discounts available—call for details. Weekends $89 for a double or single.

Bethesda, MD

Manor Inn Bethesda, 7740 Wisconsin Ave.(301-656-2100 or 800-874-0050 for reservations). Metro: Bethesda, then walk two blocks. Comfortable, well-vacuumed clone motel. Big, carpeted rooms with TVs, firm beds, framed prints, and A/C. Free continental breakfast served 6am-10am. Coin-operated laundry. Free shuttle to NIH—great for conventions. Check out by noon. Singles $69, doubles $78. Weekend deal (any day from Fri.-Mon.) $55.

American Inn of Bethesda, 8130 Wisconsin Ave. (301-656-9300 or 800-323-7081). Another clean generic inn with friendly personnel and A/C. Mattresses a bit thin, but firm. Free cable TV. Complimentary breakfast, microwave use, and pool. Check out by 12:30pm.Undergoing renovations— newer rooms are light and airy. Children under 18 stay free with parents. Singles $76, doubles $86. Awesome weekend rates: singles $52, doubles $60.

The Bethesda Ramada, 8400 Wisconsin Ave. (301-654-1000 or 800-228-2828). Walk three blocks along Wisconsin toward Bethesda from the Medical Center Metro (if Wisconsin suddenly turns into Rockville Pike., you're going in the wrong direction). Clean air-conditioned rooms with strong beds and TVs, a bit nicer than the usual decor. The marble lobby emphasizes beige. Courtyard pool. Check out by 1pm. All rooms include either two doubles or one king-size bed. Guests are charged by room, so four can stay for the price of two. Singles $72, doubles $79. Sweet weekend rates.

Arlington, VA

Quality Inn Iwo Jima, 1501 Arlington Blvd. (703-524-5000 or 800-654-2000 for reservations), on Rte. 50. Metro: Rosslyn. 10min. on foot from Metro stop. Dependable hotel with extras like air conditioning, swimming pool, washers and dryers, HBO, and free parking. Convenient to Georgetown, but a bit too far to walk. Summer singles $70, doubles $77. Fall/winter singles $80, doubles $87. Weekend rates summer $55, fall/winter $69. AAA and AARP 10% discount.

Highlander Motor Inn, 3336 Wilson Blvd. (703-524-4300). Metro: Clarendon. Orange and brown shag carpets, with two double beds in each room. Clean, but not the height of fashion. Refrigerators in rooms. Free coffee and donuts go out around 6am. Singles $45, doubles $50. Flash a copy of *Let's Go* and watch rates simmer down to a mere $41.95 for a single and $45.95 for a double. Monthly $950.

Quality Inn, 1200 North Courthouse Rd. (703-524-4000). Part of a chain of nondescript hotels. Pool and fitness facilities. Helpful staff. Out of the way if you don't have a car. Coin-operated laundry machines. Singles $45-$100, doubles $51-113 ($54 on weekends in the summer).

Holiday Inn, 1850 North Fort Myer Drive (703-522-0400). Right across from Rosslyn Metro. Friendlier than most hotel chains, with a helpful staff. Ideal for large families, since kids under 19 stay for free and kids under 12 eat for free. Nice firm beds in a comfortable, if plain, bedroom. Pool, game room, and indoor parking. Depending on the season and latest deals, rooms range from $89-99. On weekends this drops to $59-69.

West Park, 1900 North Fort Myer Drive (703-572-4814). The West Park is a little fancier than neighboring Holiday Inn, with a subdued pink and green lobby. Pool, sauna, and weight room. Complimentary parking also available. Look for the special weekend rates.

Alexandria, VA

Best Western Old Colony Inn, 625 First St. (703-548-6300). Stay in the courtyard for reasonably-priced, clean rooms; the main lobby leads to rooms that are more upscale. Near a convenience store; boasts indoor/outdoor pools and cable TV. Area is fairly safe. Complimentary shuttle to National Airport. Weekend rate $79 for up to four people. Standard rate $125.

EconoLodge, 702 N. Washington St. (703-836-5100). Neat rooms with cable TV and no-frills service. Convenient to bus stop and Metro; close to restaurants and other hotels. Singles $50. Doubles $60. Key deposit required, $10. Free coffee in the morning. Complimentary shuttle to National Airport.

Towne Motel, 808 N. Washington St. (703-548-3500). Okay, no-frills hotel (except for the working telephones, HBO, and A/C). ID required to check in. Singles $42 and $45, doubles $48. For three people $52, for four $56. 24 hr. check in.

Ramada Inn, 901 N. Fairfax St. (703-683-6000). A 15-min. walk from Braddock Rd. Metro. Pool and restaurant on hand. Single $102, double $112. On weekends rates plummet to $69 for a room sleeping four. Kids under 18 accompanied by a parent stay for free. Shuttle to service to National Airport provided.

Suburban Maryland

Comfort Inn, 16216 Frederick Rd. (301-330-0023 or 800-228-5150 for reservations), corner of Shady Grove Rd., in Gaithersburg. Metro: Shady Grove. Comfortable rooms tastefully decorated in pastels, some with desks and couches. Large bathrooms. Free shuttle service to the Metro, half a mile away. Free continental breakfast. Disabled access. Take I-270 to exit 8 onto Shady Grove Rd., turn right onto Frederick Rd. (Rte. 355). Singles $56. Doubles $62. Weekends $49. Each additional person $6.

Colonial Manor Inn, 11410 Rockville Pike (301-881-5200 or 800-881-5200), across from White Flint Mall. Metro: White Flint. Country decor marred only by fluorescent lights. Bathrooms old, but clean. 10-min. walk to the Metro or take the White Flint free shuttle to White Flint shopping mall—the hotel is right across the road. Coin-operated laundry. Singles $62. Doubles $68 (with kitchenette $78).

Camping

Capitol KOA, 768 Cecil Ave. (301-923-2771 or 301-987-7477), near Millersville. Families get back to nature, sort of. Full facilities for tents, RVs, cabins. Free pool, movies. From DC, take John Hanson Hwy. (Rte. 50) to Robert Crain Hwy. (Rte. 301, which becomes Rte. 3), and bear right onto Veterans Hwy. (Rte. 197). Go a short distance to bottom of the hill, then turn left under highway. Follow blue signs to campground. 10 mi. from Baltimore Beltway, 16 mi. from DC, 11 mi. from Annapolis. Free weekday shuttle to DC/Baltimore trains; commuter train (MARC) $6.25 round-trip to Union Station. Tent site for two $17.25. RV site $17-19. Each additional adult $3. Open April-Nov.

Greenbelt Park, 6565 Greenbelt Rd. (301-344-3948). 174 sites available for tents, trailers, and campers. Showers are down Greenbelt Rd. at the Greenbelt Recreation Center and Pool ($2). Camping limited to 5 days Memorial Day to Labor Day and 14 days the remainder of the year. Fee $6, seniors and disabled $3. 12 miles of trails teeming with deer and other wildlife. Maps and nature walk schedules available from the National Park information offices. Take the Beltway I-95 to exit 23 onto Kenilworth Ave. (Rte. 201), then head south toward Bladensburg and follow the signs to the park. You can also take the Baltimore-Washington Parkway (I-295) and exit onto Greenbelt Road (Rte. 193) and follow the signs to the park.

Cherry Hill Park, 9800 Cherry Hill Rd. (301-937-7116). The closest campground to Washington, with 400 sites and modern amenities; most sites are for RVs. Metrobus stop located on the grounds takes you to the Metrorail; cable hookup available; coin-operated laundry; heated swimming pool with whirlpool and sauna. Pets allowed. Tent site $25; RV site with electricity/water/sewer $30. Extra person $2. Reservations recommended at least 5 days in advance; call 9am-8pm. $25 deposit required. From DC take route I-95 towards Baltimore, then take exit 29B onto route 212. Follow 212 for a mile then turn onto Cherry Hill Rd. From Baltimore and elsewhere take exit 25B off of I-95 or 495. Make the first right onto Cherry Hill Rd. There are signs close to the park.

Food

DC makes up for its days as a "sleepy Southern town" with a kaleidoscope of international restaurants. Haughty European dining rooms strive to impress the expense-account crowd, while bargains from Africa, Southeast Asia, and the Americas feed a melange of immigrants from all over. Predictably, the best ethnic places attract compatriots who grew up with the cuisine. Smithsonian-goers should plan to eat dinner far away from the triceratops and the biplanes: visitors to the Mall get stuffed at (and stuffed into) mediocre cafeterias, only blocks from the respectable food on Capitol Hill. You can eat for $4 or eat well for $7 almost anywhere in DC; while Adams-Morgan is famous for budget restaurants, Dupont Circle and the Hill are worth the Metro ride, too.

It's an open secret among interns that **happy hours** provide the cheapest dinners in Washington. Bars desperate to attract early-evening drinkers set up plates, platters and tables of free appetizers; the trick is to drop by and munch, but drink little or nothing. The best seem to concentrate, along with the interns, on Capitol Hill or south of Dupont. The occasional public reception in a small museum or office lobby can also offer the courageous a free snack (especially those dressed for it). A week of nonstop nachos and mushrooms for dinner could make anyone (except an intern) sick; still, a dinner of happy-hour appetizers has salvaged many a knowing student from virtual starvation. (See *Happy Hours* below.)

Capitol Hill

The Hill's residential character means neighborhood establishments outnumber obnoxious chains. Massachusetts Avenue NE fights Pennsylvania Avenue SE for control of the restaurant scene; Massachusetts is better-looking, but Pennsylvania has sheer numbers on its side. At night, use extra caution northeast of Union Station or southeast of Lincoln Park. Government workers on the lower end of the federal pay scale tend to lunch in **government cafeterias**, whose cheap, acceptable sandwiches and salads occupy many a building basement around North Capitol St. One is the **Capitol Forum Bar and Grill,** in the sunken plaza of the building at 941 North Capitol St. (682-0060); somewhat above average for a cafeteria, this place serves burgers ($2), fries ($1), *gyros* ($4), and a salad bar ($3.49/lb). (Open Mon.-Fri. 6am-4:30pm.)

Food vendors do their thing in the block-long red brick bustle of **Eastern Market**; Washingtonians flock here for fresh produce and the rank feel of a medieval marketplace. Outside the market, fruit and flower vendors line 7th Street—even in December. The market hops on Saturdays and Sundays from around 7am to around 5pm; some say Saturday morning around 10am is the best time to shop. From the Eastern Market Metro, walk less than half a block northwest along Pennsylvania Ave., then turn right on 7th St. Over 50 eateries inhabit **Union Station**. (Metro: Union Station.) The Station's interior resembles a big, glitzy suburban mall; in the **food court** on the Lower Level, cheap take-out counters ring the walls, with burgers, pizza, sushi, bagels, and fruit shakes for under $4.

Chicken and Steak, 320 D St. NE (543-4633). Walking southeast on Massachusetts Ave. from Union Station, veer left onto D St. where it crosses Massachusetts Ave. Then walk east on D St. about one block. Ignore the spare decor and fall for the succulent chicken and steak, cooked Peruvian style *à la brasa* (grilled), at bargain prices. Delicious 1/4 chicken with plenty of fried *yucca* and salad $3.50. Half chicken with *yucca* and salad $5.25. *Chorizo* sandwich $5.25. Open Mon.-Sat. 11am-9:30pm.

Jimmy T's, 501 East Capitol St. (546-3646). At the corner of East Capitol and 5th St., under the brick octagonal turret. The paint's chipped, and the red vinyl benches look old, but it's all part of the classic loser corner diner charm. Nothing over $6. Breakfast (served all day) ranges from grits (85¢) to two eggs with ham ($4.40). Dinners (try the pepper steak) come with two vegetables ($5.25). Burgers under $3; thick shakes $1.75. Come and enjoy. Open Tues.-Fri. 6:30am-3pm, Sat. 8am-3pm, Sun. 9am-3pm.

Neil's Outrageous Deli, 208 Massachusetts Ave. NE (546-6970). Combination deli and liquor store offers creative sandwiches to go. Eat your sandwich in the grassy triangle enclosed by Massachusetts Ave., 2nd, and D St. NE. Try the "Crazy Louie," sour-dough rye topped with Dijon mustard, pastrami, turkey, and Thousand Island dressing ($4). A bristling array of sandwiches (over 23) range in price from $2-5. Cold soda 55¢, or free with a sandwich purchase after 4pm weekdays. Frozen yogurt 25¢ an ounce. Open Mon-Tues. 9am-7:30pm, Wed.-Sat. 9am-9pm.

2 Quail, 320 Massachusetts Ave. NE (543-8030), next to Café Berlin. Three restored Victorian townhouses get cutely sumptuous with flowered curtains, flowered wallpaper, and wicker room dividers; most tables set with cozy armchairs and plush, fluffy pillows. Uncategorizable, consistently excellent cuisine changes every season. May be crowded at lunch. Try the delicious cream of broccoli soup ($3.50), or the tortellini with crab meat ($10.50). Check the *Washington Blade* for coupons. Big appetizers $4-7; entrees $10-18, with an average damage at $13. Open Mon.-Thurs. 11:30am-2:30pm and 5:30-10:30pm, Fri. 11:30am-2:30pm and 5:30-11:15pm, Sat. 5:30-11:15pm, Sun. 5-10pm.

Burrito Brothers, 205 Pennsylvania Ave. SE (543-6835). Tacos and burritos to go, though you can also stand and eat at the counter. Behold the wall mural and shuffle to merengue or salsa as you order alongside government workers during weekday lunch (noon-3pm). The steak taco ($2.55), served very hot, bursts with steak, tomatoes, and beans. Tacos $2.15-2.55; burritos $2.55-3.65. Open Mon.-Sat. 11am-8pm.

Tortilla Coast, 201 Massachusetts Ave. NE (546-6768). Wildly popular Tex-Mex restaurant run by native Texans. Sit outdoors or brave colored lights and mysterious tropical scenes in the darkened dining room. Bar features zebra-stripe stools and a thatched roof. Try the mild *Quesadilla Suiza* ($7.50) or the burrito with beans and rice ($7). Big brunch Sat.-Sun. noon-3pm. Open for lunch and dinner Mon.-Thurs. 11:45am-10:30pm, Fri. 11:45am-11pm, Sat. noon-11pm, Sun. noon-10pm. Accepts most major credit cards.

American Cafe, 222 Massachusetts Ave. NE (547-8500). Next door to Tortilla Coast, the Cafe boasts a healthy selection of non-fried foods and live jazz music on Wed. and Sat. evenings. Specials include the Arizona Veggie Chili ($3) and the Chicken Caesar Salad ($5). Take out option available from market entrance. Reasonable Sunday brunch served from 10:30am-3pm ($10). Open Mon.-Thurs. 11am-11pm, Fri.-Sat. 11am-midnight, Sun. 10:30am-10pm.

Armand's Chicago Pizzeria, 226 Massachusetts Ave. NE (547-6600). Celebrated local chain features great deals on food and drink. Lunchtime all-you-can-eat pizza and salad bar $5. Daily beer specials, plus $1.25 beer and $1 slice of pizza during happy hour weekdays 4-7pm. Open Mon.-Fri. 11:30am-2:30 am, Sat. 11:30am-3:30am.

Kelley's "The Irish Times," 14 F St. NW (543-5433). Walk out of Union Station and take a right turn (west) down F St. Irish street signs, the *Irish Times*, Joyce on the wall and Yeats and Keats on the menu make this more than just another Irish pub. (Don't tell them Keats wasn't Irish.) Live music Wed.-Sat. evenings starts at 8:30pm. Lunch special $5, sandwiches around $5.25, soup $2; beer from $2.50, Irish whiskey from $4. Big deals on weekends. Open Sun.-Thurs. 10:30am-1:30am, Fri.-Sat. 10:30am-2:30am.

Cheese and Cheer, 210 7th St. SE (547-5858), north of Pennsylvania Ave. on 7th St., across from Eastern Market building. Metro: Eastern Market. Just try to utter this place's name without a glib smile breaking over your lips. Walk under the "210 Market Court" sign; the shop is down the corridor on your left. There's no place to sit, and five people would crowd the tiny takeout shop; it's the price you pay for inexpensive, authentic Russian and Eastern European food. Practice your Russian on the friendly immigrant owner, or read it on the poster of the Kremlin. Tasty *knishes*

$2, *borscht* $1.79. Ukrainian peasant bread on Fridays and Saturdays $2.89 a loaf. Plenty of meats and cheeses to buy to make your own sandwich. Lunch plate (*knish* and salad) $4.75. Open Sat.-Thurs. 8am-6:30pm, Fri. 8am-7pm.

Provisions, 218 7th St. SE (543-0694), across from the Eastern Market. Deli/coffee shop sells everything from teapots and jam to salads and sandwiches. Cafeteria style with limited seating. Gourmet sandwiches $3.25-6. Try the ever popular "218" sandwich, a sumptuous concoction of smoked ham and lingonberry jam. Quiches $3. Daily coffee specials also exist. Mon.-Fri. 7am-7pm, Sat. 8am-6pm, Sun. 10am-4pm.

The Market Lunch, 225 7th St. SE (547-8444), in the Eastern Market complex. Hailed by newspapers around DC as one of the best deals in town. The strong smells of fish and fresh meat pervade the air here, wafting over a dozen or so stools at the counter. The Lunch offers delicious food. Crab cakes ($6-9) are the local specialty, but the blueberry pancakes ($3) on Saturday mornings have people lined up around the corner. Open Tues.-Sat. 7:30am-2:30pm.

Roasters on the Hill, 666 Pennsylvania Ave. SE (543-8355). Actually hides around the corner on the 7th St. side of the building. You could sniff your way to this small shop—they roast, bump, and grind coffee daily in the store. Watch the roasting from a stool beside the counter or from a café table just outside. Friendly, energetic service. Coffee from 65¢; iced coffee 71¢ and 91¢; *espresso* from $1.15; pastries $1-2.25. Try the special bizarro cold drinks, like the Cappucino Supreme, a blend of *espresso*, milk, ice, and cinnamon, topped with shaved chocolate and whipped cream (small $1.75, large $2.25). Open Mon.-Sat. 7am-6pm, Sun. 8am-3pm.

Hunan Dynasty, 215 Pennsylvania Ave. SE (546-6161 or 546-6262). Ultra-modern surroundings include goldfish and white-collar Hill staff on power lunches. Very friendly service. Weekday lunch specials ($5.45, served until 3pm) are posted on a blackboard. Spring rolls ($2 for 2) with light crust and tender vegetables. *Kung pao chicken* $6.50. Open Mon.-Thurs. 11am-9:30pm, Fri.-Sat. 11:30am-11pm, Sun. 11:30am-10pm.

Health's A' Poppin, 2091/2 Pennsylvania Ave. SE (544-3049). A long narrow room that opens onto a long counter in the back. Kind service. They offer a mammoth selection of drinks (over 180), including over 15 kinds of water, banana and ban-apple shakes, and fresh-squeezed orange and carrot juice. The breakfast bar (7-10:30am) offers sausage, omelettes, corned beef, 2 kinds of potato, and 8 kinds of fruit at $3.15/lb. $1.85 buys toast, scrambled egg, and ham, bacon or sausage. The lunch bar (10:45am-3pm) features Chinese food and at least three kinds of sushi, while the yogurt bar dispenses with five flavors at $1.09 for 4 ounces. Sandwiches $2.70-4.75; large salads $2.70-5. Open Mon.-Fri. 7am-8pm, Sat. 7am-5pm.

Taverna the Greek Islands, 307 Pennsylvania Ave. SE (547-8360). Metro: Capitol South. Requisite white stucco walls carry the requisite Greek Tourist Bureau posters in this popular two-story establishment. Try the chef's specials, at least three options from $6. Dinners start at $9; tasty shish kabob $13. Order the *Saganaki alla Paros* (melted cheese; $5) to see 8-foot flames shoot from your plate. Happy hour on weeknights 3-7pm features special sandwich offers. Open Mon.-Sat. 11am-11:30pm, Sun. 4-9:30pm.

A.J.'s Sub, 229 Pennsylvania Ave. SE (543-5235). Personal letters of compliment from members of Congress adorn the counter; behind it, service is quick-witted, sly, and lively. Everything under $5. Burger $1.65; steak and cheese $3.85; subs $3.65-4.25; fries $1.50-3.75. Open Mon.-Fri. 10am-8pm, Sat.-Sun. 11am-4pm.

Hawk 'n Dove, 329 Pennsylvania Ave. SE (543-3300). A good bar (see *Bars*) with good bar food, which interns, regulars, and powerful politicians eagerly consume. Full menu; sandwiches $4-6.50; 14 kinds of bottled beer and 11 drafts available, $1.75 and up. Midnight breakfast served Mon.-Thurs. 11pm-1am, Fri.-Sat. 11pm-2am ($7; $9 with steak). Open Sun.-Thurs. 10am-2am, Fri.-Sat. 10am-3am.

Tune Inn, 331 1/2 Pennsylvania Ave. SE (543-2725). Metro: Capitol South. A cheaper bar (see *Bars*) with cheaper bar food. Sandwiches $2.50-4.50; Chicken dinner $4.50. Beer $1.25 for draft, $2 for bottles. $3 minimum. Breakfast available. Open Mon.-Thurs. 8am-2am, Fri.-Sat. 8am-3am, Sun. 9am-2am.

Prego, 210 7th St. SE (547-8686). Same building as Cheese and Cheer, but Prego opens onto the street. Deli boasts Italian take-out and delicious bread shipped in fresh daily ($1-2 a loaf). Also sells olive oil, olives, and Italian wines. No seating inside, but outdoor seating out front at café tables with umbrellas. Sandwiches $3.25-3.75; special "combo" sandwiches $3.25-5.25. Try the "Prego Special" stuffed with Italian cold cuts, tomatoes, lettuce, and cheese ($3.25). Open Mon.-Fri. 8:30am-7pm, Sat. 8am-7pm, Sun. noon-5pm.

Thai Roma, 313 Pennsylvania Ave. SE (544-2338 or -2339). A wild combination of Italian pastas and tomato sauces with the zest and spice of Thai food that makes area reviewers rave. A favorite spot for Hill denizens and homestead gourmands. Try the duck pizza ($9), or Italian linguini with peanut sauce ($7). Lunch entrees under $8. Reservations advised for lunch; takeout available. Open Mon.-Fri. 11:30am-10:30pm, Sat. 11:30am-11pm, Sun. 4-10pm.

Zapata's, 601 Pennsylvania Ave. SE (546-6886). Upstairs from Mr. Henry's; enter on the 6th St. side of the building. Complimentary chips, salsa, and darkness. Southwestern fare. Appetizers $2.50 to $6; try the large, crispy *quesadilla*, served hot with excellent guacamole and sour cream ($4). Entrees $7.75-11. "Texas Jailhouse Chili" $4.50. Margaritas $3.50. American-style brunch served Saturday and Sunday (10am-3pm). Open Mon.-Thurs. 5-10pm, Fri. 5-11pm, Sat. 10am-3pm and 5-11pm, Sun. 10am-3pm and 5-10pm.

Le Bon Café, 210 2nd St. SE (547-7200). Don't blink: that might just be Clarence Thomas squatting at the next table over. Off-duty Supreme Court Justices and other locals frequent this venue on many a cozy afternoon. All food made from scratch with all natural ingredients; coffee is freshly ground just before brewing. *Espresso* $1; *café au lait* $1.45-2. Buy ten *espressos*, get one free (and shake like a leaf on a tree). Breakfast pastries 75¢-$1.35 (until 10:30am). Sandwiches (served after 10:30am) $4-7. Elegant salads $3-7. Small plate-sized pizzas, good for individual meals, $4.25-6.25. Open Mon.-Fri. 7:30am-6:30pm, Sat. 9am-2pm.

Café Heartland, 637 Pennsylvania Ave. SE (543-EATS [-3287]). Laid back and comfortable eatery caters to a mixed crowd of eminent politicians and grousy locals. Brick, wood and exposed trusses give the two-story dining room a rustic feel. It's like, the Midwest, but kinder to vegetarians. Entrees come with two side dishes ($8-13). Burgers $5-7. Lunch sandwiches $3-7. Organically raised meats and chicken. Try the eggplant casserole or the vegetable enchilada, both served with two side dishes ($7). Blue-plate special changes daily—lunch $7, dinner $10. Brunch on Sat. and Sun. 10am-3pm. Open Mon.-Thurs. 11am-11pm, Fri. 11am-1am, Sat.-Sun. 10am-midnight. Kitchen closes earlier.

La Lomita Dos Restaurant, 308 Pennsylvania Ave. SE (544-0616). Metro: Capitol South. Large portions of Mexican entrees recline carefully on oval plates under carefully folded Mexican blankets within cool white stucco walls with pale green trim and many prepositional phrases. Come during lunch for cheaper prices: tacos $6-8, burritos $6-9, appetizers $1.50-5. Pay $1.50 for the sweet golden *platanos fritos* (fried plantains), served with chips and salsa. Open Mon.-Thurs. 11am-3pm and 5-10:30 pm, Fri. 11am-3pm and 5-11pm, Sat. 1-11pm, Sun. 1-10pm.

Ice Cream

Ice in Paradise, 615 Pennsylvania Ave. SE (547-1554). Deli and ice cream counters take up most of the space, but five small tables seat two people apiece. Named for the Middle Eastern dessert *Yakh-dar-behesht* ("Ice in Paradise"). They offer a large selection of Swensen's ice cream ($1.35 for a single scoop) as well as vegetarian and meat-filled sandwiches ($3-3.75). Baklava $1. Open Mon.-Fri. 10am-8pm, Sat. 11am-6pm, Sun. noon-6pm.

Bob's Famous Homemade Ice Cream, 236 Massachusetts Ave. NE (546-3860). Metro: Union Station. Bigshot lawyer Bob quit the firm to start the store in the early '80s; this is one of three tasty offshoots. Oddball flavors include Mozambique Spice, Honey Cantaloupe, and Chocolate Moose (vegetarian). Cones $1.60-2.75. Sandwiches, soups, and salads available for under $5. Open Mon.-Thurs. 11am-10:30pm, Fri. 11am-midnight, Sat. noon-midnight, Sun. noon-10:30pm.

Old Downtown

Except for Chinatown (below), the old downtown can promise diners little: upscale delis, downscale lunch counters, and crowded, bright tourist havens dominate the food scene. Try the upscale delis first. The hype-heavy **Old Post Office,** at Pennsylvania Ave. and 12th St. NW (523-5691), stuffs its concourse with ethnic-food stalls and their many patrons, most from out of town. (Open Mon.-Fri. 8am-6pm, Sat. noon-6pm. Metro: Federal Triangle.) Ubiquitous hot dog stands frequent downtown streets, posing hungry pedestrians an age-old dilemma: Half-Smoke or Super-Dog?

A.V. Ristorante, 607 New York Ave. NW(737-0550). Quite a few blocks away from the hubbub of commercial old downtown, though still frequented by suits on lunch break. Chianti bottles topheavy with melted wax, lamps turned so low they flicker on and off, huge plates of expert pasta ($6 to $10), and pizza (starting at $8 for a pie). Open Mon.-Thurs. 11:30am-11pm, Fri. 11:30am-midnight, Sat. 5pm-midnight.

Café Mozart, 1331 H St. NW (347-5732), near the National Museum for Women in the Arts. Gourmet deli proffers specialty crackers, coffees, hors-d'ouevres and tricky-to-pronounce delicacies like *schnitzel, sauerbrauten,* and *spaetzle.* Cramped storefront conceals a roomy interior.

Sandwiches ($5-7) and desserts ($3-4) are superb. Folk music Wednesday through Sunday from 6pm to 10pm. Open Mon.-Fri. 7:30am-10pm, Sat. 9am-10pm, Sun. 11am-10pm.

Los Planes de Renderos, 908 11th St. NW (347-8416) off I St. Metro: Metro Center. Good Mexican and Salvadoran cuisine comes heaping with beans and rice. Free chips and salsa forever. Try the Santa Ana—3 chicken enchiladas topped with cheese and a tangy sauce, served with refried beans and rice ($7). One meal can easily feed two. The bare one-room restaurant lacks ambience, though a small portable provides some Mexican radio. Open Mon.-Thurs. 11am-3pm and 6-10pm, Fri.-Sun. 11am-11pm.

Dutch Mill Deli, 639 Indiana Ave. NW (347-3665). Metro: Navy Memorial. Go Dutch for large, overstuffed sandwiches and outdoor dining on the porch. Busy, too. Hot sandwiches $3.95 - $5, subs $4.95. Pizza, shrimp, and clam platters on the menu. No desserts. Open Mon.-Fri. 7am-4pm, Sat. 9am-3pm.

Jan Drake's Garden Café, 401 7th St. NW (393-1150), located on Gallery Row. Metro: Metro Center. Sandwiches made to order and served hot or cold. Homey atmosphere is a relief in amongst intimidating downtown office buildings. Deli sandwiches, $3-5, regular size salads (vegetable as well as tuna and chicken) around $4. A breakfast special (scrambled eggs, meat, home fries or grits, and toast, english muffin, or bagel) is not only well balanced in an archaic sort of way but dirt cheap. Open Mon.-Fri. 7am-7pm, Sat. 8am-6pm, Sun. 11am-6pm.

American Café, 1331 Pennsylvania Ave. NW (626-0770), in the shops at National Place and National Press Building. Metro: Metro Center. This local chain has prospered for a reason: grilled sandwiches, mixed appetizer platters and a healthy array of vegetarian options (from $6). And, of course, the ubiquitous Big Star symbol. Stay for dessert, any dessert (scrumptious pies, cakes, and berries around $3). Open Sun. 10am-10pm, Mon. 11:30am-10pm, Tues.-Fri 11am-11pm, Sat. 11:30am-11pm.

Balaji Siddhartha, 1379 K St. NW (682-9090) at the corner of 14th St. Metro: Metro Center. This authentic Indian vegetarian restaurant offers cheap, spicy Indian cuisine for taking out or eating in. Try the *Mysore Masala*, a spicy lentil flour crepe of epic proportions, stuffed with onion and potato curry $4. A lunch buffet from 12pm-2pm offers a variety of soups, breads, rice, and curries for $4.99. Open Mon.-Sat. 11:30am-8:30pm, Sun. 12pm-7:30pm.

Chinatown

You don't have to dig a hole to China to find authentic Chinese food and groceries; exotic lip-smacking treats—DC's best Chinese food—ramshackle here along H St. NW. Don't be turned off by a decrepit-seeming exterior (or interior, even)—a restaurant's appearance will have little relation to its quality. Apparent dives often serve wonderful food. Chinatown's restaurants showcase the diversity of cuisines from the various regions of China: hot and spicy Hunan or Szechuan food, the sweet and mildly spiced seafood of Soochow, and the hearty, filling fare of Peking. More traditional Cantonese cooking is best sampled at *dim sum*, a Sunday afternoon tradition (though some joints offer it seven days a week). Waiters roll carts filled with assorted dishes (mostly meat, shrimp, or bean-curd buns, dough-puffs, and dumplings in bite-size servings) up and down the aisles. To partake, you simply point at what you want. (Beware of "Chinese bubblegum," a euphemism for tripe, itself a euphemism for cow or pig stomach.) At the end of the meal, the number of empty dishes on your table is tallied up (dishes run from $1-3). For regular meals, expect to shell out $3-6 for appetizers, around $7 for entrees. Metro: Gallery Place-Chinatown, for all of the following locations.

Big Wong, 610 H St. NW (638-0116 or 638-0117). Basement location makes it hard to find: from 7th and H St. NW, walk down the right side of the street with the archway to your back. Long-standing renown and wide selection; try the specialty noodle dishes. Authentic desserts include Egg Custard Tart. *Dim sum* daily 11am-3:30pm. Combination platters with rice, egg rolls, and entree around $6. Open Sun.-Wed. 11am-3am, Thurs.-Sat. 11am-4am.

Tony Cheng's Mongolian (Barbecue) Restaurant, 619 H St. NW (842-8669). Load your bowl with beef, leeks, mushrooms, sprouts, and such, then watch the cooks make it sizzle (and shrink). (One serving $6; all-you-can-eat $14). Two or more people can stir up their own feast in charcoal hotpots provided by the restaurant. (Base platter $5 per person; more meat costs extra.) Open Sun.-Thurs. 11am-11pm, Fri.-Sat. 11am-midnight.

China Doll Gourmet, 627 H St. NW (289-4755). Accept the "Chef's Suggestions"—orange beef, General Tsao's Chicken, Hunan Lamb, or Crispy Prawns with Walnuts. Famous pastries (flaky buns, jelly cakes, and almond cookies) baked on the premises. Open Sun.-Thurs. 11am-11pm, Fri.-Sat. 11am-1am.

Szechuan Gallery, 617 H St. NW (898-1180 or 898-1181). Stunning Taiwanese (mostly seafood) dishes, once hidden from English-speaking diners, have surfaced on the menu as Chef's Recommendations. Fragrant Crab (around $10) means whole crabs in spicy egg batter. Open Sun.-Thurs. 11am-10:30pm, Fri.-Sat. 11am-12:30am.

Burma Restaurant, upstairs at 740 6th St. NW (393-3453). The owner, a retired Burmese diplomat and former United Nations delegate, would love to tell you about Burma's rare cuisine, which replaces soy sauce with pickles, mild curries, and unique spices. Make it your mission at Burma to try the rice noodles with dried shrimp, fried onion, coriander, garlic, and lemon juice ($6) or the bean-curd and chopped shrimp cooked in Tabasco ($7). Open daily 11am-3pm, 6pm-10pm.

Ho Wah Restaurant, 611 H. St. NW(408-8115). For the budget-meister—$3.50 for lunch. Standard combination platters at six tables in a small room. Open Mon.-Fri. 10am-3:30pm.

Szechuan, 615 Eye St. NW (393-0130). One block from the main drag, the second-floor Szechuan sizzles; crispy orange beef ($8), *kung pao chicken* ($7), and crispy whole fish (price and fish vary by season) are old favorites. Asparagus dishes from $7 all year round. Owner shows off pix of himself with four U.S. Presidents. Open Mon.-Fri. 11am-11pm, Sat. 11am-midnight, Sun. 11am-10pm.

Li Ho Food Restaurant, 501 H St. NW (289-2059). Try the Cantonese specialities—chicken wrapped in rice paper, unshelled salted shrimp, a fish head simmered in a clay pot ($7.50), or clams in black bean sauce. Singapore-style rice noodles ($4-5) are well prepared; honey-glazed barbecued pork ($5) and 1/4 broiled chicken ($4.50) round out the cheaper side of the menu. Most entrees $6-9. Open daily 11am-11pm.

Go-Lo, 604 H St. NW (347-4656). Two large dragons will greet you from above as you enter the restaurant. Try any of the chicken entrees (around $8) or a seafood platter from their wide selection ($8.75-15.95). Open Sun.-Thurs. 11am-midnight, Fri.-Sat. 11am-4am.

White House Area/Foggy Bottom

Cheap, friendly restaurants congregate around the hungry youth of George Washington University, north of F St. and especially along Pennsylvania Ave. Closer to the White House, the chow gets more varied, but also more expensive.

Milo's, 2142 Pennsylvania Ave. NW (338-3000). GW students enjoy Euro-chic decor and Italian food—pasta ($5-8), fried mozzarella ($3), *calamari* ($5), and pizza (sm. thin crust $5.20; sm. deep dish $7; white pizza $5.20). Private parties often nab the downstairs dance floor. Monday is half-price pizza night; Wednesday is "yard" (of beer) night; Friday happy hour serves $1 beers. Live country, rock, or folk (Wed. year-round and Thurs.-Sat. during the school year). Open Mon.-Wed. 11:30am-11pm, Thurs.-Fri. 11:30am-midnight, Sat. 11:30am-2am, Sun. 5-10pm.

The Art Gallery Grille, 1712 Eye St. NW (298-6658). Metro: Farragut West. Art Deco interior and jukebox. Original Erté serigraphs, professional clientele. Breakfasts are traditional and inviting—Belgian waffles, creative granola, various omelettes ($5). DJ Thurs.-Fri. nights. Lots of fresh seafood; try the crabmeat platter ($7). Open Mon. 6:30am-11pm, Tues. and Sun. 6:30am-midnight, Thurs.-Sat. 6:30am-3am.

Balaji Siddhartha, 1379 K St. NW (682-9090). Metro: McPherson Square. Opposite Franklin Park. Deli atmosphere belies the exotic plates tailored to vegetarians and Indian food fans. Visit again on weekends, bring them back their menu, and get 10% off your meal. Curries of the day ($3) like *aloo mutter* (peas and potatoes) and *sambhar* (lentil soup with vegetables). Appetizers linger around $1.50; *kachori* (deep fried wheat bread stuffed with green peas) for $1.75. Choose from 17 desserts—combinations of mango, rice pudding, yogurt and almonds. Photos over the counter help those not acquainted with Indian food. $4.99 all-you-can-eat lunch deal is well-suited to the meager budget. Open Mon.-Sat. 11:30am-8:30pm, Sun. noon-7:30pm.

Lindy's Bon Apétit [sic], 2040 Pennsylvania Ave. NW (452-0055), near Tower Records. Metro: Foggy Bottom/GWU. Ronald Reagan once said that life at George Washington University was not complete without a bone burger from this carry-out deli. Grab a bacon cheeseburger ($3), a Monterey sandwich with refried beans, raw onions, and American cheese ($2.65), a BLT ($2.65), or 6-inch subs ($2-4). All breakfast sandwiches under $1.60. Open Mon.-Fri. 7am-8pm, Sat.-Sun. 11am-5pm.

Café Amadeus, 1300 Eye St. NW (962-8686). Metro: McPherson Square. Modern German café run by owners of Café Mozart (Café Wolfgang must be next). "Real charbroiling" in the open kitchen. Carry-out soup and sandwich special $3. Sit-down entrees $7-15. Carry out a quarter-pound burger with french fries $2.39. Happy hour weekdays (4pm-8pm) offers free appetizer with any drink. These snacks change daily but can include fried veggies, meat balls, and chicken wings. Open Mon.-Fri. 7am-10pm.

Chinacafe. A set of 4 fast-food Chinese restaurants throughout NW. Locations at 1018 Vermont Ave. NW (628-1350), 1411 K St. (393-6277), 2009 K St. (463-2129), 1723 Conn. Ave. (234-4053). The McDonald's of Chinese food. Drab grey furnishings and Hunan/Peking style food are the dominant motifs of this chain. Each restaurant offers a choice of over 30 entrees, including *Kung Pao* chicken, *lo mein*, and sweet-and-sour chicken, each $3.95. No entrees exceed $4.25. Appetizers (about $1) differ with each location. Open Mon.-Fri. 11am-9pm, Sat.-Sun. noon-9pm.

GW Deli, 2133 G St. NW (331-9391). $1-4 sandwiches (egg salad $1.75) and fresh salads make this deli popular with students. Sandwiches are deli variety—ham, turkey, pastrami, etc. Prepackaged snacks, drinks, and convenience grocery items available. Open Mon.-Fri. 6:30am-8:30pm, Sat. 8am-4pm.

Paramount Restaurant and Deli, 917 18th St. NW (223-4214). Cheap, filling breakfasts and inexpensive food bays. Self-serve salad bar with over 50 different items ($3.79/lb.). Self-serve hot Chinese food ($3.79/lb.) and sandwiches around $2. Budget travelers, take note. Open Mon.-Fri. 6:30am-8:30pm.

Holly's Cookies, 1800 G St. NW (289-6899). Move over, Mrs. Field! Around the corner from the Old Executive Office, this small sandwich shop offers mammoth cookies ($5.95/lb) in a range of flavors, from traditional oatmeal and raisin to chocolate Heath bar. Cookies are large and sweet, so have a drink handy. Open Mon.-Fri. 6am-4pm.

Sacha's Gourmet, 1917 F. St. NW (682-1622). A delicatessen with a twist. Caters to young whitecollars who flock here from 11:30 am to 1:30pm with a selection of over 100 cheeses from 13 countries. Gourmet sandwiches made from your choice of ten kinds of bread. Try the Italian Sub: Genoa salami, mortadella, caicola ham, provolone, and Italian dressing ($3.49). Design your own sandwich, from $3.25. Outdoor seating is hard to secure; be aggressive. Open Mon.-Fri. 8am-8pm, Sat 10am-4:30pm.

Treats, 1754 H St. NW (659-0558). A cheerful plum and grey spot on a rather run-down street off Penn. Ave. Counter seating. American food, with lo-cal items for the health-conscious, as well as sugary delectables. Mini pizzas $2.25, fruit shakes $1.69, individually-made sandwiches (choose from 7 different breads) $1.39. Open Mon.-Fri. 7am-5pm, Sat. 8am-4pm.

DJ's, 214 22nd St. NW. Near George Washington University. Offers a real smorgasbord of ethnic foods. The Korean chef tosses out Italian, Chinese, American, and Middle Eastern fare at record speed. A cluttered, unsophisticated diner, packed with college types thoughout the year. Lunch is extremely crowded; elbow a stiff out of the way. Most entrees under $5. Vegetarians won't be stranded here. Open Mon.-Thurs. 7:15am-8:30pm, Fri. 7:15am-5:30pm, Sat. 10am-2:30pm.

American Café Express, 1701 Pennsylvania Ave. NW (833-3434). One of a set of such restaurants around Washington. Health-conscious sandwiches on whole wheat, rye, or croissant. Vegetarians will love the Californian, a creamy concoction of avocados, Monterey jack cheese, alfalfa sprouts, tomatoes, and dressing ($3.75). For those in a hurry, catered box lunches ($5.95) are the answer. Open Mon.-Fri. 7am-6pm.

Cone E. Island, 2010 Pennsylvania Ave. (822-8460). No old-fashioned soda fountain, here. Offers a 9 calorie/oz., cholesterol free "skinny dip" as well as traditional sugar- and fat-filled favorites. Try the fudge swirl or munch on a mud pie. Sugar cones $1.47, cone sundaes $2.61.

Georgetown

Georgetown's restaurants have got pretension if you want it: tourists can feed with the powerful at inflated prices amid brass rails and autographed photos. Other restaurants are just an excuse to sell merchandise or set up an outdoor café; in the afternoon, you can sip an *espresso* and suck on the energy of the street life. Power lunchers crowd in by day, but it's the nightlife that makes Georgetown's reputation. Washingtonians come for a late dinner or dessert and stay while the bars fill and the music turns up: all-American saloons like **J. Paul's,** 3218 M St. (333-3450), double as singles bars after dark. (See *Nightlife).* Trendier Washingtonians eat in Adams-Morgan, then come here for dessert.

Some of the best (and best priced) food comes from the smaller ethnic restaurants; Indian, Ethiopian, Thai, and Vietnamese cuisine are all well-established in Georgetown. Family-run establishments are tucked downstairs in basements or up above other restaurants. Everyone thinks they've "discovered" one, but most of them have been around for years.

Booeymonger, 3265 Prospect St. NW (333-4810), corner of Potomac St. Georgetown students and residents stop by for breakfast or a quick, giant sandwich. Every sandwich seems a specialty; try the veggie pocket of cheese and vegetables in pita bread ($4.25-4.75). In peak lunch hours, the tables are packed, so grab a seat when you walk in or eat outside. Create your own sandwiches with a choice of 15 fillings and 8 breads. Free coffee refills to jump-start your morning. Open Mon.-Sun. 8am-midnight.

Olympic Carry Out, 3207 O St. NW (338-2478 or 337-1997), a block from Wisconsin Ave. Strictly carry-out and delivery, serving homemade Greek and "Mediterranean" specialties and subs. Clean, big portions, rapid service. *Gyros* and steak-and-cheese subs $3.30, *felafel* $2.75. Check for daily specials. Open Mon.-Sat. 11am-11pm, Sun. noon-10pm.

Nakeysa, 1564 Wisconsin Ave. NW (337-6500). Small but elegant Persian restaurant with salmon-colored tablecloths and napkins and fragrant flowers on every table. Beef, cornish hen, game hen, and chicken kebabs range in price from $7-12. Fine vegetarian dishes too. Try the *Fesenjan*, an exotic concoction with walnuts and tomatoes in pomegranate sauce. Take-out available. Open Mon.-Thurs. noon-10pm, Fri.-Sat. noon-11pm, Sun. noon-9pm.

Enriqueta's, 2811 M St. NW (338-7772), at the junction with Pennsylvania Ave. Famous for its lightly spiced but authentic Mexican cuisine, especially the chicken *mole*, a distinctive sauce consisting of peppers, spices, nuts, seeds, fruit, herbs—and chocolate ($13). The less adventurous can sample the *mole* before they order. Bright red, green, and yellow furniture—each chair is a different color. Open Mon.-Thurs. 11:30am-2:30pm and 5-10pm, Fri. 11:30am-2:30pm and 5-11pm, Sat. 5-11pm, Sun. 5-10pm.

Sushi-Ko, 2309 Wisconsin Ave. NW (333-4187). Authentic no-frills Japanese food prepared before your eyes. Try the affordable Maki-sushi or Temaki (over 20 kinds to choose from) for under $5. Fish offerings include the customary trout, flounder, and tuna, as well as the more exotic Uzara (with quail eggs). Order of sushi (two rolls per serving) $2-4.50. Open Tues.-Fri. noon-2:30pm, Mon.-Fri. 6pm-10:30pm; Sat. 5pm-10:30pm; Sun. 5pm-10pm.

The French Market, 1630-32 Wisconsin Ave. NW (338-4828), near Q St. Three townhouses painted blue, white, and red mimic the French flag. Ingredients for Babette's feast or just a picnic. The *boulangerie* bakes fresh baguettes; also imported cheeses, wines, canned goods, and coffees. Open Mon.-Tues. 8:30am-6pm, Wed. 8:30am-1:30pm, Thurs.-Fri. 8:30am-6pm, Sat. 7:30am-6pm.

Piccolo, 1068 31st St. NW (342-7414). Just off Wisconsin, this two-story building is easily identified by the heaving flowers cascading down the side. Head for the all-you-can-eat lunch buffet, which includes soup, salad, pasta, and seafood for $5.95. Regular entrees pricier, running $8-14. Open Mon.-Thurs. 11:30am-2:30pm, 5-11pm; Fri.-Sat. 11:30am-11:30pm; Sun 11:30am-4pm, 5-11pm.

Who's Cookin?, 1608 Wisconsin Ave. NW (625-2672), near the Texaco station. Down-home cooking, upscale customers. Hickory-smoked Alabama BBQ pork sandwiches and ribs sold alongside grilled chicken and fish and pasta salads. Daily specials from honey-glazed ham with mashed-potatoes and other vegetables to Oriental chicken salad with sesame noodles. Everything under $7. From 4pm-5pm Sat., everything is half price. Will deliver for $1.50 Mon.-Fri. 5-9pm. Open Mon.-Fri. noon-9:00pm, Sat. noon-5pm.

Vietnam-Georgetown Restaurant, 2934 M ST. NW (337-4536), and **Viet Huong,** 2928 M St. NW (337-5588) at 30th St. An economics student's dream: two neighboring restaurants in eternal competition. The spicier Vietnam-Georgetown was here first, and garners more adulatory reviews; Viet Huong is more intimate and slightly cheaper. Try *cha giú,* Vietnamese crispy egg rolls, and grilled chicken or beef on skewers. Lunch at Vietnam-Georgetown $5, dinner $7-11. Open Mon.-Thurs. 11am-11pm, Fri. 11am-midnight, Sat. noon-midnight, Sun. noon-11pm. Lunch at Viet Huong $4-6, dinner $6-11. Open Mon.-Fri. 11:30am-3pm and 5-10pm, Sat.-Sun. noon-11pm.

Fettoosh, 3277 M St. NW (342-1199). Quality Middle Eastern sandwiches provide a perennial late-night snack for Georgetown students after a night of bar-hopping. A fast-food version of Fettoosh, the flagship Middle Eastern restaurant down the street. *Felafel* $2.75, meat or spinach pies $1.25 (for five). Open daily 9am-3:30am.

Tout Va Bien, 1063 31st St. NW (965-1212). Semi-affordable French cuisine with a haute couture maitre d' to match. Feign a Parisian attitude at the black marble tables or under the vines, plants, and ceiling fans in the greenhouse. The early bird special (all entrees $11) lasts 5-6:45pm daily; the ambience is, shall we say, priceless. Open Sun.-Thurs. 11:30am-2:30pm and 5:30-10:30pm, Fri.-Sat. 11:30am-2:30pm and 5:30-11:30pm.

Café La Ruche, 1039 31st St. NW (965-2684), a block below M St. Clean, spare French café with wicker chairs and French mementos on the walls, suitable for an intimate dessert. Serves light salads ($3.25-6.25), sandwiches ($5-6.25), and a selection of vegetarian dishes, but the real treats are fresh tortes and pastries ($3-5). (Try the fruit tarts; avoid the mousse.) Weekday early-comers (5-7pm) get a soup or salad, entree, and dessert for $14. Obey the sign on the door and speak French to the proprietor. Open Mon.-Thurs. 11:30-midnight, Fri. 11:30am-1am, Sat. 10am-1 am, Sun 10am-11pm.

Zed's Ethiopian Cuisine, 3318 M St. NW (333-4710). Award-winning cuisine. Eat with your hands free from embarrassment. Use the spongy *injera* bread to pick up the *Tibbs Watt*, a spicy beef dish ($7.75), and the *Kik Alitcha*, puréed yellow split peas with onion, green pepper and garlic ($6.75). On a level with the Ethiopian food in Adams-Morgan. Open Sun.-Thurs. 11am-11pm, Fri.-Sat. 11am-2am.

Gepetto's, 2917 M St. NW (333-2602). Thin, crispy Neapolitan pizza piled high with your favorite toppings. Its 9" pie serves 2-3 people ($10.20, $1.75 for each topping). The 14" one serves 5-6 people ($15 and $2.50 per topping). Deep-dish Sicilian 9" pizza $10.70, 14" pie $16. Individual pizzas $6.25-8.25. Early-birds get 20% off, 4-6pm. Even Pinocchio wouldn't lie about this one. Open Mon.-Thurs. noon-11pm, Fri.-Sat. noon-12:30am, Sun 4-11pm. Delivery service available.

Georgetown Bagelry, 3245 M St. NW (965-1011 or 965 1012). Wait outside for the door to open at 6am with the other loyal regulars. Sit at the mahogany counter and read one of the newspapers sold here while you breakfast. Or stop by for a snack, one of the best in DC and inexpensive at 50¢ a bagel. Huge brownies and muffins ($1.50). For those on a really tight budget, day-old pastry goes for half-price. Open Mon.-Sat. 6am-9pm, Sun. 6am-7pm.

Sarinah, 1338 Wisconsin Ave. NW (337-2955). Charge through the inauspicious doorway and you'll find yourself downstairs in a tropical jungle: broad-leaved potted plants, pulpy wooden fruits, and the ceiling hides, yes, a "lush canopy of leaves." Delicious Indonesian food includes *satays,* grilled and skewered lamb, beef, chicken, or shrimp with spicy sauces ($7.90-9.95), as well as vegetarian entrees. Share with a friend to sample different dishes. Open Tues.-Sat. noon-3pm and 6-10:30pm, Sun. 6-10:30pm.

Hamburger Hamlet, 3125 M St. NW (965-6970), near Wisconsin Ave. The burly burgers come with anything and everything. Named for Rex Harrison, the Emperor Henry IV is piled so high with cheese, ham, tomato, bacon strips, and 1000-island dressing, you'll need to cut it in half to bite. Burgers are $5-6; salads, sandwiches, and seafood range from $6-12. Let the kids draw on the paper tablecloths while you wait. (Crayons provided.) Open Sun.-Thurs. 11am-midnight, Fri.-Sat. 11am-1am.

Aditi, 3299 M St. NW (625-6825), corner of 33rd St. The Sanskrit name translates as "creative power" or "abundance"; here it means "great food," but also "glacial service." Try the spicy Madras chicken curry ($9.95) and one of the *biryanis*, rice pilafs covered with a choice of chicken, lamb, shrimp, or vegetables ($9-11). Open Tues.-Thurs. 11:30am-2:30pm and 5:30-10pm, Fri.-Sat. 11:30am-2:30pm and 5:30-10:30pm.

Georgetown Café, 1623 Wisconsin Ave. NW (333-0215). Should be called the Georgetown Diner. Cheap and greasy eats, including Middle Eastern standards. Sandwiches $2-5, subs $4.75, *felafel* $4.25. Open 24hr.

Charing Cross, 3027 M St. NW (338-2141). Once a British pub, now an Italian bistro, this neighborhood favorite serves hearty standards like lasagne ($8) and linguine. Rebuilt after a fire two years ago: look for the framed patch of pre-inferno wallpaper. The bar ($1.50 draft beer) is popular with Georgetown students (see Nightlife). Restaurant open Mon.-Fri. 11:30am-midnight, Sat.-Sun. 5-midnight.

Au Pied du Cochon/Aux Fruits de Mer, 1335 Wisconsin Ave. NW (333-5440 and 333-2333). Two sister restaurants, the first serving casual French fare like salads and crepes and decorated with rustic copper pots and photos, the other serving fish and seafood in a maritime setting with an aquarium. Come by for a late snack, ($3-3.75) and a cappucino ($2.45) or a *café au lait* ($1.25). The glass-enclosed café area lets you watch the passers-by. Open 24hr.

Chadwick's, 3205 K St. NW (333-2565), under the Whitehurst Freeway. Their all-American burger special, char-broiled with fries ($2.50), is a steal. They also serve good salads and sandwiches. Open Mon.-Thurs. 11:30am-2am, Fri.-Sat. 11:30am-3am, Sun. 11am-2am.

Houston's, 1065 Wisconsin Ave. NW (338-7760). Perfect for meat-and-potato lovers. The hickory-grilled hamburgers ($6.25) and grilled chicken with ham and Monterey Jack cheese ($8.75) are served with a slew of shoestring fries. Don't try to eat light here. You may even need to bring salads ($6.25-7.50) home in a doggie bag. Lines are long, and they don't take reservations, so walk around Georgetown while you wait or crowd into the bar. Open Sun.-Thurs. 11:15am-11pm, Fri.-Sat. 11:15am-1am.

Ice Cream

Thomas Sweet, 3214 P St. NW (337-0614), at Wisconsin Ave. All the ice cream, yogurt, muffins, pocket sandwiches, and bagels made fresh daily in the store. The best ice cream in DC by a light-year. Gawk at Glenn Stratton, bass player and lead singer of the band Bruno Loves Danger, who is part-owner and often works behind the counter. Single scoop cup/cone $1.67. Hefty helpings of yogurt or ice cream mixed with fruit or candy ($3.12). Open Mon.-Thurs. 9:30am-midnight, Fri.-Sat. 9:30am-1am, Sun. 11am-midnight. These hours apply June-August; closing time might come a bit earlier after the summer.

Tout Sweet, 3000 M St. NW. Large portions of ice cream and hard-packed yogurt so creamy you'll swear it's ice cream. Thirty flavors of yogurt and ice cream, including low-fat and non-fat options. Single-scoop is $1.51. Open noon-10pm, but they may stay open later on the whim of the owner.

Cone E. Island, 2816 Pennsylvania Ave. NW (338-6778). Homemade ice cream and cones, with original flavors like Snapper, a butter-based ice cream with caramel, pecans, and chocolate chips. So sweet you'll need a drink every few bites. Wonko teen staff. Bring ice cream and coffee across the street to a film at the Biograph. $1.47 for a single-scoop cup or sugar cone, $1.70 for a single-scoop homemade cone. Open daily noon-midnight.

Glover Park

A ten-minute walk up Wisconsin Ave. from Georgetown proper, this area north of R St. boasts a small but diverse group of eateries.

Rocklands, 2418 Wisconsin Ave. NW (333-2558). South Carolina/Florida-style tangy grilled barbecue. Quarter-rack of pork ribs $4.50, BBQ pork sandwich $4. Eat at the mahogany counter or take it on the road. Pick from 100 different hot sauces; have just one or sample as extensively as your promiscuous little mouth will permit. Open Mon.-Sat. 11:30am-10pm, Sun. noon-9pm.

Austin Grill, 2404 Wisconsin Ave. NW (337-8080). This joint is hip and hopping. Even President Bush ate here once. Tex-Mex favorites like soft tacos or enchiladas ($7-8); vegetarians can also try the *migas* plate—egg with tortilla, peppers, tomato, onion, and cheese ($6). Lines are long, so enjoy the Stars and Bars, a powerful margarita worth the $4.50 price. Open Mon. 5:30pm-midnight, Tues.-Thurs. 11:30am-midnight, Fri.-Sat. 11:30am-1am, Sun. 11:30am-11:30pm.

Faccia Luna, 2400 Wisconsin Ave. NW (337-3132). Pizza crust connoisseurs, this is your Mecca. Forget pepperoni and top it with tuna, eggplant, spinach, or pesto. You can play pool here, too. 10" pie $6, 12" $7.80, 14" $9, and 16" $10.45. Open Mon.-Thurs. 11:30am-11pm, Fri.-Sat. 11:30am-midnight, Sun. 4-11pm. No credit cards.

Old Europe, 2434 Wisconsin Ave. NW (333-7600). One of the few authentic German restaurants in DC, and the older clientele look like they know it. *Bratwurst, bauernwurst,* or *weisswurst* $7.50, *wiener schnitzel* $9.25. German beers and liqueurs like Spaten, Augustiner, and Kümmel $2.75-3.25. Open Mon.-Thurs. 11:30am-3pm and 5-10:30pm, Fri.-Sat. 11:30am-3pm and 5-11pm, Sun. 4:30-10pm.

New Downtown

Lunch and dinner in the new downtown are worlds apart. Businesspeople demand cheap, decent lunches from squeaky-clean delis and Chinese-food counters like Lunchbox, Dutch Treat, China Café, and Hunan Express. Lunchtime restaurants usually deliver for free within a small radius of their store. (Pick up a monthly menu at any of the ten Lunchbox restaurants in DC for a list of changing daily specials, like baked lasagna for $3.) But beware of dinner in the new downtown: the same lawyers and lobbyists who sought a cheap lunch now spend to impress at some of Washington's best and priciest establishments. If you're careful to avoid places with minimum tabs, you can dine excellently on soups and appetizers and such—assuming you don't care what the waiters think.

Sholl's Colonial Cafeteria, 1900 K St. NW, in the Esplanade Mall. Good cooking at exceptionally low prices: chopped steak ($1.65) and plain roast beef ($1.90). These guys have been around forever; so have dozens of their patrons. Fresh food and generous portions, plus daily specials. Try the homemade pies. Open Mon.-Sat. 7am-2:30pm and 4-8pm.

The Star of Siam, 1136 19th St. NW (785-2838). Delights its diners with spicy hot curry dishes and unobtrusively fried foods. Dinner entrees from $6.25. Awesome desserts include sticky rice with coconut milk and sliced mango. Open Mon.-Sat. 11:30am-11pm, Sun. 4-10pm.

I Ricchi, 1220 19th St. NW (835-0459). Don't let the bank-busting menu or the numerous, assiduous waiters daunt you: their tasty *ribbolita,* a Tuscan bread and vegetable soup, is excellent, thick as porridge, and a meal in itself ($6.50). Try the other soups, too. Open Mon.-Fri. 11:30am-2:15pm and 5:30-10:30pm, Sat. 5:30-10:30pm.

Sabina's, 1813 M St. NW (466-5678). Return to the 50s with their all-day breakfast menu and jukebox at every table. The perfect late-night hangout. Hamburger with toppings and fries goes for $3-4. Open Sun.-Thurs. 10am-3am, Fri.-Sat. 10am-4am.

Trattu Restaurant, 1823 Jefferson Place NW (466-4570). Specializes in Florentine cuisine. Try the slightly spicy *linguine alla vongole,* made with tender fresh clams on a nestbed of linguine ($9). Open Mon.-Fri. 11:30am-2:30pm and 5:30-10pm, Sat. 5:30-10pm, Sun. 4-9pm.

Thai Kingdom, 2021 K St. NW (835-1700). Prides itself on its Gai Yang Kingdom dish—grilled chicken served with rice and several sauces ($6.50). The afternoon power-Thai crowd knows it's good. Open Mon.-Fri. 11:30am-2:30pm and 5-10pm, Sat. noon-10:30pm, Sun. 5-10pm.

Bacchus Restaurant, 1827 Jefferson Place NW (785-0734). Pages and pages of light Lebanese dishes, including several versions of fried eggplant ($3.50-5). If you've never had their "white coffee" dessert, you might receive it gratis. Open Mon.-Fri. noon-2:30pm and 6-10pm, Sat.-Sun. noon-2:30pm and 6-10:30pm.

La Prima Market Café, 950 14th St. NW (898-1140). Metro: McPherson Square. Create your own sandwich at the sandwich bar in the middle of the restaurant or try the 1001 club with turkey, ham, bacon, and avocado ($4). Vegetarians will like the vegItalian, a feast of lettuce, sprouts, tomato, and other fresh veggies. Homemade bread served upstairs. Open Mon.-Fri. 6:30am-6:30pm.

Casa Blanca, 1014 Vermont Ave. NW (393-4430). Metro: McPherson Square. Boutique serving Spanish and Peruvian specialties. Tacos ($3.50), pork or chicken tamales ($3.25), or *empanados de carne* (meat pie) for $2. Aspiring Fujimoris can go for Peruvian *pollo a la braza,* 1/4 roast chicken with salad, fried potatoes, rice, or beans ($5.50). Open daily 11am-9pm.

Health's A-Poppin! 2020 K St. NW (466-6616). Prides itself on several vegetable sandwiches, including "cool hand cuke," with cucumber, cream cheese, and olives ($2.75). Open Mon.-Fri. 7am-6pm, Sat. 11am-4pm.

Café Lausanne, 1120 20th St. NW (887-0570), just beside the mall. Serves light lunches outdoors or in. A bowl of minestrone soup comes with a basket of delicious bread for $3.50. Save room for dessert. Open daily 7am-6pm.

Angie's, 1134 19th St. NW (785-9444). Nestled unassumingly among her higher-priced neighbors, Angie offers *empanadas* (meat- and vegetable-filled turnovers) for $1-2. Open Mon.-Fri. 6:30am-7pm, Sun. 9am-5pm.

Siddhartha Vegetarian Restaurant, 1379 K St. NW (682-9090). Combines metaphysical Indian cuisine and fast-food techniques to forge an all-you-can-eat lunch buffet ($6; served daily 11:30am-2pm). Open daily 11am-8pm.

Le Palais du Chocolat, 1200 19th St. NW (659-4244), at M St. Treat your sweet tooth to a gigantic strawberry dipped in *chocolat* (75¢). Open Mon.-Fri. 8am-6:30pm, Sat. 10am-6pm.

Dupont Circle

Dupont Circle's food is more expensive but more varied than that of the funkier Adams-Morgan to the north. Cheap coffee shops, one-of-a-kind American restaurants, health-food stores, and a pricey *patisserie* or two complement the ethnic assortment. Many restaurants hang together along P St. and Connecticut Ave. on both sides of the circle.

Lauriol Plaza, 1801 18th St. NW (387-0035). Authentic Mexican food, served on a charming patio by gracious waiters. Concentrate on the left side of the menu: a tender enchilada side dish ($2) and *chili con carne* appetizer ($4) could stuff any tummy. Open Sun.-Thurs. 11:30am-11pm, Fri.-Sat. 11:30am-midnight.

Food for Thought, 1738 Connecticut Ave. NW (797-1095), two blocks from Dupont Circle. Veggie-hippie-folknik mecca with good, healthful food in a 60s atmosphere. Ten different vegetable and fruit salads, plus sandwiches and daily hot specials. Local musicians strum in the evenings, open mike every Monday. Bulletin boards announce everything from rallies to beach parties to rides to L.A. Bike messenger hangout. Bunny says: amazing gazpacho. Lunch $6-8, dinner $6-10. Open Mon. 11:30am-3pm and 5pm-12:30am; Tues.-Thurs. 11:30am-12:30am, Fri. 11:30am-2am, Sat. noon-1am, Sun. 5pm-12:30.

Dante's, 1522 14th St. NW (667-7260) at Q. St. Near the Source and Studio theaters; far from the Circle itself. Not to be missed after midnight, when punk rockers, actors, and their friends jam the place with hipness and hair. Teal and black decor complements heavenly-healthful pita sandwiches and devilish cheesecake (sandwiches $5-7, cheesecake $2.50). Try the delicious white pizza appetizer: melted provolone cheese on pita bread with Italian spices for $3.50. Don't come around here alone at night. Open Mon. 5pm-3am, Tues.-Thurs. 11:30am-3am, Fri. 11:30am-4am, Sat.-Sun. 5pm-4am.

Sala Thai, 21st and P St. NW (872-1144). Light Thai food served to many customers. Delicious crispy fish is affordable for lunch at $7. Open Mon.-Thurs. 11am-2:30pm and 5-10:30pm, Fri. 11am-2:30pm and 5-11pm, Sat. noon-11pm, Sun. 5-10:30pm.

Café Pettito, 1724 Connecticut Ave. NW (462-8771). Excellent and popular—Italian regional cooking in an understated, black-and-white-checked atmosphere. Try the tempting antipasto table ($6) and the fried Calabrian pizza. Open daily 11:30am-midnight.

Zorba's Café, 1612 20th St. NW (387-8555), by the Q St. entrance to the Dupont Circle Metro. Mediterranean folk music played for indoor and outdoor customers. Good Greek food in a self-service restaurant. Try the *yeros* plate, which comes with Zorba's excellent french fries and a small salad ($4.25). Open daily 11am-11:30pm, Sun. noon-10:30pm.

Nature's Food Basket, 1515 17th St. NW (462-7066). High-powered fruit juices and health-conscious sandwiches quickly refresh tired bodies. Smart drinks $1.75. Open Mon.-Fri. 10am-8pm, Sat.-Sun. noon-6pm.

Paru's Indian Vegetarian Restaurant, 2010 S. St. NW (483-5133). Vegetarian fast food served southern Indian style, in a quiet diner atmosphere. Try *parotta* (flat bread) with your choice of two spicy curries ($4.50). Rice platters served with vegetable pilav, raitha, paratha, papoid, and lemon pickle $7.50. Open Mon.-Sat. 11:30am-8:45pm.

Kramerbooks & Afterwords Café, 1517 Connecticut Ave. NW (387-3825). Late-night sweets behind a very good bookshop. Exorbitant *nouvelle* entrees, but Washington's best cakes, pies, and mousses ($3-4) are rich rewards for living the literary life. Cappuccino freaks should head here, too. Live music Fri.-Sun. after 10pm. Open Sun.-Thurs. 7:30am-11:45pm, Fri.-Sat. 24 hrs.

Burrito Bros., 1524 Connecticut Ave. (332-2308). Dense fare for vegetarians. Beans and rice burrito with mild salsa sauce, $2.55. Open Mon.-Fri. 7:30am-10pm, Sat. 11am-10pm, Sun. 11am-8pm.

Pan Asian Noodles & Grill, 2020 P St. NW (872-8889). Soups and unusual noodle-related dishes in two red-and-grey Art-Deco rooms on two floors. Vegetarian on request. Lunch from $6, dinner from $7. Open Mon.-Thurs. 11:30am-2:30pm and 5:30-10:30pm, Fri. 11:30am-2:30pm and 5:30-11pm, Sun. 5:30-10pm.

Crepe à la Carte, 1301 Connecticut Ave. NW (223-3300) and 1304 18th St. NW. Crepes with everything: turkey, chicken, fruit, ice cream. The *gâteau de crepes,* a stack of sweet crepes served with cream, fresh fruit, and maple syrup, makes a delicious and filling Sunday brunch at the Connecticut Ave. branch ($6). The original place on 18th St. serves crepes café-style at tables on the sidewalk. Restaurant open daily 8am-9:30pm, sun. 11am-4pm. Café open Mon.-Fri. 8am-5pm, Sat. 10am-5pm, Sun. 10am-3pm. Dinner is served at the café on the sidewalk beginning at 5pm. Brunch Sat. and Sun.

Café Luna, 1633 P St. NW (387-4005). Bustling Italian restaurant serves cool drinks to its indoor and outdoor customers; super busy in summer. Open Sun.-Thurs. 8am-11pm, Sat.-Sun. 8am-1:30am.

Enzo Trattorio, 1619 Connecticut Ave. NW (232-0404 or 232-8368). Gourmet Italian food for takeout, mostly by the pound. Lasagna $3.50/lb. Open daily 10am-11pm.

The Uptown Bakers, 3313 Connecticut Ave. NW (362-6262). Absolutely amazing breads and pastries baked on the premises, some of which you can buy day-old for half-price. Open daily 7am-9pm.

Omaha Coffee Shop, 1666 Connecticut Ave. NW (462-5300), in the basement of the office building. Dirt-cheap sandwiches: 85¢ for a grilled cheese. Open Mon.-Fri. 7am-4pm; grill closes at 3:30pm.

Bagels Etc., 2122 P St. NW (466-7171). A neighborhood bagelry with daily breakfast specials ($1-3), like a bagel with sausage, bacon, or ham, orange juice, and coffee for $2. Open Mon.-Fri. 6:30am-7:30pm, Sat. 7:30am-6pm, Sun. 7:30am-5pm.

Katmandu, 2100 Connecticut Ave. NW (483-6470). Nepalese and Kashmir cuisine. Elegantly decorated restaurant hidden away on the first floor of an apartment building. Keep an eye out for it if you don't want to miss the Katmandu chicken $6.25. Try the *momos*, mutton pieces with homemade chutney for $4. Open Mon.-Wed. 11:30am-2:30pm, Thurs.-Fri. 11:30am-2:30pm and 5-11pm, Sat. 5-11pm.

Volare Pizza, 2011 S St. NW(234-9150), three blocks north of the Circle. Nothing fancy, just solid, cheap food in large portions. Full-meal daily specials, subs and enormous *gyros* ($4-5), whole pizzas ($4-6), and greasy breakfasts ($2-3). Open daily 7am-11pm.

Trios Restaurant, 1537 17th St. NW, corner of Q St. Hardly a gourmet restaurant, but hearty breakfasts are served all day. Popular with the gay community. The 1963 March on Washington planners met in this diner. Open daily 7:30am-11:30pm.

Salad Bar Express, 1317 Connecticut Ave. NW with a back door at P St. (223-2238). The gigantic salad bar offers fresh sliced fruit and vegetables and (deceptively weighty) hot and cold Asian entrees, such as fried rice, for $3.69/lb before 4pm, $2.69 after. Open Mon.-Fri. 7am-5pm.

DC Café, 2035 P St. NW (887-5819). Superb pizza ($4.95 for a 10" pie that easily feeds two). Indoor and outdoor dining areas conveniently located near several of the Circle's well-known clubs and bars. Open daily 9am-2am.

The Pop Stop, 1513 17th St. NW (328-0880). The owner's own pop art festoons the bright walls of this new and popular café. The clientele is largely local, gay, and young; many stop by on their way to or from one of Dupont Circle's many bars and clubs. Indoors, house music simulates the club experience; outdoors, more sedate customers leaf through magazines from the "stop's" own rack. Sandwiches served with good coffee and chips will run about $4. The magazines encourage customers to linger for hours on end. Open Sun.-Thurs. 7:30am-3am, Fri. and Sat. all night.

Shaw

The immediate vicinity of 14th and U St. NW, on the area's edge near the U St./Cardozo Metro stop, is a safe source for supreme soul food, a uniquely African-American cuisine. Come during the day. The Shaw-area Metro stops (at 14th and U and at 7th and U) opened only in the summer of 1991; the hoped-for commercial revitalization has yet to take place. Still, the Metrorail system has made it easier for anyone yearning for a taste of home cooking to head on up to Shaw.

Ben's Chili Bowl, 1213 U St. NW (667-0909), at 13th St. Metro: U St./Cardozo. A venerable (30 yr. old) neighborhood hangout with a facelift—new jukebox, smooth new counters, and a molded ceiling. Spicy homemade chili—on a chili dog, served with onion, mustard, and potato chips ($1.85), on a half-smoke ($2.75), or on a 1/4 lb. burger ($2.10). Die-hards eat it plain: sm. bowl $1.90, lg. bowl $2.55. Open Mon.-Thurs. 6am-2am, Fri.-Sat. 6am-3am., Sun. noon-8pm.

Ben's Bakery and Ice Cream, 2000 14th St. NW (667-2313), on the 14th St. side of the Frank Reeves Municipal Center. Metro: U St./Cardozo. Ben's Chili Bowl diversifies. Freshly baked croissants, muffins, and rolls (89¢-$1.60) and homemade ice cream ($1.49 for a single scoop) will satisfy even the worst sugar pangs. Open Mon.-Fri. 7:30am-10pm, Sat. 11am-10pm.

Florida Avenue Grill, 1100 Florida Ave. NW, at 11th St. (265-1586). From the U St. Metro, walk east on U to 11th St., then walk north up 11th St. to Florida Ave. or take the Metrobus that runs up 11th St. Small, enduring (since 1944) diner once fed Black leaders and famous entertainers. Now their framed faces beam down at the hordes of locals who frequent the place. Don't miss the article in the first booth about a 32-year veteran Grill server: "I'd love to serve [President Reagan] chitlins," she says. "It might straighten his head out." Awesome southern-style food: breakfast with salmon cakes or spicy half-smoked sausage, eggs, grits, hotcakes, or southern biscuits ($3-$6). Lunch and dinner ($5-9). Open Mon.-Sat. 6am-9pm.

Adelis, 2017 14th St. NW (332-6599). Metro: U St./Cardozo. Lunchtime soul-food all-you-can-eat buffet ($7.50). This is straightforward old-fashioned delicious, featuring items like chicken, barbecue ribs, green beans, macaroni, chitlins, and watermelon. Add the salad bar and dessert and you'll burst right open. Open Mon.-Fri. 11:30am-4pm.

Outlaw's, 917 U St. NW (387-3978) across the street from the municipal building. Metro: U St./Cardozo. Should be the in-laws'. Family-run take-out crowds in local regulars for real, meat-laden "home-cooking." Cramped, downstairs quarters open onto the kitchen where daily specials like

Monday's liver and onions, Tuesday's meated loaf, and Thursday's Salisbury Steak are cooked up. Food is cheap too: dinners, served with 2 vegetables, $4.50-6.50; sandwiches $3-5. Open Mon.-Fri. 11am-7pm.

Hogs on the Hill, 14th and U St. NW (332-1817). Metro: U St./Cardozo. As in "big fat pigs." A plain decor offsets enticing smells from the kitchen. You'll get big portions, too. Half chickens $4; whole chickens $7. Platters, served with corn bread and two side orders, are $5-9. Choices include pork ribs, chopped BBQ beef, or chicken. Sides include collard greens, potato salad, red beans and rice, and fries. Open Mon.-Thurs. 10:30am-11pm; Fri.-Sat. 11am-2am, Sun. noon-10pm.

House of Kabob, 1361 U St. NW (234-4712). Metro: U St./Cardozo. Cheap takeout with a hurricane of kabobs. Beef shish kabob sandwich $3.50; chicken shish kabob sandwich $3; vegetable kabob sandwich $1.85; *gyros* (a.k.a. shwarma shish kabob) $3.50. Open Mon.-Fri. 11:30am-8pm, Sat. noon-7pm.

Polly's Café, 1342 U St. NW (265-8385). Metro: U St./Cardozo. Slick neighborhood restaurant/bar caters to a mixed crowd of professionals, students, and area residents. A cozy dark wood interior and a varied menu with reasonable prices draws many for Sunday brunch: omelettes, toast, home fries and a drink $6.95. Open 11:30am-2am seven days a week, special menu offerings until midnight.

Adams-Morgan

The word is out. Adams-Morgan's jambalaya of cultures can satisfy all sorts of kinky tastes, from Latin American to Ethiopian to Caribbean—all for around $7. Adams-Morgan has justifiably become DC's preferred locale for budget dining. (But as with any popular spot, some prices are climbing already.) The action radiates from 18th, Columbia, and Calvert St. NW, uphill along Columbia or down 18th. Look with suspicion on Western European restaurants here, some of which capitalize on Adams-Morgan's budget rep by charging the same old prices they'd charge downtown.

Mixtec, 1792 Columbia Rd. NW (332-1011). Popular, well-known Mexican restaurant. Two bright rooms wear neat paper lanterns and wooden Mexican chairs. Neon window sign mentions their specialty, *tacos al carbon*. The $3 version consists of two small tortillas filled with delicious beef, served with three kinds of garnish. Mixtec makes a mind-bending chicken *mole*, too. Lunch entrees, served with salad and beans, $4.50. Appetizers $2.25-4.50. Entrees are $4.50-9.95. Open Sun.-Thurs. 11am-11:30pm, Fri.-Sat. 11am-12:30am.

Cosmos Restaurant, 1801 Columbia Rd. NW (234-6203), at 18th St. Billions upon billions of dishes—Salvadoran and Mexican and subs and pizza. Not much here for the vegetarian, though. Breakfast, served until 11am, yields $3 omelets. Appetizers $1.40-3.50. Salvadoran and Mexican entrees are $4.75-6.75. Try the *yucca con chicharrones* (yucca with fried pork), served as an entree with cabbage for $4.75, or in an appetizer-sized portion with onions and tomato sauce for $3.50. Open Mon.-Wed. 7am-11pm, Thurs. 7am-2am, Fri. 7am-3am, Sat. 8am-4am, Sun. 8am-11pm.

El Pollo Primo, 2471 18th St. NW (232-5151), near Columbia Rd. By their awning shall ye know them. Second-story beige-and-brown rotisserie gives rise to moist, flavorful, tender, greaseless, cheap chicken on a big grill behind the counter. Two-piece chicken dinner with tortillas, salsa, and two side orders $3.60, three-piece dinner $4.51. Side orders include beans ($2) and rice ($2). Open Sun.-Thurs. 10:30am-9:30pm, Fri.-Sat. 10:30am-10:30pm.

Red Sea, 2463 18th St. NW (483-5000). The first of Adams-Morgan's famous Ethiopian restaurants, and still among the best. The red-painted exterior is weatherbeaten, but enticing. Placemats describe Ethiopian cuisine and climate. Use the traditional pancake bread, *injera*, to eat spicy lamb, beef, chicken, and vegetable *wats* (stews). Lunch entrees $3.70-8; dinner slightly higher. Open daily 11:30am-midnight.

Calvert Café, 1967 Calvert St. NW (232-5431), right across the Duke Ellington Bridge. Metro: Woodley Park/Zoo. Look for the brown and gold tiles; though it looks boarded-up, this landmark has lasted 30 years. Huge, unadorned platters of Middle Eastern food. Appetizers $2-4.50; dinner entrees $6-8.50. Half of a broiled chicken with Arabian rice and a salad $6. Shish kabob with rice and salad $8.50. Open daily 11:30am-11:30pm.

Meskerem, 2434 18th St. NW (462-4100). Another fine Ethiopian place, and certainly the best-looking one in Adams-Morgan. Cheery yellow three-level interior incorporates an upstairs dining gallery with Ethiopian woven tables and a view of the diners below. Appetizers $3-4.75. Meat entrees $9-11, vegetarian entrees $8-8.75. A combination of five vegetable dishes and two salads $9.45 for one, $17.50 for two. Try the *meskerem tibbs* (lamb with vegetables) $11; *yemisir watt* (lentils in hot sauce) $8.50. Open Sun.-Thurs. noon-midnight, Fri.-Sat. noon-1am.

The Islander, 1762 Columbia Rd. NW (234-4955), above a shoe store. Small Trinidadian and Caribbean restaurant over 13 years old; read about Trinidad and Tobago from the walls. Consider curried goat ($8.50) or Calypso chicken ($8). *Roti* (East Indian thin pancakes stuffed with vegetables and meat) are a bargain at $3.25-6. Platters $6.50-9.75, appetizers $2. Open Mon. 5-10pm, Tues.-Thurs. noon-10pm, Fri.-Sat. noon-11pm.

Pasta Mia Trattoria, 1790 Columbia Rd. NW (328-9114). Fresh-faced rooms and airy atrium. Big portions of delicious pasta $7; appetizers $5-6. *Tiramisu* is a dessert with cheese custard, rum- and *espresso*-soaked cake, and chocolate for only $2.50. Hot damn. Open daily 6-11pm.

Lorenzo's, 1724 Columbia Rd. NW (234-5676). Find the Latin American food in back; ignore the standard American fare up front. Black beans $1.80, with rice $2.50. Sub-sized Cuban sandwich $3.10. *Chicharrones* (fried pigskins) with *yucca* $6.79; *carne guisada* (fried pig or cow) $6.79; enchiladas and tacos, each $1.50. Open 24 hrs.

Millie and Al's, 2440 18th St. NW (387-8131). Old-time local bar and grill makes darkness its theme; the checked tablecloths barely show up. The crowd includes locals and students. Sandwiches $2-4, burgers $2-3, dinners $4.50-5. Drafts $1.50, pitchers $5.75. Mixed drinks start at $2.25. Happy hour, with reduced drink prices, Mon.-Fri. 4-7pm. Open Mon.-Thurs. 4pm-2am, Fri.-Sun. noon-2am.

El Tamarindo, 1785 Florida Ave. NW (328-3660), just east of the corner of Florida and 18th St. Be cautious after dark in this area. Superb and cheap Salvadoran and Mexican food served into the early morning. House combination plate of appetizers presents cheese *quesadillas,* nachos, a chicken wing, a *taquito,* and guacamole and sour cream, all for $6. Entrees run $5.50-9.25—*carnes de puerco al espeton* (pork brochette) served with rice and salad goes for $7; or try two tacos, served with rice and beans for $5.50. Special Salvadoran appetizers on the back page of the menu $1.25-3.25. A gungadin of a deal. Open Mon.-Thurs. 11am-2am, Fri.-Sun. 11am-5am.

Adams-Morgan Spaghetti Garden, 2317 18th St. NW (265-6665). Pick a nice evening for the rooftop dining area among the treetops of 18th St. Good, cheap pasta dishes $4.50-6.75, with a child's portion for $2.95. Lasagna with meatballs or sausage $7.75. Appetizers $1.75-4.95. Minestrone $2. Meat dishes $6.75-9, including veal marsala for $9. Open Mon.-Sat. noon-midnight.

The Argentine Grill, 2423 18th St. NW (234-1818). Chic brick, art pix, a cured cow's skin, blue fans, and a mural. The cook's as artful as the decorators, even on the low end of the menu. Lunch sandwiches are a manageable $3-7.50. Appetizers $3-6; grilled *chorizo* ($3) and *brochette de pollo* (marinated chicken cubes with vegetables, $4.75). Entrees $7.50-17; try *pollo al ajillo* (chicken in garlic sauce, $9). Sort of a classy joint—don't expect whopping portions. Open Tues.-Thurs. 11:30am-3:30pm and 5:30-10:30pm, Fri. 11:30am-3pm and 5:30pm-12:30am, Sat. 5:30pm-12:30am, Sun. 2:30-10:30pm.

El Tazumal, 2467 18th St. NW (332-6931). Ample portions of good Salvadoran and Mexican food. Large and clean interior boasts a cute bar dressed up as a small cottage with a Spanish-tile roof. Try one of the lunch specials—meat dish, corn chips, hot sauce, rice, and beans ($5.25) or the *tacos al carbon* ($6.50) or *lomo salteado* (Spanish beef strips, $9.50). Appetizers $3-5; entrees $6-9.50. Open daily 11am-11pm.

So's Your Mom, 1831 Columbia Rd. NW (462-3666). Deli with mock-New York City sensibility. Meats are shipped from the Big Apple itself; baked goods fresh daily from Baltimore. Try the "No Nonsense N.Y. Corned Beef" sandwich (with mustard, $4.15; with chopped liver and bermuda onion, $4.75). Brooklyn-style *knishes* $1. Sandwiches from $2.85 for a BLT to $4.55 for lox and cream cheese. Open Mon.-Fri. 8am-8pm, Sat. 8am-7pm, Sun. 8am-3pm.

Fish, Wings & Tings, 2418 18th St. NW (234-0322). A tiny explosion of gaudy color, zany painting, and neon lights. Perhaps DC's best Caribbean cuisine served fast-food style (sometimes with aluminum foil) with Jamaican one-plate meals. Fish, wings, and tings like curried goat. Prices aren't bad, either: entrees $5-16.50, with rice, peas, and salad. Grilled fish $10. Appetizers $3-5.50. Open Mon.-Thurs. noon-10pm, Fri.-Sat. noon-11pm.

Las Rocas, 2450 18th St. NW (387-5992 or 232-3273). Serious *barrio* atmosphere. Downstairs clients speak Spanish in a dark, cramped, sparsely decorated neighborhood bar and dining room. Upstairs dining room is more spacious. The fare is unexceptional but cheap: appetizers $3-5, *jamon serrano* (cured ham) $5, *paella* (yellow rice with seafood) $7.50. Plain lobster with butter $8. Entrees $4-9. Open Sun.-Thurs. 11am-1am, Fri.-Sat. 11am-3am.

Dahlak, 1769 U St. NW (332-6435), yet another Ethiopian restaurant. This one isn't as fancy as many of its competitors, but the food is fine. Choose from any of the individual entrees ($6.50) and you can't go wrong. Better yet, try the Dahlak combo platter with *timtimo* (a snarfy bean dish) and *zighni* (small pieces of meat in sauce), which easily feeds two ($6.50). The combo platter is served with salad and, of course, *injera,* Ethiopian sour pancake bread. Open daily 11am-2am.

Zig Zag Café, 1524 U St. NW (986-5949). A monument to kitsch, this offbeat café has brightly-colored walls postered with record jackets, a turntable (not jukebox) playing old Blondie faves, and the perfect table for smokers, featuring a phone-lighter. Sandwiches ($2.50-4) are delicious and unusual. Try the curried chicken salad sandwich with apples, raisins, and walnuts (3.50). Open Sun.-Thurs. 7:30-2am, Fri.-Sat. 7:30-4am.

Ice Cream

Ben & Jerry's, 2503 Champlain St. NW (667-6677). Nationally known hippie ice cream chain: examine the cows-eating-ice-cream mural (protected by a recent court decision) over the store before you order your Cherry Garcia. Open Mon.-Thurs. 8am-11pm, Fri. 8am-1am, Sat. 9am-1am, Sun. 11am-11pm.

Woodley Park

Popular eateries, some dirt-cheap, some wallet-smashing, gather on these two blocks of Connecticut Ave. around the Woodley Park/Zoo Metro, near the Zoo, north of Dupont Circle, and just a Calvert St. bridge away from Adams-Morgan.

Thai Taste, 2606 Connecticut Ave. NW (667-5115). DC's black-and-neon magnet for Thai food lovers. Try the fried beef with chili paste and coconut milk, then Thai iced coffee ($2). Dinner from $6. Open daily 11am-11pm.

Rajaji, 2603 Connecticut Ave. NW (265-7344). Near-total darkness complements spicy vegetarian curries ($5.95-7.95). *Very* spicy vegetarian curries. *Very, very* spicy. Open daily 11:30am-2:30pm and 5:30-10pm.

The Lebanese Taverna, 2641 Connecticut Ave. NW (265-8681). Metro: Woodley Park/Zoo. Lebanese cuisine highlights yogurt, minced veggies, lamb, and pine nuts. Relatively generous appetizers ($3.50-7) and costlier entrees (from $8.75) served in a casual outdoor or fancier indoor setting. Come here for lunch or combine appetizers to create a meal ($6.25); dinner entrees may be a little expensive ($8.75-14.50). Free parking underground on Woodley Rd. behind the restaurant. Open Mon.-Thurs. 11:30am-3pm and 5-10:30pm, Fri.-Sat. 11:30am-3pm and 5-11pm, Sun. 5:50-10pm.

Agradut-Hiya-Rabi, 3000 Connecticut Ave. NW (332-8989), across from the National Zoo entrance. Metro: Woodley Park/Zoo. Vegetarianism, among other isms; psychedelic table umbrellas complement the pic of 70s guy guru Sri Chinmoy lifting 7063 lbs. Stocks tofu products at its deli counter. A pretty convincing "B"LT $2.25, with potato chips and a pickle. Open daily 8am-8pm.

Tandoor, 2623 Connecticut Ave. NW (483-1115), next to Rajaji. Metro: Woodley Park/Zoo. Tandoor-oven and curried entrees, $4.75-8, with tasty appetizers, $1-5.50. More mainstream than Rajaji, i.e. for Western wussies who can't take the heat. Open Sun.-Thurs. 11:30am-2:30pm and 5:30-10:30pm, Fri.-Sat. 5:30-11:30pm.

Tucson Cantina, 2605 Connecticut Ave. NW (462-6410). Metro: Woodley Park/Zoo. Americans enjoy quality Mexican food in saloon-like basement or at popular outdoor tables. It's not like Arizona has a cuisine of its own, you know. Burritos $4.50. Great burgers too ($5.50)—try the Tucson burger. Over half the menu is vegetarian. Open daily noon-11pm.

Upper Northwest

No one would place Cleveland Park or Tenley Circle on the cutting edge of anything. Still, these areas have the best of both worlds: back streets almost as quiet as the suburbs, but two avenues where good food hides from the masses. Budget ethnicity dominates the food in otherwise quite white Cleveland Park, on Connecticut Ave. Friendship Heights restaurants get pricier as you approach Western Ave., more reasonable as Maryland grows more distant.

Cleveland Park

Wingmaster's Grilled Chicken and Ribs, 3514 Connecticut Ave. NW (244-1111). Metro: Cleveland Park. Tasty and cheap side orders (60¢-$1.49, $2.59 for choice of 3) complement the grilled chicken and ribs. Try the sweet and springy corn bread. Ask the owner about his adventures on the Orient Express. Open Mon.-Thurs. 11am-10pm, Fri.-Sat. 11am-11pm, Sun. noon-10pm.

Vace's Italian Deli, 3315 Connecticut Ave. NW (363-1999). Metro: Cleveland Park. A combination grocery and deli. Sells food, including white cheese pizza and homemade sausage, and foodstuffs including Nutella, a hazelnut spread. 14" New York-style pizza pie, $4.91. Open Mon.-Fri. 9am-9pm, Sat. 9am-8pm, Sun. 10am-5pm.

Indian Kitchen, 3506 Connecticut Ave. NW (966-2541). Metro: Cleveland Park. No-frills, all-you-can-eat carry-out dinner special on Sat. and Sun. ($6). Most entrees between $4 and $6. Open Mon.-Thurs. 11am-10pm, Fri.-Sun. 11am-11pm.

Marvelous Market, 2603 Connecticut Ave. NW (686-4040), at the corner of Nebraska Ave. Crams gourmet European food supplies and tempting baked goods into a tiny, well-kept and tiled store. Open Mon.-Fri. 8am-8pm, Sat. 8am-6pm, Sun. 8am-1pm.

Ivy's Place, 3520 Connecticut Ave. NW (363-7802). Metro: Cleveland Park. A mixture of Indonesian and Thai fare. The lunch special ($7) and dinner special ($9) includes soup, appetizers and a choice of entree. A good choice for vegetarians. The Thai entrees tend to be cheaper than the Indonesian ones. Open daily 3:30-10:30pm.

Yenching Palace, 3524 Conn. Ave. NW (362-8200). Metro: Cleveland Park. Semicircular booths and compelling display cases lend character to the roomy interior. You'll recognize the place by the turquoise façade. The food is great and reasonably priced. Entrees $7.75-$9.00. The 1961 Cuban Missile Crisis came to an end here, where Khrushchev and Kennedy met by proxy to finalize the Soviet missile removal (the take-out menu won't let you forget it). Open Mon.-Thurs. 1130am-11pm, Fri.-Sat. 11:30am-11:30pm, Sun. noon-11pm.

Ice Cream

Bob's Famous Homemade Ice Cream, 3510 Connecticut Ave. NW (244-4465). Metro: Cleveland Park. Flavors range from the haggard classics to erotic novelties like Java (coffee), Mozambique (cinnamon and nutmeg), peach mint, and gingersnap. The award-winning orange chocolate chip is a good choice for vegetarians—it's popular, too. Open Mon.-Fri. 7am-10:30pm, Fri. 7am-midnight, Sat. 10am-midnight, Sun. 10am-10pm.

Tenley Circle

Mediterranean Deli, 4629 41st St. NW (362-1006), just off Wisconsin Ave. above the Dancing Crab. Metro: Tenleytown. This small café dishes out some of the best and cheapest Mediterranean food in town. Vegetarian fare includes Vine Leaves, grape leaves stuffed with rice, onion, lemon and parsley ($3); sandwiches like *baba ghanouj*, an eggplant dish ($2.75), and *felafel* ($3). Choose from plates or platters. Open Mon.-Sat. 11:30am-10pm.

The Dancing Crab, 4611 Wisconsin Ave. NW (244-1882), on the corner of 41st St. Metro: Tenleytown. Locals dive in for fresh seafood, especially crab and Maryland-style crabcakes ($15). In summer Chesapeake Bay crab season, crab feasts ($15) are the law. (Mon.-Wed. 6-9pm). Climb upstairs to The Malt Shop (see *Bars and Clubs*) for a cold brew. Open Mon.-Thurs. 11am-10:30pm, Fri.-Sat. 11am-11pm, Sun. 3-10:30pm.

a.k a. Frisco's, 4115 Wisconsin Ave. NW (244- 7847) below Tenley Circle, across from Bread & Chocolate. Metro: Tenleytown. Charming deli/café with a stupid name copies San Francisco prototypes: bright and airy, decked out in the whitest of whites. Generous sandwiches test new combinations—try the Berkeley: diced turkey, extra virgin olive oil, tarragon vinegar, capers, onions, lemon pepper, tomato, and sprouts in a pita. Sandwiches substitute gourmet mustards, lemon, vinegars, relishes, and other spices for mayonnaise or salt. Sandwiches $3.50-3.75. Salads $1.80-3.75. Open Mon.-Fri. 10:30am-6pm, Sat. 10:30am-3pm.

Armand's, 4231 Wisconsin Ave. NW (686-9450). Metro: Tenleytown. Chicago-style deep-dish pizza invades Washington. Part of a chain. Sm. pizza (triple cheese) $6.35, med. $8.95 lg. $10.35. Also boasts thin crust New York-style pizza and Armand's gourmet California-style pizza with exotic toppings like Thai chicken (marinated chicken breast and a peanut ginger sauce with scallions, shredded carrots, red pepper, and bean sprouts). All-you-can eat pizza and salad bar buffet lunch, $4.99 (Mon.-Fri. 11:30am-2:30pm and Sat.-Sun. 11:30am-3pm). Happy hour promises $1 slices and $1 drafts (Mon.-Fri. 4-7pm). Open Mon.-Thurs. 11:30am-midnight, Fri.-Sat. 11:30am-1am, Sun. 11:30am-11pm. Go down the street to **Armand's take-out-only window** at 5000 Wisconsin Ave. NW (363-5500) for cheaper slices. Open Mon.-Thurs. 11am-10pm, Fri.-Sat. 11am-midnight, Sun. 11am-10pm.

Maggie's, 4237 Wisconsin Ave. NW (363-1447). Metro: Tenleytown. Families pick Armand's next door; students come here. NY-style thin-crust pizzas, Italian pasta and sub staples in a pub atmosphere. Students drink $6.50 pitchers of Rolling Rock. Small pizza $12.50, large $15.50. Sat.-Sun. (11am-3pm) salad bar and pizza, $4.49 with beverage purchase. Open Sun.-Thurs. 11am-1:30am, Fri.-Sat. 11am-2:30am.

Friendship Heights

El Tamarindo, 4910 Wisconsin Ave. NW (244-8888), near Fessenden St. Metro: Friendship Heights. Yeah, they do great Mexican staples like *enchiladas* ($5.50-7) and *chimichangas* ($6.25-7), but try the Salvadoran cuisine for a change: e.g. *pollo encebollado*, chicken sautéed with garlic butter, onion, pepper, tomato, and wine vinegar ($6.75). Open Sun.-Thurs. 11am-1am, Fri.-Sat. 11am-3am.

Booeymonger, 5252 Wisconsin Ave. NW (686-5805), at Jenifer St. Metro: Friendship Heights. Elaborate sandwiches. Try and fit your jaw around the Patty Hearst: turkey, bacon, melted provolone, and Russian dressing on an English muffin ($4.50). The puns are obscure (the English muffin and Russian dressing represent Hearst's Anglo-Saxon stock and conversion to Communism), but delicious. Order at the counter, then sit down and eat outside. Salads $4-5.25. Decent but unexciting breakfast served, too. Open Sun.-Thurs. 8am-1am, Fri.-Sat. 8am-2am.

Pleasant Peasant, in the Mazza Gallerie, an intolerable shopping mall at 5300 Wisconsin Ave. NW (364-2500). Metro: Friendship Heights. Black-and-white glossy decor and the piano player's salary push the entrees out of *Let's Go's* price range, but each dessert can feed two with a flourish. Lose your balance over the chocolate intemperance cake ($6). Open Sun.-Thurs. 11:30am-3pm and 5:30-11pm, Fri.-Sat. 11:30am-3pm and 5:30pm-midnight.

Chadwick's, 5347 Wisconsin Ave. NW (362-8040). Metro: Friendship Heights. Walk downstairs into the shade, but ask to sit in the greenhouse area out front (the glass roof rises a bit above the sidewalk). Come for Saturday's half-price burger special (Memorial Day-Labor Day 11:30am-4pm). Happy hour (Mon.-Fri. 4-7pm) $2 margaritas, $1 longnecks or glass of house wine. Sandwiches and burgers $5-9, salads $6.50. Open Mon.-Thurs. 11:30am-2am, Fri.-Sat. 11:30am-3am, Sun. 10am-2am.

American Café, 5202 Wisconsin Ave. NW (363-5400), above Booeymonger's at Jenifer St. Metro: Friendship Heights. An old stand-by for light salads and sandwiches ($4-7). Children's and Braille menus available; seniors 10% discount. Open Mon.-Thurs. 11am-11pm, Fri.-Sat. 11am-1am, Sun. 10:30am-11pm.

Yosaku, 4712 Wisconsin Ave. NW (363-4453). Metro: Friendship Heights. Moderately priced Japanese joint. Lunchtime noodle dishes $5.25-7, sushi or sashimi $6.25. Dinnertime noodles $7.50-9.50, sushi or sashimi $12. Grab ten lame friends and sing your hearts out at *karaoke,* a wildly popular Japanese pastime: you sing the lyrics, the machine provides the backing tracks (50¢ a song). Open Mon.-Thurs. 11:30am-2:30pm and 5:30-11pm, Fri. 11:30am-2:30pm and 5:30-midnight, Sat. noon-3pm and 5:30-midnight, Sun. noon-3pm and 5:30-10:30pm.

Cathedral Area

Cactus Cantina, 3300 Wisconsin Ave. NW(686-7222), at Macomb St. near the Cathedral. Recently hip due to pseudo-Texan wonk President Bush, Tex-Mex restaurants seem to follow federal guidelines, with this place no exception: yuppie crowd, irreverently playful drawings on stucco walls, and solid Tex-Mex cuisine in gut-busting portions. $6.50 for two *enchiladas*, $7.50 for three, $11 for *fajitas*. Open Sun.-Thurs. 11:30am-10:30pm, Fri.-Sat. 11:30am-midnight.

Thai Flavor, 3709 Macomb St. NW (966-0200) at Wisconsin Ave. near the National Cathedral. All-you-can-eat lunch buffet ($7), with *pad thai* (noodles, shrimp, and vegetables in a peanut sauce), egg rolls, and other Thai staples. Open for buffet Mon.-Sat. 11:30am-3pm and dinner daily 5-10:30pm.

Worth Driving To

Parkway Deli, 8317 Grubb Rd. (301-587-1427), just over the District line in Maryland. Obscure shopping center hides Washington's best deli from all but the neighborhood's knowing few—make that the knowing many; the wait for weekend breakfasts can take up to an hour. Try any sandwich ($3-7), or a bagel with nova lox ($6); the pickle bar (free after 4pm) makes national treasures of vinegar and peppercorns. Take 16th St. NW all the way north to East-West Hwy., turn left on East-West, then left onto Grubb. Open Mon. 8am-9pm, Tues.-Fri. 8am-9:30pm, Sat. 7am-9:30pm, Sun. 7am-9pm.

Bethesda

All those white-collar stiffs must have exceptional taste buds, because Bethesda's concrete renaissance has also maintained many of the DC area's best restaurants. Bethesda holds about 150 restaurants; because there are so many so close together, downtown Bethesda almost demands a pre-dinner stroll to check out menus and compare ambiences. Wander the area bounded roughly by Wisconsin Ave. on the east, Bethesda

Ave. on the south, Rugby Ave. to the north, and Arlington Rd. and Old Georgetown Rd. to the west. Since Bethesda is in Maryland, all its phone numbers are in **area code 301.**

Tastee Diner, 7731 Woodmont Ave. (652-3970), at Cheltenhem Ave., with a run-down art-deco twin in Silver Spring, MD at Colesville Rd. and Georgia Ave. Metro: Bethesda. A classic diner survival from the 50s, the Tastee puts its remodeled, glitzy imitators to shame. Moody, veteran service, wood booths, long counter, and jukeboxes at tables, all gloriously, anachronistically intact. Breakfast all day and all night: grits 95¢, hot cakes with syrup $2.65. Entrees range from $3.65-$9, but cluster around the $5 mark. Hamburgers $1.90. Daily dinner specials available Mon.-Fri. 11am-10pm, Sat.-Sun. noon-10pm. Open 24 hrs. except on Dec. 25.

Rio Grande Café, 4919 Fairmont Ave. (656-2981). Metro: Bethesda. Louder than Texas and more crowded than Mexico City—with reason. Diego Rivera-style murals depict Mexican beer, lit by Xmas lights over the bar. Appetizers are $2.25-8. $2.75 buys a huge, tasty taco. $7 buys three. *Tacos al carbon* $11, fajitas $11, or a couple of quail $11. Open Mon.-Thurs. 11am-10:30pm, Fri. 11am-11:30pm, Sat. 11:30am-11:30pm, Sun. 11:30am-10:30pm.

Bethesda Crab House, 4958 Bethesda Ave. (301-652-3382). Reserve a place, but dress casually for this extraordinary restaurant, where there is only one entree and newspapers lie as elegantly as any linen table cloth. Work up an appetite then prepare to indulge in an all-the-crab-you-can-eat feast with coleslaw and potatoes for $15. Open all year. (In the winter crabs are flown in from Louisiana.) Pitchers of beer $7.50., 16oz. sodas $1.25. One of the great institutions of Bethesda, with 32 years of experience to back it. Open Mon.-Sat. 9am-midnight, Sun. noon-midnight.

Terramar, 7800 Wisconsin Ave. (654-0888). Metro: Bethesda. Superb Nicaraguan cuisine that's pretty much affordable. The inside has the feel of a Latin American plaza without the summer heat; stucco columns divide the expansive chamber. Try the *churrasco*, grilled tenderloin with three sauces, or the *ropa vieja* (shredded beef with onions, peppers, jalapenos, and tomatoes). For *tapas* (starters) try the *repocheta*, Nicaraguan quesadillas for $2.50, *yucca fritas*, lightly fried cassava sticks for $2.25. *Tres leches* ($4) is a wonderful dessert. Latin and Spanish classical guitar Thurs.-Fri. and Sun. nights. Open Tues.-Fri. 11:30am-2:30pm and 5-10pm, Sat.-Sun. 5-10pm.

Louisiana Express, 4921 Bethesda Ave. (652-6945). White lattice and the smell of Cajun cuisine beckon to weary car dealers and buyers alike. Try the chicken jambalaya, a rice dish with chicken, tomatoes and other vegetables, and spices $4.75. Critically acclaimed crawfish bisque $3. Half a rotisserie chicken with Cajun spices, vegetable jambalaya and biscuits soft as grandma's belly $5.50. (Wowzer.) On Sundays budgeteers can feast on a concoction of scrambled eggs with ham, bacon, and sausage, on french bread with melted cheese. Open Mon.-Sat. 7:30am-11am, Sun. brunch 9am-2:30pm.

West Side Café, 4733 Bethesda Ave. (907-0808). Metro: Bethesda. New York-bred proprietors run this new storefront café beside the Artery Plaza West building. Cushions and benches cozy up to diners while overhead shelves collect small crafts. Local patrons get personal greetings: who knows, some may actually be named "Babe." Homemade soups $1.75 (cup), $2.25 (bowl). Check out the long list of sandwiches ($2.40-$5.50). Burgers $3. Breakfasts (served until 11am) under $3. Open Mon.-Fri. 7am-4pm.

Paradise Restaurant, 7141 Wisconsin Ave. (907-7500). Metro: Bethesda. "Kebob Cuisine" from a wood-burning grill. Get lost in the black, pink, and green dining room among tempting flowers, and mirrors, then regain weight at the $7 all-you-can-eat luncheon buffet consisting of soup, 6 entrees, salad, and fruit (served daily noon-3pm). Or bite into a samosa, a deep-fried pastry filled with spiced beef; get four for $5. Extra rice with entrees, free of charge. Avoid the ribs and apples. Cold appetizers $2.25-5, hot appetizers $4-7, entrees $6-11. Turkish coffee $2.50, *baklava* $2.50. Open Sun.-Thurs. noon-10pm, Fri.-Sat. noon-11pm.

Persepolis Restaurant, 7130 Wisconsin Ave. (656-9339). Metro: Bethesda. "Exquisite Persian cuisine" locked in Manichaean struggle with Paradise Restaurant across the street; everybody wins. Friendly service delivers kabobs and Middle Eastern food. All-you-can-eat lunch buffet lays down entrees, fruit, and salad for $7 (served Mon.-Sun. noon-3pm). *Hummus* and pita for $3; *chelo kabob-e kubideh* (ground sirloin of beef with onions, saffron, and seasonings) $7. Generous, friendly bartender. Open daily 11:30am-11pm.

Philadelphia Mike's, 7732 Wisconsin Ave. (656-0103 or 656-0104). Metro: Bethesda. This alone could justify the existence of Philadelphia; everything from turkey to bread is baked fresh at the store. This is the original location (two others in downtown DC). Read the dead-on rave reviews on the wall as you wait. Simple decor (green tablecloths, white tiles). Superb cheesesteaks ($3.64-7). Burgers $2-3, vegetarian sub $3.50. All-you-can-eat pizza every night from 4pm to closing, $3.50. Chowitzer. Open Mon.-Sat. 7am-10pm, Sun. 7am-9pm.

Kabul West, 4871 Cordell Ave. (986-8566), on the corner of Norfolk Ave. Metro: Bethesda. Yummy Afghan cuisine whose pleasant odors fill the rooms and permeate the Afghan rugs on the walls. Loop-de-loop for delicious, oversized *aushak* ($2.50), dumplings with creamy meat and yogurt sauce (smackdab!). Strong Afghan tea $1. Entrees and kebabs $10-15. Minimum $7 per person. Open Sun.-Thurs. 5-9:30pm, Fri.-Sat. 5-11pm.

Tako Grill, 7756 Wisconsin Ave. (652-7030). Metro: Bethesda. Dangling red lantern lures customers to this modern Japanese grill, slick with glazed wood and spattered with track lighting. Young professionals struggle with chopsticks or devour excellent if salty sushi, unfazed by mournful stares from the prominent aquaria. $6 lunch special thrusts *miso* soup, six pieces of sushi roll, and an entree at stunned consumers (Mon.-Fri. 11:30am-2pm). Also good are the *Danburi*, large steaming bowls of rice topped with noodles, vegetables, and grilled meat, with *miso* soup and a small but tasty sprout salad for $5.50. Open Mon.-Thurs. 11:30am-2pm and 5:30-9:45pm, Fri. 11:30am-2pm and 5:30-10:15pm, Sat. 5:30-10:15pm.

Peter's Carry Out, 8017 Wisconsin Ave. (656-2242). Metro: Bethesda. Unpretentious neighborhood take-out whose long orange counter, beige tiles, and humble window shame its affluent neighbors. Good food never over $5. Breakfast (until 11am) $2.50-3.75. *Gyros* $3.45, *souvlaki* $3.80, subs $2.85-4.10, sandwiches $1.50-3.45. Open Mon.-Sat. 7am-5pm.

Stromboli Family Restaurant, 7023 Wisconsin Ave. (986-1980). Metro: Bethesda. Italian standards in a Stromboli family atmosphere. Linguine (with tomato sauce and garlic bread) $4-5 during lunch, $6 during dinner), subs $4.25-5.50. Highly touted calzone $4.25. "Award-winning" small cheese pizza $3.50. Open Mon.-Thurs. 10am-10pm, Fri.-Sat. 10am-11pm, Sun. noon-9:30pm.

Chinese Express, 7613 Wisconsin Ave. (656-6111). Metro: Bethesda. Red-and-yellow awning, murals of dragons, and black-and-white TV typify this cozy, suburban Chinese place. Egg roll $1, shrimp and beef entrees $5, *kung pao chicken* and other chicken dishes $4.50. Open daily 11am-10pm, Sun. 5-9pm.

Malarky's, 7201 Wisconsin Ave. (951-9000). Weirdo upscale tack heaven. Neon signs and posters proclaiming the latest deals attract neighbors and visitors both. Avail yourself of beer and burgers, half-price, on Recession Night, every Tues. (5pm-closing). On Wednesdays, attend the free rollerblade clinic (6pm-9pm). Live rock Fri.-Sat. 9:30-11:30pm. Open Mon.-Thurs. 11:30am-1am, Friday 11:30-2am, Sat. 6pm-2am.

Ice Cream

Bob's Famous Homemade Ice Cream, 4706 Bethesda Ave. (657-2963). Metro: Bethesda. Small, clean and cool, with a counter and tables. Try the sorbet, especially pear. Ice cream from $1.62-2.28; ice-cream dishes $1.86-3.90. They also sell hot and cold sandwiches, $2.39-4.39. Open Mon.-Thurs. 7:30am-11pm, Fri. 7:30am-12:30am, Sat. 11am-12:30am, Sun. 11am-11pm.

Takoma Park

Low prices almost make up for the scarcity of restaurants on these quiet streets.

Jeyar Food Market, 308 Carroll St. (829-6625). Metro: Takoma. This Indian restaurant has one table and no air-conditioning; that's why it's takeout only. Curries $5.50, vegetarian dishes $4. Open Mon.-Thurs. 8am-9pm, Fri. 8am-sundown, Sun. 9am-7pm.

Mark's Kitchen, 7006 Carroll Ave. (270-1884). Metro: Takoma. Mark's all-American checkered tablecloths make his cuisine a pleasant cross-cultural surprise. Korean dishes gone stateside—seaweed soup or Korean steak, $6. Try the spinach salad with chicken teriyaki ($5), the dumplings ($1.75), and the curried vegetables ($3.50). Open Mon.-Sat. 8am-8:30pm, Sun. 8am-7pm.

Taliano's, 7001 Carroll Ave. (270-5515). Metro: Takoma. Subs, pasta, and pizza. Locals frequent the roomy back-room bar. Pasta and sandwiches $3.25-5.50. Call ahead about entertainment; it's a casual thing. Open Mon.-Thurs. 11:30am-10pm, Fri. 11:30am-midnight, Sat. 11:30am-11pm.

Everyday Gourmet, 6923 Laurel Ave. (270-2270). Metro: Takoma. Clean, airy deli bakes French pastries and slices up salads. Fresh flowers and a *café au lait* can brighten up any morning, and the inventive sandwiches, like ham and raspberry ($4), can fill a hungry lunchtime stomach. Dinner discount Mon.-Fri. 6-8pm. Open Mon.-Fri. 8am-8pm, Sat. 10am-5pm, Sun. 10am-2pm.

Waterfront

Next door to the wharf markets on Water St. lie the Waterfront restaurants, huge seafood establishments with the grand air of an Atlantic City boardwalk. Most, if not quite all, are exclusively for high rollers.

Negril's Jamaican Bakery, 401 M St. SW (488-3636), in the Waterside Mall (across the street from the bus stop). Chicken loaves, a cross between a calzone and a pot pie, $1.70; vegetable patties (same principle) $1.40. Open Mon.-Fri. 6:30am-7pm, Sat.

The Gangplank, 600 Water St. SW(554-5000). On a converted barge, most reasonable of the Waterfront seafood crew. Ducks waddle and paddle past the bottom deck at water level. Recently the place has expanded to include a patio cafe, cheaper than the deck, with nightly live entertainment supplied throughout the summer by extroverted croakers and a *karaoke* machine. Award-winning clam chowder $3. Upper deck open daily 11:30am-1:40pm and 5:30-9:45pm, lower deck open Sun.-Thurs. 11:30am-12:30am, Fri.-Sat. 11:30am-2am.

Hector's, in the Waterside Mall (488-1662). A distinctive ambiance created by light and shadow. Black padded stalls lit by low-hanging open lamps. Subs $4, seafood platters including fries and coleslaw $3-4, breakfast (2 eggs, bacon, homefries, and toast) $3. Open Mon.-Fri 6am-7pm, Sat.-Sun. 8am-4pm.

Arlington, VA

Those who follow immigration patterns will go beyond Washington's limits for its best ethnic food: new arrivals often settle with other immigrants and set up shop in the city's semi-suburban outskirts. If you think you've exhausted Adams-Morgan, Arlington may be the way to go. The hodgepodge of ethnic foods and shops from Rosslyn to Ballston defies glib classification. The Clarendon area, nicknamed Little Saigon, holds not only Vietnamese but worthwhile Japanese, Chinese, and Thai food. But even the name "Little Asia" would slight the nearby all-American establishments which dish out chili and ribs. Forget the whole naming business altogether and be grateful the Potomac is easier to cross than the Pacific.

Many Arlington restaurants are accessible by Metro; drivers should beware of one-way streets. From Rosslyn to Clarendon, Wilson Blvd. runs one way from Washington into Arlington; Clarendon Blvd. runs parallel to it in the other direction. Some restaurants provide parking, especially in Ballston, but street parking is usually easy enough. Remember that all phone numbers in Arlington are in the **703 area code.**

El Pollo Rico, 2912 N. Washington Blvd. (522-3220), two blocks from Wilson Blvd. Metro: Clarendon. Charcoal-broiled rotisserie chicken, Peruvian-style. Choice of two sauces here, jalapeño or a mustard mayonnaise. Eat inside on laminated butcher block tables, or take it with you. Comes with fries and cole slaw. Whole chicken $9.55, half $5.25, quarter $3.10. Open daily 11am-10pm.

Crisp 'n Juicy, 4540 Lee Highway (243-4222), near Old Dominion Dr. Don't let its fast-food name mislead you: succulent rotisserie chicken, this time Argentinian-style, marks El Pollo Rico's slightly less popular rival. Hot picante, mustard, and mild garlic homemade sauces. Counter or takeout only. Whole chicken $8.35, half $4.50, quarter $2.80. Open Mon.-Sat. 11am-10pm, Sun. 11am-9pm.

Chesapeake Seafood Crab House, 3607 Wilson Blvd. (528-8888 or 528-8896). Metro: Clarendon. A real seaside crabhouse with brown paper tablecloths and hammers to break open the crabs. Most people come here for the steamed and spiced crabs, but this Vietnamese restaurant also lists a Chinese menu and American standards like fried chicken and hush puppies. Try the crabs sautéed in black bean sauce or with ginger and scallions ($8.50). Prices for steamed crabs vary seasonally from about $10-35 a dozen according to season, size, and sex of the crab. Vegetarians get a whole page of appetizers, soups, and entrees. Don't confuse this with the similarly-named chain. Open Tues.-Sun. 11am-10pm.

Atlacatl I, 2716 N. Washington Blvd. (524-9032). A ten-minute walk from the Clarendon Metro. Calls itself a "Mexican and Salvadoran restaurant," but El Salvador carries the day: the meal starts with fried *yucca* instead of the standard tortilla chips. Combination platters include *pupusas* (thick, juicy tortillas stuffed with cheese, pork, and spicy marinated cabbage); tamales, filled with pork or sweet corn; and *pastelitos* (fried pastries filled with spicy beef). Good seafood, too. Takeout counter in front. Platters $6-7.50; seafood $8-15. Open Sun.-Thurs. 11am-10pm, Fri.-Sat. 11am-midnight.

Queen Bee, 3181 Wilson Blvd. (527-3444). Metro: Clarendon. When you see how long the line is some nights, you'll think people are waiting for concert tickets instead of Vietnamese food. Most people say you can't order wrong here, even though everyone orders the same spring rolls (*cha gio*) for appetizers ($2.50). Try the Queen Bee Seafood on Crispy Noodles with shrimp, scallops, crabmeat, squid, and vegetables ($7.50). Open daily 10am-10pm.

Red Hot and Blue, 1600 Wilson Blvd. (276-RIBS), under an office building near Pierce St. Metro: Court House. Pit barbecue direct from Memphis, with logo to match—two pigs with shades, guitars, and Elvis pompadours. The late Republican media mogul Lee Atwater, among others, licked his lips over the down-home pork BBQ ribs. Regular order $9.70, $16.70 for a full rack to feed two. Try them wet (basted with sauce), or dry (rubbed with traditional Memphis spices). Some opt for a pulled pig sandwich ($4.50). Expect a wait some weekend nights. Open Mon.-Thurs. 11am-10pm, Fri. 11am-11pm, Sat. noon-11pm, Sun. noon-10pm.

Hard Times Café, 3128 Wilson Blvd. (528-2233), across from Clarendon Metro. Used to be a rough neighborhood joint in Rockville, MD that served great chili in huge, heartburn-inducing portions; now it's renowned, upscaled, and no longer the best bargain in town, but still a good deal. Famed for Cincinnati chili with hot and sweet spices (like cinnamon), Texas chili, and vegetarian chili. Crumbly cornbread with each order. Chili $4-5.25. Open Mon.-Thurs. 11am-10pm, Fri.-Sat. 11am-11pm, Sun. 4-10pm.

Food Factory, 4221 N. Fairfax Dr. (527-2279), across from Ballston Metro; entrance in back. Ignore the name and devour the Pakistani char-broiled kebabs, which put American "shish kabobs" to shame. Tear off a piece of *nan* (tandoori bread) and wrap it around chicken, beef, or lamb on skewers ($4.50-6). All meats are *halal* (cleared by Islamic law). The overpowering smell of curry will beckon you through a side door to **Usman,** a Pakistani grocery store with *Basmati* rice, meat, spices, and sweets. To find the Factory, look for its sign across from the Ballston Metro, then walk through the parking lot and behind the dumpsters until you see the Foodsters. Open Mon.-Thurs. 11am-10pm, Fri. 11am-10pm, Sat.-Sun. noon-10pm.

Tom Sarris' Orleans House, 1213 Wilson Blvd. (524-2929). Metro: Rosslyn. Steak and fish are the specialties here. Lunch has the best deals: try the famed prime rib ($7, $8 at dinner), or crab cakes ($5). Lunch entrees cluster around $5-6. Most dinners run from $8-12. Open Mon.-Fri. 11am-11pm, Sat. 4pm-11pm, Sun. 4pm-10pm.

Pho 75, 1711 Wilson Blvd. (525-7355), near Quinn St. Metro: Court House. Full of Vietnamese people slurping *pho,* a noodle soup filling enough for a meal. Top your rice noodles in beef broth with one of eight kinds of beef, bean sprouts, chilis, and lemon. Nothing beats hot *pho.* Regular bowl $3.75, large $4.45. Open daily 9am-8pm.

Atami, 3155 Wilson Blvd. (522-4787). Metro: Clarendon. Stay as long as you like and sample both *nigiri sushi* (fish seasoned with *wasabi* horseradish on rice) and *maki sushi* (prepared with rice, fish, and vegetables rolled in seaweed). Sushi platters served with *miso* soup, salad, and rice (lunch $6, dinner $9.25). Unlimited sushi for $25—a bargain in its own exorbitant way. The Vietnamese entrees are significantly cheaper, none exceeding $7.25. Open Mon.-Thurs. 11am-10pm, Fri.-Sat. 11am-10:30pm, Sun. 4-10pm.

Rio Grande Café, 4301 N. Fairfax Dr. (528-3131). Metro: Ballston. Painted cacti and sombreros adorn the stucco walls, along with bags of rice and cases of beer. *Costillas* (spicy pork ribs) $13. Combination plates of enchiladas, tacos, *chile rellenos,* and tamales $7.25-11.50. Open Mon.-Thurs. 11am-10:30pm, Fri.-Sat. 11:30am-11:30pm, Sun. 11:30am-10:30pm.

The Cambodian Restaurant, 1727 Wilson Blvd. (522-3832), near Quinn St. Metro: Court House. Cambodian cuisine bears some resemblance to its neighbors', but the soups stand out (have your choice of seven soups, each under $2), as does the Cambodian fondue—a platter of shrimp, beef, squid, vegetables, and rice noodles skewered for dipping in a boiling broth (feeds two for $20). Dinner entrees $6.50-9.50, lunch $5.75-7.25. Open Mon.-Fri. 11am-10pm and daily 5:30-10:30pm.

Hunan Number 1, 3033 Wilson Blvd. (528-1177, -1178) about a block and a half from the Clarendon Metro. Huge bronze(like) Fu dogs perch on either side of the front porch. Try their *dim sum,* an immense and ongoing affair (it has its own menu). 27 different types, most for $2, all for under $3. Regular portions. Check the special lunch deals. Open daily 11am-2am, *dim sum* served daily 11am-3pm.

Café Saigon, 1135 N. Highland St. (243-6522 or 276-7110), across from Clarendon Metro. "French" decor. Popular dishes are the grilled pork and crispy rolls (*cha gio*) on "funny" rice noodles ($7.25) and the skewered beef with bacon, eaten with rice crepes ($9). More upscale than "Little Saigon's" other restaurants. Open Sun.-Thurs. 10am-10pm, Fri.-Sat. 10am-11pm.

International House of Pancakes, 935 Stafford St. (522-3118), corner of N. Fairfax Dr. Metro: Ballston. Insomniac legions of IHOP fanatics will find what they yearn for in the buttermilk pancakes. Chocolate chip pancakes $3.95. Say hi to Bob in the parking lot—no kidding. Open 24 hrs.

Alexandria, VA

Old Town's food scene resembles Georgetown's—but quainter and less crowded. Alexandria has reeled in and kept cheap barbecue and expensive seafood as its specialities. The well-decorated places will bust most budgets, but take heart: some tiny delis hide excellent cooking. Remember, all numbers in Alexandria have the **703 area code.**

Royal Restaurant, 734 N. Asaph St. (548-1616). Alexandria's oldest and least pretentious restaurant dishes up home-style meals and 50s jukebox hits. Sandwiches $2-5.50, omelettes $3.50-5.35, entrees $5-8. "Alexandria's Best Breakfast" menu $2-4. Those who don't want to bop to "Splish Splash" and "Under the Boardwalk" should sit to the left in the more somber setting. You *must* try the rice pudding ($1.50). Open daily 6am-9:30pm.

Lite-n-Fair, 1018 King St. (549-3717). Disguised by the modest deli façade, Ki Choi, former executive chef of the ritzy Watergate Restaurant, takes his kitchen around the world. German potato soup filled with chunks of potato and steaming with flavor ($2) is delicious, as are stir-fry chicken and shrimp dishes ($6.35). Sometimes specials, all under $7, include ginger chicken, seafood pasta, and rockfish topped with crabmeat; be sure to read the daily specials before you order. Takeout available. Open Mon.-Sat. 11am-9pm.

Generous George's Positive Pizza and Pasta Place, 3006 Duke St. (370-4303). House specialty is an invention of overindulgence—pasta-topped pizza with a puffy cheese-and-garlic crust. Toppings galore; the possibilities are endless. Kids love this place. Open Mon.-Thurs. 11am-midnight, Fri.-Sat. 11am-1am, Sun. 11am-11pm.

South Austin Grille, 801 King St. (684-8969). Moderately priced Tex-Mex in this cheery pastel hangout. *Quesadillas* stuffed with homemade *chorizo* and green chilies stand out among the appetizers. Lunch runs about $6; dinner over $10. Texas chili ($5.25) and beef and bean burritos ($8) are all popular. Open Tues.-Thurs. 11:30am-11pm, Fri.-Sat. 11:30am-midnight, Sun.-Mon. 11:30am-10pm.

Hard Times Café, 1404 King St. (683-5340). Cincinnati, Texas, and vegetarian chili (all $4) make the HTC deservedly popular. Cincinnati (the most delectable) is finely ground beef in a tomato sauce with cinnamon; Texas is coarsely ground chuck without tomatoes, mildly seasoned. A chili-spaghetti plate with beans, cheese, onions, and homemade cornbread ($5.25) would stuff anyone. Top a burger or pasta with some chili. Homemade onion rings, too. Open Mon.-Thurs. 11am-10pm, Fri.-Sat. 11am-11pm, Sun. noon-10pm.

Armand's Chicago Pizzeria, 111 King St. (683-0313). Spacious, wooden restaurant caters to families. All-you-can-eat pizza buffet and salad bar (11:30am-2:30pm) and midnight munch buffet (Fri.-Sat. 10:30pm-1am) are steals at $5; children under 7 get them at half-price. Satisfy your craving for deep-dish pizzas with all the toppings, be they pineapple or sausage (sm. $6.50-9.70, med. $9-13.25, lg. $11-15). All sandwich platters (steak, for example) under $5. Free delivery within a three-mile radius of the restaurant. Open Mon.-Fri. 11:30am-10pm, Sat. 11:30am-11pm.

King Street Blues, 112 N. Asaph St. (836-8800). A tribute to the South, with its slow-smoked ribs, pork and turkey BBQ, fresh salads, and Po'Boy sandwiches. Double-pork chili, pine-bark stew, or country-fried steak might have even a Yankee whistlin' Dixie. Entrees $5-8, lunch; $5.50-$11.50, dinner. Blue plate special ($5) changes daily. Wed. sports Virginia beef stew; Thurs. is fried chicken. Open Mon.-Thurs. 11am-10pm, Fri. 11:30am-10:30pm, Sat. 11:30am-10:30pm, Sun. 5-10pm.

Gadsby's Tavern, 134 N. Royal St. (548-1288). Tour the museum, then stop by to eat off your own pewter; waitrons in 18th-century dress deliver generous helpings of 18th-century cooking. Surprisingly good traditional tea bread and English trifle (for dessert). Lunch less expensive than dinner (lunch stew $6.50). Open daily 11:30am-3pm and 5:30-10:30pm. Tours Tues.-Sat. 10am-5pm, Sun. 1-5pm.

Old Town Sandwich Shop, 127 S. Peyton St. (684-6775). $1 bagels with cream cheese, $1-2 danishes and breakfasts, $3-4 sandwiches. Perfect for a quick bite to eat and a newspaper in the morning. Fresh food and quick service. Open Mon.-Fri. 7am-4:30pm.

le gaulois, 1106 King St. (739-9494). Moved here from downtown DC. Flavorful French entrees $7-9; fish of the day $8.50. Low-calorie entrees available. Dinner prices are steep; try to come here at lunch. Open Mon.-Thurs. 11:30am-10:30pm, Fri.-Sat. 11:30am-11pm.

Nam's River, 715 King St. (836-5910). Colonists and colonized reconcile their cuisines at this French-Vietnamese restaurant. Popular items include the tasty "river" noodles in black bean sauce and peppered mussels. Entrees $6-10, lunch; $10-16, dinner. Yikes. Open Mon.-Fri. 11:30am-2pm and 5:30-10pm, Sat.-Sun. 5:30-10pm.

Ice Cream

The Scoop Grill and Homemade Ice Cream, 110 King St. (549-4527). Funky flavors (carrot cake, for example) make this ice cream store a cut above the rest. Filled with families during the day and students at night. Burgers $2-2.50. Obviously, the ice cream is good. Small $1.65, medium $2.75, large $3.85. Open Sun.-Thurs. 8am-11pm, Fri.-Sat. 8am-midnight.

Ben & Jerry's, 103 S. Union St. (684-8866). Vermont's all-natural ice cream feeds a nightly throng of all-natural Grateful Dead fans. Bright lights, big cows. Ice cream comes in trendy flavors, from Rainforest Crunch to Cherry Garcia. Open Sun.-Thurs. 11am-11pm, Fri.-Sat. 11am-1am.

Happy Hours

Capitol Hill

Julio's, 801 Pennsylvania Ave. SE (546-0060). $2 draft beer and $1 pizza with first drink. Mon.-Thurs. 4-6:30pm.

Tiber Creek Pub, 15 E St. NW (638-0900). Inside the Bellevue Hotel. Shiny green pub serves free appetizers every 20 min. Mon.-Fri. 5-7pm.

Mickey's Patio, 406 8th St. SE (544-4842), at Pennsylvania Ave. $1.25 drafts come your way any weekday between 4 and 7pm; on Thurs. draft beers cost $1 all night. On Mondays, burgers are usually half-price. Also, half-price chili graces Wednesdays and half-price nachos enliven Thursdays, except during summer.

Hawk 'n Dove, 329 Pennsylvania Ave. SE (543-3300). 4-7pm during the week. $1.75 domestics and free hors d'oeuvres.

White House Area/Foggy Bottom

Quigley's, 1825 Eye St. NW (331-0150). Free food (chicken wings, meatballs, corn chips and salsa) Mon.-Fri. 5-7pm.

Milo's, 2142 Pennsylvania Ave. NW (338-3000). Monday is half-price pizza night; Thursday is "yard" (of beer) night; Friday happy hour serves $1 beers.

Georgetown

Champions, 1206 Wisconsin Ave. NW (965-4005), through alley. $1.60 drafts Mon.-Thurs. 5-8pm; free appetizers and $5.50 "fishbowl" drafts on Fridays. Buffalo wings on Fri.

El Torito, 3222 M St. NW (342-2290), entrance in Georgetown Park and on Wisconsin Ave., next to underground parking entrance. Food buffet (must order a drink), margaritas ($2), tacos (50¢) and drafts ($1.25) Mon.-Thurs. 4-8pm, Fri. 4-9pm.

New Downtown

The Bottom Line, 1716 Eye St. NW (298-8488). Different cheap or free food every night; free tacos, for example, along with discount drinks. Must order some drink (from $1.50), not necessarily alcoholic. Mon.-Fri. 5-7:30pm.

Stoney's Beef-N-Beer Restaurant, 1307 L St. NW (347-9163). Shuttered half-bar, half-greasy spoon wholly delights with half-price specials (pizza, steak and cheese, hamburgers) during a lengthy happy hour Mon.-Wed. 4pm-midnight.

The Madhatter, 1831 M St. NW (833-1495). Complimentary half-shell oysters speed away during the special happy hours with $1 Rolling Rocks.

Dupont Circle

The Front Page, 1333 New Hampshire Ave. NW (296-6500). Well-known for its awesome offer—variety of food with any purchase of any beverage, even a non-alcoholic one (Mon.-Fri. 5-7pm).

Bethesda

GEOZ, 7305 Waverly St. (301-907-8604). Happy hour simply made for *Let's Go* readers. Fabulous free buffet includes pasta, cheese plates, chicken wings, and the like.

Durty Nelly's, 4714 Montgomery Lane (301-652-1444). Happy hour (Mon.-Fri. 3-7pm) guzzles half-price draft beer, 2-for-1 mixed drinks, and free food (no purchase of alcohol required).

Tavern, 4824 Bethesda Ave. (654-6366). Booths. Bar. Photos. Pinball. Locals. Half-price domestic beer and free buffet (including tacos, chicken, hot dogs, and cheese). Mon.-Fri. 4-7pm.

Sights

Don't skimp on Washington's most famous sights: hundreds of thousands of tourists every year correctly decide that the Mall museums, the Capitol, and the Monuments are worth the price of a trip to DC. But the same people often leave strangely disappointed, complaining that DC holds nothing but the government, or the government plus museums. The truth usually is that the complainers didn't bother to see anything else. Before or after the inevitable Smithsonian odyssey, the rest of Washington deserves your time; away from the major monuments, DC residents go about their business in a veritable thicket of art museums, public events, ethnic communities, parks, embassies, buildings worth looking at, music worth listening to, and streets to delight and educate the attentive pedestrian. Adams-Morgan, Dupont Circle, Connecticut Ave., and Georgetown are all popular for walking around even for natives sick of the Mall. These areas can show visitors the difference (and the hidden links) between DC-as-government-town and DC's various homegrown cultures. Don't neglect the sights related to Washington's African-American community. Finally, don't feel constrained to see only what *Let's Go* mentions: we try, but we can never know everything.

Tours

Tens of thousands of out-of-towners leave DC yearly without having set foot in anything except museums and monuments. If they knew what they were missing, they might blame the guided-tour companies, which shuttle visitors from one major sight to the next, discourage them from exploring anything on foot, isolate them from actual Washingtonians, and keep them confined to central Washington. Tours also cost (the cheapest are $8.50), and most tour guides expect a tip at excursion's end. If you read this book, don't mind long walks, and can orient yourself to a new city without too much difficulty, there's no reason to take a tour.

Open-air buses and **trolleys** circulate on a fixed route; they operate on all-day tickets, so you can get off wherever it stops, then get back on when the next coach comes around. The most popular is **Tourmobile Sight-seeing,** 1000 Ohio Drive SW, (recorded messages 554-7950 and 554-7020) near the Washington Monument. Tours run mid-June to mid-Sept. 9am-6:30pm, otherwise 9:30am-4:30pm. (Standard 18-sight loop $8.50; ages 3-11 $4. To Arlington Cemetery or the Frederick Douglass home (a 2 1/2-hr. loop) $5, kids $2.50. To Mount Vernon, daily 10am, noon, and 2pm, $16.50, kids $8; price includes admission. Purchase tickets by 1pm from booth or drivers.) The orange-and-green coaches of **Old Town Trolley** (301-985-3021) pick up re-boarders along a 90-minute narrated route from the Library of Congress to the Washington Cathedral, including a stop in Georgetown. (Tickets available at the Old Post Office, Union Station, or hotels; trolleys run daily 9am-5:30pm. Tours $14, children $5.)

Other companies run specialized tours. **Scandal Tours** (783-7212) hires actors who impersonate disgraced politicians as they steer tourists from one place of infamy to the next. In good weather, the 75-minute tour stops at Gary Hart's townhouse, Watergate, and the Vista Hotel (where Mayor Barry was caught with his pants down)—fare $27. Capitol Entertainment Services (636-9203) runs standard tours of major sights, but specializes in a three-hour **Black History Tour** through Lincoln Park, Anacostia, and the Frederick Douglass home. (Tours begin from area hotels. Adults $15, children ages 5-12 $10.)

The U.S. Capitol

*It is natural enough to suppose that the center and
heart of America is the Capitol, and certainly, in its
outward aspect, the world has not many statelier or
more beautiful edifices...*
— *Nathaniel Hawthorne, 1862*

Hawthorne was no rube. The U.S. Capitol (House 225-3121; Senate 224-3121) may
no longer be America's, or even Washington's, most beautiful building, but its scale
and style still evoke the power of the republic. (Metro: Capitol South or Union Station.)
The Capitol's symmetries suggest the republic's checks and balances (or maybe a tug-
of-war between House and Senate). There are two wings, two fronts, and no back
(since all DC street coordinates begin from the compass stone in the crypt). The three-
tiered **East Front** faces the Supreme Court. From Jackson (1829) to Carter (1977),
most Presidents were inaugurated here; Reagan moved the ceremony to the newly
fixed-up **West Front,** which overlooks the Mall, a fountain and pool, a grassy plaza,
and steps and steps and steps. If there's a U.S. flag over the House wing (to your left as
you face the East Front), the House of Representatives is in session; a flag over the Senate wing (to your right) says that the Senate is too. At another, less prominent location,
harried Congressional employees raise and lower dozens of flags every day to fill constituent requests for a flag once flown above the Capitol.

Amateur architect William Thornton won a design-the-Capitol competition in 1793;
feisty expert designer Benjamin Latrobe assessed and reassembled the interior after
Congress arrived here in 1800. The British burned down the whole shebang in 1814.
The mellower Charles Bulfinch replaced Latrobe in 1818, finishing the Capitol's central section. When Congress ran out of office space around 1850, President Fillmore
tapped dome-head Thomas U. Walter to expand the edifice and erect the Rotunda.
Since then, the office of Architect of the Capitol has grown in some ways (the current
holder approves anything built within a few blocks), shrunk in others (the Capitol has
stopped expanding, so all it needs are periodic facelifts). The Capitol also regulates DC
architecture more directly: nothing built in Washington can be taller than the tip of the
dome. It's the law. Anyone glad that DC's lobbyists haven't built Manhattan-style skyscrapers has the Capitol to thank. (The Washington Monument has nothing to do with
the height limit, contrary to popular error. Neither does the National Cathedral.)

Bulfinch built the first Capitol Dome of copper-plated wood. He built big, but not big
enough for the expanded House and Senate sections; Walter, assisted by Montgomery
Meigs, executed the current cast-iron hemisphere in the 1860s. If there's light in the
dome by night, Congress is still meeting. Atop the whole edifice stands Thomas Craw-
ford's "Freedom"; her feathered helmet was a last-minute substitute for the planned
long cap worn by freed Roman slaves and French Revolutionaries. The cap was nixed
by then-Sec. of War (and future Confederate honcho) Jefferson Davis, who deemed it
an Abolitionist symbol.

*The illuminated rotunda looks fine. I like to stand
aside and look a long, long while up at the dome; it
comforts me somehow.*
— *Walt Whitman,* Specimen Days

The public entrance is through the East Front. Look up to see a possibly incongruous
trio of women—America, Hope, and Justice. (President John Quincy Adams wouldn't
let Hercules, a heathen, join them.) You will have to walk through a metal detector and
have your bags x-rayed. Through the East Portico, scrutinize Randolph Rogers's huge,
bronze **Columbus Doors**. The doors mimic Ghiberti's "Gates of Paradise" doors in
Florence, but substitute Columbus' biography for the Bible.

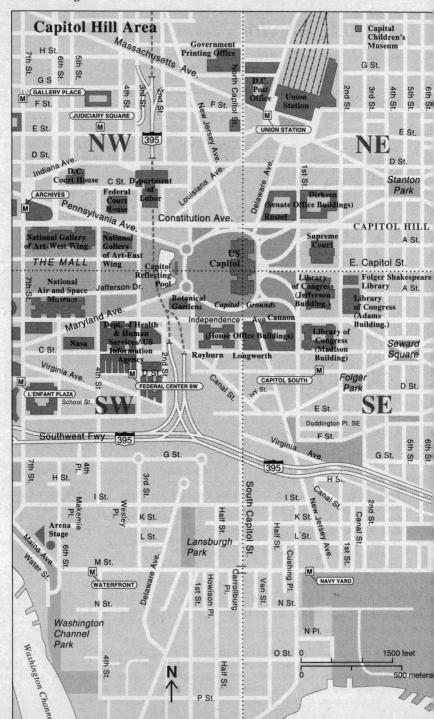

Capitol Hill Area

NW

NE

SW

SE

Massachusetts Ave.

H St.
G S
F St.
E St.
D St.

7th St.
6th St.
5th St.
4th St.
3rd St.
2nd St.

GALLERY PLACE

JUDICIARY SQUARE

395

Indiana Ave.

D.C. Court House

ARCHIVES

Pennsylvania Ave.

Federal Court House

National Gallery of Art-West Wing

National Gallery of Art-East Wing

THE MALL

National Air and Space Museum

Jefferson Dr.

C St.
D St.
Department of Labor

Constitution Ave.

Government Printing Office

North Capitol St.

New Jersey Ave.

F St.

D.C. Post Office

Union Station

UNION STATION

Louisiana Ave.

Delaware Ave.

Dirksen
(Senate Office Buildings)
Russel

Supreme Court

US Capitol

Capitol Reflecting Pool

Botanical Gardens

Capitol Grounds

Independence Ave.

Maryland Ave.

Dept. of Health & Human Services/ US Information Agency

Nasa

C St.

Virginia Ave.

L'ENFANT PLAZA

School St.

2nd St.

D St.

FEDERAL CENTER SW

(House Office Buildings)

Rayburn   Longworth

Cannon

Library of Congress (Jefferson Building)

Library of Congress (Adams Building)

Library of Congress (Madison Building)

Folger Shakespeare Library

CAPITOL SOUTH

Ivy. St.

E St.

Duddington Pl. SE

F St.

Virginia Ave.

395

Southwest Fwy.

395

G St.

7th St.
4th Pl.
Makemie Pl.
Wesley Pl.
3rd St.
Half St.

H St.
I St.
K St.
L St.

Arena Stage

6th St.

M St.

WATERFRONT

N St.

Delaware Ave.

Lansburgh Park

1st St.
Howison Pl.
Carrollburg Pl.
Van St.
Cushing Pl.

South Capitol St.

Half St.

H St.
I St.
K St.
L St.

NAVY YARD

2nd St.
Canal St.
1st St.

New Jersey Ave.

Canal St.

Washington Channel Park

4th St.

Maine Ave.

Water St.

Washington Channel

N
N St.
O St.
P St.
N Pl.

Half St.

Capital Children's Museum

G St.

2nd St.
3rd St.
4th St.
5th St.
6th St.

E St.

D St.

Stanton Park

CAPITOL HILL

A St.

E. Capitol St.

A St.

Seward Square

Folger Park

D St.

5th St.
6th St.

0   1500 feet
0   500 meters

Inside the doors, the 180-foot-high, 96-foot-wide **Rotunda** stretches and yawns. The *grisaille* (brown-and-white) frieze around the dome is mostly by Constantino Brumidi, who died three months after falling off his scaffold in 1877; in the overhead "The Apotheosis of George Washington," GW is bitten by a giant allegory as Liberty, Victory, 13 states and countless virtues (all female) attend. Eight big paintings hang below the fresco, four by John Trumbull, including "The Signing of the Declaration of Independence," which graced the ill-fated $2 bill. Busts of Presidents and others (Martin Luther King Jr.) stare up at the art. (Lincoln's head has no left ear— the sculptor claimed to represent Lincoln's unfinished life.) Statesmen from Lincoln to JFK have lain in state in the Capitol's center; at Minnesota Sen. Hubert Humphrey's service, on national TV, President Carter called him "Hubert Horatio Hornblower." Think of the Rotunda not as an art gallery but as a book of national myths, a collection of America's most self-flattering ideas. The best Rotunda-inspired work is probably William Carlos Williams' poem "It Is A Living Coral"—look it up beforehand if you dig modern poetry.

The Capitol sees over 25,000 visitors a day. Most get lost. The 19th-century design yields little logic and less help for disoriented tourists, so be an oriented one instead: pick up a map from the tour desk in the Rotunda. The desk is also the place to sign up for a **tour:** free guided tours begin here daily every 20 min. or so from 9am to 3:45pm. Ceremony and confusion reign downstairs in the Crypt area; most of the functioning rooms are upstairs from the Rotunda. If you lose your head and can't find your way, try asking one of the 1200 Capitol police: they may not be tour guides, but they know their way around.

Just south of the Rotunda is **Statuary Hall**, the first meeting place of the House of Representatives. The House changed rooms when embarrassed Members realized their chamber was also an echo chamber: stand at one edge, and you can hear anything whispered at the opposite edge. (John Quincy Adams figured this out early— the old weasel used to "sleep" at his desk while listening to his enemies converse.) In July 1864 Congress invited each state to install statues of its two most famous natives. By 1933, 65 figures threatened to cave the Hall's floor in, and the limit was rolled back to one head per state. Just 38 statues now adorn the round room.

Both the **Old Senate Chamber** and the **Old Supreme Court Chamber** were restored for the 1976 bicentennial celebration. The Old Senate Chamber is on the second (and principal) floor of the Capitol. Its door opens off the right hand side of the corridor north of the Rotunda. The comparatively modest old room might remind you of a time when oratory from the Senate floor actually mattered.

The Old Supreme Court Chamber, where the Supremes met until they got their own building across the street, is on the first floor (not the crypt level). It's another beautiful, well-fixed-up old room, this time with a more sinister history: in 1806, the ceiling handed down its opinion on architect Latrobe's assistant, crushing him when he tried to move blocks before the masonry had dried. Though it wasn't his fault, Latrobe never got over the shame.

Around the Capitol's first floor, there's plenty more worth seeing—two centuries of accumulated splendor deck the Capitol's formal sections with columns, arches, deep colors, rich patterns, nice rugs, and/or gold trim. In the downstairs **Crypt area,** souvenir counters and offices compete for attention with milling visitors. The crypt itself was built to house George Washington's body; the state of Virginia blocked the exhumation, and the tomb has stayed empty since.

There are two basic ways to see **Congress** in action. For a spectacle, but little insight, climb to the **House and Senate visitors galleries.** Americans should request a gallery pass (valid for the whole 2-year session of Congress) from the office of their Representative, Delegate or Senator: show up at his/her office or write weeks in advance. Foreign nationals should ask for a pass from the Office of the House Doorkeeper or the Senate Sergeant at Arms. Signs festoon the circuitous route to the galleries, and the Capitol's cops will prevent you from straying. In the ceremony-laden House and Senate chambers (in separate wings of the Capitol), expect a few bored-looking elected officials failing to listen to the person on the podium, who is sometimes speaking for the exclusive benefit of home-district cable TV viewers. Former House Speaker Tip O'Neill once ordered a cameraman to pan the empty chamber while an especially obnoxious Congressman was speaking, thus showing TV-land that the man was orating into the void. Snazzy desks and lecterns at the center of each semicircular chamber are reserved for the chamber's leadership. The Vice President technically presides over the Senate, though he rarely shows up; the Senate Majority Leader is actually in charge. The Speaker of the House, called "Mister Speaker," presides over the House. In the Senate chamber, notice the elementary-school flavor of the Senators' desks. The bigger, more ornate House chamber packs in all of official Washington every January for the President's annual, televised State of the Union Address. If you're lucky, there may be a vote or an argument; if the House or Senate isn't in session, all you'll see are ornate auditoria. Congress has grown too big, and its issues too complex, for floor debates to accomplish much.

The real business of Congress is conducted in **committee hearings,** all over the Capitol and the House and Senate office buildings. Most hearings are open to the public. Check the *Washington Post's* "Today in Congress" box, somewhere in the paper's A-section. Then go to the assigned rooms of the hearings that look interesting. Congressfolk sit at tables across from you, not two stories below you; rather than conduct pompous ceremonies, they debate, inquire, and consider facts and laws. Keep in mind that especially interesting hearings can get crowded, and that most hearing rooms don't have many seats. You may even get a sense of the committee members' personalities, something unavailable from TV news.

A third way to find out what Congress does is to wander around the Capitol's office space. You'll see a few real Congresspeople and plenty of important-looking imitations. Look at what offices are busy or see what you can overhear. American citizens will surely be well-received at the office of their Representative or Senator, though your chances of seeing the Member him-or-herself are slight. (A majority of Members have public offices in House or Senate office buildings, outside the Capitol itself—this may be your excuse to ride the Capitol subway.) Representatives (more than Senators) try to stay popular through constituent services, like phoning Social Security on a harried voter's behalf. Basement perks and shops in the Capitol and the House and Senate offices are generally open only to Members, who guard their privacy well. One favorite Congressional perk is the Members-only House gym, where Democrats and Republicans alike try to get 6'7" former pro standout Tom McMillan (D-Maryland) to play on their basketball team. (The basement of the Capitol itself once held a blacksmith shop, a water reservoir, and an 800-ton coal vault to keep the Members warm.)

Some unmarked rooms on the Senate side of the Capitol are used by Senators as private "hideaways." The Senate Rules Committee doles out by seniority these secret second offices; some are just oversized closets, but the best (Sen. Daniel Patrick Moynihan's (D-N.Y.), for example) are roomy, furnished offices where the Senator spends plenty of time working incommunicado. Only janitors and senators know where the hideaways are—any unmarked door could have a Senator inside. They're used to being interrupted for directions, which doesn't mean you should wander around opening doors in search of hideaways (unless you just love the Capitol Police). While most legislators use their hideaways as a second office, legends remain that these lairs have often been put to less forthright uses.

The **Senate Cafeteria**, on the second (main) floor on the Senate side of the building, is open to the public. Walk down the hallway north of the Rotunda, and you will see the cafeteria near the end of the public hallway on your right. A snack bar in the Capitol basement provides less food for less money in less time. Also in the basement is the free **Capitol subway**, which shunts Senators, Representatives, staffers, and lucky tourists between the House and Senate office buildings and the Capitol itself. If you hear a buzzer or see a red light flash, stay out of the subway and watch the Members rush to the floor for an imminent vote.

The Capitol is open daily 9am to 4:30pm, Memorial Day through Labor Day daily 9am to 8pm. Tours and special assistance for **visitors with disabilities** are available from the Special Services Office in the central first floor area known as the "crypt" (or during opening hours call 224-4048, TDD 224-4049). Tours cover the rotunda, the downstairs crypt area, and sometimes Statuary Hall.

Outside the West Front of the Capitol, at 1st St. NW, the 1922 **Grant Memorial** stands encircled and outmaneuvered by driveways and barricades. General Ulysses S. Grant, whose willingness to sustain huge losses led the Union Army to victory, contemplates war morosely in his battered uniform. Seven horsemen charge to the north, while three horses strain and tug a cannon through mud to the south. Henry Shared took 21 years to design the 252-foot-long memorial, praised today—by those who notice it—as a realistic monument to the arduous and terrible aspects of battle.

Capitol Hill

With the National Tourist Mecca, Congress, and the President to the west, and the city's worst slums to the south, Capitol Hill seems incongruously friendly; its townhouse-filled center (around East Capitol St. between 2nd St. and 11th St. NE/SE) gracefully accommodates blue-collar, white-collar, Black, Hispanic, Asian, and white people, and lawyers. Restored townhouses abut buildings in less happy conditions, and Jaguars mix freely with humbler autos. Close to the Capitol building, most pedestrians are congressional and government workers whose silk power ties connote self-importance. East of 2nd St., corner drugstores, grocery stores, and a diner (Jimmy T's) relax with the residents amid trees and lawns. You may even spot a few Congresspeople driving home, though their aides are more likely to live here than the Members themselves.

Safety in the neighborhood is indeed something of a concern; here as nowhere else, blocks can change character abruptly. Be aware of your surroundings, human and architectural. Avoid the areas east of Lincoln Park or south of Pennsylvania Ave. SE (except along 8th St.). After events at RFK Stadium, raging hordes of concertgoers proceed westward down East Capitol St.; don't be afraid to join them.

Capitol Hill's approximate boundaries are North and South Capitol Streets on the west, H St. NE on the north, RFK Stadium on the east, and the Southeast-Southwest Freeway on the south. Major sights cluster close to the Capitol building itself, including the Library of Congress, the Folger Shakespeare Library, and the Supreme Court. At dusk, head for the bars and restaurants that line Pennsylvania Ave. between 2nd St. and 7th St. SE.

The Supreme Court

The Supreme Court Building, One 1st St. NE (479-3000), across from the East Front of the Capitol Building, houses the nation's highest court. (Metro: Capitol South or Union Station.) Its nine justices are the final interpreters of the U.S. Constitution and have the power to overturn laws which go against it. Enter through the main entrance on 1st St. Architect Cass Gilbert executed the faux-Greek temple in American marble; the Court moved in in 1935. The atrium is a columned chamber sporting busts of former Chief Justices. Straight in front as you come in, literally behind the red curtain, is the Supreme Court Chamber, where the court meets to hear cases.

When the court is in session (October through June), it hears oral arguments Monday to Wednesday from 10am to 3pm for two weeks each month. Attorneys get only a half-hour each to make arguments and field questions from the Nine—conservative Justice Scalia supposedly asks the most, and the hardest, questions. There is no jury: the Supreme Court, like any appeals court, doesn't decide facts, just interprets the laws and the Constitution. Arguments are open to the public and first-come, first-served. If you show up too late to be seated, walk through the standing gallery to hear five minutes of the argument. Try to hear one; the *Washington Post*'s A-section can tell you if the court is sitting and what case they plan to hear. Tourists can hoof through the courtroom when the Justices go on vacation. In July and August, brief courtroom lectures, every hour on the half hour between 9:30am and 3:30pm, cover the history, operations, duties and architecture of the Court and its building.

The excitement continues below the court, where a videotape delivers an intelligent summary of U.S. legal history; think about the 1803 *Marbury v. Madison*, which empowered the Supreme Court to ditch unconstitutional statutes; *Dred Scott v. Sandford*, its worst decision ever; and *Brown v. Board of Education,* which desegregated public schools. The Main Exhibit Hall spews changing exhibits under the eyes of a seated, stone-faced Chief Justice John Marshall, author of *Marbury v. Madison.* The wall behind Marshall quotes his famous decisions. Walls outside the exhibit hall hold portraits of associate (non-Chief) justices. Their anonymity shows how the Court's members, compared to (say) senators, got relatively little public attention before the past few years of confirmation fights over conservative nominees Bork, Souter, Thomas *et al.* The lower level also houses a standard government **snack bar** (open 10:30am-3:30pm) and **cafeteria** (open 7:15am-10:30am and 11:30am-2pm). (Court open Mon.-Fri. 9am-4:30pm. Free.)

Library of Congress

The Library of Congress, 1st St. SE (707-5000, recorded events schedule 707-8000), between East Capitol and Independence Ave., has surpassed its original mission—to be Congress's library—and its second mission—to be the nation's library. (Metro: Capitol South.) Its current aspirations are global: it wants to be the world's library, a great repository of mankind's accumulated knowledge, with "all answers stored in a single place." The library is already the world's largest, with 20 million books and over 60 million other holdings, including Stradivarius violins, newsreels, periodicals, and phonograph records. Less than a quarter of the 20 million books are in English; most aren't even in the Roman alphabet, but in Arabic, Chinese, Japanese or other scripts.

The original library was founded in 1800, when Congress began to assemble mostly law and history books for members' personal use. The British torched them all in 1814, so Congress bought Thomas Jefferson's personal collection (6847 volumes) and started over. An 1870 copyright law guaranteed the Library a free copy of every book the United States registered, and the L of C took off. The Library occupies three buildings: the 1897 Beaux-Arts Jefferson Building, which hogs the display space; the 1939 Adams Building, across 2nd St.; and the 1980 Madison Building, a marble slab across Independence Ave. that is the largest office building in Washington, with 36 acres of floor space.

The best way to see the library is to have some research to do. All of the vast collection, including rare items, are open to anyone college age or above with a legitimate research purpose. It's a closed stack library, so they will bring the books to you. It's also a non-circulating library, so you must do your reading there. If you have no grand dissertation in the works, but still want to look at a few books, the attendants won't give you a hard time.

Those not in search of rare printed matter can still take the tour, which starts in the Madison Memorial Hall, in the Madison Building lobby across from the sales shop. After a brief talk, the tour scuttles through tunnels to the Jefferson Building, otherwise closed for renovations. Corrugated metal in the tunnels conceals a conveyor belt which runs books among the buildings. In the Jefferson Building, the Great Hall expands among grand staircases and ceiling frescoes. The octagonal Main Reading Room, with 236 desks, spreads out under a spectacular dome. Statues march in rows around the room, painted winged figures around the cupola illustrate the "stages of Human Knowledge," and a syncretic statue grafts Lincoln's head and wings onto the body of Rodin's *Thinker.* The floor has the same quiet, important, historic feeling as the House and Senate floors. (Most reading rooms open Mon.-Fri. 8:30am-9:30pm, Sat. 8:30am-5pm, Sun. 1-5pm; call 707-5000 for further information.)

The **Folger Shakespeare Library,** 201 East Capitol St. SE (544-4600), houses the world's largest collection of Shakespeariana. That's about 275,000 books and manuscripts. Unless you've got a Ph. D. and research to do, you can't see them. You can go inside the building, though, and see the Great Hall exhibition gallery, a recreated Tudor gallery with dark oak panels and carved Elizabethan doorways. The Hall houses exhibits on Shakespeare's work, the culture he inspired, and the British society he lived in. The Shakespeare Theater at the Folger is no longer at the Folger; the company, which mostly puts on Shakespeare's plays, has moved downtown to 450 7th St. NW (393-

2700). (See *Entertainment.*) During the day, tourists can peek at the theater itself, which imitates the Elizabethan Inns of Court indoor theaters, like the Blackfriars, where Shakespeare's company performed. (It does *not* imitate the more famous, and several-block-long, Globe Theater.) The Folger also sponsors high-quality readings, lectures, and concerts; call for details. Recurring highlights are the PEN/Faulkner poetry and fiction readings and the Folger Consort, a chamber music group that specializes in Renaissance works and songs. (Exhibits open Mon.-Sat. 10am-4pm; library open Mon.-Sat. 8:45am-4:45pm.)

The **Taft Memorial** stands just northwest of the Capitol on the triangular park between Constitution Ave., New Jersey Ave., and Louisiana Ave. NW. The 1958 statue of former Ohio Senator Robert A. Taft (son of President William Howard Taft) assiduously defends a large, fluted concrete obelisk. Call Taft by his nickname, "Mr. Republican." Twenty-seven bells set into the obelisk ring, like church-chimes, every 15 minutes. Interns hang out and eat lunch around the shallow moat on the low hill near the monument. After lunch, wash your hands in the flower-bedecked, monumental fountain directly north of the Capitol between Constitution Ave. and D St. NW.

Horatio Greenough's statue of a seated, shirtless George Washington, now in the National Museum of American History, once stood outside at South Capitol and E St. SE. The power plant there now incorporates the statue's pedestal, which proved too heavy to drag across the Mall; the inscription "First in War, First in Peace, First in the hearts of his countrymen" supposedly remains legible near the base of one of the power plant's walls.

On 1st St. between Independence Ave. and East Capitol St., the **Fountain of Neptune** is built around three niches in the retaining wall of the Library of Congress's main plaza. You can only see the 1897 fountain from a very narrow swath of sidewalk, but it's well worth the trouble to stop and look. Wildly twisting horses flank the central figure of Neptune, turtles spit water at Nereids (high-class mermaids), Tritons (mermen) recline half-hidden in water, and twisting snakes spit water at you in this homage to Rome's famous Trevi Fountain. Sculptor R. Hinton Perry was only 27 when he finished this marine masterpiece.

Flanking the Capitol grounds on Constitution Ave. between Delaware Ave. and 2nd St. NE, and on Independence Ave. between 1st St. SW and 2nd St. SE, are the **House and Senate Office Buildings.** (Metro: Capitol South.) (Open Mon.-Fri. 8am-7pm and whenever their respective houses of Congress are in session.) The two original buildings, the Cannon House Office Building (named for former Speaker of the House Joseph Cannon of Illinois) and the Russell Senate Office (named for Georgia Senator Richard Russell) were built in 1908 and 1909; both designed by the team of Carrere and Hastings. Two additional buildings on each side have been built since—the Longworth and Rayburn House Office Buildings and the Dirksen and Hart Senate Office Buildings.

These office buildings are hardly designed for tourists—they're needed partly because so much space in the Capitol *is* designed for tourists. Nevertheless, energetic patriots could learn a lot about how Congress works by walking through one of the buildings. House and Senate leaders command good behavior partly by controlling who gets what office; when Minnesota's freshman Sen. Paul Wellstone drove his schoolbus here to be sworn in, he angered the leadership by parking it in the Congressional lot, and consequently picked up the Senate's worst office. American citizens can find the offices of their Congresspersons without much trouble; consult the directories posted near all entrances and elevators. Once there, show proof of residence in your state and district and obtain passes to the House and Senate galleries and free information about some Washington sights. In the basement of each building is an inexpensive cafeteria open to the public during lunch hours (approximately 11am to 3pm weekdays), although access may be restricted at times to allow workers to eat more quickly. (The Rayburn Building also holds the House gym.) Check the signs posted outside each cafeteria for more information. Unless you're hearing bells (calling Senators and Representatives for a vote), you can ride the underground subway to the Capitol. Don't forget to gawk at the number of people trying to look terribly important.

Twentieth-century sculptor Alexander Calder's last work, *Mountains and Clouds,* takes up nine stories of the Hart Senate Office Building's atrium (on Constitution Ave. NE between 1st and 2nd St.). Calder died in 1976, the night after he met with architects in DC to work out the sculpture's details; the $650,000 sculpture was not completed until 1986. You can view the sculpture in its natural light from the ground floor or from the various open balconies in the building. The stable black "mountains," sculpted from sheet metal, weigh 39 tons; the mobile "clouds," made from aircraft aluminum, weigh 4300lbs. A computer controls the mobile's rotation.

Nestled up beside the Dirksen building is the **Sewall-Belmont House,** 144 Constitution Ave. NE (546-3989), one of the oldest houses in Washington and the one-time headquarters of the National Woman's Party (NWP). (Metro: Union Station.) Today the floors upstairs are a museum of the U.S. women's movement. In the entrance hall, look for busts of Susan B. Anthony, Lucretia Mott, and Elizabeth Cady Stanton. Seek out the "life-sized" statue of Joan of Arc. Friendly and knowledgeable guides will tell you all about the house, women's suffrage, and the Equal Rights movement. The museum boosts Alice Paul relentlessly, which is only fair; after all, she founded the National Woman's Party and wrote the Equal Rights Amendment back in 1923. You can see her quarters on the tour of the house, along with the banner she used to picket the White House for suffrage in 1917 and photographs of the activities of the NWP in the 1930s and '40s. (House open Tues.-Fri. 11am-3pm, Sat.-Sun. noon-4pm.) Go up the staircase and ring the bell for service; tours are unscheduled and informal.

Two blocks north of the Capitol grounds, the trains run on time at **Union Station,** 50 Massachusetts Ave. NE (371-9441 for general information). Walk northeast down Delaware Ave. from the Capitol, or take the Metro to the Union Station stop. Daniel Burnham's much-admired, monumental Beaux-Arts design took four strenuous years (1905-1908) to erect. Colonnades, archways, and huge domed ceilings equate Burnham's Washington with imperial Rome and the then-dominant train network with Roman roads. (Remember it from the shootout in *The Untouchables?*) After repeated remodelings and bizarre misuses (like a "national visitors center") throughout the 60s and 70s, Union Station has become a spotless ornament in the crown of capitalism, with a food court, chic stores and mall rats aplenty. If you have time, start reading the many inscriptions around the exterior: "Fire—Greatest of Discoveries," "The Truth Shall Make You Free," and "A Man Must Carry Knowledge With Him if He Is To Bring Home Knowledge" cap the eclectic list of Burnham's favorite profundities. The station's East Hall wall tracings copy examples from Pompeii, while its more than 120 shops and stores run the gamut from clothes to books and toys. The National Map Gallery rejoices in its extensive collection of *Let's Go* travel guides and carries maps so detailed you can almost see yourself on them. The Great Train Store robs railroad buffs of their window-shopping hours. (Retail shops open Mon.-Sat. 10am-9pm, Sunday noon-6pm.) The cavernous American Multi-Cinema operates nine movie theaters on the station's lower level near the Metro entrance. (Call 842-3757 for cinema information.) Once outside the station, look for the colorful Aztec-style mural. For food inside, see *Food*; for train information, see *Getting Here.*

Directly west of Union Station across 1st St. is the **City Post Office** (842-3812), another Burnham Beaux-Arts building, finished in 1914. (Metro: Union Station.) Italian marble and granite constitute the exterior, whose façade-obscuring scaffolds just might come down sometime in 1993. The post office still operates (through rain, snow, sleet, and renovations); enter on North Capitol St. (Open Mon.-Fri. 7am-midnight, Sat.-Sun. 7am-8pm.)

Further down on North Capitol is the **Government Printing Office** (512-0132), a large building in finely worked dark red brick. (Metro: Union Station.) The GPO contracts out most of the government's printing needs, but still prints thousands of federal documents yearly, in addition to postcards, passports, and civil service exams. Plant tours ended in the 60s, when someone realized that the electric forklifts, hot molten lead and six-foot pneumatic knives could hurt someone. To visit the bookstore, enter on the North Capitol St. side of the building. The GPO stocks what the government prints; there are Washington guidebooks, studies of U.S. history, and entertaining tomes only the U.S. Government could produce, e.g. *Design of Small Dams, Perspectives on John*

Philip Sousa, and the *Amateur-Built Aircraft Flight Testing Handbook.* You may find the government *Advisory Circulars,* the foreign country guides, or the military *Back Yard Mechanics* books actually useful. Across the hall, the **Congressional Sales Office** sells things Congress prints; the *Congressional Record* sold out in one day when a conservative Senator, debating a bill to ban pornographic 900 numbers, inserted the text of some steamy recordings into his speech. (Both stores open Mon.-Fri. 8am-5pm.)

Northeast of Union Station is the **Capital Children's Museum,** 800 3rd St. NE (675-4127), a large red-brick building that looks like a city school. (Metro: Union Station.) Enter on 3rd St. between H and Eye St. NE. Release your Smithsonian-induced tension by touching and feeling every exhibit in this huge interactive experiment of a museum. Walk through the life-size cave or try your luck at making a simple Zoetrope cartoon movie. Learn how a printing press works by printing a simple plate yourself. In the video studio, dance to music and see your image displayed or distorted on television. A model town lets children play in a miniature community complete with a bus to drive, a manhole to climb down, and a working telephone system. Also in the museum is a two-story mock-up of a Mexican Plaza; the environs, designed by Rolf Naugahyde, feature a burial site, Spanish street signs, and a place to make your own tortillas. If you're in a hurry, go first to the Mexico exhibit, the mock-up town, and the room-size maze. Because the museum is independently funded, some equipment is outdated (like the Atari 800 computers) or broken. Thus, you gotta pay to go inside. (Open daily 10am-5pm. Admission $6, children under 2 free. All children must be accompanied by an adult.)

Three blocks southeast from Union Station, down Massachusetts Ave. NE, **Stanton Park** offers benches, lots of shade, and a playground with a black rubber floor. An eclectic mix of white-collar lunchers, homeless loungers, and children playing on the playground will give you an instant sense of Capitol Hill's diversity. The park's visual anchor is a skillful equestrian statue of Nathanial Greene, Esq., a Revolutionary War Major General. Greene rides along in Continental uniform, complete with tri-cornered hat and fringed shoulder epaulets. A 1930 windstorm blew the statue off its pedestal, landing Greene, and his horse, standing on their heads in the park.

When he first moved to Washington after the Civil War, the famous abolitionist, orator, autobiographer, and African-American statesman **Frederick Douglass** lived at 316-318 A St. NE, two blocks east of the Supreme Court. Once the site of the Smithsonian Museum of African Art, the three-story grey house is now closed to the public; the museum moved to the mall, and Douglass is remembered at his larger, later home in Anacostia. The building is currently under renovation to restore it to its 1850's lustre; it will become the full-fledged Frederick Douglass Museum when restoration is completed in 1993.

From the Capitol Building, stroll east on East Capitol St. to see neighborhood life in an upscale part of Capitol Hill. A ten-block walk from the Capitol will bring you straight to the two-block square **Lincoln Park**, a good peoplewatching spot during the day. (As with all parks downtown, it becomes dangerous at night.) One statue remembers Abraham Lincoln as the Great Emancipator; another memorial, the only statue of a Black woman in DC, depicts Mary McLeod Bethune, who founded the National Council of Negro Women. The Lincoln statue was supposedly constructed solely through contributions from former slaves.

Barracks Row

To get a taste of SE Washington, try walking down 8th Street SE from the Eastern Market Metro to the Navy Yard, a stretch sometimes known as "Barracks Row." The area is properly a part of Capitol Hill, but it has a "Southeast" feel that is very different than the feeling you get walking around the Capitol and its environs. Barracks Row is usually safe during the day, but don't walk alone at night. The end of the walk will reward you with the Navy Yard.

The **Marine Barracks**, 8th and Eye St. SE (433-6060), house what are nicknamed the "Eighth and Eye Marines." The head of the Marine Corps dwells at one end of the parade ground, in a house built all the way back in 1806 (the British spared it when they torched DC in 1814). The Barracks also houses "The President's Own," the Marine Corps marching band John Philip Sousa led from 1880-92. The band now totes its Sousaphones on international tours. The infantry here, though they served in the Gulf, are mostly here for ceremony; they march at Arlington Cemetery, stand around at White House ceremonies, and guard Camp David, the President's retreat. The Eighth and Eye men and women strut their pomp at the **Friday evening parade**, at 8:45pm every Friday, May through August (see *Annual Events*).

Navy Yard

Three museums—and a destroyer you can board—stay shipshape among the booms at the Washington Navy Yard. (Metro: Navy Yard.) Enter from the gate at 9th and M St. SE, and ask directions or look at the clear maps posted near the entrance. The best of the lot, the **Navy Museum,** Building 76 (433-4882), should buoy up anyone let down by the admire-but-don't-touch Air & Space Museum on the Mall. Climb inside the space capsule, play Human Cannonball inside huge (deactivated, we assume) ship guns (3-inch, 50-caliber), jam yourself into a bathysphere used to explore the sea floor, or give orders on the bridge. *Alvin* and *Trieste* undersea vehicles hang from the ceiling next to Navy airplanes. Model ships find the museum smooth sailing; the American craft are up to 14 feet long, and their anachronistic opponents include a 1916 Austro-Hungarian warship and a Greek trireme. Fondle the life-size replicas of "Little Boy" and "Fat Man," the atomic bombs detonated over Japan at the close of WWII. A small gift shop offers souvenirs, including inexpensive sailors' hats. (Open June-Aug. Mon.-Fri. 9am-5pm, Sat.-Sun. 10am-5pm; Sept.-May Mon.-Fri. 9am-4pm, Sat.-Sun. 10am-5pm.)

Technology steams on at the unpretentious **Museum Annex** (same hours and phone as Navy Museum). The Annex is "just" a small building full of old submarines. The *Intelligent Whale* was a hand-propelled sub (!) the Navy bought in 1869. Run your hands along the *Seehund*, a well-designed mini-sub the Nazis used for coastal defense in the last days of World War II.

The *USS Barry*, a decommissioned destroyer docked a few steps from the Navy Museum, opens to the public daily 10am-5pm (no relation to the decommissioned DC mayor). Dig the decoy used during anti-submarine operations—it's a large motor which sailors threw overboard and dragged behind the ship so that noise-honing torpedoes would strike it instead of the ship's hull. You'll also get to walk through berths, control rooms, the bridge, the Captain's quarters, and the combat center. The small mess room, the largest open area in the ship, will give you boundless sympathy for the men (still no women, thanks to backward Navy restrictions) who have to live cooped up in one of these machines for months at a time. Kids will squeeze with glee up the cramped staircases.

The **Marine Corps Historical Museum,** Building 58 (433-3534), marches through Marine Corps time from the American Revolution to the present. Twenty exhibit cases tout the actions, guns, uniforms, and swords of Marines from the halls of Montezuma to the shores of Kuwait. A miscellany of Marine mementos, like the flag immortalized on Iwo Jima, dot the halls; a recent exhibit on the Persian Gulf war held captured Iraqi uniforms, explanations of battle strategy, guns, motorcycles, and lots of photographs. The museum presents an immortal antinomy: to "preserve freedom," sometimes you have to kill people. You might even talk about it, politely, with the Marines who will doubtless be perusing the exhibits next to you. (Open Mon.-Thurs. and Sat. 10am-4pm, Fri. 10am-8pm, Sun. noon-5pm; Sept.-May Mon.-Sat. 10am-4pm, Sun. noon-5pm)

The **Navy Art Gallery,** building 67 (433-3815), is a single, small gallery room with paintings of Naval action on the walls, all painted by "combat artists." These specialized artists sailed, ate canned rations, and braved gunfire with the sailors, all to record with paint and canvas the action on board. (Open Wed.-Sun. 9am-4pm.)

Smithsonian Museums

The Smithsonian is the catalogued attic of the United States. Words that might describe this country—grand, hegemonic, diverse—easily fit its mammoth museum and research institution as well. The world's largest museum complex stretches out along Washington's longest lawn, the Mall. Other exhibits are displayed in Anacostia, up Connecticut Ave. at the National Zoo, and in New York City at the Cooper-Hewitt Museum of Design and the National Museum of the American Indian; scientific branches classify and investigate from Panama to Nepal to Arizona. Smithsonian curators manage over 136 million objects, most of which you'll never see. Scientists and historians worldwide take an interest in the millions of beetles, thousands of works of art, and hundreds of airplanes that make the Smithsonian Institution outstanding in science as well as tourism. These same collections mean that the Smithsonian can assemble almost any exhibit it chooses: individual halls and chambers may tout gleaming minerals, orbital satellites, teenage fashion, or models by Rodin. Tourists throng the Mall to see the dinosaurs at Natural History, the Apollo XI capsule at Air & Space, and the luminous triangles of the East Wing building—many don't budget enough time to see much else. The clueful visitor will use at least three days to roam the ten Smithsonian buildings on the Mall, then return to his or her favorite museum; almost anything the Smithsonian chooses to show could send some visitor into hours of analytical rapture.

The Smithsonian began as the grand-spirited idea of an English scientist, James Smithson. The chemist had never visited America, but his will left 105 bags of gold sovereigns to "found at Washington, under the name of the Smithsonian Institution, an establishment for the increase and diffusion of knowledge among men." (Had Smithson's nephew had children, they would have inherited the gold instead.) Congress voted to take the money, British though it was, in 1835. The red-brick, Victorian "Castle" was institutionalized in 1855 as the Smithsonian's first permanent home; bachelor scientists boarded there along with the growing collections. The baroque Arts and Industries Building, the second-oldest, opened its doors to President Garfield's inaugural ball in 1881; the rest of the Mall splits neatly into domed neoclassical sprawl (Natural History, West Wing, Freer) and smooth, geometric modernity (Air & Space, East Wing, American History, Hirshhorn). Since 1980, new museums have had to hide below ground, casualties of space limitations. The Sackler Gallery and African Art Museums, for example, sprawl under stone entrance pavilions behind the Castle.

Orientation and Practical Information

Eleven Smithsonian buildings flank the Mall. On the north side, to the left as you face the Capitol, are the National Gallery of Art's East Wing (closest to the Capitol) and West Wing, the National Museum of Natural History, and the National Museum of American History. Closest to the Capitol on the right is the National Air & Space Museum, then the Hirshhorn, then the Arts & Industries Building (which houses the experimental gallery). The red Smithsonian Castle hides the Sackler Gallery and the National Museum of African Art in its dainty backyard garden. The renovated Freer Gallery, to re-open in May of 1993, completes the lineup of museums. At the southwest corner of the Mall, the Department of Agriculture invades Smithsonian territory with its offices, built in 1930s Federalist massiveness. Constitution Ave. (on the north) and Independence Ave. (on the south) fence the double row of museums; tour-bus-congested Jefferson and Madison Drives run east-west along the Mall itself. The Smithsonian Metro stop isn't always the best way to reach a given museum; L'Enfant Plaza (south of the Mall), Federal Triangle, and Archives (north of it) are often more convenient. Do not even begin to consider parking a private automobile in or north of the Smithsonian complex. You can probably find on-street spaces south of Independence Ave. SW, but caveat conductor: one wrong turn, and you may be irrevocably Virginia- or Anacostia-bound. If you see signs for the SE-SW Freeway, don't follow them.

All Smithsonian museums are free and wheelchair-accessible; all offer written guides in French, German, Spanish, and Japanese with some Chinese, Arabic, and Portuguese ones also available. Smithsonian museums open daily from 10am-5:30pm, with extended summer hours for the larger museums (Air & Space, Natural History; 9:30am-7:30pm); some museums close on winter weekends. Each museum features a gift shop.

Almost every museum has a restaurant, too, but you probably won't want to eat in them; some (Air & Space, American History) are overpriced, standard-fare cafeterias, and the rest (the East Wing) are overpriced cafés. Smithsonian-goers can eat cheapest and fastest from the hot-dog/half-smoke carts along Constitution and Independence Ave. Cavernous, urgently growling stomachs had best guide their possessors to the cafeteria under the National Gallery's West Wing, where the salads, sandwiches, and fruit plates are at least above average.

Allow at least three days to see the Smithsonian, even if you intend to fly through each exhibit on the Mall. The museums would take months to "finish" exploring. Choose the museums whose subjects interest you: too many visitors give up longed-for hours among the airplanes just to say they've seen the Abstract Expressionists (or vice versa). An hour in one museum is better spent than an hour dashing among three. Call 357-2700 (TDD: 357-1729) to contact a Smithsonian operator for information regarding all of the museums. For information on tours, concerts, lectures, films, and performance art, call 357-2020. Information desks in the Castle and at the museums distribute the *Smithsonian Guide for Disabled Visitors*. Most museums have two main entrances, one from the Mall and one from Constitution or Independence Ave.; the latter is often easier for wheelchairs to negotiate. Disabled visitors who call a day before their visit can obtain more extensive literature and assistance. Sight- or hearing-impaired visitors should call 786-2942 (TDD: 786-2414) at least a week in advance for special assistance.

The Mall, the U.S.'s taxpayer-supported national backyard, is a sight—or a recreation—in itself. On any sunny day hundreds of natives and out-of-towners do on it whatever they do in their own yards: sunbathe and lounge, play frisbee or football, knock down their little brothers, go fly a kite, or just get high. The sports-minded in particular may find its green (and frequently brown) acres a relief after hours of walking through refrigerated exhibits. Famous monuments occupy the Western end. Until this century, the Mall was DC's central cipher, a vacant lot in the middle of everything: slave pens occupied the space until the 1850s, and railroad tracks crossed the space at 6th St. Credit the McMillan Commission, which redesigned central Washington in 1901, for the Mall's present harmony and flatness. Near the Hirshhorn on the south side of the Mall, a merry-go-round delights everybody for only $1 a go. Thousands of people with trucks full of musical instruments, local cuisine, and overpriced fruit drinks congregate on the Mall in June and early July for the Festival of American Folklife; don't miss it if it's in session (see *Annual Events*). Other occasional celebrations, like the Fourth of July, swamp the Mall with tents and blankets.

The Smithsonian Castle, 1000 Jefferson Dr. SW (357-2700, Dial-a-Museum recording 357-2020, TDD 357-1729), holds no real exhibits, but it does have information desks, a small theater that continuously plays an impressive if tedious 20-minute introductory movie, and a crypt with James Smithson's body inside. The posh-looking, roped-off hallways lead to offices and services for Associates (who pay annual dues to be "members" of the museum). Glass cases left over from 1976 still demonstrate the history and growth of downtown and the Mall. Postcards mailed from the small 19th-century post office box by the handicapped entrance to the Castle will bear an oversized "Smithsonian" postmark. (Open 9am-5pm daily.)

National Museum of American History

> There is a statue of Washington by Greenough
> which, I believe, is very famous.
> —*A Young Traveller's Journal of A Tour in North
> and South America. (1850)*

Though Henry Ford said "History is bunk," the National Museum of American History (357-2700, TDD: 357-1563) prefers to think that history is junk: several centuries and thousands of artifacts worth of machines, textiles, photographs, vehicles, harmonicas, guns, fiber-optic cable, hats, and uncategorizable American detritus reside here behind plexiglass and plaques. When the Smithsonian inherits a quirky artifact of popular history, like Dorothy's slippers from *The Wizard of Oz* or Archie Bunker's chair, it usually ends up here. The museum, opened in 1964, was renamed the National Museum of History and Technology until 1980, and a certain techno-focus remains evident in halls like "A Material World." Recently the museum has turned politically correct with riveting new exhibits on social and cultural history. The museum's most famous displays are individual objects, like the Star-Spangled Banner; don't let the crowds around them distract you from the more informative halls of everything under the American sun.

Enter the boring rectilinear building from the Mall or from 14th St. and Constitution Ave. NW (Metro: Smithsonian or Federal Triangle). Pick up a map from an information desk and start on one of the end escalators on the top or bottom floor, then work your way clockwise through each floor. If you came in from the Mall, on the second floor, you'll face the swinging Foucault pendulum, which knocks over pegs in a circular pattern, thereby proving that the Earth rotates. When Francis Scott Key, detained on a ship in Baltimore Harbor, saw an American flag fly over Fort McHenry at dawn on Sept. 14, 1814, he knew British invaders had failed to take Baltimore; the elated Key sat down and wrote "The Star-Spangled Banner," our unsingable national anthem. The flag now hangs on the museum's second floor, behind the pendulum, where an opaque cover shields it from light damage—you can see it every hour on the half hour, when the cover is lifted.

From the building's crowded center, visitors can turn left for 20th-century African-American history in "Field to Factory," or right for 18th-century European-American history in "After the (American) Revolution." "Field to Factory" illuminates Black migration from the segregated South to Northern cities like Chicago, Cleveland, and New York between 1915 and 1940. The resettlement more or less created urban African-American culture, laid the foundations for today's Black middle class (and underclass), and generally changed the course of U.S. history and politics. Outside the exhibit entrance, seek the famous "topless" statue of George Washington. Horatio Greenough, in Florence, carved the thing by request of Congress in 1832; the statue was so big the Capitol's doors had to be removed to drag George inside, and so heavy it threatened to collapse the Capitol's floor. The sculpture was reinstalled outdoors, where snow collected in his lap and on his bare chest. The Smithsonian acquired the boondoggle in 1908.

Specialized collections of musical instruments, coins, and military paraphernalia, among other doodads, dominate the third floor. "A More Perfect Union" chronicles the World War II internment of Japanese-Americans in relentless, self-flagellating detail. Mechanical women and men will love the first floor, where entire galleries lavish their plexiglass on electricity, trains, cars, clocks, and power tools. "A Material World" takes over the central first floor, along with the museum bookstore. Electronics reign in "Information Age"; clunky early computers like EDSAC give way to microprocessors and videos and interactive software and whatnot. Unfortunately, R2D2 and C3PO, the cute robots from *Star Wars*, have been removed indefinitely. New permanent collections, such as the American pressed glass exhibit on the west wing of the second floor, and "American Encounters" (the museum's contribution to the quintecentenial of Columbus's big discovery) will figure prominently in the museum's whopping 1993 line-up. They will be joined by such temporary exhibits as "Life in America in the Nineteenth Century," "Science and American Life," and "American Women in War."

The sprawling bookstore on the lower level sells quality Smithsonian jazz and folk records. An old-fashioned, functioning U.S. Post Office and a 1910-style ice cream parlor (located in the Palm Court resting area) also enliven the first floor. The museum hosts year-round special events, including dance, music, lectures. Splendid silent (or sometimes just plain forgotten) films are screened in the Carmichael Auditorium, often for under $5. Grab a schedule at the information station near the first-floor exit. Spend at least three hours here. (Museum open daily 10am-5:30pm; June-Aug. 9:30am-7:30pm. Volunteers staff the information desks from 10am-4pm.)

National Museum of Natural History

The golden-domed Museum of Natural History (357-2700, TDD: 357-1729), built neoclassically in 1911 at 10th and Constitution Ave. (Metro: Smithsonian or Federal Triangle), considers the Earth and life on it in two-and-a-half big, crowded floors of exhibits. As with American History, several hours of gazing time are required to do the halls justice. In Victorian times, "natural history" meant geology and biology; the rarely seen tag "and National Museum of Man" licensed the curators to add anthropology exhibits. (Some displays have women in them, too.) Corridors, cases, dioramas, and hanging specimens reflect the Victorian mania to collect, catalogue, and display. Among the dusty specimens of birds and mammals, and the endless dioramas of "native peoples," you'll find some real jewels: the Hope Diamond, emeralds and rubies, and scampering, iridescent arthropods in the recently-remodeled O. Orkin Insect Zoo.

Inside the stone-floored entrance, the largest African elephant ever captured stands under dome-filtered sunshine in a hubbub of running children and slack-jawed tourists. (Don't feed her—she looks quite stuffed.) Loads of brochures at info desks to the right and left may outweigh the pachyderm herself. Skip the $3 "self-guided audio tour."

Begin at the beginning in the "Early Life" exhibit just to the right of the Mall entrance, behind the information desk. Huge dinosaur skeletons dwarf the nearby hallway, and an intriguing exhibit lets you pretend you're an archaeologist, looking by remote camera at a partially uncovered fossil. Can you remember when dinosaurs were the coolest things in the world? If not, ecstatic kids in this hall will remind you. Across the Rotunda, the revamped Ancient Seas and Sea Life exhibits reel museum-goers in under a blue whale and past a reconstructed coral reef with live coral and tropical critters. Despite their plethora of information, many of the native cultures exhibits (Asian, African, Pacific, South American, and "Native Cultures of the Americas") seem dated, static, and objectifying.

Upstairs, museum-goers worship stocks and stones: the Western Cultures gallery describes the development of ancient civilizations like Egypt and Rome. Hammurabi's code, the earliest set of written laws, regulates via cuneiform letters on a long rock. A modest mummy rests in one piece. The "Human Origin and Variation" gallery spews fascinating anthropological facts, but the galleries of minerals and gems are the real treat. Case after table after case of naturally-occurring crystals from alabaster to zirconite render the final plush room of cut gems anticlimactic, even though it includes the famous (and supposedly cursed) Hope Diamond. On your way through the corridors, get irradiated by the corner displays of fluorescent (glow-in-the-dark) rocks. Also on the second floor, at the end of the "Bones" and "Reptiles" hallways, the popular Insect Zoo pleases entomophiles with an array of live creepy-crawlies, from common and giant cockroaches (active) to exotic millipedes and walking sticks (invisibly still). The tarantula lunches on live crickets in public Monday to Friday at 10:30am, 11:30am, and 1:30pm, weekends and holidays 11:30am, 12:30pm and 1:30pm.

Those who enter the museum from the unpopular Constitution Ave. side get in on the ground floor, where temporary exhibitions strut their stuff. The floor sometimes houses innovative and meticulous displays about a particular culture ("Indonesian Village Worlds") or habitat (rainforests). Sometimes, alas, it's "75 Years of the National Park Service" instead. An escalator hauls visitors up and down from the Rotunda. Through May of 1993 at least, a quincentennial tribute to Christopher Columbus is slated for this room.

Kids can touch nearly everything in the **Discovery Room** (357-2474), hidden beyond the Sea Life at the end of the Hall of North American Mammals. The room proffers a human skeleton and various bones and stones to handle. (Open Mon.-Fri. noon-2:30pm, Sat.-Sun. 10:30am-3:30pm. Closed on major holidays.) **The Naturalist Center** (357-2804), on the ground floor to the right of the Constitution Ave. exit, provides more technical sources; they can also evaluate any "natural history object" you bring with you, though monetary appraisals are Congressionally *verboten*. (Open Mon.-Sat.

10:30am-4pm, Sun. noon-5pm.) Docents give free guided tours daily, at 10:30am and 1:30pm from Sept.-June. (Museum open daily 10am-5:30pm; June-Sept. 9:30am-7:30pm.) You may need a ticket to enter the Naturalist Center, so get one at the door; in the busy season, they usually run out of passes by early afternoon.

National Gallery Of Art: West Building

The National Gallery (737-4215) houses and hangs its world-class jumble of pre-1900 art in a domed marble temple to Western Tradition designed by the Pope himself: John Russell Pope, whose more-reverent-than-thou columns and stairs also accompany the National Archives and Jefferson Memorial. (The *New York Times* called the 1941 building "classicism boiled down to its hardest, toughest essence.") The original, Ionic-styled National Gallery building (now nicknamed the West Wing) was conceived, proposed, financed, and named by financier Andrew Mellon, who realized that other collectors would be more likely to donate to a National Gallery if it didn't bear his name. West Wing and East Wing considered as a whole are North America's most popular art museum, with over six million visitors annually (next is the Metropolitan Museum of Art in NYC, with four million). The West Building holds important work by El Greco, Raphael, Rembrandt, Vermeer, and Monet, to name a few; the "Greek Miracle," a landmark exhibition of classical sculpture from Greece of the Fifth Century BCE, featuring some objects on loan for the first time, is 1993's most important exhibit.

Enter the building from the Mall, or from 6th St. and Constitution Ave. NW (Metro: Archives); if you come in from Constitution Ave., climb the stairs inside. (At the Constitution Ave. portal, see the Zodiac symbols on the outdoor Mellon fountain.) Whichever portal you choose, you'll wind up in the round central "court" under the dome, where black marble pillars and a fountain celebrate the god Mercury. Quench your thirst for information at the relevant desk (to the left if you entered from the Mall). Sculpture-clogged hallways lead east (left) to Italian, Dutch, Spanish, German, and Flemish work, and west (right) to French, British, and finally American painting.

The West Building hangs its canvases in lots of small rooms rather than a few big ones—if you speed from one end of the building to the other, you'll miss seeing most of the paintings. West and East Garden Courts relieve the potential monotony of the Old Masters with fountains, ferns, sunlight, and benches. Leonardo da Vinci's earliest surviving portrait (and the only painting by the artist in the U.S.), *Ginevra de' Benci,* stands in the center of Gallery 6, in the West Wing's startling collection of Italian Renaissance Art. Auguste Renoir's *Girl with a Watering Can,* and other cute French Impressionist pieces hang out in Galleries 85-93, across the rotunda from the Italians. Across the hallway hangs Jacques-Louis David's unusual portrait of Napoleon standing (rather than on horseback). The museum's prize room is a hall of knock-'em-dead Dutch Masters with a few of the world's thirty-odd Vermeers. Early 20th-century American works begin in Gallery 70. Among the highlights are paintings by John Singer Sargent, George Bellows, and Winslow Homer.

The downstairs sculpture, prints and drawings, and temporary galleries lack the scope and sheer numbers of the vast upstairs collection, with its focus on European painting from the 13th century to the early 20th century. Degas' bronze dancers in tutus highlight the sculpture section. Look for Salvador Dali's science-fictional *Last Supper* in the turn of the stairway between the underground concourse and the first floor of the West Wing. Postcards, art books, and high-class cafeteria fare are yours for the money in the basement's museum shop and Garden Café. If you must eat on the Mall, this is probably the place. Even the cheapest connoisseur can exult in the guided tours, "gallery talks," free classical music concerts, and general profusion of special events, whose mercurial schedules are available at the information desk in the rotunda (as well as in the East Wing). Concerts of vocal, piano and chamber music, show up most Sundays Oct.-June at 7pm in the West Garden Court; call 842-6941 to ask about them. Expect to spend at least two hours in the West Building. (Open Mon.-Sat. 10am-5pm, Sun. 11am-6pm, with extended summer hours.)

National Gallery Of Art: East Building

Completed amid much fanfare in 1978, the "East Wing" of the National Gallery of Art (737-4215) houses (and sometimes hides) the museum's plentiful 20th-century holdings. I. M. Pei's celebrated design is the logical outcome of the idea that a building should be a work of art in itself. The smooth marble four-story gallery outlines high, interlocking triangles, glass-topped to flood the atrium with sunlight. On the one hand, the building is at once calming and innovative; it's one work of modern architecture most tourists can unstintingly admire. The design accommodates large-scale works by Alexander Calder, Anthony Caro and others created especially for the new structure. On the other hand, all those visitors admiring the atrium aren't seeing the paintings; the East Wing is extremely inefficient as an exhibit space. Large temporary exhibitions sometimes have to include spiral staircases to connect ground level to mezzanine or mezzanine to upper level. Other exhibitions are relegated to the lightless basement. Where the West Building sacrificed inherent beauty in an attempt to house large collections, Pei filled potential gallery space with air (and a Calder mobile) to make the design pleasingly bright and spacious: he succeeded, but one wonders about the price.

Enter the East Wing from Constitution Ave., Pennsylvania Ave., and 4th St. NW, from the Mall (Metro: Archives), or from the West Building of the National Gallery via the underground moving walkway. The immense red and black Calder mobile hanging in the entrance hall is the gallery's trademark; it quietly recalls the knife-edge exterior of the building itself, one of the sharpest corners in modern architecture. (According to legend, if you press the left side of your nose against the sculpture, you'll have good luck.) From the atrium, head up the escalators and through three floors and balconies of temporary shows (not always 20th-century) and/or modern art: the National Gallery owns works from most of Picasso's phases, Fauves like Matisse and Derain, Mondrian, Surrealists including Miro and Magritte, New York School types like Pollock and Newman, and an especially rich room or two of Pop artists such as Warhol, Lichtenstein, and Rauschenberg. The gallery recently inherited over 300 of the tragic, spiritual paintings of Mark Rothko; it also owns some of Matisse's famous giant paper collages, and maintains a comprehensive assortment of sculptures by the technologically-inspired American sculptor David Smith. Of course, none of this means you'll always get to see all these works. The East Building is constantly rearranging, closing, opening, and remodeling parts of itself for its temporary exhibits. Don't neglect the basement galleries, either. To see the East Wing properly takes at least an hour and a half. Outdoors, between the West and East Buildings, a scattering of glass pyramids (skylights for the underground restaurant) and a sleek fountain complement the spiffy architecture of the building itself. (Open Mon.-Sat. 10am-5pm, Sun. 11am-6pm; Fri. 10am-8pm in the summer.)

National Air & Space Museum

The National Air and Space Museum (357-2700; TDD 357-1505), on the south side of the Mall between 4th and 7th St. SW, is the world's most popular museum—7.5 million visitors a year can't be wrong. (Metro: L'Enfant Plaza.) Thirty thousand people a day (in summer) scrutinize the dangling airplanes, the Apollo XI command module, 23 exhibit galleries and the 5-story movie screen. Among the hanging aerospace vehicles, the space-age atrium also holds a rock from the moon, worn smooth by two decades of tourists' fingertips.

Air & Space is big. Very big. Everything in it will interest someone, and no one should try to see everything. Go to the information desk, get brochures and a map, and make choices before hitting the exhibits. Plan to see a movie in the middle of the day to rest your legs. A guide leads free tours of the museum at 10:15am and 1pm daily from the tour desk in the entrance gallery. Several shorter visits might be best, though the whole museum can be sampled in three hours if you race through.

Air & Space's best exhibits are its biggest—the actual planes and crafts from all eras of flight. The Wright brothers' biplane in the entrance gallery looks intimidated by all its younger kin. Actual airplanes and rockets congregate in Galleries 100 (Entrance), 114 (Space Hall), and 102 (Air Transportation). Here are the walk-through Skylab space station, the Apollo XI command module, and the walk-through DC-7. Early jet planes park on the ground in Gallery 106 (Jet Aviation). A full-scale lunar lander has touched down outside the cafeteria. In the Vertical Flight gallery (Gallery 103), the Marine Sikorsky UH-34D whirlybird takes center stage by a painted backdrop.

Sick of propellers? Soak up the science in Gallery 207 (Exploring the Planets) which shows what we know, and how we know it, about the Earth's eight orbital buddies. Gallery 211 shows how images of flight or space worm their way through all the arts, from Wagner's "Evening Star" (from the opera *Tannhaüser*) to the rock group Kiss's starshaped makeup. Gallery 102 is your ticket to Commercial Air Transportation, with old airliners like the Douglass DC-3 and an exhibit about air-traffic control. The plastic mannequins can never go on strike.

Few exhibits are interactive; most are there to be stared at, period. One salient exception is the Beyond the Limits gallery (gallery 213), where you can use a computer program to design your own airplane; another is the Sea-Air operations gallery (gallery 203) where (via computer) you can pilot a fighter, try to land it on a carrier, and, probably, crash or sink your plane.

Air & Space takes an understandable interest in mass-market science fiction. Gallery 113 (Rocketry and Space Flight) mixes the history of rockets from early Chinese experiments to the present with fictionalized notions of rocketry from popular culture. A slide show alternates "fantasy" slides, like fake pressure suits from 50s TV shows, with the real (ahem) McCoys, like EVA lunar suits from the Apollo program. Another gallery test-flies the USS Enterprise from *Star Trek*. Around such galleries, of course, genuine technology and detailed explanations show how real spacecraft get designed. The atmosphere is educational and militaristic, at times overwhelmingly so; nonetheless various video displays, the IMAX films and Star Trek exhibit can be oodles of entertainment for those wearied by endless facts and figures.

IMAX movies give spectators vertigo in the Langley Theater, home of the five-story movie screen. The screen gives effects so realistic that some viewers suffer motion sickness. The perennially popular *To Fly,* an aerial tour of America from balloons to spaceships, shows along with four other films. Buy tickets early, and stand in line a few minutes before the show starts. Headsets translate some of the IMAX films. (Films run from 9:30am to 6:45pm. Tickets $3.25, children, students, seniors $2; available at the box office on the ground floor of the museum.) A new exhibit in the museum entitled "Where Next, Columbus?" (Gallery 209) will examine the issues related to the future of space travel through a variety of films, interactive displays, and exhibits. In addition, "War Without Risk: Faith in Technology and the Lessons of Vietnam" may be seen through May 1993.

The splendid main gift shop is worth a stop: thick enthusiasts' books identify any airplane you might see overhead, fat coffee-table guides depict the museum's planes, and coloring books entice flight-minded kids. Model rockets, airplanes, and kites round out the shop. The "Flight Line" cafeteria packs in families for slightly soggy cheeseburgers ($3); the more upscale Wright Restaurant serves vegetable kebabs, chicken, swordfish, steak, and plain old pizza (lunches and entrees: $6.95-$9.95) Museum open daily 10am-5:30pm from Sept.-June;July and Aug. 9:30am-7:30pm.)

Hirshhorn Museum and Sculpture Garden

If you're convinced art ended with Picasso, stay away from the Hirshhorn Museum and Sculpture Garden, 8th St. and Independence Ave. SW (357-2700). The 4-story, slide-carousel-shaped brown building has outraged traditionalists since 1966. Each floor consists of two concentric circles, an outer ring of rooms and paintings, and an inner corridor of sculptures; from the inner circle, windows face the courtyard and its penny-collecting fountain. Built around immigrant philanthropist Joseph Hirshhorn's gifts, the museum still carries the flavor of personal preference rather than institutional design. Of the museum's architecture S. Dillon Ripley, former Secretary of the Smithsonian, once said, "If it were not controversial in almost every way it would hardly qualify as a place to house contemporary art. For it must somehow be symbolic of the material it is designed to encase." The reinforced circular structure sits on four piers, 14ft. above the ground, to create a plaza area for the display of sculpture.

The Hirshhorn's best shows are in art since 1960; no other gallery or museum in Washington pretends to keep up with its avant-garde paintings, mind-bending sculptures and mixed-media installations. Hirshhorn halls hallow 20th-century painters from Balthus to Kline to Kiefer to Stella; even visitors who could supply the missing first names might fall in love with some unknown work. D-initialed artists are especially well-featured: look for Jean Dubuffet, who mixed gravel into his paint to give it an angry, primitive feel; Willem de Kooning's manic, sketchy canvases; or Richard Diebenkorn's contemplative interiors. The museum claims the world's most comprehensive set of 19th- and 20th-century Western sculpture, including small works by Rodin and Giacometti. The second and third floors show changing parts of the museum's permanent collection. The lowest level gathers temporary exhibits, restrooms, an auditorium, and a well-intentioned but ultimately unimpressive short film on the appreciation of modern art. Susan Rothenberg's retrospective exhibition stops by here on its way across the country (Feb.-May). Enter the museum from the revolving doors at Independence Ave. Allow yourself at least an hour and a half, much more if you love modern art.

Outdoor sculpture shines in the courtyard of the museum, with aluminum and steel and bronze and silver and red creations set up artfully along the stony pavement. Those who stand under the tapering tower of steel bars to the right of the entrance (it looks like an oil derrick) and look directly up will be rewarded with a striking pattern of concentric Stars of David. Across Jefferson Dr., Hirshhorn's collection continues with the memorable Sculpture Garden on—or in—the Mall. Striking works by David Smith, Alexander Calder, Aristide Maillol, Rodin, and Giacometti ornament a pleasant terraced lawn with a shallow pool at the bottom. (Museum open daily 10am-5:30pm. Sculpture Garden open daily 7:30am-dusk. Tours of the museum Mon.-Sat. at 10:30am, noon and 1:30pm; Sun. 12:30pm, 1:30pm, 2:30pm. Sculpture tours for the blind and sign-language tours also available. Call 357-3235 for tour information.)

Arts & Industries Building

Between the Castle and the Hirshhorn, the recursive Arts and Industries Building is an exhibition of an exhibition, the 1876 Centennial Exhibition of American technology in Philadelphia. After the exhibition ended, most of the foreign exhibitors donated their shows to the U.S. government to save themselves the cost of shipping them home. Congress ordered the Smithsonian to house the inherited objects (over the museum's objections) and paid for the Arts and Industries Building, America's first national museum. Before you go in, pause for the exterior: a polychromatic, multi-style chaos of gables, arches, rails, shingles, bricks and windows, along with a flourishing garden out front, make this museum building fun just to look at. The bricks alone have more colors (and less order) than kernels on an ear of maize. Omnipresent engineer Montgomery Meigs had a hand in the design.

The dust that has gathered on some of the old-fashioned glass cases is part of this museum's charm. Light fare, like furniture and candy-making equipment, congregates near the Mall entrance; heavy machinery like an old-fashioned elevator and generator will delight advocates of steam power further back. Half an hour or so will exhaust this catalogue of Victorian technology and Gilded Age decor. The Discovery Theater presents plays especially for children, like *Winnie the Pooh* and *Binker*. An experimental gallery, facing Independence Ave. on the other side of the main fountain, showcases innovative (usually interactive) exhibits from non-profit organizations, individuals, and museums across the world. Exhibition space is available through an application process and serves as a testing ground from which exhibitors learn how to improve their shows before taking them on tour. Recent shows have included a theater installation on homelessness entitled "'Etiquette of the Undercast" and a highly interactive exhibit on psychology. The upcoming "Kid's Bridge" includes interactive videos and games, and seeks to teach children to appreciate their ethnic and racial differences (through March, 1993). Museum open daily 10am-5:30pm. Discovery performances usually Tues.-Fri.

10am and 11:30am, Sat. 11:30am and 1pm. Admission $3.50, children 12 and under $3. Call the box office at 357-1500 (voice and TDD) Mon.-Fri. 10am-4pm.

Sackler Gallery & National Museum of African Art

Built in 1987, the Sackler Gallery and the Museum of African Art hide their non-Western treasures underground, behind the Castle and below the beautifully landscaped, but unrelentingly crisp, four-acre **Enid A. Haupt Garden,** whose main entrance faces Independence Ave. and 10th St. SW. (Garden open 7am. Closing hours change with the seasons.) Metro: Smithsonian. Both museums have two underground exhibit levels ("First" above "Second") and connect to the International Gallery and the S. Dillon Ripley conference center three stories underground. A third-level connecting hall lets you walk from Sackler to African. The museums reach the outside world through paired postmodern pavilions in the Haupt Garden; if you face the Castle, the Sackler entrance will be on your left, the African entrance on your right.

The **Arthur M. Sackler Gallery,** 1050 Independence Ave. SW, (357-1300, TDD: 786-2734) showcases Sackler's extensive collection of art from China, South and Southeast Asia, and Persia. Illuminated manuscripts; Chinese and Japanese paintings from many centuries; carvings and friezes from Egypt, Phoenicia, and Sumeria; Hindu gods; and other such works repose in low light and air-conditioned majesty. An upcoming exhibit will display sculpture from Sri Lanka's Golden Age (through Nov. 1993). Allow an hour for a brisk tour of this small museum. Call ahead for tour information.

The **National Museum of African Art,** 950 Independence Ave. SW (357-4600, TDD: 357-4814), collects, catalogs, polishes, and shows off artifacts from Sub-Saharan Africa. Thoughtful exhibitions stress the insufficiency of names for an art whose artists, countries, and time periods most often cannot be known. Art objects include masks, textiles, ceremonial figures, and fascinating musical instruments, like a harp partly made of pangolin scales. A permanent display touts sophisticated bronze works from the Kingdom of Benin, in modern-day Nigeria. Temporary shows fluctuate between art-for-art's-sake ("Icons") and cultural-theoretical displays ("Africa Illustrated," Westerners' sketches of Africa). (Open daily 10am-5:30pm. Call ahead for tour information.) Allow at least an hour for the Museum of African Art.

The small **International Gallery,** 1100 Jefferson Dr. SW (357-1300, TDD: 786-2374) under the S. Dillon Ripley Center continually offers new and thoughtful temporary exhibits. Recent exhibits have featured contemporary art from Jerusalem and posters and lithographs from a politically-transformed Eastern Europe.

Freer Gallery

The Freer Gallery of Art, on the Mall at Jefferson Dr. and 12th St. SW, will re-open in May of 1993 with a marble and limestone stairway leading to a new exhibition gallery which will connect the Freer with the Sackler. The Freer collects Asian as well as Asian-inspired art (for instance, the paintings and designs of James McNeill Whistler; see his opulent "Peacock Room" when the renovated gallery welcomes guests again). The rest of the Freer collection (over 26,000 objects) is as richly historical and fabulously opulent as the Sackler's—Chinese bronzes, precious manuscripts, jade carvings and so forth reward hours upon hours of viewing and consideration. Definitely one of the great attractions of the mall.

The Mall and Environs

Exotic foliage from all continents and climates vegetates inside and outside the **U.S. Botanical Garden,** First St. and Maryland Ave. SW (225-7099). Metro: Federal Center SW. Cacti, bromeliads, and other odd-climate plants flourish indoors. Forty-minute guided tours begin at 10am and 2pm (call ahead; open June-Sept. daily 9am-8pm; Oct.-May daily 9am-5pm.) The Botanical Garden's brochure will guide pedestrians around **Bartholdi Park,** the triangular plot between First St., Independence, and Washington Ave. SW. The fruitful park tests and demonstrates gardening techniques and new varieties of plants. Carved women raise arms and lamps around the central fountain, designed by Frederic Bartholdi, who also came up with the Statue of Liberty.

Millions of listeners on every continent but this one tune in to the **Voice of America,** 330 Independence Ave. SW (619-3919, Metro: Federal Center SW), the U.S. government's overseas radio and TV organ. The guided tour shows radio announcers at home in the studio, speaking anything from English to Dari to Uzbek on the air or watching soap operas on silent TVs as they wait for the red light. (Public tours lasting 45min. begin Mon.-Fri. at 8:45am, 9:45am, 10:45am, 1:45pm and 2:45pm, except holidays.) Tours start at the C St. entrance between 3rd and 4th St.

Independence Garden, at Independence Ave. and 6th St. SW, seems refreshingly amateurish after the Botanical Gardens' world-class expertise. The block-long, somewhat overgrown urban garden cultivates corn, asparagus, and flowers, along with other vines and veggies in a do-it-yourself profusion.

Bureaucrats shop till they drop in **L'Enfant Plaza,** named for Pierre L'Enfant, the man who had the plan to lay this town down in a grid pattern. The plaza itself is an immense underground structure that takes up an entire block between 9th and 10th St. off of D St. SW. Comprised of a central area with 4 elongated tunnels, the single-floor mall offers sheer space–but not quantity. In its cavernous bowels you will find a limited selection of items from books to booze, food to fashion. There is however a video arcade, where many a government pay-hike has no doubt been squandered. The plaza's construction threatened to topple the **Dept. of Housing and Urban Development,** an unhealthy-looking X-shaped building on D St. SW between 7th and 9th. A long-standing HUD rumor holds that the building was designed to resemble a particularly admired Paris post office. Unfortunately, the HUD building was twice the size of the one in Paris; the square-cube law, which says that anything of given proportions gets weaker as it gets bigger, made the outsized HUD structure unsound from the outset.

The **Mint,** or the **Bureau of Engraving and Printing,** 14th St. and C St. SW (662-2000), just south of the Washington Monument, offers continuous tours of the presses that annually print over $20 billion worth of money and stamps. Look for the bins of shredded bills. Perhaps intoxicated with false consciousness, tourists have made this the area's longest line: skip breakfast or expect a 2-hr. wait. (Open Mon.-Fri. 9am-2pm. Moving queue; no tour guide. Free.)

Across the street from the Bureau on 14th St. SW, a crew of architects, builders and historians construct the **U.S. Holocaust Museum.** The museum remembers the Nazi murder of 16 million human beings, six million of them Jews. Exhibits and archives for historical research are set to open in 1993.

Washington Monument

DC's answer to the Eiffel Tower, the Washington Monument is a vertical altar to America's first president, where crowds of tourists sacrifice their sweat, time, and patience to ascend, descend, and take the Monument's picture along with their own. The marble-faced monument weighs 81,120 tons, stands on a foundation 126.5 square feet and 37 feet deep, and could withstand a super-tornado blowing at 145 miles per hour. Two-foot blocks of marble, along with rubble masonry, make up the base exterior; the interior support switches to New England granite about 450 feet up, then gives way to solid marble capped by a 9-inch aluminum pyramid. In 1986, DC cops left bullet holes at eye level on the Monument when they gunned down a man who parked his van here, claimed it was full of dynamite, and threatened to blow up the famous structure.

For a simple obelisk, the Monument took plenty of time and energy to build. Robert Mills' 1845 design called for a one-story, 30-column temple around the base, which would have made the Monument even more phallic. After Congress agreed to Mills' plan, construction began on July 4, 1848, but soon ran out of money; Alabama, which couldn't afford to send cash, contributed a stone instead, starting a trend that saved the monument. France, the Cherokee Nation, the American residents of Foo-Chow Foo, China, and over 100 other nations, states, towns and people sent stones. When the Vatican sent a block of Italian marble in 1854, the Know-Nothings—an anti-Catholic and anti-immigrant political party—raided the grounds and stole "the Pope's stone"; afterwards, contributions dried up. During the Civil War the half-finished obelisk was nick-named the "Beef Depot Monument" in honor of the cattle which Army quartermasters herded on the grounds. One hundred-fifty feet up, the monument's stone changes hue: when construction began again after the Civil War, and the builders returned to their favorite Maryland quarry, the layer of stones of the original color had already been used up. George Marsh, the U.S. Ambassador to Italy and an obelisk fan, nixed Mill's Doric temple in 1880; the structure, completed in 1884, opened four years later.

The first men to ascend the Monument could choose between the steam elevator and the stairs; women and children had to climb the 698 steps, since Mr. Otis' invention was considered dangerous. The stairs up the monument were a famous (and strenuous) tourist exercise until the Park Service closed them due to heart attacks (on the way up) and vandalism (on the way down). The line for the elevators, though crowded, isn't as slow as it looks; it takes 45 minutes to circle the Monument. The elevator guides whip out a comment or two before you arrive at the top. Up at the top, tiny windows offer lookout points. From 500 feet up, you can look down on all of DC's major sights. The Monument offers almost as much to see from the base than from the top: the structure itself rewards contemplation, and the queue around it offers a cross-section of America.

The Monument ascends inside a circle of flagpoles on its own landscaped block (the Monument Grounds) at Constitution Ave. and 16th St. NW, west of the Mall proper and east of the Lincoln Memorial. (Metro: Smithsonian.) A wheelchair is available on the premises for any visitor who needs it; people with disabilities may bypass the long lines. (Monument open daily 8am-midnight; September-March 9am-5pm. Free.) Restrooms and phones hang out at the bottom of the hill.

Constitution Gardens, between the Lincoln Memorial and Washington Monument, stretches out north of the Reflecting Pool with trees and grass and such. The Gardens are actually landfill: everything west of the Washington Monument and south of Constitution Ave. was once a simple swamp. On an island in a lake in the park, a granite-and-gold plate lists the signers of the Declaration of Independence.

The **Reflecting Pool**, between the Washington and Lincoln Memorials, reflects Washington's obelisk in seven million gallons of lit-up water, 24hr. a day. If you lean far enough over, it might reflect you too. Based on pools at Versailles and the Taj Mahal, the Reflecting Pool's design minimizes wind ripples while maximizing poetic effect. A demonstration big enough to surround the pool with people— like the fall 1990 abortion-rights march— makes an impressive sight indeed. South of the Reflecting Pool and visible from the road, the **DC War Memorial,** a small, rotundafied Xerox of the Jefferson one, commemorates all veterans native to Washington.

Vietnam Veterans Memorial

Maya Ying Lin, who designed the Memorial, called it "a rift in the earth—a long, polished black stone wall, emerging from and receding into the earth. The memorial is a moving composition, to be understood as one moves into and out of it; the passage itself is gradual, the descent to the origin slow, but it is at the origin that the meaning of the memorial is to be fully understood." While still an undergraduate at Yale, Lin beat 1400 contestants with her design. This subtlest of DC's memorials changes its sheen and mood between day and night. Its granite reflects the Washington and Lincoln Memorials at equal sizes. The "meaning of the memorial" lies most of all in its lists of names: 58,132 Americans died in Vietnam, and the memorial's slabs bear each one's name. Families and veterans visit the memorial to ponder and mourn; many make rubbings of their loved ones' names from the walls. Other visitors leave letters, flowers, or stranger objects; the Park Service collects the leavings for a future Smithsonian exhibit.

Some soldiers (and congresspeople) objected to the Memorial's nonmilitary appearance, so the government commissioned Frederick Hart to sculpt realistic-looking bronze troopers emerging from an unknown battlefield. From the right angle, the statues seem to stare straight at the memorial's central corner; it's as if they wanted to apologize for breaking the silence Lin's design implies. Books at both ends of the black memorial list all the names chiseled thereon, along with their panel numbers; each panel of names bears its own number. The Vietnam Veterans Memorial rises from the earth northeast of the Lincoln Memorial, north of the Reflecting Pool and south of Constitution Ave. at 22nd St. NW. (Metro: Foggy Bottom or Smithsonian.) Since it's entirely outdoors, the memorial stays "open" 24hr. every day; the park rangers leave after midnight. (Call 634-1568 for information.)

Lincoln Memorial

Anyone with a penny already knows what the Lincoln Memorial looks like; Henry Bacon's design, which placed a 130-foot wide stairway below a simple row of columns, copies the rectangular grandeur of Athens' Parthenon. A massive layer of stone atop the columns gives the building the watchful solemnity of a crypt. Though consensus demanded some memorial to Lincoln almost immediately after his assassination in 1865, the present marble temple wasn't built until 50 years afterward. The McMillan Commission, which laid out the Mall in 1902, proposed a memorial on the recently drained land called Potomac Flats; Bacon's classical design beat out several more eminent architects', like John Russell Pope's, which proposed a ziggurat and a funeral pyre. The current marble superstructure stands 80 feet high. Columns climb 44 feet to the names of thirty-six states (that's how many there were when Lincoln died) inscribed in a frieze above the columns. The names of the Lower 48 states wrap around the Memorial's roof; a plaque at the bottom of the stairs footnotes Alaska and Hawaii. The Memorial's steps have hosted many famous gatherings; Black soprano Marian Anderson sang from the steps here after she was barred from segregated Constitution Hall in 1939. Martin Luther King gave his "I Have a Dream" speech to the 1963 March on Washington crowd from these stairs.

Daniel Chester French's seated Lincoln presides over his Memorial from the inside, keeping watch over the Reflecting Pool, protest marchers, and Fourth of July fireworks. To climb the 19-foot President, even at night, is a federal offense; a closed-circuit camera will nab your scofflaw visage after the rangers have gone home. The stonecutting firm, Picirilli Bros., couldn't find a block of marble big enough for Honest Abe; instead, they joined 20 blocks so tightly you can barely see the seams. In American Sign Language, Lincoln's hands spell "A" and "L"; French, who had just finished a statue of Thomas Gallaudet, was reminding us that Lincoln signed Gallaudet College into existence. The arms of the marble seat bear Roman *fasces,* symbols of imperial power—an unfortunate choice, given Mussolini's concurrent ascension to power in Italy. Critics of the memorial argue that it weighs Lincoln's preserving the union more heavily than it does his emancipation of the slaves. Then again, so did Lincoln himself. You can read his Gettysburg address on the wall to the left of the statue; notice the "engravo" *euture* instead of *future*.

The memorial's interior looks best early in the morning, when the rising sun shines through the marble roof; builders soaked it in paraffin to improve its translucency. At night, Lincoln glows in personalized electric lights; memorial-goers can watch the Washington Monument's image shimmer in the lit Reflecting Pool and meditate from the steps. A **museum** in the memorial's base shows photos of a younger, clean-shaven Lincoln. Spelunkers supposedly roam the stalactites and stalagmites under the memorial; you can too, courtesy of the Park Service, but you have to call 425-6841 or 426-6896 and ask about touring the memorial's underground. The Memorial anchors the west end of the Mall, across the Reflecting Pool from the Washington Monument and a few blocks south along 23rd St. NW from Foggy Bottom. (Metro: Smithsonian or Foggy Bottom; it's a long walk.) Since it has no doors, the Memorial is open 24hr.; a ranger hangs around daily 8am-midnight. Free.

Jefferson Memorial

The third member of DC's white-marble triumvirate, finished in 1942, makes its debt to its forebears obvious. The open-air-room-formed-by-columns bit is a shameless steal from the Lincoln Memorial. The Thomas Jefferson Memorial's site, due south and across the Tidal Basin from the Washington Monument, makes its dome an obvious counterpoint to Washington's thin, stiff obelisk. And John Russell Pope's rotunda-centric design pays tribute to TJ's own monument to himself: his Charlottesville home, Monticello.

Pope wasn't the only one who took the construction seriously. President Franklin Roosevelt had all the trees between the memorial and the White House razed so he could watch the construction. High-society ladies tried to protect the 33 cherry trees which stood in the Monument's way by chaining themselves to the trunks; the bureaucrat in charge of construction served them coffee and tea until they had to go, then bulldozed the trees while they were in the powder room. The landscape around the Memorial, planned by Frederick Olmsted Jr. (not the Central Park guy) deserves more than a glance. The nearby basin acts as the memorial's own reflecting pool, and the raised hill offers generous views of the other monuments. Olmsted planted American hollies near the monument so Jefferson's favorite avians, mockingbirds, would hover around to eat the berries.

A 19-foot hollow bronze statue of President Jefferson rules the rotunda. In back of the statue, iconography abounds: corn and tobacco, Virginia's cash crops, grace the top of his boot. Above these crops a stack of books remembers the University of Virginia, which Jefferson founded. The interior walls quote from Jefferson's writings: the Declaration of Independence, the Virginia Statute of Religious Freedom, his Notes on Virginia, and an 1815 letter. The Declaration of Independence extract contains 11 errors, several committed to shorten the quote so it would fit on the wall. ("These Colonies" should be "these United Colonies," and "mutually pledge" should be the equally grammarless "pledge to each other.") The sentence around the top of the dome rebukes those who wrongly called T.J. an atheist. The carved squares get smaller near the top of the dome, so the ceiling looks higher than its brief 30 feet.

Today Jefferson's pocket of peacefulness is disturbed by restoration of the cracked columns around the memorial, which time, automobile exhaust, and acid rain have damaged. The memorial remains open 24hr., with the inside lights always on; you may find people playing marbles here at midnight. Park technicians answer questions 8am-midnight, except Christmas. (Call 426-6822 or 425-6821.) Jefferson's temple overlooks the Tidal Basin along DC's southwestern edge; walk to it along the Basin's rim from Independence Ave. or 14th St. SW. (Metro: L'Enfant Plaza or Smithsonian.) To drive here, take 14th St. SW (don't try it during the day).

The Jefferson Memorial overlooks Washington's most popular man-made lake, the **Tidal Basin,** where pedalboats ripple in and out of the Memorial's shadow. The lake is small enough to look at all at once, but big enough to sustain plenty of boaters; families in particular can't resist renting a two-person boat (one person must be over 16 years of age). (Boat rental 479-2426; open daily 10am-7pm; $7 per hour.)

Too famous for their own good, the Japanese **cherry trees** surround themselves with a protective ring of botanically-minded tourists during the two weeks in late March or early April when most of them (the popular *Yoshino* type) are in bloom along the Tidal Basin's rim. The cherry trees' lacy white petals have become a symbol of monumental Washington; more important, they're pretty. (A minority of *Akebono* cherry trees bloom in late April and show spare pink petals rather than profuse white ones.) The original batch of trees, sent in 1909 from Japan as a symbol of trans-Pacific friendship, arrived bearing insects and fungi and were promptly obliterated by the Department of Agriculture. The current bloomin' wonders were Japan's second try, received in 1912. After Japanese bombers attacked Pearl Harbor in 1941, irate Washingtonians took buzzsaws to several of the trees. Plaques, arranged from right to left along the Tidal Basin, tell the cherry story during their two weeks of fame each year.

Mellow **West Potomac Park** and **East Potomac Park**, both casseroles of trees, lawns, and sculptures, park themselves on either side of the Tidal Basin, along Ohio Dr. SW. The first is more popular, but the second is bigger. West Potomac Park holds summer polo games at 3pm on Sundays. (If you see empty stands, that's why). Elsewhere in the park appears to be a continuous summer volleyball tournament. Two brazen hands rise from the chthonic depths in *The Awakening*, a sculpture outdoors in East Potomac Park (though rumor says the sculpture will soon be yanked from the park). It's hard to spend more than 10 minutes south of the Lincoln Memorial without hearing military helicopters rotoring away over the Potomac: if you see one heading due north, toward the White House, it may well contain the President.

The Waterfront

Yes, Virginia, DC has a waterfront, too; all one or so mile of it south of G Street SW, along Maine Avenue and the parallel, smaller Water Street SW. Yachts congregate along the Washington Marina here, under the noses of the high-priced seafood restaurants. During the summer huge fairs occasion the arrival of hundreds of Washingtonians, kids in tow, checking out the T-shirts and food and ogling the boats. Theater-lovers will park here on the way to Arena Stage (see *Theater*).

The outstanding attraction is the **Wharf Seafood Market,** between 9th and 11th St. SW and Maine Ave. NW (next to the Memorial Bridge). Get off at the Waterfront Metro stop, on the Green Line, or walk from the L'Enfant Plaza Metro, walk two blocks to 9th St. SW from the exit at 7th and D St. SW, then walk down 9th St. (away from the Mall) to Maine Ave. No matter the season, no matter the day (except Christmas and perhaps New Year's), the vendors stand in their markets, floating platforms tied to the dock, and sell seafood galore. During low tide you'll find yourself looking down at mounds of ice cubes, coral lobsters and crawling crabs, and rows of aproned people. Almost all the fishermen sell at the wharf from about 8am to 9pm. Some places offer cooked food, spiced shrimp and crab cakes in particular; prices float under $6 for a half pound of spiced shrimp or a crabcake with fries. You can probably find a dozen steamed crabs for $12 or less, and most places accept credit cards. The seafood, most from the Chesapeake Bay, couldn't be fresher. Be warned, however: none of the markets furnish seating.

At the opposite side of Water St. from the wharf, two **touring ships** sail the harbor; the *Spirit of Washington* and the *Potomac Spirit* depart from pier 4, 6th and Water St. (554-8000). The *Potomac Spirit* motors over to George Washington's estate. (June 16-Aug. 30, Tues. and Sun. twice daily: 9am and 2pm; March 28-June 14 and Sept.1-Oct. 2, 9am cruise only.) Round trip ticket, including Mt. Vernon entrance fee $19, children ages 6-11 $11.25, children 5 and under travel free. The *Spirit of Washington* takes the scenic route through D.C., Virginia, and Maryland, passing several famous landmarks. Cruises 3 times daily: lunch $19.95-$23.95, dinner $35.95-$43.95, and moonlight party cruises $19. Children's rates available. Reservations recommended. Boarding time: lunch Tues.-Sat. 11:30, Sun. 12:30pm; dinner 6:30pm nightly; moonlight Fri.-Sat. 11pm.

Old Downtown

"Old Downtown" is an arbitrary label for the neighborhoods north of the Mall, bounded by Constitution Ave., 2nd St., New York Ave., and 15th St. NW. Federal business centers on the old downtown, where many U.S. agencies and departments do their regulating thing. But unlike its counterpart to the south of the Mall, the old downtown area also harbors a thriving commercial culture, with plenty of street vendors, luncheon spots, and pricey hotels to rival the few block-long department stores around Metro Center. This schizoid tendency reflects the area's history: 7th St. NW was DC's main commercial center during the 1800s, boasting the largest outdoor market (Center Market, opened in 1801) and the monumental Patent Office building. Washington's famous boardinghouses once packed in long-term guests of all classes here, including many Representatives (elected for only two years). Pseudo-temples and shiny offices along Pennsylvania Avenue recline above relaxing shrubbery; a few blocks north, narrow streets and fourteen-story buildings are the closest DC comes to New York-style congestion (not very). A string of low government buildings around 4th and 5th St. NW yields to Chinatown, then to slick architecture and private enterprise as you approach the recently cleaned-up 14th St.

Leaving the Judiciary Square Metro at 4th and D St. NW, turn left onto D St. and walk one block to the **DC Courthouse** (879-1010) at Indiana Ave., 5th St. and D St.

NW. This modern building can show you how the legal system really operates: suspects, lawyers, cops, and taxi drivers compete for sidewalk space outside, while lawyers rush up and down three layers of escalators inside, scampering to file their briefs in time. The DC Superior Court and the DC Court of Appeals share the building; confusingly, the Superior Court is the inferior one. Successfully pass through the metal detector and this Hall of Justice will unfold for you. You can sit in on a criminal case (check information for availability of space), eat in the cafeteria on the "C" level, or just ride the escalators. Whee. (Courthouse open Mon.-fri. 8am-6pm; free.)

On 2nd St. between D and E St., the **Community for Creative Nonviolence** runs the nation's most famous homeless shelter. The late Mitch Snyder, its founder, undertook a series of life-threatening fasts in his successful attempt to make the federal government donate the abandoned building and the money to run it. Snyder's confrontational efforts on behalf of the homeless inspired admiration and resentment all over the city; a TV movie starring Martin Sheen depicted his life. CCNV still houses hundreds of Washington's street people in its block-long tiled building, only one block from the mammoth Department of Labor.

Towards the Mall, across C St. NW, the **U.S. Courthouse** (535-3555), at 333 Constitution Ave., squats in conservative austerity on the east side of **John Marshall Park** (to the left as you face the Mall). Metro: Judiciary Square. Examine the monument to Civil War general George Meade, who led Union forces at Gettysburg, at the Constitution Ave. entrance. The federal court building opens up to the public (if you're willing to pass through a metal detector) but everything interesting requires an elevator ride: though it's legal, you may still feel like an intruder. Better-dressed lawyers and Constitutional issues stalk these marbled halls, which contain the Court of Appeals for the DC Circuit. Both civil and criminal cases are generally open to the public, depending on availability of space. Check the trial schedule in room 1825 for interesting cases. (U.S. Courthouse open Mon.-Fri. 9am-4:30pm; free.) In John Marshall Park, workaholics and alcoholics compete for a lunch bench alongside a lifelike statue of two chess players. Sit in the lap of the oversized statue of Marshall, the fourth and most important Chief Justice of the Supreme Court. Across the street, facing the East Wing of the National Gallery of Art, the small bit of park land once held the boardinghouse where poet Walt Whitman lived in 1864.

The brand-new **Canadian Embassy** (682-1740), at 501 Pennsylvania Ave. NW, deserves more than a glance. (Metro: Judiciary Square or Archives.) Its black-and-white east front (which borders Marshall Park) begins three stories off the ground, taunting gravity and opening up to pedestrians. Smooth, pale, mostly-modern side walls complement the tree-filled, terraced balconies. The embassy faces the National Gallery of Art across Pennsylvania Ave.; architect Arthur Erickson's design reconciles the National Gallery's Greek-themed West Building with the acute angles of the East Wing. Stand in the embassy's marble cupola, talk to the Doric columns, and discover the outdoor dome's unique acoustics. A gallery in the basement displays rotating exhibitions of modern Canadian art. The building also boasts a research library that may be used by appointment (made a week or two in advance). Gallery open Mon.-Fri. 10am-5pm; free.

National Building Museum

It's only proper that an architectural marvel should house the National Building Museum, which towers above F St. NW between 4th and 5th St. (Metro: Judiciary Square.) In 1881, Congress asked military architect Montgomery Meigs to design a cheap brick building for the 1,500 clerks of the Pension Bureau. The bureaucrats lucked out; Meigs' Italian-inspired edifice remains one of Washington's most beautiful. A terracotta frieze, three feet high and 1200 feet long, frames an endless parade of Union soldiers arriving to collect their pensions; look for doctors, wounded soldiers, and artillery pieces amid the crowds of infantry. Early photographer Eadward (not Edward) Muybridge, who analyzed the motions of walking and running, inspired Caspar Buberl, master of the frieze.

Inside, the expansive Great Hall exhibits a sort of budget opulence. On the one hand, its eight Corinthian columns are the world's largest; life-size busts peer down from 244 wall niches; a terra-cotta fountain is 28 feet in diameter. The Great Hall may cause visitors sensitive to scale, spectacle, and splendor to make small, almost sexual, gasping noises. It's big enough to hold a fifteen-story building. On the other hand, the columns are brick (their marble look took 4000 gallons of rose paint); the roof, partly corrugated metal, rests on iron supports. The first busts depicted famous people like Meigs, Alexander Hamilton, and Sir Walter Scott, but later architects filled empty niches with busts of federal prisoners and children from an American-Indian reservation. Still later, in the 1920s, somebody stole the busts, which the Museum replaced fifty years later. A hollow column supposedly holds secret information about President Lincoln's death. Semi-famous ghosts are also said to roam the Pension Building; the shade of pension commissioner James Tanner, who lost both feet in the Second Battle of Bull Run, traipses the halls with a distinctive limp.

Done with the building? Time for the museum: "Washington: Symbol and City," one of the NBM's first permanent exhibits, records DC's dual history. Half the exhibit covers the planning of monuments and central Washington; the other half covers DC's residential aspects. In the monument section, displays answer questions like "How Can a City Plan Be a Symbol?" and "How Grand Should the President's House Be?" Actors on tape loops read the 1872 debates over whether to run a railroad through the Mall. Other highlights include models of the rejected designs for the Washington Monument and the chance to design your own Capitol Hill rowhouse. L'Enfant Plan fans can re-write our general introduction based on the Building Museum's vast reserves of information. A new, permanent, and somewhat self-indulgent exhibit on the construction and history of the Pension Building shows in the gallery on the second floor.

The last Wednesday of each month features concerts in the Great Hall, generally by chamber ensembles or military bands. The museum also offers tours of the city, accompanied by guides who specialize in a particular architectural field. (Get a behind-the-scenes look at buildings in progress by taking a "hard-hat" tour of a construction site.) "From Mars to Main Street: American Designs, 1965-1990" (through Nov. 1993) will chronicle the federal government's role as a design client. Museum open Mon.-Fri. 10am-4pm, Sat.-Sun. noon-4pm; tours Mon.-Fri. 12:30pm, Sat.-Sun. 12:30 and 1:30. Excellent handicapped access, including exhibits for the blind. Free.)

Chinatown

DC's Chinatown is nothing to rival San Francisco's, much less New York's. Still, this five-square-block community shares enough with its larger namesakes to make it worth wandering around in. (Metro: Gallery Place-Chinatown.) Start at 7th and H St. NW; you'll know where you are by the bilingual street signs, and by the dragon-covered turquoise, red, white, yellow, and green gilded archway. Mainland Chinese money paid for the arch in the mid-80s; local leaders protested on anti-Communist grounds. Chinatown's history resembles that of Chinese districts across the nation. After the Chinese Exclusion Act of 1882 restricted immigration, barred Chinese aliens from most jobs, and banned Chinese women and children from the United States, the persecuted immigrants lived and worked near 4th St. and Pennsylvania Ave. NW. Two rival *tongs* (merchants' associations) formed to offer protection to Chinese-owned businesses. When government buildings displaced the old Chinatown, the *tongs* led the move to today's neighborhood.

Now technically bounded by 5th, 8th, F, and Eye St. NW, Chinatown is slowly shrinking under the pressure of crime and/or rising rents; the remaining shops and restaurants serve many first-generation Chinese immigrants. Shops in Chinatown resemble each other in their variety of items. Ornate but functional porcelain, teakettles, chopsticks, cards, fans, and buddhas in all sizes, colors, and stones offer a spark of culture. Often juxtaposed with tourist gadgets and souvenir gifts, these items can be hidden in the backs of stores. Don't let clutter intimidate; take the time to wander through a store to find the more authentic items. Chinatown streets usually stay safe during the day; at night, especially on weekends, bring a friend or two. (For how and where to eat in Chinatown, see *Food*.)

Over 60 "hands-on" exhibits battle for your attention at **Tech 2000,** in Techworld Plaza, 800 K St. (842-0500). From the Gallery Place Metro, turn around and walk three blocks, just past the Ramada Renaissance Hotel. Compose your own Baroque fugue from computer-friendly versions of J.S. Bach's, or play the drums on a projection screen as a high-tech camera alters your personal image. Sit down and enjoy selections from the gallery's laser disc jukebox of movies. Some of these computer programs helped plan and simulate Operation Desert Storm. Many exhibits are designed specifically to accommodate the handicapped. All of the exhibits are user-friendly; you don't have to go to MIT to understand how to use or enjoy them. In the near future, a product center will make available to the public some of the software on display. Open Tues.-Sun. 11am-5pm, winter Wed.-Sat. 11am-5pm. Admission $5, students $4, children and seniors $3. Wheelchair assistance provided upon request.

Enjoy the open air in the plaza outside the two glass wings of the technology center and hotel. A glass connecting bridge stretches overhead. The mammoth concrete building one block away from Tech 2000 is the **DC Convention Center**, whose bulk occupies four blocks and interrupts two city streets.

National Museum of American Art & National Portrait Gallery

The National Museum of American Art and the National Portrait Gallery (357-2700) share the Old Patent Office Building, a Neoclassical edifice two blocks long (American Art entrance at 8th and G St.; Portrait Gallery entrance at 8th and F). Metro: Gallery Place–Chinatown. The ubiquitous Washington temple design, complete with Doric columns, seems more appropriate to the museums, which moved here in 1968, than to the 19th-century bureaucrats the Patent Office once employed. Robert Mills, the Washington Monument's architect, designed the more delicate, less imposing south wing (now the Portrait Gallery). You'll know American Art by the fiberglass cowboy (called *Vaquero*) in front, and the Portrait Gallery by its hanging banners; a spare courtyard connects the Americans to the portraits, and allows visitors to sit and eat, smoke, or tan in the sun.

National Museum of American Art

The American art curators haven't made up their mind what their museum is for, and their loss might be your gain: the surprisingly deserted corridors include major painters from 19th-century America, an array of folk and ethnic art, and a scattering of contemporary innovators. Just inside the museum, look for the sculpture *Man on Fire*, a larger-than-life companion to *Vaquero*. Luis Jiménez based *Man on Fire* on a legend about an Aztec man burnt alive by conquistadors in 1521; his two colorful statues may represent the two faces of Mexican culture. (See *Let's Go: Mexico*.)

DC janitor James Hampton stayed up nights in an unheated garage for fifteen years to assemble the *Throne of the Third Heaven of the Nations' Millennium General Assembly*. Now on permanent display to the right of the main museum entrance, this array of sculptures may permanently alter your spiritual life. *Time* has called it "the finest work of visionary religious art produced by an American." The throne comprises 177 objects, including ruined furniture, electrical cables and dead light bulbs, sheathed in aluminum and gold foil. No one exhibited—or knew of—the work until years after Hampton died in 1964. The Throne's framework of religious symbolism would reward weeks of decoding; those with less patience than Hampton can pick up the two-page handout detailing the sculpture's history.

Choose your period of American art by choosing your floor of the museum. Folk art and early American art awaits your study to the left of the entrance on the first floor. Charles Wilson Peale and Gilbert Stuart portray the young republic and its bowls of fruit, while George Caitlin's more than 600 studies of Native Americans put the United States' westward expansion in long-overdue perspective. Classic American artists make the second floor their own. Westerners Albert Bierstadt and Thomas Moran turn the second floor lobby into Yellowstone National Park. Landscape people Thomas Cole and Frederic Church strut their stuff here. John F. Francis' calm, radiant *Luncheon Still Life* (1860) could be a depopulated Vermeer. Winslow Homer's seascapes recall the New England coast, while Childe Hassam's seascapes recall Monet. Two women fish in ironically inappropriate yellow-and-green gowns in Thomas Wilmer Dewing's *Summer* (1890).

If you still think the museum deserves the sparse crowds it gets, head to the third floor for twentieth century work: Edward Hopper (of *Night Hawks* fame) competes with the angry abstractions of Franz Kline. The calmer colors of native Washingtonian Morris Louis literally recede into the canvas in his unusual "stain paintings." More contemporary outlandishness includes a painted conglomeration of license plates and a sculpture made of blinking fiber optics on stone. Temporary exhibitions have served all of the museum's conflicting purposes, from 1988 shows of surrealist Man Ray and Lucas Samaras to an upcoming show of the hand-colored prints of Wayne Thiebaud (Nov. 1992-Feb. 1993) Open daily 10am-5:30; tours at the Museum of American Art at noon on weekdays, 2pm on weekends. Free.

National Portrait Gallery

If a museum devoted exclusively to portraiture sounds monotonous, think again; the wide range of media, periods, styles and people represented make these narrow halls more like a museum of the American character. Portraits in the Portrait Gallery come in all shapes and sizes; a Japanese wood-block print of Matthew Perry shows an artist's (accurate) conception of the American Commodore as a seaman from another land. A caricature of Rachmaninoff shows the Russian composer pensively playing piano; nearby, depictions of Theodore Roosevelt proliferate wildly.

The gallery's temporary exhibits and unmarked rooms are more fun and more varied than their staid special collections, which include a Hall of Presidents (second floor) and the Meserve Collection (third floor), featuring photos of Lincoln and those involved in his life. In the permanent collection rooms, look for the work of photographer Annie Leibovitz, a mainstay of *Rolling Stone* magazine. Seek out the visages of dancers and movie stars in the first floor's East Corridor, devoted to the performing arts. A café on the left side of the courtyard, called "Patent Pending," serves quiche and sandwiches for the hungry art-gazer (open daily for lunch, 11am-3pm). Upcoming exhibitions include "Contemporary Self-Portraits from the James Goode Collection" (July 30-Dec. 5, 1993). Produced in the 1970's and 1980's in styles as different as abstraction and photorealism, the portraits in this collection reflect the way artists like Frank Wright and Burt Silverman see themselves (duh). Also, James Vanderzee's retrospective exhibition features the artists, politicians, athletes, and entrepreneurs behind the cultural movement of the Harlem Renaissance (Oct.1993-Jan. 1994). Open daily 10am-5:30pm; tours at the Portrait Gallery 10am-3pm Mon.-Fri. by request, 11am-2pm Sat.-Sun. Free. Wheelchair access near the garage at 9th and G St.

At 901 G St. NW, across 9th St. from the National Gallery of American Art, the **Martin Luther King Jr. Memorial Library** (727-1111) is the flagship of DC's library system. The brick-and-black-glass rectangular building is the only one in Washington designed by Bauhaus celeb Mies van der Rohe; unfortunately, the city can't afford to keep the building very clean. Inside, see Don Miller's mural of Rev. King, the United States' most important civil rights leader, who led the nonviolent protests that helped end legal segregation. Or just get a library card. Local-history types will find their heaven in the Washingtoniana Room. (Open Mon.-Thurs. 9am-9pm, Fri.-Sat. 9am-5:30pm. Free.)

Pennsylvania Ave.

Pennsylvania Ave. between the White House and the Capitol, and especially between 6th and 15th St. NW, is probably the most-discussed street in Washington. New

Presidents traverse it quadrennially in the Inaugural Parade, which earns it the logical nickname "Street of Presidents"; most new Chief Executives ride in limos, but Jimmy Carter showed his energy-consciousness in 1976 by walking the 16 blocks to the White House. Before and during the Civil War era, the Avenue, which runs all the way from Northwest to Anacostia in the Southeast via the John Philip Sousa Bridge was DC's most important thoroughfare: at night, the street became "Hooker's Division," named for hard-living Union General Joseph Hooker. Here shady bars and prostitution flourished. Anyone who says the term "hooker" (for a prostitute) came from Hooker is probably just a proud native Washingtonian: the word, older than the general, most likely derives from Brooklyn (N.Y.)'s old Red Hook district.

An array of old-time Greco-Roman-Revival federal buildings includes the Federal Trade Commission at 6th St., blessed with a profusion of outdoor sculptures. (The half-naked man wrestling a horse near the eastern doorway represents the Commission controlling monopolies.) Other neoclassicisms along the avenue are the National Archives (at 8th St.), the Justice Dept. (between 9th and 10th), the taxing Internal Revenue Service (between 10th and 11th), and the Interstate Commerce Commission (between 12th and 13th). The last two buildings form the Federal Triangle complex, once the site of the notorious slum Murder Bay. The looming, blocky FBI, the charming Old Post Office, and the Willard Hotel make their contrasting marks on the avenue's wide vistas, as does the District Building at 14th and D St. NW, where Mayor Dixon tries to whip the city bureaucracy into shape. Congress invented the Pennsylvania Ave. Development Corporation in 1972 to encourage private enterprise along the government-dominated avenue; the result has been a string of offices, so a walk up the avenue on a weekday lets you survey Washington architecture and Washington office-people all at once. Small parks and plazas along the length of the street offer calm resting places for exhausted walkers. A promising nightlife seems in the works, if the development of residential buildings in the area between the Capitol and the White House, dubbed the 'Pennsylvania Quarters,' keeps pace with the increasing number of offices.

National Archives

The United States' founding documents can still be found at the National Archives, 8th St. and Constitution Ave. NW (general information 501-5000, guided tours 501-5205, library and research 501-5400). Metro: Archives/Navy Memorial. Visitors line up outside to view the original Declaration of Independence, U.S. Constitution, and Bill of Rights. Humidity-controlled, helium-filled glass cases preserve and exhibit all three documents in the central Rotunda. Every night these cases sink into the floor; the documents' nightly repose in a basement vault makes them harder to steal, slower to deteriorate, and safe from nuclear wars. Other cases flaunt papers signed by George Washington, and James Madison's handwritten corrections of Constitutional amendments. Brush up your Latin on the Magna Carta, King John of England's famous guarantee of rights to his angry barons. Long tiered steps, stone friezes, fluted columns, and mammoth bronze doors (one foot thick and 40 feet high) remind you that neoclassicist John Russell Pope, of National Gallery of Art fame, also designed the Archives. (Main exhibit area open April-Aug. 10am-9pm, Sept.-Mar. 10am-5:30pm. Free.)

The Archives preserves over four billion papers and paraphernalia from American history. Its files hold about two percent of the paper the Federal Government generates, including maps, patents, photographs, police journals, and census forms. Very few of the Archives' possessions can be displayed at one time. The Archives owns but does not display the Emancipation Proclamation, President Lincoln's slave-freeing document of 1862. Weird stuff stored here includes a portrait of Richard Nixon painted on a grain of rice; a seven-foot roll of names on a paper tape, part of an 1893 petition; a red wig worn by Watergate villain Howard Hunt; and a file of Topps baseball cards, taken as evidence in a 1960s lawsuit.

The Microfilm Room on the building's fifth floor lets visitors check military records, census records, and Confederate and Revolutionary papers. Genealogy buffs tending family trees find plenty of historical fertilizer here; professional writers, like Alex Haley (*Roots*), come here to research upcoming best-sellers. At the Central Research Library, librarians of the central research variety will track the info you need through the Archives' reams of data. (Research facilities open Mon.-Fri. 10am-10pm, Sat. 9am-5pm; enter at Pennsylvania Ave. and 8th St.)

The operations tour of the Archives can show you more; you'll have to call and arrange it in advance, though. The Archive people will show tourists the vault into which the Declaration, Constitution et al. are lowered each night, then point you to patents for an "escape coffin"; the Reagan family census; the arrest record for John Wilkes Booth; a photo of Helen Keller with President Eisenhower; and President Nixon's 1974 letter of resignation. (Call 501-5205 to join a tour; U.S. citizens may call their congresspeople instead. Tours begin 10:15am and 1:15pm daily. Free. Tour-takers enter at Pennsylvania Ave. and 8th St. Make reservations in advance.) Exhibits in 1993 include "Western Ways," a show on westward expansion in the United States (Oct. 1992-Oct. 1993) and the "The Birth of Athenian Democracy" (summer and fall 1993).

The National Archives will even play Nixon's infamous Watergate tapes for the public, though at a safe distance from the White House. A shuttle leaves the premises from the 7th street bus stop at 8am, 9:30am, 11:30am, 1:45pm, and 3:15pm for 845 Picket St., Alexandria, Va., where the tapes are stored.

The **United States Navy Memorial** (737-2300) commemorates outdoors on Pennsylvania Ave. at 8th St. NW, midway between the White House and the Capitol. Petrophiles will love the largest-ever stone map of the world, set into the floor; compass-heads will note that the map's north is exactly aligned to true north. Read the quotes along the walls or the Naval Hymn carved into the steps. The circular memorial sometimes harbors concerts by (who else?) the Navy Band. Down a stairway, the "wave wall" holds glass panels on which ships are etched. The waves lead into a Gallery deck, another nautical room that leads into a President's room. The room honors (most) presidents who have served the Navy—both Roosevelts, Kennedy, Johnson, Nixon, Ford, and Bush. (Where's Naval Academy graduate Jimmy Carter?) In the Gallery Deck, windows open on the Theater, where the movie "At Sea" flaunts its high-tech graphics. (Memorial open 24 hrs. Visitors Center open Mon.-Sat. 10am-6pm, Sun. noon-5pm.)

Greater New Hope Baptist Church, on 8th St. between H and Eye St. NW, clearly used to be the Washington Hebrew Congregation—look for the six-pointed Star of David in the stained-glass window. Founded in 1852, Washington Hebrew (now far away on Massachusetts Ave. NW) was the first Jewish congregation in DC. The 1898 synagogue building shows off its onion domes to the new Baptist tenants.

The FBI

The end of the go-go, right-wing 80s hasn't fazed the Federal Bureau of Investigation (324-3000); today's FBI still hunts Commies, freaks, druggies, and interstate felons with undiminished vigor. Serious-minded agents will show you how and why it's done on the popular FBI tour. Tour lines form on the building's outdoor plaza (tour entrance from 10th St. NW at Pennsylvania Ave.). (Metro: Federal Triangle or Archives.) Witness the nadir of Washington Modernism in the block-long J. Edgar Hoover FBI building; its beige but brutal concrete planes are at once disorienting and standoffish. J. Edgar Hoover ran the FBI for 25 years; the sexually-tormented chief gave the Bureau its deserved reputation by nabbing the nation's notorious criminals in the 30s and 40s, then drove the FBI through over a decade of political espionage, homophobic innuendo, and the hounding of left-wing figures until his death in 1971.

Tourists can't wander around the high-security interior—you must wait for the tour, which starts every fifteen minutes. Real FBI agents sport walkie-talkies (and a strange resemblance to flight attendants) as they speed you through gangster paraphernalia and photos, relics of crime bosses, confiscated marijuana and cocaine, gun displays, a kidnapper's videotaped ransom demand, and mugshots of the nation's ten most wanted criminals. Tourists have identified these felons from their mugshots on two separate occasions; each led to an arrest. At the "Say No to Drugs" display, ask yourself how many teachers the American drug-eradication budget could purchase. Other exhibits describe the FBI's achievements against spies, polluters, bank robbers, computer criminals, and the Mob. John Dillinger's death mask hangs alongside his machine gun. (The rumor about his penis is unfounded.) In the counterespionage room, see the hollow coins and pencils spies have used to hide microfilm.

The FBI's crack team of scientists will ignore you as you watch them from behind plexiglass. Forensic chemists can identify you from a single hair, or your car from a paint chip the size of a pinhead. They can track your typewriter down, too, if you still have one. A roomful of guns will shock kids and adults, as will a chamber of valuables confiscated on drug raids: given our trillion-dollar national debt, why haven't these pearls and diamonds been sold off? At tour's end, a marksman picks up an FBI-standard revolver and a Thompson submachine gun and blasts away at cardboard evildoers. Most of the audience will applaud when the shooting ends; welcome to the U.S.A.

In theory, you can park on 9th St. near the Bureau. In practice, you'd do better to take Metro or walk here from the Mall. In June and July, crowds wait up to four hours for a tour; come early in the morning or during lunch hour to shorten the wait. (Tours Mon.-Fri 8:45am-4:15pm. Free.)

"Sic semper tyrannis!" muttered Abraham Lincoln's killer, John Wilkes Booth, minutes after shooting the President during a performance at **Ford's Theatre** (426-6924), 511 10th St. NW. (Metro: Metro Center, 11th St. exit.) Recline in comfortable theater seats while Ford's guides narrate the assassination for you. Being an actor, Booth had no trouble sneaking into the theater. Lincoln's April 14, 1865 appearance at *Our American Cousin* was his first time in public since the Civil War had ended. At 10:15pm, Booth entered the President's box, shot Lincoln, then injured his leg jumping on stage. The Maryland doctor who set the broken bone was exiled to Dry Tortuga for his pains. The museum below the theatre runneth over with placards and displays. At night Ford's Theatre becomes a contemporary playhouse (see *Theater*). *Sic semper tyrannis,* by the way, means "Thus always to tyrants"—it's the motto of the state of Virginia. (Open 9am-5pm daily; tours and talks given at a quarter past the hour, 9am-noon and 2pm and 5pm. One morning and two afternoon talks serve the visually impaired; call for schedule. Free.)

The morning after the evening he was shot, President Lincoln passed away at the **Petersen House** (426-6830), 526 10th St. NW. He slept—and died—diagonally in the too-short bed. The tiny room where he died now looks as it did then, and the intimacy of the room—its dotted white curtains, low walnut bed and bureau, simple tumblers and pitchers—makes visitors seem like strangers at a wake. (Open daily 9am-5pm.)

The **Old Post Office,** at Pennsylvania Ave. and 12th St. NW (523-5691, TDD 523-5694)), sheathes a shopping mall in architectural wonder. (Metro: Federal Triangle.) Its arched windows, conical turrets and 315-foot clock tower are a standing rebuke to its sleeker contemporary neighbors. Completed in 1899, the Post Office Building was criticized by the New York Times for looking "like a cross between a cathedral and a cotton mill." The building has also been referred to as a tooth needing extraction. Today, the wayward edifice, having avoided demolition in the 1950's, houses a tiny, one-room post office, some federal office space, a multiethnic food court, shops, and a stage. Offices rise on all four sides of a ten-story empty space in which tourists and business people enjoy cheap but tasty meals. For information on the shops collectively known as the Pavilion, call 289-4224. The National Park Service can show you around the clock tower (tour info 523-5691). The tour meets at the glass elevators in the patio area, where food tables cluster. The view from the top may be DC's best, especially since the archways are open-air (wired for safety), not glassed-in or minuscule (like the Washington Monument's). Bell-ringing volunteers make the tower chime for hours on end on federal holidays. (Tower open 8am-11pm mid-April to mid-Sept.; shops open Mon.-Sat. 10am-8pm, Sunday noon-6pm.) **City Golf,** the recently-opened miniature golf course, is located in the East Atrium of the Pavillion. (Open Mon.-Thurs. 10am-11pm, Fri.-10am-midnight, Sat. 10am-11pm, Sun 10am-10pm. Adults $4.95 for 18 holes.

The red brick **New York Ave. Presbyterian Church,** at New York Ave., H St. and 13th St. NW (393-3700) exhibits relics of Abraham Lincoln's history. (Metro: Metro Center.) In a meeting room one floor below the sanctuary, Lincoln's failed proposal to compensate states which freed their slaves hangs above the settee where he drafted it.

A room next door holds letters from Mary Lincoln to the Church's then-Reverend Gurley. The sanctuary upstairs remembers Lincoln and the Union Army in stained glass; the church pew Lincoln sat in still stands, darker than its neighbors, in the second row of pews to the left. Modern Presidents who attended services here, like Carter and occasionally Reagan, have preferred to sit where Lincoln did. (Tours given from 9am-1pm by appointment; call to arrange one.)

National Museum of Women in the Arts

Once you get into the establishment, you'll have a hard time making it to the top: that's the way it's been for many talented women, and that's the way the National Museum of Women in the Arts (783-5000), at 1250 New York Ave. NW, unwittingly imitates the rest of the art world. (Metro: Metro Center.) The bottom two floors were once a Masonic Temple, and a hunt for the museum's permanent collection, which begins on the third floor, is something like an initiation rite. From outside, the NMWA resembles the neighboring office buildings; inside, sweeping staircases, pink marble and celestial chandeliers look more mansion than museum. A second-floor balcony holds changing displays of consistent interest, though varying quality—a recent celebration of Denmark included Queen Henrietta's non-earthshaking watercolors.

Climb the stairs, traverse the balcony and ascend the spare, hidden staircase to the third floor, and you'll know you've made it: women artists have come into their own during the last hundred years, and the permanent collection proves it with works by Mary Cassatt, Georgia O'Keeffe, Isabel Bishop, Frida Kahlo, and Alma Thomas. Helen Frankenthaler's expansive landscape-like canvas compels a visit: her sharp, single brushstrokes and color washes of yellow and rust won't let you look away. Audrey Flack's surreal, glossy portrait of her daughter suggests the fast-paced brutality of the teenage world. The comparatively young museum invites a flood of temporary exhibitions; peruse the museum listings in *City Paper* or the *Washington Post Weekend* section to find even more reasons why you should hurry here. (Open Mon.-Sat. 10am-5pm, Sun. noon-5pm. Requested donation $3, $2 for kids.)

Washington's branch of the **National Aquarium**, the nation's first, cowers in the basement of the Commerce Department, at 14th St. and Constitution Ave. NW (377-2825). (Metro: Federal Triangle.) Kids will stare yearningly at the sixty-odd small tanks of exotic sea creatures. The salt-water fishes' vibrant colors and wild shapes (some flat as pancakes, others round as marbles) will keep you watching. Models, placards and explanatory displays make the aquarium easy to understand without a guided tour. This National Aquarium is smaller, less sophisticated and less spectacular than the one in Baltimore; on the other hand, the air-conditioned basement provides shelter from the Washington weather. (Open daily 9am-5pm. Popular shark (Mon., Wed., Sat.) and piranha (Tue., Thurs., Sun.,) feedings 2pm daily. Admission $2, children and seniors 75¢.)

The reopened **Willard Hotel** (628-9100) spreads its silvery finery over 1401 Pennsylvania Ave. NW like an engraved announcement of its century-old marriage to the rich and influential. President Grant hung out in the hotel's carpeted, chandeliered lobby, where office-seekers and favor-seekers came to plead their cases; ever since then the Washington representatives of companies and causes have been called "lobbyists."

Pershing Park brings greenery to the corner of Pennsylvania Ave. and 15th St. NW. A statue of General John "Black Jack" Pershing, who led U.S. forces in World War I, looks triumphant among marble slabs, whose blue and pink tracings map his battles. Enjoy the peaceful birch trees and black-eyed susans and watch the ducks swim in the water.

Old downtown ends at 15th St. NW with the **Treasury Building**, a Greek Revival monolith with all the charm of an iceberg. Adding insult to injury, its north wing breaks the long arm of Pennsylvania Ave. and blocks the White House from view: to reach the President's residence, turn left (north) onto 15th St. and walk one block until Pennsylvania Ave. reappears. The White House will be on your left.

Unusual Stores

Chapters, 1512 K St. NW (347-5495). High-quality downtown bookstore satisfies literati stranded in la la lawyer land. Frequent evening readings and lectures, as well as Friday tea (with sherry and cakes). Attractive half-price book sales. Open Mon.-Fri. 10am-6:30pm, Sat. 11am-5pm.

Washington Project for the Arts, 400 7th St. NW (347-4813). Nationally and locally known contemporary artists display their work. Exhibits rotate four to five times each year. Art books, catalogues, and reference books on sale at Bookworks. Open Tues.-Sun. 10am-5pm.

Capitol Coin and Stamp Co. of Washington D.C., 1100 17th St. NW (296-0400) at L St. This small store specializes in items of philatelic interest, political pins, posters, and banners. This is probably the only place you'll still be able to buy a Barry Goldwater doll or a Cuomo/Iacocca pin. Open Mon.-Sat, 10am-6pm.

White House Area/ Foggy Bottom

Before the Civil War, when most of Washington remained undeveloped, the White House anchored its own neighborhood: socialite circles and Cabinet secretaries liked to live around Lafayette Square, across from the President's House, or slightly farther up 16th St. NW. Since World War II development on all sides has turned the White House from a center into a boundary: the blocks it occupies separate lawyer-heavy New Downtown to the north, government-heavy Old Downtown to the east, Foggy Bottom to the west, and the Mall south of the Ellipse.

Though unscrupulous writers claim all of DC was "built on a swamp," only Foggy Bottom can truthfully carry that banner. The misty, low-lying swamp air gave the neighborhood its name, then gave way to heavy industry (and its fog-resembling pollutants) in the early 20th century. During World War II, while industrial contraction and government expansion swept manufacturing out of NW, the State Department took up quarters here at 23rd and C St. NW. Just as "the Pentagon" means the Defense Department, "Foggy Bottom" has become journalese for State; the neighborhood's old name now denotes the intellectual fog and diplomatic doublespeak in which the State Department deals. Today's Foggy Bottom rolls from 18th St. NW to the Potomac River, and from Pennsylvania Ave. to Constitution Ave. Near the Mall, government departments butt headquarters with old, respectable organizations in an unbroken sprawl of gardens, columns, and statuary. Above F St., George Washington University competes for breathing room with cheap hotels and moderately-priced townhouses. Farther east, the low-rise office buildings of the New Downtown edge closer and closer to their target in the White House.

The White House

> *Never before was such a compact jam in front of the*
> *White House—all the grounds fill'd, and away out*
> *to the spacious sidewalks. I was there in the rush in-*
> *side with the crowd—surged along the passage-*
> *ways, the blue and other rooms, and through the*
> *great east room. Crowds of country people, some*
> *very funny.*
>
> *—Walt Whitman,* Specimen Days

The White House, at 1600 Pennsylvania Ave. NW (456-7041, TDD 456-6213), isn't Versailles; the President's House, with its simple columns and expansive lawns, seems a compromise between patrician lavishness and democratic simplicity. In 1792 Thomas Jefferson suggested a contest to design the President's residence. But TJ's own diagrams lost out to James Hoban's more regal plan when then-President George Washington judged the competition. John Adams was the first Chief Executive to actually live in Hoban's structure, and Jefferson himself became the first to build additions. All this work was ruined when the British burned down the house, and much of Washington, in 1814; First Lady Dolly Madison interrupted her dinner to flee the flames, taking with her one of Gilbert Stuart's famous portraits of Washington. The White House has boasted wheelchair access since at least 1933, when FDR, who needed it, took office. (He also installed a swimming pool.) Martin Van Buren, who fenced off the lawns, started keeping the White House gardens spic-and-span; 120 years later, Jacqueline Kennedy made the Rose Garden famous, allowing later journalists to call Gerald Ford's stay-at-home reelection effort the "Rose Garden Campaign" in 1976. (The voters, who never promised him a Rose Garden, replaced Ford with Jimmy Carter.)

Despite remodelings in 1902 and 1948, the central third of the Executive Mansion looks more or less as Hoban planned it (he didn't design the East and West Wings). The White House is home to press conferences, state receptions, busloads of security guards, and even the occasional Presidential nap. When the President is in town, an American flag flies over his house. The President's personal staff works on his speeches and schedules and such in the West Wing, while the First Lady's cohort occupies the East Wing. The President does his own paperwork (and sometimes makes televised speeches) in the famous Green Room. Helicopters land on the White House lawn to spirit him away to conferences and vacations. One façade stays floodlit all night for the benefit of TV news reporters. Big lawns, fences, long driveways, and closed gates make the place somewhat less accessible to terrorists, though if you wait long enough you can sometimes glimpse Bush through the bushes.

You may **tour** certain rooms at the White House after obtaining a free ticket at the ticket booth on the Ellipse, the park south of the White House on Constitution Ave. between 15th and 18th St. NW. (Tours Tues.-Sat. 10am-noon; tickets distributed starting at 8am). Disabled visitors can go straight to the Pennsylvania Ave. entrance without an admission ticket. After you get a ticket, you'll wait about two-and-a-half hours for the tour. American citizens can arrange a more comprehensive, more intimate tour of the White House through their Congresspeople: write to her or him several months in advance.

The ordinary (non-Congressional) tour is guarded, but unguided; you might try posing your questions to the Secret Service guards. In the East Wing lobby you'll survey portraits of presidents and first ladies. The hallway windows look past the tea gardens where the First Lady holds gatherings; the landscape incorporates the Rose Garden. Presidential parties, press conferences and funerals (for Harrison, Taylor, Lincoln, Harding, FDR and JFK) have taken place in the East Room, where President Cleveland got married (in 1885) and Theodore Roosevelt let his children rollerskate. The Blue Room, said to be the White House's most beautiful, frequently receives ambassadors paying their first formal visits to the President. The State Dining Room entertains large groups of guests, like the Queen of England and her entourage. Its gold and white elegance served hunter Theodore Roosevelt when he mounted his trophies there. An obsolete bomb shelter under the Treasury building, built during World War II, connects to the White House by a tunnel under the East Lawn; aides in the know use the tunnel as a quick exit to 15th St. NW. You probably won't see the President, but you can find out where he is: call 456-2343 for his daily schedule. You can get to the White House from anywhere downtown by walking towards 16th St. NW along Pennsylvania Ave. (Metro: McPherson Square, Vermont Ave. exit.)

Due south of the White House, the empty grass of **the Ellipse** sometimes fills up with political demonstrators or congregating tour groups. A small granite shaft in the Ellipse bears the names of the 18 landowners who gave up their plantations so DC could be built. Directly in front of the White House, where the green grass meets E St. NW, Washington's Zero Milestone provides tangible evidence of early surveyors.

Sometimes it's hard to tell the homeless, the political demonstrators, and the statues apart in **Lafayette Park,** across Pennsylvania Ave. from the White House. All three are more-or-less permanent presences, and the "Peace Park" denizens on the one-square-block park's southeast edge are camped out there until the U.S. gives up nukes—not soon. (Sign-toting demonstrators used to congregate on the Pennsylvania Ave. side of the White House, but the Secret Service punted them across the street.) Clark Mills' stone-faced Andrew Jackson stands in the center of the park. Wallace Stevens wrote that this statue shows that good citizens need "immunity to eloquence"; try and decide what Stevens meant as you contemplate Mills' chiselwork. (Stevens also called the horse's tail one of the world's most beautiful—go figure.) Everybody else is a Revolutionary War hero: the Marquis de Lafayette joined Jackson in 1891, on the southeast (15th and Pennsylvania) corner of the park. A half-dressed woman (France?) hands him his sword, while nude infants (the infant U.S.?) look gratefully up at him. (An old joke has the lady saying, "Give me back my clothes, and I'll give you back your sword.") Lafayette's compatriot Rochambeau takes up his post in the southwest corner. Polish Brigadier Thaddeus Kosciuszko, who fortified West Point and Saratoga for the Continental Army, defends the northeast corner, and Baron Von Steuben, who trained American troops at Valley Forge, drills pedestrians from the northwest corner.

Though Benjamin Latrobe (of U.S. Capitol fame) designed it, **Decatur House,** 748 Jackson Place NW (842-0920), retains mostly historical interest. (Metro: Farragut West.) Naval hero Stephen Decatur defeated the Barbary Pirates off the shores of Tripoli before he moved in; after only one year in his new house, Decatur died in a duel with a man he kicked out of the military. His death prompted a nationwide ban on duels. During the 1830s and 40s, hotelier John Gadsby entertained Washington's elite in the ballrooms while he kept slaves chained behind the house. In 1871 the house was purchased by Edward Beale, best remembered for having carried official news of the Gold Rush to Washington, disguised as a frontiersman. The Beales were responsible for most of the later improvements to the house, including the elegant inlaid floors and "Romantic eclectic"-style furnishing (in evidence in the upper drawing room). The first floor, furnished in the Federal style, displays Decatur's furnishings and his sword. *Life* magazine photos of parties held here decorate the tables upstairs. From the Metro, walk south on 17th St. to H St., then turn left to Jackson Place. The house is on your left, near the corner of the next block. Walk-in tours, provided immediately, last about 30 minutes. (Open Tues.-Fri. 10am-2pm, Sat.-Sun. noon-4pm. Admission $3, seniors and children $1.50. Spacious gift shop open Mon.-Fri. 10am-5:30pm, Sat. 10am-4pm.)

The **Old Executive Office Building,** on 17th St. and Penn. Ave. NW, amazes pedestrians with its gingerbread complexity; President Truman called it "the greatest monstrosity in America." Cascades of small plain columns, tall chimneys, and an endless array of mini-colonnades, pediments, and porches give the French Second Empire building its baroque distinction. Cannons flank the entrance steps. On weekdays, you'll have to stand outside and stare; since the Building continues to house White House staff workers, tours only happen on Saturdays. Tour-takers will gasp at the Indian treaty room's marble wall panels, 800-lb. bronze lamps, and gold ornamentation. Gilded domes and frilly balustrades grace much of the interior. Currently, the ornate front side is obscured by scaffolding, as extensive roof renovation is underway. The work should be completed within 5 to 10 years. (To schedule a free tour, call 395-3000.)

Blair House, 1651-53 Pennsylvania Ave. NW, across the street from the White House, houses foreign dignitaries who visit Washington; see if there's a guest by looking for Secret Service agents and diplomatic limos. President Truman lived here during White House renovations; a plaque on the wrought-iron gates remembers a guard who saved Truman from a would-be assassin.

St. John's Church, at 16th and H St. NW, across Lafayette Park, is known as the Church of Presidents; each one since Madison, Episcopalian or not, has dropped in at least once. The ubiquitous Benjamin Latrobe designed it for free; look for his half-moon windows.

The **Wilderness Society's Ansel Adams exhibit** at 900 17th St. NW (833-2300) holds over 75 poster-size prints by the American landscape photographer, including the famous *Moonrise Hernandez*. The collection is the only permanent Adams show on the East Coast. (Open Mon.-Fri. 10am-5pm. Free.)

Renwick Gallery

At 17th St. and Penn. Ave. NW, the Renwick Gallery (357-1718 or 357-2700) fills its Second Empire Mansion with some of DC's most interesting art. (Metro: Farragut

West,) The Smithsonian-owned gallery says it displays "American craft," but it's not just for macrame buffs: the first floor's temporary exhibits often show fascinating mixed-media sculptures, tapestries, and constructions by important contemporary artists. Upstairs a ballroom-sized chamber holds more traditional furniture and an uneven set of oil paintings. Translucent glass fantasies inhabit the ornate cases; look for the blown-glass fish and the lacy vases, then seek out the ebony and marble-topped cabinets. Stare for hours at *Gamefish*, a sculpture made of sailfish parts, rhinestones, poker chips and badminton birdies. Exhibitions change during the course of year; expected upcoming attractions include Albert Paley's studies of the Renwick Gallery's "Portal Gates" (Sept. 1992-March 1993); drawings by craft artists (June 1992-March 1993); "American Impressions" (March-July 1993). The first floor's contemporary exhibits change from year to year; past highlights have included a table accurately entitled *Mystery Robots Rip Off the Rain Forest*. (Open daily 10am-5:30pm. Excellent handicapped access. Free.)

Corcoran Gallery

Once housed in the Renwick's mansion, the Corcoran (628-3211) now exhibits in much larger, neoclassical quarters on 17th St. between E St. and New York Ave. NW. (Metro: Farragut West.) Frank Lloyd Wright called it "the best designed building in Washington." The Corcoran shows off American artists like portraitist John Singer Sargent, impressionist Mary Cassatt, and seascape-master Winslow Homer. Frederic Church's huge *Niagara Falls* shimmers with mist while its rainbow and horizon glow; Church was expert at copying spectacular "photographic" effects of color, light, and scale. If it sounds hokey now, it won't when you see it. The atrium holds countless marble busts. Hiram Powers' statue of a nude Greek slave made an abolitionist statement on its first nationwide tour in 1846; now electronic precautions stop modern vandals from stealing the now-depoliticized chain binding the statue. The atrium's *Veiled Nun* remains a glowing, if modest, favorite; W.W. Corcoran, the museum's founder, brought her home from Rome, and her sculptor remains anonymous.

While the permanent collection focuses on the 19th century, the Gallery's temporary exhibits seek the cutting edge of contemporary art. Four major exhibitions, not necessarily modern, sweep the second floor yearly. In 1988 the Corcoran reneged on its promise to house a touring exhibit of photography by the late Robert Mapplethorpe; the ensuing uproar over homophobia, obscenity laws, and Federal funding for the arts rendered the Corcoran notorious and made Mapplethorpe one of the best-known names in photography. Attractions for 1993 include "Karsh: American Legends" (Feb.-April), an exhibit of 20th-century African art (Feb.-April), and a show of Latin American folk art (Aug.-Oct.). Call for more detailed information. Free jazz concerts resound in the Hammer Auditorium every Wed. from 12:30-1:30pm. The Corcoran also incorporates an art school. (Open Tues.-Wed. and Fri.-Sun. 10am-5:30pm, Thurs. 10am-9pm. Suggested donation $3, students and seniors $1, families $5, under 12 free.)

If you can find the entrance at 1776 D St. NW, the **Daughters of the American Revolution** (628-1776, ext. 238) will open historical doors for you—more than 33, in fact. (Metro: Farragut West, then walk south on 17th St.) Follow a docent around the building to see 33 period rooms, each room conceived, designed, and furnished by a different state to illuminate early American life-styles. New Jersey's room copies an old-time battleship. California's tri-cultural room incorporates Chinese vases, Mexican serapes, and American horsehair furniture. New Hampshire's attic will satisfy the young'uns with its horde of antique toys. In the DAR museum, cover lovers can imagine cuddling up with the finely-made array of pre-industrial quilts. Call the Education Office for a guided tour at least two weeks in advance. (Tours Mon.-Fri. 10am-2:30pm and Sun. 1-5pm. Museum open Mon.-Fri. 8:30am-4pm and Sun. 1-5pm. Tours Mon.-Fri. 10am-3pm, Sun. 1pm-5pm. Entrance for the disabled at 1775 C St. Free.)

Adjoined to the building is **Constitution Hall,** located on 18th St. between C and D St. NW (638-2661). This 4000-seat auditorium holds concerts and ceremonies (see *Entertainment* for info on them). The U-shaped amphitheater wears the buff and blue of the DAR State seals hung from the boxes. Tapestries of Revolutionary moments, like the Boston Tea Party and George Washington's inauguration, dangle over the stage. It's been used for patriotic purposes and civic occasions, though it's most famous for an unpatriotic one: in 1939 the DAR wouldn't let African-American soprano Marian Anderson sing here, so she sang from the steps of the Lincoln Memorial.

The **Organization of American States,** at 17th St. and Constitution Ave. NW (information 458-3000; museum/gallery 458-6016), is a Latin American extravaganza: sunlight hits the concrete patio and bakes the stone benches in its air-conditioned center, where a fountain gurgles over greenery. The patio's tiles copy traditional pre-Columbian designs. During parades, like the one for Desert Storm in 1991, the OAS locks up; its position is perfect for rooftop snipers. Most OAS members are Spanish-speaking nations, so visitors will hear more Spanish than English inside. Each country gets its own parking space outside; Central American spaces may contain compact cars, but the United States one won't.

The OAS' second-floor art gallery is small but fresh, displaying 20th-century art from Central and South America. Next door is the OAS meeting room, which holds formal sessions like the United Nations'. The meetings, held largely in Spanish, welcome curious tourists; Spanishless visitors can hook up to translation machines. (Call to ask when they're in session.) Upstairs, in the Hall of the Americas, Tiffany chandeliers and windows bearing coats of arms light up the 100 foot by 65 foot room; the flags hang in alphabetical order according to their nations' Spanish names. Valiant-looking busts line the Hall of National Heroes. Downstairs and outside, the God of Flowers, Xochipilli, whom the Aztecs honored with hallucinogenic feasts and sacrificial frenzies, reclines in the **Aztec Garden**. The garden path leads to the Museum of the Americas, a collection of art from Mexico, Peru, Brazil, and other member states. The two-story building houses a permanent collection of modern art, as well as several temporary exhibits each year. (OAS open Tues.-Sat. 10am-5pm. Free.)

Completely surrounded by the American Institute of Architects, the **Octagon House,** 1799 New York Ave. NW (638-3105), continues the Foggy Bottom tradition of hiding historic houses among office buildings. (Metro: Farragut West; walk down 18th St.) The Architects occupy half the red brick mansion, but you can tour the other half. The 1799 mansion, designed by the Capitol's first architect, is a fine example of Federal-style architecture. Dolly Madison fled here when British troops torched the White House in 1814; they spared the Octagon, probably because the French Ambassador flew his nation's flag over the house. Despite its name, the house is hexagonal; a tower in one corner interrupts its geometry. The north and east walls extend to enclose a boxwood garden. The house's doors stand flush with its walls, even in the one octagonal room. The table on which the Treaty of Ghent was signed is displayed here; it's a curious furnishing, with 12 ivory-inlaid drawers marked "receipts," "bills paid," and "letters." The house holds surprises as well—a wooden commode and Bacchanalian terracotta mantelpieces. Don't miss the basement kitchen. Dolly Madison, a suicidal slave girl, and Colonel Taylor's daughter number among the ghosts said to roam the Octagon. The house is now undergoing a massive renovation project estimated to take 4 years and $4 million to complete. Detailed notices adorn the exterior to inform the public of the building's progress. On display in the cellar are a collection of artifacts uncovered by recent excavations, from old fibers and china to more recent plastic cups. (Open Tues.-Fri 10am-4pm, Sat.-Sun. noon-4pm; suggested donation $2, kids and seniors $1.)

The **American Red Cross's** (737-8300) Tiffany stained-glass windows at 18th and E St. NW deserve a few admiring minutes. Inside the East building's large bronze doors, an effusive receptionist will direct you up the marble staircase, where Hiram Powers' busts of *Faith, Hope,* and *Charity* abide. In the second-floor assembly room, Louis Tiffany's stained glass portrays figures from Spenser's *Faerie Queene:* Filomena, virtuous Una, and of course, the Redcrosse Knight. (Open Mon.-Fri. 9am-4pm. Free.)

The **Department of the Interior** (208-4743) covers a square area on C St. between 18th and 19th and extends to D St. Franklin D. Roosevelt laid the cornerstone for the building in 1936, using the same trowel George Washington employed to lay the Capitol's cornerstone in 1793. The six-wing, seven-story limestone building incorporates 16 acres of floors, two miles of corridors, and 20 high-speed elevators, and two bronze "buffalo seals" representing Interior. A cafeteria in the basement features a huge sound-proof skylit room with facilities for 1500 diners. (Open 7am-2:45pm.) The National Park Service desk spews helpful brochures about forests and outfitters. Sign in with a guard in the main entrance on 18th and C St. and walk down the hallway; to the right is the park office.

The Interior Department's museum is across from the park office, on the left side of the hallway. (Enter at 18th and C St.) Stuffed moose, deer, eagle, and bear heads welcome you to the capsule dioramas which portray the "opening" of the West. Glass cases display land patents signed by King George III, President Coolidge, and other official bestowers. Many Ansel Adams photographs show the land in its unsullied state. Paintings of wilderness scenes compete with Native American handcrafts—headdresses, tools, weapons, blankets, and baskets. (Museum open Mon.-Fri. 8am-5pm.)

The **Federal Reserve** counts its change in a heavy-set, clean-lined building on Constitution Ave. between 20th and 21st St. NW. The Federal Reserve Board and its head, Alan Greenspan, control the nation's money supply; they decide how much dough there should be and what interest rates major banks should pay when they borrow it. The actual greenbacks sleep in regional banks in Boston, New York, Cleveland, Dallas, and San Francisco (among others); this building is just where the Board meets and has its offices. Paul Cret's skimpy temple to Mammon has the settled, staid look of established wealth. An eagle on the lintel oversees hundreds of square feet of flatness in front.

Few collections of American furniture and art compare to that of the **State Department,** 21st and C St. (647-3241), whose cement HQ extends to 23rd St. (Metro: Foggy Bottom-GWU.) You must reserve a space on the 45-minute guided tour to see the inside of the State Department. The free tours fill up very quickly; call at least 2 weeks in advance. The original walls of the reception rooms were avocado-green, with floor-to-ceiling windows, wall-to-wall carpeting, and exposed steel beams. The undiplomatic decor prompted 1960s Secretary of State Dean Rusk to launch Project Americana, in which the State accumulated Boston highboys and lowboys, Chippendale chairs, paintings of Washington, and other cute items made between 1750 and 1825. There's a portrait of Thomas Jefferson in a toga; a highboy capped by a bust of political thinker John Locke; and the desk where Thomas Jefferson wrote the Declaration of Independence and Nixon signed the Constitutional Amendment (#26) giving 18-year-olds the vote. A painting of the Mayflower shows pilgrims in British Redcoats and a welcome wagon of Indians whooping hellos—oops. The Benjamin Franklin dining room makes a spectacle of itself in mauve and gold; the French carpet took a whole weekend to lay.

The **National Academy of Sciences,** at 21st and C St. NW (334-2000), holds scientific or medical exhibits (duh). A bizarre arrangement of golden pendulums and hanging globes illustrates the Earth's rotation inside. Dig the massive bronze doors at the main entrance; each of the eight panels shows important scientific personalities, from Aristotle to Pasteur. It's customary to sit in the lap of the statue of Albert Einstein, outside, and get your picture taken. The beloved physicist sits above a star map: the 28-foot field of emerald pearl granite holds metal studs that represent the planets, sun, moon, and stars. Einstein's aphorisms are carved on the back of his bench. Open Mon.-Fri. 9am-5pm.

Foggy Bottom north of F St. is the province of **George Washington University** (994-GWGW (-4949)). A desk in the Academic Center at 801 22nd St. NW gives away brochures, newspapers, and *The Big To Do*, an entertainment calendar. GWU's undergraduates often hail from abroad; its graduate schools are nationally known.

Down New Hampshire Ave. at Virginia Ave. NW, near the Kennedy Center, the man on the pedestal is Mexican hero Benito Juarez, a nineteenth-century president and author of the Mexican constitution. Juarez looks more like a scolding parent than a liberator in this standing portrait; it's not hard to imagine him saying "Don't point that thing at me!"

The Kennedy Center

Above Rock Creek Parkway, the white rectilinear **John F. Kennedy Center for the Performing Arts** (Tix. and info. 467-4600, TDD 416-8524) rises and glows like a marble sarcophagus. But don't trust your first impressions: the multi-purpose Kennedy Center can be one of the liveliest spaces in town. (Metro: Foggy Bottom-GWU, then walk away from downtown on H St. and turn left, i.e. south, onto New Hampshire Ave.; pedestrian entrance off 25th St. and New Hampshire Ave. NW.) Built in the late 1960s, the Center boasts four major stages and a film theater; its sumptuous interior rolls out wall-to-wall red carpets under mirrors, bronze busts, and crystal chandeliers. Many nations have donated materials, rooms, or free-standing art in memory of JFK. Architect Edward Durrell Stone's unique combination of modern streamlining with old-time, large-scale opulence makes it worth seeing even if you couldn't care less about most architecture. Student tickets, sometimes well-discounted, make taking in a show here possible.

Almost everything in the Kennedy Center has a self-explanatory name. State flags hang in the **Hall of States** in the order in which they joined the Union. In the **Hall of Nations,** the flags of all nations with which the U.S. has diplomatic relations hang in alphabetical order. Look for an empty pole next to Ireland's and Israel's banners to see if the Iraqi flag has been put back up. Jurgen Weber's reliefs, "America" and "War and Peace," depict the indicated subjects at each end of the Hall of Nations. Both grand halls lead to the **Grand Foyer,** which could swallow the Washington Monument with room to spare. A 7-foot bronze bust of JFK stares up and away at the eighteen ponderous Swedish chandeliers.

In the **Concert Hall,** an audience of 2750 can hear up to 200 classical musicians. The President's box includes a reception room and a banner with his seal, which hangs from the balcony when he deigns to attend. The stage was a gift from over 692 high school, college, and community organizations from the U.S., Canada, Britain, and Japan. The National Symphony Orchestra calls the KenCen Concert Hall home. Kick back in the **Israeli Lounge** on the Box Tier of the Concert Hall (that means just outside it and up the stairs). The lounge's vivid turquoise, red, yellow, and olive ceiling depicts musical instruments. Admire the Hebrew message inlaid (in 24-carat gold) in the wooden wall mosaic; intricate sepia sketches adorn the other walls. Carved from a 700-year-old tree, twelve-foot high, intricate Nigerian doors lead into the **African Room**. Tapestries, ornate bowls, print cloth, and reliefs show off the continent's traditions.

If no rehearsals are in progress, you can visit the opulent, all-red **Opera House.** Snowflake-shaped chandeliers, gifts from Austria, cover a 70-foot diameter circular space and require 1735 electric light bulbs. Japan's more sensible gift, the red silk curtain, adds to the grandeur. All those massive double doors and extra hallways, by the way, insulate the complex's theaters from the noise of planes landing at nearby National Airport. A Waterford crystal chandelier, with 4000 perfectly matched prisms, hangs from 22-carat gold leaf ceiling panels in the **South Opera Lounge.** This Lounge also holds two handwoven Spanish tapestries, copies made from paintings by Goya. When red turns to purple on the roof level, you're near the Terrace Theater, an acoustical marvel and home to an excellent chamber-music series. Art scattered about the KenCen's levels ranges from blast-damaged sheet metal polished to a glow to tapestries depicting the seven days of creation. Greece donated a bronze casting of a statue discovered beneath the Aegean Sea. Henri Matisse designed France's gift, a set of blue and white tapestries.

The **Eisenhower Theatre** is the smallest of the main floor theaters, seating only 1,100 people. The steep angle of the seats, which are made of East Indian laurel wood, to the stage can be slightly unnerving. Comic operas, classic Greek plays, and small productions are performed here. Instead of the usual presidential seal for the executive box, Eisenhower's portrait hangs here. Note that this portrait is not removed when the President is in.

The Roof Terrace Restaurant would bankrupt almost anyone, but you can walk along the outdoor **roof terrace** itself for free. Acrophiles will especially enjoy the view of the Watergate complex, the spires of Georgetown, and Theodore Roosevelt Island. The terrace becomes unbeatable around 10pm for an hour of nighttime skyline-watching. You can bring food up here, too.

For the scoop on performances at the Kennedy Center, see *Entertainment* and *Annual Events*. Superlative disabled access includes provisions for sight- and hearing-impaired audience members; all theaters are wheelchair accessible. The Center opens daily 10am-11pm. (Free tours 10am-2pm.) Parking in the commercial basement lot is available, for short and long-term visits.

Across G St. NW from the Kennedy Center, at the western end of Virginia Ave., the black-and-white half-cylinders of the **Watergate** buildings (offices, apartments, and a luxury hotel) seem to bend away from the White House, toward the Potomac River. The Watergate scandal took its name from these buildings—the office space housed the Democratic National Committee's headquarters when Nixon ordered them burgled in 1972.

Georgetown

> At Georgetown, in the suburbs, there is a Jesuit Col-
> lege, delightfully situated and so far as I had an op-
> portunity of seeing, well managed...The heights in
> this neighborhood, above the Potomac River, are
> very picturesque and are free, I should conceive,
> from some of the insalubrities of Washington.
> —*Charles Dickens,* American Notes *(1842)*

Ask a native Washingtonian for directions to Georgetown and she'll point you vaguely towards where M St. NW meets Wisconsin Ave. Ask her what it is and expect an answer even more vague than its boundaries. Georgetown is a college town and a posh real estate district, where ambassadors-in-training rub elbows with the Kissingers; it's a credit card baby's shopping nirvana; it's restaurant row *cum* club-land with no distinction between the two. Washington thinks it's pretty hip; Georgetown knows it is, painfully so.

In 1702 Queen Anne of England granted the "Rock of Dunbarton," a huge blob of land, to Ninian Beall. By the 1730s, the Beall family was complaining to the colonial government about "squatters" on its land at the edge of the Potomac. The "squatters"— Scottish merchants—founded the town of George, incorporated in 1789. The same year inaugurated Georgetown University. The port brought the new town commerce and people; as the farthest point up the Potomac a ship could travel, Georgetown proved ideal for the sorting and shipping of tobacco from Virginia and Maryland. Not until the 1800s were the Bealls fully paid for their land.

As the only existing town within the District's limits, Georgetown was the logical hangout for Washington's first bigwigs. Pierre L'Enfant stayed in Georgetown's Suter's Tavern (now destroyed) in 1791; the House of Representatives decided the election of 1800 in a "very wet" session at that tavern. While much of central Washington remained unbuilt, Georgetown prospered; most of its Federal-style buildings were erected between 1780 and 1830 when the port was thriving. You can still distinguish the smaller townhouses below Dumbarton St., built for the workers, from the larger houses of upper Georgetown.

Georgetown's incarnation as a harbor town was colorful, but short-lived. In 1828 President John Quincy Adams turned the first shovelful of dirt for the Chesapeake and Ohio (C&O) Canal. The same day Adams opened the canal dig, workers in Baltimore drove the first spike for the Baltimore and Ohio Railroad, whose steam-driven efficiency KO'd the C&O as a commercial route. Though the canal thrived in the 1870s, steam ships of the next decade couldn't fit into the harbor; after an 1889 flood, ports such as Baltimore's and Norfolk's—not to mention Southwest Washington's—rendered Geor-

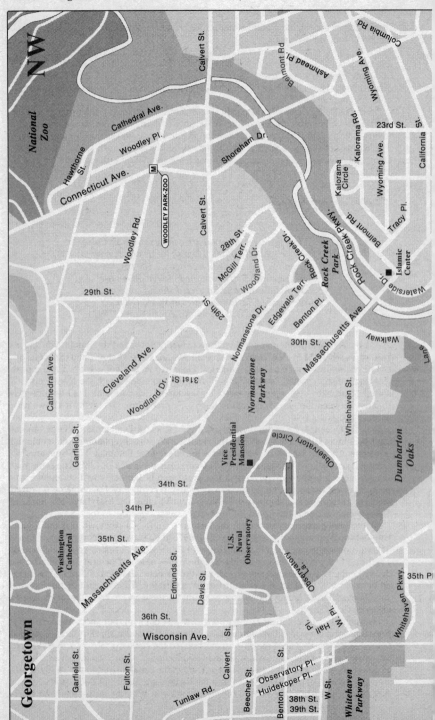

Georgetown

NW

National Zoo

Cathedral Ave.
Hawthorne St.
Woodley Pl.
Connecticut Ave.
Woodley Rd.

Calvert St.
Shoreham Dr.

WOODLEY PARK-ZOO

29th St.
Calvert St.
28th St.
McGill Terr.
Woodland Dr.
29th St.

Belmont Rd
Ashmead Pl
Columbia Rd.
Wyoming Ave.
23rd St.
California St.
Kalorama Rd.
Wyoming Ave.
Kalorama Circle
Tracy Pl.
Belmont Rd.

Rock Creek Pkwy.
Rock Creek Dr.
Rock Creek Park

Waterside Dr.
Islamic Center

Cathedral Ave.
Cleveland Ave.
Woodland Dr.
31st St.

Normanstone Dr.
Edgevale Terr.
Benton Pl.
30th St.
Massachusetts Ave.
Walkway
Lane

Normanstone Parkway

Whitehaven St.

Dumbarton Oaks

Garfield St.

Vice Presidential Mansion
Observatory Circle
34th St.
34th Pl.
35th St.

Washington Cathedral

Massachusetts Ave.

U.S. Naval Observatory

Observatory La.

35th Pl

Whitehaven Pkwy.

Garfield St.
Fulton St.
Edmunds St.
Davis St.
36th St.
Wisconsin Ave.
Calvert St.

Beecher St.
Observatory Pl.
Huidekoper Pl.
Benton St.
W. Hall Pl.
W. Pl.
W St.
38th St.
39th St.
Tunlaw Rd.

Whitehaven Parkway

getown's harbor obsolete. The canal survives as part of the national park system; long-winded bicyclists have replaced barge-pulling mules along its towpaths.

Washington's free Black population nearly doubled between 1830 and 1861, and many African-Americans moved here: DC's first Black congregation, the still-active Mt. Zion United Methodist Church (see below) also was an Underground Railroad station for slaves on their way to free Canada. As Georgetown's economy faltered, working-class Black families took quarters in historic mansions subdivided into apartments. Employed as domestics, cooks, and stable attendants to the remaining estates, over 1000 families occupied "Herring Hill" (south of P St. between Rock Creek Park and 29th St.), so called because residents subsisted on fish from the harbor. During the early 20th century Georgetown was racially integrated and unfashionable; the first Washington zoning act labeled it "industrial." But when FDR's New Deal and World War II nearly doubled the number of federal jobs, the new white-collar (and white) civil servants invaded Georgetown. Black families sold their homes, and African-American culture moved downtown.

Today only the rich can afford the inflated real estate, and only the chic feel the need to do so. Trace the history of those who have resided in Georgetown to get a feel for the shifting political winds. John F. Kennedy lived here as a U.S. Senator (at 3260 N St.). Some of the townhouses between M St. and R St. have been subdivided and rented out to Georgetown University students, but others hide backyard courtyards and Warhols in every bathroom. Hollywood has found the area's prestige, if not irresistible, at least mildly interesting: movies set at least partly in Georgetown include *The Exorcist* and *St. Elmo's Fire*.

Georgetown also serves its eponymous university, obliging the students with all-night food and late-night record stores: the combination makes Georgetown irresistible for the young and rich. Some shops are only slightly overpriced, but others are boutique-monuments to conspicuous consumption. You can browse and window-shop for free, though. Don't ignore the many historic sites, hidden on residential blocks, that are open to the public. Unfortunately, many landmarks have already been scrapped; no one knows exactly where the old Suter's Tavern was, though recent researchers claim the Pleasure Chest, a sex-toy shop, now occupies its site.

Orientation

If you try to park your car in Georgetown, you just may send your brain into gridlock—weekends are particularly infamous. The key to mental health is patience and a willingness to walk six blocks to the center of town. Try 35th St. near the university (particularly promising in summer) or Georgetown's eastern edge on the other side of Wisconsin Ave., around 28th St. Garages charge way too much. On weekend nights, choose a block and drive around in circles, scrounging for a place—raucous teens will miraculously arrive and drive their Ford off to the suburbs eventually.

When Kevin Costner, in the movie *No Way Out,* escaped Pentagon nasties by racing into the "Georgetown Metro," DC audiences laughed out loud. Persistent rumors (and rival guidebooks) claim that the Georgetown Citizens' Association vetoed a Georgetown Metro stop, illogically voting to clog their streets with other people's autos just to keep away carless proletarians. In fact, a Georgetown subway would have posed a prohibitive engineering problem—a 90-degree turn in an underground tunnel just at the water's edge. And what business would let the station take its place, or allow the excavation to obscure its storefront?

The nearest Metro stop, Foggy Bottom/GWU, is about eight long blocks from the center of Georgetown. When you exit the station, you'll find yourself facing 23rd St. NW. Turn left down 23rd and walk counterclockwise around Washington Circle, against traffic, until you reach Pennsylvania Ave., then trudge down Pennsylvania over the bridge and to M St. From Dupont Circle, just follow P St. east, past Rock Creek Park. Metrobuses #30, 32, 34, or 36 run from M St. up Wisconsin past the National Cathedral and up to Friendship Heights and the Maryland line.

Wisconsin Ave. and M St. are the main thoroughfares, and their intersection centers the neighborhood. Address numbers on Wisconsin Ave. start below M St. and go up as the avenue goes north (in this area, uphill). For most of its Georgetown length K St. is directly under the Whitehurst Freeway, thus hard to find on maps. (At twilight, enjoy the *Blade Runner*-style view of the looming Whitehurst.) East of Georgetown is the K St. Business District and, north of that, the Dupont Circle neighborhood; Rock Creek Park provides a clear boundary. M St., Pennsylvania Ave., P St., and Q St. are the only ways to Georgetown for pedestrians coming from downtown or Dupont Circle. West of Key Bridge M St. becomes Canal Road, and neon and brick abruptly give way to the trees and vines of Glover Archibold Park.

The oldest building still standing in Washington, the **Old Stone House** at 3051 M St. (426-6851) has been restored and refurbished with reproductions and relics of pre-Revolutionary Georgetown according to the alliterative inventory list of original owner Christopher Layman. Layman, a carpenter, used the front of the house as a shop, the back room as a kitchen, and upstairs for the bedrooms. Low doorways show how short, compared to us, the colonials were. Rumors that Pierre L'Enfant lived there while designing the city helped convince Congress in 1950 to protect the house. The English garden positively begs for you to stop and smell the roses, larkspurs, and poppies. The National Park Service demonstrates 18th-century cooking, bread baking, candle-making, and fabric-spinning every so often. (House open Wed.-Sun. 8am-4:30pm; garden open April-Sept. Mon.-Tues. 8am-3pm, Wed.-Sun. 8am-4:30pm. Free.)

Mount Zion Methodist Church, 1334 29th St. (234-0148) was founded in 1816 by about 125 African-Americans. The church was a stop on the Underground Railroad (the chain of hideouts for escaped slaves fleeing the South); passengers sometimes hid in a vault on the Old Methodist Burying Ground next door. Though Georgetown is largely white today, Mount Zion's congregation remains active. Behind the church at 2906 O St., the Community House, erected in 1810-11, holds old records, manuscripts, and photographs of past congregants, including Leontine Kelly, the first Black woman to become a bishop. Rev. Monroe will prove unusually helpful and infinitely knowledgeable about the church, house, and cemetery. To see the Community House and Church, call the parsonage first.

The **Mount Zion Cemetery and Female Union Band Cemetery** behind 2515-2531 Q St., remains open to the public. In 1842 the Female Union Band, a benevolent association of women, purchased this plot for the burial of free Blacks—the first African-American cemetery in DC. The Mt. Zion Methodist Church later rented (and renamed) the Old Methodist Burying Ground next door "for the sum of one dollar in hand." The two cemeteries cannot be told apart today; both are overgrown. You can still read some of the gravestones, some haunting or sad, others suffused with sweet and gentle charm.

2803 P St. seems like every other house on the block. The fence seems like every other fence. But every stake of the **Gunbarrel Fence** is really a 1767 Charlevoix rifle barrel, with the rifle stocks buried in the retaining wall. Reuben Dawes, a stonecutter, built three houses on this block of P St. in 1843 and used surplus Mexican War rifles to build his cheap fence. Some of the rifles have a small notch near the top—the rifle sight. The house inside is not open to the public.

Dumbarton Oaks

Dumbarton Oaks, 1703 32nd St. NW between R and S St. (recorded info. 338-8278, tour info. 342-3212), includes two separate must-see sights: the mansion-museum displays Byzantine and pre-Columbian art, and the terraced gardens are the best cheap date in town. (Don't confuse this estate with the entirely separate Dumbarton *House*.) The 16-acre estate is all that remains of the original Rock of Dunbarton property, out of which settlers carved the town of George. The house switched names and styles frequently since its construction in 1801; Secretary of War John Calhoun of South Carolina, later a fire-breathing secessionist, lived here from 1824-26. Robert and Mildred Bliss renovated it to accommodate the library and collections, then donated the house and gardens to Harvard University in 1940.

Don't fear the imposing gates or the solemn hush as you enter the Dumbarton Oaks building: the cold, scholarly atmosphere hides treasures. The **Garden Library** gathers rare books, references, and illustrations about landscape architecture, garden history, and botany. The **Byzantine Collection** contains bronzes, ivories, and jewelry mostly from the Byzantine Empire (326-1453AD). Scan the tapestries and pray to the marble Virgin, but don't touch the sarcophagus. Phillip Johnson's 1963 gallery holds Robert Bliss's **pre-Columbian art** collection; the eight circular glass pavilions vie in beauty with the art they contain. The gallery includes carvings and tools from the Aztec and Mayan civilizations, displayed in natural light against the backdrop of the woods outside. Try and pronounce the names of the fearsome Aztec idols before you flee to the serenity of the **Music Room.** In 1944, the Dumbarton Oaks Conference, held in this chamber, helped write the United Nations charter. The Music Room also displays El Greco's *The Visitation.* Igor Stravinsky's "Dumbarton Oaks" concerto premiered here for the Blisses' thirtieth wedding anniversary in 1934. Subscription concerts still take place in the room every winter. (Collections open Tues.-Sun. 2-5pm. Free.)

Save at least an hour for the **Dumbarton Oaks Gardens,** at 31st and R St., inside the gates of the estate; once you go in, you're guaranteed to stay that long. It's Eden. The formal gardens only occupy 10 acres; 27 acres of Dumbarton Oaks Park, 10 acres of the Danish Embassy, and the 6 acres of estate buildings and grounds insulate the garden from the fallen world outside. Start at the **orangery**, the room which protects citrus trees and delicate plants in the winter. An ornamental fig tree twines itself around the ceiling and columns to form a canopy; its roots huddle in the orangery's northwest corner. The outdoor gardens proper include several levels of terraces. The **Star Garden,** with its Zodiac-inspired statuary, served as a dining room; the **Ellipse,** a circle of sixteen foot high trees clipped into an aerial hedge, was perfect for private walks. **Rose Garden** holds the ashes of members of the Bliss family along with over 1000 roses. The numerous partitions and blocked sightlines create an atmosphere of romantic privacy, perfect for afternoon trysts: bring your own apple. On lower terraces, the gardens turn informal—**Forsythia Field** in one far corner blazes up gold each spring. Even in winter, the "bones" of the garden are serene and lovely: some trees were chosen for their distinctive branches when bare. Contemporary gardeners have added summer flowers, since the Blisses didn't bother—before air-conditioning, Washington's garden-loving elite skipped town every summer. Energetic walkers should find the 2-mile trail that leads through Rock Creek Park up to the National Zoo. (Open daily April-Oct. 2-6pm, Nov.-March 2-5pm. Admission $2, seniors and children $1; seniors free each Wed.)

George Washington's granddaughter slept at **Tudor Place,** 1605 32nd St. (965-0400). Martha Custis Peter used the $8000 her grandfather willed her to purchase the property at 1605 32nd St. and build this Neoclassical house, completed in 1816. Mrs. Peter and a friend watched the British torch Washington in 1814 from what is now the dining room. The property passed through six successive generations until the last owner, Armistead Peter III, formed a foundation to open the house to the public after his death in 1984. Visitors can see how each generation changed the house and furnishings amid unsubtle reminders of George Washington: andirons in the parlor fireplace and the tea table in the Saloon originally stood in Mount Vernon, and a portrait of George hangs opposite Peter III's. By opening the door-sized window, Tudor Place's tradition-conscious denizens could step out into the sculpture garden, wander on winding paths and recline under lattice-roofed, rose-clad pavilions. The required tour lasts about an hour, but you can hang out in the gardens indefinitely. (Open by reservation only, tours Tues.-Sat. at 10am, 11:30am, 1pm, and 2:30pm. Free; a donation of $5 is requested, $2.50 for students).

When Archbishop John Carroll learned where the new capital would be built, he rushed to found **Georgetown University** (main entrance at 37th and O St.) which opened in 1789 as the United States' first Catholic institution for higher learning. Father Patrick Healy, who became President of GU in 1873, was the first Black American to hold a Ph.D. He reorganized the college and graduate schools and began construction of the central Healy building (the one with the clock tower). Though today 57% of the 6000 undergraduates are Catholic and a Jesuit brother resides in every dorm, students of many creeds and regions attend. Georgetown's undergraduate programs are rather pre-professional. Students enroll in one of five different schools: Business, Foreign Service, Language and Linguistics, Nursing, and the College of Arts and Sciences. The distinctions are purely academic, however: students of the several schools live, study, and party together, often off-campus in one of the townhouses which line the streets near the university. (There is minimal on-campus housing.) Georgetown teams are called Hoyas, which supposedly derives from the old, half-Latin, half-Greek cheer *hoya saxa,* "what rocks" (or maybe the archaic Saxon word for embarrassing leg-stubble). If you believe that, you'll believe anything. The basketball team, perennial contenders for the national college title (they won in 1984), play at the Capital Centre in Landover, MD, since fans are far too many for a college gym. (Purchase tickets through the Capital Centre (432-0200) or the campus Athletic Department (687-4692)). Famous Hoyas include pro basketball player Patrick Ewing, New York prelate John Cardinal O'Connor, Supreme Court Justice Antonin Scalia, and Senate Majority Leader George Mitchell (D-Maine).

On campus, look for the hands on the Healy Hall clock, if they're there. Each year seniors steal them and ship them to someone famous. The new **Intercultural Center**, a ziggurat-like, modern red brick building, overlooks a small cemetery on campus—a peculiarly touching juxtaposition. During the summer the campus fills with international students, high school debaters and others on special programs—you'll see "student life," if you want to, 365 days a year. GU owns Mark Twain's manuscript of *Tom Sawyer,* but don't bother asking around: it's locked up in a rare-book library. During the school year, a student in the information booth to the left of the gate can provide you with maps and directions. Student-led tours are conducted throughout the year, generally twice a day during the summer and once daily from September to May. The admissions office's informational meeting isn't very. Call the office (in room 108 in the White-Gravner building to the right of the front gate) at 687-3800 for specific times and reservations.

The **Duke Ellington School of the Arts**, 35th and R St., is a public high school specializing in dance, music, theater, and the visual arts, like the New York high school the movie *Fame* described. Call 282-0123 to schedule a tour.

Pretend to shop for other people's art in **Spectrum Gallery**, 11132 29th St. NW (333-0954), an artists' cooperative owned and run by 29 local artists. The 29 give rotating one-person shows, so the gallery walls change every month. The gallery sells postcards and original prints. Openings are, ahem, open to the public, so check the listings in "Galleries," a schedule of events you can pick up at any local gallery. (Open Tues.-Sat. 11am-6pm, Sun. noon-5pm. Free.) The **Alif Gallery**, 1204 31st St. (337-9670) shows Arabian art and movies from Iraq, Morocco, Tunisia, Syria, Algeria, and Lebanon. Go in and pick up a schedule of events, find the openings, and snarf the free wine and cheese. Open Mon.-Fri. 10am-6pm, Sat. noon-6pm.

Georgetown Park, 3222 M St. NW (298-5577), is a ritzy shopping mall including over 150 stores, most of them costly. Its waterfalls, water fountains, underground tiled atrium, and air-conditioning make its benches relaxing for travelers tired of walking; the whole ensemble is actually quite refreshing, so long as you don't have to work there. Ask the first-floor concierge office for a map, and the lonely employees will reward you with a book of coupons. **Thomas Cook Foreign Exchange** (338-3325) on the third level, cashes travelers' checks and foreign money. Godiva Chocolatier and adult toy store The Sharper Image numbers among the mall's other denizens. Kevin Costner sprinted down these escalators in *No Way Out* before jumping on the nonexistent Metro. (Mall open Mon.-Fri. 10am-9pm, sat. 10am-7pm, Sun. noon-6pm.)

Rent a bicycle, a canoe, or, for that matter, a bike lock at **Thompson Boat Center**, 2900 Virginia Ave. NW (333-4861), next to Washington Harbor on K St. Single-speed bikes are $4 a day, $15 a week; 18-speed mountain bikes are $6 a day, $22 a week. Locks, strongly recommended, go for 50¢ a day. Canoe along the Potomac for $6 an hour or $20 per day. Kayaks are $7 an hour, $24 a day. Thompson also rents out single sculls (rowing experience required) and tandem bikes. (Open Mon.-Fri. 7am-6pm, Sat.-Sun. 8am-5pm). Rowboats, canoes, and mountain bikes can also be rented from **Fletcher's Boathouse**, 4940 Canal Rd. NW (244-0461). (Rowboats and canoes $7 per hour, $14 per day; bikes (which can only be used on the canal towpath) $5 per hour

(2hr. min.), $9 per day. some form of ID necessary as deposit. Open daily (as weather permits) 9am-7pm.

Retired from commercial use since the 1800s, the **Chesapeake & Ohio Canal** (301-299-3613) extends 185 miles from Georgetown to Cumberland, Maryland. Nature abounds along the **C&O Canal towpath**, below and parallel to M St., the dirt road along which trusty mules once pulled barges on the canal. The benches under the trees around 30th St. make a cute city lunch spot. After Georgetown, the C&O changes from a polluted relic suitable for romantic strolls to a clean waterway whose towpath accommodates gamboling families and mountain-bikers. Kayakers often practice on the water; fishermen walk the trails in search of trout or bass. The towpath, a flat and wide sandy path, grows monotonous after a few miles of running, walking, or biking, though the uniformity of this path is broken by long bridges, small waterfalls man-made and natural, and historical spots. The path is a hot, tropical, swampy area during the summer, though cooler and less crowded in the fall. To reach the canal's relatively unspoiled bits without straying too far from public transportation, take the D4 bus out along Macarthur Blvd., then turn left and walk through the subdivisions until you reach the canal.

Too tired to walk along the canal? *The Georgetown*, a **C&O canal boat** (472-4376), may be your ticket. Mules pull the passenger-filled boat down the canal two to four times daily; National Park Service guides wear 19th-century costumes, guide the boat through a lock, and explain the history of the canal. Board (and pay) for the 90-minute ride at the Foundry Mall by the canal, south of M St. at 1055 Thomas Jefferson St. NW (Boats leave mid-June to mid-Sept. at 10:30am, 1pm, and 3pm Wed.-Fri. and Sun.; 10:30am, 1pm, 3pm and 5pm Sat.; April to mid-June and mid-Sept. to Oct. at 1pm and 3pm Wed.-Fri., 10:30am, 1pm, 3pm, and 5pm Sat., and 10:30am, 1pm, and 3pm Sun. Rides $5, seniors and kids $3.50.)

For activities and sights specific to the evening, see the Georgetown section under *Nightlife*.

Stores

Georgetown is bursting at the seams with stores: these listings don't include every place to shop, only those unusually likely to delight window-shoppers and bargain-hunters. See the Appendix for more practical shopping info, like where to buy groceries or fill prescriptions in Georgetown.

Clothes

Classic Clothing, 3146 M St. NW (965-2120). Dress like your parents wish they had. Secondhand vintage clothing from the 40s, 50s, 60s and 70s, especially retro-wear bell bottoms and 50s prom dresses. Open Mon.-Wed. 10am-7pm, Thurs.-Fri. 11am-8pm, Sat. 10-7pm.

Secondhand Rose, 1516 Wisconsin Ave. NW(337-3378), near P St. Consignment shop for designer women's clothing, shoes, and accessories. Merchandise by designers such as Donna Karan, Ralph Lauren, and Yves St. Laurent, at less than third of the original price. Clothes that remain longer than a month are further discounted. Open Mon.-Sat. 10am-6pm.

Commander Salamander, 1420 Wisconsin Ave. NW (337-2265). Drop in, tune in, turn on. Funky and offbeat clothing like their line of Betsey Johnson and Perfecto motorcycle jackets—the kind of clothes which once made parents faint. Wearing their free buttons will mark you as a tourist. Open Mon.-Thurs. 10am-10pm, Fri.-Sat. 10am-11pm, Sun. noon-8pm. May close earlier on winter weekdays.

Bookstores

The Lantern Bryn Mawr Bookshop, 3222 O St. NW (333-3222). Great big gobs of used books, from rare first editions to chintzy romance novels, all priced to move. Managed by charming grannies with a passionate love of books. Hardcover (from $6) and paperbacks (from $1) share shelf space with some old jazz and classical records. For the traveler who reads on the go, this is the place to stop. Open Mon.-Fri. 11am-4pm, Sat. 11am-5pm, Sun. noon-4pm.

Periodicals, downstairs at 3109 M St. NW (333-6115). Claims to carry the largest selection of periodicals in the U.S. Foreign and specialty magazines and newspapers abound, including every nation's edition of *Vogue*. Open Mon. 11am-8pm, Tues. noon-8pm, Wed.-Sat. 11am-8pm, Sun. noon-8pm.

Another World, 1504 Wisconsin Ave. NW (333-8657), near P St. Comic recording gives a list of new comics (333-8650). Yes, Batman and Dick Tracy comic books really came before the movies. Enjoy the latest Marvel, DC, and independent comic favorites without shame. Open Mon.-Thurs. 10:30am-7pm., Fri. 11am-8pm, Sat. 11am-8pm, Sun. 11am-7pm.

Schoenhof's Foreign Books, 3160 O St. NW (338-8963). Literature in three languages: French, Spanish, and German. Books include classics and current favorites. Reference and learning material in over 60 languages, including books on tape. Open Mon.-Wed. 10am-7pm, Thurs. 10am-8pm, Fri.-Sat. 10am-7pm, Sun. noon-6pm.

Booked Up, 1209 31st St. NW (965-2344). As if you walked into someone's private library and felt underdressed for the occasion. Rare and antique books from $15-15,000 each. Open Mon.-Fri. 11am-3pm, Sat. 10am-12:30 pm.

International Bookstore, 3285 1/2 Wisconsin Ave. NW (333-5059). Suck on a cappucino ($2.25), espresso ($1.50), or soda ($1.15) as you browse through the extensive French and Arabic collection. Dictionaries available in a range of languages, along with an exciting variety of children's books, including multi-lingual copies of Tintin. Most literature $5-10. Limited selection of tapes and maps. Sit and chat about everything from books to bars with the friendly and knowledgeable staff.

Yes, 1035 31st St. NW (338-7874). No racy bestsellers or gore-soaked thrillers here. Psyche reigns supreme. Philosophy (of the soft variety), personal growth, meditation, Jung, and even a section on myths and tall-tales occupy the shelves. Videos, CDs, and tapes available, but don't look for the regular labels. Open Mon.-Thurs. 10am-7pm, Fri.-Sat. 10am-10pm, Sun. noon-6pm.

Olsson's Books and Records (see below)

Records

Orpheus Records, 3249 M St. NW (337-7970). A rock, jazz, or R&B collector's mecca: some albums have been out of print for twenty years, and are priced accordingly. Also a wide selection of cheap LPs, tapes ($5-6), and CDs ($6-10), new and used. Shipping available. Open Mon.-Sat. 11am-11pm, Sun. noon-8pm.

Olsson's Books and Records, 1239 Wisconsin Ave. NW (books 338-9544, music 338-6712). Jazz, rock, and classical LPs, cassettes, and CDs, new and used. Book selection especially strong in history, poetry and import fiction. Employees specialize in jazz, fiction, etc. Special orders, and browsers, welcome. Open Mon.-Thurs. 10am-10:45pm, Fri.-Sat. 10am-midnight, Sun. 10am-7pm.

Smash!, 3279 M St. NW (33-SMASH, 337-6274). Used to be a punk store, now it's a store that used to be a punk store. Fair assortment of local rock and "alternative" regalia; some of it quite nice. (Comparatively) cheap Doc Martens. Open Mon.-Thurs. 11am-9:30pm, Fri.-Sat. 11am-midnight, Sun. noon-6pm.

Others

The Red Balloon, 1073 Wisconsin Ave. NW (965-9394). No Ninja Turtles in here. Lots of classic toys like Slinkies, kaleidoscopes, and bubble-blowers. For ages 3 to 99, and they won't ask if you're buying it for your kid. Open Mon.-Wed. 10am-9pm, Fri.- Sat. 10am-10pm, Sun. noon-6pm.

Movie Madness, 1222 Wisconsin Ave. NW (337-7064). As many movie and music posters as can fit into a 15' by 12' room, from recent hits to old idols like Marilyn Monroe and Jimmy Dean. Postcards for the frugal. Prices $5-20. Open Mon.-Thurs. 11am-9pm, Fri.-Sat. 11am-11pm, Sun. noon-9pm.

Pleasure Chest, 1063 Wisconsin Ave. NW (333-8570). Kinkier underwear than Frederick's of Hollywood and sex toys you'd expect to find on 14th St. Leave the kids at home and stock up on panties, pasties, and massaging oils. Or don't. No one under 18 allowed. Open Mon.-Tues. 10am-10pm, Wed.-Sat. 10am-midnight, Sun. noon-7pm.

The Phoenix, 1514 Wisconsin Ave. NW (338-4404), near P St. Latin American toys like worry dolls, weird vases, and handmade silver jewelry fit for Santa Fe. Fuschia, orange, and turquoise prevail; don sunglasses before entering. Open Mon.-Sat. 10am-6pm, Sun. 1-6pm.

Georgetown Tobacco, 3144 M St. NW (338-5100), near Wisconsin Ave. Wooden Indian, tobacco leaves, and gentlemanly selections of pipe tobacco plus pipes, fountain pens, and pipe repair. One of the last vestiges of old-time sophisticated smokers; worth a look, unless you mind smelling like one yourself. Clove cigarettes for the hopelessly adolescent. Open Mon.-Sat. 10am-9pm, Sun. noon-8pm.

Little Caledonia, 1419 Wisconsin Ave. NW (333-4700). Housewares, furnishings, cards, children's toys and cute knickknacks stuff these small rooms to the gills. The controlled clutter makes every item a sort of buried treasure. Open Mon.-Sat. 10am-6pm, Sun. noon-5pm.

Appalachian Spring, 1415 Wisconsin Ave. NW (337-5780). American crafts, e.g. boxes and clocks made from tree trunks with the bark left on and impressive stained-glass kaleidoscopes. Also pewter bowls, stuffed animals, patchwork quilts, snazzy jewelry and wooden pillboxes, well-made, well-polished and, well, often expensive. Open Mon.-Fri. 10am-8pm, Sat. 10am-6pm, Sun. noon-6pm.

New Downtown

Dupont Circle melts imperceptibly into the glass-walled business district, bounded roughly by N, Eye, and 15th St. NW on the north, south, and east and Rock Creek Park on the west. While the government gets its business done in older offices to the east, the lawyers, lobbyists, and other professionals in the new downtown do their thing on behalf of every interest group around. The 13-story height limit bans NY-style claustrophobia from the District, but white-collar joggers, honking taxicabs, and street vendors hawking everything from $1 hot dogs to $3 silk ties to $100 wool rugs all signal that serious office work must take place around here. Connecticut Ave., K St., New Hampshire Ave., and 17th St. boast most of the retail and hotel hubbub, while several sights hover around M St. and Rhode Island Ave. The business of Washington is best observed in a walk down Connecticut Ave. between N and K St.; E.J. Applewhite called it "a monotonous uniformity of office buildings poured out like ice cubes."

For a kaleidoscopic glimpse of Washington, old and new, begin from the less-than-urban Vermont Ave. NW between Thomas and Logan Circles. Take the Vermont St. exit from the McPherson Square Metro and walk northeast (towards N St. NW) on Vermont Ave. Two museums fight a war of ideas on this historic, if dilapidated, neighborhood. The **Bethune Museum for Black Women's History,** 1318 Vermont Ave. NW (332-1233; Metro: McPherson Square), commemorates the life of Mary McLeod Bethune with photo exhibits on the first and second floors of her home. Bethune founded the National Council of Negro Women and advised FDR on African-American affairs. The house is also home to the Archives for Black Women's History. (Open Mon.-Fri. 10am-4:30pm. Archives open by appointment. Free.)

Just two doors away at 1322 Vermont Ave. NW, the Romanesque **Confederate Memorial Hall** once housed Confederate veterans. In a way, it still does. The articulate, impassioned docents speak balefully of "those Yankees" and proudly of "our men," and lament the statues of Union Generals Thomas and Logan which taunt the Hall from nearby traffic circles. Learn how Washington, DC fell from Southern grace after the War between the States (and don't dare call it the Civil War), or ask them if they know who Bethune was. (Open by appointment; call 483-5700 or 703-527-0237 for information. Free.)

If you continue up Vermont Ave. toward Thomas Circle, you'll find the offending general and his surprised-looking horse, who have stood together on this spot since 1879. Follow Rhode Island Ave. to 16th St. for another Union soldier, General Winfield Scott. The original equestrian statue represented Scott on his real-life mount, a mare; after its unveiling, offended veterans forced the sculptor to lend her a phallus.

At 1601 Massachusetts Ave. NW, on Scott Circle, the **Australian Embassy** (797-3000) welcomes visitors to an exhibit of excellent photographs by former Australian Ambassador to the United States, Robert Cotton. See what an embassy looks like inside. (Embassy open Mon.-Fri. 9am-9:30pm. Free.) Two blocks ahead, liberal thinkers converge on the prestigious **Brookings Institution** at 1775 Massachusetts Ave. NW. Richard Nixon once contemplated blowing up the files at Brookings, whose influence has declined since its Kennedy-era glory days.

Across Scott Circle, the **National Rifle Association Museum** at 1600 Rhode Island Ave. NW (828-6255; Metro: Farragut North) perpetuates the American obsession with guns in a display of over 1000 firearms, including Teddy Roosevelt's pistol and Ronald Reagan's flintlock. Hunting knives, several trophies, and dioramas of wild game demonstrate what a man and his rifle can kill and stuff. (Open daily 10am-4pm. Free.)

The business district becomes more businesslike as Rhode Island Ave. approaches N St. The pensive **B'nai B'rith Klutznick Museum,** 1640 Rhode Island Ave. NW (857-6583; Metro: Farragut North), which contains Jewish cultural and ritual objects of importance, including George Washington's famous letter to a Newport, RI synagogue and a display about Jewish sports stars. The security guard and accompanying bulletproof glass aren't just paranoia: terrorists held over 100 hostages in the B'nai B'rith building in 1977. (Open Sun.-Fri. 10am-4:30pm, except Jewish holidays; suggested donation $2.)

Switch religions at **St. Matthew's Cathedral** at 1725 Rhode Island Ave. NW (966-6400), one block away. The vibrant, vaulted ceiling frescoes and candle-filled chapels embrace worshippers for daily Mass, given on Sundays in Latin and Spanish. (Guided tour Sun. 2:30-4:30pm. Free.)

Past M St. on 17th St. NW, the **National Geographic Explorer's Hall** conquers the first floor of its black-and-white pin-striped building (857-7588 or 857-7689 for group tours; N.G. Society 857-7000; Metro: Farragut North.) The museum proffers working display screens, a short film, a live parrot, a globe bigger than Inglenook's rump, and fascinating changing exhibits, often by National Geographic magazine's crack photographers. (Open Mon.-Sat. 9am-5pm, Sun. 10am-5pm. Disabled access.) The courtyard on M St. which connects the National Geographic Society's office building and the museum is perfect for a brown bag lunch.

From M St., make a right on 15th St. to tour the **Washington Post** in its domineering tan building at 1150 15th St. NW (334-7969). (Metro: Farragut North.) Spin controllers, press secretaries, leakers, and flacks in this media-conscious town make the well-respected Post their #1 target. Watch the next day's edition come to life on a guided tour; you'll see the hectic news room, enormous presses, and the mock-brick-floored mailroom. The great changes in technology which this daily paper has absorbed are nearly unfathomable. They recycle, too. (One-hour tours Mon. at 10am, 11am, 1pm, and 2pm. Reservations necessary well in advance. Free; no children under 11.)

L and M Streets lead toward the shops and office buildings of Connecticut Ave. Wander around the stores, restaurants, street vendors and streets of new downtown, but don't forget to make the shortcut from 17th to Connecticut Ave. through the long, elegant, white and black marble lobby of the **Mayflower Hotel,** 1127 Connecticut Ave. NW (347-3000). Warren & Wetmore, who built Grand Central Station in New York City, also designed this high-society gem, nicknamed the "grand dame" of Washington hotels. Peek into the grand ballroom (site of every inaugural ball from Presidents Coolidge to Reagan) as you pass. Gleaming gold-colored fixtures recall the Roaring Twenties, when this hotel was the largest in the United States.

Picnic to the summer sounds of flute duets and jazz sax players in **Farragut Square**, three blocks south of Connecticut Ave. on 17th St. between Eye and K St. NW. The statue, who seems to be climbing his cannon-festooned pediment, is Admiral David Farragut, the guy who said "Damn the torpedoes—full speed ahead!" (He said it in the Battle of Mobile Bay (Alabama), in 1864, when "torpedoes" meant floating mines.)

The former Soviet Embassy mansion at 1125 16th St. NW, near K St., is now the **Embassy of the Russian Federation**. At the time *Let's Go* went to print, this and all other onetime Soviet facilities, including the new Embassy complex on Wisconsin Ave., belonged to Russia. Call them yourself (628-7551) for an update. But be warned: they don't have call waiting.

Washington's golden age of outdoor statues lasted for 50 years after the Civil War; thus it is that you can learn more than you ever wanted to know about the War Between the States by looking at DC's public sculpture. **McPherson Square,** where Vermont Ave. meets Eye, K, and 15th St. NW, promotes the memory of Gen. James McPherson, who commanded an army during Sherman's scorched-earth march through Georgia.

McPherson restrains his horse and lowers his binoculars—maybe he's just finished scouting for Southerners in the nearby White House.

Dupont Circle

Dupont Circle used to be called Washington's most diverse neighborhood; then it turned expensive and Adams-Morgan turned cool. Nevertheless, the Circle and its environs remain a haven for Washington's artsy, international, and gay communities. The neighborhood's mix of businesses and wayward pleasures makes for aesthetic delight, but a zoning commission's headache; artists, ambassadors, antique dealers, beggars, bike messengers, booksellers, restaurateurs, coiffeurs, queers, and committees all congregate within a few blocks north of N St. As the night moves in, the street crowds shift from lunching lawyers to café-hopping couples to boot-stomping skinheads. Along Connecticut Ave. north of the circle, well-groomed (and well-travelled) staffers of the *New Republic* nervously stroll past buzz-cut gay activists from ACT UP and OUT! (DC's equivalent of Queer Nation). Sidewalks scream timely social messages stenciled with spray-paint. West of Connecticut and along Massachusetts Ave., embassies from Burmese to British flap their flags, while lobbyists flap their mouths in nearby townhouse offices. Those tired of the fast lane can relax with new art in the many galleries or ogle past masters in the Phillips Collection.

Dupont Circle pushes the geographic limits of L'Enfant's plan: the streets made sense all through the nineteenth century, but no one lived on them until after the Civil War. Big-spending, fast-acting Boss Shepherd took *de facto* charge of the city in 1871, then poured money into the area around his Dupont Circle home. The Circle itself became a federal park (it still is), Connecticut Avenue got paved, and railroad tracks ran up it from downtown. When the British built their new legation at Connecticut and N in 1874, the millionaires' race to Dupont Circle began. The area kept its social prestige until the 1940s, by which time segregated Washington's Black elites had built a parallel neighborhood of their own, "Striver's Row" along U St. near 17th. As the rich fled the city, hippies moved in and made Dupont their own during the 60s and 70s, until rising real estate prices and gentrification drove them out.

The Dupont Circle neighborhood presses eagerly against its boundaries at 16th., 24th, N and S St. NW. Its only Metro stop, helpfully named Dupont Circle, can get you within walking distance of everything in the area. The D2, D4, D6 and D8 buses pass 20th and P St. on their way to Georgetown, while the L2 and L4 buses head up Connecticut Ave. Parking at night isn't hard along Massachusetts Ave.; if you must drive around during the day, try the neighborhood's eastern edge (near 16th St.) and pray. Massachusetts Ave. runs through the Circle in a pseudo-east-west way, linking the old downtown with the placid National Cathedral area. New Hampshire Ave. zooms through on its way from the Kennedy Center to NE and Takoma Park. Connecticut Ave. runs almost, but not quite, north-south to (and under) the Circle, between downtown and the Zoo; Florida Ave. branches off from Connecticut Ave. at S St. and heads for neighborhoods with more dangerous reputations. Columbia Rd. splits up with Connecticut just afterwards and steers itself toward Adams-Morgan and Mt. Pleasant. Pedestrians leaving the Dupont Circle Metro can head up Connecticut for shopping and dining, up Mass. Ave. for embassies, northwest (between the two) for paintings and hills, east to the earnest, slightly rundown 14th St. theater district, or south to the bustling charmlessness of the new downtown.

The heart of the neighborhood throbs in **Dupont Circle**, a grassy hub for the incoming spokes of six avenues and streets. Admiral DuPont's millionaire descendants moved his statue to Delaware; a fountain adorned by semi-nude goddesses now hosts the chess players, lunching office workers, drug dealers, and herds of spandexed bike messengers who populate the island. Around midday on warm-weather Sundays, a congregation of skilled percussionists fills the park with the sounds of congas.

At the **Christian Heurich Mansion,** 1307 New Hampshire Ave. NW (785-2068), on Dupont Circle, the Historical Society of Washington, DC leads visitors through the German-American beer baron's "castle on the Rhine." Exquisite woodwork renders the

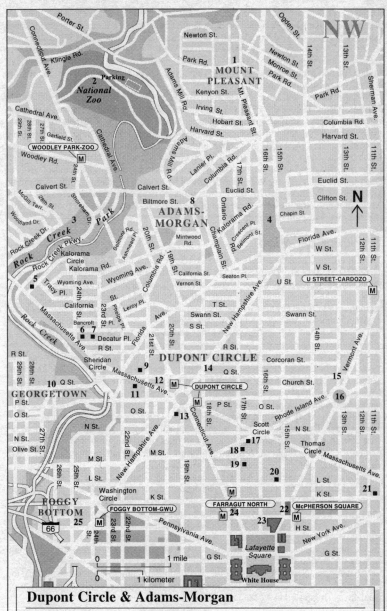

NW

N

Dupont Circle & Adams-Morgan

Romanesque mansion, designed by H.H. Richardson, worth a scan. Tours of the house permit a glimpse of the decorative arts, architecture, and domestic life of Washington at the turn of the century. (Open for hourly tours Wed.-Sat. noon-4pm. Historical Society research library, with over 100,000 items, open Wed., Fri.-Sat., 10am-4pm, but call ahead. Washingtonia Bookstore open Tues.-Sat. 10am-4pm. Admission $3, seniors $1.50, persons under 18 free.)

Massachusetts Ave. between Dupont Circle and Observatory Circle is also called **Embassy Row.** Before the 1930s, Washington socialites lined the avenue with their extravagant edifices; status-conscious diplomats found the mansions perfect for their purposes, and embassies and chanceries moved in by the dozens. Major industrialized nations have designed their own compounds (Great Britain and Japan) or moved away from downtown for more room (France and Germany); smaller or poorer countries occupy the still-grand townhouses. Identify an embassy by the national coat-of-arms or flag out front; identify an international scandal by reporters on the sidewalk. The ornate **Indonesian Embassy,** 2020 Massachusetts Ave. (775-5200), once belonged to the McLean family, the last private owners of the infamous Hope diamond (now housed in the National Museum of Natural History).

Phillips Collection

Turn left from Massachusetts Ave. to 21st St. to reach the Phillips Collection, 1600-1612 21st St. at Q St. NW (387-2151), the first museum of modern art in the U.S. and the classiest and most comfortable non-Smithsonian showplace in town. The collection grew too large for its original Victorian mansion at 1600 Massachusetts Ave.; stairs and an indoor footbridge connect it to an addition next door. The original house holds mostly American work, the addition mostly European.

The stairs to the new section stop at the second floor, where everyone gapes at Auguste Renoir's masterpiece, *Luncheon of the Boating Party.* Don't let your astonishment at recognizing a piece of art distract you from checking out some other first-rate work. Several important Van Goghs inhabit the second-floor atrium; flanking rooms hold a connoisseur's choice of French painting and several lesser-known Picassos. Changing exhibitions are shown on the third floor; since the museum owns far more than it can display, almost anything painted, drawn, or printed between 1870 and 1970 could turn up. Work of Kandinsky, Stieglitz, and O'Keefe, and others, will be on display in 1993. Downstairs, Mondrian's perpendicular works hang among the more severe canvases. In the atrium, trace the ragged lines of underappreciated San Francisco painter Richard Diebenkorn. A roomful of Mark Rothko's haunting paintings will have viewers contemplating their mortality in no time flat.

In the original wing hang American canvases by Georgia O'Keeffe, Arthur Dove, and "turbine king" Charles Sheeler. The second floor conceals Kandinsky and Klee, while the dark first floor hides a late Braque next to a piano. The collection hangs in semi-furnished rooms, among chairs and couches which, apparently, simulate the experience of visiting Mr. Phillips' home before it became a museum. Free chamber music and classical piano concerts sound off each Sunday from September to May at 5pm; check the *Washington Post's Weekend* section for information. A museum shop and café on the ground floor are new and popular additions to the collection. (Open Mon.-Sat. 10am-5pm, Sun. noon-7pm. Tours Wed. and Sat. 2pm. On weekends, admission $5, students and seniors $2.50, persons under 18 free. Admission by contribution on weekdays—suggested at weekend levels.)

Pass through the grand arched and gravel-paved entrance of **Anderson House,** 2118 Massachusetts Ave. NW (785-2040), next to the Ritz-Carlton Hotel, to see the **Museum of the Society of the Cincinnati.** Look for the pervasive egg-and-dart design along the outside moldings. The house retains the robber-baron decadence of U.S. Ambassador Larz Anderson, who built it in 1902-5; in the two-story ballroom, visitors can marvel at the marble and feel the gilt Anderson must have felt. The Society of the Cincinnati (descendants of 1770s Continental Army officers, sometimes rumored to be Freemason irregulars) makes this mansion its home base. Historical evidence of gratitude towards France, who provided crucial military aid in the Revolutionary War, reappears throughout the Cincinnati's museum. (Open Tues.-Sat. 1-4pm. Library hours Mon.-Fri. 10am-5pm. Call ahead for wheelchair information. Free.)

From the Q St. exit of the Dupont Circle Metro, walk one block north on Connecticut Ave. to R St. to reach many of Dupont Circle's 25 art galleries, which cluster between 21st and 22nd St. Occupying the nebulous territory between gallery and museum, the **Fondo del Sol Visual Arts Center,** 2112 R. St. NW (483-2777), stuck in a rickety four-story townhouse, showcases Latino art. This artist-founded Hispanic/multicultural community museum frequently features works by Native American, Afro-American, and immigrant American artists as well. Recently the center hosted a subversive quincentennial "anti-celebration" entitled "Submuloc Wohs" ("Columbus Show" spelled backwards). Saints and altars made by families in Puerto Rico and New Mexico will be displayed in an exhibit entitled "The Art of the Santero: A Living Tradition" (Jan. 1993) and "Hidden Roots," installations which re-think the aesthetics of the Americas, will also run in 1993. Check the arts listings in the *City Paper* for details. On Saturdays, Fondo del Sol presents video programs. (Open Wed.-Sun. 1-5:30pm, or by appointment. Admission $2, students $1, children free.)

Turn right from R St. onto 22nd St., then walk up the hill past Decatur Place to the tiny fountain and spreading steps. Walk uphill onto S St., turn left, pass the embassies of Laos, Ireland, and Burma (now referred to as "Myanmar" by its murderous military junta), and enter the **Textile Museum,** 2320 S St. NW (667-0441). This gallery houses two or three exhibits at a time of rare and/or intricate textiles; ethnographic displays alternate with Renwick-style shows of individual artists. As with the Renwick, it's several times more interesting than it sounds. A pleasant garden extends from the back of the house, and the museum shop sells yarn and accessories. (Museum and gift shop open Tues.-Sat. 10am-5pm, Sun. 1-5pm. Library open Wed.-Fri. 10am-5pm, Sat. 10am-2pm. Tours Sept.-June, Wed. and Sun. 2pm. Admission by contribution. Call ahead for wheelchair info.)

A few doors away, the **Woodrow Wilson House,** 2340 S St. NW (673-4034), preserves the house and memory of former President Woodrow Wilson with a detailed and informative tour of his belongings and personal history. The aging and embittered President Wilson spent his last years here after the Democrats lost the White House in 1920. (Open Tues.-Sat. 10am-4pm. Admission $3.50, students $2.50, under 12 free. Call ahead for wheelchair access.)

S St. intersects with Massachusetts Ave. at 24th St., where a diminutive statue of "Robert Emmet Irish Patriot" stands among the trees. His last words were "When my country takes her place among nations of the earth, then and not until then let my epitaph be written." Here he looks youthful and noble as he peers through the foliage at the Irish Embassy.

After years of fixing-up, the **Barney Studio House,** 2306 Massachusetts Ave. NW (357-3111), is due to reopen in 1993. Painter and salon lioness Alice Barney left her rugs and paintings and sculptures to the Smithsonian, which won't show them to you except by appointment. (Free.)

A small curved plaque on the Q St. side of **Sheridan Circle**, at Massachusetts Ave. and 24th St. NW, commemorates ex-Chilean Ambassador Orlando Letelier, killed in the 1973 by a car bomb. Letelier represented the Marxist government of Salvador Allende, which dictator Pinochet overthrew with CIA help in the same year. After the assassination was featured on the TV show *America's Most Wanted* last year, the culprit was apprehended and now awaits trial. General Philip Sheridan looks dashing and equestrian in the circle's arboreal center. From the circle, the **Dumbarton Bridge** leads Q St. pedestrians over Rock Creek Park to Georgetown via a pair of powerful but dejected-looking bronze buffaloes.

The squat, white **Japanese Embassy** reclines politely at 2520 Massachusetts Ave. NW (939-6700). On the second and fourth Thursdays of the month, the embassy allows visitors to tour the tiny tea house in back. The enthusiastic tour guide will spew interesting details about the features of the house and the Japanese tea ceremony tradition. (Call ahead to sign up for the tours, usually given at 4pm.)

Flags line the entrance to the **Islamic Center** (a.k.a. the **Mosque**), 2551 Massachusetts Ave. NW (332-8343), a brilliant white building whose stunning designs stretch to the tips of its spired ceilings. Ambassadors of several Islamic nations (Egypt, Iran, Turkey, and Afghanistan) founded the mosque after World War II. You can enter the mosque, but note that shorts are not allowed, and women must cover their head and wear sleeved clothing (no short dresses allowed). Prayers held 5 times daily. (Open daily 10am-5pm. Donation requested.)

At 3006 Massachusetts Ave. NW, the **Brazilian Embassy** (745-2700) stands up for the Third World in an uncompromising black glass box—a bit of Brasilia in Washington's greenest sector. The cubical building has won several architectural awards.

The **British Embassy**, 3100 Massachusetts Ave. NW, looks like an English country house, all done up in Queen Anne style by builder Sir Edwin Lutyens. Every May the Brit diplomats celebrate the Queen's birthday with a garden party on the south lawn, serving strawberries, Devonshire cream, and champagne. Winston Churchill's statue puts one foot on American and one foot on British soil; his right hand flashes "V for Victory," and his left hand holds a cigar and a walking stick. (Churchill's mother was American.) A time capsule in the statue's base waits desperately for 2063.

From Dupont Circle, walk up Connecticut Ave., then turn right and stroll east along R St. to discover the **House of the Temple,** 1733 16th St. NW (232-3579). Flanked by 33-ft. columns, guarded by turbaned sphinxes, utilized by Scottish Rite Masons, and designed by John Russell Pope, the ancient-looking Temple struts imposingly among the apartments and offices of lower 16th St. Pope's design copies the Mausoleum at Halicarnassus, one of the Seven Wonders of the ancient world. The ornate interior displays crowds of Masonic symbols. Downstairs, there's a reverent J. Edgar Hoover room; the ground floor is a public library (the first lending library in Washington, DC). An annex lauds famous Masons like Mozart and George Washington; upstairs, the Grand Temple lives up to its name. The 90-minute tour is a fascinating look at the quasi-religious aspects of this selective society. (Open Mon.-Fri. 9am-4pm. Free.)

Bookstores

Second Story Books, 20th and P. St. NW (659-8884). Metro: Dupont Circle. Thousands of uncatalogued, previously-read paperbacks and hardcovers. And records and posters and rare books and local music information and flyers and...just go there and browse, OK? Open daily 10am-10pm.

Kramer Books and Afterwords, 1517 Connecticut Ave. NW (387-1400). Metro: Dupont Circle. Open all night Friday and Saturday with live folk music and a small bar. Plenty of new, quality fiction. High ceilings and crowds invite browsers into a respectable history section; the cookbooks stand nearby the Afterwords Café. Open Mon.-Thurs. 7am-1am, Fri.-Sat. 24 hrs.

Kultura Books & LPs, 1621 Connecticut Ave. NW (462-2541). Metro: Dupont Circle. Nestled comfortably in a second story apartment, these secondhand books, records, and "sort-of-vintage clothing" pile up in friendly haphazardness. As you enter, note the painting-of-the-month by a local artist in the hallway. Open Mon.-Sat. 11am-8pm, Sun. noon-6pm.

Lambda Rising, 1625 Connecticut Ave. NW (462-6969). Metro: Dupont Circle. Shelves and shelves of gay and lesbian literature, with a strong section on AIDS. T-shirts, jewelry, and novelty items also available. Open daily 10am-midnight.

Lammas, 1426 21st St. NW (775-8218). Metro: Dupont Circle. Feminist and lesbian literature; smaller than Lambda Rising. Resource directories provide data on gay and lesbian life in DC. Open Mon.-Fri. 11am-9pm, Sat. 10am-9pm, Sun. noon-7pm.

Mystery Books, 1715 Connecticut Ave. NW (483-1600 or 800-955-2279). Metro: Dupont Circle. Comfortable armchairs for armchair detectives make these rooms homes for Sherlocks gone shopping. Open Mon.-Fri. 11am-7pm, Sat. 10am-6pm, Sun. noon-5pm.

Other Stores

Backstage, Inc., 2101 P St. NW (775-1488). Metro: Dupont Circle. The only theater store in town thrills thespians with stage paraphernalia from plays to theater criticism to wacky and elaborate costumes for rental. Open Mon.-Sat. 10am-6pm, Thurs. 10am-8pm.

12" Discs, 2010 P St. NW (659-2010), above the Subway sub shop. Metro: Dupont Circle. Between the salespeople, some of whom are dance-club DJs, and Gary, the irascible, literary owner, masterful knowledge and retrieval of your dance, R&B, house, or electro-pop platter is almost a sure thing. Open Mon.-Thurs. and Sat. noon-9pm, Fri. noon-midnight, Sun. 2-7pm.

Marquee, 1512 Connecticut Ave. NW (265-2355). Metro: Dupont Circle. A trendy gift shop with some unusual art and rock t-shirts, postcards, and jewelry. Open Mon.-Thurs. 11am-8pm, Fri.-Sat. 11am-10pm, Sun. noon-6pm.

Pleasure Chest, Ltd. 1710 Connecticut Ave. NW (483-3297). Metro: Dupont Circle. Lingerie, swimwear, and erotic novelty shop also offers a selection of gay and lesbian videos, books, and T-shirts. Sorta pricey. Don't be embarrassed just to go in and browse. Open Mon.-Tues. 10am-10pm, Wed.-Sat. 10am-midnight, Sun. noon-7pm.

Shaw

Shaw was once the address of choice for important African-American senators (Reconstruction-era Sen. Blanche K. Bruce), poets (Jean Toomer and Langston Hughes), musicians (Duke Ellington), journalists, and lawyers. Successful Blacks trumpeted their moves to the Strivers' Section, along U St. between 7th and 15th; a virtual Black downtown grew up along 7th St. NW. In-the-know whites joined African-American crowds to see and hear Sir Duke, Sarah Vaughan, or Charlie Parker at the Howard Theater at 6th and T, where Washingtonians like jazz singer Ella Fitzgerald began their careers. Desegregation in the 1950s played taps for the theaters and opened up other parts of the city to the Black middle-class, reducing Shaw's population and importance. The death blow came in 1968, when news of the assassination of Martin Luther King Jr. touched off three days of looting, smashing, and burning along 14th St., 7th St. and H St. NW—the former arteries of Black DC.

Shaw today is best viewed along its edges, in the Logan Circle neighborhood along 13th St. NW above M St. (Greater Shaw runs roughly between 14th and North Capitol and between M St. and Florida Ave. NW.) Some blocks remain leveled from the '68 riots. Run-down tenements, boarded-up and abandoned buildings, and crumbling store fronts abound; the Howard Theater is still a half-demolished marquee. Constant violence, usually drug-related, threatens even the residents hanging out on their stoops. Areas around housing projects are especially dangerous. At night, Shaw is not safe for the lone traveler or even small groups. Under no circumstances should you look like a tourist.

But don't give up on Shaw. Once-marvelous 14th and U Streets, notorious for prostitution in the 70s and 80s, now houses a government office building; the long-delayed Shaw Metro stations have finally opened, drawing new business like flies on sherbet. A clean-cut new storefront may stand among boarded-up windows and shambling lots; near the U St./Cardozo Metro the former now outnumber the latter. And some venerable neighborhood institutions, like Ben's Chili Bowl and the Florida Avenue Grill, have weathered the troubles along with their customers for decades. For the 14th and U business district, take the Green Line to U Street/Cardozo. Rush to the soul food restaurants, which serve the southern-derived, pork-and-greens-heavy cuisine unique to African-American culture. **Boutique Mikuba,** 1359 U St. NW (483-6877), Metro: U St./Cardozo, is a crowded store specializing in African art, jewelry, and clothing (open Mon.-Sat. 11am-8pm).

Howard University (806-6100), whose roughly 20-block campus slopes northeast from 7th and W St. NW, is America's most important historically Black university. (Metro: Shaw/Howard U.) From the Metro, walk north on 7th St., which changes into Georgia Ave. The 89-acre campus stretches to the east along 7th and Georgia. (Be very careful walking here at night, and do not walk alone.) Founded in 1867 to help newly freed slaves, the private research university now has 12,000 mostly African-American students. Ex-Supreme Court Justice Thurgood Marshall, New York Mayor David Dinkins, and novelist Toni Morrison are a few of Howard's zillions of famous alums. The campus has one of DC's highest elevations—be sure to look down on downtown while you're here. Tours (a videotape presentation, question-and-answer session, and a two-hour campus tour) are available from Monday to Friday from 10am to 3pm, by appointment only. (Call 806-2900 for scheduling.) The university library at 500 Howard Place (on the Howard campus; 806-7250) is open to the public; its Moorland-Springarn Research Center keeps the largest collection of Black literature in the United States. (Open Mon.-Thurs. 8am-midnight, Fri.-Sat. 8am-5pm; limited hours during summer months.) The College of Fine Arts, 2455 6th St. NW on the Howard Campus (806-7070 or 806-7042) houses a permanent display of African Art in its East Corridor. The constantly changing exhibits include works from the College's collection of African and African-American art. The gallery is open to the public. (Open Mon.-Fri. 9:30am-4:30pm, Sun. 1-4pm. Free.)

Adams-Morgan

Though Dupont Circle remains the liveliest of city centers, sometime in the late 80s the mantle of multicultural hipness passed to Adams-Morgan. Cool kids and the cool at heart, mostly white, arrived alongside immigrants from Mexico and El Salvador, bringing great diversity to Adams-Morgan, a neighborhood already defined by its mix of ethnic backgrounds. Slick dance, worldbeat, and rickety do-it-yourself punk venues start, change names, and fold away each year around here; even older squares have long ago discovered that a wreath of awesome ethnic food circles 18th, Columbia, and Calvert St. NW. A wealth of street carts and secondhand stores lines Columbia Rd. east of 18th St. Stroll around here in the daytime to shop or simply browse.

Poorly served by public transportation, Adams-Morgan is tough to park in, too, and jammed at night. From the Woodley Park/Zoo Metro, walk to Calvert St., turn left, and hoof east. The Duke Ellington Bridge lifts walkers stories above Rock Creek Park's treetops—take a prolonged look, then walk three blocks and fall in love with Adams-Morgan's center, the five-pronged meeting place of Columbia and 18th. Florida Avenue NW divides Dupont from Adams-Morgan on the south; Connecticut Ave. lines its western side. Church-clogged 16th St., the wide east edge, leaves Adams-Morgan behind for streets more rough; a vague north boundary, Harvard St., bears Adams-Morgan into Mount Pleasant, where a similar, but poorer, rental mix of migrants and young white-collar types survives. Signs in store windows along Mt. Pleasant St. proclaimed the neighborhood "Invincible" after the riots; so far, they seem to be right on.

Don't go to Adams-Morgan in search of a specific establishment; do go to wander around. The neighborhood is its own sight, a jambalaya of Hispanic, Caribbean, and hip/upscale cultures any city in America should envy. From the central intersection, walk south along 18th or east along Columbia to soak in the flavor and (not incidentally) eat well. As long as you stay west of 16th St. (and, at night, walk with a friend) safety should require nothing more than common sense.

Kalorama Park, nicknamed "dog-walk park," is a grass triangle between Columbia Rd., 19th St., and Kalorama Road. It houses benches, trees, a small park shelter, a playground, and basketball and tennis courts which local kids often use as soccer fields. Kids rollerskate down the hill to 19th St. Grown-ups are allowed to play here too.

Columbia Road between 16th and 18th St. is packed with **street vendors** during the summer. They sell hot dogs, African and Latin American wares, and fresh fruit. Salsa music blares from stands whose proprietors hawk cassettes of Latin music.

Three churches defend the broad intersection of Harvard, 16th, and Columbia Rd. NW. Watchful pedestrians can see the round tower of the **National Baptist Memorial Church** all the way from 18th St.—look for the cylindrical pilasters and pillars. Across the street is the Unitarian **All Souls Church,** since the mid-80s an important venue for all-ages harDCore shows. The 1921 church copies closely the 1721 Church of St.-Martin-in-the-Fields in London, a model for Anglican parishes all over the world (well, the Anglican world). The severely vertical **Unification Church** (a former Mormon Temple) reads its *Washington Times* across 16th St. from All Souls.

Grocery stores abound in Adams-Morgan, as the Hispanic residents support small corner bodegas with basic Latin American staples. The ambience and the selection of items are a sight in themselves. Make a point of visiting at least one of these places. (See *Useful Stores.*)

Meridian Hill Park lies off 16th Street between W and Euclid St. NW. High retaining walls run the two-block length of the park, which encloses a high hill carved into a rectangular, 900-foot esplanade complete with a long, impressive waterfall. The park, for all its impressive landscaping, is rather sinister; high walls and the hill block any escape except to W or Euclid St., making the lawns a mugger's paradise. Check it out in a group, during the day; stay away at night or bring your Sherman tank.

Stores

El Gavilan, 1646 Columbia Rd. NW (234-9260). Thick atmosphere. Two aisles crammed with Latin American groceries all the way up to the ceiling. Well-known and locally popular. Open Mon.-Sat. 9am-10:30pm, Sun. 9am-8:30pm.

Idle Time Books, 2410 18th St. NW (232-4774). Three floors of shelves house plenty of books for eclectic intellectuals. Open daily 11am-10pm.

Yawa, 2206 18th St. NW (483-6805). Bookstore specializing in African and African-American literature, as well as greeting cards and cool jewelry. Open Mon.-Sat. 12:30-9pm, Sun. noon-6pm.

Upper Northwest

No one would ever confuse the Bronx with Manhattan, but what's the difference between Tenleytown and Friendship Heights? All of these neighborhoods are largely residential; there are no discrete boundaries among them, though Fessenden St. NW may be said to divide Tenley from Friendship, Quebec St. to cut between the Cathedral area and Glover Park, and R St. to separate the latter from Georgetown. Connecticut Ave. parallels Wisconsin, but with a slightly more urban feel. City politicians call upper Northwest "west of the park," meaning Rock Creek Park; the moderately well-to-do (and primarily white) residents choose to live in the twilight zone between city and suburb. These neighborhoods lead Washington, D.C. in incidence of trees, parks, and private schools. The National Cathedral and the National Zoo are the outstanding sights.

These neighborhoods are easy to get around in. Connecticut Ave. connects Dupont Circle to Woodley Park, the zoo, Cleveland Park, and finally the District line at Chevy Chase Circle. Wisconsin Ave. NW runs north from Georgetown past the Cathedral, through Tenley Circle and on into Maryland. Most of the cross streets fit into DC's alphabetical order scheme—letters, then two-syllable names, then three-syllable names. Massachusetts Ave. runs northwest from downtown and Dupont Circle to the Cathedral (at Wisconsin Ave.), past American University and north to the District line at Westmoreland Circle. Nebraska Ave. connects residential areas, running southwest-northeast from AU to Wisconsin, Connecticut Ave., and finally Rock Creek Park. Western Ave., the District's northwest border, meets Wisconsin in Friendship Heights at what was once measured as the city's most polluted intersection. Military Road marches east from Wisconsin and Western to Connecticut, through Rock Creek Park, and on to 16th St. NW. All of these neighborhoods recline in the NW quadrant.

L2 and L4 buses climb Connecticut Ave. The 30, 32, 34, or 36 **Metrobus** can shuttle you all the way up Wisconsin Ave. from Georgetown; at the District line in Friendship Heights, a central Metrobus terminal lets you change buses to go into Maryland. Metro stations happen at Woodley Park, Cleveland Park, Van Ness (on Connecticut Ave.), Tenley Circle (Tenleytown Ave.), and Friendship Heights.

National Zoo

Legend has it that "pandemonium" entered the vernacular when the first giant pandas left China for Washington's National Zoological Park (673-4800 or 673-4717). Tourists and TV news magi worship the pandas, Hsing-Hsing and Ling-Ling, with special

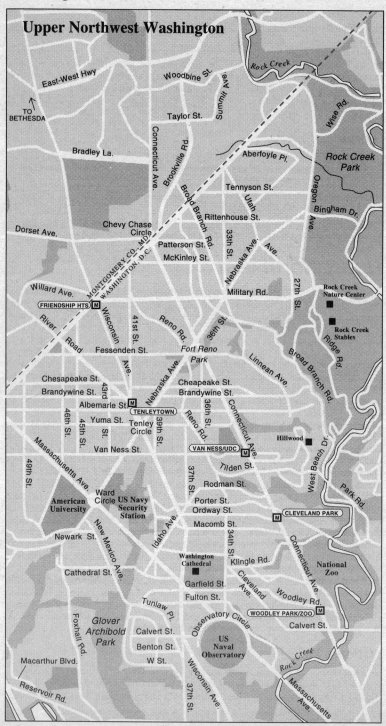

Upper Northwest Washington

fervor every spring as hopes for a healthy panda cub born in captivity are again disappointed. Gifts from Mao to Nixon, the pandas have their own concrete manger, their own keepers and even their own panda T-shirts. But they're hardly the best reason to visit the National Zoo; after the obligatory pilgrimage to the Panda House, visitors can walk over water in the new wetlands exhibit, lie down near the lions, or play St. Francis by strolling through the skyscraper-size bird cage. The zoo tries to enshrine its captives in environments they enjoy; some exhibits are even blessed with their own wooded islands.

The Zoo spreads out east from Connecticut Ave. a few blocks uphill from Calvert St. NW and the Woodley Park/Zoo Metro; follow the crowds to the entrance at 3000 Connecticut Ave. NW. For a flatter, but longer, walk, go down Connecticut from the Cleveland Park Metro. In good (i.e. not-sweltering) weather, pedestrians might enjoy walking up Connecticut from Dupont Circle (about 16 blocks). Drivers can park their worldly vehicles inside the Connecticut Ave. entrance. Dante placed the city of Pandemonium ("all demons") in Hell, predating the pandas by 700 years; on a too-hot day, the zoo might seem rather Dantesque, since most of the self-styled "biopark" is outdoors. Come here when it's heavenly outside instead.

The zoo occupies a swath of land liberated from Rock Creek Park, sprinkled with tributes to the various types of animals. Forested paths—sometimes very steep—and flat walks near the entrance pass plenty of outdoor exhibits in fields and cages, which visitors seeking the big attractions often ignore. All the paths are parts either of the blue Valley Trail (marked with bird tracks) or the red Olmsted Walk (marked with elephant feet). The more level Olmsted Walk links land-animal houses, while Valley Trail connects the bird and sealife exhibits. To see all of the exhibits, just traipse along one trail from the entrance to the far end of the zoo, near the lion-tiger hill, where you can pick up the other trail. The zoo's non-linear layout and lack of sightlines may make a map invaluable; pick one up at the info office near the entrance.

The zoo's emphasis on natural environments often has one thing in mind: sex. Some of the animals the zoo owns are endangered in their native lands, and the zoo's biologists are trying to get captive couples to reproduce and replenish the species. (Thus the fuss over pandas.) The zoo boasts about breeding the golden lion tamarin, an endangered primate native to South American rainforests. Except for the hands-on Lab exhibits, you won't see much evidence of the zoo's scientific bent—most science goes on indoors or in the zoo's satellite facilities elsewhere, while the live creatures bathe in the stares of ignorant visitors. Almost any large animal that can stand the climate will be found outdoors; the polar bears are probably sweating worse than you are. Bizarre herd animals like the okapi frequent the fenced-off hillsides. Small animals, like lizards, still live indoors. The overdue shift from bare concrete and black iron to natural settings tends to hide the residents from the visitors; the free-ranging tamarins at the zoo swing freely (and often invisibly) from limb to limb.

Valley Trail runs on down to the great flight cage, where eagles (and many other birds) hang out, past the impressively tranquil artificial wetlands where cranes, mallards, and herons shine, into the indoor Bird House. The bongo that ranges on the hill beside the flight cage looks like a balding old lady wearing high heels and bunched pantyhose. Children adore the spooky bat cave and the playful sea lions, visible above ground or (through a window) under water. Invertebrates (starfish and sea urchins and such) get their own house, the only one of its kind.

Along Olmsted Walk, rhinos, giraffes, and obscure pachyderms stretch out and stress out in a concrete barn. Look for them outside; in especially hot weather, the elephants sometimes jump in the pond, and their keepers have been known to follow suit. Visitors flock with open mouths and pointing fingers to the Great Ape and Monkey Houses, where they are tactfully ignored by the worldly primates on the other side of the glass. The Great Ape House, with its statues of animals on the roof, was once the main zoo building, back when vacationing circus animals made the zoo's winter population bulge. The split-level Panda House shows evidence of serious overattention; crowd in at feeding times (11am and 3pm) for your best glimpse of Ling-Ling.

Some of the houses contain kid-centered learning laboratories; the bird house has the BirdLab, while reptiles writhe in the hands-on HerpLab (named for herpetology, the study of reptiles). Summer Serenade concerts by the U.S. Navy band and other performers transpire on certain evenings; call the zoo for information. Both trails claim wheelchair access, though it's easier to wheel down Olmsted Walk. The zoo is accessible by bike from the Rock Creek bike path; you must lock up your wheels once you get there, though. Auto parking $1 before 10am, $3 first 3hr. thereafter, then $2 per hr. until 4:30 pm. Handicapped parking, in lots B and D, is free. (Zoo grounds open daily 8am-8pm; Oct. 16-April 14 8am-6pm; exhibit buildings open daily 9am-6pm, Sept. 16-April 9am-4:30pm. Free. Scheduled feedings listed at information desk.)

Near the Zoo

Next door to the zoo at 3133 Connecticut Ave. NW, the **Kennedy-Warren Apartments** spent the 1930s as one of Washington's fanciest addresses. The Egyptian-themed roof adornments and exterior panels on this three-section, block-long building merit some serious stares, as does the garden out front. Scooch up close to examine the robotlike eagles over the entrance.

Up Connecticut Ave. at 3400 International Drive NW, the **Intelsat headquarters** (944-6800) gleams like a science-fictional ant colony. (Metro: Van Ness/UDC.) Intelsat is a cooperative satellite producer supported by 121 countries; a high-tech tour orbits the ground floor. Pass under the prototypes and models of the Intelsat satellites, take the hokey introductory film with a grain of salt—the end contains yowzer special effects—and analyze this company that wouldn't look out of place in *Star Trek*. Fascinating. (One hour tours by appointment only, usually given Tues. 10am and Thurs. 3pm. Call ahead.)

Hillwood, 4155 Linnaean Ave. NW **(686-5807)**, once the mansion of General Foods heiress Marjorie Meriweather Post, now displays her jewels: not just pretty earrings and necklaces, but a wing of Russian decorative arts, coins, and Fabergé eggs said to be the largest outside Russia. You may have to sell your own jewels to see it, though—a two-hour tour of the newly remodeled collection costs **$10.** The price of getting in and the opulence inside may have created more than a few young socialists. Outside, 25 acres of gardens replicate England, Japan and imperial Russia in begonian glory. (Entrance to the garden is included in the tour price, or you may go at any time for $2. Call early to reserve a tour—Saturdays especially fill up months in advance. Tours Tues.-Sat. 9am, 10:30am, 1:30pm, and 3pm. Garden open Tues.-Sat. 11am-3pm.)

Washington National Cathedral

The Cathedral Church of Saint Peter and Saint Paul, also called the **Washington National Cathedral**, at Massachusetts and Wisconsin Ave. NW (364-6616 (recording) or 537-6207), took a long time getting off the ground: more than a century passed between 1791, when George Washington proposed "a great church for national purposes," and 1893, when Congress empowered a foundation to build the thing. Where to put the Cathedral, and what style to build it in, occasioned more church-state conflict: some called the chosen site, 57 acres on Mount Alto (DC's highest point), too far from government buildings. Others complained that the planned Gothic style would clash with downtown's neo-Athenian architecture. But tradition won out: the Cathedral's flying buttresses and monumental archways differ from their medieval models mainly in being cleaner, and the well-kept grounds keep the business world (if not the Wisconsin Ave. traffic) at a distance.

Building the Cathedral (the world's sixth largest) took over 80 years, from 1909 until 1990, though the Cathedral's interior spaces have been in use for decades. As Gothic architecture dictates, the Cathedral has the shape of a cross, with the nave in the main body of the church, the apse at the altar, and the transepts forming the cross-piece. Stone, mostly Indiana limestone, is the only structural material here; all details were carved from the walls by hand. The first Gothic cathedrals required centuries of human labor, and the finished products—dwarfing secular buildings—seemed themselves evidence of God; the Washington National Cathedral, whose smooth-carved walls share their scale with skyscrapers, seems less supernatural, more proof of human skill and persistence. For decades the cathedral, enshrouded by scaffolds and cranes, stood out on the Washington skyline; now finished, the limestone towers seem startlingly bare.

The Cathedral has always endeared itself to official Washington. At the cornerstone-laying ceremony in 1907, President Theodore Roosevelt showed up to speak, and every U.S. president since then has dropped by. In this political city, however, the Cathedral has sometimes risen majestically to its religious functions. Rev. Martin Luther King Jr. preached his last Sunday sermon from the Canterbury pulpit; more recently, another Nobel Peace Prize winner, Archbishop Desmond Tutu, spoke here. Christmas and Easter services attract plenty of tourists and quite a few dignitaries. Anyone can come to the regular Episcopal services (Mon.-Sat. 7:30am, noon, and 4pm, Sun. at 8am, 9am, 11am, and 4pm. also Sept.-June and special occasions Sun. 10am). Churches of all denominations can use the chapels. The Chapel of the Good Shepherd stays up till 10pm for the occasional nocturnal worshipper.

Explore the cathedral with the map available at the northwest entrance. (The **wheelchair ramp** and **restrooms** are also near this entrance.) Standing in the vast, column-filled interior, you can relax in the prismatic light, then inspect the statues and stained glass. Don't forget to descend to the crypt level or ascend to the Observation Gallery. To learn more, take the free 30-minute guided tour, led by purple-clad docents. (Tours available Mon.-Sat. 10am-3:15pm, every 15 min., Sun. 12:30-2:45pm, except on special occasions, Thanksgiving, Christmas, Palm Sunday, and Easter.)

Christian and patriotic themes find a strange truce in the many bays (as in "bay window;" each one is a sort of room formed by two columns, a stained-glass window, and the inside wall). Children can count the pennies on the floor of the Lincoln Bay. West of the Wilson bay, the "Space" window incorporates a piece of moon rock brought home in 1969 by Apollo XI astronauts. Near the main altar, one arm of a choir stall depicts the British lion crushing a Hitler-faced serpent. Stained-glass higher up on the walls tells Bible stories, from the Creation window above the main entrance to the eastern apse with the death, resurrection, and ascension of Christ.

President Woodrow Wilson's tomb juts from the south aisle (under the window commemorating him). Others buried here include: Admiral George Dewey, who captured Manila Bay during the Spanish-American War; blind and deaf education pioneer Helen Keller; her companion and teacher Anne Sullivan Macy; Larz Anderson, capitalist, diplomat, and builder of Anderson House; and Cordell Hull, secretary of state during World War II. Stone carvings and statues depict, unsurprisingly, biblical figures. One of the best, the **statue of Christian Majesty** surrounded by all the angels and archangels, sits behind the High Altar.

Downstairs, on the crypt level, burrow into the Bethlehem Chapel, the Chapel of St. Joseph of Arimathea, and the Resurrection Chapel. The Chapel of the Good Shepherd, until recently open 24hr., awaits disappointed flocks on this level as well. (Now open 6am-10pm daily; enter from the west end of the cathedral at night.) Be warned, though: the stairs to the crypt level are hardly user-friendly to handicapped persons, and may exhaust or distress those with mobility problems.

Ride the elevator (located near the main doors of the west entrance) to the **Pilgrim Observation Gallery**; get out on the top floor and turn right. You won't see pilgrims, but you will see Washington—from the highest vantage point in the city. The cathedral is still shorter than the Capitol Dome (by law all buildings must be) but the natural elevation of Mount Alto raises the gallery higher than the Capitol's tip. Check out the cathedral's narcissistic **museum** to the left of the elevator. One display lists common cathedral vocabulary, like the difference between a grotesque and a gargoyle. (Observatory open daily 9:30am-5pm, but closed during special services.)

Outside the cathedral, explore **the Close** (the technical name for the Cathedral grounds). Angels, gargoyles, and grotesques loom near the flying buttresses. Two gargoyles portray the grandchildren of one generous patron: both have broken haloes, one holds his hand in a cookie jar and another totes a broken wagon. Near the south transept, at the foot of the Pilgrim Steps, George Washington stares into the forest on a famous equestrian statue; the horse he rides is a sculpture of the world-famous racehorse Man-o-War.

The **Bishop's Garden** near the South Transept resembles a medieval walled garden. Mendel may have grown his famous pea plants in just such a garden, but no genetic experiments take place here; only herbs and roses grow in this sanctuary (open daily until dusk). Though the Garden is technically closed at night, young Washingtonian couples have taken midnight strolls here for years. On summer evenings, they also sit by Garth Fountain near the North Transept. The lights illuminating the fountain cast flowing shadows against the cathedral—the perfect romantic hideaway. Education returns to the Middle Ages at the well-connected **National Cathedral School** for Girls (NCS), established in 1899, and **St. Albans School** for Boys, founded in 1905; both educate on the Cathedral grounds. NCS's Hearst Hall relaxes in a softer Italian Renaissance style; St. Albans' Gothic excess matches the Cathedral (and the school environment) more closely. According to ex-headmaster Canon Charles Martin, "St. Alban's exists to help boys not into the Kingdom of Harvard but into the Kingdom of Heaven." We have compiled statistics on the first, but not on the second. The St. Albans tennis courts might as well be for show; they're some of the most prestigious in Washington, and require invitations.

Children and families "build" parts of their own cathedrals at the **Medieval Workshop**. Carve stone, see how a stained glass window is created, mold a gargoyle out of clay—bring the kids to the workshop before visiting the cathedral so they'll appreciate the artwork. (537-2930. Open Sat. 11am- 2pm.) The St. Albans School choir of men and boys sing at services on Sundays (9 and 11am). Carillon recitals are given every Saturday at 12:30pm, during the summer; a briefer carillon demonstration rings out after 11am services every Sunday. Check out the organ recitals after 4pm each Sunday, or to briefer organ demonstrations Wednesdays at 12:15pm (during the school year only). June and July host an irregular schedule of outdoor classical music. In late September or early October an Open Hours day resounds with organ demonstrations, choral recitals, and the only chance all year to climb the tower and see the carillon.

Public transportation can take you there, with some hassle. (Metro: Tenleytown, then take the 30, 32, 34 or 36 bus toward Georgetown; or walk up Cathedral Ave. from the equidistant Woodley Park/Zoo Metro.) Driving from downtown, take Massachusetts Ave. north and turn right on Wisconsin Ave.; the cathedral is on your immediate right. Parking is free but limited in the parking lot between the northwest and North Transept entrances and on the streets on or near the grounds. The Cathedral proper stays open daily Sept.-April 10am-4:30pm, May-Aug. 10am-9pm and is completely free. Call about disabled and hearing-impaired access.

Rock Creek Cemetery (829-0585) loads up on monuments and graves between New Hampshire Ave. NW and North Capitol St. (Enter at Rock Creek Church Rd. and Webster St. NW.) Section E of the cemetery contains Augustus Saint-Gaudens' **Adams Monument.** Henry Adams' wife Marian committed suicide by drinking photographic chemicals. Saint-Gaudens' bronze may depict her, but it's commonly called "Grief" instead: the hooded, cloaked, and seated figure seems to remember all human pain. Open daily 7:30am-dusk.

Glover Park

Busy with physicists and astronomers during the day, the **U.S. Naval Observatory** (653-1507) opens up—sort of—for guided tours on Monday nights at 8:30pm (except federal holidays). Enter the South Gate on Massachusetts Ave. next to the British Embassy. Parking is available at the gate. Arrive between 8 and 8:30pm, since only the first 90 people are allowed in. Be prepared to show identification and to go through a metal detector as you enter. Don't plan on leaving until the one-and-a-half-hour tour is over—either from concerns about spying or fear of damage to the equipment, visitors can't leave the touring party, not even to exit. The tour has three parts: a half-hour video, a visit to a 12" refracting telescope in order to view celestial objects, and a look at the super-accurate (probably very, *very* accurate) atomic clock, now back on display after a brief rest during renovations. Take the tour only if the Observatory's science and history intrigue you; your glimpse of the night sky will be all too fleeting. To experience the Observatory's timekeeping functions, set your watch by its atomic clock—call

653-1800 for the official U.S. hour, minute, and second. On the grounds of the observatory—Observatory Circle, to be exact—is the Vice President's House. Those wishing to salute our nation's handsome and genial second-in-command should stand at Massachusetts Ave. and 34th St. waiting for his motorcade to pass by on its way to a superb suburban golf course.

On the west side of Wisconsin Ave. (to the left as you walk uphill), between Calvert and Fulton St., a concrete compound hunkers down under tight security, off-limits to all comers. This amalgamation of buildings is the new **Russian Embassy complex**. The embassy's location, near the summit of Mount Alto, incensed Cold Warriors when construction began in the early 80s; as one of the highest points in Washington, the new site would be perfect for intercepting classified radio transmissions. But the right wing had its revenge when the U.S. Embassy under construction in Moscow turned out to be full of bugs. Now the complex belongs to the Russian Federation and houses Russian government workers. Don't be surprised if the complex has undergone further changes of hand by the time you read this. This.

In the same high-security vein, you'll recognize the **Israeli Embassy**, 3514 International Dr. NW at Reno Rd., by what's not there: lacking the ornate coat-of-arms, the statuary, and the refurbished-mansion look that normally signal an embassy, the Israeli delegation works securely inside a blocky concrete building whose heavy construction and difficulty of approach represent the last word in anti-terrorist architecture. Israel's archenemies, the Palestine Liberation Organization, have made such protection necessary at major Israeli installations; during the Gulf War, the embassy received an extra round of security from circling Secret Service cars.

Tenley Circle

You can recognize **Sidwell Friends School,** at Wisconsin Ave. and Rodman St. NW, by the tennis courts visible from the street. Farther up at Wisconsin and Davenport, rival **Georgetown Day H.S.** studies and plays in a tile-faced building that seems to have a bad case of measles. The multi-colored, quadrilateral construction won awards after its unveiling in 1988. Both schools lay claim to liberal philosophies, hefty tuitions and Ivy League entrees. Across Wisconsin Ave., public Woodrow Wilson H.S. serves a diverse student body; see them hang out in Fort Reno Park across Chesapeake St. at 40th St. NW. Summer punk shows in the park include embarrassing amateurs and brilliant local talent, sometimes on the same evening. (See *Music*.)

Few of these high school students stay in the neighborhood after graduation, but college could be as close as just down the street at **American University**, which fans out behind Ward Circle at Massachusetts and Nebraska Ave. NW. Among AU's few attractions are its cheap performing arts events. The movies shown during the school year for film classes, are free to visitors; some are landmarks in the history of cinema. (See *Movies*.) Theater, dance, and musical events at AU proliferate, but their quality varies; contemporary-classical composers-in-residence may give several cheap ($6 non-students) performances of their work each year. Call 885-2787 for more info on performing arts at AU.

On Nebraska Ave., east of Ward Circle, the **U.S. Naval Security station** sprawls in secrecy across several blocks of gates and low-rise brick buildings. During World War II, the Navy seized the land from a parochial school for girls. Across the street, the elegant **Japanese Chancery** (the official residence of the ambassador) reclines behind a high, white fence; if you walk by, look for limo traffic. In early spring the chancery's Japanese cherry trees blossom in peace, undisturbed by the Tidal Basin's tourists.

South of American University, hills and forests hide opulent homes along prestigious **Foxhall Road.** Glover Archibold and Battery Kemble parks rise only blocks away. A few houses, like philanthropist David Lloyd Kreeger's, hide their custom architecture behind concrete fences up to a city block long. Few tourists come this far west of Georgetown, but the neighborhood's relative isolation, and botanical proliferation, make it perfect for an afternoon walk.

Friendship Heights

The words "Friendship Heights" conjure the secret addiction of many Washingtoni-ans—ritzy stores and fabulous buys. Exit signs inside the Metro station point you in the direction of different stores. If you haven't decided exactly where to go, exit at Western Ave. and Military Rd., which puts you on street level and lets you ponder your choices. Like the neighborhood itself, the shopping areas are a mix of suburbia and downtown, blocks of street-level boutiques with malls nearby.

Beside this shopping mecca, the quaint **Washington Dolls' House & Toy Museum** cavorts at 5236 44th St. NW (244-0024) one block west of Wisconsin Ave. near Lord & Taylor's. Six rooms inside showcase a carefully researched collection of antique dolls, dolls' houses, toys, and games. The collection captures the social history of America (although some international pieces are also displayed) and attracts more adults than children. Serious collectors and the just plain curious can walk upstairs to browse: one shop offers miniature furnishings and assembled dolls' houses, while the other can help you build your own. (Wheelchair access for museum only. Admission $3, seniors over 65 $2, under 14 $1. Open Tues.-Sat. 10am-5pm, Sun. noon-5pm.)

For billions of dollars of merchandise under one roof, try **Mazza Gallerie**, 5300 Wisconsin Ave. NW (966-6114; open Mon.-Fri. 10am-8pm, Sat. 10am-6pm, Sun. noon-5pm) and the more recently opened **Chevy Chase Pavilion**, 5335 Wisconsin Ave. NW (686-6868; open Mon.-Fri. 10am-8pm, Sat. 10am-6pm, Sun noon-5pm). Ex-pensive chain stores like Neiman-Marcus, Benetton, Raleighs, Laura Ashley, and fan-cy-kitchen-gadget store Williams-Sonoma dominate these moneyed, marbled malls. On the other hand, both complexes are air-conditioned, and it can be fun to window shop. Several large department stores prey on the mall-weary: Woodward & Lothrop is directly across the street from the Metro. Lord & Taylor is on the corner of Jenifer St. and Western Ave. near Mazza Gallerie. At night after the stores close, their parking lots stay open, so you can park here and walk down Wisconsin Ave. for dinner.

Bethesda, MD

Bethesda was born of a boondocky crossroads in the early, agrarian days of Mont-gomery County. A wave of suburban housing shook the sleepy, rattletrap cowtown out of its past and set it down again on the edge of this century. Soon enough, immigrants were boring wells here and calling this soil their own. In no time various and exquisite cuisines and a healthy crop of new cultural offerings had made Bethesda an important social center. In the last decade, however, corporate real estate has beanstalked the hap-py town with uniform concrete and tiny-windowed office towers. Some of Bethesda's mid-century charm remains, but it's hidden: it will take some sniffing to uncover the stubbornly-rundown diners and silvery Art Deco shopfronts. These last relics of a once-cowprodding community depend on the stalwart support of regulars to survive.

Visitors stop in Bethesda to shop, explore the neighborhood, think about urban plan-ning, or, most of all, to eat well and cheaply; its lack of major sights hardly prevents it from being worth a visit. Just walking around in Bethesda can lead you through a ran-dom collection of outdoor modern sculpture, some of it quite worth seeing. For infor-mation on special events in Bethesda, call the **Bethesda Urban District's Special Events Line** recording at 652-8798; for their local bimonthly calendar, write to Bethes-da Urban District, 7815 Woodmont Ave., Bethesda, MD, 20814.

Bill Wainwright's *Rainbow Forest*, an aluminum-disc sculpture, sways securely above the Bethesda Metro's top escalator. Hover around it until you see the incorporat-ed holograms. The bright yellow aluminum sculpture on the plaza itself is Mary Ann Mears's *Beacon*. Crowds of up to 500 dance each Friday night between May and Sep-tember from 6-9pm in the open plaza just outside the Metro. Dancing fashions range from business suits to zebra prints to unfortunate spandex outfits. From Thanksgiving to February, outdoor ice-skaters zoom across the plaza.

A short block south of the Metro station is the **Bethesda Post Office,** 7400 Wiscon-sin Ave. (652-7401; open Mon.-Fri. 8am-6pm, Sat. 8:30am-1pm). Directly north of the

post office is the *Madonna of the Trail,* a 1929 stone memorial to the mothers of cov-
ered-wagon days. A detour west off Wisconsin Ave. will bring you to **Hampden
Square** at 4801 Hampden Lane. Around the base of the building, a shady courtyard
gives an illusion of a bit of seclusion. The columns around it suggest a Mediterranean
grotto. Tom Supensky's blue ceramic *The Wave* crashes in the center of the wall opposite the building. Raymond Kaskey's *Neptune,* a concrete rendering of the god's face,
entrances children from a nearby wall.

Farther south at 7155 Wisconsin Ave. is the **Montgomery Farm Women's Cooperative Market** (652-2291, during business hours). On Wednesdays and Saturdays between 6:30am and 3:30pm, the low white building can barely hold its bustling farmer's
market. Inside, fresh fruit competes for elbow room with vegetables, baked goods, cut
flowers, meats, preserves, and plants. The cooperative, begun in 1932, is still run entirely by farmers; the first man joined its governing board in 1968. Come in the morning to find the best produce. (Sunday fleamarket open 9am-5pm.)

National Institutes of Health

The campus of the National Institutes of Health (NIH; 496-1776) lies between Wisconsin Ave. (Rte. 355) and Old Georgetown Rd. just inside the Beltway in Bethesda.
(Metro: Medical Center.) NIH scientists and doctors are responsible for many advances
in cancer and AIDS research. Some of the buses about the grounds carry terminal patients riding to test new treatments in NIH's clinical trials. The biologically curious can
walk about the 300-acre grounds, though all the scientific action goes on indoors. From
the Metro, either walk (consult the map in the NIH kiosk outside the Metro) or take the
NIH "campus shuttle" bus to the Visitor Information Center (VIC), Building 10, Room
B1C-218, under a three-story atrium in the building's center. The VIC experiments
with a slide show, videotaped exhibits, and a working lab. (Tours leave Mon., Wed.,
and Fri. at 11am from the Little Theater. Call 496-1776 for more information. You can
also ask about walking tours of NIH.) The Foundation Bookstore, also on the lower
level of Building 10 in room BIL-101, sells some neat medical supplies such as medical sketch books and notebooks, anatomical charts, stethoscopes, and blood-pressure
cuffs (open Mon.-Fri. 8:30am-4pm). Many people come to the VIC for literature on
specific areas of disease research; more information can also be found in the National
Library of Medicine (496-6095). (Free tours Mon.-Fri. 1pm; meet in the lobby of
Building 38A. Library open Mon.-Thurs. 8:30am-9pm, Fri.-Sat. 8:30am-5pm; June-
Aug. Mon.-Fri. 8:30am-5pm, Sat. 8:30-12:30.)

Rock Creek Park

City-weary voices crying out for a wilderness can rejoice in the 15 miles of hiking
trails and bridle paths in Rock Creek Park. More like a managed forest than a landscaped city park, the 2800 acre park is a leafy home for joggers, park rangers, and a
multifarious, bustling wildlife. (Supposedly, Charles de Gaulle once mistook it for the
French Embassy's new backyard.) This opiate for nature addicts takes the shape of a
bent syringe, with the needle pointing at the Kennedy Center, and the plunger west of
16th St. NW, at the District's northern tip. Mammoth trees, covered with vines and
overgrowth, offer plenty of shade for hikers and horseback riders; Park Service experts,
operating from several open and concealed facilities in the park, track Rock Creek's animals in secret midnight expeditions using radio transmitters. Parts of the forest run
near the parkway, offering a noisy reminder of nearby city traffic, but the tiny bridges
and sporadic creeks keep wilder sections of the park all their own.

Rock Creek Parkway, which becomes Beach Drive north of Klingle Rd. NW,
traverses the park from north to south; a rapid, red-light-free commuter route in the
morning, the shoulderless Parkway can become a teenage speedway at night. North of
Dupont Circle, Calvert St., Porter and Klingle (one street with two names), Military
Rd., and West Beach Drive run east to west across the tree-filled acres. While horrid
during a snowstorm, Rock Creek Park roads make the best driving in the following

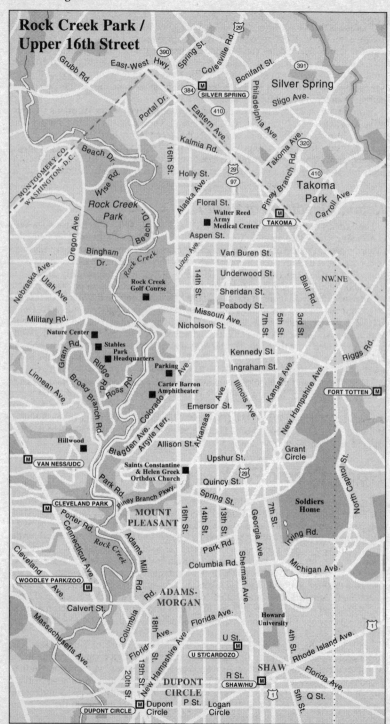

Rock Creek Park / Upper 16th Street

Silver Spring

Takoma Park

Rock Creek Park

Walter Reed Army Medical Center

Rock Creek Golf Course

Nature Center

Stables
Park Headquarters

Parking

Carter Barron Amphitheater

Hillwood

Saints Constantine & Helen Greek Orthdox Church

MOUNT PLEASANT

Grant Circle

Soldiers Home

ADAMS-MORGAN

Howard University

SHAW

DUPONT CIRCLE

Dupont Circle

Logan Circle

MONTGOMERY CO.
WASHINGTON, D.C.

NW.NE

Grubb Rd.

East-West Hwy.

Spring St.

Colesville Rd.

Bonifant St.

SILVER SPRING

Portal Dr.

Eastern Ave.

Sligo Ave.

Philadelphia Ave.

Takoma Ave.

Piney Branch Rd.

Beach Dr.

Wise Rd.

Kalmia Rd.

Holly St.

16th St.

Floral St.

Aspen St.

Alaska Ave.

Carroll Ave.

TAKOMA

Bingham Dr.

Beach Dr.

Rock Creek

Van Buren St.

Underwood St.

Sheridan St.

Peabody St.

Nicholson St.

Luzon Ave.

14th St.

Missouri Ave.

7th St.

5th St.

3rd St.

Blair Rd.

Riggs Rd.

Nebraska Ave.

Utah Ave.

Oregon Ave.

Military Rd.

Grant Rd.

Ridge Rd.

Ross Rd.

Broad Branch Rd.

Linnean Ave.

Kennedy St.

Ingraham St.

Emerson St.

Allison St.

Kansas Ave.

Illinois Ave.

Arkansas Ave.

New Hampshire Ave.

FORT TOTTEN

VAN NESS/UDC

CLEVELAND PARK

Colorado Ave.

Bladgen Ave.

Argyle Terr.

Upshur St.

Quincy St.

Spring St.

Park Rd.

Piney Branch Pkwy.

16th St.

14th St.

13th St.

Georgia Ave.

7th St.

North Capitol St.

Irving Rd.

Michigan Ave.

Porter Rd.

Connecticut Ave.

Rock Creek

Adams Mill Rd.

Park Rd.

Columbia Rd.

Sherman Ave.

Cleveland Ave.

WOODLEY PARK/ZOO

Calvert St.

Massachusetts Ave.

Columbia Rd.

18th St.

Florida Ave.

Florida Ave.

New Hampshire Ave.

U St.

U ST/CARDOZO

4th St.

Rhode Island Ave.

Florida Ave.

R St.

SHAW/HU

Q St.

5th St.

Florida St.

19th St.

20th St.

P St.

DUPONT CIRCLE

days, since the Park Service cleans them up with separate (and apparently better) snow-plows. The park divides affluent, mostly white Georgetown and upper NW from the rest of DC. While certain sections (like the "P Street Beach" slope at 23rd St. NW, a gay pickup spot) have taken on more specialized uses, the vast majority of the park is just plain old leafy, green, beautiful forest. Sporadic grassy lots along Beach Drive are designated as daytime picnic stops. (Camping in Rock Creek Park, however, is always illegal, probably dangerous, and mostly impossible anyway.)

Athletes and runners can exercise their predilections along the park's numerous trails. It's about 10° cooler inside the park than outside. Along Rock Creek Parkway, near the Omni Shoreham Hotel, is a 1.5 mile "Parcourse" **exercise trail**, complete with 18 workout stations. A four-mile run starts where Rock Creek Parkway crosses under Connecticut Ave.; run north towards Pierce Mill and retrace your route. In upper Rock Creek Park, there's a standard 11-mile run from Beach Dr. to Tilden St. to East-West Highway in Chevy Chase (except Sun. 9am-5pm, when bicycles take over the trail). Park information can be had, by mail, by phone, or in person, from the **park head-quarters** at 5000 Glover Rd. NW 20015 (426-6832), which doubles as a nature center and planetarium. **Rock Creek Horse Center** (362-0117) rents horses at $17 a ride. On weekends, the park's Nature Center (426-6828, -6829) screens films and offers a plan-etarium show. An event called "Ranger's choice" usually includes a film and an animal demonstration. Guided walks are also provided. To find out times, call ahead.

Near Rock Creek Park

Walter Reed Army Medical Center treats ill veterans and foreign dignitaries quietly in the well-integrated Shepherd Park neighborhood, on the east side of Rock Creek Park at the city's northern tip. The **Walter Reed Army Medical Museum,** 6825 16th St. NW (576-2418), studies assassinations, birth defects, military doctors, and other medical unusualness. (Take an S2 or S4 up 16th from downtown.) Lincoln and Gar-field, both shot, get their own displays in consequence. The museum's high points are its pathology displays, accompanied by case histories of the unfortunate subjects. A grisly skeleton whose bones fused to one another completely, freezing the adult owner in a seated position, is just one of the items in the Walter Reed closets. Preadolescent boys are guaranteed to think it's neat [I did—Ed.]. (Open daily 10am-5:30pm. Free.)

Takoma Park

Takoma Park straddles two lines. One is the DC line; half its own town, half a Wash-ington neighborhood, Takoma Park aspires simultaneously to small-town coziness and subdued hip. The other line divides the 60s generation from their yuppie successors: the neighbors divide evenly between tie-dyes and suit-and-ties, and most of them seem happy about the compromise. Colorful bungalows, trees, and roomy Victorian houses dominate the idyllic streetscape. Crystals, tiny Ozark harps, and South American cot-ton clutter the retail scene and fit the low-key, neo-Woodstock dress code. As any resi-dent could tell you, the town of Takoma Park declared itself a nuclear-free zone during the mid-80s height of Reaganism, joining Berkeley, CA and Madison, WI. Recently the two factions have pulled together to push for environmental reform.

There aren't major sights this far from downtown, but Takoma Park still merits a stroll-through, not to mention window-shopping and browsing. For Takoma Park's commercial heart, head up Carroll Ave. from the Takoma Metro, into the town proper. Talk to the store-keepers, peek in corners, and shop to the point of spiritual fatigue. Most of Takoma Park, and all but one of the establishments below, are in Maryland, which makes their **area code 301.**

House of Musical Traditions, 7040 Carroll Ave. (270-9090). Metro: Takoma. Probably the most outstanding shop in the DC area, the House of Musical Traditions boasts a superior collection of everything that ever went twang, wa, bong, boom, or shaka laka from Thailand to Portland; the staff might show you how to play the sturdier weird instruments. An international collection of folk, folk-rock, international, and bluegrass music, with tapes and CDs and records from Ireland, Britain, Hungary, and the Smoky Mountains (among others). Listen to Nick Drake. Tickets for area folk concerts hang out here: it's the ideal starting point for folkies trying to get their DC bearings (tickets usually $10-12; shows are usually held at the Silver Spring Unitarian Church and the Takoma Park Church). Open Tues.-Fri. noon-7pm, Sat. 11am-7pm, Sun. 11am-5pm.

Well Read Books, 7050 Carroll Ave. (270-4748). Metro: Takoma. Shelves full of used books—art hardbacks, academic paperbacks, and fiction in particular. Comics, too. All books sold at close to half-price. Open Mon.-Fri. noon-7pm, Sat.-Sun. 11-6pm.

S & A Beads, 7050 Carroll Ave. (891-2323). Metro: Takoma. African cowrie shells, cloisonné spheres, and handmade clay concoctions fill this store from floor to ceiling. Design your own chain on a bead board. Open Mon.-Fri. noon-7pm, Sat. noon-6pm, Sun. noon-5pm.

Takoma Traders, 7063 Carroll Ave. (270-0532). Metro: Takoma. Several abstract structures rise dynamically from the dying grass in front of this casual bungalow. The owners affectionately and mockingly refer to themselves as the "tacky" traders. Inside, the air-conditioning reaches two floors, one for exhibit space and the other for goods on sale. Hand-dyed cotton clothing from South America, Indian jewelry, incense burners, delicate colored hammocks, rugs, masks, and attractive prints basely and brazenly offer themselves. Next to the store, in another old bungalow, a cabinet maker works in the basement and manages the antique wing, where bargains on jewelry and chairs can be seen. Folks looking for rooms or roommates should read the message board just outside the store. Open Mon.-Sat. 11am-7pm, Sun. noon-6pm.

Green Goods, 7063 Carroll Ave. (891-1111). Metro: Takoma. An "environmental resources" establishment, Green Goods specializes in novelty items made from recycled materials like the "Tecnotes," clipboards and journals made from circuit boards. Environmentally conscious T-shirts, "earthwise" cleaners, and granola trail mix are also available. On Saturday afternoons during the winter, the store hosts activities such as folk-singing for pre-pubescent environmental activists. Open Tues.-Sun. 11am-6pm (Thurs. until 7pm).

Chuck and Dave's Books, Etc., 7001 Carroll Ave. (891-2665). Metro: Takoma. Road atlases and maps, postcards of Yeats and Camus, newspapers like the Village Voice, a decent academic book collection, and a good selection of periodicals. Jewelry, trinkets, and political pins in glass cases at the front of the store. Open Mon.-Fri. 11am-8pm, Sat., Sun. 10am-5pm.

Now and Then Vintage Store, 6939 Laurel Ave. (270-2210). Metro: Takoma. Gilded baseball hats, handmade paper, and glass moonstones proliferate in weirdness. Beach balls make faces at you as you leave. Open Mon.-Fri. 11am-7pm, Sat. 10am-6pm, Sun. 11am-4pm.

Just One, 6831 4th St. NW (202-722-1673). Metro: Takoma. Pricey but really funky clothes, designed and hand-made by the owner, are worth dropping in just to lay eyes on. Shares a building with the 100-year-old Takoma Theater. Open Tues.-Sat. 11am-7pm.

Northeast

> As you move about the city you will see that outlying
> tracts of land, once the broad receptacles of dead
> animals and where no better scavengers appeared
> than the buzzards or the crows, have been reclaimed
> and added to the city and made to blossom like the
> rose.
> —Frederick Douglass, Lecture on the National
> Capital (1877)

Northeast Washington is too big to be a neighborhood. The triangle formed by North Capitol St., East Capitol St., and the District line encloses over a quarter of the District's land area, including parts of Capitol Hill (covered under that heading) and Takoma Park and some lesser-known middle-class neighborhoods. Many parts of NE have been overwhelmed by the crack epidemic, especially near the Prince Georges County line and east of the Anacostia River. Catholic University guards (and landscapes) its acres north of Michigan Ave., off North Capitol St.; botany (the Arboretum and Kenilworth Gardens) takes up even more space east of Capitol Hill. Most of the Catholic U. students hang out on 12th St.; you might too, though not alone at night.

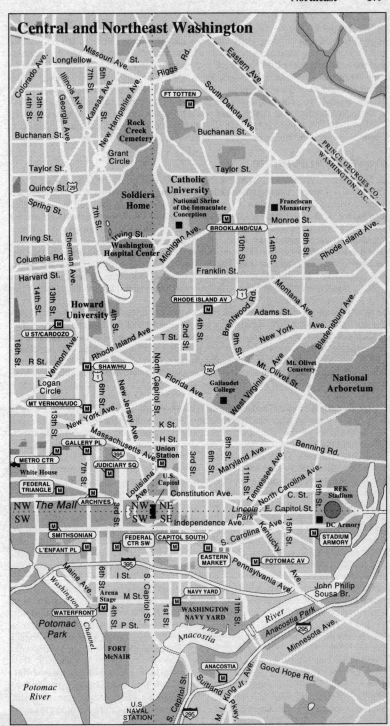

Central and Northeast Washington

North Capitol Street cruises north from the Capitol to the edge of DC at startlingly high speeds for city driving. Four roads run roughly parallel through NE on a south-west-northeast diagonal: Maryland Ave., which shoots out from the Capitol, eventually becoming Bladensburg Rd.; New York Ave., home of the cheap motel strip; Rhode Island Ave.; and Michigan Ave., which leads to the Catholic U. area. Maryland Ave. is the southernmost of the quadruplets. 13th St., which becomes Brentwood Rd. south of Rhode Island Ave., slices through the middle-class Brookland neighborhood. South Dakota Ave. parallels the District line, while off-again, on-again Eastern Ave. follows the line itself. What there is to see in NE spreads out all over the quadrant, so expect to spend some time driving or riding Metro between the clumps of sights.

National Arboretum

The National Arboretum, 24th and R St. NE (544-8733), is the U.S.'s living library of trees and flowers. A herb garden entices the cuisine-conscious, a grape arbor attracts shade-loving characters, and a circular brick walk lets pedestrians stroll the splendiferous woods. Colorful Japanese carp cavort in the lily-filled pond. Experts go berserk over the arboretum's world-class stock of *bonsai* (dwarf trees) and *penjing* (potted plants, landscaped with rocks, figurines, boats, and pagodas). Gardens, pavilions and wooden tables show off the 127 miniature flora, many of which are not only rare, but expensive (some *bonsai* cost over $10,000) and hard to keep alive. Love of the *bonsai* has engendered an international network of fanciers, cultivators, and experts; in July 1991, a mysterious thief nabbed a $1000 *bonsai* then returned it three days later in perfect condition. Go figure.

Nearly 10 miles of roads cross the arboretum's enormous landscape; the acreage is big enough to make a drive through it worthwhile. Fields of azaleas, and azalea-watchers, clog the place every spring. Drive to the arboretum if at all possible, because the surrounding area is somewhat dangerous; parking is readily accessible. The hopelessly carless can Metro themselves to Stadium-Armory, then board a B2, 3, or 4 bus. (Open Mon.-Fri. 8am-5pm, Sat.-Sun. 10am-5pm; *bonsai* collection 10am-3:30pm. Free. Visitors Center, gift shop, and information center open Mon.-Fri. 10am-3pm.)

Kenilworth Aquatic Gardens, Kenilworth Ave. and Douglas St. NE (426-6905), look best in summer, when the tropical plants bloom; come in the morning, before midday heat closes up the complex flowers. (Metro: Deanwood.) Across the Anacostia River from the National Arboretum, Kenilworth does for aquatic plants what the arboretum does for trees. There are water lilies, water hyacinth, lotus, and bamboo, to name a few; the lilies peak in June and July, the Victoria in August and September. The floating flora accompany a virtual army of turtles, frogs, waterfowl, muskrats, raccoons, and opossums. (A few blocks from the gardens, more dangerous virtual armies hold periodic turf wars. Watch your step.) A Visitors Center offers pamphlets and brochures, a tiny collection of nature art, and an aquarium exhibit. From the Deanwood Metro, tramp over a green-cage bridge, walk straight down Douglas St., and cross the parking lot. The entrance is at Anacostia Ave. and Douglas St. (Open daily 7am-5pm; Visitors Center open daily 8:30am-4:15pm. Tours at 9 and 11am; call about special tours for kids.)

Catholic University, Michigan Ave. and 4th St. NE (635-5000), is an urban anomaly, a campus in the city but not at all of the city. (Metro: Brookland/CUA.) Collegiate-gothic buildings, helplessly proliferative foliage and the traditional college quadrangle make the CUA ("Catholic University of America") grounds resemble dozens of other large universities, most of them in small towns. The student body is 80% Catholic; most professors are Catholic, too. The University gained national attention in the mid-'80s when the Vatican ordered it to fire Father Charles Curran, a liberal theologian. CUA's Hartke Theatre puts on arias for a professional-quality Summer Opera series (see *Entertainment*).

Pedestrians won't miss the **Basilica of the National Shrine of the Immaculate Conception** (526-8300), across the street from Catholic U. at Michigan Ave. and 4th St. NE. (Metro: Brookland/CUA.) The Catholic shrine's architecture crosses (ahem) sectarian boundaries; Romanesque arches support stark, Byzantine-flavored gray stone façades and a blue-and-gold onion dome that seems straight from Kiev. The bell tower beside the main entrance is cleverly disguised as an Islamic minaret. The interior continues the architectural mix 'n' match with stained-glass windows and colorful, intricate mosaics, part Byzantine, part Romanesque, and part neither. Funded in part by children who mailed in pennies, the National Shrine hosts weekly masses, which most CUA students attend. In 1990, Pope John Paul II named the shrine a minor basilica, the largest in the United States, thus adding 16 characters to its already lengthy title. (Basilica tours Mon.-Sat. 9-11am and 1-3pm, Sun. 1:30-4pm or by appointment. Free. Masses held Sat. 5:15pm, Sun. 7:30, 9, and 10:30 am, noon, 1:30 (Latin) and 4:30pm. Crypt Church masses held Sun. 7:30am; Latin mass 1:30pm. Solemn Mass held Sun. noon and 4:30pm, in the Great Upper Church. Weekday masses 7am, 7:30am, 8am, 8:30am, 12:10, and 5:15pm, in the Crypt Church. Call about holiday services. Free parking; non-free cafeteria (open daily 8am-2pm) and gift shop (open daily 8:30am-7pm.)

The peaceful **Franciscan Monastery,** 1400 Quincy St. NE (526-6800), might calm the most anxious of souls. (Metro: Brookland/CUA.) The Byzantine courtyards and shady breezeways defend monks and visitors against the secular city. Past gilded copes and chasubles worn in the 1800s reclines the church proper; the indoor exhibits blend serious religion and serious kitsch, as in the replicated tomb of Jesus, which includes the rolling rock he pushed away in the Resurrection. Red lights lead to murals depicting Christ and the Apostles, a three-dimensional mural of the crucifixion, and an ornate bronze arbor in the center of a cross. Franciscan monks show visitors through the **catacombs**, whose holy relics and wall mosaics trace Bible stories or commit hagiography. Spooky sepia-and-cream tiles show skeletons in robes reaching out to God. On deposit in the reliquaries are a collection of St. Benigus's bones wrapped in cotton; a statue of St. Cecilius, who soldiers tried unsuccessfully to decapitate; and a statue of St. Sebastian, popular with Renaissance painters, who miraculously survived being shot full of arrows by Roman soldiers. Outside, the monastery **gardens** keep tidy arbors and cave-like stone tunnels. From the Brookland/CUA Metro, take an H2 bus or walk past a bridge; a large sign will provide further directions. (Tours, guided by a Franciscan monk, run every half hour; open Mon.-Sat. 9-11am and 1-4pm, Sun. 1-4pm. Free.)

The **Brookland Gallery and Goldsmiths,** 3624 12th St. NE (526-2927), displays new African-American art, with monthly rotating exhibits of media-pastels, watercolors, oils, sculpture, and sometimes photography. (Metro: Brookland/CUA; open Tues.-Sat. noon-6pm; occasional Sunday openings with artists.)

Gallaudet University, 800 Florida Ave. NE (651-4000, TDD 651-5359), established in 1864, is still the world's only university for the deaf. (Metro: Union Station.) Protesters shouting and signing "Deaf President Now" made national news in 1989; the students got a deaf president, Dr. I. King Jordan, and the deaf community got better nationwide media attention than ever. An exhibit in the Visitors Center shows several short films and videotapes and an array of photographs (open Mon.-Fri. 9-4pm; free).

Anacostia

Anacostia began, ironically enough, as Washington's first suburb: white developers in the 1850s founded "Uniontown" on farmland across the river for white settlers disturbed by the growing working-class presence on Capitol Hill. After the Civil War, one-acre plots ($200-300) sold by the Freedmen's Bureau drew freed slaves, who founded the Barry's Farm community. Blue-collar African-Americans would cross the 11th St. bridge to work by day in the city, then return at night to build their houses by firelight. Isolation from the main city created a strong community, but made Anacostia easy to ignore; as the Black population multiplied in the 1950s, this neglect worsened—plumbing and electricity were inadequate, and the housing, education, and employment opportunities grew few and far between.

Despite the opening of the Anacostia Metro Station (on the green line), the neglected neighborhood remains largely unattractive to tourists. While community residents struggle to overcome drug-related violence, progress is slow and costly. If you prefer exploring on foot, do so here only during the day and with a friend or two. A drive down Martin Luther King, Jr. Ave. SE is much safer, though, and equally rewarding. You can see the shards of a once-strong community for yourself; people still congregate to socialize along this central artery, enriching the neighborhood with a sense of urgent vitality lacking in safer areas like Bethesda.

Look north from the parking lot of **Our Lady of Perpetual Help Church,** 1600 Morris Rd. SE, across the street from the Lucy Ellen Molten Elementary School, for a good view of downtown, the Washington Monument, the Lincoln Memorial, and the Capitol building. Watch out for the drug dealers, though; though *Washingtonian* magazine called this lot the best vantage point for gazing at the monuments, they didn't mean for anyone to roam this area on foot. The church's grounds once bolstered Fort Stanton, one of 68 Civil War installations built to guard DC. The soldiers could see all the way south to Alexandria, VA; you can, too.

The **Anacostia Museum,** 1901 Fort Place SE (287-3369; Sat.-Sun. 357-2700) focuses on African-American history and culture. Driving, take MLK Ave. SE to Morris Rd.; by bus, take the W-2 on Howard Rd. near the Metro Station and ride to Fort Place. Founded in 1967 in a former movie theater, the former "neighborhood museum" (now in modern quarters and run by the Smithsonian) holds temporary exhibits about African-American culture or history. Future exhibits will spotlight the works of sculptors Richard Hunt and Richmond Barthé ("Two Sculptors, Two Eras," Dec. 1992-Feb. 1993) and the work of the Alvin Ailey American Dance Company (March 1993-May 1993). Pick up a flyer at the Smithsonian Castle (on the Mall) to see what's showing at the museum before you make the trip out here. A small museum store sells cards, posters, and books by and about African-Americans. (Open daily 10am-5pm.)

Cedar Hill, the **Frederick Douglass Home,** 1411 W St. SE (426-5960) was the final residence of abolitionist statesman, orator, and autobiographer Frederick Douglass, who escaped from slavery in 1838, published the *North Star* newspaper in the 1840s, and served in the 1880s as a DC official and U.S. Ambassador to Haiti. Douglass broke a whites-only covenant when he bought the Old Anacostia house in 1877. Cedar Hill stays as Douglass furnished it; he must have enjoyed the view from his hilltop. Take the B-1 from Howard Rd. near the Metro station to the home. House tours every half-hour, from 9am to 4pm, begin with a movie; you then walk through the house a half hour later. (Open daily 9am-4pm; April to October, 9am-5pm. Free.)

Arlington, Virginia

Washington abandoned Arlington in 1846, when Virginia snatched back its contribution to the Federal City. Nevertheless, Arlington's inclinations remain Washingtonian. With four bridges to downtown DC as its above-ground umbilical cords, Arlington remains the Last Colony's first colony. While buildings in Washington can't rise higher than the Capitol dome, corporate high flyers take power trips in Rosslyn's skyscrapers, just across the Potomac from Georgetown. Arlington's suburban status also means more land for the taking: Arlington Cemetery, National Airport, and the Pentagon would be unthinkable in the Capital on account of their sheer size. South or west of these behemoths of business and government, thousands of commuters find Arlington's modest houses convenient. Several Asian and Hispanic communities also call Arlington County home.

Practical Information

Emergency: 911

Population: 171,000.

Visitors Center: 735 18th St., South Arlington, 22202 (358-5720). Mon.-Sat. 9am-5pm, Sun. 9am-6pm.

Greyhound: 3860 Four Mile Run Rd. (703-998-6312). Open 7:30am-7:30pm.

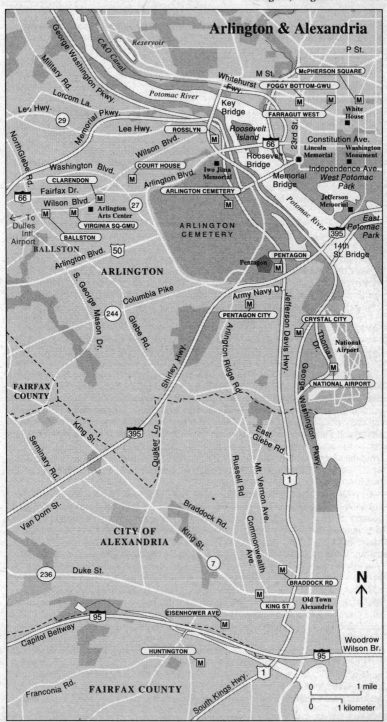

Arlington & Alexandria

P St.

M St.

Whitehurst Fwy.

McPHERSON SQUARE

FOGGY BOTTOM-GWU

Reservoir

C&O Canal

George Washington Pkwy.

Military Rd.

Lorcom La.

Lee Hwy.

NorthGlebe Rd.

29

Potomac River

Memorial Pkwy.

Lee Hwy.

Key Bridge

ROSSLYN

Roosevelt Island

FARRAGUT WEST

White House

Constitution Ave.

Lincoln Memorial

Washington Monument

Wilson Blvd.

Washington Blvd.

COURT HOUSE

CLARENDON

66

Fairfax Dr.

Wilson Blvd.

Arlington Arts Center

VIRGINIA SQ-GMU

BALLSTON

BALLSTON

Arlington Blvd.

27

Iwo Jima Memorial

Arlington Blvd.

ARLINGTON CEMETERY

Roosevelt Bridge

66

23rd St.

Memorial Bridge

Independence Ave.

West Potomac Park

Jefferson Memorial

East Potomac Park

← To Dulles Intl. Airport

50

Arlington Blvd.

ARLINGTON

S. George Mason Dr.

Columbia Pike

244

Glebe Rd.

ARLINGTON CEMETERY

Pentagon

PENTAGON

Army Navy Dr.

PENTAGON CITY

Shirley Hwy.

Arlington Ridge Rd.

Jefferson Davis Hwy.

CRYSTAL CITY

Thomas Dr.

National Airport

George Washington Pkwy.

NATIONAL AIRPORT

14th St. Bridge

395

Potomac River

FAIRFAX COUNTY

King St.

Seminary Rd.

Quaker Ln.

395

East Glebe Rd.

Russell Rd.

Mt. Vernon Ave.

Commonwealth Ave.

1

Van Dorn St.

Braddock Rd.

King St.

CITY OF ALEXANDRIA

7

BRADDOCK RD

236

Duke St.

KING ST

Old Town Alexandria

EISENHOWER AVE

95

Capitol Beltway

HUNTINGTON

Franconia Rd.

South Kings Hwy.

1

95

Woodrow Wilson Br.

FAIRFAX COUNTY

N

0   1 mile

0   1 kilometer

Helplines: **Northern Virginia Hotline**: 527-4077; **Citizens' Information**: 358-3000; **Rape Crisis**: 358-4848; **AIDS**: 800-342-2437.

Post Offices: 318 Washington Blvd. (525-4838).

Area Code: 703

Orientation

If you try to drive in Arlington for any length of time, you'll probably get lost. The original, DC-style street plan featured two- and three-syllable streets in alphabetical order (Upton, Vermont, Wakefield, Woodstock, Abingdon, Buchanan) running roughly north-south and crossed by east-west numbered streets. While these streets exist, they are often only a few blocks long; some end and pick up again miles from where they began. Since the original street plan wasn't nearly dense enough, many additional small non-perpendicular streets have defaced the map. Add the network of non-parallel, numbered routes, highways, and boulevards, designed to move commuters from downtown DC to their Fairfax bungalows, and you have non-linear, mind-bending insanity. These disorienting major roads include I-395 and the Columbia Pike (Rte. 244) in South Arlington, Arlington Blvd. (Rte. 50), Wilson Blvd., and Washington Blvd. (Rte. 237). I-66 can take you *through* Arlington, but not *to* much of it.

Fortunately, Metro and Metrobus can take you where you want to go. Buses cruise down Columbia Pike, Arlington Boulevard and Wilson Boulevard. Check with the Metro (637-7000) before you make the trip. The Metro's Orange Line can shuttle you out to most of Arlington's hot spots for ethnic cuisine. The major sights, Arlington Cemetery and the Pentagon, are just across the river at the Metro stops named for them. If you get really lost, check streets signs for "N" (north of Rte. 50, Arlington Blvd.) or "S" (south of it).

Sights

Rosslyn is just what DC's planners were trying to avoid. It's not worth a detour, but look around on your way into Georgetown or out of DC towards Little Saigon. In this mess of skyscrapers just across Key Bridge from the city, office types park underground, cross the street on two-level catwalks, and can go a whole day without touching the ground or seeing the sky. The few blocks around Wilson Blvd. and Fort Myer Dr. exhibit a computerized aridity rarely seen except in science-fiction movies; to cap it off, so to speak, the buildings are so high you can see them over the trees from DC or from the roof of the Kennedy Center. The Gannett/*USA Today,* building, in fact, looms so large it is routinely blamed for the navigation mistakes of airplanes landing at National Airport.

Crystal City, another concrete community of offices and condos, reclines (like real crystals) half-underground. (Metro: Crystal City.) Its miles of underground tunnels connect block upon block of buildings, though Metro will bring you straight to a massive underground shopping mall, the Crystal Underground. Three blocks away from the Metro in Crystal Plaza, Bldg. 3, the **Patent and Trademark Office** has all the country's millions of patents on file. People send in the strangest inventions to be patented. You can bet the Pet Rock has a patent—that is, if the red tape has gone through yet. Feel free to look up specific patents here, and then visit the **National Inventor's Hall of Fame,** 2021 Jefferson Davis Highway (557-3341), which honors Alexander Graham Bell, Charles Goodyear, Louis Pasteur, Samuel Morse, and many others. Special events take place on National Inventors Day, during a weekend on or near February 11, Thomas Edison's birthday. (Open Mon.-Fri. 8am-8pm. Free.)

Luckily, the Smithsonian museums don't have a patent on displaying exciting art. The four galleries at the **Arlington Arts Center,** 3550 Wilson Blvd. (524-1494), near the Clarendon Metro, contain paintings, drawings, sculptures, and mixed-media pieces, most of which are for sale. Classes are available in life drawing, painting, and other media. Call about the year-round Thursday evening seminars, discussion groups, and periodic poetry readings, most of which require some sort of fee or suggested donation.

Twelve artists also rent studios here. (Open Tues.-Fri. 11am-5pm, Sat.-Sun. 1-5pm. Free.)

Arlington Cemetery

The silence of Arlington National Cemetery honors those who sacrificed their lives in war. The 612 acres of rolling hills and tree-lined avenues hold the bodies of U.S. military veterans—from five-star generals to unknown soldiers. As the largest military cemetery in the U.S., Arlington National Cemetery holds 200,000 veterans and their dependents. The hundreds who visit each day aren't exactly tourists—a walk through the cemetery's endless rows of white headstones is too solemn an experience to confuse with worldly sight-seeing. Still, marble monuments to nurses, Rough Riders, and many other military groups often cross the line, sliding into memorial kitsch.

Robert E. Lee once owned an estate covering most of the cemetery grounds; the General abandoned his land when he moved to Richmond with his family to serve the Confederacy. Afterwards Union troops took over the Lees' mansion, Arlington House. Maj. Gen. Montgomery Meigs (the Pension Building guy) began to bury Union troops on the Arlington House grounds on May 13, 1864; Meigs knew the advancing Confederates would never cross sanctified land. Since then, many prominent soldiers have come to rest in peace in Arlington. Pierre L'Enfant, who laid out Washington, was reinterred here along with other soldiers from the Revolution and the War of 1812. His grave on the hillside near Arlington House overlooks the city he designed. General Philip Sheridan, who fought for the Union in the Civil War, lies near Confederate General Lee's former home; the Arlington Memorial Bridge symbolizes the reunification of the country by connecting the Lincoln Memorial with Arlington House.

Among the plain headstones of World War I soldiers lies General of the Armies John J. Pershing, commander of U.S. forces during World War I, who asked to be buried among his men. Second World War heroes include Generals George C. Marshall and Omar Bradley. Gen. Daniel "Chappie" James, who flew 78 missions in the Vietnam War, was also the highest ranking African-American officer ever, a four-star general in the Air Force. Some veterans here gained fame apart from the service: Arlington holds Joe Louis, the longest-lasting world heavyweight boxing champion in history, and Abner Doubleday, the supposed inventor of baseball, at whom the first shot in the Civil War was fired. Arctic explorers Robert E. Peary and Richard Byrd lie on the same hallowed ground as Supreme Court Justices Earl Warren and Oliver Wendell Holmes. Presidents Taft and Kennedy complete the cemetery's list of honored tombs.

Within Arlington Cemetery: Practical Information

Arlington National Cemetery is free and open to visitors from April to September daily 8am until 7pm; it closes at 5pm the remainder of the year. The cemetery is equally accessible by car or by Metro (Metro: Arlington Cemetery). To drive from downtown Washington, take Independence Ave. or Constitution Ave. and turn left onto 23rd St. to cross the Arlington Memorial Bridge. Visitors from Virginia and Maryland have a variety of options, but the easiest is probably the Beltway (I-495) to the Virginia side of the George Washington Parkway, then the Arlington Memorial Bridge. Park for $1 per hour for the first 3 hours, $2 every hour after that.

Before you enter the main gate, go to the **Visitors Center** on the left. The information booth at the center of the building dispenses maps of the grounds and booklets. A more specific gridded map is located on the inside back cover of the booklet—the cemetery is divided into squares, marked on one side by letters and the other by numbers, and each grave is identified by a section number, grave number, a grid number and letter. (President William Howard Taft, for example, is section 30, grave S-14, and grid YZ-39.5.) The winding paths are intended to provoke contemplation and reflection, but the Tourmobile's loudspeakers may destroy your elegiac mood; take the bus tour only if you have trouble walking (tour $2.75, ages 3-11 $1.25). Those wishing to find the grave of a loved one should visit the **Arlington Information Center.** Temporary passes to drive into the cemetery can also be obtained here. They will look up the location on microfiche and give you instructions on how to get there.

Tombstones note in which war the soldier fought. A sunken shield represents service in either the Civil War and Spanish-American War. Headstones with pointed instead of rounded tops signify Confederate soldiers and can be found around the Confederate Memorial in section I-23. Each day, an average of 15 burials take place; during each ceremony, the flag at Arlington House stands at half mast. For some high-ranking officers, a caisson carrying the casket leads the funeral procession.

Within Arlington Cemetery: Sights

The **Kennedy Gravesites** hold both President John F. Kennedy and his brother, Senator and Attorney General Robert F. Kennedy. John Kennedy supposedly once stood near the Arlington House, and seeing the spectacular view of Washington, declared, "I could stay here forever." He got his wish. Look for the Eternal Flame, lit by his widow at his funeral, which flickers above his simple memorial stone. Famous sentences from his inaugural speech are inscribed on a low wall near the site, reminding all who pass of the soaring eloquence of speechwriter Ted Sorensen.

The **Tomb of the Unknowns** honors all servicemen who died fighting for the United States. Unidentified soldiers from World Wars I and II, the Korean War, and the Vietnam War lie under the white marble sarcophagus overlooking the city. The famous inscription reads, "Here rests in honored glory an American soldier known but to God." Modern dental and DNA records may render finding unknown soldiers in future wars impossible; it was difficult enough to find one after Vietnam.

The Tomb is guarded 24 hours daily by delegations from the Army's Third Infantry, in dress blues and white gloves, carrying bayonets. The sentinels take 21 steps, then turn to face the Tomb for 21 seconds to symbolize the 21-gun salute, the highest military honor. You can watch the ritualized **changing of the guard** every hour, on the hour, from Oct.-March and every half-hour from April-Sept. While you're waiting, visit the **Memorial Amphitheater**. Inside, the display cases show all the plaques and medals given by national and international organizations to honor the Unknown Soldiers. Photographs of their interments line the walls. The open-air amphitheater in back holds Easter Sunrise, Memorial Day, and Veteran's Day services as well as housing other ceremonies on special occasions. Memorials near the amphitheater include the **Space Shuttle Challenger Memorial,** the **Iran Rescue Mission Memorial,** the **War Correspondents Memorial**, and the **Canadian Cross of Sacrifice**, remembering U.S. citizens in the Canadian armed forces.

"A rose is a rose is a rose," wrote Gertrude Stein; in the same vein, what seems to be a ship's mast rising out of the ground is a **ship's mast** rising out of the ground. The mast belonged to the *U.S.S Maine,* which exploded in the harbor of Havana, Cuba in 1898. The rallying cry "Remember the Maine!" helped start the Spanish-American War, though no one knows whether the Spanish caused the explosion. Polish statesman and musician Ignace Jan Paderewski was interred in the memorial until Poland became "free." He was returned to his homeland in June of 1992. To the left along Memorial Drive reclines the grave of **Audie Murphy**, the most decorated soldier of WWII.

The **Confederate Memorial** was commissioned in 1900 when a goodwill gesture set aside an area for the burial of Confederate troops. The graves of Confederate troops had been scattered around Arlington Cemetery and in cemeteries of area counties. Now they lie in one section around the Confederate Memorial. The memorial itself shows the female representation of Peace facing South and holding a plow and a pruning hook. Inscribed around the base is the passage from Isaiah, "They shall beat their swords into plowshares, and their spears into pruning hooks." A bronze frieze surrounding the base depicts Confederate soldiers leaving home, and then returning in defeat. A **Civil War Memorial** lies along Crook Walk near Arlington House. The bones of 2111 soldiers lost in the Battle of Bull Run and the route to Rappahanock lie beneath the stone sarcophagus; the remains were never identified, but their names and deaths were recorded in the Archives.

Restored **Arlington House,** built in 1802, overlooks the cemetery with the poise appropriate to a Lee possession. Enter the pastel-peach mansion at the front door, and pick up a "self-guided tour" sheet from one of the women in antebellum costume. The parlor connects through a series of arched doorways to the Family Dining Room. Up the narrow staircase, the girls' dressing room, playroom, and bedrooms contain antique dolls and clothing and such. Colonel Robert E. Lee penned his resignation from the United States Army in his bedchambers. Downstairs, you can see the White Parlor and the Morning Room, where the paintings George Custis created lean against an easel. The store room, conservatory, and Lee's office end the tour.

In front of Arlington House, Mrs. Lee's gardens and her multi-noun rose trellis pavilion are under restoration. Be sure to look beyond the gardens to the Washington skyline; your eye will also take in many memorials, including the Eternal Flame at President Kennedy's grave. You won't find Lee's grave in Arlington Cemetery: he chose to be buried at the college he helped found, Washington & Lee, in Lexington, Virginia.

If you continue down Custis Walk in front of Arlington House and out through Weitzel Gate, you can walk to the **Iwo Jima Memorial.** On the way lies President William Howard Taft's grave, to the left of the path in section 30. The walk from Weitzel Gate to the memorial takes 20 minutes, so you may prefer to drive to the junction, located between Arlington Blvd. and Ridge Rd., especially on hot days. The memorial is based on Joe Rosenthal's Pulitzer Prize-winning photograph of six Marines straining to raise the U.S. flag on Iwo Jima's Mount Suribachi. The island saw 6,321 U.S. soldiers die in battle in February of 1945, including three of the men the memorial depicts. Admiral Nimitz's comment on the battle, "Uncommon valor was a common virtue," adorns the statue's base. The U.S. flag is real, but the "flagpole" is a lead pipe—just as in the photo. The Marine Marathon begins here each year, and military concerts and parades take place in the summer Tuesdays from 7 until 8:30pm. Look at the thing from a different, non-Marine point of view to realize why this scene of butch guys with cute butts falling all over one another became a symbol of the gay rights movement in the '70s, and why it remains a gay pickup spot today.

Near the Iwo Jima Memorial rises a rectangular 127-foot-high tower which houses the **Netherlands Carillon,** a set of 49 bells made by foundries in the Netherlands to remember their liberation from the Nazis on May 5, 1945. (The rectilinear design recalls Dutch painter Piet Mondrian, who fled the Nazis for New York.) Each of the bells is engraved with a coat of arms to show who donated the money for the bell and a verse to describe the tones of the bell. The carillons are played from April to September on Saturdays from 2 to 4pm, and on national holidays. However, you can climb the towers at any time. Two bronze panthers guard the carillon, and the grounds bloom with more than 15,000 tulips each spring.

The Pentagon

If the Washington Monument's smooth obelisk symbolizes the vigor of our nation and the Capitol's classical dome represents the dignity of democratic government, the Pentagon's equipoise of concrete just shows how huge a military bureaucracy can get. On July 17, 1941, the War Department gave its planners one weekend to design a building that would hold all the capital's military offices. On Monday morning, the architects returned with the familiar five-sided monster, designed to fit in between two highways; objections to the original site, within Arlington Cemetery, forced a move to Hell's Bottom, swampy government-owned land next to the Potomac. A work force of 13,000 toiled 24 hours a day for only 16 months to create the steel-reinforced concrete building.

When the military moved in, in May 1942, the building was already too small: the Army continued to rent offices in Washington throughout World War II. As chief avatar of the military-industrial complex, the Pentagon was the natural target for the mammoth anti-Vietnam War march of 1968, which inspired poems by Robert Lowell and Norman Mailer's famous book *The Armies of the Night.* Some marchers tried to exorcise the "war demon" supposedly kept in check by the building's mystical shape. TV coverage of the marchers, who joined hands to form a huge ring around all five sides, showed the country the extent of anti-war feeling.

Today the world's largest office building boasts the world's largest parking lot and a bus terminal longer than most trains. The Pentagon has five sides, five stories, five concentric hallways, a five-acre courtyard in the center, ten radial hallways, four zip codes of its own, and $400 toilet seats. Three Washington Monuments would fit across it lengthwise. Twenty-three thousand civilians, soldiers, and sailors sprawl over 6.5 million square feet. They take the Metro or park 8,770 cars in 16 parking lots. They climb 131 stairways and ride 19 escalators to walk through 17.5 miles of corridors. Yet it only takes seven minutes to walk between any two points in the building, if you know how to read the address: 2E651, for example, is on the second floor, ring E, near corridor 6, and room 51.

You'll never have the chance to get lost on the **guided tour,** though. The Pentagon opened itself up to the public until 1972 (somebody bombed a bathroom). Now all visitors must sign in, walk through a metal detector, get X-rayed, show proper identification, and stick to the tour. The tour guide walks backwards to keep an eye on the visitors and keeps the pace so brisk that the tour is like a military music video: lots of pictures whizzing by, but very little information. Many tour-takers are veterans and servicepeople. Attentive tour-takers can learn a lot with their eyes, though. Between the memorials and exhibits, the myriad uniforms, the private shopping mall, and the motorized mini-mail carts, you'll discover the achievements, attitudes, structure, and sheer size of the United States defense establishment.

Through the metal detectors, you'll find a shopping mall with stores like Woodward & Lothrop, Fannie Mae Candies, and a barber. Don't ask about a trim, though; the mall is reserved for Pentagon employees. A film will show you the **War Room,** whose large screens light up with maps and data during national emergencies, and the **National Command Center,** but you'll never get to these basement chambers yourself. If you've seen *Dr. Strangelove* or *War Games,* though, you can already guess what they look like.

The **Commander-in-Chiefs' Corridor** depicts each U.S. President beside a montage of drawings and newspaper headlines. Another display models famous aircraft. The most recent addition to the display case is a model of the Stealth bomber, whose low-altitude flight eludes radar while its high price ($500 million a plane) provokes disgust. Used in the U.S. invasion of Panama and in the Persian Gulf, the Stealth is one of several technically secret projects the tour guide will discuss. Look for the Delta Force patch on display; the government won't even acknowledge the existence of this secret anti-terrorist team, but the Pentagon exhibits their insignia anyway.

Endless corridors commemorate exceptional soldiers, flyers, and Marines (the Navy hasn't finished its corridors yet). Other hallways celebrate military topics including General George Marshall, women in the military, Vietnam POWs, and so on. An array of state and U.S. flags ends at a spray-painted piece of the Berlin Wall, whose pro-democracy graffiti records the end of the Cold War and prepares you to leave the Pentagon behind.

Tours are free and given every half hour from May to September, Monday through Friday from 9:30am to 3:30pm except on federal holidays; from October to May, the 10:30am, 1:30pm, and 3pm tours are eliminated. No reservations are necessary, but large groups and those with special needs may reserve special tours by calling 695-1776. Non-U.S. citizens should bring their passports for the security check. Try coming early in the morning to avoid the lines and to fit in the 90-minute tour before lunch: no facilities for meals are available, *nor are restrooms open to the public during the tour.* The Pentagon has its own Metro stop; one of the Metro escalators leads directly to the tour office. The Pentagon hunkers down inside a triangle formed by three highways, Rte. 110 and 27 and I-395; those who must drive here should take the 14th St. Bridge from DC to I-395 and find the Pentagon exit about fifteen seconds into Virginia. Visitor parking is available but limited, and the walk from the lot takes a few minutes; enter through Corridor One at the South Parking Entrance.

Roosevelt Island

So you're Congress, see. And you want to build a memorial. And you want to commemorate, like, this former President. And he was mostly famous for go-get'em stuff, like leading the famous charge up San Juan Hill during the Spanish-American War, and starting the Panama Canal. (Even though he did help negotiate an end to the Russo-Japanese War.) But he was also famous for his devotion to the outdoors; for example, he created the first National Park. And there's already a famous equestrian statue of him in New York City, outside the Museum of Natural History, so you can't really just build another one. And he probably preferred the wilderness to cities like yours anyway. So you find a completely unspoiled island only about 15 minutes from downtown, and you build a statue of him on the island, and you build a parking lot, but you don't do much else. But you do set up some hiking trails, so visitors to the island can imitate TR, wander the island, see nature, and keep fit. And since nobody could pronounce "Analostan Island," you commemorate our 26th President by renaming the whole shebang Theodore Roosevelt Island.

The island's 3.1 miles of trails take about an hour to hike through; wide, flat paths make the long walk relaxing. Forests, swampy marshes, and rocky beaches number among its relatively untouched ecosystems. In the island's center, a statue of TR stands exuberantly among fountains and granite plaques engraved with bits of his speeches. (He said, "I want to see you game, boys, I want to see you brave and manly, but I also want to see you gentle and tender." He also said, "If I must choose between righteousness and peace I choose righteousness.") President Roosevelt looks slightly frustrated by his isolation: a moat surrounds his oval patio. Hikers can make a good game of searching for this statue among the paths.

Rangers will give a combined nature and historical tour if called seven days in advance; call 703-285-2600 for arrangements. Saturdays and Sundays the park rangers give a history walk, and at 2pm a nature walk is open to visitors. (No tours given in the winter season.) For ever-shifting hours and services, call 426-6922 or 285-2598. Don't confuse this Roosevelt Island with the one in New York's East River.

The commemorators obviously wanted to keep this beautiful island for themselves: it's hard to reach, especially for pedestrians. The island hides across from Georgetown and the Kennedy Center in the Potomac River; the mammoth Roosevelt Bridge (I-66) rushes several lanes of traffic across the island from DC to Virginia. Drive across the Roosevelt Bridge, take a right onto the George Washington Parkway's northbound lanes, and exit into the Roosevelt Island lot; if you see Key Bridge, you've missed it. The hopelessly carless should take the Metro to Rosslyn, then walk down N. 19th St. and look for footbridges across the highway spaghetti on the Virginia shore. From Georgetown you could walk across Key Bridge and along the bank.

Alexandria, Virginia

When Scottish tobacco merchants founded Alexandria in 1749, quaintness was not their aim: its location on the Potomac River seemed perfect for bundling up and shipping out the great weed from down south. Though included in the land grant that created DC in 1791, Alexandria stayed an independent-minded (and very Southern) shipping town; when Virginia removed it from the District of Columbia in 1846, one resident reported "great rejoicing and cannon firing." When Washington ballooned after World War II, the spreading wave of bedroom communities crashed over the town; it didn't become a sight until the 80s, when Old Town re-cobblestoned the streets, installed gardens and patios, restored over 1000 old façades, and invited tall ships and contemporary shops to share the 1700s atmosphere. On weekends, half of Northern Virginia joins a scattering of tourists to shop, stroll, and dine. Old-time sailors might enjoy some of the many pubs and clubs, but sophisticated jazzsters, angst-ridden teens, and modern singles will each find some appropriate nightlife.

Old Town Alexandria lies in the square formed by Oronoco St. on the north, the Potomac River on the east, Gibbon St. on the South, and Washington St. on the west. Restaurants, bars, small art galleries, and shops hang out here. Old Town's streets form a grid; north-south streets have random names, while east-west streets in central Old Town have royal names (King, Prince, Duke, Queen, etc.). Street layout in the rest of Alexandria has all the sense of a bowl of pasta: after all, it is northern Virginia. I-395 cuts Alexandria off from Arlington to the north, and the Beltway rushes along its south-

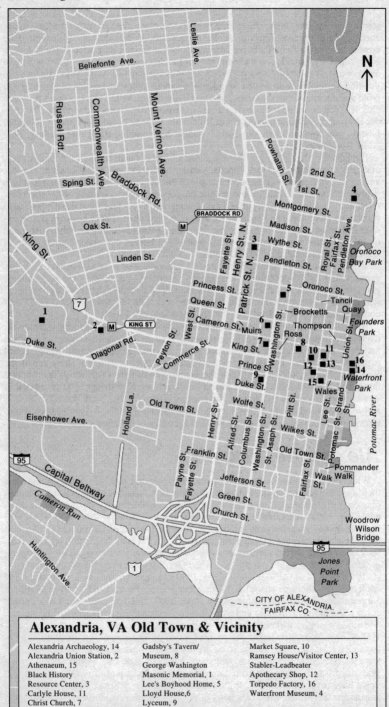

Alexandria, VA Old Town & Vicinity

Alexandria Archaeology, 14
Alexandria Union Station, 2
Athenaeum, 15
Black History
Resource Center, 3
Carlyle House, 11
Christ Church, 7

Gadsby's Tavern/
Museum, 8
George Washington
Masonic Memorial, 1
Lee's Boyhood Home, 5
Lloyd House, 6
Lyceum, 9

Market Square, 10
Ramsey House/Visitor Center, 13
Stabler-Leadbeater
Apothecary Shop, 12
Torpedo Factory, 16
Waterfront Museum, 4

ern border. King St. (Rte. 7) connects I-395 to Old Town, and the George Washington Parkway runs nearly along the river until Old Town, where it becomes Washington St. To find Old Town, from the King St. Metro, start walking down King Street (to your left as you leave the Metro; walk away from the tracks, not under them). A DASH bus also runs from the Metro to Old Town at random intervals. If you're driving, take the East King St. exit from George Washington Parkway; Old Town is about 20 minutes from downtown DC.

Practical Information

Emergency: 911

Population: 111,000.

Visitors' Information: Ramsay House, 221 King St. (838-4200). The **Alexandria Convention & Visitors Bureau** gives out street maps, DASH maps and brochures. Their $16 combination ticket for the Lloyd House, Carlyle House, Gadsby's Museum, the Lee-Fendall House and Lee's Boyhood Home saves heaps, assuming you actually plan to see them all. The ACVB also runs an Alexandria events hotline: call 838-5005 for the recording. (Open daily 9am-5pm.) **The Lyceum,** 202 Washington St. (838-4994), listed under *Sights,* also gives out maps and pamphlets.

Transportation: Amtrak: Union Station (Alexandria), 110 Callahan Dr. (836-4839). **Metro:** three Alexandria stops: Braddock Rd.; King St., close to everything; Eisenhower Ave., close to nothing. **DASH:** the local bus system. Runs throughout the city of Alexandria (75¢) and to the Pentagon ($1). Call 1-800-872-7245 for route information.

Alexandria Hospital: 379-3000. 4320 Seminary Rd., Alexandria.

Help Lines: Alexandria Hotline: 838-0900; **Drug Abuse Hotline:** 838-4455; **Alcohol Abuse Hotline:** 838-4455; **Rape Victim Companion Program:** 838-4900.

Post Offices: Park Fairfax Station, 3682 King St. (379-6017); Main Post Office, 1100 Wyeth St. (549-4201); George Washington Station, 1908 Mt. Vernon St. (549-4272).

Area Code: 703

King Street is the main thoroughfare through Old Town. It's the king of streets for eating seafood, hearing blues, jazz, rock, or country, and visiting art galleries and shops. The galleries huddle closer to the Metro, while the restaurants, like lemmings, cluster closer and closer to the river. Each Saturday the town hosts a morning fair, complete with waterfront activities, riverboat rides, and a **Farmer's Market** at 301 King St. in Market Square (838-4770; market open 5-9am). Fresh baked goods, meats, produce, and handicrafts are sold in the arcades on the south plaza of the city hall.

A walking tour of Alexandria competes with other brochures and pamphlets in the oldest house in town, the **Athenaeum,** 201 Prince St. (548-0035), which holds local and touring art shows, some of more than passing interest. The rose-colored building with its large, round columns and dignified pediment merits attention. Notice how its Greek Renaissance flair differs from the surrounding Colonial architecture. The gallery area is spacious and airy. Call for hours of opening.

The Black History Resource Center, 638 N. Alfred St. (838-4356), is the African-American community's public library. Paintings, photographs, and other memorabilia unwind Black history in Alexandria. A printed walking tour lists historical sights, including several churches, the Franklin and Armfield Slave Market, and the house of George Seaton, a free Black master carpenter who was elected to the city council and state legislature in the 1870s. The map separates Alexandria into zones by race, if you're into that kind of thing. (Open Tues.-Sat. 10am-4pm.)

Restored so faithfully that even its vivid colors are called authentic, the **Carlyle House,** 121 North Fairfax St. (549-2997), home of Scottish merchant John Carlyle, showcases Alexandria's favorite century. Carlyle patterned his home after those in 18th-century Scotland and northern England. Tours enter at the basement, where the servants lived; their white-plaster, stable-like rooms look nothing like the ornate upstairs. The second-story floors show off canvas painted to resemble marble, along with the requisite exquisite antique furniture. The last room has been left unrestored, with beams and wall exposed just as they were found. (Open Tues.-Sun. 10am-4:30pm. Tours given every half-hour. Admission $3, seniors and children $1.)

George Washington and Robert E. Lee prayed at **Christ Church,** 118 N. Washington St. (549-1450), a red-brick Colonial building with a domed steeple. A quiet, shady cemetery with well-tended gardens, it is an inviting rest stop for modern-day visitors to Alexandria. Practically as bright as the outdoors on a sunny day, the interior of the church has stark white walls and an unusual domed window behind the altar. You can also see original hand-lettered tablets containing the Apostle's Creed and the Lord's Prayer. Guided tours available. (Open Mon.-Sat. 9am-4pm., Sun. 2-4:30pm. Free.)

Robert E. Lee's Boyhood Home, 607 Oronoco St. (548-8454), contains antiques and memorabilia from several generations of the Lee family. The Revolutionary War hero, "Light Horse" Harry Lee, was the first to lease this home in 1812; Robert E. Lee went to the Quaker school next door as a young child. The inside shows family records and inventories, beautiful furnishings, weird 19th-century menswear, and a collection of dollhouses (on the sweltering third floor). United Mine Workers president John L. Lewis lived here from 1927-69. Candlelight tours are offered in December. (Open Tues.-Sat. 10am-4pm, Sun. 10am-4pm. Admission $3.)

The authentically Victorian **Lloyd House,** 220 N. Washington St. (838-4577), is primarily a genealogical library, but visitors might enjoy the drawing rooms and exhibits full of old models of clipper ships, paintings and antique books. Historians and novelists study the house's reams of historical and genealogical data. (Tours available. Open Mon.-Fri. 10am-6pm. Free.)

A newly-renovated information center, the **Lyceum,** 202 Washington St. (838-4994), shows exhibitions, audio-visual presentations, and programs on historic Alexandria; it's for the visitor who wants an in-depth historical background of many of the sites on the walking tour. The brick and stucco Greek-Revival building used to be a military hospital, a private home, and then an office building. Free parking available. Tours offered, some in Braille, but call in advance to make arrangements. (Open daily 10am-5pm.)

The **George Washington Masonic Memorial,** at 101 Callahan Drive (683-2007), at the top of King St., rises 400 ft. over Alexandria. The lofty Greek temple portico supports a steep pyramid. Look for the careful blending of all five orders of classical architecture: Doric, Ionic, and Corinthian on the three exterior levels of the tower, Composite in Memorial Hall, and Tuscan in Assembly Hall. Inside, the ninth floor claims to reproduce parts of King Solomon's Temple. Another five floors of museums celebrate George Washington and/or Masonry. Points of interest are the 17-foot bronze statue of America's first President and murals of George Washington celebrating St. John's Day and laying the cornerstone of the Capitol. A 370-year-old Persian rug valued at $1 million is also on display. A 330-foot observation deck provides a fair view of the city. Where did these guys get all their neat stuff? To go above the second floor, you must take the (free) 70-minute tour. (Tours daily 9am-3:30pm, except during "lunch hour." Open daily 9am-5pm.)

The **Stabler-Leadbeater Apothecary Shop and Museum,** 107 South Fairfax St. (836-3713), second-oldest in the country, still operates. Martha Washington's letter requesting castor oil hangs in a glass case, though no one knows why. Old-time druggists needed the shop's hundreds of colorful hand-blown bottles, mortars and pestles, powders, eyeglasses, weights, and scales, as the earnest, informative recording will attest. The museum has recently undertaken a massive project to sort through old order slips. Soon it will be known just who was sick—and from what. Senators Daniel Webster, Henry Clay, and John Calhoun supposedly had some "drug store" conversations here. And Robert E. Lee was hanging out here when he received the message to stop John Brown's insurrection at Harper's Ferry. (Open Mon.-Sat. 10am-4pm. Sun. noon-4pm. Requested donations $1.)

Over 160 artists paint, draw, and sculpt in public on two floors of the **Torpedo Factory,** 105 North Union St. (838-4565). With 83 studios, five galleries, an art school, and an archaeology lab, the art world has conquered the World War I-era munitions factory, leaving the former occupants only a small exhibit and an inert torpedo. Works from just about every mode of artistic creation await aesthetic completion or financial commodification in the myriad workshops, most of which are open to visitors. The well-lit factory has scattered chairs for seating, and a restaurant that serves salads, sandwiches, and entrees. (Open daily 10am-5pm; suggested donation box.)

On the third floor of the factory, **Alexandria Archaeology,** 105 N. Union St. (838-4399), the city's urban archaeology lab and museum, displays 18th- and 19th-century artifacts. Its ceramics, pottery, glass, and buttons have been collected and studied by the Historical Society of Alexandria. (Open Tues.-Sat. 9am-5pm; museum hours Tues.-Fri. 10am-3pm, Sat. 10am-5pm, Sun. 1-5pm.)

The **Waterfront Museum,** in the Transpotomac Canal Center, 44 Canal Center Plaza (838-4288), swims with displays about Alexandria's maritime activities from 1749 to the present. A reconstructed canal tidal lock competes with changing exhibitions. (Open Tues.-Fri. 11am-4pm, Sat. 1-4pm. Free.)

Restored to its 18th-century good looks, **Gadsby's Tavern,** 134 N. Royal St. (838-4242), allows you to see how budget travelers did it 200 years ago (when as many as four people would be assigned to a bed). Upstairs, large dancing rooms are still used today for special functions. Note the vivid colors in the largest hall, and the stairless minstrels' gallery. Open Tues.-Sat. 10pm-5pm, Sun. 1pm-5pm. Admission $3 for adults, $1 for children.

Stores

The Washington Antique Center, Ltd., 209 Madison St. (739-2484). Thirty-five antique dealers in one place, all selling 18th- to 20th-century doodads. Weekends mean free parking. Open daily 11am-6pm.

Liberation Books, 238 N. Henry St. (684-7750). All books are by or about people of African descent. Works include fiction, children's books, history, and folk mythology. Open Mon.-Thurs. 10am-8pm, Fri.-Sat. 10am-10pm.

Olsson's Books and Records, 106 S. Union St. (684-0077 books; 684-0030 music). Link in the Olsson's chain sports northern Virginia's largest collection of CDs and literature. Decent selection of local music, too. Open Mon.-Thurs. 10am-10pm, Fri.-Sat. 10am-midnight, Sun. 11-6pm.

Big Wheels Bikes, 2 Prince St. (739-2300). Situated right on the bike path, this is the most convenient place to rent mountain bikes ($5 an hour, $25 daily), 10-speeds ($4 an hour, $20 daily), or their one, precious tandem ($10 an hour, $50 daily). They will supply you with locks and helmets, when available. Credit card, passport, or driver's licence required as deposit. Payment upon returning equipment. Mon.-Fri. 11am-7pm, Sat. 10am-6pm, Sun. 11am-5pm.

Pacers, 1301 King St., Alexandria (836-1463). About 3 blocks from King St. Metro. Rollerblades for rent at $5 for 1hr., $10 for 3hrs., $15 daily. Rental includes wrist, elbow, and knee guards. Helmet $3 extra. Credit card required for rental; reserve ahead of time. Group lessons available; call for details. Open Mon.-Fri. 10am-8pm, Sat. 10am-6pm, Sun. noon-5pm.

Entertainment & Nightlife

Though Washington is not a world-class compilation of nocturnal delights on the scale of London or New York, just about anyone should be able to find a play, performance, concert, bar, club, or flick to suit their taste among DC's variegated scenes. Major culture purveyors, especially the Kennedy Center, make up for high ticket prices with student discounts and frequent low-cost or free events. Smaller theaters do things differently, and often more cheaply, along 14th St. and elsewhere, while small-scale classical music spumes from seasonal midday concert series, often at the same museums and churches you might visit as sights. Georgetown remains a big draw for its bar scene, but there's just as much happening outside as indoors.

Washington teems with annual events, listed separately under Annual Events (no duh); many of them involve or consist of theater, music, dance and/or movies, such as the American College Theater Festival, Filmfest DC, various outdoor military band concerts, Adams-Morgan Day, Malcolm X Day, the Blues Festival, and the Folklife Festival. (Bar happy hours are listed under Food.)

Theater

Arena Stage, at 6th and Maine Ave. SW (488-3300), is often called the best regional (non-New York) theater company in America. (Metro: Waterfront.) The 42-year-old theater has its own acting company and three performance spaces: the Kreeger theater and Arena Stage itself present high-quality new and used plays, and the Old Vat Theater holds smaller, more experimental performances. (Tickets $19-37; students 35% off, seniors 15% off, both except on Sat. evenings; half-price tickets usually available 90 min. before start of show.)

The prestigious **Shakespeare Theater**, at the Lansburgh, 450 7th St. NW, just off Pennsylvania Ave. (box office 393-2700), puts on, mostly, Shakespeare plays. The 1992-93 season includes *Troilus and Cressida, Hamlet, The Comedy of Errors,* and Bertolt Brecht's *Mother Courage.* Screen actor Tom Hulce (star of *Amadeus*) will appear in *Hamlet.* Call, preferably months in advance, for reservations, ticket prices, performance times, and student/senior discounts. Standing room tickets (currently $10) are available two hours before each performance. Disabled access (call at least 24hr. in advance).

At 25th St. and New Hampshire Ave., the **Kennedy Center's** (416-8000) zillions of performing-arts spaces include two theaters, the Terrace Theater and the Theater Lab; though the less-than-experimental comedy *Shear Madness* has blighted the Lab for years, the Terrace Theater stands ready for quality work. The Something New series even takes the conservative Center over the edge into performance art. Though tickets get expensive (many range from $10-50, though tickets can go all the way up to $450), all Kennedy Center productions offer half-price tickets before the start of an event and on the day of performance to students, seniors, military personnel, handicapped persons and those who can show they're poor; call 416-8340 about discount tix. Free events dot the Kennedy calendar; the American College Theater Festival, April 20-29, showcases free performances of top college productions (see Annual Events).

Thespians thrive in Washington's **14th St. theater district,** where tiny repertory companies explore and experiment with truly enjoyable results. *City Paper* provides very good coverage of this scene. If theater tickets are out of your price range, don't despair; usher. All of these regular companies need unpaid help in the aisles, and once the paying crowds are inside, ushers usually watch the play for free. Call the theaters as far in advance as you can. Woolly Mammoth, Studio, the Source, and the Church St. Theaters dwell in a borderline neighborhood east of Dupont Circle, near or on 14th St. NW between P and Q St.; not all the action is on stage, and not all the commerce goes on in ticket booths. Don't come here alone at night.

TICKETplace (842-5387), on the F St. plaza between 12th and 13th St. NW. Sells discount day-of-show tickets for theater, music, dance, and special events on a walk-up basis. Theater-related pamphlets and calendars hang out here too. Open Tues.-Fri. noon-4pm, Sat. 11am-5pm.

Woolly Mammoth, 1401 Church St. NW (393-3939). Intense, daring productions with local artists and often local playwrights. The theater encourages would-be playwrights to send in manuscripts for readings. Box office open daily noon-6pm. All kinds of cheap seats, like $10 "stampede seats" sold an hr. before curtain, and occasional pay-what-you-can shows; call to check. Tickets $15.50-21.50; students, seniors, and groups of 8 or more, 25% discount.

Studio Theater, 1333 P St. NW (332-3300). Metro: Dupont Circle. All kinds of drama and comedy on two stages (Mainstage and Second Stage) Wed.-Sun. nights. Tickets $12 for second stage productions, $18.50-25.50 for mainstage shows. Students with ID and seniors $3 off Mainstage shows; students can sometimes get half-price tickets one half hour before the show. Call 232-7267 about ushering or group discounts.

The Source Theater, 1835 14th St. NW (462-1073). The biggie; 14th St.'s oldest and most established "alternative" theater. Produces the Washington Theater Festival every summer, at various Washington locations, in addition to its regular assortment of off-Broadway shows. Tickets $15 Thurs.-Sun.; Wed. specials are two for the price of one. Students and seniors $13. Call for information on ushering programs; ushers watch for free. Box office open Mon.-Fri. 10:30am-5:30pm, Sat.-Sun. noon-5pm.

Church St. Theater, 1742 Church St. NW (265-3748). A home for roving theater companies like the Razor's Edge Rep. Tues. night shows are usually $10; weekends nights sometimes go for up to $20.

National Theatre, 1321 Pennsylvania Ave. NW (628-6161). Big-name, big-budget theater often hosts visitors from Broadway, with ticket prices to match. But the "Monday Night at the National" program puts on a variety show for free (recording 783-3372). "Saturday Morning at the National" is a separate, free series of kids' events. Help for sight- or hearing-impaired (call in advance). Some half-price tix available for disabled patrons on Tues.-Thurs. and Sun.

Ford's Theatre, 511 10th St. NW (638-2941). Where President Lincoln was assassinated, now operating on a schedule of musicals and big-budget shows. Metro: Metro Center, 11th St. exit. Box office information: 347-4833. Tickets Tues.-Thurs. and Sun. $25-28, students $17-19, seniors $12-14. Fri.-Sat. $27-30. Senior and student rush tickets available at the box office one hour before showtime for $15 each. Groups get 15-25% discounts, depending on the size (call 638-2367). All tickets $3 for matinees.

Stage Guild, at Carroll Hall, 924 G St. NW (529-2084). Horseshoe-shaped balcony, high stage and unbolted floor seats give set designers a rare opportunity. Five plays in the Sept.-May season; weekdays and matinees $15, weekend nights $18.

GALA Hispanic Theatre, 1625 Park Rd. NW (234-7174), in rickety Mount Pleasant; walk northeast on Columbia to 16th, turn left and walk three blocks to Park Rd. Turn left; GALA is behind the Sacred Heart school. The national-award-garnering Grupo de Actores Latino Americanos presents three plays by modern or classical Latin American or Spanish authors each season (Sept.-March). Plays run for one month in English and one month in Spanish, or in Spanish only. Also hosts the *Poesía en Escena* series, a program of poetry presented from the stage. Tickets $17, students and seniors $14, groups of ten or more $12. Productions Fridays and Saturdays at 8pm and Sundays at 4pm. Reservations recommended. Call Mon.-Fri. 10am-6pm.

Dance

The Dance Place, 3225 8th St. NE (269-2600). Experimental studio and theater leaps with dance, performance art, and/or music nearly every week. Controversial performers like Holly Hughes, and hot new modern-dance choreographers and companies make DC debuts here; Native American, Japanese, and ethnic dance shows join the commotion. Each June the Dance Africa DC Festival explodes with hourly free traditional dance performances from all over Africa, accompanied by an outdoor food and crafts market. Regular performances $8-10, kids around $4.

Music

Classical Music

DC is home to the well-respected **National Symphony Orchestra,** conducted by emigré cellist Mstislav Rostropovich. They perform in the **Kennedy Center,** 25th St. and New Hampshire Ave. NW (416-8000), which makes their tickets normally very expensive; on the other hand, the whole Kennedy Center rigmarole about half-price tickets applies to NSO performances. The NSO also gives three free shows a year, on Memorial Day, the Fourth of July, and Labor Day (see Annual Events). The **Washington Opera** (416-7890) also calls the Kennedy Center home. Chamber music in the Kennedy Center, though a smaller deal, is more often cheap or free, especially during the furious round of December events at the Kennedy Center, which culminates in the pre-Christmas *Messiah* sing-along. For a schedule of free events at the Kennedy Center, try their Office of Cultural Diversity (416-8090).

Wolf Trap Farm Park, 1624 Trap Rd. in Vienna, VA (703-255-1868 info; 703-218-6500 reservations), hauls in famous classical artists as well as country and folk performers for its summer outdoor concerts at the Filene Center. The cheapest tickets are around $15, though; add to that the normal inconveniences of outdoor classical music, like loud picnickers, inaudible soft passages, and the occasional passing jetliner, and you may wish you had opted for chamber music. The Center runs a shuttle from the West Falls Church Metro; you can also drive from DC, though it takes awhile.

The **Library of Congress,** 1st St. SE (concert line 707-5502), sponsors concerts in the Coolidge Auditorium, one of the finest chamber music performance spaces in the world. Concerts are currently being held elsewhere while the auditorium is being renovated. Concerts sometimes feature valuable instruments in the Library's collection, like a Stradivarius violin.

The **Summer Opera Theater Company** (526-1669; summer box office 529-3333), in Catholic University's **Hartke Theater**, runs a summer opera series better than anyone has a right to expect; operas run during July or in that month's immediate vicinity. (Tickets $15-25, $10 standing room; ushers and volunteers see the shows for free—call in advance.)

The **Washington National Cathedral's Summer Festival of Music** (537-6200) draws even atheists to free concerts in July and August, mostly chamber and choral music. The **Phillips Collection,** 1600-1612 21st St. at Q St. NW (387-2151), provides an appropriate setting for chamber music and classical piano concerts—along with bluegrass, African drumming, and other diverse offerings—each Sunday from September to May at 5pm; free, with museum admission. Check the *Washington Post's* "Weekend" section for information. **Dumbarton Church,** 3133 Dumbarton St. NW (965-2000), in Georgetown, sponsors chamber, choral, and Celtic concerts Oct.-April ($15-18; students $12-15). The **Smithsonian museums** (357-2700) also host a smorgasbord of classical performances; try to grab a schedule at the Smithsonian Castle on the Mall.

Jazz

Free lunchtime summer jazz series downtown include one at the **Corcoran Gallery,** 17th St. between E St. and New York Ave. NW (638-3211), in the Hanmer Auditorium every Wednesday at noon. (Metro: Farragut West.) Free **Wednesday Evening Big Band Concerts** (619-7222) take place on the Washington Monument Grounds from 8-10pm between June 17-August 26. The Kennedy Center and the Smithsonian, above, also put on free jazz shows.

Blues Alley, 1073 Rear Wisconsin Ave. NW (337-4141 or 337-4142), in an actual alley, below M St. Kool jazz in an intimate supper club dedicated to the art: Dizzy Gillespie chairs its music society and sponsors a youth orchestra to nurture new talent. Past performers have included Mary Wilson of the Supremes and Wynton Marsalis, but ticket prices are steep, ranging from $13-30. $7 food-or-drink minimum. Creole cuisine (entrees $14-19) served from 6pm, snacks ($2-9) served after 9:30pm. Upscale casual dress: some don tuxes on big nights. Call for reservations, showtimes, and prices or pick up a 3-month schedule.

One Step Down, 2517 Pennsylvania Ave. NW (331-8863), near M St. More casual and less expensive than Blues Alley. Local jazz Sun., Mon., and Thurs.; out-of-town talent Fri.-Sat. Jukebox well-stocked with jazz, and free jam sessions Sat.-Sun. 3:30-7:30pm. Cover $5 for local bands and $8.50-17 for out-of-towners. Usually, minimum food or drink required. Beers start at $3 and sandwiches are $3.50-6. Happy hour Mon.-Fri., 3-7pm (90¢ draft, $4.50 pitcher). Showtimes vary. Open Mon.-Fri. 10:30am-2am, Sat.-Sun. noon-3am.

Takoma Station Tavern, 6914 4th St. NW (829-1999). Metro: Takoma. African-American crowd appreciates quality jazz Monday to Saturday; on Sunday night the sound system thumps with the rub-a-dub beat of reggae. Upscale "Louisiana" or Southern cuisine—steaks, ribs, sandwiches, burgers, and salads ($5-7)—unless you count the Long Island iced tea. No cover charge. Ever. Happy hour Tues.-Sat. 6-9pm. Open Sun.-Thurs. 4pm-2am, Fri. 4pm-3am, Sat. 5pm-3am.

Live Rock, Punk, Reggae, R&B, and Folk

If you don't mind a young crowd, squeeze into a *local* rock and roll show; the DC punk scene is, or was, one of the nation's finest. To see what's up with local bands, just look at *City Paper.* (Also see Music, in our General Introduction.) The **9:30 Club** is the leading venue, but many of the best shows are all-ages (and fairly safe) gatherings in churches, rented halls, or at Fort Reno. Flyers advertise small theaters and rock-related events around Dupont Circle and Adams-Morgan—Second Story Books, 20th and P St. NW, is a good source for event announcements. (Metro: Dupont Circle.) Go-go music is best experienced at outdoor gatherings; its primary indoor venues, at this writing, may not be safe enough to recommend to average tourists.

Like any large city, Washington has arenas where devotees shell out over $20 to see acts they've seen on MTV. The biggest events hit sports arenas: **RFK Stadium** in the summer, the **Capital Centre** year-round. (See Sports.) Slightly less popular bands play **Meriweather Post Pavilion,** off Rte. 29 Columbia Pike (301-982-1800 or 301-730-2424) in Columbia, MD, under an hour from DC or Baltimore. Outdoor lawn tickets $11.50-19.50, seats inside $15.50-27.50. For tickets, call the Pavilion or Ticketron (202-432-7328 or 800-448-9009) or visit a Ticketron outlet.

George Washington University sponsors shows in **Lisner Auditorium,** 21st and H St. NW (202-994-1500). Lisner hosts plays and rock concerts by well-known but "alternative" acts (like Billy Bragg); expect tickets below $20. Summer Saturday and Sunday jazz and R&B shows occupy the outdoor, 4200-seat **Carter-Barron Amphitheater**, set into Rock Creek Park up 16th St. and Colorado Ave. NW. (426-0486; tickets around $13.50) Most of the above venues also sell tickets conveniently but expensively through Ticketron (432-7328), whose outlets exact a several-dollar service charge.

Rock, punk, and metal preempt soccer playing at **Fort Reno Park,** at Chesapeake and Belt St. NW above Wisconsin Ave. (282-0018 or 619-7225) from late June to late August. (Metro: Tenley Circle.) Most concerts feature two or three groups; some are ragged amateurs, some are seasoned scenesters, and some play wonderful, crunchy rock and roll. Find out who's scheduled (look them up in *City Paper),* then play frisbee while you flex your head. Free outdoor concerts Mon. and Thurs. at 7:30pm; for a schedule, check outside Advisory Neighborhood Commission offices at 4025 Chesapeake St. NW. On Capitol Hill, **Market 5 Gallery,** North Carolina Ave. and 7th St. SE (543-7293), also rents itself out for rock, blues, jazz, and dance. (Metro: Eastern Market.)

9:30 club, 930 F St. NW (393-0930 or 638-2008). Metro: Metro Center. DC's best local and alternative rock, since d.c. space closed down. $3 to see 3 local bands; $7-14 for nationally-known acts, which often sell out weeks in advance (box office open Mon.-Fri. 1pm-midnight). Under-21 admitted and hand-stamped. Free happy hour video cabaret Fri. from 4pm.

15 Minutes, 1030 15th St. NW (408-1855). Dark, neon-fish-scattered caverns open six nights a week for happy hour (it takes over its cafeteria neighbor's space in the evenings), and gets wilder as the night goes on. Total nuclear disaster theme: army parachutes and gas masked styro-heads hang from the ceiling. Mostly-bar on weekdays becomes mostly-dance club on weekends, with a schizophrenic assemblage of blues, jazz, and punk on different evenings. 21-plus; young crowd. Two bands and dancing in the main room on Fri. and Sat., picking up the slack left by poverty-stricken d.c. space. Sun. is "Berserk" night: wide open bar from 9pm-1am (cover $5 women, $10 men). Open Mon.-Fri. 4:30pm-2am, Sat. 9pm-3am. $6 cover on weekends.

The Bayou, 3135 K St. NW (333-2897), under the Whitehurst Freeway in Georgetown. Bands on their way up and bands on their way down, with a rough'n'ready crowd that loves them all. Music varies from metal and rock to blues and jazz. Bigger acts like the Ramones come in on weeknights; three metal bands every Friday. On Saturdays, the political satire group Gross National Product (tix and info, 783-7212) lays down the law (tickets $13.50). Some shows 18-plus. Opening act kicks off Mon.-Thurs. and Sun. 9:30pm, Fri. and Sat. after 10pm. Cover $3-20. Domestic beer $2.85. Open Sun.-Thurs. 8pm-1:30am, Fri.-Sat. 8pm-2:30am.

Kilimanjaro, 1724 California St. NW(328-3839). Dimly lit, big-deal club for international music—African, Latin, and Caribbean groups, ju-ju, reggae, and salsa DJs, with Latin music each Sun. Every Wed. his high-Go-go-ness Chuck Brown and the Soul Searchers play. Fair Caribbean food (restaurant open daily noon-4pm). No sneakers, shorts, sweats, torn jeans or tank tops. No cover Mon.-Wed., $5 cover Thurs. and Sun., $10 cover Fri. and Sat. Club open Mon.-Thurs. 5pm-2am, Fri.-Sat. 5pm-4am. Happy hour Mon.-Fri. 5-8pm.

The Birchmere, 3901 Mt. Vernon Ave. (703-549-5919), in Alexandria, VA. This low-key club features folk and blue-grass performed by live local and national acts from Mary Chapin Carpenter to NRBQ. Thursdays the bluegrass band Seldom Scene plays. There's a show almost every night; call and reserve tickets.

Comedy

Comedy Café, 1520 K St. NW (638-5653). Metro: Farragut North or McPherson Square. Johnny Carson and David Letterman have entertained here, as have Merle Hobbs and Felicia Michaels. The informal atmosphere serves up $6 sandwiches and other appetizers. Shows Fri. 8:30 and 10:30pm, Sat. 7, 9, and 11pm. Open mike Thurs. 8:30pm. Beware of strip joint downstairs. Cover $5. Call ahead for better seating and occasional deals on tix and drinks.

Chelsea's, 1055 Thomas Jefferson St. NW (298-8222), in Georgetown. Home of the Capitol Steps, a renowned political satire troupe composed of Congressional staffers, whose proximity to the absurd spectacle of national government inspires them to write and perform political parody. Worth the price if you're up on the news. Tickets are $15 with firm $10 drinks minimum ($25 total), or $35 with a four-course dinner. Free parking with dinner. Capitol Steps plays most Saturday nights from 7:30pm; arrive earlier.

Georgetown

Georgetown at night is Washington on the prowl; everyone is looking for someplace, something, or somebody. While traffic parks bumper to bumper, young Washingtonians pack the streets, roaming from bar to bar and yearning for something more real than the faux-designer purses and jewelry the street vendors hawk. Nowhere else in DC can rival Georgetown for variety of clubs: Ciccone youth, punks, ravers, folkniks, X-men, country and western fans, the underage, and the middle-aged can all find clubs that serve them without much difficulty. While diverse, Georgetown at night is probably whiter than most other nightlife centers; for the gay community, it is at best a sidelight. The area's longstanding popularity has taken its toll on food and drink prices, which are often somewhat higher than those in (say) Adams-Morgan.

Early in the evening, the streets, not the bars and clubs, are the liveliest part of Georgetown. Throngs of students, interns and young professionals share sidewalks with street musicians—some almost talented—playing anything from upended trash cans to alto sax. (Miss Teen Schnauzer is rumored to have appeared here.) As midnight approaches, the crowds move indoors; neckties are loosened and hemlines inch up to the edge of respectability. Don't neglect this neighborhood's non-alcoholic nighttime offerings: in addition to late-night ice cream at Thomas Sweet's and all-night French desserts at Au Pied du Cochon (see Food), you can take in brilliant foreign movies at the Biograph or the Key (see Movies) or do your late-night shopping at Olsson's Books and Records.

Descend Wisconsin Ave. or Thomas Jefferson St. below M St., pass under the Whitehurst Freeway, and you'll reach **Washington Harbour** on the 3000 block of K St. This glitzy, postmodern complex of stores and offices failed as a business venture, but succeeds aesthetically every night, when the sun sets over the Potomac River. Standing on the concrete riverside terrace, you can watch the unbroken line of trees on the Virginia shore change color. Walk down Thomas Jefferson St. to reach the main complex, where several restaurants incorporate outdoor cafés perfect for a late drink. **Tony and Joe's Seafood Place** (944-4545) lies on the wharf and **Sequoia** (944-4200) has its own terrace. (Beer at Tony and Joe's: $2.50-4.50 for draft, $3.25-5.50 for bottle; open Sun.-Thurs. 11am-11pm, Fri.-Sat. 11am-midnight. Beer at Sequoia: draft $3, import $3.50; mixed drinks $3.50 and up.) Late at night, look for the illuminated marble of the Kennedy Center and admire the Potomac where it reflects the city lights.

Georgetown is relatively safe at night; its residents, with their affluence and clout, attract more than enough police to direct traffic and patrol the sidewalks. If you feel especially insecure, stay on the main arteries of Wisconsin Ave. or M St. Romantic strolls along the C&O canal towpath are best attempted before 10pm; the canal's historic-landmark status means street lights along its banks are federally proscribed.

Bars and Dance Clubs

Dance clubs and bars in DC fold as fast as honest congressfolk. Of course there are some stubborn old mules that refuse to budge, and you can always count on these for an authentic hoopsmackle. Naturally, *Let's Go* lists as many clubs as possible, along with detailed information about their whereabouts, prices, special offerings, and clientele. Or just ask a young member of the local hipeoisie where he or she likes to go. Or consult the *City Paper* and other alternative papers. Some clubs move too fast to get caught in print, like the roving rave club **Parachute** (547-3400). Once a month, usually on a Saturday night, the club squats in a different abandoned warehouse around DC proper and hosts a techno freak-out. (Cover $10; must be 18 to get in, 21 to drink.) But whatever your scene—from intern-ridden Georgetown to the disco-driven gay bars of Dupont Circle—be tolerant of others and encourage them to join in the fun.

Capitol Hill

The row of bars along Pennsylvania Avenue SE from 2nd St. to 7th St. monopolizes nightlife on the Hill. This close to the Congress, weekday evenings and happy hours draw plenty of Hill workers, interns, and the occasional Member; you won't have to wait for a weekend to bar-hop to your heart's content.

Dance Clubs

Julio's, 801 Pennsylvania Ave. SE (546-0060). Metro: Eastern Market. One of Capitol Hill's only chances to dance. Good-timing waitrons in black polo shirts move smoothly and swiftly among flower centerpieces and aqua-and-pink *Miami Vice* decor, pausing only to sing along with the clamorous karaoke. Happy hour clocks in with $2 draft beer and $1 pizza slices (Mon.-Thurs. 4-6:30pm); call ahead to confirm this offer. DJs play mainstream rock Thurs. nights in summer; bands play Friday and Saturday. Softball teams and Marines from the 8th St. barracks count themselves among the regulars. Restaurant by day offers appetizers ($2.25-6), sandwiches ($5-6), and that "famous" pizza ($8-17). Crawl upstairs to play pool and video games; come tumbling back down, headlong. Cover charge $3 from 9pm on. Open Mon.-Wed. 11:30am-11pm, Thurs.-Fri. 11:30am-2am, Sat. 11:30am-2am, Sun. 10am-11pm.

Remington's, 639 Pennsylvania Ave. SE (543-3113). Caters mostly to gay men. Boogie on the ample first-floor dance floor, usually to country-western DJs and bands. The carpeted upstairs features posters of James Dean, a pool room, and a piano bar ($2 cover upstairs). Beer $1.75 and mixed drinks $2 during happy hour (Mon.-Wed. 4pm-2am). Free Country-Western dance lessons Mon. and Thurs. at 8pm. Open Mon.-Thurs. 4pm-2am, Fri. 4pm-3am, Sat. 2pm-3am, Sun. 2pm-2am.

Bars

Hawk 'n Dove, 329 Pennsylvania Ave. SE (543-3300). A Hill institution since 1967, when its several rooms separated pro- and anti-Vietnam War clients ("hawks" and "doves"). Wood-panelled walls hold antique signs, railroad lights, vintage neon signs, and even a brass bar. Interns hang out while the neighbors watch sports and singles watch each other; as in '67, different rooms serve different crowds, including one for non-smokers. The three buildings, over 100 years old, have been a blacksmith shop, a salt-water taffy plant, and DC's first gas station. Happy hour (Mon.-Thurs. 4-7pm). Sandwiches $4-6.50; Beer $1.75 and up. Fourteen kinds of bottled beer and 11 drafts available. Midnight breakfast served Mon.-Thurs. 11pm-1am, Fri.-Sat. 11pm-2am ($7; $9 with steak). Sat.-Sun. brunch 10am-3:30pm offers a screwdriver, mimosa, or bloody mary for $1.95. Open Sun.-Thurs. 10am-2am, Fri.-Sat. 10pm-3am, Sun. 3pm-2am.

Tune Inn, 331 1/2 Pennsylvania Ave. SE (543-2725). Metro: Capitol South. Unpretentious fun has meant slumming at the Tune Inn since 1933; *Esquire* calls it one of America's 100 best bars. Clients range from congressional workers to construction workers to students. Walls hold mounted fish, game heads, and sports trophies. Sandwiches $2.50-4.25; chicken dinner $4.50. Beer $1.25 for draft, $2 for bottles. $3 minimum. Open Mon.-Thurs. 8am-2am, Fri.-Sat. 8am-3am, Sun. 9am-2am.

Kelley's "The Irish Times," 14 F St. NW (543-5433). Walk out of Union Station and take a right turn (west) down F St. Irish street signs, the *Irish Times*, Joyce on the wall, and Yeats and Keats on the menu make this more than just another Irish pub. (Don't tell them Keats wasn't Irish.) Live music Wed.-Sat. evenings. Sandwiches $5.25, soup $2; beer from $2.50, Irish whiskey from $4. Open Sun.-Thurs. 10:30am-1:30am, Fri.-Sat. 10:30am-2:30am.

Taverna the Greek Islands, 307 Pennsylvania Ave. SE (547-8360). Metro: Capitol South. First-floor bar complements two floors of dining (see Food) with comfortable service and a familiar, jovial young crowd. Look for fresh mint sprigs from the boss's garden in vases at the bar. Happy hour (Mon.-Fri. 3:30-7:30pm) brings $1.85 mixed drinks and $1 draft beer. Bar usually offers a "sandwich special;" call to find out. Open Mon.-Sat. 11am-midnight, Sun. 4-11pm.

The Li'l Pub, 655 Pennsylvania Ave. SE (543-5526). Neighborhood pub distinguished by a friendly and diverse crowd (Black and white, gay and straight), yellow stucco walls, and a large framed photo of a customer being accosted by a stripper. Faroutski! Their "best burgers on the hill" weigh 9-11 oz. before cooking ($3.25). Beer $1.75 and up. 50¢ off drinks during happy hour, weekdays 4pm-7pm. Open Mon.-Thurs. 11:30am-2am, Fri.-Sat. 11:30am-3am, Sun. 1:30pm-2am. Open Sun.-Thurs. 11:30am-2am, Fri.-Sat. 11:30am-3am.

Duddington's, 319 Pennsylvania Ave. SE (544-3500). Watch sports upstairs on the big-screen TV, or downstairs around an octagonal, free-standing bar vaguely reminiscent of the Pisano pulpits in Florence and Siena. (See *Let's Go: Italy.*) Happy hour (Mon.-Fri. 5-8pm) features $1 draft beer. Sandwiches are $4.35-7.35. All-you-can-eat salad and hot-food buffet is $6 during lunch (11am-3pm), $8 during dinner (5-10pm). The downstairs crowd includes interns, softball teams, and Marines. Open Mon.-Thurs. 11am-2am, Fri. 11am-3am, Sat. 10am-3am, Sun. 10am-2am.

White House Area/ Foggy Bottom

The nightlife here resembles the daylife: older workers looking to relax find one set of spots, GWU students rock out in another.

Bars

Mr. Henry's Washington Circle, 2134 Pennsylvania Ave. NW (337-0222). Metro: Foggy Bottom/GWU. Plush red wallpaper and centuries-old *Sunday Telegraph* clippings—all in chronological order—grace this pseudo-Victorian saloon. Youthful crowd comes for jukebox or DJ Thurs.-Sat. nights. There's also an outdoor porch area for eating, or sordid carousing. Open Sun.-Thurs. 11am-1am, Fri.-Sat. 11am-2am.

Red Lion, 2000 Pennsylvania Ave. NW (659-0444). Metro: Foggy Bottom/GWU. Mellow hangout for GW students. This small balcony offers perfect people-watching. Large deli sandwiches ($4-6). Happy hour (Mon.-Fri. 4-7pm): pitchers $4.25. Open Mon.-Thurs. 11am-2am, Fri. 11am-3am, Sat. 8pm-3am. Flexible hours during the summer.

Quigley's, 1825 Eye St. NW (331-0150). Metro: Farragut West. Relax upstairs or boogie down below. College-age and professional crowds. Free food (chicken wings, meatballs, corn chips and salsa) at happy hour (daily 4-7pm). Regular entrees $7-8 at the cheapest. DJ plays Thurs.-Sat. starting at 9pm. Open Mon.-Wed. 11:30am-midnight, Thurs. 11:30am-1:30am, Fri. 11:30am-2:30am, Sat. 9pm-2:30am.

Georgetown

Bars

Champions, 1206 Wisconsin Ave. NW (965-4005), through an alley. Strapping jocks abound. Signed photos of sports stars on the wall, Redskins (football) and Capitals (hockey) players stop by, and "the big game" is always on TV. Around 11pm young singles (mid-20s to mid-30s) replace aging armchair quarterbacks. Europeans come by to gawk, and can you blame them? Champions' buffalo wings may be the best in town ($5 for 8). Don't bother trying to get in if you're underage. Top-40 hits and oldies, dance music. Tuesday is Karaoke Night, and buffalo wings go for 30¢ a piece. Happy hour Mon.-Thurs. 5-8pm, $1.60 drafts. $6.50 "fishbowl" drafts on Fridays. Draft beer normally $2.35. One drink minimum, but no cover on Friday and Saturday nights. Open Sun.-Thurs. 5pm-1:30am, Fri.-Sat. 5pm-2:30am.

The Tombs, 1226 36th St. NW (337-6668), corner of Prospect St. next to 1789. Recognize the bar? Designers for the movie *St. Elmo's Fire* based a stage set on it. Georgetown U. students drop in for burgers and beer; smell both as you walk downstairs. Older lunch clientele; justly crowded at night. Sunday's hopping dance nights cost $3 at the door (free with Georgetown ID); no cover other nights. Dollar drafts and $6 pitchers. Burgers and sandwiches $4.75-7. Open Mon.-Sat. 10am-2am, Sun. 10am-2am.

Charing Cross, 3027 M St. NW (338-2141). Collegians pound beers in here early, then head down the street to Garrett's. Clean-cut prep school types are the norm, with summer interns filling in when the college regulars leave. $2.50 for draft beer ($1.50 during 11pm-closing happy hour—pitchers $5, too). Mon.-Fri. 5-7pm. Open Mon.-Fri. 11:30am-2am, Sat.-Sun. 5pm-3am.

Garrett's, 3003 M St. NW (333-1033). Up the street from Charing Cross; fluid movement between the two. G-town's most popular bar is a body-to-body all-night frat party. If you can move or see, look for the "Hemingway" rhino, shot by one of Ernest's wives. No cover charge. Open Sun.-Thurs. 11:30am-2am, Fri.-Sat. 11:30am-3am.

J. Paul's, 3218 M St. NW (333-3450). King of the Georgetown restaurant/saloons—it even has its own house brand of ale (16oz. bottle $3.25). Beers range from $3 to $4.50, clientele ranges from twenties to forties. Casual and bustling; come in for a beer with friends. No cover charge. Open Sun.-Thurs. 11:30am-2am, Fri.-Sat. 11:30am-3am.

Third Edition, 1218 Wisconsin Ave. NW (333-3700). Five bars, including a dance floor and house music upstairs and a tiki bar outside where reggae plays. Older crowd sticks to the bar downstairs. Come before 9pm on the weekends to eat and to avoid the $4 admission charge and the lines. Draft $2.75, domestic bottles $3, imported bottles $4. Originator of the potent GBS shooter ($4). Men must wear collared shirts; no sandals, no cutoff shorts, and no hats. Open Mon.-Thurs. 11:30am-1:30am, Fri.-Sat. 11:30am-2:30am, Sun. 9:30am-1:30am.

The Hennessy, 3263 M St. NW (342-0406). Towards the Georgetown University end of M St., and—unsurprisingly—filled with sweaty collegiate bods humping to a mix of music from reggae to top 40. Daily $1 drafts until 11:30pm. Weekend cover charge $3. Open Sun.-Thurs. 11am-1:30am, Fri.-Sat. 11am-2:30am.

Grog and Tankard, 2408 Wisconsin Ave. NW (333-3114), in Glover Park, north of Georgetown proper. Sounds like a motorcycle joint, but attracts college kids from American University and Georgetown. Monday: Grateful Dead night; Tuesday: acoustic blues for an older crowd; Wednesday: local progressive bands. Show starts around 9:30pm, cover about $6 depending on band. $2 draft, $7.50 pitcher. Open daily 5pm-2am.

The Saloon, 3239 M St. NW (338-4900). Two of the best things in life: live jazz by local musicians and more than 75 different kinds of beer (a stunning 18 on tap). Prices range from $2.25 for domestic draft to $16.50 for the Belgian St. Sebastian Crockale. House draft only 95¢ every day from 3pm-7:30pm. Tuesday offers a special 10 oz. sirloin with fries and salad for carnivores—only $6.25. Cover Tues.-Thurs. $2, Fri.-Sat. $3; free Sun.-Mon. and before 8pm every night. No muscle shirts or sweats allowed. Open Sun.-Thurs. 3pm-2am, Fri.-Sat. 3pm-3am, Sun. 3pm-2am.

Dylan's Café, 3251 Prospect St. NW (337-0593), above Morton's near corner of Wisconsin Ave. Artsy, mellow café suitable for deep, meaningful conversations over wine or beer ($2.25 draft). Local progressive or 60s-70s cover bands. Cover $2 for popular acts. Music starts at 9:30pm. Open Tues.-Sun. 11am-2am.

Dance Clubs

Paper Moon, 1069 31st St. NW (965-6666). This Italian restaurant by day transforms into a dance club full of slithery, sweat-coated bodies on Fri.-Sat. nights from 11pm-3am (cover $5). European crowd goes crazy for the top-40 sound. Drinks $3.50 and up.

Winston's, 3295 M St. NW (333-3150). So many men, so little hair. Marines and Navy come for R&R; Georgetown, American, and George Washington University guys crowd in. 18 and over welcome. Over 21, no cover. For the under-age, cover changes during the week depending on what specials are being offered and to whom (plan on paying $5-7). Get here before 11pm and reap the benefits: draft beer $1.25 (usually $1.90). No tank tops, no cutoffs. Open Sun.-Thurs. 8pm-1:30am, Fri.-Sat. 8pm-2:30am.

Anastasia's, 3204 M St. NW (751-2220), above Banana Republic on the corner of Wisconsin Ave. Look for the strobe lights and sashaying people from the sidewalk outside. Videos play non-stop on the scattered TVs—top-40 and oldies. Must be 18 Sun.-Thurs., 21 Fri.-Sat. Cover charge around $7, but changes throughout the week. Tuesday is Ladies Night, with $1.25 drafts and shooters for all until midnight. Wed.-Mon. $1.75 draft and $2.75 domestic bottle. No torn jeans, tank tops, flip-flops, sweats, or hats. Open Sun.-Thurs. 9pm-2am, Fri.-Sat. 9pm-3am.

New Downtown

Downtown nightlife doesn't begin to rumble until the weekend, when the pot of standard bars, go-go bars, industrial, punk, jazz, and reggae clubs, and entertainment-seeking teenagers begins to percolate. Nightlife thrives along F St. between 9th and 10th St., but don't expect the street life of Georgetown to come calling: the action is strictly indoors.

Bars

The Ritz, 919 E St. NW (638-2582). Older crowd. 1500 people can pack themselves into the five rooms filled with a fashionably-dressed upmarket crowd—"proper attire is required." Music ranges from jazz, classic soul, and Motown to international music, calypso, progressive R&B, and reggae. Tables are set up for relaxing and drinking while listening to the music. Open Thurs. 5-10pm, Fri. 5pm-3am (happy hour 5-8pm), Sat. 9pm-4am, Sun. 10pm-2am. Free Thurs., cover Fri. (after 8pm), and Sat. $10, Sun. $6.

Stoney's Beef-N-Beer Restaurant, 1307 L St. NW (347-9163). Shuttered half-bar, half-greasy spoon delights its regulars with half-price specials (pizza, steak and cheese, hamburgers) during a lengthy happy hour (Mon.-Wed. 4pm-midnight). Open Mon.-Fri. 9am-midnight, Sat.-Sun. 10:30am-midnight.

The Madhatter, 1831 M St. NW (833-1495). Swells with collegiate patrons during the school year. Complimentary half-shell oysters speed away during the special happy hours with $1 Rolling Rocks. Open Mon.-Thurs. 11:30am-1:15am, Fri. 11:30am-3am, Sat. 11am-3am, Sun. 11am-1:15am.

The Midtown Bar and Grill, 1827 M St. NW (331-1827). Frequent $1 drinks for women. Advertised all-you-can-eat barbecue specials ($9). Open Mon.-Fri. 11:30am-3am, Sat. 11am-3am. Sun. brunch 10am-4pm.

Dance Clubs

Fifth Colvmn, 915 F St. NW (393-3632). Euro-crowd brings serious disco into the trendy '90s. Milli Vanilli and Prince have been spotted here. Art exhibits change every four months. Splashy "underwater" decor in a converted bank, with fish tanks, fast-paced dizzying films, and lights. House music shakes the basement; quieter bar upstairs. Look for the four stone columns outside: the line to get in is the fifth. The week's line-up reads like a hip house music menu: No cover Mon.-Tues. for hardcore techno and underground house; Wed. $6 for hip-hop and acid jazz; Thurs. $8 for European house; Fri. more Eurohouse, $5 before midnight, $7 after; Sat. $8 New York freestyle house. Sunday is gay techno night (cover $6). Open daily 10pm-whenever.

The Roxy, 1214 18th St. NW (296-9292). Alternates on the weekends between smoke-filled industrial noise (Wed. and Fri.) and reggae music (Thurs. and Sat.). Look for $1-off-cover coupons which frequently appear in area book and record stores. Free before 10pm Wed. and Fri., after 10pm cover: 18-20 yrs. $3, 21 and over $5. Thurs. $6, Sat. $7.) Open Wed.-Thurs. and Sat. 9pm-2am, Fri. 9pm-3am.

The Dome, 21st and M St. NW (487-4180), below ground with an outdoor bar upstairs. Students flock to the crowded, top-40 dance floor. Open Mon.-Thurs. 9pm-2am, Fri.-Sat. 9pm-3am, Sun. 9pm-1:30am. Standard cover $5, but goes as high as $10 for men, $5 for women on Sundays. Free Wednesdays. Young crowd.

Dupont Circle

Gay Clubs

J.R.'s, 1519 17th St. NW (328-0090). Metro: Dupont Circle. An upscale but down-home brick and varnished wood bar, with wood floors, stained glass windows, and a DJ in a choir stall overlooking the tank of "guppies" (gay urban professionals). Open Sun.-Thurs. 11am-2am, Fri.-Sat. 11am-3pm.

Friends, 2122 P St. NW (822-8909). Low-key piano bar. Daily cocktail hour (4-9pm) features weekly drink specials $1.50. Fri.-Sat. cover $3. Open Sun.-Thurs. 4pm-2am, Fri.-Sat. 4pm-3am. Restaurant open Sun.-Thurs. 6pm-10:30pm, Fri.-Sat. 6pm-11pm. Early-bird special (6-8pm) includes entree, caesar salad, and a glass of the house wine for $8.95

Mr. P's, 2147 P St. NW (293-1064). Caters to an older crowd. Despite the dance floor and nimble DJ, the men here are more interested in getting plastered or just plain cruising. Spacious back balcony allows to you to drink outdoors. Open Mon.-Thurs. 3pm-2am, Fri.-Sat. 3pm-3am, Sun. noon-2am.

Fraternity House, at 2122 P St. NW (223-4917), in the alley between 21st and 22d St. Metro: Dupont Circle. The "Frat House" attracts ethnically-mixed crowd of young gay men. Strobe lights, disco balls, and hard core house beats pump and flicker as the guys dance the night away amid bookshelves and mirrored walls. Happy hour sports $1.50 domestic beer and mixed drinks (4-9pm). Cover Wed.-Thurs. $2, Fri.-Sat. $4. Open Sun. 8pm-2am, Mon.-Wed. 4pm-2am, Thurs. 4pm-4am, Fri. 4pm-5am, Sat. 8pm-5am.

Badlands, 1415 22nd St. NW (296-0505), off P St. A predominately white and older crowd rocks to the beat of pop dance music and some house. Cover: Sun. and Tues. $1, Thurs. $3, Fri.-Sat. $5. Open Sun.-Thurs. 9pm-1:45am, Fri. 8pm-.2:45am, Sat. 9pm-2:45am.

Other Clubs

Brickskeller, 1523 22nd St. NW (293-1885). Metro: Dupont Circle. Deserves its reputation for "the world's largest selection of beer"—over 500 brands, plus thousands of defunct labels on display upstairs and downstairs. Read the menu for beer listings "from Aass to Zywiece" and multilingual toasts from Albanian ("Gezuar") to Zulu ("Oogy Wawa"). Open Mon.-Thurs. 11:30am-2am, Fri. 11:30am-2:30am, Sat. 6pm-2:30am, Sun. 6pm-1:30am.

The Fox and Hounds, 1537 17th St. NW (232-6307). Metro: Dupont Circle. Local residents claim it owns the best jukebox in DC; judge for yourself—it certainly never stops playing. Early-twenties crowd races here for strong drinks and shoulder-to-shoulder company. Open Sun.-Thurs. 11am-2am, Fri.-Sat. 11am-3am. Patio open Sun.-Thurs. 11am-12:30am, Fri.-Sat. 11am-2am.

El Bodegón, 1637 R St. NW (667-1710), near 17th St. Metro: Dupont Circle. As close to Spain in America as you'll get. Cool stucco walls hung with pottery and tile; garlic, peppers, and curing hams (complete with little cups to catch the drippings) dangle from wood beams. Flamenco music on tape during the day, live starting about 8:30 every night. Enjoy the show and the atmosphere—forget the entrees ($15-25) and nosh *tapas* (Spanish appetizers) instead. *Tapas* $3-7, dinner appetizers $4.50-12. Smack your lips on the *Empanadillas* (pastries stuffed with spiced ground beef; $4.50). Open Mon.-Fri. 11:30am-2:30pm and 5:30-10:30pm, Sat. 5:30-11pm.

The Front Page, 1333 New Hampshire Ave. NW (296-6500). Metro: Dupont Circle. Well-known among the intern crowd for its generous Thursday happy hours (5-7pm). Open daily 11:30am-1:30am; bar closes earlier if business slows.

Chicago Club, on Dupont Circle NW (463-8888), by the 19th St. entrance. Multiple personalities serve a specific clientele (yuppies, gay men, women) each night of the week. On Friday night, the club changes its name to **Dakar** and plays West African music. The decor is black, gray and red, the dance floor small. Small, eclectic following sometimes blossoms after midnight. Call the recording for the club's profile on a given night. IDs checked at door. Open Sun.-Thurs. 9pm-2am, Fri.-Sat. 9pm-3am. Cover Thurs. and Sun. $5, Wed. $7, Fri.-Sat. $8.

Adams-Morgan

Though the nightlife isn't super-cheap budget, Adams-Morgan's multi-purpose nightspots are popular with twentysomething club-hoppers.

Bars and Dance Clubs

Café Atlantico, 1819 Columbia Rd. NW (575-2233). A new, slick Caribbean grill dressed up as a Pacifico nightclub, with track lights, mirrors, and a DJ blasting international music. Good but expensive food, with specials as low as $8. Appetizers $4.25-6, *tostones* (fried plantains) $2.75. Caribbean mixed drinks $4.75. Beer from $3.50. Open Sun.-Mon. 5:30-10pm, Tues.-Thurs. 5:30-11pm, Fri.-Sat. 5:30pm-midnight.

Mr. Henry's, 1836 Columbia Rd. NW (797-8882). Dark bar with dark wood furniture; mixed gay and straight clientele. Mr. Henry discovered Roberta Flack here; skip open mic night. Nightly live entertainment, from jazz piano to stand-up comedy to open-mike nights. Draft beer $1.75-2.75. Appetizers $1.75-4.25. Sandwiches $4.75-6. Open daily 11am-2am. Often open 24hr. on weekends.

Cities, 2424 18th St. NW (328-7194) and **IKON** (483-2882), on the second floor. Cities' packed restaurant 'n bar stays hip, or tries to, by changing decor and menu every eight months or so to mimic a different city. The versatile chef keeps her job through all the culinary mutations; the chic decor hints at out-of-range entrees, but the menu's low end satisfies, too. (Appetizers $3.50-6; entrees $8.50-15). **IKON**'s decor would never think of changing—the dance club's patrons come for the gabled ceiling, techno-lights in motion, purple fluorescence, and murals of a tranquil, dreamy beach. In the barroom funky wood tables brawl with leopard skin benches beside a spectacular, view-from-the-'copter-style full-length window. Beers from $3.75. Cover Wed.-Thurs. $7, Fri.-Sat. $8. Cities open Mon.-Fri. 5pm-2am, Sat. 5pm-3am, Sun. 11am-2am. IKON open Wed.-Thurs. 9:30pm-2am, Fri.-Sat. 9:30pm-4am. Restaurant closes at 11pm.

Café Heaven and **Café Hell**, 2327 18th St. NW (667--4355). Hell's downstairs, Heaven's upstairs, so the ground-floor Italian restaurant must be *purgatorio*. In Hell, smoke blurs the funky gold tables and loud music emanates from spooky, yellow-backlit masks. It's every high schooler's dream of a New York café and bar. Heaven looks rather like an old townhouse: scuffed wood floor, comfy couches, a small bar, and three TVs. But the dance floor throbs to pounding beats, and Heaven's back patio is crowded with timid souls who can't take the noise. No cover charge unless a band is playing. Beers from $3; half price during happy hour (6:30-8:30pm in Hell). Dancing starts daily about 9pm. Open Sun.-Thurs. 6:30pm-2am, Fri.-Sat. 6:30pm-3am.

Café Lautrec, 2431 18th St. NW (265-6436). Semi-sophisticated restaurant/bar/café boasts Parisian art and great coffees. High school kids may come to feel the chic, but lots of others come for the live jazz every night (starting around 9pm), tap dancing on the bar (Thurs.-Sat. nights), or coffee and conversation. The musicians struggle among jammed-together tables—"intimate" is hardly an adequate description. Vocalist Sat. No cover, but $6 food/drink minimum Thurs.-Sat. after 10pm. Beers from $3; appetizers $4.50-5.50; desserts $2.75-3.50. Open Sun.-Thurs. 5pm-2am, Fri.-Sat. 5pm-3am.

Opera, 1777 Columbia Rd. NW (751-2200). Urban hipsters spin on the roomy, lighted dance floor and balconies. Wednesday is Ladies' Night. Dress is casual; cover $6. Thursday is Euro

204 Entertainment & Nightlife

night, when clientele is about 20% gay. Cover $5. Each Friday picks an ethnic theme; cover around $8. Saturday's elegant Latin night features hot, live Latin music and $10 cover; suits or ties encouraged—along with sweats or baseball hats. Beer from $3.50. Café in back serves "succulent Latin food" until closing. Open Wed.-Thurs. 9pm-2am, Fri.-Sat. 9pm-4am.

Upper Northwest

Bars

Ireland's 4 Provinces, 3412 Connecticut Ave. NW (244-0860). Metro: Cleveland Park. Draws a foot-tapping family crowd to communal tables and small stage with Irish and folk music five or six nights a week. Outdoor café-style seating, too. Open Sun.-Thurs. 4pm-2am, Fri.-Sat. 4pm-3am. Fri.-Sat. cover $2.

Oxford Tavern, 3000 Connecticut Ave. NW (232-4225), across the street from the Zoo. Metro: Woodley Park/Zoo. The "Zoo Bar" ladles out beer after beer to a collegiate crowd. A DJ plays on Fri. nights, and a live band Thurs. and Sat. There's nothing special about this bar except that everybody seems to come here. Open Sun.-Thurs. 9:30am-2am, Fri.-Sat. 9:30am-3am.

The Malt Shop, 4611 Wisconsin Ave. NW (244-1882), at 41st St. above the Dancing Crab. Get yourself a brew and watch the game on TV with the regulars. In the good old days, the Redskins drank here after taping "Redskin Sideline" down the street at WUSA-TV. Because they didn't want to say they were going to a bar, they said they were going to a malt shop. Hence the name. Ogle pictures of famous 'Skins on the theme wall along with Dennis Quaid's flagging penis. $2 draft, $2.25 imported bottles, and $6.25 pitchers. Open Mon.-Fri. 4pm-12:30am, Sat-Sun. noon-1:30am.

Quigley's, 3201 New Mexico Ave. NW (966-0500), off Nebraska Ave. Metro: Tenleytown. American restaurant by day: burgers ($6), sandwiches ($5-8), and salads ($5-8.50)—American U. hangout by night. Students come for half-price burgers ($3.50) and $6 pitchers on Sunday nights from 6 to 11pm, and to visit their friends who staff the place. Tues. $1.50 Bud, $5.50 pitchers. Last Tues. of each month brings half-price food to the bar from 1-5pm. Open Mon.-Sat. 11:30am-1:30am, Sun. 11:30am-12:30am.

Bethesda, MD

Bars and Clubs

Tequila Sunrise Café, 7940 Wisconsin Ave. (907-6536). Metro: Bethesda. Outdoor cantina, bar, and patio (heated in winter) wouldn't fail as a movie set. Happy hour (Mon.-Fri. 4-7pm) offers $1 off drinks and a buffet of free appetizers. Potent margaritas $4. Draft beer from $2. Open Sun.-Mon. 4:30pm-1am, Tues.-Wed. 11am-1am, Thurs.-Sat. 11am-2am.

Nantucket Landing, 4723 Elm St. (654-7979). Cool place for ceiling buffs. Fancy food by day, fancy bar by night, with molded ceiling and a stained-glass ceiling vault. By night the crowd retains an excitable high-school feel (though none are under 21; this place *cards*). Happy hour (Mon.-Fri. 4-7pm) celebrates half-price drinks and free pizza. Drafts $2.75, but $1 on Wednesdays. Mixed drinks from $3.50. Dance music from 10pm. Appetizers $2.50-5. Burgers $4.50-6. Open Mon.-Thurs. 11:30am-1am, Fri. 11:30am-2am, Sat. 5pm-2am.

Durty Nelly's, 4714 Montgomery Lane (652-1444). Long bar where the neighborhood hangs out. Outdoor patio and bar in back. Happy hour (Mon.-Fri. 3-7pm) features half-price draft beer, 2-for-1 mixed drinks, and free food. Beers $3-3.50, burgers $5.75-6.25, sandwiches $5.25-6.25. Live rock'n roll and blues entertainment every night; for the very bold or very shit-faced, open mike every Mon. night. Open Mon.-Thurs. 11:30am-1am, Fri.-Sat. 11:30am-2am.

GEOZ, 7305 Waverly St. NW (907-8604). Hot new club goes all-out with charcoal-grey walls and aquamarine neon. Dance floor totes a smoke machine and a laser thang. A lower room drinks and dines, and a hard-to-find side room shoots pool. Must be 21 to enter. Boogie every night to a variety of music. Happy hour was simply made for *Let's Go* readers, who will be found huddling around the fabulous free buffet, overflowing with pasta, cheese plates, chicken wings, etc. Drafts $1.25, mixed drinks from $1.95. Free parking. Open Mon.-Thurs. 11am-1:30am, Fri. 11am-2:30am, Sat. 7pm-2:30am.

Also see the **Bethesda Cinema 'n Drafthouse,** below under Movies.

Northeast

Kitty O'Shea, 3514 12th St. NE (636-9882). Irish *noir* bar where locals play pool in the smoky dimness. Grab a $3.50 burger or munch on Kitty's giant appetizers ($1-2). Open Sun.-Thurs. 3pm-2am, Fri.-Sat. 3pm-3am.

Breeze's Metro Club, 2335 Bladensburg Rd., NE (526-8880). Go-go got going here. The scene varies from night to night, but count on Thurs.-Sat. for music from some of go-go's original masters (cover $3; 19 and over; open 9pm-2am). Call to find out about times, prices, and themes for other nights.

Worth Driving To

Roratonga Rodeo, 2771 Wilson Blvd., in Arlington, VA (703-525-8646) Metro: Clarendon. Live acoustic sets on Thurs., Sat., Sun., and the occasional Wed. night. Wurlitzer jukebox made from a '59 Cadillac blares everything from Johnny Cash to the Buzzcocks. How could you not drop in? 18- to 20-year-olds welcome. Happy hour 5-8pm, free nachos and salsa or chips depending on the pitcher; Rolling Rock pitchers $5. A selection of 66 beers, 12 of which are on tap. No cover. Shows begin at 9pm, 8pm on Sun. Open Sat.-Thurs. 5pm-2am, Fri. 4pm-2am.

TRACKS, 1111 First St. SE at M St. (488-3320). Fri. night is "college night" on TRACKS' broad neonized dance floor, with min. age 18 and a mixed (gay and straight, African-American and white) crowd. On Sun. night gay African-American men make up much of the dance floor's large population, though all are welcome. Closes 5-6am weekends. Cheap beer ($2 a glass, $3 per pitcher weeknights) and many special events—pick up the TRACKS newsletter in Dupont Circle stores for the week's calendar. Popular club, but dangerous surrounding neighborhood; don't go without a car. No cover Mon.-Tues. and nightly before 9pm; cover Wed.-Thurs. and Sun. $3; Fri.-Sat. $5.

Old Town Alexandria, VA

Bars and Clubs

Ireland's Own, 132 North Royal St. (549-4535). High-spirited pub and restaurant whose nightly live Irish entertainment fills Old Town's largest patio. Even the owner sings along on weekends. A visit from Ronnie hasn't been forgotten: a sign reading "Reagan's corner" hangs on a beam near the bar. Open daily 11am-whenever, depending on the crowd. Last call 1:30am.

The Basin St. Lounge, 219 King St. (549-0035). Live jazz in a restored 18th-century living room. Plush armchairs fill nightly with a thirtysomething crowd for the Creole jazz, fusion (weekends), or contemporary jazz spin-offs. Sun. anyone can join in. Ask the bartenders about Edna, the friendly ghost. Under-21 welcome, but not served. Cover Sun.-Thurs. $3, Fri.-Sat. $5, special shows $6.

French Quarter Café, 808 King St. (683-2803). Gay-owned and operated, as the window's pink triangle attests, but not exclusively gay—a happening contemporary bar and dance club. Wall caricatures of Michelangelos wear jeans, since the original, naked murals endangered the liquor license; the blue jeans' labels name the agent who blew the whistle. Young professional crowd hangs with a DJ and 90s music upstairs at the bar and dance floor. Entrees usually over $8, appetizers $6. Special prices 3-7pm. Wed. is Ladies' Night, when women occupy the bar upstairs. Open Mon.-Fri. 3pm-12:30am, Sat.-Sun. 3pm-1:30am.

Laughing Lizard, 1325 King St. (548-2582), upstairs from Terlitzksy's Deli. Rocks loudly past 1am. Spontaneous (i.e. Steve Burt freestyle) dancing to rock or reggae in front of the bar area. College-dorm decor; school T-shirts abound. Order lizard legs (sm. $4, lg. $7), a $5 sandwich, a $3 burger, or an 8-inch pizza ($6). Shows Fri. and Sat. nights at 8:30pm and 10:30pm. Cover $6. Open mike Mon. and Wed. Variable cover $2-6. Young crowd. Open Tues.-Sat. 6pm-2am.

Tiffany Tavern, 1116 King St. (836-8844). Homey and laid-back. Tues. and Wed. nights are open-mike; Thurs.-Sat. welcomes live entertainment with no cover. Bluegrass dominates. Heavy wood interior and big bar. Happy hour Mon.-Sat. 5-8pm. Sandwiches $5-6, omelettes $5-6, and entrees $6-9 for lunch, $8-12 for dinner. Bluegrass/country Fri. and Sat. nights. Open Mon.-Thurs. 11:30am-2:30pm and 5pm-midnight; Fri. 11:30a-2:30pm and 5pm-2am; Sat. 5pm-2am.

Metropolis, 1755 Duke St. (519-9400). Metro: King St. Generic but trendy suburban dance club/bar that mostly features a mix of basic techno and progressive dance music. A daily happy hour runs from 4:30-7:30pm. The club proper opens Thurs.-Sat. at 9; things shut down at 3 on Sat., 2 on the other two nights. Cover varies, increasing as the weekend progresses. The attached restaurant serves "American cuisine." 11:30am-10:00pm weekdays, 5-11 Sat. and Sun.

Movies

DC is awash with movie theaters; *Let's Go* lists only theaters with unusual programming or discounts. Check the *Washington Post* "Style" or "Show" sections for all the film that's fit to print.

The Smithsonian's **Hirshhorn Museum** (357-2700), on the Mall at Independence Ave. and 8th St. SW, runs three separate pseudo-weekly free film series: foreign and independent films at night (usually 8pm), documentaries about modern and contemporary art, and animated matinees for kids. Grab a "Calendar" brochure when you visit the Hirshhorn; the back pages should contain the film schedule. The **Smithsonian's Museum of American History** also hosts classic and art films, sometimes with a talk before the flick. The excellent **American Film Institute** (828-4000), at the Kennedy Center, shows classic American, foreign, and avant-garde films, usually two per night.

American University film classes show movies most Mondays through Thursdays at 5:30 and 8:10pm, free and open to the public; for a schedule, call 885-2040 (8:30am-5pm) or send a self-addressed stamped envelope to AU at 4400 Massachusetts Ave. NW, Washington, DC 20016, attn. Media Center MCG 319.

Biograph, 2819 M St. NW (333-2696). First-run independents, foreign films and classics. Film festivals frequent; the eclectic is the norm. Animation festivals and Peter Greenaway (of *Cook, Thief, Wife, Lover* fame) films are highlights. Not to go here would be a serious cultural blunder; some film buffs even have lifetime passes. Improv comedy on weekends at midnight. Occasional daytime porn keeps the theater afloat. Newsletter gives dates, times, and future programming. Bring all the food you want inside. Admission $5, seniors and children $2.50. Handicapped access.

Key Theatre, 1222 Wisconsin Ave. (1 bl. north of M St.) NW (333-5100). First-run art films every critic raves about; subtitled films and exclusive showings offer plenty of chances to polish up your French. Admission $6.50, over 65 $4, under 12 $3, most matinees $3.50.

Bethesda Cinema 'n Drafthouse, 7719 Wisconsin Ave. (656-3337). Metro: Bethesda. Glorious art-deco exterior; inside, see second-run movies among rows of bars and bar stools. Beer, wine, and deli food served while you watch. Sound like fun? It is. BCnD evokes the days when going to a movie was a great social event, instead of a chance to watch glorified TV with 300 of your closest friends. Admission Sun. and Tues.-Thurs. $3, Mon. $1, Fri.-Sat. $4. Live midnight comedy Fri. and Sat. Beers from $1.75, wine from $2 per glass. 9" pizza $5, chili dogs $4, buffalo wings $6. Must be 21 to get in. Showtimes Sun.-Thurs. 7:30pm and 9:45pm, Fri.-Sat. 7:15pm and 9:45pm, but call to confirm.

Outer Circle, 4849 Wisconsin Ave. NW (244-3116), across the street from Safeway. First-run foreign films, some exclusive engagements. If the Key isn't showing it, this place will. Admission $6.50, seniors $4, children $3.25. All shows before 6pm, $3.25.

Cineplex Odeon Jenifer 1&2, 5252 Wisconsin Ave. NW (452-1155). Shows second-run movies, after they've been in major theaters but before they hit the video stores. $1 a seat at all times.

Sports

Opportunities for sports addicts abound in the Washington area. The **Georgetown Hoyas** (basketball) pack the **Capital Centre** in a bad season and turn tickets to gold in a good one. (They won it all in 1987.) Their professional counterparts, the **Bullets,** also play at the Capital Centre, as do the **Capitals** (NHL hockey); tickets are easier to get for these two teams. The **Redskins** wore Superbowl rings home in 1982, 1987, and 1992, and fans flock religiously to **Robert F. Kennedy Stadium** to see them—especially when the Dallas Cowboys are in town. (Call Capital Centre at 547-9077. It is located between Landover Rd. and Central Ave., in Landover, MD. Take the Beltway (I-95) to exits 15 or 17 and follow signs to the arena. Call RFK Stadium, 2001 E. Capitol St. SE (547-9077) for tickets; if it's the 'Skins you want to see, be prepared to wait a few years.)

Bicyclists ought to love Washington, though Washington won't love them back: the diminishing fraternity of bike messengers—skillful, speeding spandex blurs who weave through frustrated downtown traffic to deliver documents—has forever changed bicyclists' image in DC. (The messengers themselves may be on the way out, thanks to the advent of fax machines.) Cyclists who plan to brave Virginia should try the 18.5-mi. **Mount Vernon Trail** which starts on Theodore Roosevelt Island and follows the Potomac River and the George Washington Parkway past Arlington, through Old Town Alexandria, and to its namesake, George Washington's mansion. Trail maps await in Great Falls Park (Virginia), at Thompson Boat Center on the edge of Georgetown, and from the National Park Service. Two bike trail maps are ADC's **Washington Area Bike Map** (962-3200) or call for free maps from the **National Park Service** (619-7222). The incredibly diligent West Coast folks at Ten Speed Press, Box 7123, Berkeley, CA have compiled the thick but pocket-sized and map-packed tome *Touring the Washington, DC Area by Bicycle*, $13.20 by mail, $10.95 by any other means. (Their idea of "the Washington, DC area" is DC plus most of Maryland and Virginia.) Get a Kryptonite or similar lock when riding in any urban area, and wear a helmet anywhere. Helmetlessness is illegal in Maryland (in DC and VA, it's merely life-threatening). For bicycle rental, see Practical Information.

Those who choose to traverse Washington on their own unaided feet will find the C&O canal and Rock Creek Park relatively **jogger**-friendly—at least before dusk. Near the Tidal Basin, along the canal, on the Mt. Vernon Trail, and down Constitution Ave. near the Vietnam Veteran's Memorial are especially good areas. Serious runners may want to enter the **Marine Corps Marathon,** on November 1, which starts at the Iwo Jima Memorial in Arlington Cemetery and continues through most of downtown Washington. Call 703-690-3431 to register; there is a $22 entrance fee.

In the summer heat, swimming is a must, and the city obediently provides free, public pools. Try the **Georgetown Pool,** off Wisconsin Ave. at Q and 34th Sts. (open in summer Mon.-Fri. 11am-7pm, Sat.-Sun. noon-7pm), or the indoor **Reed Pool** (673-7771; open Mon.-Fri. 1:30-4:30pm open swim and 5-7pm adult swim).

For those who would rather be on the water than in it, **Fletcher's Boathouse,** 4940 Canal Rd. NW (244-0461), rents rowboats and canoes (open Mon.-Fri. 9am-7pm; Sat.-Sun. 7:30am-7:30pm; rowboats $7 per hour, $14 per day; canoes $7 per hour, $13 per day). The **Thompson Boathouse** (333-4861) rents canoes, rowboats, and sailboats (open Mon.-Fri. 7am-6pm, Sat.-Sun. 8am-5pm; canoes and rowboats $6 per hr., sailboats $12 per hr.). The **Tidal Basin Boathouse,** near the Jefferson Memorial (484-0206), rents two-person paddle boats (open daily 10am-6:30pm; $7 per hour). Experienced kayakers can rent boats at Great Falls Park in Virginia. (See also Sights: Georgetown.)

You can usually pick up a game of **volleyball** or **softball** on summer weekends or evenings on the Mall near the Washington Monument.

When it gets cold enough, there is **ice skating** for free on the Reflecting Pool in front of the Lincoln Memorial and on the C&O Canal (ask the National Park Service, 619-7222); and for a fee at the National Sculpture Garden Rink, 9th St. and Constitution Ave., NW (371-5340; Metro: Smithsonian) and Pershing Park, 14th St. and Pennsylvania Ave. NW (737-6938; Metro: Federal Triangle). Both are around $4; call about skate rentals.

Shopping

This book lists many individual stores by neighborhood under Sights (for books, records, clothes, and gewgaws) or under Useful Stores (for groceries, drugstores, maps, and such). See Dupont Circle for books and records, Adams-Morgan for books and food, and Georgetown or Old Town Alexandria for clothes or almost anything else.

Maybe it's the steaming summers that drive so many desperate Washingtonians to the air-conditioned American fools' paradise known as a shopping mall. Or maybe it's just a healthy interest in architecture and urban ethnography. Or a hankering for a good time at the arcade, on the food court, or in the discount denim outlet. Whatever which way, Georgetown would like to think that it has mastered the art of mall-building—the ritzy **Georgetown Park,** 3222 M St. NW (342-8180 or 298-5577), shines, even underground, but the price tags attached to its chic wares are usually outrageous. (Mall open

Mon.-Fri. 10am-9pm, Sat. 10am-7pm, Sun. noon-6pm.) **Mazza Gallerie**, 5300 Wisconsin Ave. (966-6114; open Mon.-Fri. 10am-8pm, Sat. 10am-6pm, Sun. noon-5pm) and **Chevy Chase Pavilion**, 5335 Wisconsin Ave. (686-6868; open Mon.-Fri. 10am-8pm, Sat. 10am-6pm, Sun noon-5pm) certainly give Georgetown a run for its money. Don't be deceived, though, you'll probably find the same stores in them all. Three more clones, **Tyson's Galleria I and II,** 2001 International Dr., McLean, VA (703-827-7700; open Mon.-Sat. 10am-9:30pm, Suñ. noon-6pm) and **White Flint Mall,** 11301 Rockville Pike, Rockville, MD(Metro: White Flint) fled the city, but will still most probably have the clothing, jewelry item, or gadget that you're looking for. Both Tysons solicit shoppers at Rte. 7 and Rte. 123, off the Beltway at exit 10B or 11B; mall-crazed Metro-users can take the 26T bus to Tysons from the Dunn Loring stop, which might take over an hour all told. (It should be noted, for the record, that the North American covered-mall, in addition to harboring scores of big-chain price-busters, often makes for an afternoon or evening of superb people-watching.) For those made paranoid by the mall revolution, several large department stores have maintained their independence. Try **Woodward & Lothrop,** 11th and F St. NW (879-8375), directly across the street from the Friendship Heights Metro (open Mon.-Sat. 10am-8pm, Sun. 11am-5pm), or **Lord & Taylor,** 5255 Western Ave. NW (362-9600), on the corner of Jenifer St. and Western Ave. (open Mon.-Fri. 10am-9pm, Sat. 10am-7pm, Sun. noon-6pm).

Daytripping from DC

It's no accident Congress lets out for the summer. The torrid sun and roiling humidity can really zonk those unaccustomed to overexertion. If you too are fortunate enough to have time off from work, we recommend getting out of the sweltering city air and heading for the cool Atlantic or the shade of a Virginia park. If you're looking for a change of urban pace, why not try Baltimore? *Let's Go* provides detailed information on what to do, where to stay, and how to get back from these varied getaways. (See Getting Around and Practical Information, below.)

Listed below, in order of increasing travel time from DC, are some suggested day-trips. The last few entries should perhaps be considered weekend-trips.

Mt. Vernon, Fairfax County, VA: 30min. driving; 1hr. by tourbus; 1hr. and 30min. by boat.

Baltimore, MD: 45min. driving; 30-40min. by train; 55min. by bus.

Annapolis, MD: 45min.-1hr. driving; 40min. by bus.

Fredericksburg, VA: 1hr. driving; 1hr. by train; 1hr. and 30min. by bus.

Harper's Ferry, WV: 1hr. and 30min. driving; 1hr. and 5min. by train.

Richmond, VA: 2hr. driving; 2hr. by train; 2hr. and 15min. by bus.

Charlottesville, VA: 2hr. and 30min. driving; 2hr. and 15min. by train; 2hr. and 30min. by bus.

Rehoboth, DE: 2 hrs. and 30min.-3hr. driving; 3hr. and 30min. by bus.

Williamsburg, VA: 3hr. driving; 3hr. and 15min. by train; 4hr. by bus.

Virginia Beach, VA: 4hr. driving; 5hr. by train (includes bus connection); 6hr. and 30min. by bus.

Fairfax County, Virginia

What tourists see in Fairfax has little to do with the everyday life of the people who live here. This largest of Washington suburbs prospered throughout the 80s, as white- and blue-collar immigration turned farms into suburbs, country roads into congested six-lane highways, and vacant lands to office complex upon shopping mall upon parking lot. Some feared uncontrolled development, commercial expansion, and dependence on highways would turn Fairfax into a postmodern City of Quartz à la Los Angeles. County executive and Democrat Audrey Moore, elected to beat back the real estate moguls, has yet to placate the county's commuter voters in the face of a rough economy. Meanwhile, the people keep moving in; Reston, one of the nation's most successful "planned communities," now boasts its very own juvenile delinquents (called "bundumplings" in the local parlance) and an outdoor shopping plaza, not unlike a sterilized Georgetown.

For visitors who aren't traffic engineers, though, the real sights of Fairfax belong more to the 18th than to the 20th century. When Philadelphia was still the nation's capital, aristocratic planters like George Washington and George Mason luxed out in Fairfax country estates and profited from Virginia's omnipresent cash crop, tobacco. In the 1780s, the anti-federalist pressures that produced the Bill of Rights emerged first and loudest from these Virginia slave owners. One farm is even responsible for DC's historically unpopular location. According to legend, George Washington, asked to pick a spot along the Potomac for the new national capital, chose the land closest to Mount Vernon, his home. Restored colonial-era plantations compete for your tourist dollar with porticoes, porches, pigsties, and patisseries. Few of these estates still produce crops, though the county's southern and western reaches preserve plenty of rural land. Some green space opens up to the public; parks and forests near the Potomac, west of Washington, make for a peaceful break from the budget travel circuit. Cheap, too.

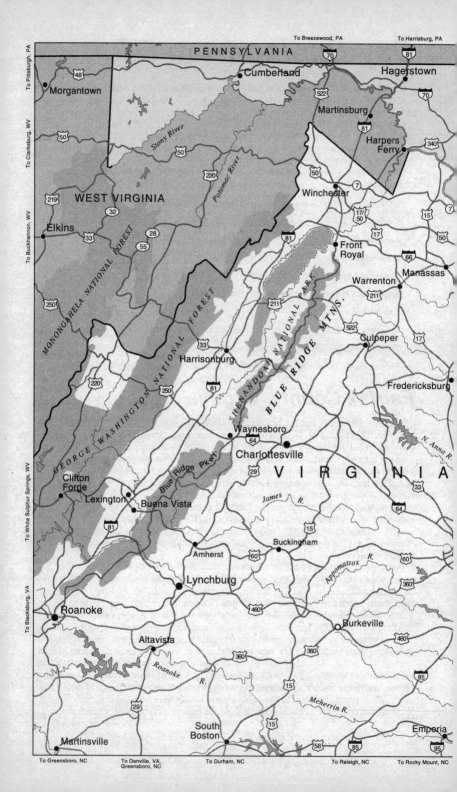

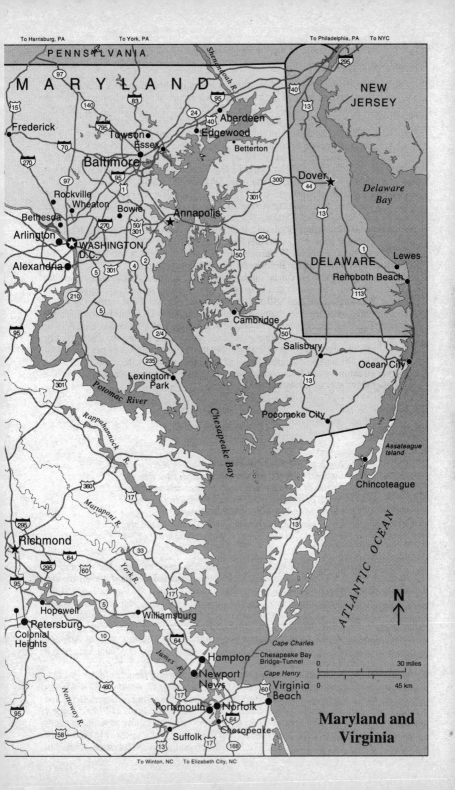

Getting Around

Fairfax doesn't exactly lack public transportation, but long distances and a scarcity of Metro stops make busing to Fairfax sights an adventure of up to two hours each way. Arlington's George Washington Parkway winds speedily southward to an end near Mount Vernon, then becomes Mount Vernon Memorial Highway in northeast Fairfax. Rte. 1, the Jefferson Davis Highway, named for the President of the Confederacy, heads southwest from Arlington through Fairfax in an endless strip of motels and fast food, then heads south, like the Union Army, on to Richmond. Interstate 395 becomes I-95 beyond the Beltway; the northern Virginia leg, named the Shirley Highway, is sometimes called "the world's longest parking lot." Alexandria's Duke St. continues west to become the Little River Turnpike (Rte. 236). Lee Hwy. (Rte. 29) and Arlington Blvd. (Rte. 50) run east-west, joining Arlington to Fairfax City; after Fairfax City, Lee marches west to Manassas National Battlefield Park. Georgetown Pike, a cross-river continuation of MacArthur Boulevard in NW Washington, takes river rats northwest along the Potomac River to Great Falls Park. The Beltway (I-495 west of Springfield, VA, I-95 east of it) encircles Washington from a safe distance, while the Dulles Toll Road (Rte. 267) runs from the Beltway to Dulles Airport (surprise).

Driving in Fairfax County can be mighty confusing; call your destination and ask for detailed directions. Remember that Fairfax's roads, though numerous enough to stymie longtime Washingtonians, are still far too few to handle rush-hour traffic. On weekdays, don't drive here from DC between 4pm and 7pm, or to DC from Fairfax between 6am and 9am. During approximately these hours, parts of I-66 become HOV-3 or HOV-4; it stands for "High Occupancy Vehicle," and you're asking for a hefty ticket, bigboy, if you're caught in an HOV lane without the requisite number of people in your car. (Look for the backseat mannequins and inflatable dolls [Yeah, right—Ed.] some desperate commuters use to circumvent this rule.) Farther out, towards many of the sights, highways may give way to rural byways.

Sights

Mount Vernon

> Not a soul intruded upon the privacy of the visit to
> the tomb… Not a murmur was heard, save the
> strains of solemn music, and the deep and measured
> sound of artillery, which awoke the echoes around
> the hallowed heights of Mount Vernon.
> —George Washington Parke Custis, describing
> Lafayette's visit (1824).

George Washington slept here. As did Bushrod. The tours, exhibits, and restorations at Mount Vernon, the Washington estate, can seem staid and worshipful even by Virginia standards. Still, the Washington mansion and plantation are impressive, and the care taken to find period furnishings, detail the house's history, and document Washington's life represents one of the triumphs of scholarly Americana. And George Washington once cut a fine, heroic figure: from Parson Weems' popular biography (the source of the cherry-tree fable) to literati like Whitman and Thoreau, most of America revered George Washington throughout the 19th-century. A tour of Mount Vernon is a good way to recall their excitement.

When George Washington inherited the 2,000 acre property from his father in 1754, only a small farmhouse stood on the spot. After his marriage to wealthy widow Martha in 1759, George converted it into a 20-room mansion fit for a king (or a president) and bought four adjacent farms, which Martha sold off after his death in 1799. Nephew Bushrod Washington took over in 1802; soon afterwards, the family gave up on keeping the mansion shipshape, offering to sell it to the federal government or to the state of Virginia. Neither accepted the offer. The Mount Vernon Ladies' Association, formed in

1853, bought the property in 1858, and Mount Vernon ladies—obviously a special breed—have been organizing restoration and upkeep of the plantation ever since.

Before you join the crowds inside, stop to check out the mansion's Georgian exterior. From far away, the façade passes for stone; in fact, clever builders painted the pine boards, then sprinkled the wet wood with sand to give the house a stony face. Grab a map of Mount Vernon's grounds at the entrance gate. Mount Vernon claims not to have a guided tour, but attendants in each room will answer any and all of your questions about the estate—if they have time. On busy days, it's all they can do to keep prodding the line forward. In colonial America, men supervised the interior decoration, so you can judge Washington's taste for yourself as you walk through the house. Prussian blue and vivid green walls shine with their original hues, and most of the furniture and decorations in the house are the genuine belongings of Washington. When the lack of air-conditioning gets you hot under the collar, you can look forward to the piazza in back of the house, where a superior view of the Potomac River accompanies a cooling breeze from the water.

The first room you enter once hosted the Washingtons' parties. In the hall, look for the key to the Bastille, a relic of the French Revolution. Washington received it in 1790 from his close friend the Marquis de Lafayette; don't ask how Lafayette nabbed the key. Inside the common parlor, check out the harpsichord of Martha Washington's granddaughter Nelly Custis. Upstairs, see where Lafayette slept, then inspect the bedroom of George and Martha Washington (*tee hee*). George died in this room, and lots of his stuff is still here. Note his initialed name plate hammered onto the foot locker at the end of the bed—over the initials of the original owner. The third floor is open only during the fall and winter months.

The tour ends downstairs in Washington's study, pantry, and kitchen. The pantry stored food for the whole household, its 300 slaves, and the Washingtons' house guests; if it seems too puny to have fed them all, it was—the main kitchen stood apart from the house so stove fires wouldn't burn them both down. An archaeological dig behind the kitchen is now sifting the garbage dump, as archaeologists are wont to do.

Fans of smokehouses, washhouses, or outhouses can relieve themselves behind the kitchen. A gravel path leads to **George and Martha Washington's tomb**; consult your map, read the signs, and beware of poison ivy and disease-carrying ticks. Don't expect to get too close to the Founder of His Country; George and Martha's stone sarcophogi are in a mausoleum behind a sturdy iron gate. Washington family members, like grandniece Bushrod, are also buried in the graveyard; more interesting is the quiet, graveless "slave burial ground" nearby, which now includes a long-overdue memorial to the slaves.

Stop at the wharf for a close-up look at the Potomac, or go back to the house and sit in the back porch chairs for a panoramic view. The estate also holds botanical gardens to walk through and 18th-century vegetable gardens to look at; the Mount Vernon fields once grew corn, wheat, tobacco, and, according to author Robert Anton Wilson, smokable marijuana. Only the corn remains at the **Mount Vernon Museum**, near the slave quarters' greenhouse to the left of the house; stop in for more Washingtoniana, including his swords, his toothbrush, her wedding slippers, and Houdon's 1785 bust of George Washington. Restrooms await you beneath the Museum. Dig the exhibitions at the **Museum Annex** next door.

The cafeteria-style **Creamery** sells soft drinks (95¢), small hamburgers ($1.80), and french fries ($1.10). The **Mount Vernon Inn** serves a genuine lunch. Try the distinctive peanut and chestnut soup ($1.75); lunchtime sandwiches run between $4.50 and $5.75. Dinner at the Inn costs between $12 and $17.50. (Open Mon.-Sat. 11am-3:30pm and 5-9pm, Sun. 11:30am-4pm.) Picnic on the banks of the Potomac at **Riverside Picnic Area** located a short distance away by car on George Washington Parkway.

To drive to Mount Vernon, take the Beltway (I-495) to the George Washington Parkway on the Virginia side and follow the parkway to Mount Vernon's circular driveway. Parking in the Mount Vernon lot is free for four hours. The 18.5-mile Mount Vernon Trail for bicycles starts on Theodore Roosevelt Island and ends here (see Sports). You can use public transportation, too: take the Metro to Huntington on the Blue/Yellow line and catch the 11P bus. If all else fails, you can get there by water. The *Potomac*

Spirit runs from late March through October. The 90-minute trip takes you from Pier 4 on 6th and Waterstreet (a short walk from Waterfront metro) to the dock at Mt. Vernon. The boat leaves Washington Tues.-Sun. at 9am and 2pm from June 16-Aug. 30. In early spring and fall, cruises are less frequent and depart only at 9am. Round trip fare including Mt. Vernon entrance fee $19, senior citizens $17.25, children 6-11 $11.25. For information call 554-8000, or listen to the recording at 554-1542.

Crowds at Mount Vernon get out of hand in July or August; during those months, try to show up on a weekday morning. There is no air-conditioning at Mt. Vernon, though the breeze from the river makes it bearable on even the hottest of days. The complex is open daily 9am-5pm; Nov.-Feb. 9am-4pm; admission $7, over 61 $6, ages 6-11 $3. Call 703-780-2000 for more information.

Gunston Hall

Spend the extra ten minutes on the road to Mount Vernon and stop by this plantation first. Thankfully skipped by the Tourmobile route, Gunston Hall gives a relaxed tour, which focuses as much on 18th-century living as on the plantation's one-time owner, George Mason. Especially for travelers with children, Gunston Hall will prove less crowded and at least as interesting as its more-famous neighbor.

George Mason hung with George Washington and James Madison, two other Virginia plantation aristocrats; but after they revolted against British rule, George Mason found the alternatives almost as revolting. With the outbreak of the American Revolution, the Second Continental Congress called for each colony to establish its own constitution. Mason prefaced Virginia's, the first of its kind, with his own document—the Virginia Declaration of Rights. Three weeks after the appearance of the Virginia Declaration, Thomas Jefferson used similar wording in the Declaration of Independence. Mason refused to sign the U.S. Constitution because it had no bill of rights; he helped convince Congress to add the first ten amendments (now the Bill of Rights) to the Constitution.

While you're waiting for the guided tour to leave (they do so every half hour), look around the museum in the visitors' building. The displays provide short, informative discussions about the life of the Mason family at Gunston Hall, using the family as a springboard from which to discuss 18th-century colonial life. Try reading the page of the family bible recording births and deaths, especially the touching eulogy George Mason wrote for his wife Ann.

Depending on your tour guide, you may hear about Mason's political importance, about women and children in the household, or about the exquisite architecture. Pause under the arched columns at the top of the stairs: George Mason's design for the mansion proved structurally unsound, so the builders added these columns. The tour also highlights William Buckland's work on the house; an English indentured craftsman, Buckland helped out here from 1755 to 1759. Trace his woodwork in the Palladian Room, or sun yourself on the octagonal porch.

Behind the house, an English boxwood garden grows in formal geometric patterns. Stroll through the quiet garden, or walk down to the wharf on the Potomac River. Because this area abuts the Mason Neck National Wildlife Refuge, it's a great place to bird watch. In the meadow in front of the house, stunted sheep from Hog Island (in the Chesapeake Bay) haven't evolved much since the 18th century. Gunston Hall also sports the inevitable schoolhouse, kitchen, laundry, smokehouse, and dairy. On George Mason Day, in early May, costumed actors play members of the Mason household and demonstrate colonial life. A **Kite Festival** in March numbers among other annual events here; call 703-550-9220 for more info.

The only practical way to reach Gunston Hall is by car. Follow the directions to Mount Vernon, but where George Washington Memorial Parkway ends at the circular driveway of Mount Vernon, Mount Vernon Memorial Highway begins. Drive on Mount Vernon Highway until you hit Route 1, also called Richmond Highway. You'll pass Fort Belvoir, but keep going until you hit Gunston Rd. (Rte. 242). A few miles down the road on your left is Gunston Hall. Parking is plentiful. Gunston Hall is open daily from 9:30am to 5pm, except on Thanksgiving, Christmas, and New Year's Day, with the last tour beginning at 4:30pm and the grounds closing at 6pm. (Admission $5, seniors 60 and over $4, students grades 1-12 $1.50.) No wheelchair access.

Near George Mason's house, strain your neck birdwatching at the aptly named **Mason Neck National Wildlife Refuge,** a mile down Gunston Rd. (Rte. 242) from Gunston Hall. (Open 8am-dark. Free.) Hike through forest, grasslands, and marshes while you try to photograph bald eagles, great blue herons, beavers, and otters. No fires, camping, hunting, or fishing allowed.

The Wildlife Refuge may bore the skedaddle out of kids; take them instead to the **Pohick Bay Regional Park** (703-339-6100) also along Gunston Rd. The facilities include the largest swimming pool on the east coast, a marina with sail- and paddleboat rentals, an 18-hole golf course, miniature golf, picnic tables, a four-mile bridle path, and 200 campsites. Belber! (Open daily 8am-dark, swimming pool open only Memorial Day to Labor Day; admission $4 per vehicle, $8 per vehicle with 10 or more passengers. Swimming fee $3.25, ages 2-11 and over 59 $2.75. Golf green (339-8585) fees Mon.-Fri. $16, Sat.-Sun. $20.)

Pope-Leighey House and Woodlawn Plantation

From the Woodlawn Plantation parking lot, a clear path points you to Woodlawn, but a sign for **Pope-Leighey House** directs you across the parking lot and into the woods. Take the road less traveled and admire Pope-Leighey first: plantations loiter on every Virginia street corner, but only one other Frank Lloyd Wright house of this kind is now open to the public. Wright is America's most celebrated architect (there's even a Paul Simon song about him) for good reason: his spare, innovative and efficient houses of the mid-20th century set a new standard for designers worldwide.

The Pope-Leighey place is one of his Usonian houses, designed for inhabitants of moderate means. ("Usonia" was utopian author Samuel Butler's euphemism for the United States of North America; here, it also suggests "usable," "usefulness," "us," "anyone," and "Houston.") Commissioned in 1939, the $7,000 house served a family of four. When devious highway planners sent Route 66 through the house's original location in Falls Church, VA, Mrs. Robert Leighey rescued it by donating it to the National Trust for Historic Preservation in 1964.

The 25 Usonian houses Wright built follow his famous design precept in their organic unity with their environments: here cypress, glass, and brick blend with the surrounding forest. The flat roof and long lines of the wood siding and mortar joints of the brick (the vertical mortar between the bricks have been colored red) add to this horizontal feeling. Look for the unique Usonian designs on the house's high windows, which stand out only when the windows are propped open.

The **guided tour** (every half hour) probes the interior. Pope-Leighey covers only 1200-square feet, but Wright's genius makes it seem surprisingly roomy. Two patios and large windows on either end make the living and dining rooms seem to extend outdoors. Take a closer look at the modern geometric furniture: it's made of plywood. Wright intended it as furniture most people could afford to build for themselves. The two bedrooms also seem larger because their closets hold, and hide, the bureaus. Seek no storage space under the house's flat roof; Wright considered attics and basements wasteful.

Woodlawn Plantation was daughter-in-law Nelly Custis' wedding present from George Washington—2000 acres of his Mount Vernon lands. The gift included his grist mill and a distillery, all for use during his life and to be inherited upon his death. After he gave up the presidency, Washington asked nephew Lawrence Lewis to join him at Mount Vernon and serve as secretary and host to the many guests that still visited the plantation. Less than a year later, Lewis asked for Nelly's hand. Married by candlelight on February 22, 1799, George Washington's last birthday, the couple soon engaged William Thornton, the architect of the U.S. Capitol, to design and build a house on the land Washington gave them.

Woodlawn looks suspiciously like Mount Vernon. Nelly and Lawrence moved most of their furniture here from Mount Vernon, then cut down trees near the house to create a view of the Potomac like their uncle's. The house even has a "Lafayette Bedroom," named for the famous family friend. Look for stuffed birds mounted on the wall in their son Lorenzo's bedroom. Woodlawn also reflects its post-Lewis owners, anti-slavery Quakers and Baptists, playwright Paul Kester and his 60 cats, and Senator and Mrs. Oscar Underwood of Alabama. A guided tour gives more details.

(Woodlawn open daily 9:30am-4:30pm with the last tour given at 4pm and the grounds closing at 5pm, except on Thanksgiving, Christmas, and New Year's Day; admission $5, high school students and seniors over 65 $3.50. Pope-Leighey is open daily March-Dec. 9:30am-4:30pm; admission to Pope-Leighey House $4, students through 12th grade and senior citizens over 65 $3. Admission to both $8, students and seniors $6. Wheelchair access limited; call 703-780-4000 for details.)

To drive to Pope-Leighey House and Woodlawn Plantation, continue down Mount Vernon Highway from Mount Vernon and cross Route 1, also called Richmond Highway. The road through the intersection leads to the parking lot. If you are coming from Gunston Hall, take Gunston Rd. and turn right onto Route 1. Then turn left at the light marking the intersection with Mount Vernon Highway.

Explore the same scenery the nation's founders savored at **Great Falls Park** (VA info. 703-285-2964, MD info. 301-492-6246). Go **hiking** along the waterside paths and see what remains of the canal George Washington's Patowmack Company built in the late 18th century to transport goods to Georgetown. The canal operated for 26 years, but just as the C&O Canal Company bought the Patowmack Canal and connected it to theirs, railroads bypassed canals as the favored form of transport. You can still see the thickly overgrown locks of the Patowmack and the ruins of Matildaville, a canal town that flourished here from 1790 to the 1820s. Hoof it to the Visitors Center for hiking-trail maps.

Some of the best **whitewater boating** east of the Mississippi rushes along this stretch of the Potomac River, but only experienced boaters should try it. Serious **rock climbers** get vertical on Great Falls' bare granite; the Park Service asks all climbers to register first at the Visitors Center. Many people enjoy scrambling over the rocks that line the river, though the Park Service would rather they kept to the paths; every so often someone tumbles sidelong into the Potomac. Even devoted rock-scramblers should steer clear of the river; the surprisingly strong currents drown about seven people yearly, some of them expert swimmers. Special **ranger walks** are offered daily throughout the year; the Breakfast with the Birds walk, for example, each Sunday at 8am, samples the area's birds and bagels (B.Y.O. Bagels).

If **fishing** lures you, come here to catch and eat catfish or carp; cast your line between the two overlook points to the right of the Visitors Center. Use cut herring, nightcrawlers, and clam snouts fished on the bottom for bait. Anyone over 16 must have a fishing license (5-day licenses $6, seniors $1). Call the Visitors Center in advance for a list of locations in Virginia and Maryland where you can purchase one. (Forget about taking a Metrobus here, though.) To drive to Great Falls, take the Beltway I-495 to exit 13, the Georgetown Pike (Rte. 193). Turn right at Old Dominion Drive (Rte. 738). (Open daily 9am-dark, except on Christmas. Entrance fee $3 per vehicle, $1 per person without a vehicle, free for those under 17 and over 61.)

Let your childhood dreams, or just your children, out at the **Pet Farm Park**, 1228 Hunter Mill Rd. (703-759-3636), geared for children under 12. Stroke and feed everyday and exotic animals—try and do that at the National Zoo. Some animals run free in the courtyard, such as goats, a cockatoo, a pot-bellied piglet, and a buzzcockling. Ride Sukari, the African elephant, for $2, or jump on a free hayride and circle the bison-laden field. You won't have to pet them—promise. From Great Falls, turn right onto Georgetown Pike (Rte. 193). After several miles, take a left onto Springvale Rd. After crossing Leesburg Pike (Rte. 7), turn left on Hunter Mill Rd. The park will be on the right. (Park open spring and fall Mon.-Fri. 10am-3pm, Sat.-Sun. 10am-5pm. Summer Mon.-Fri. 10am-5pm, Sat.-Sun. 10am-5:30pm. Weekday admission $6, seniors and children 2-12 $5. Weekend admission $7 and seniors and children 2-12 $6. Animal food 50¢ a cone.)

Just a few miles away, on Colvin Run Rd., **Colvin Run Mill Park** (703-759-2771) recalls even simpler pleasures. Watch a member of the Northern Virginia Wood Carvers sculpt from wood (every other Sunday noon-4pm, call 703-534-1845 for a schedule), then try your own hand at it from a plank you can purchase for a few dollars. Make people guess what animal you're trying to create. If you're afraid of sharp objects, take a tour through the operating 19th-century water-powered grist mill and the miller's house. (Tours Wed.-Mon. 11am-5pm every hour with the last tour at 4pm. Adults $3, seniors $1.50, children $1.) Enjoy the park every day until dark for free. To drive there, take Leesburg Pike (Rte. 7) to Colvin Run Rd.

Concealed among the fields and homes of suburban Langley, VA is the most interesting Washington sight you'll never see; the new headquarters of the **Central Intelligence Agency,** which supervises the United States' spy network, is most emphatically closed to tourists. One in every $200 spent on new government buildings must pay for "public art"; though its grounds are hardly public, the CIA HQ's builders followed the rules by commissioning sculptor Jim Sanborn to create a flat, green wall-like sculpture stamped with thousands of letters and numbers. Only ex-CIA head William Webster and Sanborn know their secret meaning. Every two years or so, nonviolent mass protests block the CIA's driveways, keeping the spooks from driving to work.

Suburban Maryland

The satellite towns and bedroom suburbs in Montgomery and Prince Georges Counties resemble with disturbing accuracy the parts of DC they border: from estate-rich Potomac to downtrodden Seat Pleasant, every segment of Washington has its quieter suburban counterpart. Lower Montgomery County's parks rival Rock Creek Park in NW; NASA is Prince Georges' counterpart to NE Washington's spread-out installations like Catholic U. and the Soldiers' Home. Where SE boasts Bolling Air Force Base, southern Prince Georges retaliates with Andrews AFB. Much of the green on a Montgomery County map turns out to represent country clubs; the typical county resident shops at gourmet supermarkets, flaunts her children's school—private or public, high school or college—on an Audi or Saab, and golfs away the weekend. Of course, the county is more complicated than that, incorporating aging Silver Spring, high-tech Rockville, and neo-urban Bethesda along with ritzy Potomac. Prince Georges County is Montgomery's blue-collar cousin, with less dough and fewer executive homesteads. The Maryland suburbs are far too spread-out (unless you count Bethesda) to merit the random explorations common to city sight-seeing; those who burn to explore Montgomery and Prince Georges Counties should pick a destination and get hold of a car somehow.

Getting Around

Public transportation in the area is designed for people going to and from their cars. The Metro's Red Line zooms all the way out past Rockville, depositing shoppers at White Flint Mall and commuters conveniently beside their vehicles. The Red Line follows Rte. 355, which starts in DC as Wisconsin Ave., turns into Rockville Pike after Bethesda, changes again to Hungerford Dr., and finally settles on Gaithersburg Rd. The Capital Beltway links Montgomery to Prince Georges to Alexandria to Fairfax to Montgomery County again. The Baltimore-Washington Parkway cuts through Prince Georges, zipping past the Beltway and NASA in Greenbelt. U.S. 1 heads north as always through NE Washington, Prince Georges County, and College Park, home of the University of Maryland.

Food

Four Rivers, 184 Rollins Ave. (301-230-2900), off Rockville Pike (Rte. 355), corner of E. Jefferson. The name is a Chinese pun on "Szechuan." Some say it's better than any Chinese food in the city. Try the fried *calamari* for an appetizer, then move on to shrimp stir-fried with their shells and heads still on. (Krakatoa!) If you have a larger group, order one of the whole fish ($13). Stir-fried Chinese veggies and shredded pork in hot sauce ($7.75) is also tasty. Open Sun.-Thurs. 11:30am-10pm, Fri.-Sat. 11:30am-11pm.

Chop Stix, 4A N. Washington St. (301-762-8810), off Hungerford Dr. (Rte. 355), in the shopping center at N. Washington St. The silly name belies great homemade noodle dishes like spicy beef noodle soup ($4.50), house noodle soup ($4.75) with shrimp, chicken, bean curd, egg, and bamboo shoots, and house lo mein ($4.50 lunch, $6 dinner). All entrees under $5.25 for lunch, $8 for dinner. Each bowl makes a satisfying meal by itself. Very casual—order at the counter and seat yourself at one of the formica tables or along the counter. Open Sun.-Thurs. 11am-9pm, Fri.-Sat. 11am-10pm.

Ambrosia, 1765 Rockville Pike (301-881-3636). Crowded, casual neighborhood restaurant just slightly more formal than a diner. Popular for the Greek specialties, especially *gyro* and *souvlaki* sandwiches ($3.55) and the *mousaka* ($6.75). Good thin-crust pizza just $7.25 (feeds 2-3). Subs, $3-4. Restaurant and carry-out open Mon.-Sat. 7am-1:30am.

India Grill, 1761 Rockville Pike (301-468-2222). Indian restaurant (duh) serving reliable basics, mostly for carry-out. Stay for the all-you-can-eat buffet ($5 lunch, $8 dinner). 8 different Indian breads, 89¢-$2. Extensive vegetarian menu ($4-6). Open Mon.-Sat. 11am-3pm and 5-10pm, Sun. noon-8pm.

Wurzburg Haus, 7236 Muncaster Mill Rd. (301-330-0402), between Rockville and Gaithersburg. Take I-270 to Shady Grove Rd. North, turning right onto Muncaster Mill Rd. Located in the Red Mill Shopping Center. People travel long and far to reach this German restaurant, which serves rich, hearty dishes in big, gullet-busting portions. The best of the great appetizers is the goulash soup ($3.75), better before dinner than as dinner. Try the *wurst* ($9-10) and the veal with mushrooms and cream sauce. Wonderful homemade bread and German beers. Open Mon.-Thurs. 11:30am-9pm, Fri. 11:30am-10pm, Sat. noon-10pm.

Roy's Place, 2 E. Diamond Ave. (301-948-5548), in Gaithersburg. Take time to read the whole menu and you might never eat. Even the waitresses admit they haven't read the 180 sandwiches named after local celebrities in great detail. Try the Rat Burger, topped with ratatouille ($4.50), or Francine the Obscure, made with broiled tongue, sharp cheese, tomato, and garlic mayo ($5.60). Open Mon.-Thurs. 11am-11pm, Fri.-Sat. 11am-midnight, Sun. noon-11pm. Wheelchair access.

Sights: Montgomery County

The 53-acre, outdoor **Brookside Gardens,** 1500 Glenallen Rd. (301-949-8230), offers lush tropical greenery, a Japanese teahouse and garden, an aquatic garden complete with ducks and geese riding lily-pads, and a fragrance garden where you can smell the lavender and taste the mint. The Trial Gardens, which change every season, are definitely the hottest attraction; themes have included "A Child's Garden of Verses," with plants like the pickled peppers of which Peter Piper picked a peck. The Conservatories house seasonal displays such as Easter lilies in April and chrysanthemums in November. (Conservatory open daily 10am-5pm; grounds open daily 9am-sunset.)

The nearby **Wheaton Regional Park,** 1400 Glenallen Rd., offers hikes, bicycle tours, canoeing, and crafts at the **Nature Center,** (301-946-9071; open Tues.-Sat. 9am-5pm, Sun. 1-5pm). Guided horse tours leave every Sunday at noon, 1pm, and 2pm (301-622-3311; horse rides $10 per hour, by reservation only). Or tour the grounds on your own, on foot, on bike trails, or on horseback. Wheelchairs can traverse the paved bike trails, though these can get pretty steep. There's a children's playground complete with a small farm, an antique 1915 carousel, and a miniature train ride through two miles of park (carousel and train open April-Aug. Mon.-Fri. 10am-4:30pm, Sat.-Sun. 10am-5pm; carousel tickets 70¢, train tickets 95¢). Skating is also available in the indoor ice rink (skate rentals $2). To get to the park, take the Beltway I-495 to exit 31 Georgia Ave. (Rte. 97) right onto Randolph Rd., then right again to Glenallen Rd. (Park admission Mon.-Fri. $3.25, under 17 $2.25; Sat.-Sun. and holidays $4, under 17 $3; seniors $2. Call for schedule, Nov.-March 301-649-2703, April-Oct. 301-649-3640.)

The **National Capital Trolley Museum,** on Bonifant Rd. in Wheaton (301-384-6088), lets you ride the original Washington and Maryland trolleys that were once the primary form of public transportation. The 20-minute ride includes a tour which explains the history of streetcars in DC and fills you in about the specific streetcar in which you are riding. Trains run every half hour, so take a look at the museum while you wait for the next ride. The centerpiece of the exhibit thrills children big and small: a made-to-scale replica of the Calvert County trolley line (push a button and watch it wind around the tracks). The last active trolley finished its run on Jan. 28, 1962. To get to the Trolley Museum, take New Hampshire Ave. left onto Bonifant Rd. (Open Sat.-Sun. 11am-3pm, Memorial Day, July 4th, and Labor Day noon-5pm; also open July-Aug. Wed. 11am-3pm; closed Dec. 15-Jan. 1. Trolley rides $2, under 18 $1.50.)

Just outside the Beltway lies the **Church of Jesus Christ of Latter Day Saints Temple,** (301-587-0144), better known as the Mormon Temple. The white-and-gold, multi-spired church looks more like a wizard's residence than a conventional place of worship; a few years ago, the nearby graffito "Surrender Dorothy!" stunned all Washington with its appropriateness. Composed entirely of Alabama marble, the building has no windows; thin slabs of marble let soft light inside. The spires crowning the temple are steel fused with liquid gold. Moroni, the son of the prophet Mormon, stands 18 feet tall on top of a spire and is made of brass and gold leaf. Since the dedication of the temple in 1974, no non-Mormons are allowed inside (it was open for one month between its completion and dedication). Even atheists can still take a 30-minute tour of the Visitors Center, including laser disc shows about Mormon. There's a dazzling display of lights and stuff at Christmastime. Get off I-495 at exit 33 and onto Connecticut Ave. going north, then turn immediately onto Beach Rd., which winds through Rock Creek Park. Turn left onto Stoneybrook Rd., and the Temple is on the left. (Visitors Center open daily 10am-9pm. Free.)

Glen Echo Park, just down MacArthur east of the Clara Barton House (301-492-6282 or 301-492-6229), is an old turn-of-the-century amusement park; enjoy the relics. Pack a lunch and then eat a picnic in the old Bumper Car pavilion, ride the restored 1921 Dentzel Carousel (May-Sept. Sat.-Sun. noon-6pm and Wed. 10am-2pm; rides 50¢), or check out the wealth of local art at the gallery on site (320-5331; open daily 10am-5pm). Kids can take in a puppet performance (320-6668; shows Wed. and Thurs. 10 and 11:30am, Sat. 11am, 1pm, 2:30pm, tickets $4) or dare to experience a show at the Adventure Theatre. (Shows Sat.-Sun. 1:30 and 3:30pm; tickets $4.50. For information call 301-320-5331 daily 10am-4pm. Reservations recommended; call 320-6668 Wed.-Fri. 9:30am-3:30pm and Sat.-Sun. 10:30am-3:30pm.)

Smaller than Great Falls Park on the Virginia side of the Potomac, Maryland's **Great Falls Park** (301-299-2026) includes part of the Chesapeake & Ohio Canal, whose towpath makes a perfect jogging and biking trail with a great view of the kayakers below. Only knee-deep water separates reasonable Maryland from the wild, green Virginia border. About seven people drown each year by falling from the sharp-looking rock formations. A 90-minute cruise of the canal on the mule-drawn *Canal Clipper,* including a demonstration of the lock system and a history of the canal told by guides in period costume, is more fun than it sounds and safer than rock climbing. Barge tours leave from the Canal Museum at 11710 MacArthur Blvd., in Potomac. To reach Great Falls Park, take MacArthur Blvd. westward until it ends. (Barge tours June-Sept. Wed.-Sun. 10:30am, 1pm, 3pm, and on Sun. 5pm; April-early June and late Sept.-Oct. Sat.-Sun. only. Tickets $4, seniors $3, children $2.50. Park open sunrise to sunset, vehicle admission $3, pedestrians $1, seniors free.)

At the very busy intersection of Rockville Pike (Rte. 355) and Viers Mill Rd. **F. Scott** and **Zelda Fitzgerald** lie in the graveyard of St. Mary's Church. Admirers throw flowers beside *The Great Gatsby*'s famous last sentence: "So we beat on, boats against the current, borne back ceaselessly into the past."

In the far northern outskirts of the county near Poolesville, several family farms huck their wares in their front yards. Take I-270 to W. Montgomery Ave. (Rte. 28), which becomes Darnestown Rd. Continue west until you pass Beallsville Ave.; another mile down the road on your left will be Peachtree Rd. On this corner, **Lewis Orchards,** 18900 Peachtree Rd. (301-349-4101) sells corn, cucumber, tomatoes, squash, green peppers, several types of apples, and a slew of other home-grown vegetables and fruits. Go and seek out the white peach; this sweetest and juiciest peach, grown only in Maryland and southern Pennsylvania, can be had for two weeks in mid-July and again near the end of August. (Two quarts cost about $4, four quarts $6, and half a bushel $18, but prices vary. Call ahead to find out when the white peaches will be ready to pick—you might be allowed to pick your own.) **Horine's Orchard,** 19211 Peachtree Rd. (301-972-8755), just another quarter mile further, has a less extensive selection, but often sells the same or better quality at cheaper prices. The farms' proximity lets buyers compare before purchasing. (Lewis Orchards open July-Nov. daily 9am-6:30pm; Horine's Orchard open July-Nov. daily 9am-6pm.)

Sights: Prince Georges County

The 200-acre **Oxen Hill Farm** separates the sheep from the goats on the corner of I-295 and I-95. This traditional 19th-century working farm invites its guests to join in its many activities. Cow-milking takes place at 10:30am and 4pm, while chicken feeding and egg gathering take place at 2pm. (Sorry, folks: no duck dunking). The barns also shelter rabbits, ducks, turkeys, and donkeys, along with their respective redolences. Take a half-mile walk along the woodlot trail, or try the hayride. Sometimes butter-churning and ice cream-making demonstrations are scheduled as well. To reach Oxen Hill Farm from downtown, take South Capitol St., which becomes Indian Head Highway, and turn right onto Oxen Hill Rd. just after passing I-95. Finally, turn right onto Bald Eagle Dr. to reach the farm. You can also take the Beltway I-95 to exit 3-A onto Oxen Hill Rd. (Call 301-839-1177 for a recording of directions and the program schedule; call 301-839-1176 from 2:30-4pm for specifics or to organize a more formal tour. Open daily 9am-5pm. Free.)

Fort Washington Park (301-763-4600) gathers the requisite woods and grass to its military-historical bosom at the confluence of Piscataway Creek and the Potomac River. The two-waterway view will bliss you out; you can see Mount Vernon from the hill, and the six-mile trail along the water's edge provides a peaceful escape from the city. Rangers tour the fort in Civil War-era costume hourly every weekend. Aspiring military historians should check out the Endicott system—eight batteries strategically built around the fort, each with different types of weapons to repel all classes of enemy naval vessels. Informal tours are offered on weekdays by request. A 7-minute film reviews the fort's history. To reach Fort Washington Park, take South Capitol St., which becomes Indian Head Hwy., and turn right onto Fort Washington Rd. You can also take the Beltway I-95 to exit 3, turning right onto Indian Head Pkwy. Turn right off of the parkway onto Fort Washington Rd. (Park open daily 8am-dark; fort open 9am-5pm; Visitors Center open daily 10am-4:30pm. Admission $3 per vehicle, $1 per pedestrian, biker, or motorcyclist, seniors free. After 4:30pm every one gets in free.)

Space cases go ballistic at the **NASA/Goddard Space Flight Center** (301-286-8981). The tour covers, among other buildings in the complex, the Test and Evaluation Facility, the NASA Communications Network, and control centers for satellites. The Visitors Center itself has permanent exhibits reminiscent of the Smithsonian's Air and Space Museum. Hands-on activities show kids robotics, the mission of the Space Shuttle, the Hubble Space Telescope, and the uses of a space station. Don't bother with the drive unless you plan to take the tour. To get here take the Baltimore-Washington Pkwy. (I-295) and exit onto Greenbelt Rd. Follow the signs to the Visitors Center. (Open July 4-Labor Day daily 10am-4pm, the rest of the year only Wed.-Sun. Free. Guided tours 4:30am and 2:30pm daily; also free.)

The Rest of Virginia

If Virginia seems obsessed with its past, it has good reason: the white settlement of North America, the shame and legacy of the slave trade, American independence, the aristocratic farsightedness of the early United States, and even the Civil War might all be said to have their roots in Virginia. English colonists founded Jamestown in 1607; the New World's first African-American slaves joined them unwillingly only thirteen years later. While George Washington was still battling Native Americans in the French and Indian War, Thomas Jefferson scribbled away about religious and political freedom in the colonial capital, lavish Williamsburg. Virginian James Madison traveled to Philadelphia in 1787 with drafts of the Constitution, and Virginian George Mason led the campaign for a Bill of Rights. Meanwhile, eastern Virginia's Tidewater aristocracy dominated the state for a century, maintaining a rigid, gracious culture of slave-dependent plantations. It all went kablooey in the Civil War, when Union and Confederate armies pushed one another around the state on the way to Appomattox.

Virginia has mostly left the Old South it once led, but a host of Confederate street names, Robert E. Lee parks, fixed-up plantations, and battlefields exhibit to excess the world before 1865. In Richmond, where Patrick Henry boomed, "Give me liberty or give me death," nostalgia and horror compete in the Confederate Museum. Nostalgia climaxes in Colonial Williamsburg, where guides in 18th-century dress show sweating tourists around the restored 18th-century capital. Virginia Beach caters to the sunny side of the visitor's vacation and relaxation reigns over the region. Much of the state remains farmland, with tobacco a major crop. But Virginia's culture is certainly changing: several Old Dominion cities celebrate Confederate generals Jackson and Lee and civil rights leader Martin Luther King on one fair-minded local holiday.

Shenandoah National Park

Before 1926, when Congress authorized the establishment of **Shenandoah National Park,** the area held a series of rocky, threadbare farms along the Blue Ridge Mountains. Congress specified that no federal money be spent on land for the national park, so the enthusiastic state of Virginia appropriated over $1 million, while the people of the state donated the rest. School children sent pennies. Thirteen years later, the farmers and their families had been booted off their lands and the area returned to its "natural" state. Forests replaced fields, wild deer and bear drove out the cows and pigs, and a two-lane highway, Skyline Drive—complete with intermittent viewing points where Sunday drivers can stop and gawk—steamrolled over the dirt roads.

And stop and gawk the roadhounds do. On clear days drivers and hikers can look out over miles of unspoiled ridges and treetops. In summer, the cool mountain air offers a respite from Virginia's typical heat and humidity. Go early in June to see mountain laurel blooming in the highlands. In the fall, Skyline Drive and its lodges bloom with tourists enjoying the magnificent fall foliage. The narrow park stretches almost 75 miles along the Blue Ridge Mountains, parallel to and south of the wilder George Washington National Forest.

Practical Information

Emergency (in park): 800-732-0911 or 703-999-2226, or contact the nearest ranger. Collect calls accepted; dial the area code.

Park Information: 999-2266 for 24-hr. recorded message; 999-2227 or 999-2229 for general information. Mailing address: Superintendent, Shenandoah National Park, Rte. 4, P.O. Box 348, Luray, VA 22835.

Visitor Information: Dickey Ridge Visitors Center, mile 4.6 (635-3566), closest to the north entrance. Daily nature interpretation programs. Open April-Nov. daily 9am-5pm. **Byrd Visitors Center,** mile 50 (999-3282), in the center of the park. Movie and museum explain the history of the Blue Ridge range and its mountain culture. Open March-Dec. daily 9am-5pm; Jan.-Feb. weekends only. Both stations offer changing exhibits on the park, free pamphlets, the AMC guides, daily posted weather updates, and ranger-led nature hikes.

Area Code: 703.

Shenandoah, properly experienced, is a three-dimensional *manifestation*, not just a three-hour car-ride at the irksome 35 m.p.h. speed limit. The Technicolor mountains—bluish and covered with deciduous flora in the summer, smeared with reds, oranges, and yellows in the fall—deserve, if not a probing hike, at least a look from the stone walls of the overlooks. The drive runs 105 miles south from Front Royal to Rockfish Gap. Overlooks provide picnic areas or rest stops for hikers; map boards carry data about trail conditions. The drive closes immediately, during and after periods of bad weather. Most facilities hibernate from November through March. (Entrance $5 per vehicle, $2 per hiker, biker, or bus passenger; pass good for seven days; free for seniors and the disabled.)

Miles along Skyline Drive are measured north to south, by mileposts on the east side of the road. There's no public transportation inside the park. Within the park, hitching opportunities are rare; outside the park, hitching is illegal. **Greyhound** sends buses from DC to Waynesboro, near the park's southern entrance, twice daily ($35, $65 round-trip), but no bus or train serves Front Royal. Rockfish Gap is only 25 mi. from Charlottesville on Rte. 64. You can also drive to Shenandoah from DC; take Rte. 66

west to 340 south to Front Royal. The 70-minute trip offers views of the mountains from either side.

When planning to stay more than a day, purchase the *Park Guide* ($1), a booklet containing all the park regulations, trail lists, and a description of the area's geological history. The *Guide to Skyline Drive* ($5.50), what the park rangers call the Blue Bible, provides information on accommodations and activities. The free *Shenandoah Overlook* newspaper reports seasonal and weekly events as well as practical information within the park. All three publications are available at the Visitors Center.

Accommodations and Camping

On Highway Route 601 South, the **Bear's Den AYH/HI Youth Hostel** (554-8708) provides a woodsy stone lodge for travelers, with two ten-bed dormitory rooms. (Write Bear's Den AYH-Hostel, Postal Route 1, Box 288, Bluemont, VA 22012.) There is no train or bus service; those with a car should exit from Rte. 7 onto Hwy 601 South and proceed for about one-half mile. Turn right at the entrance—look for a stone gate, and proceed up the hostel driveway for another half-mile. The friendly staff offers information about nearby activities, including hiking, birdwatching, fishing, rafting and tubing, cycling, winery tours, antiquing, and swimming. There's a dining room, a clean self-service kitchen, on-site parking, and a laundry room. (Check-in 5-9pm only; front gate locked at 10pm. Quiet hours at 10pm. Check-out by 9:30am. Members $8, non-members $11; winter months members $9, non-members $10. Sheet sleeping sack $1. Camping $4 per person. Reservations recommended.)

The park maintains two lodges, **Skyland** (mile 42) and **Big Meadows** (mile 51) with rooms comparable to motel rooms, but with cabin-like exteriors; the large windows allow you views of the craggy valleys below, and the patios provide outdoor seating. Skyland (999-2211 or 800-999-4714) offers brown and green wood-furnished cabins (Sun.-Thurs. $38-68, Fri.-Sat. $40-70; Oct. $43-73) and slightly more upscale motel rooms (doubles $68; $5 for each extra person). Skyland closes from December through March. Big Meadows (999-2222 or 800-999-4714) offers similar cabins and motel rooms in a smaller complex (cabin doubles $59, motel rooms from $44; $3 more in Oct.). Big Meadow shuts down from November to April. Lewis Mountain sports a well-kept set of cabins with front porches and private baths (one room $50, two rooms with connecting cabin $73. Each additional person $5. Surcharge $6 in October). All three locations charge an extra $2 or more on Friday and Saturday nights. Reservations are usually necessary for all of these accommodations (up to six months in advance for the fall season); write ARA-Virginia Sky-Line, P.O. Box 727, Luray, VA 22835.

The park service keeps four major campgrounds: **Matthew Arm** (mile 22); **Big Meadows** (mile 51); **Lewis Mountain** (mile 58); and **Loft Mountain** (mile 80). All have stores, laundry facilities, and showers (no hookups). Heavily wooded and uncluttered by mobile homes, Lewis Mountain makes for the happiest tenters. All sites cost $9 except the reservations-only Big Meadows ($11); call the Visitors Center to check on availability.

Back-country camping is free, but you must obtain a permit at a park entrance, a Visitors Center, one of the ranger stations, or the park headquarters halfway between Thornton Gap and Luray on U.S. 211. Back-country campers must set up 25 yards from a water supply and out of sight of any trail, road overlook, cabin, or other campsite. Since open fires are prohibited, bring cold food or a stove; boil water, bring iodine pills, or drink bottled water, because some creeks are infected. Illegal camping carries a $50 fine. Hikers on the Appalachian Trail can make use of primitive open shelters, the three-sided structures with stone fireplaces strewn along the trail at approximately seven-mile intervals. At full shelters, campers will often move over to make room for a new arrival. These shelters are reserved for through-hikers with three or more nights in different locations stamped on their camping permits; casual hikers are now banned from them. The Potomac Appalachian Trail Club maintains six cabins in back-country areas of the park. You must reserve in advance by writing to the club at 1718 N St. NW, WDC 20036 (202-638-5306). The cabins contain bunk beds, water, and stoves; you must bring lanterns and food. (Sun.-Thurs. $3 per person, Fri.-Sat. $14 per group; one party member must be at least 21.)

Hikes and Activities

The **Appalachian Trail** runs the length of the park. Trail map and the AMC guide can be obtained at the Visitors Center. The AMC puts out three detailed topographic maps (each $5) covering different parts of the park. Purchase all three and get a trail guide, descriptions, and suggestions on time budgeting ($16). Brochures that cover the popular hikes are available free. Responsible campers should remember to avoid lighting fires and use stoves instead, and leave no litter behind. Overnight hikers should remember the unpredictability of outdoor weather. Be sure to get the Park Service package of brochures and advice, in Shenandoah or out of it, before you begin a long hike.

Old Rag Mountain, 5 miles from mile 45, is only 3291 feet high; but the 7.2-mile loop up the mountain is quite fierce. The hike is steep, involving scrambling, scrunching, and squeezing over and between granite, and at many points tempts with discouraging "false summits." Bring lots of water and energy food. There are nice spots for camping all around the summit area, so avoid the main campground. Perhaps a less demanding climb is **Little Devil Stairs**, at Mile 19; also a 7-mile loop, this hike rises through a rocky gorge 100 ft.-high on both sides. The hike is easy down, but strenuous going up.

The **Whiteoak Canyon** trail beckons from its own parking lot at mile 42.6. The trail to the canyon is easy and the waterfalls spectacular. The shady area, with great boulders under tall hemlocks, cascades and pools, rock walls, and five more waterfalls, is a must-visit. The rushing waters of the Whiteoak Canyon are home to trout galore. The Visitors Centers hawk a five-day fishing license ($6), but hordes of regulations hem in the catch. The five-mile trail leads into a semi-open area, once an apple orchard, now more of a crabapple orchard. From Whiteoak Canyon, the **Limberlost** trail slithers into a hemlock forest. At mile 50.7, **Dark Hollow Trail** takes about half an hour to lead you to a gorgeous array of falls—the closest to Skyline Drive in the whole park. The trail descends further (up to an hour's walk) to the base of the falls, where water drops 70 feet over the crumbling stone of an ancient lava flow. There's also a hike to the Big Meadows swamp, swelling with wildflowers. Bigfoot.

Drivers should enjoy **Mary's Rock Tunnel** (mile 32), where the road goes straight through almost 700 feet of solid rock. **Hogback Overlook,** from mile 20.8 to mile 21, offers short and easy hikes and spectacular views of the smooth Shenandoah River and its bosom companion, the Shenandoah Valley; on a clear day, you can look endlessly on eleven bends in the river. The nearest bend is more than half a mile below the overlook.

Horse and pony riding from Skyland Lodge competes with driving and hiking. One-hour horse rides will show some scenic vistas. (Reservations can be made one day in advance at Skyland stables from 8:30am-3:30pm; after 3:30pm, reservations can be made at the front desk at Skyland.) Thirty-minute pony rides cost $16; a 2 1/2-hr. ride to White Oak Falls is $32 (available daily 9am-3pm).

Take a break from hiking or driving at one of Shenandoah's seven **picnic areas,** awaiting you at Dickey Ridge (mile 5), Elkwallow (mile 24), Pinnacles (mile 37), Big Meadows (mile 51), Lewis Mountain (mile 58), South River (mile 63), and Loft Mountain (mile 80). All have tables, fireplaces, water fountains, and comfort stations. If you forget to pack a picnic basket, swing by the **Panorama Restaurant** (mile 31.5) for an overpriced meal and a view. (Sandwiches $2-3. Dinners $6-14. Open April-Nov. daily 9am-7pm.)

Outside the Park

The **Shenandoah Caverns,** Shenandoah Caverns, VA (477-3115), are the only caverns in Virginia with an elevator for the disabled. The caverns tout an iridescent panoply of stalactites, stalagmites, and other weirdo rock formations. "Rainbow Lake" and the amusing "Capitol Dome" figure among the underground formations. (Open daily 9am-6pm; tour $7, ages 8-14 $3.50, under 8 free.) **Skyline Caverns,** Front Royal, VA, (635-4545 or 800-635-4599), has built a reputation on its dependable anthodites, whose white spikes defy gravity and grow in all directions—but only at a rate of one inch per seven thousand years. The caverns are located fifteen minutes from the junction of U.S. 211. The tour lasts one hour. (Open daily 9am-5pm. Tour $8, ages 6-12 $4, under 6 free.)

Canoe and rafting trips take off daily from the **Shenandoah Canoe and Tube Voyagers**, at the Massanutten Resort (433-1109 from 9am-1pm or 433-9457; ask for Keith in the evening). The Voyagers are less than 20 miles west of the Parkway on Route 33. (3- to 4-hour trips, tubing $12 per person, canoeing $19 per person.) **The Downriver Canoe Co.** (703-635-5526) P.O. Box 10, Rte. 1, Box 256-A, in Bentonville, is for the serious canoer: canoe trips stretch from 3 miles to 150 plus miles. From the Skyline Drive, mile 20, follow 211 west for 8 miles, then north onto Rte. 340 for 14 miles to Bentonville. Turn right onto 613, 1 mile. (Prices vary with length of trip. 3 miles $25 per canoe; 40 miles, $110 per canoe.)

Charlottesville

This college town (population: 42,000) in the Blue Ridge foothills proudly bears the stamp of its patron, Thomas Jefferson. The college he founded, the University of Virginia (pronounced you-vee-AY) dominates the town, supporting both the pubs and writers like Peter Taylor and Pulitzer Prize-winning poet Rita Dove. Visitors get steered to Monticello, the cleverly constructed classical mansion Mr. Jefferson designed for himself. Even C-ville itself, low-lying, friendly, hip, and compact, seems to reflect the third President's dream of well-informed, culturally-aware citizens who choose to live close to the land. In recent years Charlottesville has become the favorite small town of actors, writers, and billionaires: Muhammad Ali, Sam Shepard, and Jessica Lange all call it home. Shenandoah National Park beckons to wilderness-lovers northeast of the town; oenophiles can head to the suburbs for the ten wineries of "Virginia's wine capital." The Corner neighborhood near UVA has bookstores to browse in and countless cheap eats, but most commercial action and nightlife happens in downtown proper, around E. Main St.

Practical Information

Emergency: 911. **Campus Police:** 4-1766 on a UVA campus phone.

Visitor Information: Chamber of Commerce, 415 E. Market St. (295-3141), within walking distance of Amtrak, Greyhound/Trailways, and historic downtown. Open daily 9am-5pm. **Charlottesville/Abermarle Convention and Visitors Bureau,** P.O. Box 161, Rte. 20 near I-64 (977-1783). Statewide brochures, maps (Virginia and Charlottesville); same information as Chamber of Commerce. Lodging reservations made. Take bus #8 (Piedmont Community College) from 5th St. and Market St. By car, take Market St., which borders the Downtown Mall on the North, and head east. Make a right on E. High St., then a left on Monticello Ave., which turns into I-20. Visitors Bureau on right. Combination tickets to Monticello, Michie Tavern, and Ash Lawn-Highland ($16; seniors and children $14.50) available. Open daily 9:30am-5:30pm. **University of Virginia Information Center** (924-1019), at the rotunda in the center of campus. Few brochures, map of the university. Information on campus tours. Student helpers answer questions in **Newcomb Hall** at UVA; university brochures available. Open daily 9am-10pm. Larger **University Center,** off U.S. 250 west—follow signs (924-7166). Transport schedules, entertainment guides, and hints on budget accommodations. Answers phone "Campus Police." Campus maps. Open 24 hrs.

Amtrak: 810 W. Main St. (800-872-7245 or 296-4559), 7 blocks from downtown. To Washington, DC ($22, 3hr. trip, make reservations as far as possible in advance) and New York ($81, takes 7-8hr.).

Greyhound/Trailways: 310 Main St. (295-5131), within 3 blocks of historic downtown. To Richmond ($11.50, 1 1/2hr.), Washington, DC ($20.50, 3hr.), Norfolk ($29.50, 4hr.), and Lynchburg ($12.50, 1 1/2hr.).

Public Transport: Charlottesville Transit Service (296-7433). Bus service within city limits, including most hotels and UVA campus locations. Buses operate Mon.-Sat. 6:20am-7pm. Maps available at both information centers, Chamber of Commerce, and the UVA student center in Newcomb Hall. Fare 60¢, seniors and disabled 30¢, under 6 free. The more frequent blue University of Virginia buses require UVA ID or long-term pass to board. **Yellow Cab:** 295-4131. To Monticello $12.

Post Office: 1155 Seminole Trail (Rte. 29). Open Mon.-Fri. 8am-5:30pm, Sat. 8am-2pm. **ZIP code:** 22906.

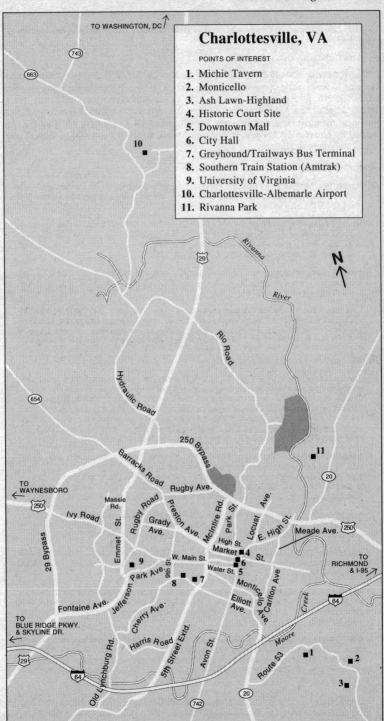

TO WASHINGTON, DC

Charlottesville, VA

POINTS OF INTEREST

1. Michie Tavern
2. Monticello
3. Ash Lawn-Highland
4. Historic Court Site
5. Downtown Mall
6. City Hall
7. Greyhound/Trailways Bus Terminal
8. Southern Train Station (Amtrak)
9. University of Virginia
10. Charlottesville-Albemarle Airport
11. Rivanna Park

N

Rivanna River

Rio Road

Hydraulic Road

250 Bypass

Barracks Road

Rugby Ave.

TO WAYNESBORO

Massie Rd.

Ivy Road

Rugby Road

Emmet St.

Grady Ave.

Preston Ave.

McIntire Rd.

Park St.

Locust Ave.

Meade Ave.

29 Bypass

9th St.

W. Main St.

High St.

Market St.

Water St.

E. High St.

Jefferson Park Ave.

Fontaine Ave.

Cherry Ave.

Harris Road

5th Street Extd.

Avon St.

Elliott Ave.

Monticello Ave.

Carlton Ave.

Moore Creek

TO RICHMOND & I-95

TO BLUE RIDGE PKWY. & SKYLINE DR.

Old Lynchburg Rd.

Route 53

Help Lines: Region 10 Community Services Hotline: 972-1800. **Lesbian and Gay Hotline:** 971-4942.

Area Code: 804

Charlottesville rests in the delta formed by Rte. 29, Rte. 250, and I-64. Streets number east to west, using compass directions; 5th St. NW is 10 blocks from (and parallel to) 5th St. NE. Streets running east-west across the numbered streets are neither parallel nor logically named. Charlottesville has two downtowns; **the Corner** on the west side near the university, and **Historic Downtown** about a mile east. The two are connected by **University Avenue**, running east-west, which becomes **Main Street** after the Corner ends at a bridge.

Accommodations

Budget Inn, 140 Emmet St. (Rte. 29; 293-5141). Near the university. Forty comfortable, hotel-quality rooms, clean and air-conditioned with private baths and TVs. Discounts for seniors. Singles $32-35. Doubles $40-45. Each additional person $5.

Howard Johnson's, 1309 West Main St. (296-8121), at the end of the Corner, toward downtown and next to Cavalier diner. Near the UVA hospital. Air-conditioned, well-kept rooms; dim hallways. Sixth floor is non-smoking. Outdoor pool; TVs in rooms. Singles $57. Doubles $67; each extra person $9. Senior discounts approx. $10 off.

Econo-Lodge. 400 Emmet St. (296-2104). Outdoor pool and standard rooms with TVs. Surrounding area is noise-polluted, but the hotel is set far enough off the road to be fairly quiet. Singles $40. Doubles $49. Two to a bed, $43.

Camping: Charlottesville KOA Kampground, P.O. Box 144, 22901 (296-9881, for info 336-9881, for reservations). All campsites are shaded. Recreation hall with video games, a pavilion, and a pool (open Mon.-Sat. 10am-8pm). Fishing (not wading or swimming) allowed. Camping season is March 15-Nov. 15. Check-in after 1pm, check-out before noon. Sites $16, hook-up $18.

Food

The Hardware Store, 316 E. Main St. (977-1518), near the middle of the outdoor "mall." Bar atmosphere, but weirder: beers served in glass boots, appetizers in mini basketball courts, and condiments in toolboxes. Collectors would drool over the 1898 building's antique collection. An American grill with an eclectic set of entrees, from Ratatouille Gratinée ($5) to crepes, both sweet ($1.50-4) and salty ($4-6). Sandwiches $3-7. Thirty different cakes or pies baked fresh each day: try the rich Russian coffee cake $2.15, raspberry nut torte $2.25, or Heath bar cheesecake $3.25. Open Mon. 10am-5pm, Tues.-Thurs. 10am-9pm, Fri.-Sat. 10am-11pm.

Garden Gourmet, 811 West Main St. (295-9991). Northern California circa 1967, with vegetarians, hippies, burners, and an unusual air of friendliness. Homemade 7-grain bread, salad dressings, and creative vegetarian sandwiches ($3-5) and plates ($4-6). Wooden booths accompany artwork by the owner's family and staff. Nightly folk music. Open Mon.-Thurs. 11:30am-2pm, 5:30-9pm; Fri. 11:30am-2pm, 5:30-10pm; Sat. noon-3pm, 5:30-10pm.

Macado's, 1505 University Ave. (971-3558). Excellent sandwiches ($3.95-4.50) and homemade desserts. Features pinball machine and candy store. Rockin' bar upstairs, where Edgar Allan Poe once lived. Take advantage of the long hours. Open daily 11am-2am.

The Howlin' Pig at Zipper's, 1202 W. Main St. (295-7060). Zoinks. Used to be just a bar, now a Southern barbecue. Look for the black and white checked tables out front. Pulled pork or pulled chicken sandwich $3.50. Open daily 5pm-11pm.

The Tavern, 1140 Emmet St. (295-0404). "Where tourists, townspeople, and students meet" is painted in white letters atop this inconspicuous building. A breakfast Eden; its banana-nut, bacon, or fruit-filled homemade pancakes ($3.50) are a full meal. UVA jocks buy kegs here, too. Open daily 7am-3pm.

The Nook, 415 E. Main St. (295-6665). Modest American diner with a varied clientele. On a hot night, eat outside near a small fountain. Famous Nook Burger Plate—good-sized juicy burger with waffle fries and coleslaw, no skimping, $4.25. Regular hamburger with chips and a pickle, $2; tuna or chicken salad, $3. Fast service. Open Mon.-Fri. 7:30am-7:45pm; Sat. 9:30am-3:30pm.

Sights

Most activity on the spacious **University of Virginia** campus clusters around the **Lawn** and down fraternity-lined **Rugby Road.** Through his telescope, Mr. Jefferson watched the construction of the University from the windows of Monticello. You can return the favor with a glimpse of Monticello from the **Lawn**, a terraced green carpet which unrolls down the middle of the university. Call UVA students first-, second-, third- or fourth-years, never freshmen or sophomores. During the year, students study and play along the Lawn; the tiny dorm rooms which face it are awarded only to distinguished fourth-years (less than 10%). Professors live in the Lawn's pavilions; Mr. Jefferson designed each one in a different architectural style so students could see them all without having to tour the capitals of Europe. (See *Let's Go: Europe.*) Lawn tours, led by student volunteers, leave on the hour at the Rotunda from 10am-4pm, except at noon (call 924-7969 for info); printed maps available.

Mr. Jefferson was especially proud of the Pantheon-style dome of the **Rotunda**; the Rotunda's natural lighting and numerous windows makes it an ideal spot for quiet reflection. The **Old Cabell Building** across the Lawn from the Rotunda houses an auditorium with impressive acoustics. On its wall, a reproduction of Raphael's mural *The School of Athens* depicts Jefferson's vision of student-faculty harmony. The **Bayley Art Museum,** Rugby Rd. (924-3592), hosts visiting exhibits to complement its small permanent collection, which holds one of Rodin's castings of *The Kiss*. Look for the annual spring flower show and other special festivals. (Open Tues.-Sun. 1-5pm.) Students show off their art in **Fayerweather Hall,** next door to the Bayley Art Museum on Rugby Rd. (924-6123). Professors show off theirs in the **McGuffey Art Center,** 201 Second St. NW (295-7973). (Open Tues.-Sat. 10-5pm, Sun. 1-5pm. Free. Disabled access.)

The **Downtown Mall** is a brick thoroughfare lined with restaurants and shops. Students make the mall a part of nightlife, but it caters to a diverse crowd of locals, tourists, and neighborhood characters as well. A kiosk near the fountain, the center of the mall, has posters with club schedules—e.g. what's going on at TRAX or other downtown hotspots. At 110 D-Mall, **The Movie Palace** shows current flicks for only $2. (Fruitscrootie!) Other eateries, bars, and specialty stores provide places to savor smells and browse. **The Book Cellar,** 316E. Main St. (979-7787), a well-lit, comfortable place to browse, houses a large half-price collection of literary and academic books. (Open Mon. 10am-5pm, Tues.-Fri. 10am-7pm, Fri.-Sat. 10am-9pm.)

Mr. Jefferson's more-classical-than-thou design for his home, **Monticello** (295-8181), derives from the work of 16th-century Italian architect Andrea Palladio. TJ oversaw every stage of the designing and building and collected gadgets for the inside on his travels. Jefferson found (or invented?), for example, a compass which registers wind direction through a weathervane on the roof. Those familiar with the Jefferson Memorial in DC won't be surprised by Monticello's columns and central dome. Mr. Jefferson loved silver goblets, parquet flooring, and marble statuary. The statesman filled his airy tea room with likenesses of his heroes and contemporaries. Busts of Franklin, Lafayette, Washington, and John Paul Jones (probably the naval hero, not the Zeppelin bassist) copy the Houdon originals Jefferson bought in Paris.

There's nary a non-picturesque spot on Monticello's landscape; from the west lawn, a round-about floral walk leads to a magnificent hillside view. Mr. Jefferson's slaves, whom his will emancipated, lived and labored in the vegetable garden. The garden's view takes in Montalto, the "high mountain" on which Jefferson wanted to build an observation tower. Tours of Monticello begin every five minutes during the day, but the wait can be as long as 90 minutes on summer Saturdays. Come early. (Open March-Oct. 8am-5pm; Nov.-Feb. 9am-4:30pm; tickets $7, seniors $6, ages 6-11 $3.)

Minutes away (take a right turn to Rte. 795) is **Ashlawn** (293-9539), the 500-acre former plantation home of President James Monroe. More quaint and less imposing than Monticello, Ashlawn boasts outdoor views to rival its domed neighbor's. The current owners, the College of William and Mary, have turned Ashlawn into a Monroe museum. Ashlawn's peacocks stroll the gardens and lawn while making curious noises through their beaks. Tempting smells spill from a small hutch where a chef offers free demonstrations of open-hearth cooking. (Open March-Oct. daily 9am-6pm; Nov.-Feb. daily 10am-5pm; tour $6, seniors $5.50, ages 6-11 $2.)

In the **Box Gardens** behind Ashlawn, English-language opera highlights the **Summer Festival of the Arts** (tickets $14, seniors $13, students $10, and $1 more on Sat.;

box office 293-8000; open Tues.-Sun. 10am-5pm). A 45-minute intermission allows for a picnic supper, which can be self-supplied or provided by Festive Fare (296-5496) at $8 per person. Ashlawn also hosts **Music at Twilight** (tickets $9, seniors $8, students $6), including New Orleans jazz, Cajun music, blues, and swing. Combination tickets for the performance, house tour, and picnic supper are available ($22).

Down the road from Monticello on Rte. 53, is **Michie** ("mick-ee") **Tavern** (977-1234), with an operating grist mill and a general store. You can tour the 200-year-old establishment (tour $5, seniors $4.50, ages 6-11 $1); potted history recordings help visitors who explore the rooms. (Tours run daily 9am-5pm.) Jefferson's daughter supposedly fled the tavern after improperly teaching a man to waltz in the ballroom. **The Ordinary** (977-1235), located in the tavern, serves up a fixed $9 buffet of fried chicken, beans, cornbread, and other dishes (ages 6-11 $3). Eat outside in good weather. (Open daily 11:15am-3:30pm.)

Nightlife

Charlottesville loves jazz, doesn't mind rock 'n roll, and in general supports quite a few pubs. Around the Downtown Mall, omnipresent posters and the free *C-ville Review* can tell you who plays where when.

The Blue Ridge Brewery Co., 709 Main St. (977-0017). Down-home bar/lounge run by two brothers, a brewmaster and a chef. Light and dark beer brewed on the premises with water from the Blue Ridge Mountains. Dreamy appetizers include hot, tangy "creamy trout wontons" ($3). Specials on blue crabs and fresh steamed shrimp Sun.-Thurs. Entrees $7-15. Open Mon.-Fri. 11:30am-2pm and 5-10pm; Sat.-Sun. 11:30am-3pm and 5-10pm; bar open until 2am.

The Court Square Tavern, 500 Court Sq. (296-6111). Drink your way around the world, with over 100 imported beers. Open Mon.-Sat. 11:30am-midnight, Sun. 5:30pm-midnight.

TRAX, 122 11th St. (295-8729). Rock and jazz acts, national (Wynton Marsalis, the Ramones), and local. Spacious enough to dance or hang out. Attracts both students and townies. Cover $8-15. Look for a monthly flyer and call ahead for show information.

Richmond

Capital of the short-lived Confederate States of America, Richmond (population: 213,000) keeps one face turned towards its Civil War past, with numerous museums and restored houses showing everything from troop movements to tablecloths belonging to Confederate President Jefferson Davis. But in districts like the sprawling, beautiful Fan and formerly industrial Shockoe Bottom, another Richmond rears its coiffed and powdered head with relaxed cultural savvy and excellent, inexpensive food.

Richmond's urban area is the shape of a closed ladies' fan placed east to west: the center is the **State Capitol,** the short handle to the east is Court End and Shockoe Bottom, and the long western blade begins downtown and becomes the Fan neighborhood. Streets form a grid pattern but are not named logically except for 1st (west) through 14th (east) St. downtown. Both I-95, leading north to Washington, DC and I-195, parallel to the James River, encircle the urban area. Route 64 heads northwest to Charlottesville and southeast to Williamsburg.

Practical Information

Emergency: 911

Visitor Information: Richmond Visitors Center, 1700 Robin Hood Rd. (358-5511), exit 14 off I-95/64, in a converted train depot. Helpful 6-min. video introduces the city's various attractions. Reserves accommodations, sometimes at heavy ($10-20) discounts. Arranges walking tours and provides quality maps. Open Memorial Day-Labor Day daily 9am-7pm; off-season 9am-5pm. Brochure-only branch office at 301 E. Main St. downtown. **State of Virginia Visitors Center** in the **Bell Tower,** 101 N. 9th St. (786-4484), on Capitol Square. Open Mon.-Fri. 8:15am-5pm.

Trains: Amtrak, far away at 7519 Staple Mills Rd. (264-9194 or 800-872-7245). To: Washington, DC ($21, 2hr.), Williamsburg ($9,1 1/4hr.), Virginia Beach ($18, 3hr., the last third of the trip on a shuttle), New York City ($78, 7hr.), Baltimore ($28, 3hr.), Philadelphia ($45, 4 3/4 hr.).

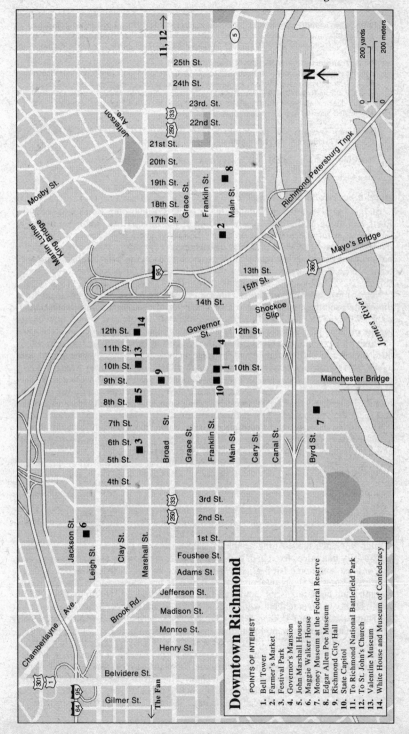

Downtown Richmond

POINTS OF INTEREST

1. Bell Tower
2. Farmer's Market
3. Festival Park
4. Governor's Mansion
5. John Marshall House
6. Maggie Walker House
7. Money Museum at the Federal Reserve
8. Edgar Allen Poe Museum
9. Richmond City Hall
10. State Capitol
11. To Richmond National Battlefield Park
12. To St. John's Church
13. Valentine Museum
14. White House and Museum of Confederacy

Buses: Greyhound/Trailways: 2910 N. Boulevard (353-8903). To get downtown from here, walk two blocks to the Visitors Center or take GRTC bus #24 north. To: Washington, DC ($17.50, 2 1/2hr.); Charlottesville ($11.50, 1 1/2hr.), Williamsburg ($9, 1hr.), Norfolk, VA ($18, 3hr.).

Public Transport: Greater Richmond Transit Co, 101 S. Davis St. (358-4782). Maps available in the basement of city hall, 900 E. Broad St., and in the Yellow Pages. Fare 75¢ (exact change required), transfers 10-50¢. Buses serve most of Richmond infrequently, downtown frequently; most leave from Broad St. downtown. Bus #24 goes south to Broad St. and downtown. Free trolleys provide dependable, if limited, service to downtown and Shockoe Slip 10am-4pm daily, with an extended Shockoe Slip schedule from 5pm-midnight.

Help Lines: Travelers Aid, 648-1767. Rape Crisis Hotline, 643-0888 (24 hrs.). Gay Hotline, 353-3626. Psychiatric Crisis Intervention, 780-8003 or 648-9225.

Post Office: 10th and Main St. (783-0825). Open Mon.-Fri. 7:30am-5pm. ZIP code: 23219.

Area Code: 804.

Accommodations and Camping

Budget motels around Richmond cluster along Williamsburg Rd., on the edge of town, and along Midlothian Turnpike south of the James River; public transport to these areas is infrequent at best. As usual, the farther away from downtown you stay, the less you pay. The Visitors Center distributes an extensive accommodations guide, but many of the prices are outdated. A trustworthy Motel 6, 5704 Williamsburg Rd., Sandston (222-7600), sleeps about six miles east on Rte. 60, across from the airport. (Singles $27. Doubles $33. Take the #7 "Seven Pines" bus.).

Nearer town, the Massad House Hotel, 11 N. 4th St. (648-2893), four blocks from the capital, shuttles its guests via a 1940s elevator to charming, comfortable-enough rooms with shower and TV. Since these are the only inexpensive rooms downtown, they're often booked; in summer call at least a week ahead. (Singles $33. Doubles $40.)

Three miles from the center of town, the Executive Inn, 5215 W. Broad St. (288-4011 or 800-542-2801), offers grand (by motel standards) but slightly faded rooms and a pool. Bus #6 runs frequently into town. (Singles $41. Doubles $45-48. Free breakfast, pool and healthclub facilities.) Most of Richmond's B&B's are converted mansions along Monument Ave. (rooms $60-125). Call Lyn M. Benson at Bensonhouse of Richmond (353-6900) weekdays between 10am and 6pm or Abbey Hill Bed and Breakfast (330-4656 or 355-5855) for more information.

The closest campground, Pocahontas State Park, 10300 Beach Rd. (796-4255), about ten miles south on Rte. 10 and Rte. 655, offers showers, biking, boating, lakes, and a huge pool. (Sites $8.50. No hookups. Pool admission $2, ages 3-12 $1.50.) Reserve a site by phone through Ticketron (490-3939), but be forewarned of the service charge ($4.50-6).

Food

Richmond's many good budget restaurants laze inconspicuously among the shady trees and well-kept porches in the spread-out, gentrified Fan district (bordered by Monument Ave., Main St., Laurel St., and Boulevard). Downtown is chock full of cheap regular-guy lunch spots. At the wondrous 3rd St. Diner, at the corner of 3rd and Main (788-4750), find prices fixed in days of yore. The $2 meatless breakfast (two eggs, biscuit or toast, and home fries, grits or Virginia fried apples) is served all day, and the waitresses know all the regulars by name. (Open 24 hrs., closed Mon. 2am-7am.) Anglophiles and homesick Brits should head for Penny Lane, 207 N. 7th St. (780-1682), a delightfully exaggerated pub with flags on the walls and soccer on the telly. Live music Thurs.-Sat. 9:30pm-1:30am. (Open Sun.-Wed. 11am-4pm and 5-11pm, Thurs.-Sat. 11am-4pm and 5pm-1:30am. In summer, open Mon.-Fri. 11am-2am, Sat. 5pm-2am.)

The Commercial Café, 111 N. Robinson St. (353-7110), serves the best barbecue in this barbecue-grizzled town. Sandwiches start at $5, but cavernous stomachs will order the ribs—the "Taster" ($7) is quite filling, and the plates ($9-14) can be shared. (Open daily 5-11pm; in summer Tues.-Sun. 5-11pm.) The Texas-Wisconsin Border Café, 1501 W. Main St. (355-2907), features chili, potato pancakes, and *chalupas*. Look for the signs above the bar which read "Dixie Inn," "Secede," and "Eat Cheese or Die." At night the café becomes a popular bar. (Lunches $4-6. Dinners $6-10. Open daily 11am-2am.) **Piccola's**, at the corner of W. Main St. and Harrison (355-3111). Virginia Commonwealth University students rave about their cheap and delicious pizza, calzones ($3.15), and jumbo sandwiches ($3.25-4.50). (Open Mon.-Thurs. 11am-midnight, Fri.-Sat. 11am-2am, and Sun. 3pm-midnight.) **Helen's Inn**, 2527 W. Main St. (354-9659). Funny-faced figurines of the famous line the windowsills of this otherwise unassuming restaurant. Helen has tantalizingly cheap, standard-fare burgers ($2-4) and subs ($3-5). (Open Mon.-Fri. 11am-6pm, Sat. 11am-5pm.)

The **Shockoe Slip** district—from Main, Canal, and Cary St. between 10th and 14th St.—features fancy shops in restored and newly painted warehouses, but few bargains. At the **farmer's market**, outdoors at N. 17th and E. Main St., pick up fresh fruit, vegetables, meat, and maybe even a farmer or two. **E. Cary St. Fish Market** (782-2311), a bonanza of fresh seafood in blue-and-white-checked decor, touts its trademark peppery clam chowder ($1.25/bowl; open daily for dining 11:15am-midnight; drinks served until 2am).

Sights

Ever since Patrick Henry boasted "Give me liberty or give me death" in Richmond's **St. John's Church**, 2401 E. Broad St. (648-5015), the river city has been quoting, memorializing, and bronzing its historical heroes. Sundays at 2pm from the last Sunday in May through the first in September an actor recreates the famous 1775 speech, given when the church served as the site of a Revolutionary Convention. You must take a tour to see the church. (Tours given Mon.-Sat. 10am-3:30pm, Sun. 1-3:30pm; admission $2, students $1.) Larger-than-life statues of George Washington and Thomas Jefferson grace the **State Capitol** grounds (786-4344). Jefferson designed the neoclassical edifice after a Roman temple in France. Attendants arrange free tours. (Open daily 9am-5pm.) For more sculpture, follow Franklin Ave. from the capitol until it becomes Monument Ave., lined with trees, gracious old houses, and towering statues of Confederate heroes. Robert E. Lee, who survived the war, faces his beloved South; Stonewall Jackson, who didn't, glares North.

The **Court End** district stretches north and east of the capitol to Clay and College Streets and guards Richmond's most distinctive historical sights. The **Confederate Museum**, 1202 E. Clay St. (649-1861), remembers the Civil War from the losing side with the world's largest Confederate artifact collection. The main floor leads visitors through the military history of the Civil War; the basement displays guns and flags of the Confederacy; and the top floor houses temporary exhibits on such topics as African-American life in the antebellum South. The Museum also runs one-hour tours through the **White House of the Confederacy**, next door (ask at the museum desk). Statues of Tragedy and Comedy grace the White House's front door. (Open daily 10am-5pm; Tours Mon., Wed., and Fri.-Sat. 10:30am-4:30pm, Tues. and Thurs. 11:30am-4:30pm, Sun. 1:15-4:30pm. Admission to museum or tour $4, seniors $3.50, students $2.50, under 13 $2.25; museum and tour $7, seniors $6, students $5, under 13 $3.50.)

The **Valentine Museum**, 1015 Clay St. (649-0711), exhibits—surprise—local and Southern social and cultural history. Admission price includes a tour of the just-renovated Wickham-Valentine. (Open Mon.-Sat. 10am-5pm, Sun. noon-5pm. Admission $3.50, seniors $3, students $2.75, ages 7-12 $1.50.) Combination "Court End" tickets to the Confederate Museum, White House of the Confederacy, John Marshall House, and Valentine Museum (all within easy walking distance of each other) $9, seniors and students $8.50, under 13 $4.

Four blocks from the intersection of Monument Ave. and N. Boulevard stands the Southeast's largest art museum, the **Virginia Museum of Fine Arts**, 2800 Grove Ave. (367-0844). The museum possesses a gorgeous collection (the largest outside Russia) of Fabergé jewelry and Easter eggs made for Russian Tsars, a fine showing of U.S. contemporary art, and what might just be the largest collection of horse sculpture and painting in North America. Zillionaire Paul Mellon, whose dough established the museum, was also a horse admirer; his Mellon Galleries include the only sofas in the entire edifice. (Open Tues.-Sat. 11am-5pm, Thurs. 11am-8pm in the North Wing Galleries, Sun. 1-5pm. Donations requested.)

Fine-arts students at VCU call the **Anderson Gallery**, 907 1/2 West Franklin St. (367-1522), their home. The Fan district gallery features experimental artwork by national and international artists, as well as periodic exhibitions by VCU students and faculty. Anderson's museum shop contains quirky little *objets d'art* for as little as 10¢. (Usually open Tues.-Fri. 10am-5pm, Sat.-Sun. 1-5pm. Call ahead to be sure. Free.)

The **Maggie L. Walker National Historic Site**, 110 1/2 E. Leigh St. (780-1380), commemorates the life of an ex-slave's gifted daughter. Physically disabled, Walker advocated Black women's rights and was the founder and president of a bank. (House tours Wed.-Sun. 9am-5pm. Free.) The two floors of the **Black History Museum and Cultural Center of Virginia**, 00 (yes, 00) Clay St. (780-9093) showcase sparse but informative exhibits on individual African-Americans. Upstairs are profiles of and articles by Maggie Walker and the Rev. John Jasper. (Open Mon.-Fri. 9am-4pm, but call first to confirm. Free.)

Walking tours are organized by the **Historic Richmond Foundation**. There are three main tours: **Old Richmond Today** ($15, kids $12), **Civil War Battlefields** ($20, kids $10, only on Sundays) and the **Civil War City** (Mon.-Sat., April-Oct. $18, kids $14). Call 780-0107 for reservations and departure times or 643-7407 for info.

All of the above sites and more can be seen from the **Cultural Link Trolley** (358-5511 for more info). Connecting 34 of the Capital's most fascinating cultural and historic landmarks, the trolleys run from 10am-5pm on Sat. and from noon-5pm on Sun. ($5).

Richmond's early 20th-century rebuilders were fond of the grand Art Deco style and the **Jefferson Hotel,** at Franklin and Adams St. (788-8000), is a prime example. The hotel opens up its grand piano for free to the public nightly from 8pm-midnight, provided there's no convention upstairs. Serious players only (no "Chopsticks"); ask the manager at **T.J.'s** downstairs for permission to tinkle on the ivories. At the **Byrd Theatre**, 2908 W. Cary St. (353-9911), you can view Hollywood's latest in extraordinary style: marble balconies, enormous stained-glass windows, and a Wurlitzer Organ that rises from the floor to entertain before each show.

Civil War buffs should brave the trip to the city's boundaries to inspect the **Richmond National Battlefield Park,** 3215 E. Broad St. (226-1981). The Chimborazo Visitors Center, located in a former Civil War hospital, has an educational film and exhibits about the Civil War, as well as maps detailing the battlefields and fortifications surrounding the city. (Open daily 9am-5pm. Free.)

There are free concerts here in the summer; check *Style Weekly,* a free magazine available at the Visitors Center and around town. Free entertainment often finds a home in **Dogwood Dell,** an outdoor theater below the Carillon World War I Memorial on the 100-acre Maymont grounds. (Grounds open daily 10am-5pm. For a recording of concert information, call 358-3355.)

Entertainment

Crowds cluster in Shockoe Slip and, to a lesser extent, throughout the Fan. At night, the **Paradise Café,** at Strawberry and W. Main St. (358-6759), in the Fan district, is a combination popular café, bar, and upstairs stage show, starring Richmond's original comedy troupe **Shadowcast Theaterworks** (open Mon.-Sat. 11:30am-2am, Sun. noon-midnight; shows Wed. 9pm, Thurs. 8pm, but call 755-6716 to check times; admission $4). Down in the Slip, the **Tobacco Company Club**, downstairs from the restaurant at 1201 E. Cary St. (782-9555), comes alive with top-40 music and no cover charge. (Open Tues.-Sat. 8pm-2am.) Next door, at 1045 12th St., **Matt's British Pub and Comedy Club** (643-5653) lives up to its name with stand-up puds at 8pm and 11pm. (Open Tues.-Sat. 8pm-2am.)

For live theater and concerts, Richmonders travel south of Shockoe Slip to the **Flood Zone,** 11 S. 18th St. (643-6006), which offers a combination of big-name and off-beat acts (ticket office open Tues.-Fri. 10am-6pm. Tickets $6-20, depending upon the show). **The Metro,** 727 W. Broad St. (649-4952), features local progressive bands most nights.

You'll need a car and a strong stomach to visit **King's Dominion** (876-5900), a world-class amusement park 20 miles north of the city on I-95, but it's definitely worth the trip. Among its many rides lurks a new six-loop steel rollercoaster, the Anaconda. The newest edition to the park is the wet Hurricane Reef with pools, slides, and water-spouting mushrooms. (Rides open daily 10:30am-10pm; Labor Day-Memorial Day Sat.-Sun. 10am-8pm. Admission $23.95, over 55 $17, ages 3-6 $15.95.)

Williamsburg

At the end of the 17th century, when English aristocrats wore brocades and wigs, Williamsburg (current population: 13,000) was the capital of Virginia. During the Revolutionary War, the capital moved to Richmond, taking with it much of Williamsburg's grandeur. John D. Rockefeller, Jr. began pouring funds into the distressed city in 1926, restoring part of the town as a colonial village. His foundation still runs the restored section, a five-by-seven block town-within-a-town called Colonial Williamsburg, where fife and drum corps parade and cobblers, bookbinders, blacksmiths, and clock-makers go about their tasks using 200-year-old methods.

Street-side Punch and Judy shows, evenings of 18th-century theater, and militia reviews are just part of everyday business in Williamsburg. Though the fascinating and beautiful ex-capital claims to be a faithfully restored version of its 18th-century self, don't look for dirt roads, open sewers, or African slaves. Williamsburg also prides itself on William & Mary, the second-oldest college in the United States. Outside Williamsburg, Virginia's other big tourist sights lie in wait; history buffs should see Yorktown, Jamestown, or one of the restored plantations, while amusement park fans should head to Busch Gardens.

Practical Information

Emergency: 911.

Visitor Information: **Williamsburg Area Convention & Visitors Bureau,** 201 Penniman Rd. (253-0192), half a mile northwest of the transportation center. Free *Visitor's Guide to Virginia's Historic Triangle.* Open Mon.-Fri. 8:30am-5pm. **Tourist Visitors Center,** Rte. 132-132y (800-447-8679), 1 mi. northeast of the train station. Tickets and transportation to Colonial Williamsburg. Operated by the Colonial Williamsburg Foundation. Maps and guides to the historic district, including a guide for the disabled, available upstairs. Information, including prices and discounts on Virginia sights, available downstairs. Open daily 8am-8pm.

Transportation Center: at the end of N. Boundary St., across from the fire station. **Amtrak,** 229-8750 or 800-872-7245. To: New York ($79, 7hr.), Washington, DC ($28, 3 1/2hr.), Philadelphia ($58, 6hr.), Baltimore ($33, 5hr.), Richmond ($9, 1 1/2hr.), Virginia Beach ($13, 2hr.). Open Mon.-Tues. and Fri. 7am-9pm, Wed.-Thurs. and Sat. 7am-2:30pm, Sun. 1:30-9pm. **Greyhound/ Trailways,** 229-1460. Ticket office open Mon.-Fri. 8am-6pm, Sat.-Sun. 8am-4pm. To: Richmond ($9.50, 1hr.), Norfolk ($19.50, 2hr.), Washington, DC ($19.50, 4hr.). **James City County Transit (JCCT),** 220-1621. Service along Rte. 60, from Merchants Sq. in the Historic District, west to Williamsburg Pottery, or east past Busch Gardens. No service to Yorktown or Jamestown. Operates Mon.-Sat. 6:15am-6:20pm. Fare $1 plus 25¢ per zone change; exact change required.

Bike Rentals: **Bikes Unlimited,** 759 Scotland Ave. (229-4620), rents for $10 per day, with $5 deposit. Open Mon.-Fri. 9am-7pm, Sat. 9am-5pm, Sun. noon-4pm. **Bikesmith of Williamsburg,** 515 York Rd., rents single-speed bikes at $8.50 for 4 hr., $11.50 for the day.

Williamsburg Limousine Service: 877-0279. Both the local taxi and the cheapest guided tours. To Busch Gardens or Carter's Grove $8 round-trip. Guided tours to Jamestown ($19.50), Yorktown ($17.50), or both ($35), with admission fees included. Will take you to and from your Williamsburg lodgings. Make reservations for tours at least 24 hrs. in advance; call between 9am-1am.

Post Office, 425 N. Boundary St. (229-4668). Open Mon.-Fri. 9am-5pm, Sat. 10am-noon.

ZIP codes: 23185 (Williamsburg), 23690 (Yorktown), and 23081 (Jamestown).

Area Code: 804.

Williamsburg lies some 50 miles southeast of Richmond between Jamestown (10 mi. away) and Yorktown (14 mi. away). The Colonial Parkway, which connects Williamsburg, Jamestown, and Yorktown, has no commercial buildings along its route, which helps to preserve an unspoiled atmosphere. Travelers should visit in late fall or early spring to avoid the crowds, high temperature, and humidity of summer. Also, if you want to go to Colonial Williamsburg, don't follow the signs (they lead to the Visitors Center); instead take the Lafayette St. exit off the Colonial Pkwy. You'll be surprised at how easy it is to park.

Accommodations and Camping

The few bargains in the Williamsburg area lie along Rte. 60 west or Rte. 31 south to-ward Jamestown. From Memorial Day to Labor Day, rooms are scarce and prices high-er, so try to call at least two weeks in advance. Centrally located, family-run guest houses are clean, comfortable, cheap, and friendly alternatives to hotels. For a com-plete listing of accommodations, pick up a free copy of the *Visitors Guide to Virginia's Historic Triangle* at the convention bureau, *not* at the CWF Visitors Center (see Practi-cal Information).

The closest hostel, **Sangraal-by-the-Sea Youth Hostel (AYH/HI),** Rte. 626 (776-6500), near Urbanna, is 30 mi. away. They do provide rides to bus or train stations dur-ing business hours, but don't expect a daily ride to Williamsburg. (Singles $10, non-members more. Call ahead.) Closer to Williamsburg, guest houses are your best bet: some don't require reservations, but all expect you to call ahead, and most expect cus-tomers to avoid rowdiness and behave like house guests.

Only five minutes from the historic district, **Lewis Guest House,** 809 Lafayette St. (229-6116), frequently rents the upstairs unit with private entrance, kitchen and bath to a single person or couple for $25 a night. The friendly proprietor keeps a very short dog. One block away is **Mrs. H.J. Carter,** 903 Lafayette St. (229-1117). Dust mice wouldn't dare hide under the four-poster beds in these airy singles ($25) and doubles ($28). Be forewarned: Mrs. Carter will not let unmarried men and women sleep in the same bed. **The Elms,** 708 Richmond Rd. (229-1551), offers elegant, colorful, antique-furnished rooms to one or two visitors for $20. Both houses sleep eight. **Holland's Sleepy Lodge,** 211 Harrison Ave. (253-6476), rents one blue room at a time ($25). Ho-tels close to the historic district, especially chain- or foundation-owned hotels, do not come cheap. **The Southern Comfort Inn,** 1220 Richmond Rd. (229-8913), a ten-minute walk from William & Mary, has clean, ordinary rooms with colonial-looking façades and a pool. (Singles $25-30. Doubles $30-35.)

Several campsites blanket the area. **Anvil Campgrounds,** 5243 Moretown Rd. (526-2300), 3 miles north of the Colonial Williamsburg Information Center on Rte. 60, boasts a swimming pool, bathhouse, recreational hall, and store. (Sites $14-15, with hookup $21.) **Brass Lantern Campsites,** 1782 Jamestown Rd. (229-4320 or 229-9089), charges $10, with full hookup $14.

Food and Nightlife

Though Colonial Williamsburg proper contains several authentic-looking "taverns," few are cheap and most require reservations and forbid tank tops. For less pomp and more rustic circumstance, pack a picnic from one of the supermarkets clustered around the **Williamsburg Shopping Center,** at the intersection of Richmond Rd. and Lafay-ette St., or try the fast-food strip along Rte. 60. The **farmer's market** at Lafayette and North Henry St. sells cheap seafood or vegetables, depending on the farmer.

Chowning's Tavern, on Duke of Gloucester St. If you really have to eat in the historic district, you can wait in line for stew, sandwiches, or the misleading "Welsh Rabbit" (bread in cheese and beer sauce with ham) from $6. (Open daily 11:30am-3:30pm and 4pm-1am.) Join in the gambols after 9pm at Chowning's: costumed waiters serve mixed drinks, sing 18th-century ballads, and teach patrons how to play out-dated dice and card games.

The Old Chickahominy House, 1211 Jamestown Rd. (229-4689), rests over a mile from the his-toric district. Share the antiques and dried-flowered decor with pewter-haired locals whose ances-tors survived "Starvation Winter" in Jamestown. Miss Melinda's "complete luncheon" of Virginia ham served on hot biscuits, fruit salad, a slice of delectable homemade pie, and iced tea or coffee ($4.95) will fill you up for hours. Expect a 20-30 min. wait for lunch. (Open daily 8:30-10:15am and 11:30am-2:15pm.)

Paul's Deli Restaurant and Pizza, 761 Scotland St. (229-8976), a summer hangout for errant, leftover William and Mary students, sells crisp stromboli for two ($5.50-8.75) and filling subs ($3-5). The hot Italian subs are lipsmackers. (Open daily 10am-2am.)

Greenleafe Café, next door to Paul's Deli (220-3405), half-way upscale, serves sandwiches, salads, and the like ($5-10) and sways after 9pm on Tuesday (cover $2) to the quiet sounds of live folk music. Locals and students eat at a 20% discount. (Open daily 10:30am-2am.)

College Delly Restaurant, 336 Richmond Rd. (229-6627), faithfully delivers sandwiches and subs. The "Holly" (a bacon, roast beef, and turkey sub) can serve one hungry person or two delicate ones for $4. (Open daily 10:30am-2am; free delivery within limited area 6pm-1am.)

Sights

Unless you plan to apply to W&M, you've probably come to see the restored gardens and buildings, crafts, tours, and costumed actors in the historic district also known as **Colonial Williamsburg.** The Colonial Williamsburg Foundation (CWF) owns nearly everything in the historic district, from the **Governor's Palace** to the lemonade stands and even most of the houses marked "private home." A **Patriot's Pass** gains admission for one year to all the town's attractions (except Bassett Hall), to nearby Carter's Grove Plantation, and a one-hour guided tour ($28, ages 6-12 $17); a **Royal Governor's Pass** lasts the length of your visit and covers all the attractions in the town itself, the Governor's Palace, and the **Wallace Decorative Arts Museum** ($25.50, ages 6-12 $15.25); a one-day **Basic Admission Ticket** lets you into any of the historic area exhibits but none of the museums ($23, ages 6-12 $13.75). Buy them at the CWF Visitors Center or from booths in town.

"Doing" the historic district without a ticket definitely saves money; for no charge you can walk the streets, ogle the buildings, march behind the fife and drum corps, lock yourself in the stocks, and even use the restrooms. Some old-time shops that actually sell goods—notably **McKenzie Apothecary** by the Palace Green—are open to the public. Outdoor events, including a mid-day cannon-firing, are listed in the weekly *Visitor's Companion,* given away to ticket-holders—many of whom conveniently leave it where non-ticket-holders can pick it up.

Take one of the guided walking tours trampling Colonial Williamsburg night and day. The poorly-named but fascinating "Other Half" tour relates the experience of Africans and African-Americans (tours given March-Sept.; separate ticket ostensibly required). A two-hour tour called "Stepping into the Past" is designed especially for families (daily, $3).

Those willing to pay shouldn't miss the **Governor's Palace,** on the Palace Green. This mansion housed the appointed governors of the Virginia colony until the last one fled in 1775. Reconstructed colonial sidearms and ceremonial sabers line the reconstructed walls, and the garden includes a hedge maze. (Open daily 9am-5pm. Separate admission $14.)

Spreading west from the corner of Richmond and Jamestown Rd., the other focal point of Williamsburg, **The College of William & Mary,** is the second-oldest college in the U.S. Chartered in 1693, the college educated Presidents Jefferson, Monroe, and Tyler. The **Sir Christopher Wren Building,** also restored with Rockefeller money, is the oldest classroom building in the country. The Wren building faces the old Capitol, a mile away, at the other end of Colonial Williamsburg's main drag, **Duke of Gloucester St.** Nearby, the shops at **Merchant Square** sprawl a hair's breadth from the historic district. Park here and walk straight into the restored town proper.

Near Williamsburg

Jamestown and **Yorktown** are both important in the U.S. colonial story. The National Park System provides free, well-administered visitor's guides to the two areas, which sport two attractions each: the feds run Jamestown National Park and Yorktown Colonial Park, while Virginia operates the flashier Yorktown Victory Center and Jamestown Settlement. Combination tickets to Yorktown Victory Center and to Jamestown Settlement are available at either site for $10.25.

At the **Jamestown National Park** you'll see remains of the first permanent English settlement of 1607 and exhibits explaining colonial life. At the Visitors Center, skip the hokey film and catch a "living history" walking tour on which a guide portraying one of the colonists describes the Jamestown way of life. Call ahead (229-1733) for information since "living history" guides sometimes take the day off. (Site open daily 8:30am-dark; off-season 9am-5:30pm. Entrance fee $5 per car, $2 per hiker or bicyclist.)

Sniff around also at the nearby **Jamestown Settlement** (229-1607), a museum commemorating the Jamestown settlement, with changing exhibits, a reconstruction of James Fort, a Native American village, and full-scale replicas of the three ships which brought the original settlers to Jamestown in 1607. The 20-minute "dramatic film" lives up to its name and fills in the settlement's history, including an embarrassed treatment of settler relations with the indigenous Powhatan tribe. (Open daily 9am-5pm. Admission $7, under 13 $3.50.)

The British defeat at Yorktown signalled the end of the Revolutionary War. British General Charles Lord Cornwallis and his men seized the town for use as a port in 1781, but were stranded when the French fleet blocked the sea approaches. Colonists and French troops soon surrounded and stormed it, so the British soldiers surrendered. Yorktown's **Colonial Park** (898-3400) vividly recreates this last significant battle of the war with an engaging film, dioramas, and a smart-looking electric map (behind the information center). The park also maintains the remnants of the original trenches built by the British; guided tours of the British defense line are given throughout the day. Take a 7-mi. automobile journey 'round the battlefield; rent a tape cassette and recorder for $2 in the Visitors Center, to listen while you drive. (Open daily 8:30am-6pm; last tape rented at 5pm.)

The **Yorktown Victory Center** (887-1776), one block from Rte. 17 on Rte. 238, offers a museum brimming with items from the Revolutionary War, as well as a film and an intriguing "living history" exhibit: in an encampment in front of the center, a troop of soldiers from the Continental Army of 1781 takes a well-deserved break from active combat. Feel free to ask them about tomorrow's march or last week's massacre. (Open daily 9am-5pm. Admission $5.25, under 13 $2.75.) Pay careful attention to the importance of tobacco in the survival of these first successful settlements and towns.

Without a car, you won't find a cheap way to get to Jamestown or Yorktown; since the "towns" are tourist sights, guided tours provide the only transportation. With **Williamsburg Limousine** (877-0279), a group of at least four people can see both Jamestown attractions in the morning ($19.50 per person), both Yorktown sights in the afternoon ($17.50 per person), or take the whole day and see it all ($35). The unlined **Colonial Parkway** makes a beautiful biking route, but beware of inattentive motorists. You can rent a bike for $10 a day (plus a $5 deposit) at **Bikes Limited**, 759 Scotland Ave. (229-4620), in Williamsburg. (Open Mon.-Fri. 9am-7pm, Sat. 9am-5pm, Sun. noon-4pm.)

The James River **plantations,** built near the water to facilitate the planters' commercial and social life, buttressed the slave-holding Virginia aristocracy. Tour guides at **Carter's Grove Plantation,** 6 miles east of Williamsburg on Rte. 60, show off the restored house and fields. The last owners doubled the size of the original 18th-century building while trying to keep its colonial "feel." The Carter's Grove complex also includes reconstructed 18th-century slave quarters and, in front of the house, an archeological dig. The brand-new **Winthrop Rockefeller Archeological Museum,** built unobtrusively into a hillside, provides a fascinating case-study look at archeology.

Williamsburg Limousine (see above) offers daily round-trip tours from Colonial Williamsburg to the plantation ($8), but if you can, bike from South England Street in Colonial Williamsburg along the one-way, seven-mile, wooded **Carter's Grove Country Road**. (Plantation open daily 9am-5pm, Nov.-Dec. 9am-4pm; museum open daily 9am-5pm; slave quarters open daily 9am-5pm; Country Road open daily 8:30am-4pm, Nov.-Dec. 8:30am-3pm. Plantation admission $8, ages 6-12 $5, free with CWF Patriot's Pass.)

Berkeley Plantation (829-6018), halfway between Richmond and Williamsburg on Rte. 5, hosted the first Thanksgiving in 1619 and later saw the birth of U.S. President William Henry Harrison. Union Soldiers camped on the grounds here in 1862; one of them wrote the famous bugle tune *Taps*. Pause at the terraced box-wood gardens, which stretch from the original 1726 brick building to the James River. (House open daily 9am-5pm; grounds open 8am-5pm. Admission to house and ground $8, seniors $7.20, ages 6-16 $5. Admission to grounds $4, seniors $3.60, ages 6-16 $2.)

When you tire of history, head to **Busch Gardens: The Old Country,** 3 miles east of Williamsburg on Rte. 60 (253-3350). You'll be flung, splashed, and throttled by the various shows and rides. Each section of the park represents a European nation; trains and sky-cars connect the sections. **Questor,** a new ride, brings roller coasters into the video age, while trained birds prance in "Fethered Follies." The Loch Ness Monster rollercoaster is an enduring classic. Williamsburg Limousine and local buses serve Busch Gardens (see Practical Information above). (Open mid-March through Oct. daily 10am-midnight. Admission $24.95. Parking $3.)

A free monorail from Busch Gardens takes you to the **Anheuser-Busch Brewery** (253-3600), where tourists can get two free cups of Busch beer. Accessible from Interstate 64. (Open daily 10am-4pm. Free.)

Virginia Beach

Aaah, the beach. Gaze upon endless miles of water, sand, and sky; inhale the perfume of the tide; listen to the insistent rhythm of the waves. Then turn around and face the boardwalk.

Virginia Beach (population: 375,000) is unabashedly immersed in the present. Rows of hotels and motels, ice cream stands, surf shops and fast-food joints flank the golden coastline, and swarms of cruising college students and servicemen descend upon the beach resort every summer.

Practical Information

Emergency: 911.

Visitor Information: Virginia Beach Visitors Center, 22nd and Parks Ave. (425-7511 or 800-446-8038), across the street from the Center for the Arts. Helps you find budget accommodations and gives information on area sights. Open in summer daily 9am-8pm; Labor Day-Memorial Day daily 9am-5pm.

Public Transportation: Greyhound, 1017 Laskin Rd. (422-2998), connects with Norfolk, Williamsburg, and Richmond, and with Maryland via the Bridge Tunnel. To: Washington, DC ($36, 6 1/2hr.), Richmond ($21, 3 1/2hr.), Williamsburg ($12.50, 2 1/2hr.) The nearest **Amtrak** Station (245-3589 or 800-872-7245), in Newport News, provides free 45-min. bus service to and from the Radisson Hotel at 19th St. and Pavilion Drive in Virginia Beach, but you must have a train ticket to get on the bus. To: Washington, DC ($41, 5 1/2hr.), New York City ($79, 9hr.), Philadelphia ($68, 8hr.), Baltimore ($47, 7hr.), Richmond ($18, 3hr.), Williamsburg ($13, 2hr.).

Local Transportation: The **Virginia Beach Transit/Trolley Information Center** (428-3388) provides complete information on area transportation and tours, including trolleys, buses, and ferries. In summer, the **Atlantic Avenue Trolley** runs from Rudee Inlet to 42nd St. (Memorial Day-Labor Day daily noon-midnight; fare 50¢, seniors and disabled 25¢.) Other trolleys run along the boardwalk, the North Seashore, and to Lynnhaven Mall.

Bike Rentals: North End Cyclery, at Laskin Rd. and Arctic Ave. Open 10am-7pm. Bikes $3.50 per hr. or $15 per day. Moped Rentals, Inc., 21st St. and Pacific Ave. Open in summer daily 9am-midnight. Bikes $7 per 90 min., mopeds $22.50 per 90 min.

Post Office: 24th and Atlantic Ave. (428-2821). Open Mon.-Fri. 8am-11am and noon-4:30pm. **ZIP code:** 23458.

Area Code: 804.

Virginia Beach is confusing to get to, but easy to get around. Drivers from the north can take Interstate 64 south from Richmond through the Bay Bridge Tunnel into Norfolk, then get on Rte. 44 (the Virginia Beach-Norfolk Expressway), which delivers them straight to 22nd St. and the beach. Virginia Beach's street grid pits east-west numbered streets (from 1st to around 90th) against north-south avenues (Atlantic, Pacific, Arctic and Baltic) parallel to the beach.

Accommodations and Camping

Finding a cheap place to stay in Virginia Beach is like finding…well, like finding Angie's (see below). Atlantic Avenue and Pacific Avenue run parallel to the ocean front, buzz with activity during the summer, and boast the most desirable hotels; reserve as far in advance as possible. If you're traveling in a group, shop around for "efficiency rate" apartments which sometimes rent cheaply by the week.

Angie's Guest Cottage-Bed and Breakfast and AYH/HI Hostel, 302 24th St. (428-4690), still ranks as the best place to stay on the entire Virginia Coast. Barbara Yates (who also answers to "Angie") and her team welcome guests with exceptional warmth; they won't turn anyone away. They'll pick you up from the train station, go out of their way to help guests with job-and house-hunting, and may, in fact, themselves be a reason to visit Virginia Beach. (Open April 1-Oct. 1, March and Oct. with reservations. Memorial Day-Labor Day $10.50, non-members $13.50. Off-season $7.55, non-members $10.55. Linen $2. Kitchen and lockers available.) If you stay in the guest cottage, breakfast is included. (Doubles $44-62.) Call 10am-10pm for reservations.

An alternative is the **Ocean Palms Motel,** 30th St. and Arctic Ave. (428-8362 or 428-5357; singles $40). Or try the **Viking Motel,** 2700 Atlantic Ave. (428-7116, 800-828-3063 for reservations), just a block from the beach. (Singles from $45, off-season $25. Doubles from $60, off season $25.)

You can camp at the **Seashore State Park,** about 8 miles north of town on U.S. 60 (481-2131; 490-3939 for reservations), which has some juicy spots ($14). Because of its desirable location amid sand dunes and cypress trees, the park is very popular, so call two to three weeks ahead (during business hours) for reservations. (Park open 8am-dusk; take the North Seashore Trolley.) **KOA,** 1240 General Booth Blvd. (428-1444), runs a quiet campground with free bus service to the beach and boardwalk. (Sites $22, with hook-up $24. Comfortable and Kapacious 1-room cabins $38.) **Holiday Travel Park,** 1075 General Booth Blvd. (425-0249), is a mega-campground with 1000 sites, 4 pools, and miniature golf. (Sites $23, $27 with hookup.)

Food

Junk-food slughogs will love Virginia Beach, thanks to the jumble of fast-food joints along boardwalk and main drags. But don't let the neon glare blind you to restaurants with a more local flavor. **The Jewish Mother,** 3108 Pacific Ave. (422-5430), is one of the most popular eateries in town. The JM dotes on her customers with quiche, omelettes, crepes ($5-9), deli sandwiches ($4-6), and desserts ($2-4). At night it's a popular (and cheap) live-music bar. (Open daily 9am-3am.) **The Raven,** 1200 Atlantic Ave. (425-9556), lays out well-prepared seafood, steaks, and salad in a tinted-glass greenhouse setting. You can eat outdoors when it's warm. Sandwiches and burgers $4-6, dinners $9-15. (Open daily 11am-2pm.) **Giovanni's Pasta Pizza Palace,** 2006 Atlantic Ave. (425-1575), serves tasty Italian pastas, pizzas, and hot grinders. Lunches and dinners $5-7. (Open daily noon-11pm.)

Buy produce at **Virginia Beach Farmer's Market,** 1989 Landstown Rd. (427-4395; open daily 9am-6:30pm; open until dark in winter). At 31st St. (Luskin Rd.) and Baltic Ave., the **Farm Fresh Supermarket** salad bar, stocked with fresh fruit, pastas, and frozen yogurt at $2.39/lb., is a cheap alternative. (Open 24 hrs.)

Nightlife

On summer nights, it's a good idea for women to avoid walking the boardwalk alone; deadbeats sometimes congregate here. In darkness the beach becomes a haunt for lovers, while singles hover around the bars and clubs between 17th and 23rd St. along Pacific and Atlantic Ave. Locals favor **Chicho's** (422-6011) and the **Edge**, along Atlantic Ave. between 20th and 21st Streets. Dress code: T-shirts; short, tight dresses; tanned skin. Bartenders shout to one another underneath videos of surfing competitions and bungee jumping, while hopeful patrons run their eyes up and down their neighbors' figures. (Chicho's open Mon.-Fri. 5pm-2am, Sat.-Sun. 1pm-2am; no cover charge. The Edge open daily 4pm-1:30am; no cover.) Cheap drinks, live bands and graffiti-covered walls mingle and get mellow at the Jewish Mother (see Food). Most bars are open until

2am and in the morning you're liable to find puke-splattered partyboys passed out on the nice clean boardwalk. Clubs like **Peabody's** at the corner of 21st St. and Pacific Ave. feature neon lighting and live bands playing a variety of music. (Open 7pm-2am. Cover $5.)

Sights

The main sights here are the beach and its muscle-clad sun-worshippers, but museum-seekers can start with the **Virginia Marine Science Museum,** 717 General Booth Blvd. (425-3476), which traces marine life from mountain ponds to the Sargasso Sea. The Ocean Drive simulates the porthole view from an underwater investigative ship. (Open daily 9am-5pm, extended hours in summer. Admission $3.50, seniors and children $2.75.) Right off the beach at 24th St. in a former life-saving service station (the predecessor to the U.S. Coast Guard) stands the cozy **Life-Saving Museum of Virginia.** Earnest tour guides can tell you more than you ever thought you wanted to know about the origins of the Coast Guard. (Open in summer Mon.-Sat. 10am-5pm, Sun. noon-5pm; Sept.-May. Tues.-Sat. 10am-5pm, Sun. noon-5pm. Admission $2.50, over 60 and military personnel $2, ages 6-18 $1).

Virginia Beach is biker-friendly, with bike paths along the boardwalk and some of the larger streets. Rent a bike in one of the many stands near the boardwalk (about $5/hr.), then ask for the **Virginia Beach Bikeway Map** at the Visitors Center. If you're feeling athletic, bike south down the coast to **Sandbridge Beach,** where the locals hang out to avoid crowds of tourists; take the bike trail through the **Back Bay National Wildlife Refuge**. Or bike north to calm, self-descriptive **Seashore State Park.**

On the way back from Seashore State Park, test your psychic ability at the Visitors Center of the **Edgar Cayce Association for Research and Enlightenment,** 67th St. and Atlantic Ave. (428-3588), dedicated to psychic potential and holistic health. (Open Mon.-Sat. 9am-5:30pm, Sun. 1-6pm. June-Aug. Mon.-Sat. 9am-10pm, Sun. 1-10pm.)

Near Virginia Beach: Norfolk

Navy-heavy Norfolk (population: 286,000) is Virginia Beach's sister city. Slow, expensive city buses connect the two; don't bother. If you want to see more than one of the tourist sights in Norfolk, buy a **"Discover Tidewater" passport** for the **TRT Trolley** at the Virginia Beach Visitors Center or at the blue-and-white information booth at 24th and Atlantic Ave., in Virginia Beach (623-3222). With a one-day passport ($6; children, seniors and persons with disabilities $3.50) in your hand, you can catch a trolley into Norfolk every half-hour from the dome at 19th St. and Pacific Ave.

The **Chrysler Museum,** Olney Rd. and Mewbray Arch (622-1211), is Norfolk's jewel, offering an eclectic collection ranging from decorative art to religious icons. Occidental art hangs in chronological order; viewers begin in the 14th century and end in the 20th. Grab a map at the information desk and begin upstairs, proceeding clockwise around the courtyard. Don't miss the photography gallery and the 8,000-piece collection of glassware. (Open Tues.-Sat. 10am-4pm, Sun. 1-5pm. Free.) The museum is a stop on the "Discover Tidewater" trolley tour, but you can also take the #20 Bus (one-way fare $2.60).

Armchair admirals will love the **Norfolk Naval Base,** which contains the **Hampton Roads Naval Museum.** This humongous naval base keeps Norfolk's economy afloat—the Persian Gulf war, which sent the sailors away, meant economic disaster. Stroll down the pier to see the massive gray hulks of the U.S.'s crack warships. Come early; the hours are tricky. The tour office at 9809 Hampton Rd. (444-7955) opens daily from 8am-4pm and the museum opens daily from 9am-4pm, but be there before 3 or you'll be turned away. (Ship tours Saturday only, 1-4:30pm.) The "Discover Tidewater" passport includes this tour in its package, but you can also purchase a separate Norfolk Naval Base ticket ($4.50, seniors, disabled persons, and children under 12 $2.25). The driver will need a visitors' pass; get one across Hampton Rd. at Gate 5.

The Rest of Maryland

Used to be everyone knew what Maryland was about. There was the Chesapeake Bay, a picturesque, shellfish-rich estuary running straight through from the ocean north to Pennsylvania. On the rural Eastern Shore, small-town Marylanders captured crabs and raised tobacco. Across the bay in Baltimore, workers ate the crabs, loaded the ships, ran the factories and joined the club of blue-collar port cities from Cleveland to Providence. Then the federal government expanded, industry shrank, and Maryland had a new, slender core: not the Bay, but the Baltimore-Washington Parkway. Suburbs grew up and down the corridor, Baltimore cleaned up its smokestack act and the Old Line State acquired a new, liberal urbanity. As DC's homogenized commuter suburbs break the limits of Montgomery and Prince Georges Counties, Baltimore revels in its polyglot immensity, and Annapolis, the capital, stays small-town. The mountains and mines of the western panhandle are still ignored after all these years, geographic and cultural kin to West Virginia. If anything brings this state together, it may be a sense of proportion: forest and fields seem very exhaustible, rivers and islands aren't too big to explore, and cities—and their problems—are too small to seem endless. Even the Chesapeake Bay has changed: after centuries of living off it, Maryland must clean it up, and the Free State's license plates now read "Save the Bay."

Baltimore

Once a center of East Coast shipping and industry, "Bawlmer" (population: 751,000) declined structurally and economically from the late 1950s to the mid-70s. Its renaissance began as Mayor Donald Schefer launched a program to clean up pollution, restore old buildings, and convert the Inner Harbor into a tourist playground. Today, Harborplace has inspired dozens of lookalike waterfront malls along the eastern seaboard. Run by the articulate Kurt Schmoke, modern Baltimore still serves as Maryland's urban core, and old-time, shirtsleeve Bawlmer endures in the quiet limelight of Anne Tyler's novels. Near the downtown skyscrapers, old ethnic neighborhoods like Little Italy front Baltimore's signature row houses, whose unique façades are microcosms of the larger city—polished marble stoops represent the shiny Inner Harbor, while straightforward brick fits the proud and gritty urban environs. After the superb National Aquarium, try a stroll uphill to Mt. Vernon or through Fell's Point during the day. North of downtown, prestigious Johns Hopkins University generates pre-meds, philosophers, and some of the nation's best lacrosse teams.

Practical Information

Emergency: 911

Visitor Information: Baltimore Area Visitors Centers, 300 W. Pratt St. (837-INFO (-4636) or 800-282-6632), at N. Howard St. 4 blocks from Harborplace. Pick up a map, an *MTA Ride Guide*, and a *Quick City Guide*, a quarterly glossy with excellent maps and event listings. Open daily 9am-5pm. An **information booth** on the west shoreline of the Inner Harbor is often crowded. Open daily 10am-6pm. A **satellite booth at Penn Station** provides basic information, usually open late Fri. evenings, weekday mornings, and all day Sun.

Travelers Aid: 685-3569 (Mon.-Fri. 8:30am-4:30pm), or 685-5874 a 24hr. hotline. Desks at Penn Station (open Mon.-Thurs. 9am-noon, Fri. 9am-9pm, Sat. 9am-1pm, Sun. 10am-5pm) and the Baltimore-Washington Airport (open Mon.-Fri. 9am-9pm, Sat.-Sun. 9am-5pm).

Baltimore-Washington International Airport (BWI): 859-7100. On I-195 off the Baltimore-Washington Expressway (I-295), about 10 mi. south of the city center. Use BWI as your gateway to Baltimore or Washington, DC. Take MTA bus #230 downtown. Airport shuttles to hotels (859-0800) run daily every half hour 7am-midnight (to downtown Baltimore $8). Trains from BWI Airport run to Baltimore ($6, $9 Metroliner. MARC trains are considerably cheaper but are also slower and only run Mon.-Fri., $2.75). To Washington, DC ($10, $15 Metroliner MARC $4.25). BWI train office 410-672-6167.

Amtrak: Penn Station, 1515 N. Charles St. (800-872-7245), at Mt. Royal Ave. Easily accessible by bus #3, 11, or 18 from Charles Station, downtown. Trains run about every half hour to: New York ($59, $81 Metroliner), Washington DC ($12, $21 Metroliner), and Philadelphia ($27, $41

Metroliner). Ticket window open daily 5:30am-9:30pm, self-serve machines open 24hr. (credit card only).

Greyhound: Two locations: downtown at 210 W. Fayette St. (752-0868), near N. Howard St.; 5625 O'Donnell St. (744-9311), 3 mi. east of downtown near I-95. Frequent connections to: New York ($39 one-way, $70 round-trip), Washington, DC ($8.50, $16 round-trip), and Philadelphia ($15, $28 round-trip). Open 24hr.

Public Transport: Mass Transit Administration (MTA), 300 W. Lexington St. (539-5000 for recorded bus and Metro info., 333-3434 main office), near N. Howard St. Additional numbers: 760-4554 toll-free in Annapolis, 800-543-9809 elsewhere in Maryland and in DC. Operator answers Mon.-Fri. 6am-11pm, Sat. 8:30am-5pm. Bus and rapid-rail service to most major sights in the city; service to outlying areas is more complicated. Bus #230 serves the airport. Free MTA Ride Guide available at any visitor information center. Some buses run 24 hrs. **Metro** operates Mon.-Fri. 5am-midnight, Sat. 8am-midnight, Sun. 11am-7pm. Bus fare $1.10, transfers 10¢; Metro base rate $1.10.

Taxi: Yellow Cab, 685-1212; **G.T.P. Inc.** (to and from BWI airport), 859-1103.

Baltimore Trolley Tours: 410-752-2015. Tours and transportation to major sights in Baltimore. One-day pass good for unlimited boarding along the 90-min. loop. Trolleys every 30 minutes, daily 10am-4pm. Adults $9, children $4.50.

Car Rental: Thrifty Car Rental, BWI Airport (768-4900), and 2030 N. Howard St. (783-0300), 9 blocks from Penn Station; also call 800-367-2277 (24 hours). Economy cars from $34 per weekday, $22 per weekend, and $169 weekly. Unlimited mileage. Under 25 $10 extra per day. Airport branch open 6am-midnight. Must be 21 with a credit card. **Rent-A-Wreck,** 9006 Liberty Rd., and 5901 Pulaski Highway in Glen Burnie near the Beltway (325-2757). They do the "rent," you do the rest. From $20-30 per day, 50 free mi. 19 cents each additional mi. Must be 21. With cash payments, required $150 deposit and a Maryland driver's license. Open Mon.-Fri. 8am-4pm.

Help Lines: Sexual Assault and Domestic Violence Hotline, 828-6390. **Gay and Lesbian Hotline and Information,** 837-8888. Gay bars, meetings, and special events; operators daily 7:30-10:30pm, recording all other times.

Post Office: 900 E. Fayette St., 655-9832. **ZIP Code:** 21233.

Area Code: 301.

Baltimore is plagued by one-way streets. Pratt St. (which runs east across the Inner Harbor) and Charles St. (which runs north from the west corner of the Harbor) divide the city into quarters. Streets parallel to Pratt St. get "West" or "East" globbed onto their names, depending on which side of Charles St. a given block is. North-south streets get dubbed "North" or "South" of Pratt St. Interstates and signs deposit tourists at the Inner Harbor, near Pratt and Charles. The museum-heavy Mount Vernon neighborhood, reached by city buses #3, 9 and 11, exhibits itself up Charles St., north of the Inner Harbor, around Monument and Centre Ave. Little Italy hangs its hat a few blocks east of the Inner Harbor, past the Jones Falls Expressway; walk or drive east to Broadway, then turn right (south) and motor a few blocks to reach happening, bar-happy Fell's Point. The Visitors Center dishes out a good bus and road map.

Baltimore dangles in central Maryland, 100 mi. south of Philadelphia and about 150 mi. up the Chesapeake Bay from the Atlantic Ocean. The Jones Falls Expressway (I-83) halves the city with its southern end at the Inner Harbor, while the Baltimore Beltway (I-695) circles the city. I-95 cuts across the southwest corner of the city as a shortcut to the wide arc of that section of the Beltway. During rush hour, these interstates get slower than a whale on downers. Blue and green signs point drivers to tourist attractions. To drive from Washington, DC to Baltimore, take the Washington Beltway (I-495) to I-95 at exit 27 or to the Baltimore-Washington Expressway at exit 22. The two highways run roughly parallel. Take the Russell St. exit to reach the Inner Harbor. Without traffic, the trip will take less than an hour.

Accommodations and Camping

Expensive chain hotels dominate the Inner Harbor; for more reasonable options downtown, call **Amanda's Bed and Breakfast Reservation Service,** 1428 Park Ave. (225-0001 or 800-899-7533). The personalized service will match you with B&Bs in private homes, small inns, or yachts that suit your needs, whether you're allergic to cats

Madison Street
Monument St.
MOUNT VERNON
Penn Station
3
Greyhound Bus Terminal
Centre St.
4
5
6
Hamilton St.
Franklin St.
7
8
Mulberry St.
Pleasant St.
Saratoga St.
Pleasant St.
LEXINGTON MARKET
Josephine St.
Lexington St.
Marion   St.
Lexington St.
9
Fayette   St.
2
Baltimore St.
CHARLES CENTER
Redwood St.
Baltimore Arena
Lombard St.
14
Pratt Street
1
Camden Station
Camden St.
15
Orioles Stadium
Conway St.
Inner Harbor
Barre St.
Welcome St.
Lee St.
York St.
Hill
Hughes St.
19
Hughes St.
Key Highway
Montgomery St.
Churchill St.
Henrietta St.
Warren St.

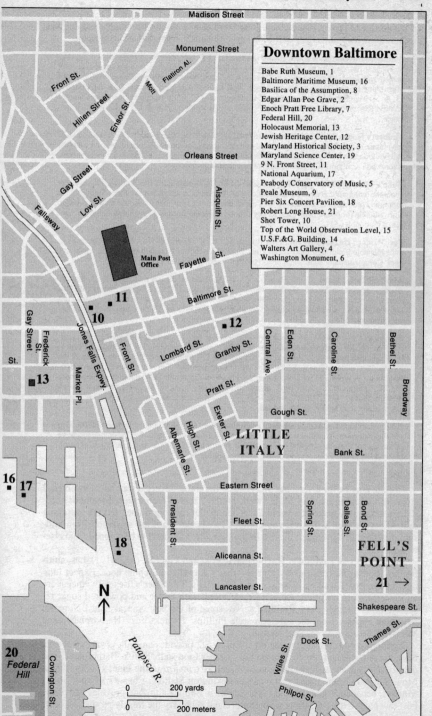

Madison Street
Monument Street

Front St.
Flatiron Al.
Mott
Hillen Street
Ensor St.

Orleans Street

Gay Street
Low St.

Fallsway

Alsquith St.

Main Post Office

Fayette St.

Downtown Baltimore

Babe Ruth Museum, 1
Baltimore Maritime Museum, 16
Basilica of the Assumption, 8
Edgar Allan Poe Grave, 2
Enoch Pratt Free Library, 7
Federal Hill, 20
Holocaust Memorial, 13
Jewish Heritage Center, 12
Maryland Historical Society, 3
Maryland Science Center, 19
9 N. Front Street, 11
National Aquarium, 17
Peabody Conservatory of Music, 5
Peale Museum, 9
Pier Six Concert Pavilion, 18
Robert Long House, 21
Shot Tower, 10
Top of the World Observation Level, 15
U.S.F.&G. Building, 14
Walters Art Gallery, 4
Washington Monument, 6

Baltimore St.

■ 11
10 ■

Jones Falls Expwy.

Gay Street

Frederick St.

St.

■ 13

Market Pl.

Front St.

Lombard St.

■ 12

Granby St.

Central Ave.

Eden St.

Caroline St.

Bethel St.

Pratt St.

Gough St.

Broadway

High St.

Exeter St.

**LITTLE
ITALY**

Bank St.

Albemarle St.

Eastern Street

16 ■
17 ■

President St.

Fleet St.

Spring St.

Dallas St.

Bond St.

**FELL'S
POINT**

18 ■

Aliceanna St.

Lancaster St.

21 →

N
↑

Shakespeare St.

20
*Federal
Hill*

Covington St.

Patapsco R.

Wills St.

Dock St.

Thames St.

Philpot St.

0   200 yards

0   200 meters

or would like to have a private bath. Rates start at $75 a night for singles and doubles. Reservations recommended. Call Mon.-Fri. 8:30am-5:30pm, Sat. 8:30am-noon.

Baltimore International Youth Hostel (AYH/HI), 17 W. Mulberry St. (576-8880), at Cathedral St. Elegant 19th-century brownstone provides 48 beds in dorms, kitchen, laundry, and lounge with baby grand piano. Window-unit A/C. Max. stay 3 nights, later with manager's approval. Lockout 10am-5pm. Curfew 11pm. Chores required. Near bus and Amtrak terminals. Take MTA bus #3, 11, or 18. Members $10, non-members $13. Sheet rental $2. Fully-equipped kitchen and laundry facility. Reservations recommended, especially in the summer; deposit advised 2 weeks in advance.

Mulberry House, 111 W. Mulberry St. (576-0111), downtown near Cathedral St. Fixed-up 1830 townhouse overflowing with antiques. All four doubles professionally decorated, two in Federalist and Victorian styles. Large modern baths are shared. Grand piano available in the sitting room. Rooms $65. Call hosts Curt and Charlotte Jeschke for reservations.

Duke's Motel, 7905 Pulaski Highway (686-0400), in Rosedale off the Beltway. Don't worry about the bulletproof glass in the front office—all the motels around here have them. Simple, clean rooms and probably the best deal on the Pulaski Hwy. motel strip, though slightly more expensive. Only suitable for people with cars. $2 key deposit and some form of ID required. Cable TV. Singles $36, doubles $41.

Best Western Harbor City Inn, 1701 Russell St. (727-3400 or 800-528-1234), near Beltway in unfashionable South Baltimore about 1 mi. from Inner Harbor. Standard rooms, free cable, and pool. Complementary continental breakfast. Free parking. Singles $53, doubles $55.

Abbey Schaefer Hotel, 722 St. Paul St. (332-0405). Right on the bus route from Penn. Station. slightly decrepit but functional rooms with working bathrooms. Great location. Rooms with "the works," attached bathroom and air conditioning $44. Rooms good for two people. For extras, roll out bed $8. Rooms without an attached bath $39. Rooms without A/C are even cheaper. $2 key deposit required.

Camping: Capitol KOA, 768 Cecil Ave. (923-2771 or 987-7477), near Millersville. Full facilities for tents, RVs, cabins. Free pool, movies. Family atmosphere. From DC take route 3 North to 97 North, then bear over to Veterans Highway (Route 178 south). Short distance to bottom of the hill, turn left under highway. Follow blue signs to campground. Ten miles from Baltimore Beltway, 16 mi. from DC, 11 mi. from Annapolis. Free weekday shuttle to Washington and Baltimore MARC Trains ($6.25 round trip). Shuttle leaves campground at 8am, departs Penn station 4:50pm. Tent site for 2 $19, RV site $20-$28. $4 per additional adult. Open April-Nov. Open until 10pm in summer, 8pm in spring and fall.

B&B: Maryland Bed and Breakfast Association, Box 23324: Baltimore, Maryland 21203. Skip the cheap floral prints, pastel walls, and thin mints—bed and breakfasts offer the double incentive of having comfortable, original rooms and full, hearty breakfasts. For particulars pick up a brochure at the visitor's center or write to the above address.

Food

Virginia may be for lovers, but Maryland is for crabs—every restaurant, convenience store, diner, cafeteria, and Mom (well, almost) serves crab cakes. Steamed, hard-shelled crabs may make you wield a wooden mallet for your dinner, but the seasoning rubbed on the shell will keep you going. Chesapeake crabs are in season from mid-summer through November; the rest of the year, the crabs tend to be shipped from elsewhere.

The Light Street Pavilion at **Harborplace,** Pratt and Light St. (332-4191), has multifarious foodstuffs to suit every tourist—that's why they all come here. Expect long lines and crowded walkways between the food stalls. **Thrasher's** fries with vinegar are an Eastern Shore tradition. **Anna's** Fried Dough with butter and powdered sugar resemble puffy funnel cakes. **Phillips'** serves some of the best crabcakes in Baltimore; buy them cheaper from the cafeteria-style Phillips' Express line. (Harborplace open Mon.-Sat. 10am-9:30pm, Sun. noon-8pm.)

Lexington Market, on Lexington at Eutaw St., provides an endless variety of produce, fresh meat, and seafood, as well as cheaper food stalls than at Harborplace. The quality may not be as high, but you can't get $1 *tempura* in the Inner Harbor. (Open Mon.-Sat. 6am-6pm. Take the subway to Lexington Station or bus #7.) **Cross Street Market,** between S. Charles and Light Streets in South Baltimore, provides one of the best raw bars in the city, along with produce and such. Try the freshly ground coconut, a specialty. Old South Baltimore families still run many stalls: the sixth generation bakes fresh bread at **Muhly's Bakery,** 1115 S. Charles St., though no longer for 5¢.

Food: Little Italy and Fell's Point

Bertha's Dining Room, 734 S. Broadway (327-5795), corner of Lancaster. Obey the bumper stickers and "Eat Bertha's Mussels." Gorge yourself on the black-shelled bivalves ($7) while sitting at butcher block tables. Locals of all ages crowd in to hear jazz bands play Mon.-Wed. and Fri.-Sat. nights. Ninety sorts of beer and ale ($1-6). Restaurant entrance on Lancaster St., wheelchair accessible. Kitchen open Sun.-Thurs. 11:30am-11pm, Fri.-Sat. 11:30am-midnight. Bar until 2am. Come for afternoon tea (make a reservation): share a platter of scones and assorted tarts with homemade whipped cream for only $7.40.

Café Madeira, 1623 Thames St. (675-7105). A "European style" dessert café whose owner reinvents the menu daily. Try a fruit tart or a slice of chocolate espresso cake ($3-5). Iced cappucino $1.50. Light lunches $1.50-5. Open Tues.-Thurs. 8am-10pm, Fri. 8am-midnight, Sat. noon-midnight, Sun. noon-6pm.

Al Pacino Café, 609 S. Broadway (327-0005). Egyptian pizza from a wood-burning oven to a hip young crowd of Method actors who imitate Al in the narrow dining room. Gourmet toppings like squid, rabbit sausage, and pignoli nuts. There may be a gun in the bathroom—if you know where to look. (Small pizza $6-8, med. $8-11, lg. $12-16.) Open Sun.-Thurs. 11am-midnight, Fri.-Sat. 11am-3am.

Obrycki's, 1727 E. Pratt St. (732-6399), near Broadway; take bus #7 or 10. Some of Balto's best crabs served every and any way—steamed, broiled, sauteed, or in crab cakes. Sandwiches $5-10. Steamed hard shell crabs $20-46 per dozen depending on size. Expect lines on weekends. Open Mon.-Fri. 12-11pm, Sat. 2-11pm, Sun. 2-9:30pm.

Food: Mount Vernon

Kawasaki, 413 N. Charles St. (659-7600). Best sushi in Balto, some say. Cozy, simple decor, with Japanese prints on the wall and low tables with cushions for seats. Park your motorcycle, take off your shoes, wriggle your toes, and make yourself at home. *A la carte* sushi $2.50-9, combinations $9-18. Open Mon.-Thurs. 11:30am-2:30pm and 5-11pm, Fri. 11:30am-2:30pm and 5pm-1am, Sat. 5pm-1am.

Buddies, 313 N. Charles St. (332-4200). Extensive salad bar with over 80 items (Mon.-Fri. 11am-2:30pm; $2.95 per lb.) and pile-driving sandwiches ($5-7). Jazz quartet draws in loyal locals and visitors of all ages (Thurs.-Sat. 9:30pm-1am). Domestic draft $1.60, imports $3-5. Happy Hour 4-7pm with an assortment of free food stuffs and 2-for-1 drinks. Show ID on Tues. nights and get $1 drafts. Open Sun.-Wed. 11am-1am, Thurs.-Sat. 11am-2am. Food served daily until 12:30am.

No Da Ji, 2501 N. Charles St. (235-4846 or 889-8621). New management. Japanese, Chinese and Korean cuisine in a sleek black and plum setting. Korean and Chinese dishes start from $7, Japanese sushi around $2. Don't order before looking at their great specials. Open Mon.-Sat. 11am-11pm, Sun. noon-10pm.

Louie's Bookstore Café, 518 N. Charles St. (962-1222), just up the street from the youth hostel. Upscale bookstore with extensive sections on music and philosophy. Lively café is upbeat and low key, home to half-starved artists and crunchy, indy-rock tourists. Live music at night. Sandwiches and burgers around $4-6. Entrees $8-10. Vegetarian available. Lunch is cheap; the dinner scene is groovier. Open Mon. 11:30am-midnight, Tues.-Thurs. 11:30am-1am, Fri.-Sat. 11:30am-2am, Sun. 10:30am-midnight.

Food: Farther out

Ikaros, 4805 Eastern Ave. (633-3750), 2 mi. east of downtown; take bus #10. This spawn of East Baltimore's Greek community is perfect for cheapskate romantics. Try *avgolemono* soup with egg, lemon, beef, and rice ($1.25) and spinach and feta pies ($2). Greek salads big enough for a meal ($4.50). Other specialties are *mousaka* ($6.25) and *kalamari* ($9). Open Sun.-Mon. and Wed.-Thurs. 11am-10pm, Fri.-Sat. 11am-11pm.

Bo Brooks, 5415 Belair Rd. (488-8144), Moravia Rd. exit off the Beltway. Maybe it does have Baltimore's "Best Steamed Crabs" ($20 per dozen) and crabcakes (from $5.50); it's hard to tell, what with the popular, tacky white dining room, and orange plastic chairs. Bo knows marketing techniques, as the T-shirts ("Bo Knows Crabs") prove. Take-out menu, but only at dinner. Draft beer $1.15. Imports $2. Open Mon.-Fri. 11:30am-3pm and 5-10:30pm, Sat. 5-11pm, Sun. 3:30-9:30pm.

Haussner's, 3242 Eastern Ave. (410-327-8365), at S. Clinton; take bus #10. An East Baltimore institution; cute paintings crowd the huge dining room, including some Rembrandt, Gainsborough, Whistler, and Winslow Homer copies. Central European cuisine like fresh pig knuckle and *sauerbraten* (meat stewed in vinegar and juices) $10, sandwiches $4 and up; big portions. Try their famous strawberry pie ($3.50), or get other freshly baked goods to go. No shorts after 3pm; lines for dinner on weekends. Open Tues.-Sat. 11am-10pm. Full menu all day long.

Sights

Most tourists start at the Inner Harbor, and all too many finish there. Baltimore's harbor terminates with a bang in a five-square-block body of water bounded on three sides by the National Aquarium, Harborplace, the Maryland Science Museum, and a bevy of boardable old and new ships; visitors roam the horseshoe-shaped perimeter and neglect the real neighborhoods to the east and north. But the **National Aquarium,** Pier 3, 501 E. Pratt St. (576-3800), makes the whole Inner Harbor worthwhile. Multi-level exhibits and tanks show off rare fish, big fat fish, red fish, and blue fish along with the biology and ecology of oceans, rivers, and rainforests. The angular building's glass-pyramid roof looks down on Harborplace from 157 feet up, and its exterior tiles copy nautical flag codes. "Wings Under Water" shines on 50 species of rays (including the playful manta) on the first level (fed daily 10:45am and 2pm), while levels 2, 3, and 4 spiral over central tanks and through various aquatic communities. The Icelandic coast vibrates with cheeky puffins and an undersea kelp forest (fed daily 11am, 1:30pm, and 3pm). The Children's Cove on level 4 lets kids and adults handle intertidal marine animals in the Touching Pool. Level 5 (inside the glass pyramid) is a steamy tropical rainforest; piranhas, parrots, and a pair of two-toed sloths peer through the dense foliage. Subtle eco-propaganda on the walls shows how we've gunked up our rivers and seas. Exit down a four-story series of ramps inside a 13-foot deep, doughnut-shaped tank simulating a coral reef—it's like scuba-diving without getting wet. Below this tank lurk sharks of all shapes and sizes, close enough to touch without losing a hand [Aaaah!— Ed.] The Marine Mammal Pavilion touts dolphins and whales, including an amphitheater with performances à la Sea World. Arrive before 9am to avoid long lines; on weekends buy a ticket from the booth outside and return at the time printed on the ticket (usually 1/2 hr. later, but up to 3 1/2hr. in summer). Tickets can also be purchased in advance from TicketMaster (800-481-7328 in Baltimore; 202-432-7328 in Washington, DC) with a small service fee. Expect to spend three hours in the Aquarium. Excellent disabled access through separate entrance; call ahead. (Open Mon.-Thurs. 9am-5pm and Fri.-Sun. 9am-8pm; Sept.-May Sat.-Thurs. 10am-5pm, Fri. 10am-8pm. Admission $11.50, seniors $9.50, ages 3-11 $7.50, under 3 free. Sept.-May Fri. after 5pm, admission $2.)

Several ships bob in the harbor by the aquarium, among them the musty frigate **Constellation** (539-1797), which shows walk-through visitors the joys and travails of life in an old sailing ship. The first commissioned ship of the U.S. Navy, the Constellation sailed from 1797 until 1945, serving in the War of 1812, the Civil War, and as a flagship of the Pacific Fleet during World War II. Go below decks to see (and aim) the cannons. (Powzer!) (Open daily 10am-8pm, May-June and Sept.-Oct. 10am-6pm, Nov.-April 10am-4pm. Admission $3, seniors $2, ages 6-15 $1.50, active military $1, children under 6 free.) Also moored in the harbor, U.S.S. Torsk submarine, which sank the last Japanese combatant ships of WWII, and the lightship Chesapeake, a floating navigational lighthouse, make up the **Baltimore Maritime Museum** 9396-9304) at Pier III. (In contrast to the Constellation's wooden decks and sails, these two ships are thoroughly modern vessels. 396-9304. Open daily 9:30am-4:30pm; admission $3, seniors $2.50, children 12 and under $1.50, active military free.)

If imitation is the sincerest form of flattery, **Harborplace** is Baltimore's most flattered building. When then-Mayor Schaefer and developer James Rouse decided to make the Inner Harbor tourist-friendly, they started by building an air-conditioned shopping mall at the water's edge; Harborplace was the first and maybe the best of the pier-pavilions now also in New York, Detroit, and San Francisco. Stop by Harborplace's **Pratt Street Pavilion** and the **Gallery,** across the street on the corner of Pratt and Light Streets, for a little wharfside shopping and air-conditioned bliss (332-4191; open Mon.-Sat. 10am-10pm, Sun. noon-8pm). See *Food* for the superior food court.

At the Inner Harbor's far edge lurks the **Maryland Science Center,** 601 Light St. (685-5225), where children can learn basic principles of chemistry and physics cleverly disguised as hands-on games and activities. The Energy Place tires them out with pulleys and levers, while the Structures exhibit allows children to explore architecture and the arts of building. The IMAX Theater's five-story screen stuns audiences; the planetarium is pretty neat, too. On summer weekends, come in the morning before the lines get too long. (Open Mon.-Thurs. 10am-6pm, Fri.-Sun. 10am-8pm; Sept.-May Mon.-Fri. 10am-5pm, Sat. 10am-5pm, Sun. noon-6pm. Admission $8, children, seniors, military $5.50. Separate IMAX shows Fri.-Sat. evenings $5.)

In South Baltimore on Key Highway, **Federal Hill Park** offers a view of the Inner Harbor from across the water as well as a look at the more mundane shipping and warehouse sections. A party of 3,000 guests celebrated the adoption of the Federal Constitution by the Maryland Senate in April 1788 at this site. During the Civil War, cannons on the hill guarded the harbor and an observation tower warned of incoming ships. But the biggest threat to the Union came from the other direction. Much of Baltimore was fiercely pro-Confederate; the state song "Maryland, My Maryland" warns the city, "The despot's heel is on thy shore"—guess who? Abe Lincoln. The old tunnels around Federal Hill, sometimes taken for Union passages to Fort McHenry, are really just old iron and clay mines.

Some of Baltimore's best restored homes lie to the west of Federal Hill. **Montgomery Street** gives perhaps the best example, with its grand façades and cobblestone streets. To the east along Key Highway, dilapidated warehouses loom along the shore. The industrial behemoth at 1415 Key Highway holds the **Baltimore Museum of Industry** (727-4808) in one of its warehouses. (Take bus #19x or 20x.) The museum displays the inventions which made Baltimore an industrial center; in a weird throwback to the good old days of child labor, children can run the many working machines. The star exhibit is the oyster cannery, which canned from 1865 to 1985. Children can shuck oysters, fill the cans, or print the labels. The "foreman" pays each child in tokens, redeemable only at the General Store; John L. Lewis would not be pleased. (Open Tues.-Fri. and Sun. noon-5pm, Sat. 10am-5pm; Sept.-May. Thurs.-Fri. and Sun. noon-5pm, Sat. 10am-5pm. Admission $3, students and seniors $2, families $10.)

Fort McHenry National Monument (962-4290), located at the foot of E. Fort Ave. off Rte. 2 (Hanover St.) and Lawrence Ave. (take bus #1), commemorates its victory against British forces in the War of 1812. This famous battle of Sept. 12-14, 1814, inspired Francis Scott Key to write "The Star Spangled Banner." Admission ($1, seniors and under 17 free) includes entrance to the museum, a way-too-long film, and a tour of the fort. Rangers in costume give tours every hour on the half-hour. A flag flies over the fort all day, but *the* flag hangs in the Smithsonian Museum of American History in Washington, DC. Take the bus #1 or a narrated cruise from the inner harbor (round trip $4.40). (Open daily 8am-8pm; Sept.-May 8am-5pm, admission $1. Wheelchair-accessible; film captioned for the hearing impaired. Ample parking.)

A few museums dwell among the row houses east of the Inner Harbor. The **Babe Ruth Birthplace and Baseball Center,** 216 Emory St. (727-1539; take bus #31), off the 600 block of W. Pratt, remembers the "Sultan of Swat." Some exhibits pitch to diehards only, like the alcove recalling each of his 714 home runs. Others swing at a wider audience with Maryland baseball memorabilia; one display documents the amazing Oriole climb from last place in 1988 to "almost first" in 1989. Chalk 1991 up to almost last place again, guys. (Open daily 10am-5pm, on game nights until 7pm; Nov.-March 10am-4pm. Admission $4, seniors $2.50, under 16 $1.50.)

Itself once a station for the Baltimore & Ohio Railroad, the **B&O Railroad Museum,** 901 W. Pratt St. (752-2388; take bus #31), looks out on train tracks where dining cars, Pullman sleepers, and mail cars park themselves for your touring frenzy. Inside the museum, three films chug through the history of railroads. The Roundhouse captures historic trains and replicas thereof, including the 1829 "Tom Thumb," the first American steam-driven locomotive. Don't miss the extensive model train display. (Open daily 10am-5pm. Admission $5, seniors $4, ages 5-18 $3, under 5 free.)

The divine Edgar sleeps evermore in the **Edgar Allan Poe Grave** in the Westminster Churchyard (328-7228), at Fayette and Greene St. (Tours every first and third Friday evening and Saturday morning of the month.) Every year on the anniversary of Poe's death (Oct. 7, 1849), a mysterious visitor dressed in black decorates his grave with cognac and roses. Edgar Allan Poe came into this world at the **Edgar Allan Poe House** (328-7228), now in a somewhat seedy area at 203 Amity St. off Saratoga St. (bus #15 or 23). It wasn't called that at the time. The short-lived, mustachioed, 1830s author virtually invented the horror tale and the detective story; he also penned macabre, extravagantly vacant poems. The tour ushers Poe-heads through the writer's biography and around the tell-tale original furniture. (Poe house open Wed.-Sat. noon-3:45pm; admission $2, under 13 $1.) The **H.L. Mencken House,** 1524 Hollins St. near Gilmore St. (396-7997), reached by bus #2 or 20, does the birthplace/commemorative thing for the essayist, wit, and social critic whose *American Spectator* improved the vocabularies and soured the outlooks of thousands of 1920s readers. The Sage of Baltimore would probably frown on the attention paid to *his* original furniture. (Mencken house open Wed.-Sun. 10am-5pm, Nov.-March 10am-4pm, tours weekends on the hour; admission $1.75, seniors and college students $1.25, ages 6-18 75¢, under 6 free, family $5.)

The **Mount Vernon** neighborhood, a mix of hip and stiff-upper-lip, is one of Baltimore's cultural cores. Its center is Baltimore's own **Washington Monument**, designed by Robert Mills, who later planned the more famous Monument in DC. The older monument shows a 16-ft. tall General Washington resigning his commission as Commander of the Continental Army. Vertiginously carved atop a 160-foot column, the statue suggests that Washington never lost his poise. Take bus #3 or 31 up N. Charles St. to reach the sights in this area. A few blocks south of the Washington Monument, the **Basilica of the Assumption**, sometimes called America's most beautiful building, basks at the corner of Cathedral and Mulberry Streets. Benjamin Latrobe, who helped design the U.S. Capitol, planned the Basilica in 1806. The first Roman Catholic church in the United States, it mixes Greek Revival lines with an octagonal base and Kremlin-style twin onion domes in a strange cultural assemblage. No one knows how the domes got there, since Latrobe's original plans called for round towers. (Open Mon.-Fri. 7-9am and 11am-1pm, Sat. 7-9am and 4-6pm, Sun. 7am-6pm. Free tours available at noon on the second and fourth Sun. every month. Call 727-3564 to arrange for other times.)

Baltimore's best museum, the **Walters Art Gallery,** 600 N. Charles St. at Centre (547-9000), keeps one of the largest private collections in the world, spanning 50 centuries. The museum's biggest deal is the Ancient Art collection on the second level, with sculptures, jewelry, and metalwork from Egypt, Greece, and Rome. Seven marble sarcophagi with intricate relief carvings are of a type found in only two known collections (the other is the National Museum in Rome). Children will dig the Egyptian mummies and mummy cases. The third level holds medieval art from the Byzantine, Romanesque, and Gothic periods, especially jewelry and metalwork. Paintings on the third and fourth levels give a nod to every European school between the 12th and the 19th centuries. Particular strengths are the Italian works and Impressionists, including Manet's *At the Café* and Monet's *Springtime.* **Hackerman House,** the flashy new addition to the Walters on the third level, accumulates art from China, Korea, Japan, India, and Southeast Asia. The early Buddhist sculptures from China are very rare, as are the Japanese decorative arts of the late 18th and 19th century. Some of the finest examples of the often-copied Ming Dynasty Peachbloom Vases can be found here. (Open Tues.-Sun. 11am-5pm. Admission $4, seniors $3, students and children under 18 free; Wed. free. Tours given Wed. 12:30pm and Sun. 2pm.)

Across the street from the Walters at 1 E. Mount Vernon Place, the **Peabody Conservatory of Music** (659-8124), attracts classical musicians and students from everywhere. Founded in 1857, the conservatory is the oldest school in the United States for classical musicians. The beauty of the neo-Renaissance façade continues inside: the six-tiered library with cast-iron columns and railings and a cold, smooth marble floor will leave you awe-struck. Writer John Dos Passos loved the room so much he did most of his research here. During the school year, the concert hall in the west wing holds weekly concerts by students, faculty, and visiting artists; call for information. (Conservatory library open Mon.-Sat. 9am-5pm. Free.) **The Baltimore School for the Arts,** 712 Cathedral St. (396-1185), once the Alcazar Hotel, now teaches public high school students talented in the performing arts. Tours by appointment, but the exhibitions in the Alcazar Gallery are open to the public.

Approximately three miles north of the harbor on N. Charles St. (bus #3, 9, or 11), **Johns Hopkins University** spreads out from 33rd St. The beautiful campus lies on a 140-acre wooded lot that was originally the Homewood estate of Charles Carroll, Jr., the son of a signer of the Declaration of Independence. Free tours of the campus are available at the Office of Admissions in Garland Hall (May-Sept. Mon.-Fri. 10am, noon, and 3pm; up to six times each day during the academic year. Call 338-8171 for times and to reserve Sat. tours.) Two historic houses administered by the university also lie on the campus. **Homewood** (338-5589), the elegant house belonging to Carroll, displays 18th and 19th-century furnishings, some originals to the house; **Evergreen House** (516-0895), seated on 26 acres north of the main campus on N. Charles St., shows the mansion, private theatre, carriage house, and gardens of Ambassador John Work Garrett and family. (Homewood open Mon.-Fri. 11am-5pm, Sun. noon-4pm; admission $5, Hopkins students 1/2 price, under 12 free; tours offered every hour 10am-3pm. Evergreen open Sun. 1-4pm, Mon.-Fri. 10am-3pm; admission $5, students 1/2 price, Hopkins students free; tours offered every hour 10am-3pm.) **The Lacrosse Hall of Fame Museum**, 113 West University Parkway (410-235-6882), squats at the end of the Johns Hopkins Lacrosse fields. Opened in 1992, this low white building contains trophies, jerseys, a display on the evolution of the lacrosse stick and helmet, and countless pictures of snarling men and sweating women leaping at each other. Adults $2, students $1. (Open Mon.-Fri. 9am-5pm, Sat. 10am-3pm.)

To the west of campus at N. Charles and 31st St., the **Baltimore Museum of Art** (396-7100 or 396-7101) exhibits a fine collection of Americana and modern art, including several pieces by Andy Warhol. The collection also strives to impress with paintings or sculpture by Matisse, Picasso, Renoir and Van Gogh. Two adjacent sculpture gardens of 20th-century works make wonderful picnic grounds as well. In residence at the museum, the **Baltimore Film Forum** shows classic and current American, foreign, and independent films on Thurs. and Fri. at 8pm (admission $5); pick up a schedule at the museum or call 889-1993. (Museum open Tues.-Wed. and Fri. 10am-4pm, Thurs. 10am-7pm, Sat.-Sun. 11am-6pm. Admission $4.50, seniors and full-time students $3.50; Thurs. free, ages 4-18 $1.50, under 3 free. Metered parking available. Wheelchairs available.)

Off Jones Falls Parkway on Druid Park Lake Drive, **Druid Hill Park** (396-6106) contains the **Baltimore Zoo** (366-5466), a spectacular Palm Tree Conservatory, and a lake surrounded by lush greenery. The zoo features elephants in a simulated savannah, Siberian tigers, and a waterfall. The Children's Zoo imports farm animals and animals from the Maryland wilds, like otters and crafty woodchucks. Children can also ride a carousel and a "zoo choo" train (rides $1.25). Open Monday-Friday 10am-4:20pm. Children's Zoo and Conservatory close 15 minutes earlier; everything closes early in winter. Admission $6.50, seniors and ages 2-15 $3.50, under 2 free. Kids under 15 go for free on the first Saturday of each month.

In the eastern section of downtown, the **Peale Museum,** 225 Holliday St. (396-1149), is one of Baltimore's City Life Museums. Once the location of the old city hall, the Peale Museum was built by portrait painter Rembrandt Peale in honor of his father Charles Wilson Peale in 1814, making it the oldest museum building in the U.S. A permanent exhibit of more than 40 portraits painted by the Peale family (Rembrandt was just the most famous son) as well as some traveling exhibits are housed there. (Open Tues.-Sat. 10am-4pm, Sun. noon-4pm.)

The rest of the City Life Museums (other than H.L. Mencken House) line up in **"Museum Row"** at 800 E. Lombard St. (396-4545). On your way there, peer up at the **Shot Tower** on the corner of E. Fayette St. and Jones Falls Expressway. The Shot Tower looks like a huge smokestack; molten lead, dropped from the top, shaped itself into shotgun pellets as it fell and cooled. **Carroll Mansion** (396-3523) belonged to Charles Carroll, signer of the Declaration of Independence; it shows a signal example of the lifestyle of a mid-19th century upper-class family. In contrast, **1840 House,** the rowhouse next door, was home to a craftsman's family of the same time period. The **Center for Urban Archaeology** shows how archaeologists work to uncover the lipstick traces of a city's history. (Open Tues.-Sat. 10am-5pm, Sun. noon-5pm; museum closes at 4pm in winter. Admission $4 to all four museums, $1.75 to one museum; seniors $3 for all, $1.25 for one; ages 6-18 $2 for all, 75¢ for one. Sat. free 10am-1pm.)

The **Jewish Heritage Center** is a three building complex located at 15 Lloyd St. (732-6400). On the left, the **Lloyd Street Synagogue,** built in 1845, was Maryland's first synagogue; the **B'nai Israel Synagogue,** the building on the far right, was founded in 1876 to preserve Orthodox religious practices; and between the two synagogues, the **Jewish Historical Society of Maryland** has established a library and museum to house documents, photographs, and objects reflecting Maryland Jewish history. The center studies in the heart of East Baltimore, where Maryland's first Jews settled. (Open Tues.-Thurs. and Sun. noon-4pm, other times by appointment. Library open by appointment. Admission $2; kids free.) A few blocks away on a hillside at Gay and Water Streets, the concrete **Holocaust Memorial** remembers the six million Jews who died in the concentration camps of WWII. On the other side of the hill, facing Lombard St., a statue of flames engulfing the bodies of the Nazis' victims will shock you, especially after the less emotional symbolism of the memorial. The base of the statue quotes George Santayana: "Those who forget the past are condemned to repeat it."

For Baltimore's historic districts, take bus #7 or 10 from Pratt St. to Albemarle St. to reach **Little Italy,** or ride the same buses to Broadway and walk down four blocks to **Fell's Point.** Italians emigrated from Genoa to the U.S. in the early 19th-century and helped establish Little Italy in Baltimore, but the largest influx of Italians rode south from New York on the B&O Railroad in the 1850s. Hoping to earn enough money to go west and find their fortune in gold, many settled permanently in Baltimore instead. The neighborhood around Albemarle, Fawn, and High Streets is still predominantly Italian, even if the restaurant clientele no longer are; many of the brownstones have stayed in one family for generations. Fell's Point, by the harbor, imitates old Baltimore with cobblestone streets, quaint shops, and historic pubs.

Useful Stores

St. Paul's Wash, 702 St. Paul St. (727-0843). Right across from the Abbey Schaeffer Hotel. 50¢ for soap. Washers $1, dryers 25¢. Coffee while you wait 25¢ (lighten it with Cremora™). Drop off service available. Open daily 7am-11pm.

Metro Coin-up Laundry, 1700 N. Charles St. (547-5655). Across the street from Penn. Station. Clean and comfortable place to do laundry. Washing powder 50¢. Washers $1.25, dryers 25¢. Roller baskets available. Suspended TV helps to pass the time between loads. Open Mon.-Sat. 7am-8pm, Sun. 8am-6pm.

Entertainment and Nightlife

The **Pier Six Concert Pavilion** (625-4230) at—where else?—Pier 6 in the Inner Harbor presents big-name musical acts at 8pm from late July to the end of September. Get tickets at the Mechanic Theatre Box Office Oct.-May, then at the pavilion or through TeleCharge (625-1400 or 800-638-2444) for the rest of the summer ($12-25). Sit on Pier 5, near Harborplace, and overhear the music for free. The **Baltimore Symphony Orchestra** under conductor David Zinman plays at Meyerhoff Symphony Hall, 1212 Cathedral St. (783-8000), from September to May and during their July Summerfest. (Tickets $15-45; box office open Mon.-Fri. 10am-6pm, Sat.-Sun. noon-5pm, and 1 hr. before performance.) The Lyric Opera House down the street at Mt. Royal and Cathedral Streets (685-5086) hosts the **Baltimore Opera Company** from September to May. Broadway hits get a tune-up at the **Morris Mechanic Theatre**, Baltimore and N. Charles Streets (625-1400). All these venues are wheelchair-friendly.

The **Theatre Project,** 45 W. Preston St. (752-8558), near Maryland St. experiments with theater, poetry, music and/or dance Wednesday to Saturday at 8pm and Sunday at 3pm. (Tickets $14, seniors, students and starving artists $8; box office open Tues. noon-5pm, Wed.-Sat. 1-9pm, Sun. noon-4pm; charge tickets (752-8558)). The **Arena Players,** a Black theater group, show musicals, comedies, drama, and dance at McCullough St. and Martin Luther King, Jr. Blvd. (728-6500). The **Baltimore Arts United (BAU) House,** 1713 N. Charles St. (659-5520), near Lanvale, hosts frequent jazz concerts, poetry readings, local art shows, chamber music, and rock 'n roll (tickets $4-7).

The supper club **Blues Alley,** 1225 Cathedral St. (837-2288), showcases world-renowned artists such as Wynton Marsalis, Sarah Vaughan, and Dizzy Gillespie. (Same management as the DC Blues Alley.) Shows are at 8 and 10pm, with a midnight show on Friday and Saturday. The **Left Bank Jazz Society** (945-2266) can tell you what's happening jazz-wise every week.

The **Showcase of Nations Ethnic Festivals** celebrates Baltimore's ethnic neighborhoods with a different culture each week from June through September. Though somewhat generic, the fairs are always fun, vending international fare and the inescapable crab cakes and beer. Most events happen at **Festival Hall,** W. Pratt and Sharp Streets. (Call 752-8632 or 800-282-6632.)

The beloved Baltimore Orioles now play at their new stadium at **Camden Yards**, just a few blocks from the Inner Harbor at the corner of Russell and Camden Streets. Bawlmer holds its breath for the yearly ups and downs of the O's with an attention no other city could ever *hope* to match.

Bars

The Hippo, 1 W. Eager St. (547-0069). Baltimore's largest and most popular gay bar, with pool tables, videos, and a packed dance floor. The first Sunday of every month is Ladies' Tea (6-9pm); Wednesday is R&B; Thursday is Men's Night. Cover varies. Saloon open daily 3pm-2am. Dance bar open Wed.-Sat. 10pm-2am. Video bar open Thurs.-Sat. 10pm-2am.

Orpheus, 1003 E. Pratt St. (276-5599), corner of S. Exeter St. Theme decor changes every two months; crowded dance floor with balcony upstairs. Regular DJ Thurs., Sat., and Sun. nights; guest DJs with their own followings during the rest of the week. Mon. is insomnia night; $3 cover for 18-21 year-olds, all night; $1 cover for 21 and over, before 11pm; after 11pm $2. Wed. is drink and drown night; there's no cover and $5 will buy you all you can drink, you gurgling codger. Must be 18 and over for Wed.-Sat. Sun. is teen night (cover $5). Dress code: "wild." Domestic beer from $2, imports $3, mixed drinks $2. Open Mon., Wed.-Sat. 9pm-2am, Sun. 7:30pm-1am.

Fat Tuesday's, 34 Market Place (727-4822), in the Brokerage. Hot pink and turquoise loosens the collars of young professionals. Famous for 30-odd frozen drinks like the Jungle Juice and Colada 151 (made with 151 rum) dispensed like Tastee-Freez from a row of churning machines ($3.25-5). Free samples. Happy hour (Mon.-Fri. 4-7pm) features draft beer, wine, or shooters for $1; drafts regularly $1.75, wine $2. Live music Tues., and Thurs. No cover on Tues.; $2 cover on Thurs. Open Mon.-Fri. 3pm-2am, Sat.-Sun. 1pm-2am.

Allegro, 1101 Cathedral St. (837-3906), near Chase St. in the theater district. Mix of gay and straight. Mellow happy hour (Mon.-Sat. 6-8pm, Sun. 4-8pm) with 2-for-1 beers and mixed drinks; a younger crowd gathers when the DJ starts at 9pm. Disco and top-40 dance music nightly. Tuesday is men's night; Thursday is women's night; Wednesday is 70s disco night; drag shows happen periodically. Cover $2. Domestic draft $2.25, or mixed drinks $2.50. Open daily 6pm-2am.

The Sanctuary, 723 S. Broadway (327-8800), in Fell's Point. Biggest and hottest dance club in Fell's Point. Holds 450, fishbowl-style—huge main floor and a balcony above for spectators and public dancers. Palm trees, flashing lights, and fluorescent paint-splattered walls. Thurs.-Sat. is "progressive" music; Sun. is top-40. Happy hour Fri.-Sun. 8:30-10:30pm features 2-for-1 drinks. Four bars serve 16 oz. draft for $2.25. No cover during happy hour; cover changes daily after 10:30pm. No tanks, midriff shirts, or cutoffs. Open Thurs.-Sun. 8:30pm-1:30am.

Baltimore's Original Sports Bar, 34 Market Place (244-0135), the Brokerage. Total entertainment: 50 TVs, a batting cage, video games, pinball, foozball, pool tables, and darts. Boxing ring doubles as a dance floor. Volleyball court outside on patio. Hot damn. On some Wed. evenings and on Fri. 5-7pm you can feast off of their sumptuous 30ft.-long buffet. Happy hour Mon.-Fri. 4-8pm includes $1 draft, $1.50 bottled domestics. Drafts usually $1.50, bottled imports $3, mixed drinks $2.50. Live music on Thurs. and Fri. nights. Cover on Thurs. nights $1, on Fri. before 8pm $2, after that $3. Kids welcome on Sat.-Sun. noon-6pm.

Max's on Broadway, 735 S. Broadway (276-2850, concert schedule 675-6297), at Lancaster St. in Fell's Point. Alternative rock leavened with occasional jazz &/or blues. National acts like Echo and the Bunnymen, Lowen Navarro, and Arrested Development on weeknights. Fri.-Sat. features cover bands and Gordon Mill kicks off the week with Mon. Night Madness (tickets $3-5). Most shows start around 9:30pm, doors open at least an hour before. Tickets at the club or Ticketmaster (800-481-7328). Drinks run between $2.75-5.25.

Annapolis

Like an antique car with brand-new shiny parts, Annapolis both flaunts and hides its age. Though the major industry here is the government of Maryland, forget about office buildings and stuffed shirts; instead of a downtown, Annapolis has a historic waterfront district. Narrow streets, flanked by restored 18th-century brick, run downhill to the crowded, commercial, and weirdly clean docks, where yachts relax on the water, along with their tanned and summery owners. Crew-cut "middies" (students) from the Naval Academy mingle with longer-haired students from St. John's and affluent couples here for "weekend getaways." A real town (however slender) slumbers beneath the trellises; if all the gardens and plaques get you down, walk down to the docks, buy an ice cream, and stare awhile at the soft bobbing of the masts.

Settled in 1649, Annapolis thrived as capital of the colony of Maryland; all those fine Georgian (18th-century British-style) houses once held colonial aristocrats (and their slaves). Annapolis made real history when the 1783-84 Continental Congress here ratified the Treaty of Paris, making the end of the American Revolution official. After its 1790 stint as temporary capital of the U.S. (hot on the heels of Philadelphia, New York City, and Trenton, N.J.), Annapolis relinquished the national limelight, satisfied with being Maryland's capital and a Chesapeake Bay port.

Annapolis' interesting quarter extends south and east from two landmarks: Church Circle, home of St. Anne's Episcopal Church, and State Circle, site of the Maryland State House, where the Continental Congress met. School Street, in a blatantly unconstitutional move, connects Church and State. Maryland Avenue runs from the State House to the Naval Academy, Main Street (where food and entertainment congregate), through Church Circle to the docks. Those lost in Annapolis can reorient themselves by looking for the State House dome or the St. Anne's spire. Annapolis is compact and easily walkable, provided you can find a parking space.

Practical Information

Annapolis fishes off U.S. 50 (also known as U.S. 301) 30 mi. east of Washington, DC, and 30 mi. southeast of Baltimore. From DC take U.S. 50 east to Rte. 70 (Rowe Blvd.) and follow signs to the historic district. From Baltimore, follow Rte. 3 south to U.S. 50 west, cross Severn River Bridge, then take Rte. 70.

Baltimore's excellent **Mass Transit Administration** (539-5000, call during business hours) makes frequent runs from downtown Baltimore to Annapolis. (Express bus #210 runs during rush hour Mon.-Fri. 6:10am-8:10am, 4:15pm-6:45pm, 1 hr., $2.45. Local bus #14 Mon.-Fri. 5am-10pm, Sat. 6:40am-10:20pm, Sun. 6:40am-8pm, 90min., $1.95.) **Greyhound/Trailways** connects Annapolis with Washington, DC (4 per day, 40min., $9.50) and with towns on the far side of the Chesapeake Bay. Call Greyhound/Trailways (565-2662) for current fares and schedules. The **Annapolis Department of Public Transportation,** 160 Duke of Gloucester St. (263-7964), operates a web of city buses connecting the historic district with the rest of town (Mon.-Sat. 6:15am-7pm; from 7pm-10pm only the Brown line runs) including the "Shopper Dropper," a park-and-ride from the Navy/Marine stadium parking lot (off Rte. 70) to the historic district (Mon.-Fri. 10am-6pm every half hour, 75¢).

Annapolis swims with offices, tours, and booths to help visitors. If you're planning your trip ahead of time, write to the **Annapolis and Anne Arundel County Conference & Visitor's Bureau**, One Annapolis St. (280-0445), for brochures and information. (Open Mon.- Fri. 9am-5:30pm). On-the-spot questions can be answered at the information desk at the State House (974-3000) or the dockside visitors booth (268-8687). (State House open Mon.-Fri. 9am-5pm; visitors booth open daily 10am-5pm).

Accommodations

In this self-consciously quaint town, bed and breakfasts abound. Hostels and motels are harder to come by. After wandering around, however, you probably won't want to sleep in anything less cozy than a bed and breakfast anyway. The Visitor's Information Centers have brochures for B&Bs and hotels in the area. Try to reserve a room in advance, especially if you're travelling during the busy summer months. Amanda's Bed

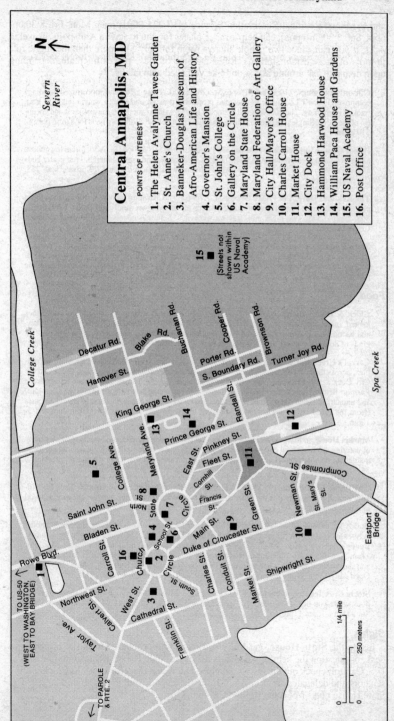

Central Annapolis, MD

POINTS OF INTEREST

1. The Helen Avalynne Tawes Garden
2. St. Anne's Church
3. Banneker-Douglas Museum of Afro-American Life and History
4. Governor's Mansion
5. St. John's College
6. Gallery on the Circle
7. Maryland State House
8. Maryland Federation of Art Gallery
9. City Hall/Mayor's Office
10. Charles Carroll House
11. Market House
12. City Dock
13. Hammond Harwood House
14. William Paca House and Gardens
15. US Naval Academy
16. Post Office

Severn River

College Creek

Spa Creek

15 (Streets not shown within US Naval Academy)

Decatur Rd.

Blake Rd.

Buchanan Rd.

Hanover St.

Porter Rd.

Cooper Rd.

S. Boundary Rd.

Turner Joy Rd.

Brownson Rd.

King George St.

Randall St.

Prince George St.

13

14

East St.

Pinkney St.

Fleet St.

Cornhill St.

Francis St.

Compromise St.

12

11

Newman St.

St. Mary's St.

5

College Ave.

Maryland Ave.

Saint John St.

North St.

State Circle

8

7

Bladen St.

School St.

4

6

9

Green St.

16

Church Circle

2

Main St.

Duke of Gloucester St.

10

Carroll St.

Northwest St.

West St.

South St.

Charles St.

Conduit St.

Market St.

Shipwright St.

Eastport Bridge

Calvert St.

Cathedral St.

Franklin St.

3

Taylor Ave.

Rowe Blvd.

1

(WEST TO WASHINGTON, EAST TO BAY BRIDGE)

TO US-50

TO PAROLE & RTE. 2

N

1/4 mile

250 meters

and Breakfast Regional Reservation Service (410-225-0001; open Mon.-Fri. 8:30am-6pm, Sat. 8:30am-noon), can help arrange places for you to stay in Annapolis. Travel in pairs, if you can, since two people share a room for only $10 more than the single rate in most of these establishments. Rates at some of these places fluctuate, depending upon demand: ask around and sound like you need convincing.

Gibson's Lodgings, 110 Prince George St. (268-5555). Three clean and modernized buildings comprise Gibson's Lodgings; the bearded proprietor runs around with a walkie-talkie to keep track of everything. The 200-year-old Patterson House, with six rooms, is the quaintest and cheapest of the three. Single range from $58-88, doubles from $68-98. Rollaway beds for a third person, $10 extra.

Prince George Inn Bed & Breakfast, 232 Prince George St. (263-6418). A Victorian townhouse as polished and preserved as Annapolis façades—but cozier and more cluttered. Four poster beds and wood floors. Closed Jan. to mid-April. Rooms with a shared bath $75, private bath $85. Check-in 4-6pm.

The Ark and Dove, 149 Prince George St. (268-6277). Charming wooden furniture includes a player piano downstairs. Teeny townhouse keeps afloat with two rooms and shared bath. Single $65. Double $75. Two-night min. stay on weekends. Seniors/students with ID discounted $5. Check in 2pm.

Shaw's Fancy Bed and Breakfast, 161 Green St. (410-263-0320). Don't worry about the For Sale in front—it's been there for years. The owners are planning to expand if they don't sell soon. A beautiful house with all the finer touches—tubs with feet, terrycloth robes, and a swing on the porch. Rates from $75 for 2 people to $130 for a suite that lodges up to 4 people.

Food

Chick & Ruth's Delly, 165 Main St. (269-6737). A cheeky Annapolis institution, with dishes named, often satirically, for local and national politicians. Try the Dan Quayle—a ham, turkey, and bacon sandwich on rye. The all-day breakfast menu includes unlimited coffee. Twenty-two kinds of donuts for under $1. Some kosher food. Open 24hr.

Carrol's Creek Bar & Café, 410 Severn Ave. (263-8102), in the Annapolis City Marina Complex, across the Eastport Bridge from Annapolis proper. Spectacular views of Spa Creek and the City Dock across the water. When the weather cooperates, you can sit on the patio to watch the Eastport Bridge come up and the sun go down. Order from the Lite Fare menu (served after 4pm) and munch unlimited dinner rolls. May be packed on weekends. Snails in a nest of angel hair pasta (from the Lite Fare menu) $6. Open Mon.-Sat. 11:30pm and 5-10pm; Sun. 10am-2pm and 3-10pm.

Market House, in Market Place, at City Dock, at the corner of Randall and Pinkney St. A variety of eateries, from seafood bars to frozen yogurt shops, meet under one roof. No seating available inside, but the dock makes a great picnic bench. Crabcakes and oysters (a Chesapeake specialty) $4; clams $2.49. Open Mon.-Thurs. 9am-6pm, Fri.-Sat. 9am-7pm, Sun 10am-7pm.

Old Towne Restaurant, 105 Main St. (268-8703). Pink floral curtains frame the Main St. window, dim ship's lanterns line the walls, and the drab-diorama decor disguises the cheapest seafood in downtown Annapolis. Crab cakes $5, broiled herbed scallops $7. Open daily 11am-9pm.

Buddy's Crabs & Ribs, 100 Main St. (626-1100), on the second floor above Banana Republic. Aggressively happy decor in aquamarine tones and white trellis. On Sundays, come for quantity; Buddy's boasts a Sunday breakfast buffet from 8:30am-1pm ($6, children under 5 free). Mon.-Fri. 11am-3pm, offers five different entrees as part of an all-you-can-eat lunch buffet for $6. Staunch and starving seafood lovers can belly up to the happy hour Raw Bar Buffet ($7), Mon.-Fri. 4-7pm. Open daily 11am-11pm. Steep stairs make wheelchair access tough or impossible.

Storm Bros. Ice Cream Factory, 130 Dock St. (263-3376), offers a great view of the ships at the dock while you lick up 39 flavors of ice cream and 3 flavors of yogurt. $1 for one scoop. Open Sun.-Thurs. 10am-11pm, Fri.-Sat. 10am-midnight.

Sights

Inside the **State House,** get Maryland maps and brochures from the information desk, or question the helpful volunteers behind it. State House architecture mimics the U.S. Capitol; check out the history exhibits, and watch the state legislature bicker if the senators and delegates are in session (from the second Wed. in Jan. to mid-April). The State House gives free tours from 10am-4pm. Open daily 9am-5pm.

From State Circle, follow Maryland Ave. to meet up with historic buildings. The **Hammond-Harwood House** hams it up at 19 Maryland Ave., at King George St. (269-1714). This elegant 1774 building, the last one designed by colonial architect William Buckland, became the first one preserved as a museum when St. John's College bought it in 1926. The museum keeps up period decor down to the candlesticks. (Open Nov.-March Mon., Wed.-Sat. 10am-4pm, Sun. 1pm-4pm; April-Oct. Mon., Wed.-Sat. 10am-5pm, Sun. 2-5pm. Tours on the hour; last tour an hour before closing. Admission $3.50, ages 6-18 $2.50, uniformed armed service personnel free.)

A right onto King George St., then another onto Martin St. reveals an unimposing parking lot and the sign for the **William Paca Garden,** 1 Martin St. (267-6656; from Baltimore, 269-0601). Turn right onto East St., past the Brice House, and turn right again onto Prince George St. for the entrance to the companion museum, the **William Paca House,** 186 Prince George St. (263-5553). William Paca (pronounced PAY-ka), an early governor of Maryland, was one of the signers of the Declaration of Independence. Visitors to his beautifully restored estate find a 1765 grandfather clock still ticking inside and trellises, water lilies, and gazebos outdoors. Preservationists rescued the garden from under a bus station and parking lot. Tours whenever enough people gather; come at least an hour before closing. (House open April-Oct. Mon., Wed.-Sat. 10am-5pm, Sun. noon-5pm; Nov.-March Mon., Wed.-Sat. 10am-4pm, Sun. noon-4pm. Free.)

Up East St. and towards State Circle, you'll see Pinkney St. on your left. **Shiplap House,** 18 Pinkney St. (run by Historic Annapolis Tours, 267-8149), a charming, little tavern, built c. 1715, might be the oldest surviving building in the city. (Open for tours by appointment; walk-ins can be accommodated. Call Historic Tours for details.)

From Shiplap, follow the smell of food and the sound of tourists down Pinkney St. towards the **City Dock**. Restaurants line the waterfront, a convenient information desk provides answers to tourists' questions, and boats leave on maritime tours every hour during summer. (See *Practical Information* for maritime tours info.) Tell the Naval Academy ships, farther away, apart from the small private ones, or watch the yachtsmen congregate and flex; the docks easily earn their nickname, "Ego Alley."

Main St., full of tiny shops and eateries, stretches from here back up to Church Circle. In an old church adjacent to Church Circle, the **Banneker-Douglass Museum,** 84 Franklin St. (974-2893), houses temporary exhibits and photographs about African-American life and history.

From Church Circle, walk along College Avenue past St. John's St., and turn left onto the campus of **St. John's College,** where students share an identical four-year "Great Books" curriculum, eschewing contemporary textbooks for the hallowed tomes of Western civilization. If academic freedom is nil, at least geographic freedom exists; St. John's students can read their Aristotle, Euclid, and Thucydides either in Annapolis or at the newer campus in Santa Fe, New Mexico. Sometime in the early 1980s, cocksure midshipmen boasted that they could beat St. John's at any team sport; St. John's picked croquet, won the first match, and now leads the annual series seven to three. (Go team!) (For information on the May matches, call 263-2371.) From the quad at St. John's, take College Ave. to King George St. and follow King George down to Gate One of the institution whose name means Annapolis: the Naval Academy.

At the **U.S. Naval Academy,** harried, short-haired "plebes" (first-year students) in official sailor dress try desperately to remember the words of the navy fight songs while the rest of the undergraduates, "middies" (midshipmen), go about their business. Naval Academy graduates become U.S. Navy officers and must serve as officers for several years. President Jimmy Carter graduated from Annapolis; more recently the institution has made headlines for expelling its gay and lesbian students. The rigorously planned and expansive campus includes plenty of green lawns and long docks at the water's edge; even in summer, a brigade of students and officers sticks around to work and drill, oblivious to visitors.

Bancroft Hall, an imposing stone structure about three blocks long, houses the entire student body, making it the world's largest dormitory. Its mammoth steps, stonework and arched entranceways follow its function as a cathedral of discipline. In the yard outside Bancroft Hall, witness the middies' noon lineup and formations. For good luck, kiss the bronze statue of Tecumseh that stands out front. From a balcony inside the high, stone lobby of Bancroft Hall, survey the campus, or inspect an uninhabited model middie's dorm room. (The rest of Bancroft Hall is closed to tourists.) **King Hall,** the academy's gargantuan dining hall, turns madhouse at lunchtime, serving the entire brigade in under four minutes. The hall even has its own brand of ketchup. You'll have to watch lunch from the outside, though.

Elsewhere on campus, the Naval Museum in **Preble Hall** has a simple collection of naval artifacts (open Mon.-Sat. 9am-4:45 pm, Sun. 11am-4:45pm. Free). Walking tours of the academy begin at the **Ricketts Hall** Visitors Center (263-6933) directly inside the gates of the academy at the end of Maryland Ave. (Tours March-May 10am-3pm on the hr.; June-Labor Day 9:30am-4pm on the half hr.; Labor Day-Thanksgiving Day 10am-3pm on the hr. Fee $3, ages 6-12 $1, under 6 free.)

Throughout the summer, the Academy provides entertainment for the general public, from parades and sporting events to movies and concerts. The schedule of events is published in the Trident, the Academy's newspaper which can be obtained by request at the Visitor's Center.

Nightlife

Small town by day, Annapolis stays small town by night, though it has its share of local pubs, particularly along Severn Ave. in Eastport. Call 268-8687 for information on free concerts at the city dock. For light entertainment, try the **Annapolis Summer Garden Theatre,** 143 Compromise St. (268-0809), at City Dock. (Performances Thurs.-Sun. evenings, beginning after dark—around 8:45pm. Tickets Thurs. and Sun. $9, Fri.-Sat. $10; seniors and students $7.) Afterwards, head to the popular **Ram's Head Tavern,** 33 West St. (268-4545), where imported bottled beer from Belgium, Czechoslovakia, New Zealand, Denmark, and so on heads for hordes of thirsty customers (open daily 11am-2am). Locals swear by **Marmaduke's Pub,** on Severn Ave. at 3rd (269-5420), across the bridge from the dock in Eastport. Sailors flock here Wednesday nights to watch videos of their races. (Open daily 11:30am-2am. No cover downstairs. Weekend piano bar upstairs, cover $2.50.) If you drive to Marmaduke's, take the Eastport Bridge and ignore the detour signs—they apply only to trucks. **Armadillo's,** 132 Dock St. (268-6680), hosts live bands every night from 9:30pm-1:30am. Behind the concert platform, you can sit upstairs and watch the harbor (open daily 11am-1am).

Rehoboth Beach, Delaware

With a minimum of advance planning, you can join the committees of vacationing bureaucrats from DC who convene at the sand reefs of Rehoboth Beach on hot summer weekends, to tan, mix, and mingle with anyone who may donate to a future campaign (or to an evening of good fun). (Rehoboth is also a minor-league gay cruising scene.) The **Chamber of Commerce,** in the restored train station at 501 Rehoboth Ave. (800-441-1329 or 227-2233 for information), provides brochures. (Open Mon.-Fri. 9am-4:30pm, Sat. 9am-1pm.)

At the **County Squire,** 17 Rehoboth Ave. (227-3985), you can talk with locals over one of the complete dinner specials (about $7). The breakfast special ($3) is served all day; the cheesesteak is hot, hot, hot ($3.95). (Open daily 7am-1am.) **Thrasher's** has served fries, and only fries, in enormous paper tubs ($3-5.75) for over 60 years. Bite too hastily into one of the tangy peanut-oil-soaked potato treats and understand how the place got its name. Locations on either side of the main drag, at 7 and 10 Rehoboth Ave., make it impossible to miss. (Open daily 11am-11pm.) Escape to **Nicola's Pizza,** at 8 N. 1st St. (227-6211), for Nic-o-boli—pizza fixin's rolled in dough and tossed in the oven ($4-6)—or for some of the best 'za on the East Coast ($2.50-9.50). (Open Sun.-Thurs. 11am-10:30pm, Fri.-Sat. 11am-2:30am.)

For inexpensive lodging, walk one block from the boardwalk to **The Lord Baltimore,** 16 Baltimore Ave. (227-2855), which has clean, antiquated, practically beachfront rooms. (Singles and doubles $30-60. Call ahead; it's popular.) Or walk a little farther from the beach to the cluster of guest houses on the side lanes off 1st St., just north of Rehoboth Ave. **The Abbey Inn,** 31 Maryland Ave. (227-7023), is what the proprietress calls "an old fashioned tourist home." This warm place always has a local staff and a friendly conversation waiting on the front porch. Call for reservations at least one week in advance, especially in summer. (2 day min. stay. Doubles from $40.) The **Big Oaks Family Campground,** P.O. Box 53 (645-6838), sprawls at the intersection of Rte. 1 and 270. (Sites $16.50, with hookup, $18.50.)

Founded in 1613 by the Zwaanendael colony from Hoorn, Holland, nearby **Lewes** (pronounced "LOO-iss") rightly touts itself as Delaware's first town. To learn about Lewes, simply walk around. To read more about it, try the Lewes **Chamber of Commerce** (645-8073), in the Fisher Marine House on King's Hwy. (Open Mon.-Sat. 10am-3pm.) The **Lighthouse Restaurant,** on Fisherman's Wharf (645-6271) just over the drawbridge in Lewes, occasionally serves brilliant food. Try the Grilled Swordfish ($13.95) with homemade bread. (Open Sun.-Fri. 5am-9pm, Sat. 4am-10pm.) Due east from Lewes, on the Atlantic Ocean, lurks the secluded **Cape Henlopen State Park** (645-8983), home to a seabird nesting colony, sparkling white "walking dunes," and campsites (645-2103) available on a first-come, first-serve basis (sites $13; open April-Oct.).

Greyhound/Trailways serves Lewes (flag stop at the parking lot for Tom Best's on Rte. 1; no phone) and Rehoboth Beach (227-7223; small station at 251 Rehoboth Ave.). Buses run to: Washington (3.5hr., $29.60); Baltimore (3.5hr., $25.50); and Philadelphia (4hr., $27.55). To get around within Rehoboth, use the free shuttle transport run by the **Ruddertowne Complex** (227-3888; May 27-Sept. 2 daily 3pm-midnight), which serves points between Rehoboth and Dewey Beaches, including a stop at Rehoboth Ave.

To drive to Rehoboth Beach from DC, take I-595 to and past Annapolis, MD over the Chesapeake Bay Bridge; continue east to U.S. 50, then southeast a short distance to Rte. 404. Follow Rte. 404 through Delaware (where it's also sometimes named Rte. 18 and U.S. 9) to where it meets Rte. 1; turn right (southeast) and drive to the town. It's a 2-to-3hr. drive. For Lewes, don't turn onto Rte. 1— follow 404 all the way there. Rehoboth's **post office** is at 179 Rehoboth Ave. (227-8406; open Mon.-Fri. 9am-5pm, Sat. 9am-noon). The **ZIP code** for Lewes and Rehoboth Beach is 19971; Delaware's **area code** is 302.

Harper's Ferry, West Virginia

> *Through these striking passages, its force of course*
> *augmented by the slope, the waters roar, and rush,*
> *and foam; sometimes, meeting with an obstructing*
> *rock, they spout up in sheets of spray, with a noise*
> *like thunder; at other times, where it is clear of*
> *rocks they glide with a fearful rapidity, down to-*
> *wards the village of Harper's Ferry, where, making*
> *a sudden turn, they form a sort of whirlpool.*
> *—A Young Traveller's Journal of Travels in the*
> *United States in the Year 1850*

Strangely enough, the very thing that helped sink Harper's Ferry as a town—the October, 1859 raid on the U.S. armory by radical abolitionist John Brown and his 21-man "army of liberation"—has caused its rebirth as an historic attraction. Before the raid, Harper's Ferry thrived as a military and industrial town because of its prime location, where the Shenandoah River meets the Potomac. John Brown descended on the town to gather arms for a slave insurrection; federal troops under then-Col. Robert E. Lee foiled his plans and shot most of the raiders, including Brown's three sons. Brown himself was tried and hanged (for treason against Virginia) two months later. The insurrection (eulogized by Ralph Waldo Emerson in a lecture called "John Brown") convinced many people that real change would require direct, violent action; Brown's incendiary example helped spark the Civil War. The war, in turn, destroyed the town; retreating troops burned the armory down, and Harper's Ferry endured two years of siege before a series of floods finally KO'd it. The spectacular view from Harper's Ferry's many overlooks may be worth more than all the history exhibits combined.

Harper's Ferry National Park has restored many of the town's buildings in their original, 1850's style. (In those days the town flourished with a population of 3200; today the number is a mere 400.) Stop first at the **Visitors Center** (535-6298) just inside the park entrance off Rte. 340; park rangers will hand you a map of the area, tell you more about the park, and show you a long movie about John Brown. The Visitors Center also provides free 30-to-90 minute **tours** guided by park rangers daily 10am-3pm throughout the summer. Keep your ears open for evening programs throughout the summer. The National Park and Visitors Center are open daily Sept.-May 8:30am-5pm, June-Aug. 8:30am-6pm. Admission fee $5 per car, $2 per hiker or bicyclist good for seven consecutive days (though it's unlikely anyone would care to stay that long). Free lifetime pass for seniors 62 and over, just like at every other National Park. If you drive, park near the Visitors Center; you'll get ticketed any closer to town. The shuttle bus from parking lot to town scoots along every 15 minutes.

Across the street from the Harper's Ferry entrance is the **West VA Welcome Center**, unaffiliated with the Ferry but great for anything in-state; get info on accommodations, restaurants, and activities such as white water rafting. The place is often mistaken for the Harper's Visitor's Center, and the staff are accustomed to directing visitors across the road.

The bus from the parking lot stops at **Shenandoah Street.** Browse through the renovated blacksmith's shop, ready-made clothing store, and general store. Wince as the blacksmith hammers at real iron, fired in a furnace; the stores contain replicas of nineteenth-century goods. Guides in period costume explain the vagaries of the Industrial Revolution. The **Park Service Book Store,** also on Shenandoah St., carries a large collection of books on life in Harper's Ferry, including literature on the Civil War and on wildlife in the National Park. (Open daily 9am-4:45pm.)

Turning left off Shenandoah St. onto High St., you'll find a slew of antique stores, souvenir shops, cafés, and ice cream stores. Most of these are standard fare, and you'd be best to avoid them. If you're really hungry, try the **Garden of Food** (535-2202), on High St., which serves salads and sandwiches ($3-7) either indoors or outside on the patio. (Open Mon.-Fri. 11am-6pm, Sat.-Sun. 11am-7pm.) And if your sweet tooth starts aching, stop at the **Old Tyme Fudge Shop,** which sells an array of fudges ($1.45 1/4lb., $2.85 1/2lb., $5.50 1lb.; open Tues.-Fri. 9am-5pm, Sat.-Sun. 9am-6pm.) The **Back Street Café,** Potomac St. (725-8019), doubles as a burger joint (burgers and hot dogs under $2.25) and a offbeat guide service; "Ghost Tours" of the town are offered weekend nights. (Tours May-Nov. 8 Fri.-Sun. 8pm; tours cost $2. Reservations recommended in Oct. Café open daily 10am-5pm. A few 3-speed bikes are for ready rent near the Back Street Café ($3 per hr. and $15 per day).

Uphill, stairs on High Street lead to the footpath to **Jefferson Rock**; experience awe and vertigo as you look out on the three states (Virginia, Maryland, and West Virginia) and two rivers (Shenandoah and Potomac) below. Thomas Jefferson declared the experience "worth a voyage across the Atlantic." The old, abandoned campus of **Storer University,** one of America's first Black colleges, moulders on Filmore St.

Those who prefer nature to history have several options, including hiking and boating. The **Maryland Heights Trail** offers some of the best views in the Blue Ridge Mountains and winds past cliffs worthy of experienced rock climbers. Climbers must register at the Visitors Center. Maryland Heights is just a leg of the continental millipede that is the Appalachian Trail, which runs from Maine to Georgia. **Appalachian Trail Conference Headquarters** (535-6331), at the corner of Washington and Jackson St., offers catalogues to its members featuring good deals on hiking books. (Open May-Oct. Mon.-Fri. 9am-5pm, Sat.-Sun. 9am-4pm. Membership $25, students and seniors $18. Write to P.O. Box 807 or call.) The less adventurous can walk along the **Chesapeake & Ohio Canal Towpath**.

Water fanatics should contact **Blue Ridge Outfitters** (725-3444), a few miles west of Harper's Ferry on Rte. 340N; they arrange excursions ranging from four-hour canoe trips on the Shenandoah to three-day whitewater raft rides on Virginia's toughest waterways. Prices start on weekdays at $40 for either a canoe or a seat on a half-day raft trip.

(Open daily 8am-7pm.) **River & Trail Outfitters** (695-5177), 604 Valley Rd. off Rte. 340 at the blinking light, rents canoes, inner tubes, and rafts in addition to organizing guided trips. ($40 per day per canoe; raft trips $42 per person; tubing $22.50 per day.) They also organize cross-country skiing weekends ($199) and day trips ($60). Call ahead for reservations.

Hikers can try the **Harper's Ferry AYH/HI Hostel**, 19123 Sandy Hook Rd. (301-834-7652), off Keep Tryst Rd. in Knoxville, MD, for cheap accommodations. Meet a rugged through-hiker or two, about halfway on her 2020-mile Appalachian Trail Odyssey. This renovated auction house, standing high above the Potomac, has 36 beds in two dormitory rooms. Train service to Harper's Ferry, WV, two miles from the hostel, and Brunswick, 3 miles. Limited parking. Lockout is between 9am and 5pm. Limited parking. (Members $8, non-members $12 Oct. 16-Dec. and Feb.-April 14 $9. Sheets are included in the price. Camping $7 per person. Check-in only 5-9pm, max. 3 nights, 50% reservation deposit.)

The **Comfort Inn** at Rte. 340 and Union St. (535-6391; reservations 800-228-5150), a ten-minute walk from town, offers dependable rooms and serves coffee and doughnuts each morning—it also has wheelchair-accessible and non-smoking rooms. (From Mon.-Thurs. singles $47, doubles $54. From Fri.-Sun. singles $51, doubles $58.)

You can camp along the C&O Canal, where sites lie five miles apart, or in one of the five Maryland state park campgrounds lying within 30 miles of Harper's Ferry. **Greenbrier State Park** (301-791-4767) lies a few miles north of Boonsboro on Rte. 66 between exits 35 and 42 on I-70 ($12; open April-Nov.). Far closer is the commercial **Camp Resort,** Rte. 3, Box 1300 (535-6895), adjacent to the entrance to Harper's Ferry National Park. (Sites $18 for two people, with water and electric hookup $21; each additional person $4, under 17 $2. Registration fee $3 per person.)

A natural stop for hikers on the Appalachian Trail, Harper's Ferry also makes a convenient day trip from Washington. The drive to Harper's Ferry from DC takes 1hr. and 30min. by car. Take I-270 north to Rte. 340 west. **Amtrak** (800-872-7245) only goes to Harper's Ferry from DC in the afternoon and back to DC in the morning. Call for reservations ($13 one-way, $20-26 round-trip--depending on availability). The closest **Greyhound** bus stations are half-hour drives away in Winchester, VA and Frederick, MD.

If time allows, drive an extra few miles north to **Antietam National Battlefield**, where the bloodiest day of the Civil War was fought after skirmishing at Harper's Ferry. On September 17, 1862, 12,410 Union and 10,700 Confederate soldiers lost their lives as Confederate Gen. Robert E. Lee tried and failed to penetrate the North against the army of Union General George B. McClellan. The nominal Union victory provided President Abraham Lincoln with the opportunity to issue the Emancipation Proclamation, which freed all slaves in those states still in rebellion against the United States on January 1, 1863. Start the tour at the Visitor's Center open daily 8:30am-6pm; glance in at their museum of artifacts used in the battle, and catch the introductory film on the battle. Films run 9am-5pm on the hour. Grab a free map for a self-guided tour of the battlefield, or rent a tape ($4) for a detailed account of who was slaughtered and why. Battlefield fee $1 per person. To get to Antietam from Harper's Ferry, take Route 340 North to Route 67 heading towards Boonsboro. Stay on Rte. 67 North until you reach Rte. 65; follow 65 to Antietam.

   Harper's Ferry's ZIP code is 25425; the **area code** is 304. **Knoxville, MD's ZIP code** is 21758.

Appendix A: Annual Events

*Yesterday the Fourth of July was celebrated in a
style of magnificence never before witnessed in this
city: it was ushered in by twenty-four cannon.*
—Anne Royall, Sketches of Life and History in the
United States *(1826)*

Washington's seasons runneth over with special events; in spring and summer, periodic parades, marches, and festivals block off streets and clog the Mall with booths and banners. Lovers of historic homes and/or military bands can easily fill their calendars with diversions, but everyone should find something interesting. Street festivals tout the crafts and food of one or more ethnic groups (the best, Adams-Morgan Day, probably covers around twenty). The Black community celebrates a string of African-American cultural festivals, like Malcolm X Day in Anacostia Park, while cuddle-punks come together for the Pop Loser festival. The blooming of Washington's Japanese cherry trees, whose famous white petals ring the Tidal Basin in spring, ensures a civic frenzy of parades and recitals; the blossoms themselves, though, are pretty enough to be the main attraction.

Remember that some of the best (and, by definition, the most spontaneous) special events don't get planned a year in advance and can't be listed in *Let's Go*. Outdoor rock concerts, demonstrations, marches, and rallies can leap into existence only days after the news event that inspires them, promoted by street posters and word of mouth. Attempt to distinguish between tiny wanko-extremist gatherings and larger, more reasonable demonstrations; definitely try to see or take part in one of the latter. Occasionally a giant rally will let hundreds of thousands of people loose around the Mall to show the government their cause means business. Abortion-rights groups are especially good at this—if Roe v. Wade (the Supreme Court decision legalizing abortion) is overturned anytime soon, pro-choice forces could conceivably send one million protesters to DC.

The Fourth of July

On the nation's birthday, the capital throws an all-day bash; events get better as the day goes on. In mid-morning a costumed orator reads the country's birth certificate, the Declaration of Independence, from the steps of the National Archives at 7th St. and Constitution Ave. NW (501-5000). A noisy demonstration of colonial-era militia segues at noon into the old-fashioned **Fourth of July parade** (789-7000), along Constitution Ave. to 17th St. NW. (Tourists line the sidewalks by 11:30am; arrive early.) High school bands, veterans, baton twirlers, horses, and marchers from as far as South America celebrate the country's existence. The uniforms get worse, but the music gets better if you sojourn up Pennsylvania Ave. to the **DC Free Jazz Festival** (783-0360), 1-8pm in the Freedom Plaza park between 13th and 14th St. NW. ("Free Jazz" means that the concerts don't cost anything, not that you'll be treated to spaced-out twelve-tone tunes.) Caribbean-food and BBQ stands rim the crowd, and even the surly skatepunk gallery shuts up and makes way for the international jazz.

The **Festival of American Folklife** occupies the Mall during the day, but the Fourth must be the worst (most crowded) time to go. See the Festival another day; leave downtown, but come back for the fireworks. The tradition of big-name rock acts on the Mall is, alas, temporarily over; it had its moment in the sun when then-Secretary of the Interior James Watt tried to ban the Beach Boys in the early 80s. (He said they brought "the wrong element.") The **National Symphony** (416-8100) plays patriotic music on the Capitol's West Lawn from 8pm, but if you sit there you won't get a good view of the 9:15pm fireworks, best observed from the grounds of the Washington Monument. Bring friends and a blanket, arrive by 6:30pm for a decent spot, and face west (away from the Capitol, towards the Lincoln Memorial). For a memorable if slightly guilty pleasure on Independence Day, befriend a White House intern and squeeze an invitation to the White House Lawn; spread out in front of the balcony for a front-row view of the Bushes.

It's much easier to attend all these ceremonies without a car. The Metro usually extends its hours (and lowers its fare) on July 4th to accommodate the swarms, and walking home from the fireworks is part of the experience. (See how "might makes right" when the crowd decides to cross the street.) This is something worth changing your travel plans to attend.

Summer-long Events

Marine Corps Tuesday Evening Sunset Parades, May 26-Aug. 25, at the Iwo Jima Memorial, with the U.S. Marine Drum and Bugle Corps and Silent Drill team (433-3173). Metro: Arlington Cemetery. Starts at 7pm; free shuttle bus service from Arlington Cemetery Visitors Center starting at 6pm. Free.

Marine Corps Friday Evening Parades, May 8-Aug. 28, at the Marine Barracks, 8th and Eye St. SE (433-6060). Metro: Eastern Market. The Eighth and Eye Marines strut their pomp at 8:45pm sharp: Marine Corps band music, a procession of soldiers (all between 5'11" and 6'1"), the Marine mascot (a bulldog) and a spotlit figure bugling *Taps* into the night. Free, but reserve over three weeks in advance. Free parking and shuttle bus from the Navy Yard at 9th and M St. SE.

Sunday Polo Matches, every Sunday afternoon on the field east of the Lincoln Memorial (619-7222). May 2pm; June 3pm; July-Aug. 4pm; Sept.-Oct. 3pm. Free.

U.S. Military Band Summer Concert Series, in and around the Mall every summer evening Memorial Day through Labor Day at 8pm. Army Band: 703-696-3399. Marine Band: 433-4011. Navy Band: 433-2525. Air Force Band: 767-5658.

Annual Events

Robert E. Lee's Birthday, Jan. 19 (703-557-0613). Metro: Arlington Cemetery. At the house he used to live in, Arlington House in the Cemetery. 19th-century music, old-time Southern food, and a show of the house. 1:30-4pm. Free.

Martin Luther King Jr.'s Birthday, observed Jan. 20 (619-7222). Wreaths laid down and the "I Have a Dream" speech re-spoken at the Lincoln Memorial. Choirs, guest speakers, and military color guard. 11am. Free.

Abraham Lincoln's Birthday, observed Feb. 12. (619-7222). Laying down of the wreaths and booming out of the Gettysburg address from the cold steps of the Lincoln Memorial. Free.

Chinese New Year Parade, mid-Feb., down H St. NW between 5th and 8th St. Metro: Gallery Place. Firecrackers, lions, drums, and dragons make the normally tame streets of Chinatown—all six of them—explode with delight. Free.

Mount Vernon Open House, Feb. 15 (703-780-2000). Free admission to Mount Vernon, fife and drums on the green, and the obligatory wreath-laying. Don't take any wooden teeth. 9am-4pm. Free. Do a little dance.

George Washington's Birthday Parade, Feb. 15, through Old Town Alexandria (703-838-4200). Rather self-explanatory. Free.

U.S. Army Band 70th Anniversary Concert, March 2, at the Kennedy Center (703-696-3399). Metro: Foggy Bottom/GWU. Top brass, so to speak (duh); also choral music. Free.

Festival of St. Patrick, March 12-17 (347-1450). Irish culture proliferates at 924 G St. NW, with books'n'musicians'n'dancers. Metro: Gallery Place. Free.

Bach Marathon, March 21, at Chevy Chase Presbyterian Church, 1 Chevy Chase Circle NW (363-2202). For J.S. (Papa) Bach's birthday, 10 organists play JSB's works on the church's massive pipe organ. Take an "L" bus up Connecticut Ave. from the Van Ness or Cleveland Park Metro. Refreshments. 1-7pm. Free.

St. Patrick's Day Parade, March 15, downtown on Constitution Ave. NW (301-424-2200). Dancers, bands, bagpipes, and floats start at 1pm. Free.

U.S. Botanic Gardens' Easter Flower Show, March 20-April 18 (225-8333). Metro: Federal Center SW. Colorful. Free.

Smithsonian Kite Festival, March 27 (357-3244). Metro: Smithsonian. Go fly a kite or watch designers of all ages at the Washington Monument grounds compete for prizes and trophies from 10am-4pm. Free.

Save the Children/Marvin Gaye Day, April 25. Metro: Gallery Place. Go-go, jazz, and gospel music, food, and festing in the outdoor "downtown mall" on F St. NW between 7th and 9th St., behind the National Museum of American Art.

National Cherry Blossom Festival, April 5-12, all over town; contact the festival committee (737-2599) or the Convention and Visitors Assn. (789-7000), or just read the *Washington Post.* Official Washington goes bonkers over the pretty, white Japanese blossoms, expected to appear most heavily during this week. Expensive tickets (728-1135) necessary for the April 11 Parade down Constitution Ave. NW from 7th to 17th St. Other events (some free) include fireworks, a fashion show, free concerts in downtown parks, the Japanese Lantern Lighting Ceremony, the Cherry Blossom Ball, and an annual Marathon Race.

Easter Sunrise Service, April 11, at Arlington Cemetery's Memorial Amphitheater (475-0856). Free.

White House Easter Egg Roll, April 12, on the White House South Lawn (456-2200). Metro: McPherson Sq. For kids 8 and under; bring your adult. Famous egg roll usually brings out the President and the press for perfect photo opportunities with all-American kids; you'll have to stand in line. Eggs provided; entertainment scheduled. Enter at the southeast gate of the White House on East Executive Ave. 10am-2pm. Free.

American College Theater Festival, last week in April (25th-30th), at the Kennedy Center (416-8000). A jury chooses the nation's best college shows, which go on at the Kennedy Center. All shows are free; line up for tickets at 10am on Jan. 20 in the Kennedy Center's Grand Foyer, or just show up on the night of a show; you'll probably get in.

Washington Craft Show, April 15-18, at the Smithsonian's Departmental Auditorium, 14th St. and Constitution Ave. NW (357-4000). Metro: Federal Triangle. A sales exhibition of fine handcrafted objects; 100 exhibitors in fiber, ceramics, glass, jewelry, leather, metal, paper, textiles and wood, chosen by cunning experts. Entrance fee $6.

Duke Ellington Birthday Celebration, April 24 (April 26 rain date), at Freedom Plaza, 13th St. and Pennsylvania Ave. NW (331-9404). Metro: Federal Triangle. The DC-born jazz star deserves this celebration, which prominently showcases his music. Noon-6pm. Free.

Shakespeare's Birthday Celebration, April 24, at the Folger Shakespeare Library, 201 E. Capitol St. SE (544-7077). Metro: Capitol South. Exhibits, plays, Elizabethan music, food, and children's events. Don't be misled: the Bard's actual birthday is April 23. 11am-4pm. Free.

Potomac International Regatta, late April (333-3838). Handsome crew hunks from Oxford, Cambridge, and various American schools erg down the Potomac. Best seen from the Washington Harbor complex, below K St. in Georgetown.

Filmfest DC, early May (727-2396), in artsy movie houses all over town. Dozens of international and local art films premiere. Check the *Washington Post* and *City Paper* for film schedules/locations.

Chesapeake Bay Bridge Walk, early May (301-563-7104), from the Marine Corps Stadium in Annapolis, MD. Take a shuttle bus to the east end of the bridge and walk back west. It's 4.3 miles just to get back where you came from. If hundreds of your best friends walked over a bridge, would you do it, too? Free.

Andrews Air Force Base Air Show, first or second weekend in May; call for exact dates (301-568-5995 or 301-981-4424). The base, in Camp Springs. MD, opens up for visitors and aerobatics. Army parachutists plummet and recover; Blue Angels and Thunderbirds demo teams zoom and swerve under the clouds. Don't try this at home, kids. To reach the base, take the Beltway I-95 to exit 9. Turn right onto Allentown Rd. and follow the signs. Free, and crowded.

Greek Spring Festival, May 14-16, at Saints Constantine and Helen Greek Orthodox Church, 4115 16th St. NW (829-2910). Greek food, music, dance, etc. Noon-9pm. Free.

Malcolm X Day, May 22, in Anacostia Park along the Anacostia River in SE (Fax 543-1649). A daylong festival honoring the slain Black leader Malcolm X. Food, speakers, and "Harambe Village" (three tents of exhibits) complement gospel, African, Caribbean, blues, and go-go music; premier go-go-ists E.U. dropped by last year. Noon-7pm. Free.

National Symphony Orchestra Memorial Day Weekend Concert, May 24 (rain date: May 25), on the West Lawn of the U.S. Capitol (416-8100 or 619-7222). Metro: Federal Center SW. 8pm. Free.

Memorial Day Jazz Festival, May 24, in Old Town Alexandria, VA (703-838-4200). Local big bands. Noon-7pm. Free.

Memorial Day Ceremonies at Arlington Cemetery, May 24 (475-0856). Metro: Arlington Cemetery. Wreaths at John F. Kennedy's tomb, at the Tomb of the Unknown Soldier, and services in Memorial Amphitheater; the President himself will show up and talk. Free.

Memorial Day Ceremonies at the Vietnam Veterans Memorial, May 24 (619-7222). Wreath-laying, speeches, military bands, and a keynote address. Free. 11am.

Dupont-Kalorama Museum Walk Day, June 5 (387-2151). Metro: Dupont Circle. Eight museums north of Dupont Circle seek publicity, including the Textile Museum, Anderson House, and the Fondo del Sol Arts Center. Music, historic house tours, food, crafts, etc. Free.

Gay Pride Day, June (298-0970; call for exact date). Big march through downtown for gay and lesbian consciousness and rights. Starts at 16th and W St. (Metro: U St./Cardozo); ends in a festival at the Francis School, 24th and 25th St. Festival entrance $5 on the day, advance purchase at Blockbuster Video in Dupont Circle $3.

Philippine Independence Day Parade and Fair, June 12 (call Philippine Embassy, 202-488-1414, for info). Parade: Pennsylvania Ave. NW from 4th St. to 13th St. Fair: Freedom Plaza at 13th St. and Pennsylvania Ave. Free.

Dance Africa DC, June 13-16, at Dance Place, 3225 8th St. NE (269-1600). Metro: Brookland/CUA. International dancers cut nice figures. Some shows free, others not.

Bloomsday Marathon *Ulysses* Reading, June 15-16, at Kelly's Irish Times pub, 14 F St. NW (543-5433). Metro: Union Station. Annual read-through of Joyce's greatest novel draws crowds of literary and/or Irish notables. Starts around 11am on June 15 and ends in the early morning of the 16th—the same days as the setting of the novel. Free.

Festival of American Folklife, June 25-29 and July 2-5, on the Mall (357-2700). Huge Smithsonian-run fair demonstrates the crafts, customs, food and music of a few selected states, territories and/or foreign countries to over a million visitors, with musicians, performers, and craftspeople imported from the featured regions. The 1992 Festival went gaga over Columbus's visit to the New World. Free.

Fourth of July—hoo boy. Lots of events, most of them magnificent; the Fourth has its own paragraphs, above.

Bastille Day Waiters' Race, July 14, starting at Pennsylvania Ave. and 20th St. NW. Metro: Foggy Bottom/GWU. Waiters carry champagne glasses on trays and demonstrate their juggling ability for a grand-prize trip to Paris. Dominique's Restaurant (452-1132) sponsors. Noon-4:00pm. Free.

Virginia Scottish Games, July 24-25, 3901 W. Braddock Rd. in Alexandria, VA on the grounds of Episcopal High School (703-838-4200). Two-day annual Scottish festival is one of America's largest, with Highland dancing, kilts, tartans, sheepdogs, bagpiping, national professional heptathlon, animal events, fiddling competitions, and Scottish foods, goods, and genealogy. Tickets $9 per day. Free shuttle from King St. Metro back to the games.

Latin American Festival, July, on the Washington Monument grounds (724-4091; call for exact date). Metro: Smithsonian. Free food, music, dance, and theatre from 40 Latin American nations.

Latin and Jazz Festival, Aug 7, at Freedom Plaza, 13th St. and Pennsylvania Ave. NW (331-9404). Metro: Federal Triangle. Continuous live jazz and ethnic food, noon-6pm. (By the same people who organize the Duke Ellington Birthday Celebration.)

Civil War Living History Day, mid-August, at Fort Ward Museum and Park, 4301 W. Braddock Rd., Alexandria, VA (703-838-4848). Torchlight tours of Union and Confederate camps. Soldiers reenact camp life and perform artillery drills. These reenactment guys don't tire. Free.

U.S. Army Band's *1812 Overture,* Aug., on the Washington Monument grounds (703-696-3399; call for exact date). Metro: Smithsonian. Actually Tchaikovsky's *1812 Overture,* but the Army Band—along with the Salute Gun platoon of the 3rd U.S. Infantry—performs the work. 8pm. Free.

Navy Band Children's Lollipop Concert, Aug. 19, on the Washington Monument grounds (433-2525). Metro: Smithsonian. The U.S. Navy band plays for kids. 8pm. Free.

National Frisbee Festival, Labor Day weekend, Sept. 3-5, on the Mall near the Air & Space Museum (301-645-5043). Metro: Smithsonian. The largest non-competitive frisbee festival in the U.S., with frisbee studs and disc-catching dogs. Free.

African Cultural Festival, Sept. 19, at Freedom Plaza, 14th St. and Pennsylvania Ave. NW (667-5775). Metro: Federal Triangle. African cooking, sounds, movement, and stuff for sale. Noon-7pm. Free.

DC Blues Festival, early Sept., in Anacostia Park, across the eponymous river in SE (724-4091 or 301-483-0871; call for exact date). Top blues people twang, wail, and moan. Free.

Black Family Reunion, early Sept., on the Mall (659-2372' call for exact date). "Celebration of the Black family" with music, food and exhibits. Free.

National Symphony Orchestra Labor Day Weekend Concert, Sept. 5 (rain date: Sept. 6), on the West Lawn of the U.S. Capitol (416-8100 or 619-7222). Metro: Federal Center SW. 8pm. Free.

Kennedy Center Open House, mid-Sept. (416-8000). A one-day hodgepodge of classical, jazz, folk and ethnic music, dance, drama, and film from DC performers including members of the National Symphony Orchestra. Free.

Adams-Morgan Day, Sept. 13, along 18th St., Columbia Rd., and Florida Ave. NW in the aforementioned neighborhood (332-3292). Live music on three or four stages (check out the go-go band), stuff for sale, and the wondrous kaleidoscope of ethnic food for which Adams-Morgan is justly famous. Free, all day, always jammin', and consequently always jammed with pedestrians.

Saints Constantine and Helen Greek Orthodox Church Bazaar, Sept. 18-20, 4115 16th St. NW (829-2910). Greek food, crafts, and dancing. Free.

White House Fall Garden Tours, mid-Oct. (456-2200). Like the spring garden tours, but this time with military band music. Free, but fills up fast; call them beforehand.

Veteran's Day Ceremonies, Nov. 11, around Arlington Cemetery (475-0843). Metro: Arlington Cemetery. Solemn ceremony with military bands honors the nation's war dead. Service in the Memorial Amphitheater. The President or a substitute lays a wreath at the Tomb of the Unknown Soldier. Ceremonies begin at 11am. Free. Vietnam Veterans Memorial also holds ceremonies (619-7222; free).

Kennedy Center Holiday Celebration, throughout December (416-8000). Musical events colonize the Kennedy Center from Dec. 1 to the New Year. Free performances include classical chamber, choral, cello and "Tubachristmas" concerts, a gospel music concert (tickets given away a few weeks in advance), and the hugely popular sing-along to Handel's *Messiah,* for which thousands of classical-music groupies stand in line all day to get tickets.

Woodlawn Plantation Christmas, early Dec. at Woodlawn Plantation, 9000 Richmond Highway, Alexandria, VA (703-780-4000). Recreates an early-1800's Xmas; log fires, rides, and drink. Call for days and times, but make reservations early (by November). About $6.

People's Christmas Tree Lighting, 1st or 2nd Wed./Thurs. of Dec. on the Capitol's West Lawn (224-3069). Metro: Federal Center SW. Congress lights its own Christmas tree while the military band plays on. 6pm. Free.

National Christmas Tree Lighting/Pageant of Peace, Dec. 16 (3rd Thurs. in Dec.)-Jan. 1, on the Ellipse south of the White House (619-7222). Metro: McPherson Sq. The President switches on a Christmas tree, a Hanukkah Menorah, and possibly other electrical objects at 5:30pm on Dec. 10; the Ellipse hosts choral music, a Nativity scene, a burning yule log, and lit-up trees from 50 states until the New Year crashes in. Free.

Washington National Cathedral Christmas Celebration and Services, Dec. 24-25, at the Cathedral, Massachusetts and Wisconsin Ave. NW (536-6200). Christmas carols and seasonal choral music during the day, but the nighttime service is more famous. Dec. 24: pageant 4pm, service 10pm. Dec. 25: service 9am. Free.

White House Christmas Candlelight Tours, Dec. 26-28 (456-2200). See the Christmas decorations between 6-8pm. Free, but fills up fast; get to the White House a few hours early.

New Year's Eve Celebration at the Old Post Office Pavilion, Dec. 31, 1100 Pennsylvania Ave. NW (289-4224). Crowded, festive outdoor and indoor New Year's party emulates NYC's Times Square—complete with pickpockets. The giant Love Stamp drops from the clock tower at midnight. (Several years ago, then-Mayor Barry counted down "5-4-3-2-1...Merry Christmas!" No wonder they caught him.) Free.

Appendix B: Useful Stores

Grocery Stores

Capitol Hill Supermarket, 241 Massachusetts Ave. NE (543-7428), at 3rd St. Metro: Union Station. A corner grocery store offering fruit, water, juices, cold cuts, a few wines, and fresh sandwiches ($1.75-3.50), in addition to basic supplies. Five aisles. Open Mon.-Sat. 8am-8pm, Sun. 8am-5pm.

Congress Market, 421 East Capitol St. NE at 5th St. Metro: Eastern Market. Corner grocery serves the neighborhood along East Capitol St. between the Capitol building and Lincoln Park. Two aisles display drinks, ice cream, some fruit, beer and wine, and basic foodstuffs. Open Mon.-Sat. 7:30am-11:30pm, Sun. 7:30am-11pm.

11-M Corner, 1133 11th St. (898-0344), corner of 11th and M St. One block from AYH/HI. Metro: Metro Center or Mt. Vernon Sq. Pure convenience; no fresh items. Prepackaged foods. People may feel uncomfortable alone in this area after dark. Open daily 8am-10pm.

Capitol Market, 1231 11th St. NE (289-1336), near N St. Metro: Metro Center or Mt. Vernon Sq./UDC. A supermarket, super for fresh veggies. People may feel uncomfortable alone in this area. Open Mon.-Sat. 9am-8pm, Sun. 9am-6pm.

Da Hua Market, 623 H. St. NW (371-8888). Metro: Gallery Place. Chinese market with fresh vegetables as well as almost every canned and bottled good a Chinese kitchen would need. Open Fri.-Wed. 10am-8:30pm, Thurs. 10am-7:30pm.

Neam's Market, 3217 P St. NW (338-4694), in Georgetown. Clean, upscale butcher, deli, and grocer. Some prices are very Georgetown, but others are reasonable. Open Mon.-Fri. 8am-7pm, Sat. 8am-6pm.

Schele's, 1331 29th St. NW at Dumbarton St. (333-4143), in Georgetown. Mom-and-Pop grocery is the second oldest store in Georgetown (at almost 100 years. running). Open Mon.-Sat. 8am-8pm, Sun. 9am-6pm.

Americana Grocery, 1813 Columbia Rd. NW, in Adams-Morgan. Five clean aisles stocked with flair—fresh meats, fruits, vegetables, dry goods, and cookware. Large store area (the storefront takes up three smaller shop windows) allows for a more extensive and carefully organized selection than other local grocery stores. Open Mon.-Thurs. 8:30am-7pm, Fri.-Sat. 8:30am-8pm, Sun. 8:30am-5pm.

El Gavilan, 1646 Columbia Rd. NW (234-9260), in Adams-Morgan. Thick atmosphere. A small store with two aisles crammed with Latin American groceries all the way up to the ceiling. A well-known and popular store in the area. Open Mon.-Sat. 7am-10pm, Sun. 7am-8pm.

Merkato Market, 2116 18th St. NW (483-9499), In Adams-Morgan. Down a narrow flight of stairs. Look for the green sign. Named for the huge market in Addis Ababa, the Ethiopian capital. Small, airy store with two low-rise aisles stocked with Ethiopian food. Sniff around—you'll know they specialize in spices. Open Mon.-Sat. 10am-9pm, Sun. 11am-9pm.

Safeway, 1747 Columbia Rd. NW (667-0774). The Adams-Morgan Safeway. A big supermarket, not noticeably ethnic. Open Mon.-Sat. 7am-midnight, Sun. 7am-10pm.

Joe's Mini-Supermarket, 3527 12th St. NE (529-6922). Metro: Brookland/CUA. Fresh vegetables and fruits enhance this oversized convenience store. Open daily 6am-8:30pm.

Murry's Steaks and Fine Foods, 12th St. and Newton St. NE (635-0926). Metro: Brookland/CUA. Fine foods, nope; cheap foods, yup. Open Mon. 10am-8pm, Tues.-Fri. 9am-8pm, Sat. 9-7.

Takoma Grocery Market, 7056 Carroll St. NE (270-2024), in Takoma Park. Metro: Takoma. Midway between a grocery and convenience store with a small collection of fresh fruit and vegetables as well as all other packaged items. Open Mon.-Sat. 8am-9pm, Sun. 8:30am-8pm.

Indian and Middle Eastern Foods, 7007 Laurel St. NE, in Takoma Park. Metro: Takoma. Noodles and cracked wheat in packages ($2). Spices and foodstuffs that Indian chefs would find difficult to obtain elsewhere. Open Mon.-Fri. 10am-7pm, Sat-Sun. 10am-5pm.

Health Food

Yours Naturally, 1523 L St. NW (457-0175). Metro: Farragut North. Carries all the Washington African-American newspapers, in addition to every vitamin imaginable. Cramped, neighborly quarters also house health foods and all-natural products. Open Mon.-Sat. 10am-7pm.

Yes! Natural Gourmet, 3425 Connecticut Ave. NW (363-1559). Surprise. Natural foods, including a variety of grains and nuts by weight. Open Mon.-Thurs. 9am-9pm, Fri.-Sat. 9am-8pm, Sun. 10am-6pm.

Nature Food Centres, 1079 Wisconsin Ave. NW (338-2185), in Georgetown. "All-natural" products and health foods, including herbs, vitamins, juices, nuts, cereals, and soybean ice cream. Open Mon.-Sat. 10am-9pm, Sun. 10am-6pm.

Drugstores

Foer's Pharmacy, 1800 I St. NW (783-1344), in Foggy Bottom. A professional outfit. Open Mon.-Fri. 8:30am-5:30pm, Sat. 9am-1am.

People's Drug, 661 Pennsylvania Ave. NE (543-3305), on Capitol Hill. Filled with shampoo, stationary, over-the-counter drugs, and other supplies. Open Mon.-Sat. 8am-9pm, Sun. 10am-6pm.

White House Area/Foggy Bottom: 14th St. and Thomas Circle (628-0720). Five blocks from AYH/HI. Be careful after dark. Open 24 hrs. **Georgetown:** Wisconsin Ave. and O St. NW (337-4848). Open Mon.-Sat. 8am-10pm, Sun. 10am-6pm. **New Downtown:** 717 14th St. NW (737-9525). Open 24 hrs. **Dupont Circle:** 7 Dupont Circle (785-1466). Open 24 hrs.

Cleaners/Laundromats

Penn Cleaners, 650 Pennsylvania Ave. SE (675-4677), on Capitol Hill. Metro: Eastern Market. Cleaning that comes in before 10am can be available after 4pm the same day. Minor shoe repairs performed speedily. Open Mon.-Fri. 7:30am-7pm, Sat. 9am-5pm.

Lustre Cleaners, 2100 Pennsylvania Ave. NW (429-0591), in Foggy Bottom. Open Mon.-Fri. 7:30am-7pm, Sat. 7:30am-6pm.

Swift Cleaners, 1220 L. St. (842-5132) and 1208 E. St. NW (347-5019). Same-day dry-cleaning. Open Mon.-Sat. 9am-6pm.

J & M Dry Cleaners and Shoe Repair, 1906 I St. NW (457-9838), in White House Area/Foggy Bottom. Keys made here and watches repaired. Open Mon.-Fri. 7:30am-6:30pm, Sat. 10am-2pm.

Royal #1 Cleaners, 3336 M St. NW (298-6561), in Georgetown. 99¢ men's shirts if you bring in at least three. Dresses $6.25. Open Mon.-Fri. 7am-7pm, Sat. 7:30am-5pm.

Georgetown Cleaners, 1070 1/2 31st St. NW (965-9655). Dry cleaning and shoe repair. Dresses $5.20, blouses $3.15, shirts $2.35. Same-day service if brought in before 10am. Open Mon.-Fri. 8am-7pm, Sat. 9am-6pm.

Bubblez Laundromat, 3208 Mt. Pleasant St. NW, in Adams-Morgan. Around 35 washing machines, with dryers to match. Don't come alone at night, especially carrying a load of dirty clothes in both arms. Open daily 8am-10pm.

Laundromat, 1730 Columbia Rd. NW, in Adams-Morgan. Ten washers and dryers, and a TV to pass the time. Open Mon.-Fri. 7am-10pm, Sat.-Sun. 6am-10pm.

Dry Cleaners, 5019 Wisconsin Ave. NW (364-2952), in the Upper Northwest. Shirts $1 (same-day service $1.40), blouses $3.75, dresses $7.25. Open Mon.-Fri. 7:30am-7:30pm, Sat. 8am-5pm.

Twelfth Street Cleaners, 3525 12th St. NE (526-7836), in Northeast. Dry cleaning, not street cleaning. Mon.-Fri. 8am-6:30pm, Sat. 8am-6pm.

4th St. Cleaners, 520 Rhode Island Ave. NE (832-1303), in Takoma Park. One-day service. Open Mon.-Fri. 7am-7pm, Sat. 8am-6pm.

Tailors

Capitol Tailors, 2 8th St. SE (544-3640), on Capitol Hill. A friendly neighborhood place. Owner is on a first-name basis with her customers. Same-day service for cleaning: in by 9:30am, out by 5pm. The tailor on the premises can try to accommodate rush mending orders. Open Mon.-Fri. 7:30am-7pm, Sat. 9am-5pm.

Photo Developing

Colorfax, 600 Pennsylvania Ave. SE (544-0104), on Capitol Hill. Metro: Eastern Market. Offer a variety of developing services. Same day service (in by 11am, out by 5:30pm) is available for Kodak Colorprint film ($13.88 for 24 exposures, $18.39 for 36 exposures). Open Mon.-Fri. 9am-6pm, Sat. 10am-2pm.

Optical Supplies

United Optical, 645 Pennsylvania Ave. SE (547-0956), in the "Market Place" complex. Metro: Eastern Market. Like most optical places, they can fix a broken eyeglass screw in a couple of minutes for no charge. Open Tues.-Fri. 9am-5pm, Sat. 9am-2pm. Closed Mon.

Travel Supplies

AYH/HI Travel Center, 11th and K St. NW (783-4943), underneath the AYH/HI Hostel. Metro: Metro Center or Mt. Vernon Square. Travel guides, backpacks, and other equipment for using your new *Let's Go* books. AYH/IYHF discounts. Open Mon.-Sat. 9am-6pm.

The Rand McNally Map Store, 1200 Connecticut Ave. NW (223-6751). Globes, maps, books, and stuff galore for the backpacker or motorist. Open Mon.-Fri. 9am-6:30pm, Thurs. 9am-7:30pm, Sat. 10am-6pm.

Flowers

Dupont Flowers, 1534 14th St. NW (797-7600), next to Café Rondo. Metro: Dupont Circle. Don't blink; you might miss this tiny store overflowing with fresh flowers. $6 for a bunch of ektachrome daisies, in season. Open Mon.-Sat. 9am-8pm, Sun. 10am-6pm.

Appendix C: Late-Night Washington

Though the federal schedule tends toward the 9-to-5, enough of DC stays up all night to make the city insomniac-friendly. While the museums shut their doors after the sun goes down, some national monuments stay open 24 hrs.: a nocturnal tour of the **monuments** will let you bypass the crowds and see the nighttime spotlights as they wax eloquent across the marble. The **Jefferson Memorial** is particularly nice for midnight monument- and star-gazing on its lawn by the Tidal Basin (though you'll need a car to get there and back). The **Kennedy Center's** scenic roof stays open till 11pm and doesn't charge admission. Savor the late-night café culture in collegiate form in Georgetown at **Au Pied du Cochon/Aux Fruits de Mer** (open 24 hrs.) or at punkoid hipster **Dante's,** 14th and Q St. NW (open till 3am weekdays, 4am weekends). The greasy, honest **Georgetown Café,** 1623 Wisconsin Ave. NW, is also open 24 hrs. In Dupont Circle, **Kramerbooks & Afterwords** bookstore/café sticks around 24 hrs. a day, but only if the day is Friday or Saturday. **Sabina's,** 1813 M St. NW, open till 3am (Sun.-Thurs.) or 4am (Fri.-Sat.), beckons with 1950s vinyl downtown; two **Tastee Diners,** 7731 Woodmont Ave. in Bethesda (vinyl version) and Colesville and Georgia Ave. in Silver Spring, MD (Art-Deco aluminum spaceship version) veritably incarnate the 50s, 24 immortal hrs. a day. Adams-Morgan's **El Tamarindo,** 1785 Florida Ave. NW, though not on a wonderful block, keeps its eyes open until 2am (Mon.-Thurs.) or even till 5am (Fri.-Sun.) On Capitol Hill, **Café Heartland,** 637 Pennsylvania Ave. SE, stays open till 2am daily; **Kelley's "The Irish Times," The Dubliner, Hawk 'n Dove,** and the **Tune Inn** are bar/restaurants that stay up even later. In Chinatown, **Big Wong,** 610 H St. NW, doesn't shut down till at least 3am nightly; several other Chinatown restaurants open till 3am Thursday to Sunday. In driving through late-night downtown Washington, stay away from 14th and L St. NW; prostitutes congregate in this area, and slow-moving Johns behind the wheel create late-night gridlock in this neighborhood. Unless you're looking for some action, roll up your windows as you drive on by.

INDEX